370.

KT-154-549

# Psychology and the Teacher

## 8th Edition

| DATE DUE | | | |
|---|---|---|---|
| | | | |
| | | | |
| | | | |
| | | | |
| | | | |
| | | | |
| | | | |
| | | | |
| | | | |
| | | | |
| | | | |
| | | | |

LIBRARY & INFORMATION SERVICE
TEES, ESK & WEAR VALLEYS
NHS FOUNDATION TRUST

DEMCO

**Also available from Continuum**

# Psychology and the Teacher

## 8th Edition

## Dennis Child

**Professor of Educational Psychology (Emeritus)**
**University of Leeds**

continuum

**Continuum International Publishing Group**
The Tower Building                                80 Maiden Lane, Suite 704
11 York Road                                      New York, NY 10038
SE1 7NX

www.continuumbooks.com

© Dennis Child 2007

First edition published 1973
Subsequent editions 1977, 1981, 1986, 1993, 1997, 2004

All rights reserved. No part of this publication may be reproduced or transmitted in any form or by any means, electronic or mechanical, including photocopying, recording or any information storage or retrieval system, without prior permission in writing from the publishers.

Dennis Child has asserted his right under the Copyright, Designs and Patents Act, 1988, to be identified as Author of this work

**British Library Cataloguing-in-Publication Data**
A catalogue record for this book is available from the British Library.

ISBN: 0-8264-8716-5 (paperback)
      0-8264-8715-7 (hardback)

**Library of Congress Cataloging-in-Publication Data**
A catalog record for this book is available from the Library of Congress.

Typeset by TechBooks International, New Delhi, India
Printed and bound in Great Britain by The Cromwell Press, Trowbridge, wiltshire.

# Contents

## Part Three  Learning

**viii** Contents

## Part Six  Educational Research and Test Design

# Preface to 1st Edition

The presentational style of the book has remained more or less the same since the First Edition and the time has come for an overhaul. The biggest changes, referred to in the next paragraphs, involve the creation of 'Sections' which bring together inter-related chapters; also, there is a reappraisal of 'Notes and References' and 'Enquiry and Discussion' entries at the end of every chapter.

There are some major psychological themes running through most teacher education syllabuses. The six sections, Introduction to the importance of psychology in education, Development, Learning, Individual Differences, Educational Research and Assessment, and Classroom and Curriculum Management reflect these themes. To adapt the book for this thematic approach and improve the flow of presentation, a rearrangement of chapters and their content has been necessary.

In all earlier editions, the 'Notes and References' contained both additional material and straightforward references. These have now been separated. 'Notes' remain because smaller print size enables me to pack in some interesting additional material which students have found useful as a starting point for essays, projects and dissertations. 'References' have been removed to the end of the book to create a conventional reference list.

School practice is much longer than in the past. Therefore, time spent in university has to be well organized and purposefully directed. To this end, I have rewritten the entries under 'Tutorial Enquiry and Discussion' for use in group and tutorial meetings, hoping that students will bring their classroom experiences to bear on the questions raised.

A new entry at the end of every chapter, 'Implications for Teachers', is an attempt to highlight the crucial issues in the chapter. This is a chastening exercise for any author. Out of many thousands of words and hundreds of ideas, what should be the key issues on which to focus our attention? I hope I have managed to pick some relevant ones. Tutors will doubtless have others 'up their sleeves'!

In the five years since the Sixth Edition there have been several critical changes in government policies which rendered some parts of the text out of date. This is particularly true of educational assessment, the curriculum and children with special needs – all of great interest to psychologists. Rapid progress in the study of brain activity using scanning techniques has also led to some fascinating developments in our knowledge of brain activity accompanying speaking and thinking.

Changes in our attitudes towards children with special needs have been marked. Whether of high or low ability, it is now recognized that we are committed to particular mainstream educational provision. These changes are reflected in chapter revisions.

The number of specialist books on the market is becoming burdensome for students and tutors. Selecting relevant and readable material has become a science. I have tried to select some of the most recent, but tutors and students need to be vigilant in directing their attention to well-written, informative examples. This also applies to the avalanche of Internet material. I hope this new edition provides a good starting point.

Dennis Child
University of Leeds
December 2002

# Preface to 8th Edition

The place of psychology in our understanding of human behaviour in learning and teaching is undoubtedly as significant today for the teacher as it ever was. Detailed studies of individual differences in behaviour and experience – a central psychology, have a crucial part to play in teachers' understanding of those whose learning they are hoping to guide and influence.

Since this book first appeared in the early 1970s, we have seen increased emphasis on tracking the progress of every pupil in the state educational system. There are vastly increased numbers moving to further and higher education, with a wider spread of ability and motivation. Greater opportunities exist for those who want to return to education. Changes in lifestyles at school, work and leisure are in evidence. All these factors, and more, have had a huge impact on individual learning and teaching processes.

Wherever such changes have affected the way we interact with our pupils, this edition of *Psychology and the Teacher* has new coverage. The education of those with special needs, across the whole intellectual spectrum, has become a concern of the mainstream teacher, as has the greater understanding of the effects of social and cultural differences on behaviour and development, and so in turn teaching and learning. In response, this new edition now has more coverage on nature and nurture, and their causes and effects, to help teachers in their role. Gender differences also receive much more coverage in this edition, particularly in the areas of development, intelligence and assessment. For early years practitioners, and all others keen to see how experience in the early years can impact on later life, there is more on play theory in Chapter 8. Since the 7th edition, research about the teaching of reading (a debate about phonic methods) has been in the minds of primary school teachers – Chapter 5 now offers a comprehensive overview.

As we enter the 21st century, the huge impact of research in genetics and brain functioning has to be reckoned with. Education is concerned with influence. Therefore, knowing what we are most and least likely to be able to influence in the behaviour of human beings is of paramount importance to us as teachers, be it interest in our subject, regard for other human beings or capability in performing certain tasks. Consequently, I have added more to the sections on neuroscience and genetics and their possible applications in education. This again includes a consideration of sex and gender differences.

In terms of presentation, this 8th edition has been much improved to guide the reader to information of interest as and when it is sought, and to make the text ever more accessible and user-friendly. At the top of each chapter is a full contents outline, and a list of key implications the contents have for the teacher. Bulleted lists now replace some prose;

background information (optional, but used by many students as a starting point for more detailed projects and essays) appears in boxes as 'Further reading'; references are more abundant and lists of useful websites are provided. In all, it is hoped to make the book comprehensive, yet easy on the eye. One of the greatest compliments a student can pass to a textbook author is 'your book was very useful and readable'.

The professional standards for qualified teacher status (QTS) required by the Department for Education and Skills (DfES) contain many criteria needing psychological knowledge. Where this is the case, the book should assist student teachers in satisfying the QTS requirements.

As ever, I am thankful to many people who have commented on the content and presentation of the book. I have tried to meet their comments within the constraints of trying to keep the book manageable in content and size.

Dennis Child
University of Leeds
February 2006

# Part One
## INTRODUCTION

# Psychology and Education

## Implications for teachers

- Education has turned to social sciences, particularly psychology, for a knowledge base about learning and teaching.
- Psychology is an extensive subject. Many of the branches now offer some guidance to teachers and this has developed into the applied area of educational psychology.
- Because of the particularly complex nature of education, care has to be taken in using research findings directly from psychology. This is taken up again in Chapter 17.
- Guesswork as the basis for professional practice in classrooms is insufficient for a teacher. Therefore, research has been a primary source of information.

*Psychology interests people because it asks questions that touch virtually every aspect of our lives.*
(Smith *et al.*, in *Atkinson and Hilgard's Introduction to Psychology*, 2003, p. 2)

# The study of psychology

Understanding ourselves and others has probably always been a human preoccupation. Certainly from the time when the first written record appeared; it showed that we have a deep interest in human and animal behaviour. Yet, until relatively recently our ideas have been almost entirely unsystematic and unrepresentative. Even in daily life we casually watch others or listen with prejudiced ears to conversation, and from this build up crude notions about human beings. Early explorers of human nature engaged in what is now known as 'armchair theorizing'. For example, Hippocrates and Galen, many centuries ago, speculated about different typologies of human personality without collecting experimental evidence. Later, Jean-Jacques Rousseau, in his book *Emile*, theorized about child development. However, this kind of theorizing has been replaced, from the nineteenth century onwards, by serious attempts to adopt and adapt the methods of the natural sciences in order to make the study of behaviour more systematic (Cohen *et al.* 2000). Other research methods have appeared during the last century and these are discussed in Chapter 17.

In 1869, Sir Francis Galton published a book, *Hereditary Genius*, in which he applied statistical procedures to the study of intelligence. This marked the beginning of the movement for applying scientific and mathematical methods to the study of human behaviour, and made Galton the founder of psychological studies of individual differences. In 1879, Wilhelm Wundt, a German physiologist, turned his scientific training to the study of psychology and established the first experimental psychology laboratory. At the turn of the last century, Sigmund Freud tried to build a model of the causes and cures of mental illness from careful observations of his patients (case study methods) and thereby founded the school of psychoanalysis.

Psychology is concerned with a wide area of interest. It has been defined as the systematic study of animal and human behaviour (observable and mental processes) and covers all kinds of pursuits, from making dogs salivate at the sound of a bell to a study of the growth of intelligent behaviour in humans. The term 'behaviour' includes all those aspects of human activity which we can observe: in effect, it represents the outward life of individuals that is public knowledge and which can be noted dispassionately. But behaviour also involves personal experience, which can be studied only by asking individuals to express their feelings and thoughts. For example, frequently we sit motionless while watching television or solving a problem 'in our heads'. Yet our senses and brains are operating or 'behaving'. To discover anything about this internal action we would have to seek out some physiological method of 'tapping' the nervous system (see scanning techniques in Chapter 2) alongside asking individuals to relate their experiences (Chapter 17). This method of introspection – attempting to expose the private knowledge of persons by asking them to recount their conscious experiences, attitudes, opinions or values – is regarded with suspicion by some (for arguments for and against, see Richer 1975 and Hebb 1974), but it does constitute a widely used technique in several fields of psychology (Cohen *et al.* 2000).

# Approaches to psychology

Contemporary general textbooks, (e.g., Smith *et al.* 2003) identify five perspectives in the study of psychology. Only brief mention will be made here of the approaches, but all of them appear regularly in this textbook. They are:

- Psycho-biological
- Behaviourist
- Cognitive
- Psychodynamic (Clinical)
- Phenomenological (Subjectivist).

The *psycho-biological* perspective places emphasis on the central fact that the human body is composed of chemicals. The chemicals associated with the brain and central nervous system are especially responsible for influencing behaviour not just of humans but all animals. One example from a vastly expanding body of work in this field is that of neuro-psychologists exploring the link between the brain and behaviour.

*Behaviourist* perspectives became very influential in the field of education in the latter half of the twentieth century. Observable behaviour is central to the behaviourist's concerns. The activities of 'out-of-sight' nervous systems or feelings are not of much direct interest to the behaviourist.

*Cognitive* perspectives, almost as a reaction to behaviourism, are especially directed to the internal processes assumed to accompany observable human behaviour, such as thinking, remembering, decision-making, problem-solving and so on.

*Psychodynamic* (sometimes called *clinical* or *psychoanalytic*) perspectives have emanated from Freud and his successors (neo-Freudians) who concentrate on the possible roots of human behaviour in subconscious or unconscious motives. These motives are assumed to have their origins in the interaction between inborn instincts and child-rearing practices.

Finally, *phenomenological* (or *subjectivist*) perspectives emphasize the here-and-now, subjective experiences of humans, in stark contrast to the mechanistic beliefs of the other four approaches outlined above. Humans have centre stage as the 'actors' rather than the 'acted upon'. These five psychological perspectives are influential to a greater or lesser degree in the following branches of psychology.

# Branches of psychology

The study of animal or human behaviour can take many forms. They are:

- Animal
- Human
- Physiological
- Social
- Psychology of individual differences
- Developmental.

Some psychologists are concerned with general principles about *animal* or *human psychology* without particular regard for the application of these principles. Just as the physicist attempts to discover the laws which govern planetary motion, so the psychologist tries to discover the laws which govern learning in organisms. At this broad level, the psychologist concentrates on *animal* behaviour, either for its own sake or in the belief that, if humans have emerged from the animal kingdom as part of the evolutionary process, we will have brought with us some of the characteristics of animals. Therefore a study of animals might give a clue, at a rudimentary level, to human nature.

Some psychologists prefer to look at the *physiological psychology* of animals and humans by studying body structures and their bearing on behaviour. In Chapter 2, which is about the brain and the central nervous system, we shall find many examples of physiology being used to discern body-behaviour connections. This process is called *reductionism*. The primary interest is in the *internal biological agencies* which influence behaviour.

*Social psychology*, the study of social institutions and their impact on the behaviour of individuals, concentrates on *external agencies*, such as families, schools or communities, which influence people. Researchers in this field would investigate such topics as the role of the headteacher in a school or the effects of family background on the achievement of children at school.

The *psychology of individual differences* is concerned with the systematic study of, for example, traits, types and abilities associated with personality, motivation and intelligence. Psychologists in this area often use *multivariate* (lots of variables) statistics to search for the underlying factors which combine to form traits or abilities (Child 2006).

*Developmental psychology* is yet another example of a broad field of interest, in which the physical, emotional and intellectual characteristics and development of children, from the prenatal stage onwards, are studied. Clearly, educational specialists draw extensively on this knowledge for its possible relevance to teaching. A particularly informative book for teachers on child development is Bee and Boyd (2004).

These branches contribute to applied fields, which have become quite numerous. Some examples are:

- Clinical psychology and counselling
- Occupational psychology and ergonomics
- Industrial psychology
- Forensic psychology
- Cybernetics
- Cognitive neuroscience
- Sports psychology
- Educational psychology.

*Clinical psychology and counselling* involve the study of abnormal mental life and are of interest to psychiatrists, clinical psychologists and counsellors in, for example, school and college settings. The findings from clinical psychology have sometimes offered useful criteria for defining the attributes of normal mental life.

*Occupational psychology* has grown rapidly into a prominent applied field. Examples are the study of such problems as vocational development, stress in the work place, job satisfaction and human efficiency in the workplace (*human factors* or *ergonomics*). Chapter 13 is devoted to the problem of vocational development and guidance in schools.

Other examples of applied branches are *industrial psychology*, which is concerned with psychological factors in the work place, *forensic psychology*, which involves the use of psychological knowledge in crime detection, and *cybernetics*, which is the study of machine simulation of human functions, e.g. the automatic pilot in aircraft.

Two recent interdisciplinary applied fields are *cognitive neuroscience*, which is concerned with relationships between cognitive functioning and brain activity using scanning techniques (Blakemore and Frith 2000 – see Chapter 2), and *sports psychology*, which uses a knowledge of psychology to help individuals and teams in improving their performance in various sports.

Finally, and of particular benefit to student teachers and others engaged in work involving young people, we have the applied field of *educational psychology*.

# Educational psychology

## A definition

Traditionally, educational psychology has endeavoured to apply the findings of general, social, developmental and child psychology and individual differences to assist in a better understanding of learning processes, which include social and moral, as well as academic learning. It seeks to discover, by studying the mental, physical, social and emotional behaviour of children and adults, the factors which influence the quality and quantity of learning. Ideally it offers to replace 'common sense' or trial-and-error notions of learning and teaching with a variety of hypotheses regarding learners and learning environments derived from systematic studies of individuals in those environments. The application of psychology in education, therefore, gives us a means of appraising individual children's similarities and differences and should enable us to create more efficient learning environments for them. It provides us with a means of making evaluations of our own strengths and weaknesses as learners and teachers and is a useful background for anyone concerned with the young. It might also help us as parents or in the context of our daily lives and dealing with others (Glaser 1973).

At this point, we need to distinguish between the use of 'educational psychology' as broadly defined above and its specific use to describe the professional application as in special educational needs. It is possible to become qualified as a specialist in educational, clinical or occupational psychology applied in educational settings. In Chapter 11 we shall meet with the work of *educational psychologists* with children having special educational needs.

It is important to remember that most of the concepts used in psychology and consequently applied in education are *invented* and not *discovered*. They are invented to account for human behaviour. Discoveries have followed showing that some concepts are influenced by biological (e.g. the brain) and cultural factors. The concept of intelligence is a good example. Psychologists invented it in the nineteenth century. They defined what they meant by it and proceeded to seek out measures to suit the definition. It was then found that intelligence measures are affected by, for instance, brain damage and educational experiences.

In this book an attempt is made to define and elaborate those aspects of psychology which would seem to illuminate the work of those dealing with young people. Psychology teaches us about people – how they think, respond and feel, why they behave as they do and what initiates and sustains their actions. Such fundamental processes are so central to our understanding of children's learning that they cannot help but form a substantial part of a course in teacher education. We cannot rely on our independent observations alone. When we observe children in class or at play, it is deceptively easy to draw conclusions based on isolated incidents and to make generalizations about all children from these incidents. This is called *anecdotal evidence*. It is sometimes helpful as a starting point for more systematic observations or as confirmation of a general principle, but anecdotes cannot serve as the sole criterion for making decisions about children's education. Instead, psychologists try to formulate generalizations based on representative groups of people, ideally *in situ*, or on animals, where they think the findings can be transferred validly to human situations. Here the problem is to convert a generalization into a form which makes it useful for teachers, or other professionals whose work involves them with people, to apply in individual cases. However, there are problems with tightly controlled experiments involving children and we shall discuss these in Chapter 17.

# What this book is about

There are so many questions of common concern to psychologists, teachers and social, youth and community workers that a single book could not possibly touch on them all. Therefore value judgements have to be made about the most important contributions. It is also hoped that each student will get some personal satisfaction from the text.

The book is divided into six parts reflecting the most important aspects of psychology relevant to education. Part One contains the present chapter which introduces the reader to the subject.

Part Two contains four chapters dealing with various aspects of human development. They focus on physical, perceptual, cognitive and language growth in children and young people. By starting with a consideration of the brain and the central nervous system, we are recognizing that the physical and mental lives of children have their origins in biological mechanisms. The fascinating story of brain function and its possible connection with day-to-day learning skills and problems is beginning to unfold. We are now learning some of the specifics of how the nervous system is related to mental functioning, memory and emotional development, and this is a source of feverish research activity. Although at present the findings offer teachers no direct help in dealing with children, knowledge of the biological mechanisms provides a background context in which they can consider the behaviour processes of their charges. The next chapter raises important issues connected with perception and attention in learning and development. Chapter 4 focuses on the important area of cognitive development, including the teaching of thinking skills in children, while Chapter 5 concentrates on language acquisition, including the influence of home and school.

Part Three brings together chapters on learning and motivation. Chapters 6 and 7 summarize what the major theorists have had to say about the processes of learning and memory. Although these theoretical explanations offer a wide and sometimes difficult range of suggestions, teachers who study and understand them are more likely to structure classroom activities to promote effective learning. Chapter 8 highlights some of the conditions which determine variations in levels of motivation, both in terms of individual differences and in the environmental settings of the child.

Part Four deals with a range of psychological factors which make us different from each other and affect our abilities to cope with many aspects of learning. Chapter 9 deals with individual differences in intelligence, Chapters 10 and 11 highlight the needs of gifted children and those with special educational needs, whilst Chapter 12 focuses on personality. Chapter 13 examines social, emotional and vocational guidance which is, perhaps, of more concern to those in secondary and higher education. Exciting new developments in these areas continue to shed light for everyone whose work entails communicating with and helping individuals, each of whom possesses a unique blend of mental, emotional, physical and social attributes. For teachers, behavioural and emotional variability is the order of the day, especially in these days of inclusion. The teacher, therefore, must know what to look for and what action to take.

Part Five brings together three chapters at the hard end of teaching. They introduce students to such important considerations as classroom management, the curriculum and educational assessment. Chapter 14 considers the key elements of effective teaching while Chapter 15 discusses curriculum development and planning. With quality assurance, increased use of standardized materials, such as SATs, and a greater concern for more students to reach standards sufficient for entry to further and higher education, comes greater responsibility on the part of teachers to acquire a thorough knowledge of the art and science of assessment and evaluation. Examining the work of children is a skilled task and psychology provides a sound basis for the reliable and valid examination of children's progress and achievement. This is covered in Chapter 16.

Finally, Part Six examines some quantitative topics met with in reading and understanding the literature and in assessing pupils. Chapters 17 and 18 are tough chapters and really need to be read alongside specialist texts.

In addition to the 'Summary' at the end of each chapter, there is a section for 'Tutorial enquiry and discussion', intended to focus the reader's thinking and give some ideas for discussions in lectures, tutorials or in school.

## Summary

Psychology is the study of overt and covert behaviour in humans and animals and therefore has an obvious contribution to make to our understanding of education problems relating to the learner, the processes of learning and the conditions of learning. Much of the information in educational psychology has been applied from specialist branches such as developmental, social, physiological and clinical psychology. As a scientific enterprise, the psychology of education still has a long way to go and consequently the message of this chapter has been one of cautious optimism for the application of psychology to the daily routines of the teacher. While it cannot provide unequivocal or black and white answers to the teacher's problems, nevertheless it does provide an essential ingredient in the decision-making processes of classroom practice.

## Tutorial enquiry and discussion

(a) Consider the dangers of being influenced by first impressions when faced with a group of children with differing abilities, personalities and social experiences.

(b) From your experience of being in schools and using material in your college library, identify the current sources and methods used by teachers in keeping up to date in the psychology of education.

(c) Examine some of the most influential educational experiences which you had as a pupil and explore the psychological significance of them.

(d) Discuss the ways in which psychology can assist you in your role as a teacher. See also the articles on this subject in *The Psychologist*, British Psychological Society, March 1993.

## References

Bee, H. and Boyd, D. (2004), *The Developing Child* (10th edn). Boston, MA: Pearson and AB.

Blakemore, Sarah-Jayne and Frith, U. (2000), *The Implications of Recent Developments in Neuroscience for Research on Teaching and Learning*. London: Institute of Cognitive Neuroscience.

Child, D. (2006), *The Essentials of Factor Analysis* (3rd edn). London: Continuum.

Cohen, L., Manion, L. and Morrison, K. (2000), *Research Methods in Education* (5th edn). London: Routledge Falmer.

Galton, F. (1869), *Hereditary Genius*. London: Macmillan.

Glaser, R. (1973), 'Educational psychology and education', *American Journal of Psychology*, 28, 557–66.

Hebb, D.O. (1974), 'What psychology is about', *American Psychologist*, 29, 71–9.

*Psychologist, The* (March 1993). Leicester: British Psychological Society.

Richer, J. (1975), 'Two types of agreement – two types of psychology', *British Psychological Society Bulletin*, 28, 342–5.

Smith, E. E., Nolen-Hoeksema, S., Frederickson, B. L., Loftus, G. R., Bem, D. J. and Maren, S. (2003), *Atkinson and Hilgard's Introduction to Psychology* (14th edn). Belmont, CA: Wadsworth/Thomson.

## Further reading

For more technical detail in psychology, readers should refer to the following:

Bee, H. and Boyd, D. (2004), *The Developing Child* (10th edn). Boston, MA: Pearson and AB.

Medcof, J. and Roth, J. (eds) (1991, first printed 1979), *Approaches to Psychology* (10th international edn). Milton Keynes: Open University Press.

Shorrocks-Taylor, D. (ed.) (1998), *Directions in Educational Psychology*. London: Whurr.

Smith, E. E., Nolen-Hoeksema, S., Frederickson, B. L., Loftus, G. R., Bem, D. J. and Maren, S. (2003), *Atkinson and Hilgard's Introduction to Psychology* (14th edn). Belmont, CA: Wadsworth/Thomson.

## Useful websites

http://www.tta.gov.uk/qualifyingtoteach
Teacher Training Agency (tta)

# Part Two
## DEVELOPMENT

# The Nervous System

## Chapter Outline

# Implications for teachers

- Learning is both a function of the brain and central nervous system (BCNS) and a central concern of teachers. Some knowledge of interplay between these is therefore important.
- As we progress into the twenty-first century, more connections are going to be made between learning and the nervous system (e.g. neuroscience).
- Some aspects of poor achievement (thought to be about 5 per cent) and abnormal behaviour have their origins in physical disorders of the BCNS.
- Recognizing and allowing for differences in educational provision is important.
- In an inclusive education system, professional help is often needed with particular pupils with physiologically-based cognitive and behavioural disorders.
- Increasingly, the literature for teachers assumes a knowledge of the BCNS.
- If the development of the BCNS is a key to learning (e.g. critical and sensitive periods, literacy, numeracy), both teachers and parents are crucial agents.

*It seems to me totally plausible that in 40 or so years' time, it will be possible to walk into a successor of my current research laboratory and have a sensible discussion with an artificially conscious system ... You can make a neural system which can store experience and it will have feelings, albeit of a machine-like kind.*

(Igor Aleksander, 1996, *Impossible Minds*)

Human behaviour is an extremely complex affair. The variety of possible human experiences and their impact on our development is in itself a vastly intricate subject. At the core of the problem is an organism whose biological and chemical equipment sets the scene for the immense potentialities of each person's lifestyle. The advances since the 1970s, when the present book first appeared – particularly in neural structure, functioning and chemistry, computer science and scanning techniques of the brain – have been so remarkable that contemporary scientists are willing to make claims such as that at the head of this chapter (Aleksander 1996 and 2000).

On the other hand, there are those who believe that despite years of endeavour by scientists, we are not much nearer to creating a machine which can be regarded as being 'conscious'. The British Association of Science at its conference in 1996 devoted a large slice of time to a debate on this subject. Sir Roger Penrose (1991, 1994), a pessimist, concluded that 'The neuron level of description that provides the currently fashionable picture of the brain and mind is a mere *shadow* of the deeper level of action – and it is at this level where we must seek the physical basis of the *mind*' (see Highfield and Coveney (1995) for a summary of the arguments). Aleksander (1996) disagreed with Penrose (1991, 1994). Aleksander was for the motion and Penrose against. This may seem far removed from the concerns of teachers. But it isn't. There is no doubt that discoveries surrounding the functioning and chemistry of the nervous system are going to have a crucial impact on the way we attempt to resolve behavioural problems in thinking, memory, attention, aggressive behaviour, etc.

One clear consequence of these scientific discoveries is our greater understanding of principles and problems relating to human behaviour. It is now firmly established that certain body structures are closely linked to the behaviour we can observe in animals and humans. The central nervous system, in particular the brain, is undoubtedly the most important structure in this respect. Injuries to specific parts of the brain, as we shall see presently, cause specific behaviour changes and disorders; severing nerve fibres in the front part of the brain can bring about obvious and sometimes radical changes in the personality of individuals; abnormalities in brain or nerve structures at birth bring with them a corresponding variation in, or absence of, behaviour consistent with normal brains. There is the substantial role of chemicals in the neurons (Carlson 2005) affecting many aspects of our behaviour. But our knowledge of the precise causal connections between behaviour and body mechanisms is far from complete. For instance, we have only a gross notion of the part played by the brain in thinking, emotional activity, perceiving and memory, despite advances in scanning the active brain. Nevertheless, what little we do know is important for any student of human behaviour.

# Organization of the nervous system

The two bodily control systems of particular interest are the nervous and endocrine systems. At present we will look at the reception, transmission and control mechanisms of the nervous system. For a detailed but readable description of the structure and functioning of these systems the student is recommended to read a basic text in physiological psychology (Chapter 2 in Smith *et al.* 2003; see also Carlson 2005).

The nervous system has been classified in several ways, the classifications depending on the location or function of the various portions of the system. Common to all these classifications is the *central nervous system* (often abbreviated to CNS), comprising the brain, brain stem and spinal cord, and the *peripheral nervous system* (PNS). The CNS is a central mass of nerve cells which integrates messages received from *receptors* and then sends out responses to the *effectors*. These messages are sent through the nerve fibre system of the peripheral nervous system.

The PNS is composed of two functional parts called the *somatic* (or *voluntary*) nervous system and the *autonomic* (or *involuntary*) nervous system. The somatic nervous system supplies the sense organs with nerve fibres to the CNS (*receptor fibres*) and from the CNS to the muscles (*effector fibres*). It is responsible for: (a) transmitting impulses set up in the

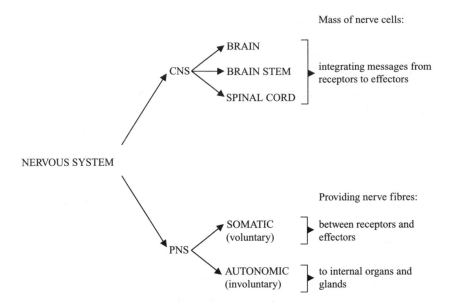

Mass of nerve cells:

BRAIN

CNS — BRAIN STEM    integrating messages from
                    receptors to effectors

SPINAL CORD

NERVOUS SYSTEM

Providing nerve fibres:

SOMATIC        between receptors and
(voluntary)    effectors

PNS

AUTONOMIC      to internal organs and
(involuntary)  glands

**Figure 2.1** Diagram of structure and functions of the brain.

sense organs by external or internal stimuli (sights, sounds, sources of pain, etc.) to the brain (interpreting and responding to these receptor impulses is done within the brain) and (b) transmitting the effector impulses from the brain through the spinal cord to muscles which then contract if required. The final phase represents a response to the stimulus.

The somatic nervous system can be brought under the direct control of an individual. When a hungry child sees an inviting apple he or she might reach out, pick it up and eat it. The stimulus through the sense of sight has set up impulses transmitted through the optic nerve fibres to the brain, from which the effector impulses are transmitted to bring about an appropriate response pattern of muscular movements necessary for grasping and lifting the apple. Conduction paths from sense organs in other parts of the body, e.g. pain, temperature and kinaesthetic sensory regions (the *periphery*) pass through the spinal cord to the brain and back to the musculature by the same nerve but different fibres.

This, of course, is an over-simplified version of what goes on inside our bodies. The effects of socialization, to mention just one complication, may prevent the child from taking the apple if it belongs to someone else. Something intervenes between the stimulus and the response to inhibit the child from taking the apple. What precisely goes on in the brain in this case is still a mystery. In our discussion on motives we shall raise the matter again.

There is a way in which the receptor and effector organs are connected directly without necessarily involving interpretative functioning of the brain. This is called the *reflex arc.*

Humans and some higher animals are born with certain reflexes such as swallowing, eye blinking, sneezing, coughing and knee jerking in response to the presence of threatening stimuli. A puff of wind directed at the eye will cause the lids to close automatically to protect the delicate surface of the eye. Swallowing prevents unwanted particles from passing into the air passages leading to the lungs.

The other important system, the *autonomic nervous system* (ANS), supplies the glands and various organs of the body. As the term implies, the autonomic, self-controlling, in-voluntary system operates without a conscious effort on the part of the individual. Organs such as the heart, lungs, stomach, intestines, bladder, blood vessels in the skin (respon-sible for blushing and pallor effects) and glands (tear, hair follicle, sweat and salivary) continue to throb, expand, contract, open, close and secrete quite independently of our conscious control. Routine operations that are managed by the system have their ori-gins in the hypothalamus (see pp. 28–9) and pass from there to the organs via the spinal cord. Two divisions known as the *sympathetic* and the *parasympathetic* have been iden-tified. The sympathetic portion innervates and stimulates organs which enable the or-ganism to respond rapidly, especially in circumstances which spell danger or create fear. A frightening experience, as readers will know, causes increased and irregular breathing and heartbeat, sweating, pallor and the hair to stand on end. The extra supply of oxy-gen and release of energy-giving chemicals (glucose from liver glycogen, for instance) provide the excess energy which enables the organism to escape or fight. The parasym-pathetic section also innervates the same organs, but has the opposite effect on them, by acting as a braking system to the sympathetic nerves and slowing down the body mechanisms.

Implicit in all we said in the previous paragraph is the assumption that the organs reg-ulated by the autonomic nervous system may not be brought under the control of the will. This, however, is not the case. At a simple level, it is possible to arrest lung action and bring about a change in heartbeat. More sophisticated control is achieved by those on the stage, who can think themselves into emotive states (weeping, anger) without really 'feeling like it'. Devotees of yoga are able to control their metabolic rates so as to reduce the amount of oxygen needed for body functioning. Several yogis have been known to survive in confined spaces for much longer than would be possible in normal circumstances. Controlled experi-ments in the United States by N. E. Miller (1978) support the view that autonomic functions are susceptible to conscious control. By a system of rewards in the form of a pleasant buzzer sound, he encouraged high-blood-pressure patients to think about reducing their heart rate. When the heart rate had reached a predetermined lower level, the buzzer sounded. In this way the patients were able to lower the rate to quite a marked extent. This process, by which a person regulates a normally involuntary body function (heartbeat, brainwaves, blood pressure, breathing, certain muscles) by the use of information from internal organs, is known as *biofeedback* (Carroll 1984). It is rapidly becoming a most important development in medical science for pain and stress control. Further uses to which biofeedback has been put are in the control of breathing during bronchitic or asthmatic attacks, by regulating air-passage sizes, and in the relief of tension headaches by controlling a forehead muscle which tightens during certain kinds of stress along with scalp and neck muscles (Thorpe and Olson 1997).

This model has also been used to explain some *psychosomatic* disorders. One example, familiar to parents and teachers, is the child who because of fear (an exam, a distressing episode with a teacher) may claim to feel sick. The fear causes physical changes, some of which involve paleness and stomach contraction (even sickness). These symptoms are read by the parents as illness and the child is kept at home. This successful event – of being allowed to stay home from school – may reinforce subsequent similar fearful occasions when the child begins to develop more chronic symptoms. These are often inadvertently learned responses to fear (Miller 1978).

# Receptors

Our waking lives are filled with testing the environment with our senses. In fact, our continued existence depends on our sensitivity to the environment and the appropriateness of our responses. To receive this information from the surroundings, there are groups of cells which are receptive to light, sound, touch, taste, smell, movement, heat and the like. The cells are known as *receptors*, and some groups of cells form the sense organs, such as the eyes, ears, taste buds on the tongue and 'olfactory' areas in the nose; less obvious receptors of pain, temperature change and movement (kinaesthetic sense) are widely distributed both on the surface and inside the body. The complex structure of these organs is a subject which need not detain us here (Smith *et al.* 2003).

In general terms, a receptor cell will operate when there is a change or difference in the environment. The change is known as a *stimulus*. The difference in light intensity between the dark letters and the white background of this page enables you to observe the stimulus of the letters. When an object vibrates sufficiently it sets up a disturbance in the surrounding air. The disturbance spreads out in all directions from the source and, on striking the eardrum, sets it in sympathetic motion. In turn this is transmitted to the sound-sensitive receptors in the inner ear. A change in pressure or temperature on the body surface is soon detected. Where a change does not reach a perceivable *threshold*, obviously it will not be detected. By 'threshold' we mean a level of stimulation below or above which we are not aware of the stimulus, and this constitutes the first clear source of individual differences. Regular background stimulation, e.g. the ticking of a clock or the pressure of clothes on the body, often goes unnoticed. This provides a sound reason why teachers should vary their voices and take note of the colours used on blackboards or visual aids. There are also variations in the threshold levels from one person to the next. It is thought that some people have low pain thresholds and soon succumb by showing marked anxiety symptoms. Some children are more upset by pain than others, although, as we saw above, the differences probably arise as much from experiential as from constitutional sources.

## Vision

It has been shown that vision in the newborn is very rudimentary. A baby's eyes are sensitive to light and they can adapt to darkness. Colour discrimination may also develop very quickly in the first few months. But the eye lenses cannot alter (accommodate) readily to focus on objects at different distances. The eye movements are not coordinated. In fact, each eye can move independently at first in a fashion disturbing to unsuspecting mothers and fathers. They need not worry, because it is not an abnormality and eye movements ultimately become coordinated.

*Colour blindness* is a genetically transmitted inability to distinguish particular colours. The commonest form, *protanopia*, involves red and green. Sufferers see the world in yellows and blues. Red and green colours are seen as shades of yellow. Four in every hundred people are colour blind, so on average there will be one pupil in every class you might take who is unable to distinguish some portions of those colourful visual aids so lovingly prepared. Many visual aids used by teachers rely on colour code differences for effect. Teachers should make absolutely certain that *all* pupils appreciate the differences.

There are several ways in which the eyes move according to their usage. *Pursuit movements* occur when we watch a moving object such as a car. *Compensatory movements* happen when we fix our attention on an object and move our heads from side to side. A third kind of movement is *convergence* or *divergence*, when an object travels towards or away from an observer. Finally, and most significant for the teacher of reading, is *saccadic movement*, which occurs when the eye moves along a line of print, and *fixates* when it pauses. The present sentence might require, on average, eight to ten eye movements, one every two words. But the length and difficulty of the words, coupled with the reading speed of a person, will govern the number of eye movements required by each person. The following sentences demonstrate the possible positions at which the eyes fixate as they jump along the line of words. The fixation points are shown as black dots.

The 'visual span' (the number of words taken in at each fixation point) of a slow reader is small, and the movements would look something like this:

· · · · · · · · ·<br>
The eye only sees when it is stationary.

For a fast reader, the following might apply:

· · · · · · · ·<br>
Therefore the more you take in at each jump the bigger can be the jumps.

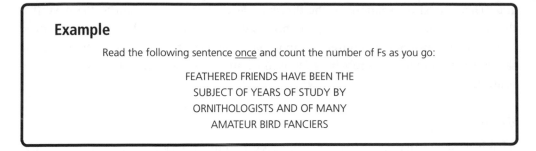

**Example**

Read the following sentence <u>once</u> and count the number of Fs as you go:

FEATHERED FRIENDS HAVE BEEN THE
SUBJECT OF YEARS OF STUDY BY
ORNITHOLOGISTS AND OF MANY
AMATEUR BIRD FANCIERS

Most people get three or four. Now take your time and see if you can find six. Possibly the faster you read originally, the fewer you would see. The eye skips along the lines and may not even fixate on short words such as OF.

Reading efficiency, among other things, is related to saccadic movement because the distance between each fixation of the eye will govern the pace of reading – but *not* necessarily the understanding of the reading material. Pace (Carver 1990) is also affected by other mechanical aspects such as fixing for long periods at each point, using too many jerky forward and backward movements over the words already viewed, or by the arrangement of the print. Courses for improving reading speed concentrate some of their time on these factors. Further discussion on reading appears in Chapter 5.

## Hearing

Research involving babies as subjects is plainly a precarious business. Because they cannot communicate verbally and since their motor skills are still rudimentary, it is not always possible to plot the progress in some aspects of their development. Response to sounds seems to be fairly general, in that babies do not appear to discriminate readily between types of sound. Of course they react to sounds of varying intensity. Loud sounds may produce a 'startle' reaction, although there could be dissimilar reactions to the same loud sound. But we have to wait until babies are several months old before they begin to respond to their mothers' voices in a way that differs from their responses to other similar sounds.

Hearing and sight are the two important communication senses for the teacher. Faulty hearing or eyesight in children can, and often does, go unnoticed by parents and teachers. The effect of these deficiencies on learning is obvious. The teacher can do much to improve the situation by judiciously placing children who have partial hearing or seeing defects in suitable positions in the classroom. Teachers should refer serious cases to the appropriate professionals. (See Chapter 5 for references to the education of hearing impaired children.)

## Touch

The sense of touch in infancy is our first hard evidence of reality. We probably underrate the importance of tactile experience for our children. Our preoccupation with the written and spoken word has led to our neglecting the sense of touch, which includes the detection of pressure, pain and temperature. Many primary school teachers now give their children opportunities to manipulate various materials or identify objects hidden from view using only the sense of touch, as in the 'feeling' boxes or bags used in primary schools. Some regions of the body are devoid of pain; some areas are more sensitive to pressure than others. The fingertips are particularly sensitive, whilst the sole of the foot is comparatively less discriminating.

For further discussion of sensation and perception, see the beginning of Chapter 3.

# Transmission

Reception of stimuli from outside or inside the body is only the beginning. Impulses set up by the receptors need to be conveyed to the brain for interpretation and possible response.

The impulses are the result of electrical and chemical changes passing along the length of the nerve fibres with great rapidity. The slowest is around one metre per second and the fastest approaches 100 metres per second (over 200 mph). Witness the speed with which a pinprick which excites the pain receptors on the body will give rise to withdrawal of that area from the painful stimulus.

The tissues making up the nervous system are living cells of various shapes and sizes, depending on the work they do. Our bodies contain many billions of these cells. Scientists are now able to study their structure using the powerful magnifying properties of the electron microscope. A nerve is composed of numerous long fibres, the length depending on the distance between the brain and the receptor. A single cell within the fibre is called a *neuron*. Neurons are most important nerve cells. There is no doubt that they are central in brain functioning and are involved in sensory activity, thinking and memory.

Figure 2.2 gives a diagrammatic view of a neuron magnified many times. It consists of a *cell body* with fine hair-like processes called *dendrites* and a drawn-out portion, the *axon*, which gives the nerve fibre its length. The axon is surrounded by the *myelin sheath*, which both protects the fibre and speeds up the transmission of the impulses. The processes at the end of the axon consist of small buttons or *synaptic terminals*. They form connections with the next neuron or with muscle fibres (end plates). The dendrites from one cell interlace with the synaptic knobs from an adjacent cell. Note from the diagram that they do not actually touch the dendrites. The minute gap (roughly a millionth of an inch) is known as the *synaptic gap* or *cleft* and the surrounding area as the *synapse*. Electrical impulses are conveyed along the neurons by means of electrical potential differences between the inside and the outside of the neuron membrane. On reaching the synaptic gap, the signal, which has passed down the axon by means of electrical charges, now passes across the gap by chemical transmission. This is achieved by the *synaptic vesicles* which are tiny spherical pockets in the synaptic terminals. On reaching the surface of the terminal (Figure 2.2), they release molecules of chemicals (neuropeptides) known as *neurotransmitters* and these

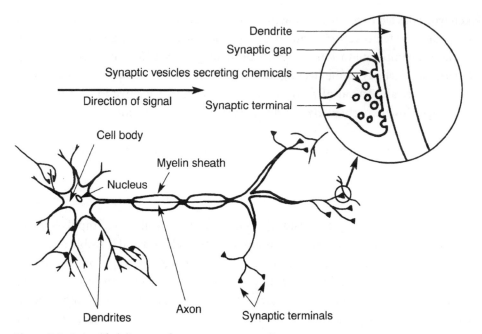

**Figure 2.2** A simplifed diagram of a neuron or nerve cell.

diffuse across the synaptic gap to be taken up by the *receptor molecules* at the surface of the next neuron. Over 70 such neurotransmitters have been identified in different parts of the body performing different functions (for a clear summary, see Smith *et al.* 2003).

There are about 100 billion neurons and synapses in the human brain. In early child-hood there is a rapid proliferation of connections between the neurons and synapses. This is followed by a period when unused connections become redundant whilst used ones remain. This process is called *synaptogenesis*. Clearly, answers to questions about this experience-dependent process, such as critical and sensitive periods, enriched en-vironments, timing of presentation of new experiences, are crucial (Blakemore 2000, http//:www.parliament.uk/parliamentary_offices/post/pubs2000.cfm then choose Report 140).

The combination of the neurotransmitter and receptor molecules creates electrical charges. The sum of these charges gives an electrical impulse which either excites or inhibits the dendrite processes of the receiving neuron. It is the magnitude of the electrical impulse created by these charges which governs whether the resultant impulse will or will not pass along the receiving neuron. This is known as *facilitation* (or *excitation*) or *inhibition*. There appear to be no half measures. The neuron either fires or it does not fire, a phenomenon known as the 'all or nothing' principle. The chances of an impulse reaching the brain depend on the strength of the incoming signals, so the stronger the signal the more rapid is the impulse rate. The presence of inhibitory processes enables many possible courses of action (or simple inaction). It also helps to deal with all the extraneous perceptions in the field of view or hearing by eliminating them and preventing the brain from having to cope with an excess of information from the senses.

As mentioned above, many neurotransmitters and receptors have been identified and particular ones play a crucial part in medical conditions and drug taking. This new area of study has been called *molecular psychology* (Franklin 1987). For example, degenerative conditions such as Alzheimer's and Parkinson's diseases have been described in terms of transmitter and receptor malfunctioning. *Attention deficit hyperactivity disorder* (ADHD) has been linked to neurotransmitter deficiencies. This knowledge has also been applied to relieving conditions such as schizophrenia and to studying the effects of drugs such as cocaine, amphetamines, tranquillisers and LSD (Kruk and Pycock 1991).

# The brain

## Overall structure

The brain is a massive concentration of nerve cells representing about a third of all the nerve cells in the body. The outer layer, or *cortex*, consists of many folds (*convolutions*) of large (*fissures*) and small (*sulci*; the singular is *sulcus*) grooves so as to confine a large surface area into a small volume. About two-thirds of the surface is to be found in the grooves and the total surface area is about two-and-a-half square feet. The finished article looks like a walnut. Brain tissue has one of two shades depending on its composition. Where there is an abundance of nerve cells the resulting tissue is called grey matter. The outer cortex consists of *grey matter*. Where there are many nerve fibres, which are normally surrounded by a white sheath, the tissue is called *white matter*. The cells require a constant and rich supply of oxygen, otherwise they develop serious and permanent malfunction within one or two minutes. In instances where oxygen supply is limited, as when the windpipe is blocked or, more directly, in stroke conditions, serious and permanent mental impairment can result. Well-ventilated classroom conditions are an obvious necessity to enable normal oxygen supply and the reduction of carbon dioxide for efficient brain activity.

Viewed from the side, as shown in Figure 2.3(a), there are two conspicuous folds, the *central* and *lateral fissures*, which act as convenient boundary lines from which to describe the divisions of the brain. Bear in mind that we are looking only at one side. The other side, because of the approximate bilateral symmetry of the body, looks very much the same.

The deep fold running across the top and a little way down the sides is the *central fissure*. The second, at the sides, is the *lateral fissure* (or fissure of Sylvius). Figure 2.3(a) also gives an idea of the positions of these fissures. Viewed from above (Figure 2.4, page 32), the brain appears to be divided into two equal parts by a deep groove, the *median fissure*, running the length of the brain with a connecting band of fibres, called the *corpus callosum*, linking the *cerebral hemispheres* (see later). Using these fissures as boundary lines, Figure 2.3(a)

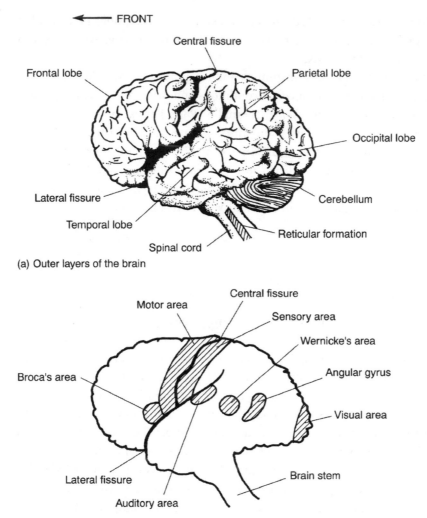

(a) Outer layers of the brain

(b) Some important areas on the surface of the brain

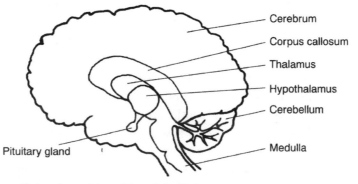

(c) Diagrammatic locations of some internal structures

**Figure 2.3** Structure–function relationships of the brain (left side).

shows how the surface cortex has been divided into *frontal, parietal, temporal* and *occipital* regions, or lobes. These lobes have corresponding partners on the other side of the brain. It is worth noting that these are only broad divisions partly reminiscent of the functional aspects of the brain.

If the brain is divided down the median fissure to expose the central organs, we find the termination of the spinal cord forming the brain stem and at the rear we find the *cerebellum*. It has been known for some time that the cerebellum coordinates fine movement of the body, but more recent research (Beatty 1995) indicates a further function in collaboration with the frontal lobes in language and reasoning. The cortical region normally enveloping the brain stem (sometimes referred to as the *cerebrum*) can be seen as a thick and extensive covering of nerve cells. A curious crossover of nerve fibres occurs between each side of the brain so that the left-hand side supplies the right-hand side of the body and vice versa for the other side. Consequently, damage to the motor region (Figure 2.3(b)) on one side of the brain will bring about a corresponding malfunctioning of the motor activity on the opposite side of the body.

## The brain stem

In Figure 2.3(b) the brain stem is shown as a deep-seated portion at the core of the brain and in an evolutionary sense it is the oldest part of the brain. Crudely, it is a hollow tube of nerve tissue at the top of the spinal cord through which all impulses from the cord must pass *en route* to the brain. It consists of two areas, the *medulla* on the outside (controlling breathing and posture), surrounding the inner core or *reticular formation* which lines the hollow tube and runs through to connect with the hypothalamus and thalamus. The reticular formation has two systems, the *descending reticular system* for motor functions and the *ascending reticular activating system* (ARAS) for sensory functions. This latter system is of particular importance. In broad terms its function is to monitor the impulses coming from the senses. Stimuli are selected or ignored so as to prevent overloading the brain with too much incoming information. *Selective attention*, therefore, is accomplished by the ARAS. Interestingly, the receipt of sensory information is necessary for normal functioning of the brain. If sensory cues are eliminated, as in many experiments where the subject's arms are encased in tubes and the eyes and ears are shut off from the surrounding stimuli, the subject becomes disorientated and distressed.

### Further reading

Students at McGill University (Bexton *et al.* 1954; also Lilly 1956) were bribed with money to undergo this kind of experiment, only to abandon it after a day because of intense frustration. It seems, then, that we must have sensory stimulation or spontaneous body activity. Humans and

$\longrightarrow$

animals must satisfy what appears to be their basic need to explore, driven by curiosity. This fact has obvious implications for the teacher, who must take advantage of the ready-made inquisitive nature of children.

The brain stem is also related to the cycle of sleep and wakefulness. Different areas of the stem appear to be responsible for the states of waking, sleeping and dreaming. Considerable research stretching back many years has focused on arousal and sleep (Horne 1988; Webb 1975) and its effects on both physical and mental performance. In the normal mechanism of sleep and waking there appears to be a built-in *biological clock*, known as *circadian rhythm* and controlled by the hypothalamus. It has its first settings laid down both by the control of the individual and by unconscious habits formed in childhood and the daily light and dark cycle, although scientists have shown that we have a natural cycle of 24.9 hours. Babies spend a fair proportion of their lives snoozing or sleeping during the day, and the habit carries over to schools and colleges. Reception and primary class teachers are well acquainted with their children dropping off during the afternoon and often have 'time out' sessions for children to sleep. Secondary school and college teachers will not be surprised at the news that about a third of their students fall asleep at least once a week during lessons (Smith *et al.* 2003), presumably despite the riveting lesson content and presentation!

By attaching electrodes to various points on the scalp and face (eyes, ears, chin) and recording the brain activity (using the EEG) and facial movements just before, during and just after sleep, it has been possible to identify five stages of sleep. Four of these stages (*slow-wave* or NREM sleep) are a progression from shallow to deep sleep. The other stage, different in several ways from the slow-wave, is detected from *rapid eye movements* (REM, hence the alternative name for slow-wave is non-REM or NREM). In sleep, we slip from one stage to another, not necessarily the next stage, during the night. Deeper sleep tends to occur earlier and REM sleep later in a normal period of sleep. Consolidation of recent learning occurs during REM periods (Karni *et al.* 1994). A connection between this phenomenon and subliminal learning using tape recordings playing during sleep has still to be made.

## Hypothalamus

Near the top of the brain stem and close to the pituitary gland we find the hypothalamus. This organ, by its control of the autonomic nervous system (see ANS, Figure 2.5 p. 37) and the endocrine gland system, contributes to starting, maintaining and stopping behaviour associated with satisfying the basic body needs such as food, water intake, sexual activity and temperature control. The balance between need and satisfaction is called *homeostasis*. When 'fuel' is running low in our bodies, the homeostatic balance is said to be disturbed. Sensations of hunger leading to food-seeking activity will occur until eating restores the balance. The hypothalamus also exerts some control over the activities of the pituitary gland, which is an endocrine gland controlling the hormone-producing glands of the body.

There is good reason for believing that the hypothalamus acts like a thermostat in controlling appetites by switching the controls of hunger, thirst, temperature, etc. on and off in response to body chemistry. This control is sometimes referred to as the *appestat*.

---

### Further reading

Research in the 1950s and 1960s (Anand and Brobeck 1951; Delgado 1969 and 1987; giving fascinating detail of physical control of the brain) using mild electrode stimulation of the brain (ESB) led to identifying the sites in the hypothalamus that are responsible for excitation accompanying hunger, thirst, body temperature variation, sex, pleasure and aggression.

---

As ever in science, these ESB findings were too simplistic to fit the facts. It is now clear that other regions of the brain and brain stem are involved in the control of physiological needs. Variations in complexity become apparent when one compares thirst and hunger. The former largely involves one substance – water. Hunger, on the other hand, involves many substances (proteins, fats, carbohydrates, vitamins, minerals, etc.) which have to be present in a chemically balanced body. Again, reproduction requires two people. Thus sexual behaviour is partly a function of physiological urges and partly culturally defined.

## Thalamus

The thalamus surrounds the top of the brain stem and has nerve connections from its position deep in the brain cortex in the roof of the brain. Fibres from all sense organs except the olfactory organs (the nose in humans) pass through this region. It provides a centre for sorting and directing information from sensory organs to specific sensory and motor regions in the roof of the brain (Figure 2.3(b)). It also plays a part in the control of sleep and wakefulness.

## The limbic system

The limbic system (difficult to show in a simple diagram) appears as a lining to the roof of the brain and surrounds the top of the brain stem. The important functional units are the hippocampus, amygdala and the septal area and cingulate gyrus which work in harmony with the hypothalamus. Damage or stimulation to these units gives rise to perceptual changes and disorders such as an inability to distinguish visual cues (caused when the cortex in contact with these units is removed), impairment of recent memory (hippocampus) and the disappearance of avoidance behaviour, as when a person no longer appears to be afraid of painful stimuli (amygdala). The hippocampus is not fully developed in infancy, which provides a possible reason for *infantile amnesia*, that is our inability to remember incidents from the first few years of life. Broadly speaking, the limbic system exercises some control over motivational and emotional behaviour and pain perception.

## Cerebellum (or little brain)

The conspicuous lump of tissue at the rear of the brain and under the occipital lobes (see Figure 2.3(a)) is known as the *cerebellum*. ESB studies by Eccles (1953, 1978), using micro-electrodes, attempted a minute exploration of this part of the cat brain. His conclusion was that it is responsible for the control of movement in routine activities such as walking and balancing. Damage to this region leads to coarse, clumsy and inaccurate movements. Eccles refined his method to such a point that he could detect information from a particular part of the body through the nerves to a specific cell in the cerebellum.

It now appears that the cerebellum is also connected to the frontal lobes (Beatty 1995) and is concerned with language and reasoning (Middleton and Strick 1994), thus suggesting a coordinating function in both physical and mental processes.

## Cerebral hemispheres

In this brief, whistle-stop tour of the brain we have now reached the extensive outer cover, described above as a highly convoluted grey mass of nerve cells. The outer layer is called the *cerebral cortex*, and has a conspicuous median fold that appears to divide the brain into two *cerebral hemispheres*. We also note four regions which will help us in defining some of the functions associated with the cortex (see Figure 2.3(a)).

First notice the *motor* and *sensory* areas bordering the central fissure (Figure 2.3(b)). The motor strip, of all brain regions, has been explored in great detail by, for example, Wilder Penfield (e.g. Penfield and Rasmussen 1950). Motor control of the left toe can be located at the top of the strip in the median fissure in the *right* hemisphere and, as we work down the strip, motor-control regions progress from the lower to the upper parts of the left-hand side of the body. The sensory strip on the other side of the central fissure is responsible for the senses of touch, pain and kinaesthesia. Note the separate regions for sight and hearing. A knock on the back of the head will make one 'see stars', because the visual area impinges on the rear of the skull.

Regions outside these areas are known as the association areas. They are divided into the *frontal association area*, sited in the frontal lobes, and the PTO *association area*, made up from portions of the **P**arietal, **T**emporal and **O**ccipital lobes.

The frontal association area has eluded the efforts of scientists to determine with any precision the purposes of the tissues beyond their role in problem-solving and emotional behaviour. In adult humans, extensive damage to frontal tissue seems in most cases to have had little effect on performance in conventional intelligence tests. Hebb (1973), on the other hand, has noted that similar kinds of damage in children appear to have a lasting effect. It may be that frontal tissue is particularly relevant in establishing, in a diffuse manner, intellectual schemas in children. Damage at this stage will have a more potent, lasting effect on intelligent behaviour than when the schemas are well established and dependent on a wide distribution in the brain tissues. Psychologists seem agreed that the frontal lobes are connected with the processes involved in problem solving. Certainly the size of the frontal lobes seems to be proportional to the intellectual complexity of animals. But this by itself does not tell us much about the workings of the lobes.

Operations in the frontal region can affect personality. *Frontal leucotomy*, severing certain connections between the frontal lobes and radioactive 'seeds' planted in specific locations in this area of the brain have been used in the past to alleviate patients suffering from acute conditions such as depressive states.

The PTO association area governed by the thalamus covers those remaining portions of the brain, chiefly the parietal, temporal and occipital lobes not already mentioned. Damage to the cognitive association cortex results in speech and language deficiencies known collectively as *aphasias*. Sensory and motor aphasias are possible. On the sensory side we find *auditory aphasia* – an inability to understand speech – and *visual aphasia* (*alexia*), an inability to read or understand the written language. This does not mean that all children who cannot read suffer from brain damage in this region. Far from it, for there may be many other causes. Motor aphasia appears in three forms: *verbal* (cannot pronounce words), *manual* (cannot write) and *nominal* (cannot name objects).

# Brain size and laterality

## Size

Despite superficial appearances, the brain is **not** symmetrical either in size or function. Usually, the left hemisphere is larger and contains more long nerve fibres (and therefore more neurones) than the right hemisphere. On average, the male brain is larger and weighs more than the female brain. Overall body size does play some part, but even when size is controlled for (taking men and women of the same size or using the ratio of brain size to body size), male brains work out to be larger then those of females. Consequently, males possess four billion more neurons in the cortex region. In some females, parts of the corpus callosum are proportionally larger than in males, and there are correspondingly more nerve fibres connecting the cerebral hemispheres.

Whether these differences in size confer disadvantages or advantages has still to be worked out in detail, but, as we shall see in later sections, there appear to be correlations with performance in language processing (females are, on average, better than males) and visuo-spatial tasks (males, on average, do better). There are also differences in *empathizing* and *systemizing* skills (see the next section).

## Laterality

### Language functioning

Not only do the cerebral hemispheres differ in size, but also in function. Referring back to Figure 2.3(b) giving the left-hand view of the brain, three areas are identified *on this side only* which are related to the aphasic conditions mentioned previously. These are *Broca's* and

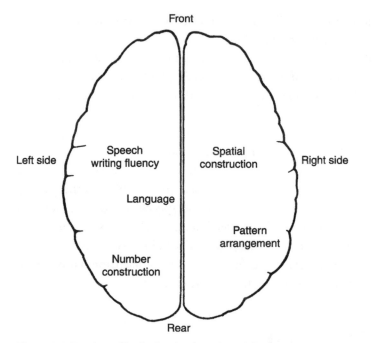

**Figure 2.4** Top view of brain showing lateral specialization.

*Wernicke's areas* and the *angular gyrus*. The top view in Figure 2.4, left side, translates these into the corresponding language functions associated with these areas. They are speech, writing, language usage and calculation. The same locations on the right side have different functions relating to spatial and pattern arrangements.

These lateral differences first came to light in the nineteenth century when the French physician Paul Broca in the 1860s noted that damage to a particular point on the left frontal lobe was accompanied by a speech disorder where people had great difficulty saying words. They tended to speak in a slow and tortuous way. Some words were omitted and others, like nouns, had plurals removed. But they could understand what others were saying. The disorder is sometimes referred to as *expressive aphasia* – disruption of articulation but not comprehension.

Carl Wernicke in Germany in the mid-1870s found that those who had damage to an area in the left temporal lobe could not understand words they had been able to before damage. Hearing words was not a problem, but understanding them and producing correct word order was difficult. This disorder is known as *receptive aphasia.*

He went on to produce a model of language functioning which was only slightly modified by Geschwind (1979; Geschwind and Galaburda 1987) to become the Wernicke-Geschwind model of language expression and understanding. The three areas of Broca, Wernicke and the angular gyrus are connected. There is also a connection between these and the motor, auditory and visual areas, depending on whether the language is being spoken, heard or seen. This distinction is very important when considering the findings of scanning techniques to be discussed presently. Broca's area stores the 'know-how' for articulating words and sends messages to that part of the motor region responsible for articulation (muscles of the lips, tongue and voice-box). Hence, any defect of the Broca area prevents proper expression of words (production). Wernicke's area stores auditory codes and word meanings. When someone else speaks, the auditory area is stimulated and the results are sent to Wernicke's area for interpretation (comprehension).

A popular theory is that the two operations just described can be linked together. If someone heard a spoken word and was asked to repeat it, the sequence would be:

> ear (to hear the word) → auditory area → Wernicke's area (interpretation code) → Broca's area (articulation code) → motor area → speech organs (to say the word).

The angular gyrus helps in the process of linking the written word (transmitted from the visual or occipital area) with the sound of the word stored in Wernicke's area. If someone is shown a written word and asked to repeat it, the sequence would be:

> eye (to see the word) → visual area → Wernicke's area (interpretation) → Broca's area → motor area → speech organs (to say the word).

In the next section we shall mention the new techniques of *scanning*. These have confirmed that Broca's and Wernicke's areas do not operate independently. Moreover, these researchers in neuroscience (Kutas 2000) no longer think in simplistic terms of Broca's area equating only with production or syntax or rule-based processes (e.g. regular verbs), and Wernicke's only with semantics or comprehension or memory store for exceptions (e.g. irregular verbs); they interact. Further, some workers (Deacon 1996) have suggested that both areas consist of sub-areas. As ever, the plot just gets more complex as our techniques get more refined (see Figure 2.5, page 37).

There is clear evidence for further differentiation of the right and left sides of the brain. Figure 2.4 shows the main areas located so far. The pioneer in this area of split-brain research is the 1981 Nobel prize winner R. W. Sperry (Springer and Deutsch 1997). Studies with brain-damaged patients, for example those in whom the corpus callosum had been severed, show other important lateral differentiations. The left side controls written and spoken language, spelling, reading and calculation; the right side controls spatial perceptual functions (patterns and geometric constructions). These different functions have also been confirmed using imaging techniques.

Penfield has used ESB methods to tap the temporal lobes. From his work, patients have claimed to experience vivid flashbacks to their past. He supposes this to be evidence that the brain retains in the interpretive cortex a record of conscious experience which can be revived randomly with electrical stimulation. Removal of the temporal cortex impairs visual learning where discrimination is required, for instance where coloured or shaped objects have become linked with food rewards in animal experiments. Symptoms similar to those described for a malfunctioning limbic system are also in evidence.

### Sex differences

A further differentiation of both sex and brain function was summarized by Baron-Cohen (2003). He distinguishes between *empathy* and *systemizing*. Empathizing is 'the drive to identify another person's emotions and thoughts and to respond to them with an appropriate emotion'. Systemizing is 'the drive to analyse, explore and construct a system. The systemizer intuitively figures out how things work, or extracts the underlying rules that govern the behaviour of a system'. He shows these to be normally distributed in the population, but *on average* females score higher on empathy and males higher on systemizing.

Using evidence from brain structure and functioning, genetics, sex hormone studies (particularly testosterone) and custom-made tests of empathy and systemizing, he concludes that 'the female brain is predominantly hard-wired for empathy. The male brain is predominantly hard-wired for understanding and building systems'.

The upshot of this work has implications for language, intelligence testing, giftedness and special needs (autism in particular), personality, academic achievement and choosing a career, all of which are mentioned later in the book.

# Discovering how the brain works

In the previous section, we took a brief look at some important structures in the brain and gave one or two ways in which scientists have studied how the brain functions. We shall now look at the range of common methods used by researchers in exploring brain-behaviour connections using both humans and animals as subjects (clearly summarized in Beatty 1995). Methods used are:

- Post-mortem operations following brain injury and disease
- Brain lesion analysis using animals
- Electrical activity of the brain
- Electrical stimulation of the brain
- Neurochemistry
- Brain imaging and scanning.

*Post-mortem operations* following the death of a brain-injured or brain-diseased patient can often reveal a link between behavioural patterns prior to death and the damaged portion of the brain. With conspicuous nerve tracts it is possible to trace the paths using careful dissection techniques. Hebb's work, to be mentioned in the section on intelligence (Hebb 1942) was amongst the first to show that substantial proportions of the frontal regions of the brain in adults could be removed without seriously diminishing intellectual performance, although the same is *not* true of children.

Using animals (or as an outcome of human brain surgery, injury or disease), portions of brain tissue can be affected or removed. Observations of specific aspects of behaviour are made before and after and any change in behaviour noted. In humans, this is often a chance affair depending on there being some useful pre-lesion data (a *lesion* is damage or injury to tissue). Destruction of tissue can also be done using chemicals, radioactive substances and hot or freezing probes. The use of these methods is referred to as *brain lesion analysis.*

*Electrical activity* in the brain is also used. As we saw above, the impulses in the nervous system are the outcome of electrical and chemical changes, and the surface of the brain exhibits voltage changes which can be picked up using small plate-like electrodes placed against the scalp. These voltage changes are translated and recorded as a wavy ink-line drawn by a pen moving along a rotating drum. The instrument is known as the *electroencephalogram* (EEG). The size of the waves and the number per unit of time are employed to estimate the level of arousal of the brain.

*Electrical stimulation of the brain* (ESB), where an external electrical impulse is passed through electrodes which have been implanted in specific regions of the brain, has been most successful in identifying functions of deep regions of the brain as well as in studying emotion in animals (Delgado 1987). Probes can be used, while an animal (or human) is conscious and without pain, to detect the activity of individual cells. This has been accomplished using microelectrodes small enough to penetrate single cells and capable of movements of a few thousandths of a millimetre. A new method by Claus *et al.* (1990) has been established using magnetic fields to induce electrical impulses in specific regions of the brain. The beauty of this method is that it does not require any contact with brain tissue and can be operated from outside the skull.

As the human body is physically a 'bag of chemicals', it would be surprising if chemicals could not be used to identify some behavioural functions. This has led to a branch of science called *neurochemistry*. For example, by introducing drugs into the body at specific points, indeed into one cell using tiny injection tubes if required, behaviour can be affected and observed.

A remarkable advance in recent years has been the technique known as *brain imaging* or *scanning*. It enables us to visualize the activities of the human brain. From this, we can discover more about how the active brain functions when a person is given certain tasks. The techniques have proved to be particularly helpful where animal research is of no assistance, such as the processes involved in using language or memory (Smith and Jonides 1994). Apart from pinpointing specific areas of the brain involved when we are cognitively busy and identifying individual difference in learning, these methods have confirmed that most activities in perception, attention, memory and language are not the property of a single area of the brain, but several. Further, the technique should help us to make early diagnoses of special educational needs.

Knowledge of the technicalities of the various sophisticated brain-scanning devices is not necessary. Sufficient to say that there are, broadly, three types of machine in common usage, abbreviated to CAT, PET and MRI. CAT means Computerized Axial Tomography; PET is Positron Emission Tomography; and MRI is Magnetic Resonance Imaging. *Tomo* is Greek for *slice* and that is what it is all about – taking pictures of successive slices of the brain as quickly as possible. Sometimes we see MRI shown as fMRI, the f representing *function*. The difference between MRI and fMRI is important because it distinguishes the use of imaging for *structural* or *functional* purposes. Neurologists investigating such diseases as Alzheimer's or brain tumours are concerned chiefly with structural differences and changes from normal. Functional techniques are concerned with what happens in the brain when given a task.

It is the functioning brain (fMRI scans) that is of particular interest to teachers. For example, when cognitive tasks are undertaken, the accompanying neural activity can be detected because there are corresponding blood flow changes in the brain. By taking many images of very thin slices, bit by bit across the whole or part of the brain, radioactivity, blood flow or magnetic field changes in the brain are detected. The results can be recomposed into two- or three-dimensional images of the working brain as X-rays, photographs or on a computer screen. Note that often more than one area in the brain is involved and the activity may not necessarily be bilateral in the brain. We noticed in Figure 2.4 that many locations do not function identically in each hemisphere of the brain. Figure 2.5 is a sketch of a slice down the left side of the brain through the areas involved in reading (motor, temporal, parietal and visual). What happens is that the blood flow is affected by the action of reading and this creates 'hot spots' picked up on radiographic plates or computer screens. Neurological texts often show these in shades of red, yellow and green.

These techniques are widely used in medicine for locating and identifying problems in the brain such as tumours, shrinkage and blood clots. But there is growing interest in the application of neuroscience in the processes of learning and teaching (Goswami 2004; Hall 2005). For example, Blakemore and Frith (2000, and website reference) at the Institute of Cognitive Neuroscience, London wrote a comprehensive consultation document on ways in which educators and neuroscientists might collaborate on research problems of interest to both parties. A TLRP (Teaching and Learning Research Programme of the ESRC) report on the document contains several important questions relating to education (see website reference for Blakemore and Frith).

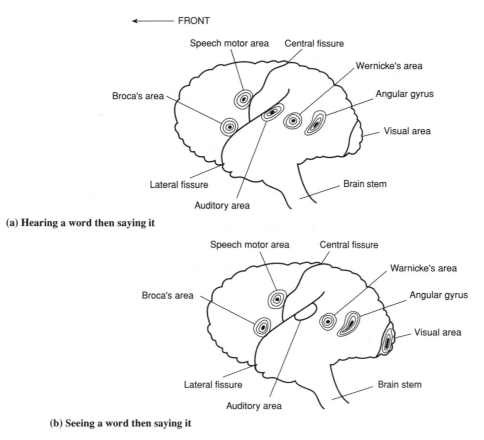

(a) **Hearing a word then saying it**

(b) **Seeing a word then saying it**

**Figure 2.5** Diagrammatic left side view of 'hot spot' areas seen in scans of the functioning brain.

# Memory and the brain

Memory is one of those eye-catching subjects of interest to most of us and its study has been the centre of considerable research effort over the years. At a simple, but inaccurate level, the workings of the brain in the recall of information have been likened to a computer's storage banks. The analogy breaks down when we realize that information stored in a computer has a precise location and is retrieved in exactly the same form each time. 'Information' storage in the brain seems to be much more diffuse and can be of different natures, as in short-term or long-term memory (see also Broadbent's filter theory in Chapter 3).

The brain operates in complex physical and chemical ways. Questions such as: How and where are memories stored? How long do memories last? Are different sorts of information stored in different places in the brain? These are the core research themes at present. Chapters 3 and 7 include further discussion of these questions. For the moment, our concern will be to indicate any physiological support for locations in the brain of (i) the processes of learning and memory, (ii) long- and short-term memory and (iii) storage of different kinds of information.

The early classical experiments of Lashley (1929) in the 1920s were unsuccessful in finding locations. He concluded that the whole brain was involved (and that learning should be impossible!). Using brain-scanning techniques, we now know that learning new information (encoding) involves activity in the right hemisphere, and recalling past memories (retrieval) involves the left hemisphere (Shallice 1988, Shallice *et al.* 1994).

Different locations for the operation of long- and short-term memory are now established (Maguire *et al.* 1996, 2000). We now know that if the hippocampus (part of the limbic system) is destroyed, individuals can no longer lay down long-term memories. This is especially true of spatial memories. Memories previous to damage are preserved and short-term memories such as recalling a telephone number for a few minutes are still possible, but lasting learning is not possible without the agency of the hippocampus. We have also seen various aphasic conditions when the PTO association area is damaged and the impairment of visual learning when the temporal cortex is removed.

The third area of interest poses the question of whether there are varying kinds of information which are dealt with in different parts of and in varying ways by the brain. It seems that retaining facts, for example, what is printed on this page, requires a different kind of memory function to retaining skills, for example, motor learning such as driving a car. We shall return to this when discussing *explicit* and *implicit* memory in Chapter 7.

Another intriguing advance is the prospect of a chemical explanation of learning and memory. The electrical activity in the brain can be detected using the EEG, and there is no doubt about chemical processes occurring in the synaptic clefts. Further, when animals are taught to run a maze and the animals' temperatures are lowered to halt the electrical activity, the animals can still remember how to complete the maze task. This has forced scientists to conclude that memory storage is likely to depend on chemical as well as electrical factors. Baldwin, at Cambridge, has injected into the brains of goats drugs contrived to have a disruptive effect on electrical activity; yet this has no effect on short-term memory, and thus strengthens the case for a chemical theory of learning. Also, research into the role of the hippocampus has shown the importance of the neuroreceptor NMDA (N-methyl-D-aspartate) in establishing increased responsiveness of neurons in the process of forming new memories (well summarized in Carlson 2005).

## Emotion and the brain

You have just settled down in the carriage of a train. The train begins to move off and suddenly you notice your suitcase standing on the platform. Intense feelings quickly take over, along with a sudden burst of action or frozen dread. Our language is rich with expressions one might use to describe your state of mind and body – astonishment, alarm, panic, despair and many others. In cases of this kind we are said to be experiencing emotions. Disgust, joy, hopefulness, pity and a whole range of experiences from highly pleasant to deeply unpleasant sensations are described, although the hard evidence from physiology or psychology for the separate existence of these supposed emotional states is not yet available. One simple classification by Watson (1931) embraced fear, rage (anger) and love. More recently, some (Ekman *et al.* 1983; Levenson *et al.* 1992) have postulated that, as neonates, we experience only excitement, which becomes differentiated as we grow older into positive emotions (such as happiness, surprise, disgust) and negative emotions (such as anger, fear and sadness).

All these reactions, whether we attempt to distinguish different patterns of response for dissimilar circumstances or not, have their beginnings in internal physiological changes assisted by the sympathetic nervous system and endocrine secretions. A general definition of emotion would be that it is a condition giving rise to 'physiological and psychological responses that influence perception, learning and performance' (Murray 1964). The endocrine glands secrete special chemicals called hormones into the bloodstream. The glands are ductless; in other words, they pass their secretions directly into the bloodstream without the aid of tubular ducts (in contrast, say, to the salivary glands, which secrete through ducts into the mouth). Deficiencies or excesses of the hormonal secretions give rise to various diseases, the nature of which can be read about in any standard biology textbook containing human physiology.

## The important glands, their position and the function of their hormones

- Pituitary suspended beneath the hypothalamus controls the action of the endocrine system
- Thyroid in the front of the neck secretes thyroxine, which aids in growth and metabolic control
- Adrenals near each kidney continuously secrete adrenaline and noradrenaline to mobilize various organs already mentioned in connection with the ANS; testosterone is also secreted which explains why females produce it; adrenals also exude excessive quantities of the hormones in emergency and emotive states
- Pancreas level with kidneys secretes insulin, which is responsible for sugar control in the body; the well-known disease of diabetes occurs when insufficient insulin is secreted, therefore, the body must be supplied artificially by injecting insulin into the bloodstream
- Gonads the sex organs of testes – secrete testosterone, and the ovaries secrete oestrogen and progesterone; these secretions control the appearance and maintenance of secondary sexual characteristics such as face, chest and pubic hair, voice breaking and body stature in men, and the menstrual cycle and breast formation in women

From the middle of the nineteenth century a classical interpretation of emotive activity and responses was that, after a stimulus which is interpreted as threatening or pleasing has been received, the body reacts via the nervous and endocrine systems and these give rise to feelings of emotion. Fear, anger, joy and tenderness were said to be the outcome of body secretions and nerve action. Fear was then made manifest by increased breathing and heartbeat, drying of the mouth, hair on end and so forth.

Lange and James (1922) contested this hypothesis independently and suggested quite the reverse. They maintained that the outward reaction of the body to an emotive stimulus – running, crying, fighting – gave rise to sensations of fear, anger, etc., expressed in the well-known James–Lange theory of emotion. James, summarizing his views, says 'we are afraid because we run, we do not run because we are afraid'.

Cannon (1929) provided evidence to confound the James–Lange theory. When the nerve connections between the organs influenced by the autonomic system and brain are severed, organisms still show fear, rage, affection and other emotional states. The Cannon–Bard theory (again, independent investigators coming to much the same conclusions from their researches) was proposed. According to this, the impulses from incoming stimuli pass through the thalamus, sensitizing it and passing the impulses to the cortex, organs and muscles. The cortex input represents conscious knowledge of an emotive state and the feelings which accompany emotions. The organs and muscles would be responding at the same time.

A more recent theory, the Schachter–Singer theory, has been proposed by Schachter (1971), who believes that emotion results from the interaction of cognitive factors and physiological arousal. Feedback to the brain from physiological activity sets up an un-differentiated state of arousal. The emotion felt by the person depends on the circum-stances existing at the time and the source which the person believes to be the cause of the activity. Past experience is thought to play a part in 'labelling' the source. Thus, if a person insults you, you become aroused and from previous experience you associate anger (or embarrassment) with the feeling of arousal. This view has its critics (Reisenzein 1983).

*Appraisal* theories (Ellsworth 1991) are the most recent addition to a growing list of views about the origins of emotive behaviour. Broadly, they propose that people appraise situations and not their physiological state. For example, one of the theories suggests that an emotion such as fear might arise from appraising a situation as threatening; again, disgust might arise from viewing a situation as horrific. One clear advantage of this theory is its allowance for cultural differences. For instance, members of some cultures have a fear of dogs, which they regard as disease-ridden and dangerous. As another example, members of other cultures might feel disgust at being offered a leaf full of fried caterpillars for lunch.

From our viewpoint, it is probably more helpful to think of emotional behaviour in terms of three dimensions in preference to numerous specific states which are loosely tied

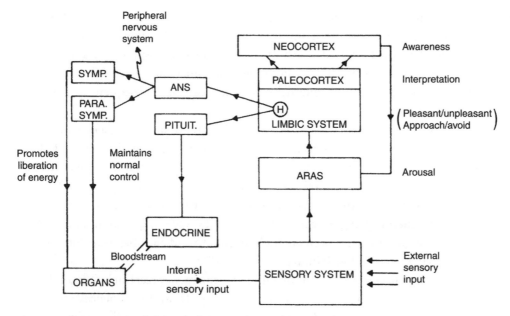

**Figure 2.6** Representational diagram of emotional arousal sequence (H =hypothalamus).

in our minds to ill-defined terms which exist in our language to describe our feelings. The three dimensions proposed by Murray (1964) are intensity, pleasantness-unpleasantness and approach-avoidance. Intensity is related to the level of arousal and is widely recognized by psychologists (see the section on drive and performance in Chapter 8). The second dimension helps to remind us of the infinite variety of experiences, from complete ecstasy to utter terror (while being vaguely reminiscent of the hedonistic theory of man as a pleasure-seeking, pain-avoiding animal). The third dimension concerns the feelings of attraction towards, or repulsion from, emotively charged objects or situations. Fear arising from unpleasant experience may give rise to either fight or flight.

Returning to the place of the brain in emotional response, we know that two systems are involved. One is the limbic system, including parts of the thalamus and hypothalamus, and the inner portion of the cortex (old cortex or paleocortex). Stimulation of this system, as we have observed, is associated with fear, anger, aggression and many other reactions. The other is the ascending reticular activating system (ARAS) in the brain stem, already identified earlier in the chapter as responsible for arousing the cortex and moderating messages from the sensory systems. Its function is not directive, but energizing.

The sequence of events might be easier to follow by looking at Figure 2.6. A sensory stimulus is received by receptor organs (bottom right in the figure) and transmitted to the brain via the ARAS. Arousal of the latter is noted by the cortex and also by the hypothalamus in the limbic system. As the hypothalamus transmits to the ANS and pituitary gland, the sympathetic and endocrine systems are alerted. Organs which might aid in escape by providing additional sources of energy are activated, and this is recorded by internal sensory systems. Thus we are made aware not only of the external stimulus, but also of our internal body reactions. The exact point at which the body as a whole responds by approaching or avoiding the stimulus is not fully understood, but it may take place when the ARAS is arousing the cortex along with internal emotional reactions subsequent to ANS and pituitary stimulation.

The utility of emotional states is clear. In a stressful situation – taking a driving test or going into one's first classroom full of children to be taught – increased supplies of blood sugar are released from the liver to provide extra fuel for physical and mental activity. Hormones are also released to convert fats and proteins into sugar. Typical reactions to threatening stimuli begin to appear, such as increased heartbeat and breathing (to supply the muscles with energy-giving oxygen). Other activities, such as digestion, decline. The mouth dries up to increase the capacity of both the mouth and air tubes. Capillaries in the skin contract to lessen blood loss if injury occurs.

All these reactions have survival value by aiding the 'emergency reaction' (Cannon 1929). They provide the extra resources to fight or flee. Many stressful experiences cannot be reacted to physically and prolonged stress of this kind can lead to serious physical and psychological disturbances (ulcers, cognitive impairment, lack of confidence). But not all stressful experiences end up as harmful. Apart from providing useful supplies of energy, stress in small, intermittent doses can be of benefit in producing, over time, *stress tolerance*, a 'hardening' process which enables a person to become toughened to further stresses of the same or similar kind (Dienstbier 1989).

A discussion of stress in teaching will be taken up in Chapter 8.

# Heredity and environments

A question which intrigues us all is the relative influence of inherited characteristics and life's experiences when they interact to make us what we are. All manner of terms have been given to the two contenders – nature and nurture, inherited and acquired, heredity and environment. The fact that they are both involved in the vast majority of human attributes is no longer questioned, but the extent of each contribution is still in dispute. The reason is that it is so hard to measure the proportion. The following paragraphs expand a little on the issues.

## Inheritance

Starting with heredity, an important biological fact is that the human race has a vast pool of characteristics, which can be transmitted from generation to generation during the process of reproducing its kind. In our discussions of such complex human qualities as intelligence and personality we will frequently have cause to wonder to what extent the potential for individual characteristics is inherited and to what extent the life experiences of individuals shape the outcome of these inherited properties. At this stage it is necessary to give readers a brief idea of the biological mechanisms of inheritance.

It is common knowledge that the basic structures for reproducing human characteristics are the germ cells (female ovum, or egg, and male sperm). Within each is found a nucleus which contains the *chromosome*s (46 in the normal cell, 23 contributed from each parent). These are long, thread-like structures, chains of chemicals, consisting of units from which all our inherited characteristics are derived. Every chromosome is numbered.

These basic units for the transmission of characteristics from parent to offspring are called *genes*. Using powerful chemical and electron-microscope techniques, biologists have found that each gene has a unique chemical composition, with a specific purpose and location along the chromosome. A worldwide research, the Human Genome Project, dedicated to mapping the entire gene function and its location on every chromosome, has recently completed its task (a useful website for the Human Genome Project is http://www.genome.gov/10001772). What a job, as there are upwards of 30, 000 genes in the human cell (at least 700 genes on each chromosome). The mechanism of gene reproduction and interaction is a rather detailed biological phenomenon which need not concern us here, but we do need to discuss the broad ideas underlying the transmission of physical and mental characteristics.

Some traits relate to one gene only. Others are related to several genes – *polygenic* traits. For example, blood type and many diseases are 'monogenic'. Height, eye colour, intelligence and personality are examples of polygenic traits. Some genes are *dominant* and some are *recessive*. So if one parent contributed a gene for brown eyes (dominant colour) and the other parent's contribution was for blue eyes (recessive colour), that child would have brown eyes. Note that the offspring do not exhibit a mixture of the parents' gene contributions. In other words, if dad contributes a brown-eye gene and mum a blue-eye gene, the son or daughter will *not* inherit a mixture – hazel eyes. However, as eye colour is polygenic, there would be several bits of jigsaw to piece together to determine the final eye colour of the offspring.

Each parent carries in the germ cells certain possibilities for a given characteristic which he or she, in turn, has inherited from parents. So there is some element of luck attached to the specific characteristic which has been 'drawn' from the parents' gene pools. As indicated above, should the contributions from the parents conflict, the dominant gene prevails. At the same time, the child now possesses the dominant gene from one side *and* the recessive gene from the other. When the child is about to pass on the characteristics, once more there will be two possibilities (see Bee and Boyd, 2004, for a clear description of inheritance).

One way of regarding the process of evolution and inheritance is to think of the genes, with their enormous potential for variety, as a *population*. Within this population we would find a pool of characteristics for a given trait ranging between extremes. For example, high to low reading disability, length of limbs or body (polygenic, by the way) or hair colour, from black (dominant) to blond (recessive). Each new generation brings with it a selection from this gene pool supplied by parents, grandparents, etc. Strains which are beneficial to survival will continue, while other strains which are maladaptive will die out. This is, crudely, the Darwinian theory of the survival of the fittest, by which the natural environment will support only those best suited to that environment. This reshuffling of gene content is one way of producing variety in a species.

There is a second method called *mutation*, which arises from sudden, often accidental, alterations in the gene structure and gives rise to unique characteristics. Mutations are known to be caused by exposure to radioactive fall-out, and many examples have been reported from the A-bomb aftermath in Japan. Fortunately, in well-established species, most mutations do not survive.

An intriguing example of positive adaptation by a harmful mutant is provided by the resistance of certain strains of bacteria to streptomycin. Normally, a population of a bacterium called *E. coli* can be destroyed when exposed to streptomycin. However, very occasionally a mutant appears which is quite resistant. The fact that it is a mutant strain and not a question of the bacteria becoming resistant has been shown quite conclusively. Flu epidemics arise from mutant strains (witness the bird flu with the possibility of transferring to humans).

There are now many well-established anomalies in both physical and mental characteristics arising from faulty chromosomal and gene structure. Several are of concern to teachers (Atkinson and Hornby 2002). *Attention deficit hyperactivity disorder* (ADHD) *Down's syndrome, autism, Obsessive-Compulsive disorder* (OCD) and *Asperger's syndrome* (AS) all have a genetic component and teachers will meet up with cases during their careers. For example, Down's syndrome, caused by an anomaly in chromosome 21, is well known and exhibits several distinct facial and body features, such as upward-slanting eyelids, conspicuous tongue and unusual fingerprints. There are frequently intellectual disadvantages, some quite severe. This connection between chromosomal defect and mental ability is used as evidence in support of the argument that the gene pool contains a factor (or factors) relating to human intelligence. Another piece of evidence comes from the study of autism, a polygenic disorder. Bailey *et al.* (1998) showed that chromosome 7 is linked to the characteristics associated with autism (e.g., impairment of empathic, social and communication skills plus obsessional behaviour), yet the cognitive component could range widely from seriously impaired to very bright. This issue, termed the *autism spectrum*, is taken up in Chapter 11. In reading ability, Plomin *et al.* (2001) say that 'different genetic factors affect reading disability and reading ability' (p. 146). Reading disability appears to be associated with chromosomes 6 and 15. Reading ability, on the other hand, overlaps with general cognitive ability and is much more widely dispersed amongst the chromosomes.

## Environments – physical and social

Another fact is that the surrounding conditions within which a person grows, both physical and social, can have lasting effects on his or her development and behaviour. From Freudian child-rearing practices to behaviourist conditioning, the emphasis is on environmental influences. Even the most extreme reductionists (Chapter 1) accept that environmental changes are influential. As teachers, we can only do our job if we believe that education, formal or informal, is all about creating environments which can have a lasting beneficial effect on the development of those we teach; so teachers are insatiable environmentalists.

But environments are there from the start. Genes and chromosomes exist in environments. They persist the egg and sperm, and and into the womb, and thence to the outside world where a vast array of environments await the neonate.

Two commonly used biological terms are *genotype* and *phenotype*. The *genotype* refers to the precise genetic characteristics of individuals that are transferred in the genes of the parents at fertilization. The many human characteristics transferred from generation to generation by the genes are the biological blueprints of physical, cognitive (mental processes) and affective (emotions and feelings) features.

The *phenotype* results from the interaction between the genotype and environmental effects from conception onwards. Thus, by the time the child is born, he or she has already experienced environmental influences on phenotypic development.

Inherited physical, cognitive and affective characteristics (such as intelligence and personality) differ in the extent to which they can be examined. With the help of scanning techniques, physical changes can now be observed in the womb from the moment of conception, but not so with cognitive and affective changes. However, Mother Nature has provided several natural research projects of which the comparison of identical twins reared together and apart is one. The impact of accidental damage to specific parts of the human body and brain is another.

The concept of the phenotype is frequently misused, and confused with *acquired* characteristics. A young plant which is undernourished or short of light or water does not grow into a healthy plant, so the genotypic potential has been distorted by environmental conditions to give a phenotype. The essential features of the genotype are still there, however, and a weedy, undernourished cabbage can still be distinguished from a weedy, undernourished pea. Similarly, 'undernourished' children, exposed to physical and/or mental impoverishment, are less likely to realise their full potential.

On the other hand, we can acquire certain skills, habits or physical injuries during life which are 'one off'. They die with us and are not transmitted to our children. Similarly, if peas from the pod of our undernourished pea plant are planted and reared properly, they will grow into healthy peas. According to conventional genetics, if we cut off the tails of successive generations of mice, we would *never*, no matter how many times we did it, produce a tailless generation. This can happen only by mutation (that is, distortion of the genetic material).

However, a new branch of genetics, *epigenetics*, has raised doubts about the infallibility of the expression 'we do not inherit acquired characteristics' (to get the flavour and some information about epigenetics, put this term into a web search). Research involving rare medical conditions (Angelman's syndrome/Prader-Willi syndrome), famine, high stress (post-traumatic stress disorder) and exposure to chemical toxins such as fertilizers has shown that environmental exposure information can be passed on in the genes. If these traumatic events occur at critical periods in the formation of eggs or sperms, the relevant genes can be 'switched off'. The effects are sex-linked because the traumatic event usually happens to either a female (at egg formation in the mother's womb) or male (puberty), but not both. Angelman's syndrome results when gene 15 in the mother's egg is 'switched'. Prader-Willi syndrome involves the same gene, but in the father's sperm. For females the critical period is the last third of pregnancy. For males it is the time immediately before puberty.

The idea that there is a genetic memory (*genomic imprinting*) for stressful environmental events, captured in the egg or sperm, then carried to the next, and possibly a subsequent, generation has serious implications for genetics, psychology and education. To begin with, the 30,000 genes now become a fraction of the story. If they can be switched on or off by environmental conditions, there is a consequent increase in, and explanation for, the variability of human characteristics. Metaphorically, you are what your mother, father, grandmother, grandfather, etc. ate and not just what you eat. Research into high-profile, world catastrophes seems to support the drift of epigenetic theories. Women involved in the Twin Towers bombing who were pregnant at the time, and survivors of the holocaust and their offspring have been the subjects of these investigations. At present, the implications for education remain largely at a descriptive level – 'why' children are as they are and not 'what' we can do about it.

## The impact of nature and nurture (Plomin *et al.* 2001 and Plomin 2004)

The areas of psychology associated with genetics is called *behavioural genetics* (Plomin *et al.* 2001) and we shall meet up with the subject again in discussions of intelligence and personality. There is appreciable discord amongst psychologists as to the relative influences of genetics and the environment. At present, the prevailing thoughts are that whatever the relative effects of these two sources, the genetic components in subjects of interest to psychologists are predominantly dependent on several rather than one gene – polygenic. Therefore the inheritance of intelligence is far subtler than that of some physical characteristics. The environment also plays a significant part in providing numerous alternative scenarios within which intellectual potential is allowed to develop. This point will be taken up in Chapter 9.

## Sex and gender

It is important to distinguish between two commonly used terms in psychology – sex and gender. Technically, the term *sex* refers to the biological differences between male and female, and according to some specialists (e.g., Baron-Cohen 2003) is defined at various levels. The levels are:

- Genetic
- Gonadal
- Genital
- Brain type
- Sex-type behaviour.

The most basic level is *genetic* which results from the combination of 'X' and 'Y' chromosomes (23 pairs in each cell, making 46 in all). In the 23rd chromosome of females, the pair consists of two 'X' chromosomes, which give X or X on division. Males have an XY chromosome giving X or Y on division. The male's sperm dictates the sex because if his Y half meets up with either of the female's X chromosomes, the baby will be a boy. The X combinations all lead to female children. So, statistically, there should be as many girls as boys. However, the acidity or alkalinity of fluids within a female vagina when sperm is present can affect the survival prospects of male X or Y carrying sperms (see Bee and Boyd, 2004, for a good description). At present it seems that the proportion of females to males in Britain is 51: 49.

Each of the next four levels sees overlapping of male and female characteristics. So to varying extents we all carry characteristics typical of both sexes – rather like two overlapping normal distributions of maleness and femaleness.

A good example is the *gonadal* sex level, defined by males carrying, predominantly, hormone-producing testes (testosterone) and females, predominantly, the hormone-producing ovaries (oestrogen and progesterone). However, from medical conditions of abnormally high or low hormone presence, or injections of male or female hormones, corresponding variations in brain type (see next paragraph) and sex-type behaviour appear. Adrenal androgen, a testosterone-related substance, is secreted by the adrenal glands in both sexes and thus it is present in females.

*Genital* sex is defined by males having a penis and females a vagina. The *brain type* level distinguishes males, who, on average, have stronger systemizing skills than females, and females who, on average, have stronger empathizing skills than males. The final level, *sex-typical behaviour*, according to Baron-Cohen (2003), builds up from differences in all the foregoing levels. Males, for instance, with predominantly systemizing brains, are more inclined to 'analyse, explore and construct a system'. They like 'things' and facts and get turned on by 'gadgets, CD collections and football league results'. Some research has shown that testosterone aids spatial awareness. Females, on the other hand, with predominantly empathizing brains, are more interested and able to 'identify another person's emotions and thoughts, and to respond to them with an appropriate emotion'. They are more likely to get involved in 'caring for friends, worrying about their feelings and striving for intimacy'.

They are tuned in to people and relationships. It is important to emphasize that these are generalizations; 'on average' males and females exhibit these differences.

A Darwinian view would be that these distinctions between the male and female have survival value and may be regarded as strengths for the continuation of our species. Women, on average, do better in some things (e.g., caring) and men, on average, do better in others (e.g., planning, exploring and mastering the environment) and this division of human activity has contributed to the survival of the species in the environments into which we have been born – so far. Our inventions in the future may make the differences less relevant, but for the moment, the differences are still critical.

In addition to biologically determined differences between the sexes, societies superimpose roles and expectations for each sex. *Gender* is the term we now use for the identity associated with male or female behaviour and is socially rather than biologically defined, although it may have its origins in the latter. The distinction between sex-typical behaviour, as discussed above, and gender identity behaviour is blurred. Theoretically, sex-typical behaviour results from internal physical differences (we cannot help it), whereas our perceived gender is dictated by the roles expected of us in our native culture. Given a completely free hand, girls tend to choose dolls and boys to choose weapons or construction kits. Is this a biologically-based sex preference, a culturally determined choice, or both? Discuss! The evidence is strong for a biological starting point strengthened by cultural role modelling (Baron-Cohen 2003).

Whatever the sources of these sex and gender differences, they exist. Teachers have an obligation to ensure that they do not prejudice or jeopardize the life-chances of their students. We have to be aware of the need to compensate in our educational provision whenever necessary. As we shall see, the brain-type sex differences can account for variations in, for example, school performance or occupational choice and consequently require skilful teaching strategies to enable boys and girls to realize their full potential.

## Maturation

The nature/nurture, heredity/environment distinction has an added complication – maturation. Part of our inheritance involves a systematic growth of physical and mental characteristics. Maturational changes are going to take place, whatever. It is the circumstances in which they take place that govern the final form of the characteristics. The origins of these changes are separated into *maturation* and *learning*. Maturation is the term we use to describe the inherent tendency in all members of a species to grow and age in an ordered sequence of events. The changes should occur in the absence of experience, although adverse or beneficial experiences (environment) can affect the maturational process – and this is called *learning*. Witness the steady increase in the average height of humans during the past century, particularly females. This has resulted, amongst other things, from improved diets and healthcare methods. We have learned from our researches that diet and healthcare enable us to come nearer to our potential best.

*Learning* is the process which helps in our striving towards our maturational best. It results from environmental influences, that is, influences external to us which can affect the extent of physical, intellectual and emotional development. And knowledge of these influences is the primary concern of teachers. The combination of maturational 'givens' and learning 'opportunities' make us what we are.

The physical growth pattern of children is a clear example of maturation. However, there are other kinds of development said to be maturational. Skill in locomotion, which starts with crawling and ends in walking, is one. Gesell and Ilg (1949) studied the motor development of children and postulated several landmarks of motor competence in normal development. Norms of physical development along with information about differences occurring between children from dissimilar socioeconomic backgrounds are now established (Bee and Boyd 2004, Davie *et al.* 1972). Regarding these backgrounds, Davie and his colleagues concluded that equality of educational opportunity cannot be achieved solely by improving our educational institutions. The child is often handicapped as a result of basic educational deficits at home before ever reaching school age.

There are dozens of general and specific texts on child development including cognitive, social, emotional, moral and aesthetic as well as physical aspects. For an overview, see a standard text such as Bee and Boyd, 2004.

## Summary

The mind has puzzled philosophers and psychologists for centuries. Study of the functioning of the central nervous system implies an assumption that we may discover some biological explanations for our behaviour, although this idea should be tempered with the possibility that our behaviour is more than the sum of the actions of our physiological parts, and that conscious life is more than an epiphenomenon arising from body functioning.

Certainly the important body mechanisms which bring us into sensory contact with, and help us to respond to, our surroundings are located in the central nervous system. A brief description of the structure of the CNS was given to illustrate the nature of the systems. In this description we looked at the receptor, transmission and brain processes, relating them to activities of general interest to teachers.

Several sections were concerned with behaviour and the most significant parts of the brain. Whilst this has no direct bearing on the day-to-day workings of an educational system, nevertheless it provides a background of factual information which fits the physical body into a behavioural context. Some of this may be quite difficult for the non-biologist, though an attempt should be made to understand the functioning of the brain stem, homeostasis and the hypothalamus, the higher regions of the brain including aphasic conditions, bilaterality and sex-linked functioning of the brain.

Memory and brain action involved a somewhat speculative look at current theories intended to give the reader a glimpse into the research of the near future. The subject of memory comes up again in Chapters 3 and 7. Emotion and the brain were dealt with from the point of view of the arousal sequence involving hypothalamus action and the organization of the sympathetic and parasympathetic nervous systems. The topic of arousal appears again in Chapters 3 and 8.

With the introduction of refined scanning techniques of the active human brain, it is now possible to map the actions during various processes of direct interest to teachers such as memory, use of language, emotion. But many questions are going to involve collaboration between the neuroscientists and educators, questions such as: Is accelerated teaching a neurologically damaging or beneficial activity? What are the critical and sensitive periods for particular subjects? What are the effects on brain development of serious emotional disturbance?

The final two sections on heredity and environments and maturation were included in this 'biological' chapter as a basis for later elaboration of such important considerations as intelligence, personality, cognitive and language development and the earlier theories of vocational development.

## Tutorial enquiry and discussion

(a) Read the relevant parts of Bee and Boyd (2004) and Davie *et al.* (1972) and use these as starting points to consider the physical growth, sensory development and the use made of medical services in relation to socioeconomic background.

(b) Discuss in seminar the distinction between maturation and learning. Of what significance is this distinction to the teacher?

(c) Discuss with tutors the action that must be taken when a teacher finds children in the classroom who suffer from sensory and related defects. Which professionals should be approached and how are they accessed?

(d) What questions should teachers be asking the neuroscientists to investigate (Blakemore and Frith 2000)? A report obtained using the website information at the end of the chapter raises questions such as 'What is the neurological basis of cognitive development stages?', 'What is the effect of experience on neurological development?', 'what specific neural structures are implicated in specific skills, strategies and aptitudes?', 'What are the neurological substrates of creativity, multiple intelligences and aptitudes?'

(e) How important is a consideration of sex differences in the education of children at your chosen age group (see Baron-Cohen 2003)?

## References

Aleksander, I. (1996), *Impossible Minds*. London: Imperial College Press.

Aleksander, I. (2000), *How to Build a Mind*. London: Weidenfeld and Nicolson.

Anand, B. D. and Brobeck, J. R. (1951), 'Hypothalamic control of food intake', *Yale Journal of Biological Medicine*, 24, 123–40.

Atkinson, M. and Hornby, G. (2002), *Mental Health Handbook for Schools*. London: Routledge Falmer.

Bailey, A., Le Couteur, A. and Rutter, M. and the International Molecular Genetic Consortium (1998), 'A full genome screen for autism with evidence for linkage to a region on chromosome 7q'. *Human Molecular Genetics*, 7, 571–8.

Baron-Cohen, S. (2003), *The Essential Difference: Men, Women and the Extreme Male Brain*. London: Allan Lane (and Penguin Books).

Beatty, Jackson (1995), *Principles of Behavioral Neuroscience*. Madison: Brown and Benchmark.

Bee, H. and Boyd, D. (2004), *The Developing Child* (10th edn). Boston, MA: Pearson and AB.

Bexton, W. H., Heron, W. and Scott, T. H. (1954), 'Effect of decreased variation in the sensory environment', *Canadian Journal of Psychology*, 8, 70–6.

Blakemore, Sarah-Jayne and Frith, U. (2000), *The Implications of Recent Developments in Neuroscience for Research on Teaching and Learning*. London: Institute of Cognitive Neuroscience.

Cannon, W. B. (1929), *Bodily Changes in Pain, Hunger, Fear and Rage*. New York: Appleton-Century-Crofts.

Carlson, N. R. (2005), *Foundations of Physiological Psychology* (6th edn). Boston: Allyn and Bacon.

Carroll, D. (1984), *Biofeedback in Practice*. London: Longman.

Carver, R. P. (1990), *Reading Rate: A Review of Research and Theory*. London: Academic Press.

Claus, D., Murray, N. M. F., Spitzer, A. and Flügel, D. (1990), 'The influence of stimulus type on the magnetic excitation of nerve structures', *Electroencephaly and Clinical Neurophysiology*, 75, 342–9.

Davie, R., Butler, N. and Goldstein, H. (1972), *From Birth to Seven*. London: Longman.

Deacon, T.W. (1996) 'Prefrontal cortex and symbolic learning: why a brain capable of language evolved only once', in B. M. Velichkovsky and D. M. Rumbaugh (eds), *Communication Meaning*. Mahuah, NJ: Erlbaum.

Delgado, J. M. R. (1969), *Physical Control of the Mind*. New York: Harper Row.

Delgado, J. M. R. (1987), 'Electrical stimulation of the brain', in G. Adelman (ed.), *Encyclopedia of Neuroscience* (Vol. 1). Boston: Birkhauser.

Dienstbier, R. A. (1989), 'Arousal and physiological toughness: implications for mental and physical health', *Psychological Review*, 96, 84–100.

Eccles, J. C. (1953), *The Neurophysiological Basis of the Mind*. Oxford: Oxford University Press.

Eccles, J. C. (1978), *The Understanding of the Brain* (2nd edn). New York: McGraw-Hill.

Ekman, P., Levenson, R. W. and Friesen, W. V. (1983), 'Autonomic nervous system activity distinguishes among emotions', *Science*, 221, 1208–10.

Ellsworth, P. (1991), 'Some implications of cognitive appraisals on theories of emotion', in K. T. Strongman (ed.), *International Review of Studies on Emotion* (Vol. 1). New York: Wiley.

Franklin, J. (1987), *Molecules of the Mind*. New York: Atheneum.

Geschwind, N. (1979), 'Specializations of the human brain', *Scientific American*, 241, 180–99.

Geschwind, N. and Galaburda, A. M. (1987), *Central Lateralization*. Cambridge, MA: MIT Press.

Gesell, G. A. and Ilg, F. L. (1949), *Child Development*. New York: Harper.

Goswami, U. (2004), 'Neuroscience and education', *British Journal of Educational Psychology*, 74, 1–14.

Hall, J. (2005), *A Review of the Contribution of Brain Science to Teaching and Learning*. SCRE Research Report No. 121. Edinburgh: The Scottish Council for Research in Education.

Hebb, D. O. (1942), 'The effect of early and later brain injury upon test scores, and the nature of normal adult intelligence', *Proceedings of the American Philosophical Society*, 85, 275–92.

Hebb, D. O. (1973), *The Organization of Behavior* (9th impression). New York: Wiley.

Highfield, R. and Coveney, P. (1995), *Frontiers of Complexity*. London: Faber.

Horne, J. A. (1988), *Why We Sleep: The Functions of Sleep in Humans and Other Mammals*. Oxford: Oxford University Press.

Karni, A., Tanne, D., Rubenstein, B. S., Askenasy, J. J. M. and Sagi, D. (1994), 'Dependence on REM sleep of overnight improvement of a perceptual skill', *Science*, 265, 679–82.

Kruk, Z. L. and Pycock, C. J. (1991), *Neurotransmitters and Drugs* (3rd edn). London: Chapman and Hall.

Kutas, Marta (2000), 'Current thinking on language structures', in M. S. Gazzaniga (ed.), *Cognitive Neuroscience: A Reader*. Malden, MA. and Oxford: Blackwell.

Lange, C. and James, C. (1922), *The Emotions*. Baltimore: Williams and Wilkins.

Lashley, K. (1929), *Brain Mechanisms and Intelligence*. Chicago: University of Chicago Press.

Levenson, R. W., Ekman, P., Heider, K. and Friesen, W. V. (1992), 'Emotion and autonomic nervous system activity in an Indonesian Culture', *Journal of Personality and Social Psychology*, 62, 927– 88.

Lilly, J. C. (1956), 'Mental effects of reduction of ordinary levels of physical stimuli on intact, healthy persons', *Psychiatric Research Report*, 5, 1–9.

Maguire, E. A., Frackowiak, R. S. and Frith, C. D. (1996), 'Learning to find your way around: a role for the human hippocampal formation', *Proceedings of the Royal Society of London (B): Biological Sciences*, 263, 1745–50.

Maguire, E. A., Gadian, D. S., Johnsrude, I. S., Good, C. D., Ashburner, J., Frackowiak, R. S. and Frith, C. D. (2000), 'Navigation related structural change in the hippocampi of taxi drivers', *Proceedings NASciences (USA)*, 97(8), 4398–403.

Middleton, F. A. and Strick, P. L. (1994), 'Anatomic evidence for cerebellar and basal ganglia involvement in higher cognitive function', *Science*, 266, 458–63.

Miller, N. E. (1978), 'Biofeedback and visceral learning', *Annual Review of Psychology*, 29, 373–404.

Murray, E. J. (1964), *Motivation and Emotion*. Englewood Cliffs, NJ: Prentice-Hall.

Penfield, W. and Rasmussen, T. (1950), *The Cerebral Cortex of Man*. New York: Macmillan.

Penrose, Roger (1991), *The Emperor's New Mind*. London: Viking Penguin.

Penrose, Roger (1994), *Shadows of the Mind*. Oxford: Oxford University Press.

Plomin, R., DeFries, J. C., McClearn, G. E. and McGuffin, P. (2001), *Behavioral Genetics* (4th edn). New York: Worth.

Plomin, R. (2004), *Nature and Nurture: An Introduction to Human Behavioural Genetics*. Belmont, CA: Wadsworth.

Reisenzein, R. (1983), 'The Schachter theory of emotion: two decades later', *Psychological Bulletin*, 94, 239–64.

Schachter, S. (1971), *Emotion, Obesity and Crime*. New York: Academic Press.

Shallice, T. (1988), *From Neuropsychology to Mental Structure*. Cambridge: Cambridge University Press.

Shallice, T., Fletcher, P. C., Frith, C. D., Grasby, P., Frackowiak, R. S. and Dolan, R. J. (1994), 'Brain regions associated with acquisition and retrieval of verbal episodic memory', *Nature*, 368, 633–5.

Smith, E. E., Nolen-Hoeksema, S., Frederickson, B. L., Loftus, G. R., Bem, D. J. and Maren, S. (2003), *Atkinson and Hilgard's Introduction to Psychology* (14th edn). Belmont, CA: Wadsworth/Thomson.

Smith, E. E. and Jonides, J. (1994), 'Neuropsychological studies of working memory', in M. S. Gazzaniga (ed.), *The Cognitive Neurosciences*. Cambridge, MA: MIT Press.

Springer, S. P. and Deutsch, G. (1997), *Left Side, Right Side* (5th edn). New York: Freeman.

Thorpe, G. L. and Olson, S. L. (1997), *Behavior Therapy: Concepts, Procedures, Approaches* (2nd edn). Boston, MA: Allyn and Bacon.

Watson, J. B. (1931), *Behaviourism*. London: Routledge and Kegan Paul.

Webb, W. B. (1975), *The Gentle Tyrant*. Englewood Cliffs, NJ: Prentice-Hall.

## Further reading

Bee, H. and Boyd, D. (2004), *The Developing Child* (10th edn). Boston, MA: Pearson and AB.

Blakemore, Sarah-Jayne and Frith, U. (2000), *The Implications of Recent Developments in Neuroscience for Research on Teaching and Learning*. London: Institute of Cognitive Neuroscience.

Carlson, N. R. (2005), *Foundations of Physiological Psychology* (6th edn). Boston: Allyn and Bacon.

Gale, A. and Edwards, J. A. (eds) (1983), *Physiological Correlates of Human Behaviour*. Vol. 1: *Basic Issues*. Vol. 2: *Attention and Performance*. Vol. 3: *Individual Differences and Psychopathology*. London: Academic Press.

Plomin, R., DeFries, J. C., McClearn, G. E. and McGuffin, P. (2001), *Behavioral Genetics* (4th edn). New York: Worth.

Plomin, R. (2004), *Nature and Nurture: An Introduction to Human Behavioural Genetics*. Belmont, CA: Wadsworth.

Smith, E. E., Nolen-Hoeksema, S., Frederickson, B. L., Loftus, G. R., Bem, D. J. and Maren, S. (2003), *Atkinson and Hilgard's Introduction to Psychology* (14th edn). Belmont, CA: Wadsworth/Thomson.

## Useful Websites

http//:www.parliament.uk/parliamentary_offices/post/pubs2000.cfm then choose Report 140.

Blakemore, Sarah-Jayne (2000), *Early Learning Years*. In POST (Parliamentary Office of Science and Technology) Report 140, June. London.

Blakemore, Sarah-Jayne and Frith, U (2000), a TLRP (Teaching and Learning Research Programme of the ESRC) report (Desforges) on the document contains several important questions relating to education.

For those with Internet facilities, sources of documentation can be obtained by putting 'blakemore frith neuroscience education' in the search dialogue box.

http://www.genome.gov/10001772.

Human Genome Project website.

# Attention and Perception

## Implications for teachers

- Attracting children's interest and attention is central to the role of the teacher.

- Holding attention is as important as attracting pupils' attention. Teacher movement, voice, using various sensory channels and developing teacher–learner interaction are amongst the important ways of holding attention.

- Effective presentation should take into account orientation (providing a lesson framework), set induction (gearing up to a good start to the lesson), motivation set (finding ways of motivating students), cognitive set (arranging material so that it links with previous knowledge and flows into the new material of the lesson) and educational set (allowing for differences between conceptual and factual material).

- There is considerable value in teachers learning about human perception. The section 'Perception and the teacher' lists many useful ideas.

- Physical and social deprivations can seriously affect attention in school.

*We see things not as they are but as we are.*

(Kant)

The ceaseless, simultaneous bombardment of stimuli on the sense organs, and their subsequent treatment in the nervous system and brain, were mentioned in the previous chapter without considering the prevention of overloading (see, for example, the section on the brain stem in Chapter 2). Clearly we could not possibly cope with every stimulus that falls on the eyes in a given instant, let alone those falling on all the other senses at the same time. Just consider for a moment some aspects of what is happening around you at this very instant. Our eyes are taking in the print impressions (and we hope the brain is *encoding* and translating them into meaningful patterns!), as well as the peripheral images of other nearby objects on the table or of your hand gripping the book. We may be the victims of audible noises from other students, vehicles, building in progress and so on. There may be perfume or other chemicals in the air. Our bodies are experiencing pressure from contact with clothes, and objects such as this book, the chair and the table. Along with many other sensory possibilities, the brain would have to deal with a phenomenal number of sensations. The study of attention is concerned with finding an answer to the question of how the body manages so many signals and why an individual selects certain stimuli for attention and ignores others.

Again, having selected stimuli for attention, what do we make of them? If, for example, we looked at the same object or listened to the same piece of music, would we interpret the sensory stimuli in precisely the same way? It is more than likely that we would not. There may be cultural differences in the way we perceive objects because of differences in our sensory experience (see the section on illusions later in the chapter), or the combinations of notes in the music may be recognized as a tune by some and simply seem an indescribable, formless noise to others. Most important is the fact that the interpretation of present sensory information is dependent of our past experiences. A consideration of sensory interpretation, or perception, will be the second major concern in this chapter.

# The meaning of sensation, attention and perception

First let us distinguish between three terms that are sometimes confused, and which will frequently recur in this chapter. They are sensation, attention and perception. *Sensation* is said to occur when any sense organ (eye, ear, nose, skin containing pressure and pain cells) receives a stimulus from the external or internal environment. This can, and frequently does, occur without our knowledge. Sound waves, for instance, are impinging on the eardrum and causing disturbances which we do not register. If you listen attentively for a moment you will soon discover many sounds which would have passed you by had you not made a search for them.

With so many senses being activated at the same time, how is it that we are aware of only one stimulus at a time? One possible explanation is that a selection mechanism operates which is either voluntary (where we make a deliberate effort and search for a particular kind of stimulus) or involuntary (where some peculiar quality of the stimulus arrests our attention). The ability of human beings to process some part of the incoming sensations to the sense organs and to ignore everything else is referred to as *attention* (Goldstein 2002).

Receiving and attending to a noise or the touch of a material is only part of the story, because we need to interpret the selected sensations in the light of the present context and our past experience. This internal analysis and integration of sensations by the brain is termed *perception*. Although these three terms are defined separately, it is clear from the definitions that they are closely connected and constitute an integral part of human information-processing.

A common and inaccurate belief is that the sensations picked up from our surroundings are selected, received, interpreted and reproduced by the brain like a photograph or tape recording of sights and sounds – as if there were a little man sitting in the recesses of the brain making exact reproductions of incoming signals. This is not the case. The physical images received by the sense organs must first be translated (*encoded* – see the next section on Broadbent's filter theory) into a form compatible with nerve impulses previously received and stored so that the incoming impulses can be matched with past experience. Consider how many ways you have experienced the concept 'rose' – spoken word, written word, touch, smell, sight, etc. In the spoken word alone you will have heard many accents, voice pitches and intensities, but all have been transformed to a common code. So there is wide latitude within which sensory experience is given a common meaning (*perceptual constancy*). Therefore the nervous system must carry out appreciable transformations of the input of physical images in order for perception to take place.

# Attention

At the end of the nineteenth century, James (1890) generated considerable interest among psychologists in the topic of attention. Experimentation was not his strong point, but his insights into the processes of attention and perception served until the early 1950s, when Broadbent (1987) revitalized interest with his seminal researches and speculations.

As you sit reading this book, just turn your mind to your foot. First notice that you will not be able to concentrate on your foot and what you are reading at the same time. Now focus on the fact that your shoe, if you are wearing one, is pressing against parts of your foot. There are odours in the air and sounds around you. None of these pressures, smells or sounds occurred to you until you searched for them (but see *involuntary attention* in the next paragraph). This is *selective* or *voluntary* attention, that is, when an individual is actively seeking some signals and ignoring others. Sometimes the term is used to describe search behaviour, as in vigilance tasks where the individual is required to identify specified signals on a screen or clock. For auditory signals, a common research technique is to pass messages into each ear (sometimes different) through earphones (*shadowing*). This technique has been used in an attempt to verify sex differences in the bilateral action of the brain. For example, the female brain seems more capable than the male brain of *multi-tasking* under certain circumstances (see the next section on shadowing).

Sometimes our attention is demanded rather than controlled (*involuntary attention*), as when we hear a loud or unusual sound, see contrasting colours on a blackboard or sense a harsh smell. Factors influencing attention are discussed later in the chapter. The work we shall describe below deals essentially with selective, purposeful attention.

## Broadbent's filter theory

Broadbent's work (1975) on selective attention has been a productive model. Basically, the filter model (Broadbent 1987; see Figure 3.1) is taken from communication theory, including much of the jargon and attempts to explain how selective attention is managed. The sense organs and nervous system receiving and transmitting impulses are referred to as the *input channels*. Several input channels are operating simultaneously in parallel. However, the amount of information passing along the channels is far too much for the brain to cope with at any one time because overloading would occur if all the information was assimilated. Thus, to regulate the intake Broadbent supposes that there is a filter followed by a bottleneck (*limited-capacity channel*) which selects some of the incoming impulses for processing in the brain. The input not selected may be held in a *short-term storage* system and can be taken out of store provided this is done within a very short time (a few seconds at the most). However, the stored input signals grow weaker with time and when 'a line becomes available' for one impulse through the limited capacity channel, the remaining stored impulses suffer a further weakening effect. The phenomenon of short-term memory accounts for both our ability to recall a very recent incident and the deficit in information when it has been stored for a short time compared with the moment of reception. In other

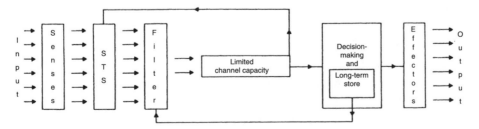

**Figure 3.1** Adapted from D. E. Broadbent, *Perception and Communication*, Oxford University Press, London, 1987. (STS = short-term store.)

words, we have a temporary and limited capacity for remembering events which the sense organs have received but to which we have not given our immediate attention.

Transmissions through the limited capacity channel are said to be processed by a perceptual system possessing at least the *long-term memory* store and a *decision-making system*. The latter is subsequently responsible for *effector* activity and *output*.

Several modifications have been recommended to accommodate subsequent research findings. For example, the model assumes that selection of input takes place *before* the interpretation of its meaning, which confines the selection to the physical sensory characteristics of the input. Treisman (1964) questioned this stage at which Broadbent places selection and argued from her researches that a more complex analytical mechanism operates to filter out levels of increasing complexity. Thus, starting with physical characteristics, let us say of spoken sentences, one voice sound is chosen from all others. Then comes a test of that sound for syllables, words, grammatical structure and finally meaning. Therefore the sentence input is progressively attended to and defined. Peripheral input is stored temporarily in the short-term memory and *attenuated* ('subdued' or 'reduced' in value).

Some recent experimentation in perception has involved the technique of *shadowing*. This means presenting aurally through headphones a message which the listener has to repeat while some other distraction (often another message) is given in the same ear, in both ears or in the opposite ear to the shadowed message. Moray (1969), a leader in this field, describes several shadowing experiments. Also using auditory stimulation through earphones, the issue of sex differences in laterality mentioned in Chapter 2 is of significance in language performance. Evidence (Shaywitz *et al.* 1995) confirms that females used both right and left sides of the brain in a language task, whilst males used only the left side (Broca's area). This is taken up again in Chapter 5.

Craik and Lockhart (1972) proposed three levels into which information might be translated (*encoded*) in readiness for storage in the long-term memory. This subject is developed further in Chapter 7. These are *visual/auditory*, *syntactic* and *semantic* levels, forming a hierarchy. At the simplest level a visual or auditory stimulus is received and processed for storage. If we give a young person an unfamiliar word, for example 'braise', the pattern of letters or the sound of the word could be stored, but without meaning. However, if we placed the word correctly in a phrase, additional meaning could be given to it. For example, 'you can braise meat' tells the child that the word is a verb – something can be done when you braise – but it does not convey a definition of the word. To do this would require a definitive statement making semantic-level processing possible, for example 'you can braise meat by frying it quickly and then stewing it in water'. This information will probably not be stored in isolation from previous knowledge: it will most likely be *accommodated* (cf. Piaget in Chapter 4) into previous similar kinds of knowledge about cooking methods.

All three levels of process occur in the classroom. Learning without understanding of isolated visual and auditory stimuli is not uncommon. For example, in learning the shapes and sounds of the alphabet or the numbers, there is no inherent logic in the link between the sight and sound of the symbols. Teachers would be wise to consider the level in the hierarchy of the work they are giving to pupils in order to assess the steps needed to arrive at an understanding of the material being taught.

## Attention and the brain

Study of damage to the brain was the popular way by which neuroscientists managed to locate which part or parts of the brain were involved when we attend to things around us. With the rapid progress in brain-scanning techniques in the past few years, we have a more precise knowledge of locations. By injecting substances which pass to the brain tissue or identifying increased blood flow, the active parts of the brain are located (e.g. by using PET (positron emission tomography) or fMRI (functional Magnetic Resonance Imaging) – see Figure 2.5, Chapter 2).

When we select and attend visually to external objects, the sensory inputs are dealt with as two separate factors in two different parts of the brain – *localization* and *recognition*. Localization (spatial) refers to the position of the objects in space. It is crucial that we are able to locate objects so that we can navigate our bodies towards, around and between objects to grasp, avoid or manipulate them. Given location tasks, a person's PET scan shows activity in the parietal cortex and hippocampus (see Chapter 2, Maguire *et al.* (1996 and 2000)). Because the parietal cortex is near the back of the brain, the area responsive to localization activity is known as the *posterior system.*

The other function of recognition is concerned with the attributes of the located object, such as size, shape, colour and texture. As this function activates tissue towards the front of the brain (anterior cyngulate), it is referred to as the *anterior system* (Posner and Raichle 1994, Posner and Dehaene 1994). These locations have been verified following accidental damage to the relevant part of the brain.

## The factors which influence attention

Workers in this field are agreed that both the observer and the stimulus possess character-istics which are likely to influence attention. The following are of particular relevance for the teacher. For convenience let us divide them into external and internal factors.

### External factors

The most important are as follows:

(a)   Selection of information does not occur in a random fashion. The *intensity* of a stimulus, for instance, can attract attention. Loud noises, bright colours, strong odours and high pressure on the skin are compelling stimuli.

(b)   *Novel* stimuli attract attention. Any unusual or irregular event is liable to distract us. The reason for using italics in a textbook or colour on a blackboard is to draw your eye to key concepts by printing the words in an irregular form. Ringing the changes of methods of presenting subject matter in school has obvious possibilities of catching children's attention.

(c) A *variable* or *changing stimulus* demands our attention. Animals stalking their prey (cats for instance) move as little as possible so as not to attract attention. Teachers quickly discover how to use their voices by changing the intonation frequently. Wall charts and aids should be changed regularly, otherwise they no longer attract the children's interest: the children become *adapted* to the aids in the same way as happens with the ticking of a clock to which one becomes accustomed and takes for granted.

(d) *Regularity* of stimuli presented in space (spatial) or time (temporal) has an effect on attention. Distributed presentations, again to avoid becoming adapted, have a better chance of becoming noticed than rapid, regular presentations.

(e) Certain *colours* are more attractive than others. Infants are much more interested in coloured than in grey backgrounds, and both children and adults pay more attention to red and white designs than to black and white ones.

(f) *High sounds* are more likely to be listened to than low sounds when the two are presented simultaneously.

(g) *Conditioned* and habitual stimuli are likely to be picked out from other stimuli. When your name is spoken in the midst of other names or conversation. You are more likely to pick it out. This is called the 'cocktail party' effect because it is often possible to hear a familiar phrase or name over and above the noisy chatter at a party.

(h) *Cueing* involves the deliberate use of clues or hints which direct attention to a stimulus. Teachers frequently use cues to orientate pupils. For example, verbal cues such as 'watch this' and 'note that' or physical cues such as pointing or demonstrating are employed.

### Internal factors

Physical and mental dispositions are necessarily important influences on attentiveness. The fact that people in identical or very similar physical circumstances display striking differences in the degree to which they attend to stimuli is partly a matter of internal dispositions. The following are among the most important:

(a) Interest, or the lack of it as in boredom, is clearly a factor likely to influence attention. Events in which a child has already gained an interest are more likely to attract attention than events which have not previously been of interest. Attitudes and prejudices also affect the extent to which we are drawn to pay heed to events or ideas.

(b) Physical or social *deprivations* pertaining to basic human needs (see Chapter 8) have marked effects on the direction and intensity of attention. Sensory deprivation for any length of time can have a disorientating effect. It affects both physical and mental capacities. Feelings of being off balance, hallucinations, irritability and being unable to concentrate or to solve problems are some of the effects. Those subjected to experiments (frequently university students) in which they wear translucent goggles, gloves, long cardboard cuffs on their arms and are asked to sit still in one position find the sensory deprivation unbearable after a time. Some students, despite a handsome financial inducement, had to abandon the experiment (Zubek 1969, Heron *et al.* 1956). Suedfeld and Coren (1989) have shown that reduced stimulation under controlled conditions can help to reduce sleeplessness and tension headaches.

Extreme deprivation frequently leads to excessive orientation of all the senses towards the satisfaction of the deprived need. Excessive starvation ultimately gives rise to all manner of unusual manifestations where the individual dreams of, fights for, has hallucinations about and directs all physical and mental energies towards food (see the Minnesota Starvation Studies, Chapter 8).

(c)  *Fatigue* and *illness* have detrimental effects on attentiveness. It stands to reason that, as our physical reserves become depleted, our vigilance in any sense modality will be correspondingly reduced. Fatigue can occur in a general way where the whole body is affected, or it can occur in one or some of the senses which have been overused. A child who is short of sleep or exhausted from strenuous physical or mental activity is unlikely to attend in class. This can be related to *span of attention* (see also Chapters 7 and 12), in which it can be shown that we differ in the extent to which we can concentrate on or cope with sheer quantity of information. One wonders how many children become swamped with information, thus lessening their capacity for attention.

(d)  In Chapter 8 on motivation (and subsequently in our discussions of personality) we shall meet with a theory of drive which states that performance improves with increased *arousal* up to a point. Beyond this point, performance begins to deteriorate until, at high levels of arousal, the quality of performances is extremely poor. A graph of this relationship (Chapter 8, Figure 8.5) approximates to an inverted U-shape. Attention is also thought to be affected in a similar way as the arousal level increases. A basic level is needed in the first place for attention to be attracted (a threshold of arousal) and once this level has been passed the individual's attention increases usefully. Beyond an optimum level, which varies with the sense in use and the intensity of the external and internal factors mentioned above, attention becomes adversely affected.

(e)  The *attention needs* mentioned in Chapter 8 – curiosity, exploration and manipulation – are clearly influential in directing attention.

(f)  Our attention is most frequently drawn to those activities or ideas which we least expect. *Expectation* is an important factor in directing attention (see Chapter 8). This is also related to several external factors mentioned above.

(g) *Personality characteristics* have a differential influence. Students will be introduced later to a theory of personality structure involving several personality types, and one type, defined by the dimension of extraversion and introversion, will be considered in more detail then. For the present, it is enough to point out that many behavioural distinctions exist between extraverts and introverts. Extraverts need more *involuntary rest pauses* while performing tasks requiring concentration. Consequently their vigilance suffers in comparison with introverts, who do not require so many pauses. Extraverts also accumulate inhibition to the continuation of a repetitive task and therefore cannot attend as consistently as introverts (Eysenck, 1967, Gale and Edwards 1983, Gale and Eysenck 1992). The sensory thresholds (levels of stimulation required for us to be aware of the stimulus, mentioned in Chapter 2) tend to be lower for introverts than for extraverts. The implications for the class teacher are that children with extravert qualities are more likely to wilt and become distracted during long periods of attentive activity and to work at a lower level of sensory susceptibility than introverts.

## Set

The notion of *set induction* is a useful one in the context of attention-seeking applied by teachers in their work (Woodworth and Marquis 1949). *Set* is a term used by some psychologists to describe the state of readiness to receive a stimulus. *Induction* relates to the process of trying to encourage set. Teachers are obviously in the business of inducing various kinds of readiness in the classroom. We have already had an example of one kind of set inducer in cueing (a behaviourist term originally) which is a direct call for attention ('Watch', 'Pay attention, John'). Another example is Ausubel's *advance organizers*. These are ideas fed to learners at the beginning of a lesson in order to give structure to what is to follow and to help the learner in organizing the material.

Several kinds of set have been defined (Hargie *et al.* 1994). These are *motivational, perceptual, social, cognitive* and *educational*. Hargie *et al.* give a fuller indication of the intentions of set induction in all these forms:

- to induce in participants a state of readiness appropriate to the task which is to follow, through establishing rapport, gaining attention and arousing motivation
- to ascertain the expectations of the participants and the extent of their knowledge about the topic to be considered
- to indicate to participants what might be reasonable objectives for the task to follow
- to explain to participants what one's functions are, and what limitations may accompany these functions
- to establish links with previous encounters (during follow-up sessions)
- to ascertain the extent of the participants' knowledge of the topic to be discussed.

These are obviously of prime importance to teachers and will be applied in the next section. In general, *motivational set* refers to those aspects of, in this case, the learning environments used to gain the attention of learners. The list of external factors above indicates some of the more important stimulants. *Perceptual set* has to do with how a person perceives the personal attributes of others and how this might influence performance. The teacher has an important role to play in making sure that the setting is conducive to learning. Impressions of the teacher, other children and the school organization have, in some cases, had an effect on the performance of children. *Social set* refers to the interrelations which set the scene for learning, for example the social rituals (or graces) such as welcoming, smiling, using voice or eye contact. *Cognitive set* relates to mental preparedness – creating a comprehensive framework for the lesson to follow (cf. Ausubel's advance organizers). Finally, *educational set* concerns the learning style preferences contrasting 'factual set' learners and 'conceptual set' learners (Siegel and Siegel 1965). These style preferences will influence the readiness of children to participate in different lesson methods (rote learning, theoretical or analytical sessions).

## Attention and the teacher – getting 'set'

The process of catching and holding attention starts when a teacher first meets a class. Experience teaches us how easy it is to get off on the wrong foot with someone else. A casual word or gesture can so easily be misunderstood. This effect can be multiplied in a class of children. The flow and 'feel' of a lesson or part of a lesson is often established at the beginning, and if matters go wrong, it is difficult to recover. Social psychologists have made some interesting studies of social interaction (Cohen and Manion 1981), and they have stressed the importance of verbal and non-verbal communication in the classroom – the verbal, visual or auditory uses which begin, accompany and sometimes set a seal on a relationship. These have grown into extremely complex and problematic topics in recent years. For help about the beginning of a lesson, the research is more descriptive than instructive for the student teacher, and we are generally forced back to anecdotal experience of others (teachers, tutors, other students).

### Meeting a class for the first time

As with most new encounters, meeting a class for the very first time frequently creates appreciable tensions in both the teacher and the class. Most experienced teachers appear to support the time-honoured method of 'start as you mean to go on' because 'well begun is half done'. Perhaps the emphasis in starting with a new class should be a strong rather than a weak one. Whatever else, you will be acting out a role. Teaching 30 to 40 young people in one place at one time is not a natural human activity. It requires some acting out. As the first impressions tend to last for some time, it would not be out of place to take on the role of a confident and competent person who is in control of the situation.

Age and the kind of school play a part in the way children respond to teachers, but some children try to develop expertise in detecting and working on the 'soft spots' of teachers. The further up the educational system one goes, the more blatant is the pursuit of chinks in the teacher's armour.

Acting is an important skill in classroom life. Some events are larger than life and our responses are correspondingly exaggerated. Anyone with an audience has to work on them in order to make them receptive. Teachers need to act out events which help to establish a good working environment, sensitive to children, but at the same time making it clear that it is not in anyone's interests to have any nonsense. Being firm, friendly and fair, but avoiding being overpowering or oppressive requires great skill and self-discipline.

### Starting a lesson or new topic

The first step, as indicated in the last section, is capturing the pupils' attention, followed by four of the various kinds of set outlined by Hargie *et al.* (1994). These steps are:

- orientation
- social set
- motivational set
- cognitive set
- educational set.

*Orientation* involves gaining attention and providing the framework for what is to come. In both primary and secondary schools, the transition from one lesson to the next involves tension and effort on the part of the teacher. In secondary schools this is made additionally difficult, because the change frequently involves a new class – they come to you or you go to them. Whichever is the case, never allow too much time to be idled away. If the pupils are coming to your room, be there first and make sure they are occupied on arrival. Stragglers are inevitable when children have to move from one classroom to another, and occupational therapy for those who arrive first is necessary. When you go to them, the problems may be greater, especially if they have been left without a teacher for a while.

When the class is assembled, a teacher must ensure that they are all attending before launching into the lesson. Casual beginnings with some children not listening can easily deteriorate into unproductive, often noisy and half-hearted effort. Capturing the interests and attention of pupils is a skilled activity and should be quite deliberately rehearsed and practised. The process of gearing pupils up and coaxing them to learn was introduced above as *set induction*. The methods used are intended to establish the right frame of reference and mind for what will follow in the lesson, and it is about getting learners ready and 'set' to go, and excited to hear more.

One of the first tasks of settling a class down involves *social set*. It is the opening relationship of pleasantries, smiles, gestures, etc. to set the tone. Most of the time the teacher can slip from these beginnings to the first stage of the lesson. Occasionally, gentle persuasion to gain attention fails and snappier methods are needed. For example, when pupils return from an exciting event, some time is needed for them to cool down. Whatever the methods used (hand clap, louder voice, 'I'm waiting' techniques), be careful not to get trapped into prolonged efforts to gain attention. They tend to take the edge off what is to follow and give an impression that you have not got a grip on matters. If you have to use these methods frequently, begin to wonder why and get advice.

*Motivational set* is clearly amongst the most important. The use of novel, surprising, provocative stimuli are ways of introducing topics. Starting with a knotty, but fascinating problem, an example, specimen or actual object is quite common. Uncharacteristic (but not bizarre) approaches have their place, such as commencing with mime or a rehearsed entré where one of the pupils might start the lesson. Do not overdo one method, lest the novelty wears off.

*Cognitive set* is a complex idea. It incorporates those aspects at the beginning of a lesson or new part of a lesson which encourage mental preparedness. For cognitive set we need to (a) provide a link with previous work (transition from the familiar to the unfamiliar), (b) gain information about previous knowledge, experience and expectations of the learners, and (c) give structure to, and an outline of, what is coming in the lesson, i.e. the advance organizer of Ausubel (see Chapter 6). An advance organizer is introductory information (concepts, ideas) given to learners to increase their understanding of the lesson and to enhance their prospects of organizing the new material. There are occasions, however, when it is quite possible to start with a semi-structured or guided discovery method in which pupils will be required to organize and make sense of the information available. This is possible, for instance, when a process is being explored and the content is already well established or is not important for the process. Observation sessions in science, for example, can be conducted in this way. Certain topics lend themselves to guided discovery techniques (e.g. in science, social science and environmental studies), although it is important to point out that learners need careful guidance in the methods of 'discovery'. The method must be learned. Again, there are occasions when one might not want to give a preview in case the 'cat gets out of the bag'. There are times when a teacher wants to build up an argument, scenario or pose a problem with the gradual help of the learners.

*Educational set* is a particularly interesting concept, because it refers to the distinctions between various learning styles. The extremes, defined in the research of Siegel and Siegel (1965), are '*conceptually set* subjects [who] were adversely affected by emphasizing factual rather than conceptual acquisition; conversely, *factually-set* subjects [who] were adversely affected by emphasizing conceptual rather than factual acquisition'. Learners' reactions to subjects, parts of subjects, teaching methods, various forms of examination and general study methods will be influenced by educational set. The difference between the extremes of factually-set and conceptually-set learners is that the former are predisposed to learn factual content and the latter conceptual content. This question is raised again in discussions of learning and teaching styles.

## Keeping attention

In the previous section we looked at ways of attracting attention. Interest is now turned to ways of holding the attention of learners. Setting tasks which are long and tedious, usually when there is little opportunity for teacher guidance in large classes, would be fatal. Ways have to be found which provide *progression* and *interaction* (with content or other people) for each individual (not an easy task in large classes) and varying sensory input.

From the teacher's viewpoint, as we said in the section on motivational set, providing novel, variable, challenging and relevant stimuli in a lively way should continue throughout the lesson. There are also presentational factors such as voice, gesture, enthusiasm, use of eyes and other non-verbal cues, movement of the teacher in the classroom, deployment of aids, grouping and regrouping of the class, all of which provide stimulus variation.

Stimulus variation is vitally important in classroom activity. The following list of activities indicates ways in which a teacher can use tactics to bring about stimulus variation. Observe an experienced teacher, noting which tactics are used.

(a) Movement of teacher in the classroom:
   - around the class
   - when speaking to the class
   - gestures (lively, still, etc.)
   - eye contact
   - any other movements which hinder or help the progress of the lesson.
(b) Voice–speech pattern:
   - variation, and when this happens
   - response to different kinds of pupil behaviour
   - how language is used to attract attention (focusing behaviour).
(c) Using alternative sensory channels:
   - use of visual aids
   - looking, listening, speaking, reading on the part of pupil
   - other kinds of aids – demonstration, model making, manipulating objects, scientific apparatus, etc.
(d) Teacher–learner interaction (e.g., see work by Galton *et al.* 1980, 1999)
   - class grouping
   - how much teacher–group interaction
   - how much teacher–pupil interaction
   - how much pupil–pupil interaction, and what kinds of interaction are helpful.

From the learner's point of view, there are some obvious reasons which lead to flagging attention and motivation, such as loss of interest, boring presentation, inability to cope with the level of work presented or the work being too easy. Two other causes, given high motivation, are *fatigue* and *span of attention.*

Judgements have to be made by the teacher as to the limit of physical and mental activity the learner can tolerate. These judgements are based on a knowledge of the learner's physical and mental development, abilities, previous knowledge and understanding. Interestingly, the conventional length of lessons in this country is a matter of history and not the outcome of research into the optimum time for exposure to a particular subject. Teachers will need to be vigilant in deciding on the most productive exposure time by watching reactions and getting feedback from children.

'Span of attention' deals with the extent of a person's ability to cope with the quantity of information presented. Do we swamp some learners by choosing too much material? The span of attention is also influenced by personality factors. Extravert personalities tend not to be able to concentrate for as long as introverts. This information is only helpful as background information – awareness of possible strengths or limitations in the make-up of learners. For those who possess extreme personality profiles, the style of working has to be looked at in order to be compatible with that profile. Self-awareness of limitations or strengths is helped by teachers prepared to discuss (tactfully) with learners the range of possibilities. Breaks and transitions to other kinds of activities require careful management by the teacher.

A largely biological problem appearing before age seven and mentioned briefly in the last chapter (and Chapter 11) is *attention deficit hyperactivity disorder* (ADHD). This is often a complex of inattention, hyperactivity and impulsivity (Atkinson and Hornby 2002) and is one of the commonest debilitating problems met with by teachers. The disorder is not clearly understood and the definition a matter of debate, but the incidence is thought to be around two per cent. It is much more frequent in boys than girls (some give 7:1). Most teachers will meet a pupil with ADHD on average once in a year group.

The symptoms of inattention include inability to give close attention or to maintain attention; the pupil does not listen, has difficulty with instructions and organizing and completing tasks, is easily distracted and forgetful. Professional help is really needed for this disorder. A combination of low-dose medication (optional in some cases) coupled with intervention programmes involving parents, teachers and psychologists gives temporary help. Unattended in childhood, ADHD can lead to disruptive, aggressive, antisocial and sometimes delinquent behaviour.

# Perception

We cannot help making sense of our world. How this might be done varies from one person to another. The basic sensory signals from objects are the same, but the way we apprehend them differs because of the circumstances in which similar sensory experiences have occurred. The newborn child with crude sensory equipment and next to no backlog of experience against which to evaluate incoming signals builds up, from recurring stimulus patterns presented in a multitude of sizes, shapes, colours, distance from the eye, etc., a perception of its surroundings.

## The nature of perception

In a previous section entitled 'Attention and the brain' (p. 59), recent knowledge of which parts of the brain are involved in the two central functions of *localization* and *recognition* was outlined. In addition, there is a third important requirement in ensuring satisfactory perception – *perceptual constancy*. This is the ability of our sensory system to allow for lightness, colour, shape and distance and thereby keep constant the image received.

The most researched sense has been that of sight, but physiologists believe the general principles apply to the other senses. The visual cortex at the rear of the brain deals with location and recognition by involving two different regions. After passing through the rear visual region, the localization impulses pass to the upper part of the brain; recognition impulses pass to the lower part (Kosslyn and Koenig 1995). A similar division of labour, it will be recalled, happens in the process of attention.

### *Localization*

What helps our senses to locate an object? We use what is called *figure and ground*. In locating an object, it is necessary to be able to isolate, using any of the senses, that object (the figure) from its surroundings (the background or 'ground'). To do this, we scan a scene or listen to sounds and pick out particular features which become the figure. The background against which the figure is observed is known as the ground. Thus, in identifying a shape, the contour outline is most important. It is probably aspects of the figure which pass through the filter to the brain and the immediate ground which is stored temporarily in the short-term memory. Figure–ground discrimination applies in all the sense modalities. For example, music can be picked out and understood against a background of other moderate sounds. Tomato sauce is identified against a background of other foods in one's mouth. When one tries to discriminate one taste from another, they successively take on figure and ground by conscious selection.

Attempts to find a figure against a background are usually not difficult, but occasionally we can be deceived. Figure 3.2(a) in one instance is seen as a candlestick, and in the next as profiles of two faces looking at each other. Note the decisiveness with which the figure is *either* a candlestick *or* faces, and not a mixture of both. We automatically select a figure. Moreover, when it is a candlestick the brain fills in the lines at the top and bottom. You may even get the impression that the candlestick is of a brighter nature than the surrounding white page, so strong is the tendency to distinguish figure from ground in terms of previous

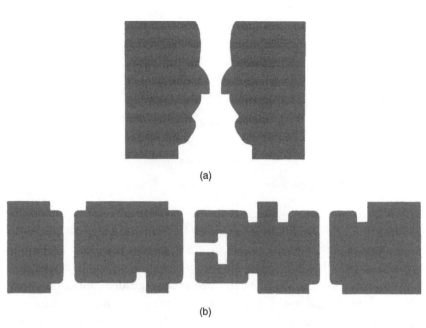

(a)

(b)

**Figure 3.2** Figure-ground reversal.

models (in this case a candlestick). Figure 3.2(b) has a similar effect. You may at first notice only meaningless shapes like a plan of a housing estate, but it should transpose into a word which will suddenly leap out of the page when you realize what it is.

Another important feature influencing the localization of objects is how they are grouped and organized. An influential school of thought was founded in Germany in the early twentieth century, and held that perceptual organization is inborn. Psychologists such as Wertheimer, Koffka and Köhler created a movement known as the *Gestalt School* of psychology. The word 'Gestalt' is German for 'pattern' or 'form' and the theory emphasizes our ability to perceive patterns as *wholes*. The motto for this movement could well be that 'the whole is more than the sum of the parts'. In other words, we perceive and give meaning to objects by their characteristics *in toto* and not by considering a jumble of the parts which go to make up the total figure. Several criteria affect the meaning we ascribe to objects. Four arrangements seem to be of primary assistance in recognizing and determining the dominant pattern of the figure in order to form a 'good' pattern, or gestalt. The formation of 'good' perceptual patterns is referred to as the *Law of Prägnanz*. They are similarity, proximity, continuity and closure.

- *Similarity* – where a figure consists of similar elements we tend to group them to form a pattern. Details such as similar shape, size and colour tend to be grouped. In Figure 3.3(a) we are more likely to see four columns of Xs or Os than rows of XOXO, even though we normally read horizontally. We prefer to order and arrange similar objects in rows rather than at random to avoid the uncomfortable sensation which

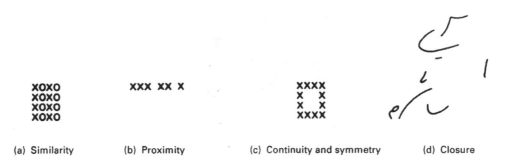

(a) Similarity          (b) Proximity          (c) Continuity and symmetry          (d) Closure

**Figure 3.3** Patterns which assist in forming gestalten.

randomness creates. Instruments, for example violins in an orchestra, are heard as an entity and not as separate instruments.

- *Proximity* – proximity applies where similar objects appear close together. In Figure 3.3(b) the pattern would most probably be described as three groups containing three, two and one Xs respectively, and not as six crosses. The Morse code relies on the differential proximity of dots and dashes. However, note the importance of context in the interpretation of perceptions. Once the idea of a code is given, the penny drops.

- *Continuity and symmetry* – similar parts of a figure which appear in lines (straight or curved) tend to stand out. When they make recognizable shapes such as circles or squares they become conspicuous. The illustration given in Figure 3.3(c) will be seen as a square not as twelve Xs. We spontaneously join up the Xs to make lines. Music is perceived as a continuous rather than a separate system of sounds.

- *Closure* – Closed or partially closed figures are more readily perceived than open figures, except when the open figure has an acquired meaning such as the letters of the alphabet (for example, letter C is open but is recognized as a letter). Figure 3.3(d) is incomplete, but doubtless it will be recognized from previous models as a man's face. In this recognizable instance we have closed the figure in order to give it a familiar meaning.

## Recognition

To locate an object, there have to be distinguishing features or attributes which the observer recognizes. A white dot against an identical white background cannot be identified – unless it moves or changes one of its attributes. We use criteria such as shape, size, colour, light and shade, texture. Of these, shape is very important. The attributes are actually processed in different sub-regions of that part of the visual cortex dealing with recognition. One hypothesis to explain how we recognize natural shapes starts with familiar geometrical shapes (*geons*, short for *geometrical ions*) such as cubes, cylinders, wedges and spheres as the basis for recognizing more complex forms (Biederman 1990). Figure 3.3(d) is an example that provides sufficient geons for us to recognise it as a face, pipe and hat.

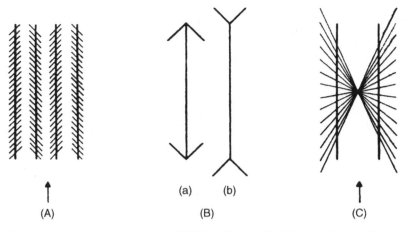

**Figure 3.4** Three common illusions: (A) Zöllner illusion; (B) Müller-Lyer illusion; (C) Hering illusion.

## Visual illusions and perceptual constancy

Evidence that we tend to perceive in 'gestalten' rather than by building up the separate elements of an object is provided from the study of *visual illusions*. They are false perceptions of reality. The three illusions of Figure 3.4 are well known. If the book is held so that you are looking along the vertical lines of (A) from the bottom edge of the page they will be seen to be straight and parallel. (B) is the Müller–Lyer illusion, with (a) and (b) exactly the same length. In the third illustration (C), it looks as though the lines are curved. But if you look along them from the direction of the arrow they will be seen to be parallel and straight. Even when we know the details it is still impossible to compensate. One explanation for the illusion (Gregory 1996 and 1998) is that we are compensating for perspective. Take the Müller–Lyer illusion (B). The outward-pointing arrows (a) could be taken as a near corner jutting out, and (b) could be taken as a far corner. Consequently we compensate for this possible perspective by perceiving the drawing (b) as larger than it is. *Perceptual constancy* is another case of compensation where we allow for the distance of an object from our sense organs when judging its magnitude. A man seen at a distance may look as if he is 200 mm high, but we allow for the distance.

Actually, the more experience we have of perspective in our daily routines, the more we are taken in by illusions. African tribes who live in round huts are apparently less prone to the Müller–Lyer effect. The essential point about illusions is that, no matter how hard we try, it is impossible to separate out the parts of the figures. Invariably we perceive the figure as a whole.

Bruner and Goodman (1947) found that young children from poor socioeconomic conditions tended to underestimate the size of coins, whilst children from favourable conditions were accurate in their judgements. Bruner and Goodman regarded this as evidence for cultural experience being a significant influence on perception. Selective attention as an

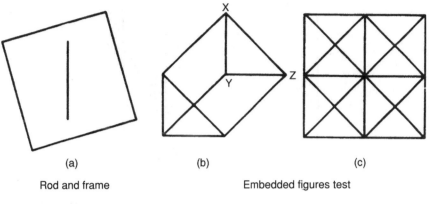

(a)                    (b)                         (c)

Rod and frame          Embedded figures test

**Figure 3.5** Witkin's tests.

outcome of a particular upbringing (e.g. parents who encourage their children to observe the behaviour of animals) is similarly thought to be a factor in perceptual development.

## Perceptual style

In Chapter 12, we shall discuss in some detail the broader definition of style – characteristic ways in which cognitive, motivational and temperamental factors influence a person's problem-solving techniques. Here we shall concentrate on one aspect of cognitive style, that is *perceptual style*. Witkin (1962) has shown that people vary in their perceptual styles, that is, their characteristic patterns of perceiving in the process of problem-solving. Two famous experiments, the rod and frame and the embedded figures tests, were used to detect differences between individuals. The rod and frame consists of an illuminated rod placed inside an illuminated frame in a dark room (Figure 3.5(a)). Both can be adjusted independently and they are set at different angles from which an individual is required to adjust the rod until he or she believes the rod to be vertical. Some people are sufficiently influenced by the frame as to be thrown off the vertical. Others seem, however, to be able to ignore the frame. The former are referred to by Witkin as *field-dependent* and the latter as *field-independent*. In other words, some people are more affected in their perceptual judgements of a figure (the rod) by the ground (the frame) than others are. Another method used by Witkin was the Embedded Figures Test, which consists of several shapes similar to Figure 3.5(b) and (c) from which an individual is asked to trace the shape in (b) by drawing over the corresponding lines in (c).

Research from Witkin and his associates onwards (summarized in Vernon 1969; also see Wapner and Demick 1991) show that there are differences between field-dependent and field-independent children. Field-independent children tend to be better at cognitive tasks which are spatial. They tend to head towards science and maths subjects. In temperament they tend to be more assertive and independent. Females tend to be field-dependent.

## The search for meaning

One dominant conclusion from the research is that human beings are not passive receptor organisms of incoming stimuli. We try to make sense of the stimuli in terms of the context and our previous experience. At a simple level, this is shown by the examples given above in defining the Law of Prägnanz. A few dotted lines or marks are transformed into recognizable shapes, faces, etc. There is yet another example of how we, according to gestalt psychologists, set up hypotheses from the sensory information received. In Figure 3.5(b), is the face XYZ of the triangular prism the front face or the rear face? (This effect is sometimes illustrated with a cube – Necker's cube.) You will find that in one instance the face XYZ is at the front, the next instance it is at the back of the prism. You are trying out hypotheses about a three-dimensional problem drawn in two dimensions – and there is no solution. Therefore, you are switching from one possible solution to the other.

Our perceptions are influenced not only by the immediate sensory data, but by the context and our previous experience. If you were given several sounds such as 'dit dit dit dah dah dah dit dit dit' you would probably say first that they were groups of three sounds, the first three and last three being identical. If it was a lesson on Morse code, you would be searching for some further interpretation of the letters represented by the code (the context has been defined). If you have sufficient experience with the code you would probably conclude that it spells out 'SOS' – the distress signal.

A theory by Neisser (1976 and 1982) summarizes the way in which the stimulus, context and past experience combine to give a perceived 'best guess' at the 'meaning' of a stimulus. He refers to this as *analysis-by-synthesis*. The stimulus input, say the sight of an object, is received and a guess – a hypothesis – is made about the identity of the object from the context, previous experience and expectations. The main features of the object are then compared with the information retrieved from memory and a decision made as to whether the object is familiar or not. If not, a fresh guess and search is made of previous memories until recognition or abandonment. The meaning associated with the input from the object is provided by the person observing and not from the object itself.

## Perception and the teacher

We have still much to learn about perception in human beings, but what we do know of value to a teacher will now be summarized.

(a) The idea of the Law of Prägnanz in perceptual matters is thought to apply equally well to mental activity. Having clear organization and classification of intellectual experience therefore would obey the same rules as perceptual phenomena; therefore the field of learning should have structure.

(b) Pupils should be given opportunities to use closure. This amounts to leaving something for pupils actively to complete for themselves. Attempting to give meaningful structure to concepts helps to implant them in long-term memory (see the work of Piaget, as discussed in Chapter 4).

(c) Perception always depends on previous experience. Therefore, it is essential to start from a point in the presentation of material which enables the pupil to call on previous experience (advance organizers). Understanding, rather than rote learning, is important in the formation of clear perceptions and is more likely to assist in long-term memory. However, 'understanding' is not always possible as, for instance, when learning letters of the alphabet or numbers. The teacher should emphasize that the learning process consists of discovering meanings, building up patterns of knowledge and meaningful relations (Morton 1967).

(d) Some have argued that learning by getting the total picture rather than learning material piecemeal is more efficient. Methods of learning a poem by rereading it through until it is learned, or the 'look and say' (and not the 'phonic') method of reading, are based on 'whole' rather than 'part' learning. However, the generalization is questionable. A lot would depend on the type and extent of material to be assimilated. As we shall see from Miller's work (see Chapter 7), 'chunking' does have its place in learning, and even then there are limitations to the amount of channel capacity.

(e) The extent to which young children perceive their surroundings and themselves is subject to developmental limitations. Piaget has proposed that the child *centres* on a particular dimension of the sensory field to the exclusion of all others. In two-dimensional or three-dimensional problems the young child is not able to escape from the single dimension to make judgements about changes or constancies in such matters as volume and area (see Chapter 4).

(f) There are individual differences in the way pupils perceive the process of problem-solving. 'Perceptual styles' is a developing area which could have an influence on the teaching styles adopted.

(g) False perceptions can arise because:
- Sensory information is inadequate or inaccurate. Auditory, visual or tactile materials should be plentiful, appropriate and unambiguous.
- Attention is not full or the direction is misguided: we have already given several reasons why attention might stray. Another cause may be that too much latitude is provided in the perceptual field, so models cannot begin to be formulated.
- The existing percepts are inadequate for incoming sensory experience. This should soon be evident to the teacher who is evaluating his or her work as an ongoing process.
- The wrong 'set' is present; that is, the pupil is looking out for, or picking up, the wrong cues.

As an illustration of the role played by visual perception in school, we might consider some of the concepts dealt with in geography and geology. In both these subjects there is a need to imagine shapes in three dimensions, usually from two-dimensional information. For example, the interpretation of a contour map requires some effort to convert the contour lines into an elevation. Equally, the orientation of a map for direction finding, or the transfer of information from an aerial photograph to a map (or vice versa), requires spatial visualization skills. The term *graphicacy* has been used to describe communication of spatial information that cannot be conveyed adequately by verbal and numerical means. Thus, map and photograph readings would be regarded as forms of graphicacy (Chadwick 1978).

## Summary

Sensory reception, attention and analysis have an important place in the work of teachers. Needless to say, without the pupils' attention the teacher might as well retire. But gaining their attention is not just a question of insisting on their looking at and listening to what is going on. There are many factors conspiring to distract or fatigue the child at a more subtle level than this. We have noted that external factors such as intense, novel, changeable, colourful, high-pitched and conditioned stimuli can operate to assist or defeat the teacher's intentions. Internal variables of interest, fatigue, need deprivation, arousal state and personality qualities are likewise of relevance.

Memory was considered in Chapter 2 from the viewpoint of physiological functioning. We explored the subject using a speculative model derived from Broadbent's filter theory of attention. A development of this by Craik and Lockhart (1972) proposes three levels of translation of incoming information for storage in long-term memory – visual auditory, syntactic and semantic. The forms most likely to prevail in the encoding of the information are non-verbal and verbal symbolic images. In considering the use of these in the classroom, teachers might give thought to the non-verbal material used for illustration and the level of verbal communication most appropriate to the lesson content in terms of past work done and new content to be taught.

Of the theories of perception, the most influential to date has been that proposed by the Gestalt School. Perceptual discrimination is seen to be more than just the sum of sensory experiences. Questions of interpretation are often distorted by the acquired perceptual characteristics of one's culture or sub-culture (i.e. we learn *how* to look at things and *what* to look at as an outcome of cultural inheritance). The deceptions of illusions are partly a question of cultural experience. It is also believed that social-class background can affect the perceptions of children (Bruner and Goodman 1947).

Finally, we gave several suggestions from research on perception which should be of assistance to the teacher. These included: set induction; the importance of structure in the presentation of material; the need to leave children to complete some part of their learning, provided they are in possession of sufficient knowledge to do this (closure); the importance of starting with familiar perceptual experience from which to derive the unfamiliar; 'whole' learning, in some cases, as more valuable then learning 'in bits'; a consideration of the developmental level of the child; and some common sources of false perceptions.

## Tutorial enquiry and discussion

(a) In tutorials see if you can devise a series of small-scale experiments to show that the intensity, novelty, variability, distributed regularity, colour and conditioned stimuli are effective in attention-seeking. Explore ways in which this information might be used in classrooms.

(b) On teaching practice and in tutorials observe and consider various ways of starting lessons. List your observations under the three headings of social, motivational and cognitive set.
  - *Social set.* Were there any pleasantries to begin with? What form did they take? How did the learners react to different kinds of opening relationships? Which appealed to you?
  - *Motivational set.* How did the teacher initially obtain attention from the class? How did the lesson begin? What was the reaction of the learners?
  - *Cognitive set.* How was the lesson put into context (if it was)? Did the teacher try to fit present knowledge into previous knowledge?

(c) Build into your earliest teaching experiences a systematic plan of different beginnings to lessons. Experiment in order to discover ways which feel most comfortable for you and rewarding for the learners.

(d) Examine in the literature and discuss in tutorials the important differences in the extent to which we use our senses (e.g. whether we tend to use our eyes more than our ears). Do we tend to learn through one sense more than another? How could your findings help in deciding on the arrangement and emphases of lesson presentation? Are there differences according to the age of pupils?

(e) Read through the suggestions given under the heading of 'Perception and the teacher' and use these in your observations at school. Analyse the content and presentation of lessons or class activities with these in mind. Try to seek out examples for each suggestion.

## References

Atkinson, M. and Hornby, G. (2002), *Mental Health Handbook for Schools*. London: Routledge Falmer.

Biederman, I. (1990), 'Higher-level vision', in D. N. Osherson, S. M. Kosslyn and J. M. Hollerbach (eds), *An Invitation to Cognitive Science: Visual Cognition and Action* (Vol. 2). Cambridge, MA: MIT Press.

Broadbent, D. E. (1975), 'Cognitive psychology and education', *British Journal of Educational Psychology*, 45, 162–76.

Broadbent, D. E. (1987), *Perception and Communication*. London: Oxford University Press.

Bruner, J. S. and Goodman, C.C. (1947), 'Value and need as organizing factors in perception', *Journal of Abnormal and Social Psychology*, 42, 33–44.

Chadwick, P. (1978), 'Some aspects of the development of geological thinking', *Geology Teaching*, 3, 142–8.

Cohen, L. and Manion, L. (1981), *Perspectives in Classrooms and Schools*. Eastbourne: Holt, Rinehart and Winston.

Craik, F. I. M. and Lockhart, R. S. (1972), 'Levels of processing: a framework for memory research', *Journal of Verbal Learning and Verbal Behavior*, 11, 671–84.

Eysenck, H. J. (1967), *The Biological Basis of Personality*. Springfield, IL: Thomas.

Gale, A. and Edwards, J. A. (eds) (1983), *Physiological Correlates of Human Behaviour. Vol. 1: Basic Issues. Vol. 2: Attention and Performance. Vol. 3: Individual Differences and Psychopathology*. London: Academic Press.

Gale, A. and Eysenck, M. W. (eds) (1992), *Handbook of Individual Differences: A Biological Perspective*. London: Wiley.

Galton, M. J. and Simon, B. (eds) (1980), *Progress and Performance in the Primary Classroom*. London: Routledge and Kegan Paul.

Galton, M. J., Simon, B. and Croll, P. (1980), *Inside the Primary Classroom*. London: Routledge and Kegan Paul.

Galton, M. J., Hargreaves, L., Comber, C. and Wall, D. with Pell, S. (1999), *Inside the Primary Classroom: 20 Years On*. London: Routledge.

Goldstein, E. B. (2002), *Sensation and Perception* (6th edn). Pacific Grove: Wadsworth and Thomson.

Gregory, R. L. (1996), 'Twenty-five years after "The Intelligent Eye"', *Psychologist*, 10, 452–5.

Gregory, R. L. (1998), *Eye and Brain: The Psychology of Seeing* (5th edn). Oxford: Oxford University Press.

Hargie, O., Saunders, C. and Dickson, D. (1994), *Social Skills in Interpersonal Communication* (3rd edn). London: Routledge.

Heron, W., Doane, B. K. and Scott, T. H. (1956), 'Visual disturbances after prolonged perceptual isolation', *Canadian Journal of Psychology*, 10, 13–16.

James, W. (1890), *The Principles of Psychology* (Vol. 1). New York: Holt.

Kosslyn, S. M. and Koenig, O. (1995), *Wet Mind: The New Cognitive Neuroscience* (2nd edn). New York: Free Press.

Maguire, E. A., Frackowiak, R. S. and Frith, C. D. (1996), 'Learning to find your way around: a role for the human hippocampal formation', *Proceedings of the Royal Society of London (B): Biological Sciences*, 263, 1745–50.

Maguire, E. A., Gadian, D. S., Johnsrude, I. S., Good, C. D., Ashburner, J., Frackowiak, R. S. and Frith, C. D. (2000), 'Navigation related structural change in the hippocampi of taxi drivers', *Proceedings NASciences (USA)*, 97(8), 4398–403.

Moray, N. (1969), *Listening and Attention* (2nd edn). London: Penguin.

Morton, J. (1967), 'A singular lack of incidental learning', *Nature*, 215, 203–4.

Neisser, U. (1976), *Cognition and Reality: Principles and Implications of Cognitive Psychology*. San Francisco: Freeman.

Neisser, U. (1982), *Memory Observed*. San Francisco: Freeman.

Posner, M. I. and Dehaene, S. (1994), 'Attentional networks', *Trends in Neuroscience*, 17, 75–9.

Posner, M. I. and Raichle, M. E. (1994), *Images of Mind*. New York: Scientific American Library.

Shaywitz, B., Shaywitz, S., Pugh, K., Constables, R., Skudlarski, P., Fulbright, R., Bronen, R., Fletcher, J., Shankweiler, D., Katz, L. and Gore, J. (1995), 'Sex differences in the functional organization of the brain for language', *Nature*, 373, 607–9.

Siegel, L. and Siegel, L. C. (1965), 'Educational set: a determinant of acquisition', *Journal of Educational Psychology*, 56, 1–12.

Suedfeld, P. and Coren, S. (1989), 'Perceptual isolation, sensory deprivation and rest', *Canadian Psychology*, 30, 17–29.

Treisman, A. M. (1964), 'Verbal cues, language and meaning in selective attention', *American Journal of Psychology*, 77, 215–6.

Vernon, P. E. (1969), *Intelligence and Cultural Environment*. London: Methuen.

Wapner, S. and Demick, J. (eds) (1991), *Field Dependence-independence: Cognitive Style across the Life Span*. Hillsdale, NJ: Erlbaum.

Witkin, H. A. (1962), *Psychological Differentiation: Studies of Development*. New York: Wiley.

Woodworth, R. S. and Marquis, D. G. (1949), *Psychology*. London: Methuen.

Zubek, J. P. (1969), *Sensory Deprivation: Fifteen Years of Research*. New York: Appleton-Century-Crofts.

## Further reading

Coren, S., Ward, L. M. and Enns, J. T. (2004), *Sensation and Perception* (6th edn). Chichester: Wiley.

Eysenck, M. W. and Keane, M. (2005), *Cognitive Psychology* (5th edn). Hove: Psychology Press.

Hargie, O., Saunders, C. and Dickson, D. (2004), *Skilled Interpersonal Communication: Research, Theory and Practice* (4th edn). London: Routledge.

# Concept Formation and Cognitive Development

## Implications for teachers

- Concept formation and attainment are of central interest to teachers. Their lives are spent finding ways of helping their students to achieve concept understanding.

- A study of how concepts develop is important to all teachers no matter at which level they teach or, if relevant, what subject specialism.

- The substantial contributions of Piaget and Vygotsky have influenced teaching methods and should be studied.

- Though criticism surrounds the theories of cognitive development, there remains much of value in them.

- Language plays a substantial part in concept development and formation (see Chapter 5).

In Chapters 3 and 7, we assume the existence of internal mental processes as a necessary step in the analysis of sensory experiences. One simplified interpretation suggested is a long-term store of past experiences which are made available when we need to appraise incoming signals, the outcome of which is to regulate our behaviour. The mental activity which we assume is taking place is defined by the familiar term *thinking* (Sternberg and Smith 1988, Baron 2000). Vinacke (1952) suggests that thinking involves 'internal processes which bring the organization laid down in past learning to bear upon responses to current situations, and which shape these responses in keeping with inner needs'. The existence of these inner processes is supported from observations we make of our own thought processes (introspection) and from the simple fact that our responses to problem situations have much more in them than the original information with which we are provided. Brain scanning during problem-solving also exhibits changes in blood flow.

Unfortunately, 'thinking' has become a confused and multipurpose term; it has even come to mean different things to different psychologists. Peel (1960) presented a number of different ways in which the term 'thinking' had been used.

## Further reading

He classified them under four headings:

- *thematic* – imaginative thinking in creative writing, painting or music, where one is not bound by a given problem
- *explanatory* – describing and explaining events and things
- *productive* – applying knowledge in new situations, giving rise to new inventions or products
- *co-ordinating* or *integrative* thinking – seen in the discovery of new theories and systems of thought.

However, a useful, broad distinction which we can draw is between *perceptual* and *ideational* thinking. Perceptual thinking is the term we apply to the mental activity occurring during problem-solving which relies on the presence of the object or objects involved in the problem. For example, much of Piaget's work with very young children calls for an understanding of perceptual thinking (see later in the chapter). Ideational thinking, on the other hand, is much more complex and relies on the existence of a symbolic form such as a language or number system, and does not necessarily rely on the presence of cues from the environment. The work of Sperry, mentioned in Chapter 2, points to a further distinction in ideational thinking between *spatial* and *verbal* thinking specific to right and left hemispheres of the brain.

We shall meet both these types of thinking in our discussion of concept formation later in the chapter. But first we must turn to a consideration of the means whereby thinking is made possible.

# Concepts

## Theories and definitions

If we were not able to classify the things and events around us we would find it impossible to carry out the simplest task, let alone the highly complicated mental operations of which we are capable. To attempt to treat all objects or events as unique would lead to an unmanageable task when it came to trying to comprehend and represent our environment. Instead we categorize objects and events. From accumulated experience we learn to group characteristics which are common to particular objects or events, even though these characteristics are only roughly similar; for example, 'chairs' come in various shapes and sizes, colours, numbers of legs, but they are given the name 'chair'. The end product is a concept – an idea consisting of attributes that are sufficiently similar as to be grouped together. For example, flowers (like the chairs above) come in many forms, but they have properties in common: they all serve the same purpose in providing for the production of seeds; they have, by and large, similar structures such as petals, stamen and pollen grains. These *critical attributes* which connect one flower with the next enable the category 'flower' to be formed.

But how do we arrive at critical attributes? *Classical* theory (Howard 1987), which goes back to Greek philosophy, claims that we abstract from experience the defining features (attributes) of the concept. In the 'chair' example above, the defining features might be the surface to sit on, legs solid enough to support weight of a body, etc. To define a concept, the common features have to be sought and these are then applied to any new exemplar. Unfortunately, the clarity with which a concept can be defined ranges from near certainty to hazy probability. An example of a 'certain' (sometimes called a classical) concept is 'virgin' or 'earth's moon'. The defining attributes of both these concepts are clear and referred to as *core* properties. However, most concepts are probabilistic. Take, for instance, the 'chair' exemplar above. Where does a beanbag fit into the definition? It is used as a chair, but it certainly hasn't many of the features we normally associate with a chair. Again, take the concept 'table'. There are many objects we call a table. The predominant characteristic is a flat surface with some means of support. But the range of variations – in the shape and size of the surface, its colour, height from the ground, material from which it is made and the kind of support – is tremendous. The permutations and combinations of characteristics at first seem to defy generalization, yet we are able to apply the concept 'table'.

To account for the possible variation in a concept, a *prototype* theory was postulated (Smith and Medin 1981). A prototype is an idealization which brings all the attributes together. No example of the concept need necessarily possess *all* the attributes. In the chair example above, a beanbag has no legs and no flat surface to sit on, but it does support the weight of the body quite comfortably. It is largely a question of whether an exemplar shares sufficient features to qualify as an example of a concept. Defining a prototype depends upon specifying which features 'on average' consistently turn up (Howard 1987).

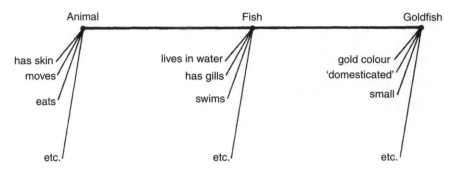

**Figure 4.1** Hierarchical theory of concepts – an illustration.

In addition to accumulating characteristics of particular concepts from observation, other people, reading, etc., we also establish relationships between them. Several theories have developed, amongst which the *hierarchical* (and, more recently, the *spreading activation*) theory has common currency (Smith and Medin 1981, Medin and Smith 1984).

For instance, a 'goldfish' is a sub-set of 'fish', which is a sub-set of 'animal'. These networks of concepts can be arranged hierarchically and consist of *nodes* which represent key concepts. The information 'stored' at these nodes (this is clearly an information-processing model) is illustrated in Figure 4.1.

The characteristics common to the vast majority of fish would be stored only at the 'fish' node. Attributes which distinguish one variety of fish from another would be stored at the lowest node. Exceptions to the generality of fish would have to be learned as a technical distinction.

A recent modified view by Collins and Loftus (1975), which tries to meet a number of weaknesses in the hierarchical theory, is called the *spreading activation* theory. This relies on semantic relatedness and distance. Nodes are used as described above but in a network rather than a hierarchy. The theory is quite complex, but put in its crudest form it depends on the strength of links between nodes for the process of concept characterization. When a concept is presented a node is activated and this activity spreads out to neighbouring nodes. By a process of 'true'/'false' decisions at the nearby nodes, evidence is accumulated to define the presented concept.

This process has been used to explain the acquisition of concepts as a form of hypothesis-testing (Bourne *et al.* 1979). But there are many unresolved problems as to the 'how' of concept formation. Young children, for instance, are particularly prone to overgeneralization and this is assumed to be the result of not having learned the criteria for the limits to be imposed in forming a classification. Any part of a plant, be it a leaf, root, stem or whatever, is likely to be labelled as a flower. By the same token, all men *may* be 'daddies' to a young child because the critical attributes of fatherhood have not yet been established in the child's mind, only 'maleness'.

Families find these over-generalizations endearing and most have amusing examples, oft repeated and sometimes to the embarrassment of the children involved. The two-year-old daughter of the author's neighbour saw, on different occasions, mothers breast-feeding their babies. Shortly afterwards the youngster was seen trying to put her nipple in her doll's mouth, and enquired of mother why the doll wasn't feeding, and where was her milk? The grandchildren of the author provide numerous examples. He went with Thomas at the age of 18 months to a zoo. Thomas was in the process of learning about animals, their names and the sounds they make. On seeing wolves, he said, 'Uf! Uf!' – an understandable error. His granddaughter, Natasha, at two-and-a-half went to see some horses in a paddock at the back of the house. She pointed to them and said 'big doggies'.

At a more advanced level, refined distinctions will be necessary before a child can distinguish between different kinds of flowers and between 'daddies'. The argument surrounding this point is whether the child has not assimilated the criteria because he or she lacks the necessary level of mental maturity or because *we* have not discovered how to put it over to young children in a manner they can understand.

The speed and inevitability of concept attainment in the young, despite varied child-rearing practices and in some cases alarming cultural disadvantages, have led many to believe that we are born with a predisposition to order our perceptions into concepts. However, though the *act* of concept formation might be inborn, the substance of the concepts is acquired from experience and it is this vital point which is of concern to teachers. Both parents and teachers constitute reference groups for assisting children in establishing concept attributes.

## Imagery

It is believed that in the early stages, some concepts become established as images. *Imagery* is the term we use to describe calling up a mental replica (using any sense modality) of an object or event which we have previously experienced. If we said 'call up the image of a ringing bell', you would imagine the sound of an actual bell which you had heard sometime in the past. Bruner (see Chapter 5, 'Cognitive growth and representation') supposes that we actually recall a composite sound by combining previous similar experiences. He calls this *iconic* representation. Piaget (later in this chapter) refers to imagery as *internalized imitation*; in other words, we take in the actual sensory events and reproduce some aspects of them on request. *Eidetic imagery* is an extreme case of the ability to recall a sensory event in great detail. This is done by casting an actual image of what is seen on to a surface and using it to identify parts of the total scene. Children are especially gifted (about 6 per cent) in exhibiting the skill. Probably the talent becomes redundant because it is not put to use. The phenomenon is sometimes known as 'photographic memory', although it seems unlikely that the images are as perfect as a photograph.

Images can be used as the basis for simple reasoning. For example, the simpler scientific and geometrical concepts involving apparatus and figural arrangements can occasionally be manipulated as an image in our minds. It is also possible that animals use imagery as an aid in their responses. They also try out their reactions to the environment physically rather than by manipulating mental concepts because, it is believed, animals have more highly developed and organized sensory organs than humans do.

Scanning techniques have made some significant contributions to our knowledge of imagery (Blakemore and Frith 2000). For example, scanning has shown that the same parts of the brain are involved when imagining an object as when we actually look at the same object. Vivid or frightening images (e.g. mutilated bodies) have an effect on some physiological functions such as heart rate, skin temperature and conductance – the more frightening the image, the more the brain is stimulated. This is also related to the phenomenon of *biofeedback* (met with in Chapter 2) where the emotional and physiological state of a person can be regulated and controlled by the individual, thus affecting the physiological functioning of the body.

The important point is that the extent to which a person can control emotional states is influenced by their ability to use imagery. Problems such as stress are partly influenced by a person's ability to form and use images, although it has to be emphasized that these abilities vary greatly from person to person.

## Abstract concepts

But many concepts cannot even be imagined because they are far too complex or abstract. We cannot imagine 'energy' or 'honesty'. We might be able to conjure up an image of a body moving and therefore possessing energy, or perhaps the picture of someone stealing (and by implication what an honest person should not do), but these are only instances (*exemplars*) of some aspect of the concepts. People's ability to deal with problems in the absence of material evidence or mental images and to reach higher levels of complexity in appreciation of and response to the environment (in contrast to animals) is due entirely to the use of *symbolic languages*. These include number systems, musical notation, etc., as well as the spoken and written word. By classifying and labelling with words and phrases, humans can represent the world economically, while at the same time freeing themselves from the need for material evidence in our reasoning. Through the acquisition of concepts, from the simplest discrimination and classification of objects to the complex moral, mathematical or scientific concepts, we order our experiences. In the process, language plays a vital role, and we shall devote the next chapter to a consideration of this aspect. For the time being it is important to remember that words are not concepts: they only stand for concepts. In the case of class concepts a word is a label which represents, symbolically, a class of objects or events.

## Propositional and imaginal thought

Another way of expressing the distinction drawn by Sperry (Chapter 2) between spatial and verbal thinking is *propositional* and *imaginal* thought processes. Much of the description above revolves around *propositional thinking* in which we appear to use language 'in our minds'. To use language, we have to rely on concepts. Our propositional thinking rests on the strength of the concepts we have available for use in our language repertoire. 'Reasoning' is often used as an alternative term for propositional thinking. If we asked you to tell us the difference between night and day, what would go on in your mind? Whatever else, you would be thinking about light and dark, time concepts, sun movements and so on – all propositional thinking.

But suppose we asked you to tell us what your favourite teacher looked like. Your first thoughts would deal with the decision about what qualities are necessary to become a favourite teacher of yours – what did she/he have to be and do in order to become your favourite. These would be propositional thoughts. On the other hand, you might start trying to recall the faces of teachers from your past and present. This is a quite different use of your memory because instead of 'language in your mind', you are relying on visual images. This is referred to as *imaginal thought* and is a very powerful tool in the hands of teachers. Generally, any question which asks for a description (visual, auditory, tactile, smell, taste and kinaesthetic) will rely on images rather than concepts derived from propositions. Where a question relies on sensory experiences, imaginal thought will be used (e.g. your mind's eye or ear). Try these. Where would the hands of a clock be if the time is quarter past one? If your local church has bells, how many are there? Distinguish between the feel of silk and sharkskin. How does it feel when you touch your toes? All the answers will depend to some extent on recalled sensory experiences. We shall see later that Gardner (1999) suggested kinaesthetic intelligence, where we have different sensitivities to body movement. Dancers and those good at sports would probably have high values of this ability.

## Some characteristics of concepts

To help us in our understanding of the development of thinking in children, let us first take a closer look at some of the more important characteristics of concepts (Vinacke 1952).

(a)  They are not the actual sensory events, but representations of some aspects of these events (prototypes). With most concepts there are wide margins of attribute acceptability, for example a leaf can be small, glossy, dark green and prickly like a holly leaf or large, dull, light green and harmless like a chestnut leaf. In some cases the boundaries which distinguish concepts are hazy and ill defined (some of the abstract concepts we have to deal with in the study of human behaviour are of this nature), but generally speaking there is a large measure of agreement in the definition of most class concepts within a given culture.

(b) Concepts are dependent upon previous experience. We have noted that home background and educational opportunity are possible variables in the formation of concepts. Likewise there are emotional as well as perceptual connections associated with concept formation (see (e) (ii) below on the intentional use of concepts).

(c) Concepts are symbolic in human beings. The concept 'bee' can be called to mind from numerous stimulus sources. The sight of the insect or the word 'bee', a relentless droning sound, honey, a piece of music ('The Flight of the Bumble Bee') can all trigger off the concept 'bee'. Words, numbers, chemical symbols or physical formulae have symbolic significance beyond the simple meaning normally associated with the actual symbol. For the chemist, the symbol 'O' is not just a circle: it represents the element oxygen. Sometimes objects have complex symbolic meaning, for example the crucifix, a V sign or road signs. The same symbols can have totally different cultural significance. A 'thumbs up' in Britain generally means OK, but on the continent (Italy for example) it has the same meaning as raising the middle finger in Britain.

(d) Concepts can form 'horizontal' or 'vertical' organizations. An example of a horizontal classification would be if we were to give children some examples of reptiles – snakes, lizards, crocodiles and dinosaurs. They all belong to the same major group of animals because they possess certain attributes in common. However, they also differ in several other respects, thus permitting us to classify them into separate groups *within* the same level in the animal kingdom.

Vertical classification results from the presence of hierarchies, that is, categories which increase in complexity as we proceed through the classification. A dog belongs to the family of animals called *canis*, which is subordinate to the order of animals called *carnivora* (along with cats, bears, otters and seals), which is subordinate to the class of animals called *mammals*, which in turn are *vertebrates* (with backbones), which are *animals*. You will notice the increasing inclusiveness of the groups as we pass up the hierarchy of the animal kingdom (see Figure 4.1).

Some higher-order concepts are very complicated. Try working out the number of subordinate concepts required to understand the concept of 'force', the theorem of Pythagoras, the Ten Commandments or the causes which led to the fall of the Roman Empire.

(e) Concepts function in at least two ways: extensionally and intentionally.

 (i) The *extensional* use of concepts applies where the meaning given is the widely acknowledged one defined in terms which are patently clear to anyone observing the object or event. Concept usage arises from common agreement and acceptance of the objective attributes of the object. A particular variety of plant or animal, let us say a lupin or a giraffe, has a 'public' meaning which we all accept.

(ii) The *intentional* use of concepts can vary considerably from one person to another. In this case the concept is defined as a result of personal, subjective experiences accompanying the formation of the concept. A rose might arouse pleasant associations or unpleasant ones if one has suffered the thorns during pruning. A botanist might view the plant from a technical standpoint, an artist from a creative, aesthetic angle, and a cricket fan in Lancashire as an emblem of the county in the 'Roses match'. In all these cases, special significance which has no universal acceptance has become attached to the object.

(f) Some concepts can be irrational. Superstitions (black cats, ladders, opening an umbrella indoors, lucky numbers and colours) provide many illustrations of irrational concepts. Their origins are obscure.

(g) Many concepts are formed without our conscious awareness. Values established by our culture and which regulate our daily conduct have often been formed as habits in our childhood without our realizing it. Aversions and prejudices frequently are stamped into our repertoire of responses in this way. Dislike of animals, racial prejudice and attitudes towards religion or politics are planted imperceptibly during a lifetime.

In our discussion of concepts it has been argued that concept formation is dependent upon several psychological processes. First, a young child, by whatever means, has to be able to *differentiate* the attributes of the environment. By this we mean that the child must have sufficient perceptual skills to distinguish the characteristics observed in order even to begin the formation of categories. As we observed before, young children may refer to all men as 'daddy' or all four-legged creatures as 'doggy', possibly because of the child's inability to limit the scope of generalizations, because he or she has not yet learned the rules of differentiation, or because the concepts are formed but the child has not yet learned how to use the words.

Second, having consolidated an ability to differentiate features, children have to perceive *grouping*, that is, they need to recognize structural or functional similarities. Finally, they have to *categorize* the groupings into hierarchies, thus devising classes of experience with increasing levels of complexity and abstractness.

# Piaget's theory of cognitive development

Contemporary views on the nature of cognitive development have been vastly influenced by the work of one man. This was Jean Piaget (1896–1980), once a biologist, who turned his energies to a study of the evolution of children's thinking. His impetus from the Universities of Paris and Geneva has led to a worldwide search for important factors in concept development. His particular line of thinking and the abundant research it has generated is sometimes known as the *Geneva School* of thought to distinguish it from the *Harvard School* in the United States typified by the work of Bruner, the *Russian School,* founded by Vygotsky and Luria, and the *Anglo-Saxon School* in Britain. His findings probably have done more to influence educational practices in Britain than most theories (Piaget 1952, 1970; Inhelder and Piaget 1958). He would have claimed that *epistemology,* that is, the study of how we know what we know and the extent of this knowledge, was his primary interest.

His initial method of investigation was the clinical approach: detailed face-to-face discussion, observation and questioning of individual children in many problem situations (he used his own children in the first experiments in the 1920s). It aims to discover, by analysing performance and verbal introspections, the quality and nature of children's concept attainment at a particular time in their lives. The work has led to a descriptive analysis of development of basic physical, logical, mathematical and moral concepts from birth to adolescence (concept growth in such things as number, time, space, velocity, geometry, chance and morality). At heart, his theory is:

- a genetic one, in that higher processes are seen to evolve from biological mechanisms which are rooted in the development of an individual's nervous system (compare this view with that of Hebb 1973; also see Bartlett 1932).
- a maturational one, because he believes that the processes of concept formation follow an invariant pattern through several clearly definable stages which emerge during specific age ranges.
- an hierarchical one, in that the stages he proposes *must* be experienced and passed through in a given order before any subsequent stages of development are possible.

Piaget also maintained that three factors are of special importance in ensuring the appearance of the stages of cognitive development. These are: (a) biological factors, which account for the regularity and inevitability of the stages he postulates in much the same way as we see the appearance of sexual characteristics during a given period in the development of boys and girls before we are justified in saying they are physically mature adults; (b) educational and cultural transmission, which, according to Piaget, account for the discrepancies in the chronological ages at which his stages appear as we pass from one individual to another; and (c) the activities in which children engage. Piaget took an 'active' rather than a 'passive' view of the part played by children in their own development. The child's self-directed motor activity is seen as a necessity in cognitive development.

His earlier preoccupation with biology and logic was reflected in the widespread use he made of the technical language used in these subjects. It will be necessary, therefore, to sort out some of these terms before we describe his developmental theory.

In the first days of life, a baby responds to the surroundings by reflex activity which, as we know, is *not* acquired. Very soon, the baby develops beyond reflex action and begins to react to the surroundings in a way which leads us to suspect purposeful behaviour. The baby seeks the mother's nipple, grasps objects in contact with the palm of its hands; general body movement begins to show signs of coordination. These actions, which become organized into distinct patterns of behaviour, Piaget referred to as *schemata* ('schema' is the singular, 'schemata' or 'schemas' the plural). Note that the key to the formation of schemata is *action* on the part of the baby in attempting to adapt to the demands of the environment. Once a schema has appeared, it becomes directed to similar, parallel situations, rather like transfer of training (see Chapter 7). For example, arm movement, grasping, then lifting towards the mouth is a cycle of activity which is likely to happen to any object which comes within the child's range.

The process described in the last paragraph, of incorporating new perceptions either to form new schemata or integrating them into existing schemata, was termed assimilation by Piaget (analogous to humans taking in a variety of foods which the body uses to build into existing tissue). When the child is capable of modifying existing schemata to meet new environmental demands, it is said to experience *accommodation*. (Using the biological analogy again, the infant being weaned from milk to solids will have to accommodate the change in the nature of the food in order to assimilate the food for use by the body.)

In summary, Piaget considered that conceptual growth occurs because the child, while actively attempting to adapt to the environment, organizes actions into schemata through the processes of assimilation and accommodation.

A *schema* is an important element in Piaget's theory. Bartlett (1932) coined the expression to describe 'an active organization of past actions'. Hebb (1973) uses *cell assemblies* as the counterpart of Piaget's schemata. In effect, the mental framework of past experiences is the substance of Broadbent's long-term memory store (see Chapters 3 and 7). When the actions become replaced by symbols (words, numbers, etc.), they become known as *representational schemata*. When a child is able to represent the world mentally, by means of memory, imagery or symbolic language, it is said to have *internalized* these experiences.

Thought or thinking, according to Piaget, has its origins in actions physically performed and then internalized. Bluntly then, thought is internalized actions. The starting point of cognitive development, therefore, must be activity on the part of the neonate, not passive reception of sensory data. The child's striving to adapt and structure experiences enables patterns of actions to be formed. At a primitive level, the patterns may be simple perceptual patterns which become internalized. When these are recalled, they reappear as images of the original experience. We have already mentioned this phenomenon as imagery (internalized imitation).

Once symbolic language frees children from the need to manipulate raw reality in order to form schemata, they can begin to develop logical thinking and are able to reason using representations of facts. The ability to carry out activities in one's imagination is known as an *operation* and, as we shall see presently, a child's growth to intellectual maturity depends on its capacity to carry out these mental operations. This reminds us of the distinction between perceptual and ideational thinking mentioned at the beginning of the chapter.

In the developmental description which follows, we shall see how Piaget accounts for the gradual unfolding of thinking skills, starting with simple sensory and motor activities in babyhood and gradually being superseded by internal representation of actions carried out by the child; then, through the agency of language, reaching the highest form of logical thinking, at first in the presence of objective evidence and finally by mental reasoning.

## Piaget's stages of development

Beard (1969) or Phillips (1979) give dated, but excellent summaries.

We argued above that Piaget's theory was genetic, maturational and hierarchical. Adaptation takes place in a set sequence of stages associated with successive mental (not chronological) ages. Several schemes representing the stages exist. The outline in Table 4.1 are the two most popular.

**Table 4.1** Outline of Piaget's stages of development

| Period | Stage | Mental age range in years |
|---|---|---|
| Sensori-motor | I Sensori-motor | 0–2 |
| Preparation for, | II Pre-operational | |
| and use of, | (A) Pre-conceptual | 2–4 |
| concrete operations | (B) Intuitive | 4–7 |
| (or latency) | III Concrete operations | 7–11 |
| Formal operations | IV Formal operations | 11 onwards |

### I: The sensori-motor stage (mental age approximately 0–2 years)

Developmentally, the first two years of life are very important and full. So much is achieved in motor and mental skills by way of walking, talking, playing and establishing a self-identity. Yet, at birth, actions are severely limited to reflex grasping, sucking and general body movement. Within the first months, the reflexes become adapted to very simple tasks. The first schemata involve grasping or sucking anything which comes in contact with hand or mouth.

As the senses and limb movements rapidly improve and coordinate, cycles of activity are discovered and repeated by the infant. For example, the baby may combine an arm movement with placing thumb in mouth and sucking it. These cycles of action Piaget calls *primary circular reactions*. They are significant because their appearance gives the first clues to the existence of a primitive memory. Note, however, that the voluntary motions of the infant are extensions of reflex action and not purposive movements. Equally, the movements are directed towards the baby's own body rather than objects outside it. These rudimentary habitual schemata are called 'primary' because they are at first built into the baby's inherent reflex systems.

Soon new activities appear, with less and less apparent connection with reflexes. Around four to eight months the baby begins to direct its activities towards objects outside the body, and this enlarges the range of actions. Increasing visual-motor coordination enables the child to carry out these tasks. With each new object, the baby carries out party pieces with schemata already assimilated. These are called *secondary circular reactions*, where patterns of action become generalized to any object within reach. Up to one year of age the secondary circular reactions are coordinated and applied to new situations. There is every sign of purposeful behaviour as sequences of movements seem to be directed towards the attainment of goals. For example, the infant will move objects out of the way to obtain a desired toy, which implies that schemata are being assimilated and co-ordinated by combining secondary circular reactions.

Accommodation has played a minor role up to this point. The child has been preoccupied with the assimilation of schemata. Initially, when an object is hidden, even in the presence of the child, it will not be pursued – out of sight, out of mind! There is no suggestion of reasoning as we know it. Life is all go!

From 12 to 18 months, however, the child becomes capable of inventing new ways of attaining ends. Circular reactions may be repeated with several variations. In other words the child is beginning to accommodate to new situations by modifying and experimenting with existing schemata. These are called *tertiary circular reactions*.

Towards the end of the sensori-motor stage, the child is beginning to represent the world in mental images and symbols. The onset of language enables the child to represent objects in their absence. Playing bricks become cars or real building bricks in the child's imagination. Play becomes very important. For Piaget, play enables the child to assimilate. Imitation, on the other hand, is an example of accommodation, because the child is attempting to modify behaviour to become someone or something else. *Deferred imitation* is the ability to copy someone else in their absence and represents a great advance, because it shows that the child is now able to form images of events which can be recalled for future reference.

## II A: Pre-conceptual stage (mental age approximately 2–4 years)

The direct link between sensory experiences and motor activity, so apparent in the first of Piaget's stages, gradually becomes obscured by the intermediate process of mental activity. This occurs largely because the child is internalizing imitations and actions.

As the term 'pre-conceptual' implies, children are not yet able to formulate concepts in the same way as older children and adults. Concept formation which relies on abstracting and discriminating the characteristics of objects or situations in order to form generalizations is known as *inductive* reasoning. Where generalizations are used to describe particular instances, we call the process *deductive* reasoning. Children at this stage tend neither to induction nor to deduction. Instead, they use *transductive* reasoning. By this Piaget means that children reason by going from one particular instance to another particular instance in order to form *pre-concepts*.

One or two illustrations of transductive reasoning should help to show how preconcepts are formed. My daughter, Louise, at three years six months saw her mother combing her hair. She said, 'Mummy is combing her hair. She is going shopping.' I asked her why Mummy was going shopping and apparently she had noticed that on the previous day the two events had been linked. Louise had reasoned transductively by going from the particular to the particular. Mummy combs her hair on many occasions for many reasons – similarly she goes out on many occasions – but the coincidence of these two events had created a pre-concept. In summary, A occurs with B once, therefore A occurs with B always. The pre-concept 'all men are daddies' has been formed by the child who has used only one characteristic (voice, clothing or features) which all men have in common. We tend to play on this fact in the Father Christmas confidence trick. Young children are not sophisticated enough to distinguish between the men dressed up and appearing in different places. For very young children, they are all one person. Piaget thus claims that the child cannot successfully form classes of objects.

The period is also progressively dominated by symbolic play – dolls become babies, flowers become rows of children. Similarly, imitation of what other people are doing is in evidence. *Egocentricism* predominates because the child is unable to view things from another person's point of view. The child does not appreciate that if he or she and another person were looking at an object from different angles, the two views would be different. We shall see the importance of egocentric speech (rehearsing with oneself) in the next chapter.

Some research (Povey and Hill 1975, Donaldson 1978, Bryant 1982) has cast some doubt on the inevitability of pre-concepts. Piaget's theory, being essentially maturational and hierarchical, assumes a systematic unfolding of ability. But the central role of language, very much a social activity, may have been undervalued by Piaget and his followers, not only as a source of variation between children's concept development but also as the vehicle by which children convey their ability to form concepts. This point will arise again under 'Some criticisms of Piaget's theory', later in the chapter.

### II B: Intuitive stage (mental age approximately 4–7 years)
The child begins this period of intellectual development very much dependent upon su-perficial perceptions of the environment. Ideas are formed impressionistically – hence the name 'intuitive' stage. This arises because the child appears to be unable to account for all aspects of a situation simultaneously. Also, the outlook is dominated by the perceptual field, in that the youngster fixates on one dimension of an object or event to the exclusion of all others. Piaget calls this phenomenon *centring*. The child grasps only one relationship at a time.

> ## Example
>
> A simple experiment described by Piaget will demonstrate the notion of centring. Two plasticine balls are rolled until the child agrees that they are the same size. One ball is then chosen and rolled into a sausage shape, as in Figure 4.2, and put alongside the other ball. If a five-year-old is asked if they are the same size (or whether one ball has more plasticine in it than the other), the child will most frequently say that the sausage is bigger. If asked why, the child usually says, 'because it is longer'. Occasionally a long, narrow shape is taken as being smaller because it is narrower. In the first case the child has 'centred' on the length dimension of the sausage shape and has compared it with the width of the ball to arrive at the conclusion that the former is more. In the second case, where there are claims that the sausage is smaller, the child has centred on the width.

To explain this, Piaget says that children, by centring on a single aspect of a problem and ignoring all others, lack the ability for *conservation of quantity* (plasticine or water would be described as a 'continuous' quantity, beads as a 'discontinuous' quantity). An inability to conserve arises because at this stage of their development children seem unable to reverse the situations they are observing. While watching a ball being rolled into a sausage shape, they 'centre' on one dimension changing in length without being capable of reversing the

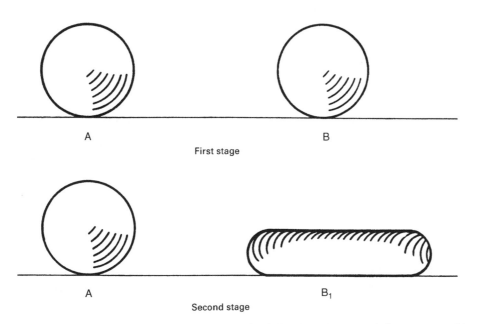

**Figure 4.2** To demonstrate conservation using balls of Plasticine. First stage: balls appear equal in quantity. Second stage: to conservers, balls are still accepted as equal in quantity: to non-conservers, $B_1$ is more or less than A.

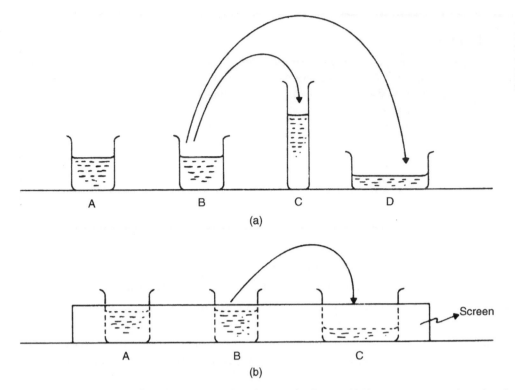

**Figure 4.3** Conservation of continuous quantities using vessels of water. (a) The conserver appreciates that the quantities in C and D are the same as in A. The non-conserver says there is more in C and less in D when they are compared with A. (b) Bruner's experiment.

process back to the point of origin and realizing that the actual quantity of material is unchanged.

Another example of irreversibility in a conservation experiment is afforded by filling two identical vessels with water to the same level. They must be accepted by the child as similar in level. One vessel is taken and the contents poured into a vessel of a different shape – tall and thin or small and squat, as in Figure 4.3(a). Children who cannot reverse and therefore conserve would claim that there was more liquid in vessel C than in A (or less in D than in A). When asked why, the children soon display that they have centred on length or width without compensating for changes in the other dimensions.

An interesting modification reported by Bruner (1964) is shown in Figure 4.3(b). The third vessel, C, was chosen to be the same height as the other two and all but the tops of the vessels hidden from view using a screen. When asked which vessel, A or C, had the most drink in it, younger children (four- to five-year-olds) did no better than chance (half were correct), 90 per cent of the five- to six-year-olds got the correct answer, while 100 per cent of six- to seven-year-olds came up with the answer. It would seem that the younger children who can see what is going on are overwhelmingly influenced by the perceptual field and, when this is partly removed, they resort to intuitive guesswork.

According to Piaget, the act of repeating the sequence of activities performed in these experiments in one direction makes it very difficult for the child to reverse the process. Therefore, reversibility is a central skill which frees the child from intuitive impressions, enabling an appreciation of the *invariance* of materials undergoing a change in physical dimensions without changes in total quantity.

---

## Example

Some of these experiments look so simple to the adult, and the child's errors so incredibly naïve. In an experiment of Piaget's, several sweets or counters are arranged in equal rows, some for the child, and an opposite row for another person.

child

. . . . .

. . . . .

other person

When the child's row is spread out thus:

. . . . .

. . . . .

the child will say, if at the intuitive level of development, that he or she has more than the other person. A contracted row is said to be smaller and contain less. We again meet up with a transitivity problem involving invariance similar to those described in the body of the textbook. The child uses length as the criterion of quantity and is immediately faced with a conflict of hypotheses.

Bryant (1971, Bryant and Trabasso 1971) attempted to remove the conflict. If the arrangement of counters is such that the child has more, as indicated in the illustration beneath:

. . . . . . .

. . . . .

the child will, even at the intuitive level, set up the correct hypothesis by saying he or she has more than the other person (by, as yet, some unsubstantiated method). If the second state is now made indeterminate by placing the counters in two identical glass containers such that they appear the same height (in other words, two counters have not made an appreciable difference to the height), the child, according to Bryant, still says that he or she has more than the other person, regardless of the fact that it can be seen that the heights are equal. Why? Because, says Bryant, the child has been able to establish a 'definite hypothesis' at the first stage, can appreciate the invariance principle in the transformation to the second stage and is not so perceptually dominated at this second stage as to say that the quantities are equal when the heights are equal. When equal numbers of counters are used in the same experiment but are arranged to give unequal lengths in the rows, as in the second part of the illustration at the beginning of this note, the child sets up the incorrect, but definite, hypothesis of a difference in the quantities and maintains it throughout even though, as in the first case, the heights in the glass vessels look equal. Bryant's conclusion is that we ought to concentrate on how children arrive at definite hypotheses rather than debate the invariance issue.

Bryant has questioned the basic assumptions of conservation and has offered alternative explanations which have far-reaching implications for education if they are correct. The central issue is the question of invariance. Piaget, as we have seen, claimed that children who cannot conserve have not yet learned the invariance principle. Bryant challenges this position in the following way. In all the conservation experiments there are usually three steps. First, the child establishes a hypothesis about the equality of the plasticine balls or amounts of liquid as in our particular examples. In other words, the child appreciates that $A = B$ (for plasticine in Figure 4.2 and for the vessels of water in Figure 4.3(a). Furthermore, there is consistency in the appraisal of equality which shows success in making a definite hypothesis. At the next step, the child applies the invariance principle such that the child sees $B = B_1$ (plasticine) or $B = C$ or $D$ (water). Finally, to solve the problem correctly, the child coordinates these first two stages to establish a final hypothesis that $A = B$ (plasticine) or $A = C$ or $D$ (water).

Unfortunately young children without knowledge of counting, weighing or measuring must rely on some other criterion, possibly estimates of length or width in the case of the experiments above. Therefore there is a conflict of hypotheses between the first ($A = B$ using length) and the last ($A$ is not equal to $B$, $C$ or $D$, again using length). Faced with this conflict, the child chooses the most recent deduction and says that $A$ is not equal to $B$, $C$ or $D$. Bryant goes on to substantiate his conflict-hypothesis theory by experiment (see above in small print). His major conclusion is an optimistic one for education because, unlike Piaget, he believes that teaching hypothesis-testing and memory-training would serve a useful purpose. 'Piaget's experiments effectively demonstrate that young children find transitivity problems difficult, but these difficulties are simply the result of *inadequate strategies of recall*' (emphasis added). In effect, we must teach children how 'to distinguish correct hypotheses about quantities and numbers from incorrect ones' and thus avoid failures of memory (not to be confused with failures in logical thinking).

### III: Concrete operations (mental age approximately 7–11 years)

As we have seen, an operation for Piaget is internalized action. At first children's reasoning is tied almost exclusively to concrete experience. They may be able to formulate in the mind a hypothesis which takes them one step beyond the concrete evidence available to them, but they are largely dependent on the perceptual facts before them. The child at this stage *describes* the environment; at the highest levels of abstract reasoning he or she tries to *explain* it. This distinction will be clarified later in the section describing the pendulum experiment.

Conservation, irrespective of number, shape or quantity transformations, is crucial for reasoning at the concrete stage of operations. For example, children would have to be aware that no matter how one presented the problem $2 + 4 + 3(4 + 2 + 3$, etc.) it would still add up to the same quantity. Similarly, they would need to achieve reversal of number to solve any combination of the problem $2 \times 6 = 12$ or $12/6 = 2$ or $12/2 = 6$, all of which require a knowledge of reversal. There are numerous properties capable of being conserved and these, according to Piaget, appear in a particular sequence. Conservation of substance, for instance, occurs around the age of seven to eight years and precedes the conservation of weight (around nine to eleven years), which in turn precedes the conservation of volume (at about twelve years of age). Number conservation appears before area. Another essential process mentioned previously is that of *decentring*. This involves the realization that the same fundamental quantity, be it number, volume, area, weight or whatever, exists no matter how the dimensions might be altered; the child's attention is no longer fixed on one dimension.

A second important operation in the development of concepts is the formation of consistent *classifications*. Previously we saw how the child tended to form pre-concepts by passing from the particular to the particular (transductive reasoning). Now, the formation of valid concepts depends on accurate sorting out of similar and irrelevant properties.

Allied to classification is another process known as *seriation*; that is, the ability to cope with the ordering of similar objects according to, say, size or position. A child who can count (cardination) may not be capable of appreciating the ordering of objects (ordination). Given six sweets arranged in a row, the pre-conceptual mind may not be able to select the fourth from a specified end. Classification and ordination are plainly interdependent, so much so that a child is not able to operate at the concrete level until able to cope with both these processes. Seeing relationships between groups and understanding similarity and subordination of classes are essential skills (Beard 1969, pp. 81–3; Phillips 1979, pp. 69–75) in concrete operational thinking.

There is still a failure to distinguish between hypothesis and reality. At a more advanced stage of cognitive development, a person will test a hypothesis against evidence, whereas in the latency period of concrete operations the person will often adjust the facts to meet the hypothesis. This kind of operation is known as making *assumptive realities*.

One particular assumptive reality is described by Elkind (1973) who observes an interesting egocentric characteristic which he refers to as *cognitive conceit*. Up to this time children have tended to take the wisdom of adults on trust. However, during the period of concrete operations they come to recognize that adults are not infallible. They are sometimes wrong and the child is sometimes right. But this becomes distorted: if adults are wrong in one or two things they are wrong in most things, while if children at this stage are correct in one thing they think they will be correct in almost everything – hence cognitive conceit. In support of his contention, Elkind points to children's literature and cartoons, which are replete with examples of children outwitting adults – *Peter Pan*, *Emile and the Detectives*, *Tom Sawyer*, *Alice in Wonderland*, *Winnie the Pooh* (with the numbskull bear as adult and the cool, clever Christopher Robin as the child), *Tom* (adult) and *Jerry* (child). The kind of verse which tickles children's fancy often pokes fun at what many adults take to be serious, for example the Church and royalty, and Elkind cites several examples, including one from the short reign of Edward VIII, Duke of Windsor:

> Hark the herald angels sing,
> Mrs Simpson's swiped our King.

Another which springs to mind and is calculated to arouse adults of religious conviction is 'while shepherds wash their socks by night', etc. As with other Piagetian stages, it is held that the characteristics may continue to reappear later, and examples of 'assumptive realities' therefore can be found in adult behaviour.

### IV: Formal operations (mental age approximately 11 onwards)

Nine- and ten-year-olds are quite capable of dealing with concepts involving such things as weight, number, area, distance or temperature provided they can operate in the presence of concrete referents. Concepts involving an understanding of, for instance, volume, density, justice or cruelty are not well formed. These require more subtle levels of reasoning which we call *formal operations*. These highest levels of thinking of which individuals are capable develop once they can follow the *form* of an argument without needing the concrete materials making up the substance of the argument.

At the formal level of operations, individuals can reason hypothetically and in the absence of material evidence. They set up hypotheses and test these to determine real solutions to problems amongst a number of possible solutions. This is known as *hypothetico-deductive reasoning*.

To illustrate the difficulties in hypothesis-testing experienced by children at the concrete stage as contrasted with those at the formal level, let us take an actual illustration. The author's son, Paul, at nine years six months was given the pendulum problem originally used by Inhelder and Piaget (1958). With one or two minor modifications from the original experiment this consisted of a length of string with a lump of plasticine on the end. The string could be changed in length and more plasticine made available for adding to, or removing from, the existing lump. Paul was required to discover the factor or factors which governed the time of swing of the pendulum we had made.

His first reaction was to say that the further one pulls the lump to one side before release the longer it takes to slow down because gravity (a concept vaguely mentioned at home and school) gradually pulls it 'slower and slower towards the middle' (of the swing). After a good deal of somewhat random exploration with the length of the string, amount of plasticine and method of release (either pushing with different forces or releasing freely) and with little regard for accurate measurement, he concluded that altering the length of the string, weight on the end, force of release and 'gravity' would change the time of swing. It was then put to him that of the possible variables he had suggested, only one made much difference to the time of swing; how, then, would he set about discovering which of the four variables he had suggested was the important one?

His first proposition was to alter the length of the string while varying the 'push'. What happens to the other variables? He would include those as well. After some trials and tribulations trying to arrange an experiment involving all the variables at once, he concluded, 'I'm completely lost. There are too many, what do you call them, variables.'

Paul's responses were typical of concrete operational thinking. He was capable of sorting out the factors which might vary by making direct observations of the apparatus. He pinpointed length, weight, gravity and method of release. He could also carry out seriation: as the string gets longer and longer, the pendulum swings slower and slower. But he could not at this stage manage to *test hypotheses* which were unambiguous by considering only one variable while holding the others constant. In fact, he became confused at the prospect of having to change the variables simultaneously. For formal operations he would need not only to theorize about the *possible* influences of all factors, but then to design an experiment to test the influence of each one in a systematic way while keeping the others invariant.

There is a second characteristic of formal reasoning, not too well illustrated by the pendulum experiment; that is, the *setting up of hypotheses* (Lunzer *et al.*, Vol. 2, 1968). We saw how hypotheses were tested in the experiment, but the relevant variables were fairly obvious and the child has no need to go much beyond the raw materials in front of him or her to discover the attributes necessary for hypothesis-testing. Length, weight or 'push' are self-evident. Frequently, formal reasoning requires more subtle processes of abstracting the important criteria from the objective evidence. Moreover, the reasoning must go beyond the tangible and perceivable to the construction of propositions about objects and events from the attributes extracted. Piaget calls these 'second-order operations' to distinguish them from the 'first-order operations' of the concrete stage. Second-order operations, then, are operations on first-order operations. Problems involving proportion require second-order operations because we must first establish the relationship from the information given (first-order), and use this to discover a second relationship.

Some extremely interesting research by Driver and co-workers (1983, Driver *et al.* 1985, 1996) suggests that:

> by the time children are taught science in school, their expectations or beliefs about natural phenomena may be well developed. In some cases these intuitions are in keeping with the ideas pupils will meet in their science lessons. They may be poorly articulated but they provide a base on which formal learning can build. However, in other cases the accepted theory may be counter-intuitive with pupils' own beliefs and expectations differing in significant ways from those to be taught. (Driver 1983)

These beliefs Driver refers to as *alternative frameworks*. One important aspect of this is that as children begin to test hypotheses and attempt to explain what they are observing, the alternative frameworks may well, if they are inaccurate, be counter-productive in a child's formulation of scientific principles.

The view underpinning the findings of Driver and others is referred to as *constructivism*. This means that the learner actively constructs both the knowledge acquired and the strategies used to acquire it. The illustration above of Paul trying to handle the pendulum problem is a good example of a learner bringing his previous experiences and inventions to the present situation. Paul's own previous observation, deduction and other people's ideas are all brought to bear. The constructivist view is in stark contrast to the *transmission* view of learning where it is assumed that a person's knowledge is assimilated from the words and actions of others in demonstrating a point. If children in a classroom were shown the pendulum experiment, transmissionists would assume that the children would take up some or all the points as delivered by the teacher. According to the constructivist view, there would be as many interpretations of what is happening as there are children in the classroom.

Constructivism has been particularly prevalent in science and mathematics. Cobb (1988; also see Lee 1990) rightly reminds us that not only the pupils but also the teachers bring to their task a lifetime of their own internal structures and experiences. Consequently, he believes:

> the teacher who points to mathematical structures is consciously reflecting on mathematical objects that he or she has previously constructed. Because teachers and students each construct their own meanings for words and events in the context of the ongoing interaction it is readily apparent why communication often breaks down, why teachers and students frequently talk past each other. The constructivist's problem is to account for successful communication.

## Some criticisms of Piaget's theory

Like so many theories in psychology, Piaget's has not been without its critics. Most texts contain a critical section. In addition to Bryant above (1971, 1975, 1982), there are Donaldson (1978), Modgil and Modgil (1982), Brown and Desforges (1979). For a balanced overview, see Sutherland (1992). Before pointing to the implications of his work, we must first consider the most common objections raised by psychologists.

(a)  Some American psychologists have been very sceptical of the clinical methods Piaget adopted to establish his views. They are said to depend too much on the verbal introspections of immature minds. Behaviourists much prefer evidence to be independent of attitudes and self-reports. Nevertheless, replications using representative samples and all kinds of adaptations to overcome the shortcomings of introspection have yielded results which are very similar and coherent. Children from very different social and ethnic backgrounds with varying degrees of verbal talent still appear to give the developmental pattern described by Piaget.

(b)  Inevitably, the haste to formulate a neat and tidy unfolding of events at prescribed 'ages and stages' in the child's development overlooked the part played by differences in mental and environmental factors, but the stages propounded are not so rigidly coupled with age (Lovell and Ogilvie 1960, 1961). The conservation of substance, for instance, appears at different ages in children. Moreover, appearance of the ability to conserve in a child is not sudden or all-embracing. There is a gradual emergence of the ability to conserve which varies from one property to the next. This point has considerable value for teachers. Individual differences in children's conceptual development will greatly influence the design of the curriculum by the teacher who is aware of the criteria for determining when certain conceptual possibilities can be entertained.

(c) Some (Bruner 1966, Bryant 1971, 1982) place greater emphasis on the part played by experience than Piaget. It is argued that the consistency of the stages is a function of the regularity of a culture's child-rearing patterns rather than of some in-built and inevitable sequence of development. Also an inability to carry out the kinds of tasks set by Piaget and his followers may arise from insufficient information rather than from lack of ability as a function of maturation. However, 'training programmes' designed to ring the changes of these patterns and accelerate development have not, as yet, produced more than minor deviations in Piaget's developmental sequence.

(d) The role of language has been paramount in the process of trying to discover from children the course of their cognitive functioning and growth. In fact, some of Piaget's original experiments are almost entirely dependent on the child's understanding of the verbal instructions. For example, questions such as 'Are all the primroses some of the flowers?' or 'Are all the ladies some of the people?' are quite semantic tongue-twisters for a child of four years (and probably several adults). Povey and Hill (1975), for example, using children in the age range two to four years, found with pictorial material that the children had acquired some specific and generic concepts. The term 'pre-conceptual' stage, according to them, implies, wrongly, that children cannot form concepts. Whilst they may make errors in conceptual judgements (decentring, transductive reasoning), nevertheless they do form correct concepts and apply them (see also the discussion of 'virtuous errors', mentioned by Herriot (1971), in Chapter 5, in which children have established rules of language for plurals or past tenses).

(e) Piaget offers no adequate explanation of cognitive development. A descriptive structure is given, but no satisfactory means of making predictions from it of structural change.

(f) The bulk of Piaget's theorizing has been applied to mathematics and science, with much less regard for other school subjects. Naturally, concept formation extends far beyond the bounds of maths and science, and this has to some extent been rectified over the past few years by an increase in research and curriculum development in other areas of interest to schools.

> **Further reading**
>
> Several workers have looked at concept growth in particular subject areas. Some are listed below (full references at the end of the chapter) to give the reader an idea of the scope of research in the later half of the last century when work in this area was thriving. Have a look at Wallace (1965, concept growth and attainment), Goldman (1964, religious concepts) Peatling (1982), Jahoda (1963, concepts of time and history), Lovell (1968, mathematical and scientific concepts), Shayer (1978), Sloan (1969, children's conception of musical scales), Jahoda (1969, concepts of country and nationality), Hallam (1969, history), Kay (1968, moral development), Kohlberg and Lickona (1986, ethical development).

# Implications of Piaget's work for the teacher

Whilst bearing in mind these limitations of Piaget's work, we can still learn much of service in teaching. Some of the more relevant aspects are discussed below.

(a) The existence of a maturational unfolding of conceptual skills being linked with certain periods in the lives of children has an obvious bearing on curriculum planning (Furth and Wachs 1974). Piaget is quite clear in his belief that neurological development and a progression of concept-forming skills must appear before full intellectual maturation is possible. The theory implies that certain periods are critical in mental growth. Teachers should, therefore, have some awareness of the range of possibilities in the concept formation of their children. As contemporary research shows, this does not mean that we must stick rigidly to a programme of teaching based exclusively on Piaget's sequence of concept development. Such a philosophy is too pessimistic if it leads us to sit back and wait for the next stage to appear. We should continue to explore teaching environments crucial to concept formation and hypothesis testing. In this respect, mental age is a more valid concept than chronological age because we are concerned here with intellectual and not physical development.

(b) Teaching at middle and upper school level should begin from concrete considerations, building up, where applicable, to more abstract reasoning. This is reflected in many teaching programmes in mathematics and science which begin with experimental, practical aspects before attempting deductive work. Science and mathematics organizations are very much concerned with this approach.

(c) The idea of active participation is in keeping with Piaget's view that concept formation arises from the internalization of actions. Building up schemata requires practical experience of concrete situations, as far as possible, to encourage active assimilation and accommodation.

(d)    Research also suggests that explanation should accompany experience. Children should be helped to realize how hypotheses are reached.

(e)    It is probably true to say that most of us, for most of the time, are operating at the concrete level. Less able secondary school children may rarely, if ever, reach the heights of abstract thinking (Lovell 1961). Even university students have their problems (Abercrombie 1990). Discretion must be exercised in the presentation of abstract concepts, particularly where they are of such an order of abstraction as to require an understanding of several subordinate concepts.

(f)    With primary school children and less able secondary school children, be on the lookout for intuitive, pre-operational thinking. Again, practical as well as verbal experience must assist the formation of concepts. Note also that operational thinking in some aspects of schoolwork is by no means an indication of similar competence in other related aspects. Remember that research has shown marked irregularities for individuals in both the character and the level of concept attainment.

(g)    Cognitive development is a cumulative process. The hierarchical nature requires the formation of lower-order schemata on which more advanced work can be built. If, therefore, cognitive frameworks depend on what has preceded, it is important to regulate the difficulty level and order of presentation of material. To apply an ordered sequence of work is to admit that we can monitor children's progress. Therefore we can use the pattern of development in each child as a means of assessing attainment both in respect of the child's own progress and in relation to the expectations of his or her mental age group.

(h)    Verbalization is very important. Language aids internalization and consequently the formation of concepts. Verbal interchange between teacher and child or parent and child constitutes an important communication channel by which the world is defined. More will be said about its role in the next chapter.

# Information-processing approach to cognitive development

An alternative approach to cognitive development has been presented by Klahr and Wallace (1976) which uses the theory of information processes as the model. Children are assumed to be born with processes enabling them to 'construct' their world as a result of experience and interaction with the environment. One major difference between this approach and Piaget's is that the former attempts to cast light on the *process* of mental activity.

Using the model to be described in Chapter 7, memory is one of the key concepts. It would seem reasonable to assume that in order to handle the variety and quantity of incoming stimuli, the human being must possess innate processes which enable a search for consistency and structure in the information received by the senses. This makes the process of coping with large quantities of information easier because it can be 'chunked' (see Chapter 7). These innate capacities are believed by Wallace to be *discrimination processes* activated by the flow of stimuli from the environment, processes for the *detection of regularities in structures* and, thirdly, *problem-solving processes.* The information built up in the memory in this way then acts as a guide to coding of further input.

Some psychologists (Mandler 1983) who favour the information-processing approach would retain the stages, but relate them to specific areas of study where intellectual differences have been shown to occur (see Chapter 9 on intelligence). So the progress in mathematics might be much faster for some than for others. Other psychologists go further, such as Klahr (1982) who rejects the 'stages' approach in favour of a continuous and variable developmental approach.

# Concept attainment

## Vygotsky (1896–1934)

Piaget is by no means the only person to attempt an analysis of concept formation, but there are differences in emphasis which distinguish the researchers in this field. Piaget was interested in the structural side of concept growth, but other psychologists, notably Vygotsky and Bruner, have concentrated more on function than structure.

### Social constructivism

Another difference between Piaget and Vygotsky is the greater stress placed by the former on biological adaptation which accounted for the systematic unfolding of development, whereas Vygotsky placed emphasis on social influences, sometimes called *social constructivism.* This is not to deny Piaget's belief in the importance of educational and cultural transmission which he thought would partially account for some of the discrepancies in development, but his theory was genetic and maturational, both depending largely on physiological properties.

Vygotsky, in his short life of 37 years, was a most prolific researcher living in Russia early in the twentieth century (see Moll 1990). He postulated that human mental activity was the result of cultural learning using social signs. The culture into which a child was born was the source of concepts to be internalized and this affected the physiological functioning of the brain. Tools such as language, number and art were seen as the means by which a culture would conceptualize, organize and transmit thinking. Therefore, our thinking processes are a product of the culture in which we happen to be born.

He (Vygotsky 1962, reprint) carried out several ingenious investigations into concept formation using a method which did not depend on language skills already acquired by the child. His main purpose was to show a relationship between language and thought across widely differing cultures, and recent revitalization of interest in his work originates from his views about the link between language and thought. Recent evidence (Kivilu and Rogers 1998) using attribution theory (see Chapter 8) has verified that children from different cultures attribute their school achievement successes to different factors. Kenyan children think that external factors, such as how they were taught, are most important compared with children from Western cultures who think that internal factors, such as personal effort and ability, count.

---

### Further reading

Briefly, Vygotsky's materials consisted of 22 wooden blocks varying in colour, shape, height and size. These *attributes*, as they are called, occurred in a variety of combinations derived from five colours, six shapes (square, triangle, circle, semi-circle, six-sided figure and trapezium), two heights (tall or flat) and two sizes of horizontal surface (large or small). Each block had a nonsense syllable written on the underside so that the subject could not see it. Only four syllables were used, LAG, BIK, MUR and CEV, representing specific combinations of attributes (e.g. LAG is written on all tall, large blocks). Colour is not used as an attribute but is included as a distraction. The experimenter thinks of a concept and exposes a syllable on the underside of one block (called the *sample*) and asks the subject to pick out all the other blocks having the same syllable on them – that is, the subject must deduce the critical attributes of the block which make up the concept (in this case tallness and largeness). When a wrong choice is made the experimenter shows the subject an inaccurate block and the game proceeds until the subject tracks down the concept.

---

## Vygotsky and concept formation

In the course of his research Vygotsky and his co-workers arrived at conclusions about concept formation in close agreement with those of Piaget. Three stages were isolated: first, there is the *vague syncretic* ('syncretic' in this context means random rather than reasoned groupings of blocks), in which the child at an early stage of development piles the blocks into heaps without any recognizable order. The groupings result from trial and error, random arrangement or from the nearness of the blocks.

The second stage is called thinking in *complexes*. These are a kind of primitive concept in which the child groups attributes by criteria which are not the recognized properties which could be used for the classification of the concepts. Five sub-stages were identified. Classification of the blocks was drawn up: (a) according to one common characteristic – *associative complexes*; (b) in collections like a square, a circle and a semi-circle (similar to the idea of having a knife, fork and spoon); (c) as *chain complexes*, where the child first picks out some triangles and notices that the last one chosen was, say, green and this in turn makes the child's next series of selections green, etc.; (d) as *diffuse complexes*, consisting of chains which are unrelated, such as green–blue–black, and so forth; and (e) as *pseudo-concepts*, which arise when the child perceives superficial similarities based on the physical properties of objects without having grasped the full significance of a concept. The formation of pseudo-concepts is not spontaneous, but is determined by the meaning given to a word by adults. In effect, the pseudo-concept is the product of mechanical and rote learning without an understanding of the underlying attributes, and led Vygotsky to place more weight on the role of cultural experience in concept formation than Piaget.

The third stage identified by Vygotsky is called the *potential concept* stage, in which the child can cope with one attribute at a time but is not yet able to manipulate all the attributes at once. Maturity in concept attainment is reached when the child can do this.

The description of how children progressed from haphazard grouping through pseudo-concept to full concept formation is illuminating. One can spot the grave difficulties presented to the infant and primary school child when faced with classification problems. We must be wary of creating too many pseudo-concepts using drill methods without first providing a rationale. Verbal labels are too readily acquired from adults with insufficient exemplars to aid in the construction of class concepts. Children often use terms which give the appearance of understanding, yet on closer inspection it becomes obvious that they do not really know the concepts involved.

### Scaffolding

Progression depends on how thoroughly the child has mastered the 'building blocks' leading to an understanding of particular concepts. The kind of support from knowledgeable others (adults or peers) which Vygotsky had in mind he called *scaffolding*. A tutor provides help at significant points in development and gradually removes support as the child succeeds. Scaffold teaching is therefore a matter of judging how much and when support is needed. But this support has to happen at a period in development when the child is capable of benefiting from help. The appropriate period (similar in some ways to critical, or sensitivity, period theory) is referred to by Vygotsky as the *zone of proximal development*. Students will recognize, behind these technical terms, some common good practices in teaching. A good example of scaffolding is provided in the 'reading recovery' programme of Marie Clay (next chapter).

The suggestion of peers as 'knowledgeable others' in the last paragraph raises the importance of children sharing their knowledge. This is sometimes referred to as *peer tutoring* or *reciprocal teaching* (Rosenshine and Meister 1994).

A shift in the last century to the use of structured apparatus (Cuisenaire rods, coloured discs, Dienes apparatus, colour factor) was an attempt to recognize the need to establish an understanding of number operations as well as manipulative skills with numbers (Mercer 1991).

## Bruner's strategies

We have dealt in some detail with concept development from birth to mid-adolescence. We shall now look briefly at some work which attempts to answer the question of how adolescents and adults, who already have well-formed concepts, expand on these in order to acquire more elaborate concepts. Bruner and his colleagues (Bruner *et al.* 1965, Thomson 1959) devised a method seeking to discover the routes used by people who are attempting to expand, modify and adapt existing concepts to meet new demands.

To do this, Bruner, like Vygotsky, used objects with several attributes; using well-defined attributes such as colour, shape, size or number which can have different values and combining these to create concepts which were drawn on cards, Bruner asked subjects to deduce the concept which he had chosen.

Peel (1960) provides a reduced version of the task in his book *The Pupil's Thinking.* Using verbal reports from subjects and by watching the direction taken by them in trying to arrive at a solution, Bruner distinguished two broad strategies or plans of action. These are *scanning* and *focusing* strategies.

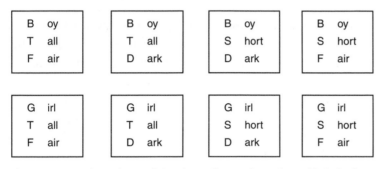

**Figure 4.4** Sample cards containing the attributes of sex, size and hair shade.

## Example

To elucidate their meaning, let us take a simple illustration. We shall use three attributes of human beings, each with two values. These are sex (boy (B) and girl (G)), size (tall (T) and short (S)) and hair colour (fair (F) and dark (D)). To simplify the presentation, each attribute value will be given a letter of the alphabet; these are shown after each value. Cards containing these attributes are then presented to someone as displayed in Figure 4.4. We have used words instead of a card carrying a picture of the attributes. The cards contain all the possible combinations of the three attributes. Given the values, we can arrange them to form concepts containing three, two or one attribute values. Thus with the values:

B oy   G irl
T all   S hort
F air   D ark

we can get the following combinations:
eight 3-attribute concepts by combining (see Figure 4.4)

BTF, BTD, BSD, BSF
GTF, GTD, GSD, GSF

$\longrightarrow$

twelve 2-attribute concepts by combining

BT, BF, BS, BD, GT, GF, GS, GD, TF, TD, SF, SD

six 1-attribute concepts from

B, G, T, S, F, D

making 26 concepts in all.

The tester now thinks of one of the concepts (let us say the 2-attribute concept of *fair girl*, GF) without telling the subject. The former then selects one of the eight cards (the sample card) which includes the concept (let us say card GSF). The subject tries to deduce the concept by pointing to another card which is thought to be another instance of the concept. The tester answers 'yes' or 'no' to the selections until the subject is able to specify the precise combination of attributes making up the concept.

The strategies observed by Bruner, in the scanning strategies a boy, say, works out hypotheses from the information given. In the case above, he has been shown GSF and he can now assess the combinations of attributes still open to him. Of the concepts, there are seven remaining possibilities: GSF, GS, GF, SF, G, S, F. With these in mind, he can adopt a completely logical approach known as *simultaneous scanning* by holding in mind all the combinations while setting up further hypotheses. To cut down the range of options still further, let us say the subject now chooses GTF, to which the experimenter says 'yes' because it contains GF. The number of alternatives is now reduced, since the only common values in the two selections GSF and GTF are G and F. This, therefore, leaves three concepts, namely girls (G), fair girls (GF) and fairness (F). By a process of elimination, it would not take long to track down the correct concept.

However, simultaneous scanning can be a tedious and uneconomic procedure putting a premium on having a good memory, especially when there are a lot of attributes. A less exacting variation is *successive scanning*, by which a person takes one step at a time. In our example, at the stage where GTF is picked, the subject would then go on to look at each attribute in turn, noting the positive instances only (in simultaneous scanning, negative instances are also taken into account). Guesswork and anticipation (two popular ploys with us all) are used in the early stages of this method.

Focusing does not involve hypothesis-testing. The individual proceeds by altering one attribute value at a time (*conservative focusing*, which can be a long-winded affair) or more than one attribute at a time (*focus gambling*). The safest, or most conservative, method is to change and test the attribute values one at a time. In our example using GSF as the sample card, if one wished to test the presence of *girl* in a concept one might point to the card containing BSF. By this means, one is holding SF constant. Building up to two and three values, if necessary, will finally enable the concept to be specified. The focus gambler, as the term implies, chances an arm by varying two attributes at each choice to test, in the first place, for single attribute concepts. One might, in our example, offer BSD as the first choice to test the significance of the size attribute. Lack of success would lead one to test double and ultimately treble attribute concepts.

Teachers will soon recognize the tactics employed by pupils (and themselves) in trying to solve problems involving attribute discrimination. The more concrete methods of successive scanning, particularly the focusing methods, are the commonest. Note the rapid increase in task difficulty as one increases the number of attributes. At any level of mental operations it is important to avoid unduly overloading the problems with variables where simultaneous scanning is important (many physics problems, for example, can be approached in this way, such as the pendulum experiment mentioned earlier). There is also a suggestion (Wetherick 1969) that strategies adopted by individuals are a function of the conditions in which they work. As a laboratory exercise, the games mentioned above are more likely to induce focusing techniques, while everyday problems appear to encourage scanning. As yet, research has not been able to provide any precise information about the appropriateness of strategies for particular kinds of problem.

## Summary

Much of our experience is assimilated in the form of concepts and expressed in a symbolic form, as in verbal and mathematical modes. Thus, by the processes of forming categories and discriminating between the critical attributes of objects and events, we can organize our percepts and employ symbol forms to represent these experiences. Concepts have several distinctive characteristics, of which the following are among the most important. Concepts:

- are representations with wide margins in defining the critical attributes of objects and events
- are subject to experiential influences
- are symbolic
- can be used either in a way which is widely accepted by everyone (extentionally), or in a highly personal way (intentionally)
- form hierarchies of increasing complexity (think of the classification of animals as an illustration of hierarchical structure)
- can be irrational, as in superstitions and phobias
- may be formed without the conscious knowledge of an individual.

Concept formation has been one of the special provinces of the Swiss psychologist, Jean Piaget. His researches led him to postulate a theory of qualitative changes during cognitive development from birth to adolescence which take place in a definite, inevitable sequence of maturational steps starting with biological mechanisms and culminating in a highly developed system of abstract operations. The child, while striving to come to terms with the surroundings, organizes activities into schemata by the processes of assimilation and accommodation. Piaget suggested four stages from birth to maturity, consisting of the sensori-motor, pre-operational (composed of pre-conceptual and intuitive sub-stages), concrete operations and formal operations.

A particular contribution of Piaget's theory to the educational scene is in drawing attention to the child as an active participant in concept-learning processes. Moreover, curriculum planning needs to be informed by the stages he postulated, but without being too rigid and ignoring either the variations in individual concept growth or the potential of children for concept formation. With new topics at any stage, one should proceed from the concrete and practical to the more difficult abstract. With younger children there may be little success in going beyond the concrete aspects of a topic. Where concepts are cumulative, the order of presentation must be worked out carefully so as to build up schemata in a logical and orderly sequence.

Language is most important for the internalization of concepts. The work of Vygotsky pays attention to the build-up of concepts alongside the acquisition of verbal symbols representing the concepts. His developmental theory was similar in many respects to that of Piaget, but see Chapter 5 for a discussion of the function of language in concept growth. Bruner's main interest was to elucidate the thinking strategies of adults who already had a grasp of concepts. He concluded that there are four basic ways of attaining concepts, in the form of simultaneous scanning, successive scanning, conservative focusing and focus gambling.

## Tutorial enquiry and discussion

(a) With care, several of Piaget's original experiments can be repeated with children. The materials are usually inexpensive and readily available. Try to choose a range of ages likely to include children from each stage of cognitive development. As a guide to materials, procedures and characteristic findings see K. R. Fogelman's book, *Piagetian Tests for the Primary School* and Furth and Wachs (1974). Do not forget to let the children know where they have gone wrong once the experimentation has been completed. You will find this a particularly exacting task, especially where the developmental stage of the child clearly falls short of that required for an understanding of the problem; however, see (b) first.

(b) Much very pointed criticism has been levelled at Piaget's work. The critical references in the text should be read and a careful analysis made of these criticisms preferably *before* trying out any experiments.

(c) Explore Bruner's strategies using materials indicated in Peel's (1960) *The Pupil's Thinking*.

(d) The same as (c) can be done for Vygotsky's ideas – see Moll (1990) and Mercer (1991).

(e) Examine in terms of learning and teaching techniques the theories of concept growth associated with subjects of interest to you (see 'Further reading' on p. 102).

# References

Abercrombie, M. L. J. (1990), *The Anatomy of Judgement*. New York: Columbia University Press.

Baron, J. (2000), *Thinking and Deciding* (3rd edn). Cambridge: Cambridge University Press.

Bartlett, F. C. (1932), *Remembering*. London: Cambridge University Press.

Beard, R. M. (1969), *An Outline of Piaget's Developmental Psychology*. London: Routledge and Kegan Paul.

Blakemore, S.-J. and Frith, U. (2000), *The Implications of Recent Developments in Neuroscience for Research on Teaching and Learning*. London: Institute of Cognitive Neuroscience.

Bourne, L. E., Dominowsky, R. L. and Loftus, E. F. (1979), *Cognitive Processes*. Englewood Cliffs, NJ: Prentice-Hall.

Brown, G. and Desforges, C. (1979), *Piaget's Theory: A Psychological Critique*. London: Routledge and Kegan Paul.

Bruner, J. S. (1964), 'The course of cognitive growth', *American Psychologist*, 19, 1–15.

Bruner, J. S. (1966), *Towards a Theory of Instruction*. New York: Norton.

Bruner, J. S., Goodnow, J. J. and Austin, J. A. (1965), *A Study of Thinking*. New York: Wiley.

Bryant, P. E. (1971), 'Cognitive development', *British Medical Bulletin*, 27, 200–5.

Bryant, P. E. (1975), *Perception and Understanding in Young Children*. Andover: Methuen.

Bryant, P. E. (ed.) (1982), *Piaget: Issues and Experiments*. London: British Psychological Society.

Bryant, P. E. and Trabasso, T. (1971), 'Transitive inferences and memory in young children', *Nature*, 232, 456–8.

Cobb, P. (1988), 'The tension between theories of learning and instruction in mathematics education', *Educational Psychology*, 23, 87–103.

Collins, A. M. and Loftus, E. F. (1975), 'A spreading activation theory of semantic processing', *Psychological Review*, 82, 407–28.

Donaldson, M. (1978), *Children's Minds*. London: Fontana.

Driver, R. (1983), *The Pupil as Scientist?* Milton Keynes: Open University.

Driver, R., Guesne, E. and Tiberghien, A. (eds) (1985), *Children's Ideas in Science*. Milton Keynes: Open University.

Driver, R., Leach, J., Millar, R. and Scott, P. (1996), *Young People's Images of Science*. Buckingham: Open University Press.

Elkind, D. (1973), 'Cognitive structure in latency behavior', in J. C. Westman (ed.), *Individual Differences in Children*. New York: Wiley.

Fogelman, K. R. (1970), *Piagetian Tests for the Primary School*. Slough: NFER.

Furth, H. G. and Wachs, H. (1974), *Thinking Goes to School*. New York: Oxford University Press.

Gardner, H. (1999), *Intelligence Reframed: Multiple Intelligences for the 21st century*. New York: Basic Books.

Goldman, R. (1964), *Religious Thinking from Childhood to Adolescence*. London: Routledge and Kegan Paul.

Hallam, R. (1969), 'Piaget and the teaching of history', *Educational Research*, 12, 3–12.

Hebb, D. O. (1973), *The Organization of Behavior* (9th impression). New York: Wiley.

Herriot, P. (1971), *Language and Teaching: A Psychological View*. London: Methuen.

Howard, R. W. (1987), *Concepts and Schemata: An Introduction*. London: Cassell.

Inhelder, B. and Piaget, J. (1958), *The Growth of Logical Thinking from Childhood to Adolescence*. London: Routledge and Kegan Paul.

Jahoda, G. (1963), 'Children's concepts of time and history', *Education Review*, 15, 87–104.

Jahoda, G. (1969), 'The development of children's ideas about country and nationality', *British Journal of Educational Psychology*, 33, 47–60 and 143–53.

Kay, W. (1968), *Moral Development: A Psychological Study of Moral Growth from Childhood to Adolescence*. London: Allen and Unwin.

Kivilu, J. and Rogers, W. (1998), 'A multi-level analysis of cultural experience and gender influences on causal attributions to perceived performance in mathematics', *British Journal of Educational Psychology*, 68, 25–37.

Klahr, D. (1982), 'Nonmonotone assessment of monotone development: an information processing analysis', in S. Straus (ed.), *U-Shaped Behavioral Growth*. New York: Academic Press.

Klahr, D. and Wallace, J. G. (1976), *Cognitive Development: An Information Processing View*. New Jersey: Lawrence Erlbaum.

Kohlberg, L. and Lickona, T. (1986), *The Stages of Ethical Development: From Childhood through Old Age*. New York: Harper and Row.

Lee, V. (ed.) (1990), *Children's Learning in School*. Sevenoaks: Hodder and Stoughton.

Lovell, K. (1961), 'A follow-up study of Inhelder and Piaget's The Growth of Logical Thinking', *British Journal of Psychology*, 52, 143–54.

Lovell, K. (1968), *The Growth of Basic Mathematical and Scientific Concepts in Children*. London: University of London Press.

Lovell, K. and Ogilvie, E. (1960), 'A study of the conservation of substance in the junior school child', *British Journal of Educational Psychology*, 30, 109–18.

Lovell, K. and Ogilvie, E. (1961), 'A study of the conservation of weight in the junior school child', *British Journal of Educational Psychology*, 31, 138–44.

Lunzer, E. A. (1968), 'Formal reasoning', in E. A. Lunzer and J. F. Morris (eds), *Development in Human Learning* (Vol. 2). London: Staples.

Mandler, J. (1983), 'Representation', in P. H. Mussen (ed.), *Handbook of Child Psychology*. New York: Wiley.

Medin, D. L. and Smith, E. E. (1984), 'Concepts and concept formation', *Annual Review of Psychology*, 35, 113–38.

Mercer, N. (1991), 'Accounting for what goes on in classrooms: what have neo-Vygotskians got to offer?', *Education Section Review* (British Psychological Society), 15(2), 61–7.

Modgil, S. and Modgil, C. (1982), *Jean Piaget: Consensus and Controversy*. New York: Praeger.

Moll, L. C. (ed.) (1990), *Vygotsky and Education: Instructional Implications and Applications of Sociohistorical Psychology*. Cambridge: Cambridge University Press.

Peatling, J. H. (1982), 'On beyond Goldman: religious thinking in the 1970s', in J. M. Hull (ed.), *New Directions in Religious Education*. London: Falmer Press.

Peel, E. A. (1960), *The Pupil's Thinking*. London: Oldbourne.

Phillips, J. L. (jnr) (1979), *The Origins of Intellect: Piaget's Theory*. San Francisco: Freeman.

Piaget, J. (1952), *The Child's Conception of Number*. London: Routledge.

Piaget, J. (1970), *Science of Education and the Psychology of the Child*. London: Longman.

Povey, R. and Hill, E. (1975), 'Can pre-school children form concepts?', *Educational Research*, 17, 180–92.

Rosenshine, B. and Meister, C. (1994), 'Reciprocal teaching: a review of research', *Review of Educational Research*, 64, 479–530.

Shayer, M. (1978), 'The need for a science of science teaching', *Education in Chemistry*, 15, 150–1.

Sloan, W. B. (1969), 'The child's conception of musical scales: a study based on the developmental theory of Piaget', MSc dissertation (unpublished), University of Bradford.

Smith, E. E. and Medin, D. L. (1981), *Categories and Concepts*. Harvard, MA: Harvard University Press.

Sternberg, R. J. and Smith, E. E. (eds) (1988), *The Psychology of Human Thought*. Cambridge: Cambridge University Press.

Sutherland, P. (1992), *Cognitive Development Today: Piaget and His Critics*. London: Chapman.

Thomson, R. (1959), *The Psychology of Thinking*. London: Penguin.

Vinacke, W. E. (1952), *The Psychology of Thinking*. New York: McGraw-Hill.

Vygotsky, L. S. (1962), *Thought and Language* (trans E. Haufmann and C. Vakar). Cambridge, MA: MIT Press.

Wallace, J. G. (1965), *Concept Growth and the Education of the Child*. Slough: NFER.

Wetherick, N. E. (1969), 'Bruner's concept of strategy: an experiment and a critique', *Journal of Genetic Psychology*, 81, 53–8.

## Further reading

Brown, G. and Desforges, C. (1979), *Piaget's Theory: A Psychological Critique*. London: Routledge and Kegan Paul.

Cohen, D. (1983), *Piaget: Critique and Reassessment*. London: Croom Helm.

Donaldson, M. (1978), *Children's Minds*. London: Fontana.

Donaldson, M. (1992), *Human Minds: An Exploration*. New York: Viking Penguin.

Meadows, S. (2005), *The Child as Thinker: The Acquisition and Development of Cognition in Children* (2nd edn). London: Routledge.

Sutherland, P. (1992), *Cognitive Development Today: Piaget and his Critics*. London: Chapman.

Wood, D. (1998), *How Children Think and Learn* (2nd edn). Oxford: Blackwell.

# Language, Literacy and Numeracy

## Implications for teachers

- Thinking and the language we think in are central to school activities in all subjects.
- Effective communication, whether verbal or non-verbal, is at the core of our work as teachers. Therefore, some knowledge of the findings of psychologists in this area is important.
- Literacy and numeracy in both primary and secondary education are now centre-pieces of government policy. Several principles discussed in this chapter have their roots in psychology.
- Knowledge of the functions of spoken language, its onset and acquisition are particularly important to primary school teachers who will be required to teach literacy.
- Knowing something about vocabulary growth is valuable both to teachers and parents.

*Everything that can be said can be said clearly.*
(Wittgenstein)

Language is one of our finest human assets. For an introductory text on language, see Paul (2001). Many essentially human activities spring from this unique characteristic by which we become detached from our physical world. As far as we can tell, animals normally go into action because they are prompted by physical stimuli (internal as well as external). A cat stalks a bird which has attracted attention; a dog begs for food when it can smell or see it, when feeding rituals are set in motion or as a result of 'feeling' hungry. In contrast, humans can indulge in reveries which take them well beyond the present reality into the realms of abstract thought. They communicate to themselves in some symbolic form. Moreover, they can communicate their ideas to others by using these symbolic forms. These two uses of language, personal and social communication, are very important for teachers because their work is built around the efficient communication of ideas. The importance of language competence and the role of teachers in making sure that such competence is relentlessly encouraged in schools are the concern of both the teaching profession and the Department for Education and Skills (DfES). From the Bullock Report in the 1970s (see later in this chapter) onwards, there has been growing concern about standards of literacy.

In Chapter 2, when exploring the regions of the brain involved in language, we noted that defects in Broca's area prevent the *production* of words. Wernicke's area stores auditory codes and word meanings and is involved in *comprehension*, that is, interpretation of incoming sounds. These two activities are at the centre of language usage.

How far is language solely a human activity? Animals can, of course, communicate – ants, bees and primates afford well-known examples of animal contact – but the level is basic. It is habitual, situation-specific and initiated by internal or external physical cues which are not symbolic. Primates have systems of sounds for survival and emotional needs (grunts, howls) which are *not* symbolic. But the vocalizing apparatus of the primates does not seem to be able to produce the vast range of meaningful characteristic vocalizations of human beings. Viki, a chimpanzee belonging to the American psychologists C. and K. Hayes, took six years of hard labour to learn four rather imperfectly spoken words. (See also the work of the Gardners 1969, 1972; Premack 1971, 1985; Savage-Rumbaugh *et al.* 1993.) So language as we know it is essentially a human activity. With human beings, once the ground rules are laid down, competence to assimilate a spoken language is comparatively rapid. In addition, human communication has the potential for creating new meanings and having duality of meaning for identical or similar sounds.

# Characteristics of spoken language

Language has been defined as the term denoting 'the psychological processes which regulate speech' (Herriot 1976). Speech is language behaviour by the articulation of sound patterns.

Talk involves using speech to communicate experience and convey meanings. The two basic requirements of a language are that it is symbolic and systematic. We tend to regard language in a somewhat atomistic fashion by looking upon it as a collection of words strung together in sentences, each word having a separate identity and meaning. This is a false way of looking at language. In fact, the words are brought together in special ways to give a highly systematic order from which we get a meaning. Similarly, there is no one meaning for each word in a sentence. The meaning we ascribe to a sentence can change from one context to another. For example, 'What on earth are you doing for Heaven's sake (!)(?)' could be taken in two ways, depending on whether it is a show of annoyance or a priest after souls. Altering the position of words in a sentence alters the sense of the sentence, even though the same words are there. 'The sun is shining' is not the same as 'Is the sun shining?' Language, then, is not random behaviour, but is systematic, where certain orderings are accepted as having prescribed meanings.

In producing and comprehending language there are three levels identified by linguists, namely, sounds (*phonemes*), word units (*morphemes*), building up to give sentences which have meaning (*semantics*).

The raw materials of each language are the basic sounds. These give the character of the language and form one method of distinguishing different languages. The *phoneme* (see Crystal (1987) or Paul (2001) for basic texts on language structure and function) is the term we use for the perceived basic speech sounds of a language. We say 'perceived' because the latitude in pronunciation within a culture may vary widely, but all have the same interpretation (compare how a broad Scot, Londoner, Geordie or Lancastrian would say 'night'). Certain phonemes are specific to a language. 'Th' (as in 'the') in the English language has no equivalent phoneme in French. The French pronounce it as 'z', to begin with, because, as one au pair girl from France put it, 'I say "z" instead of "th" so zat I don't bite ze tongue.' There are about 50 phonemes in Standard English.

Phonemic utterances are put together to form *morphemes*, which are the smallest units of a language with a grammatical purpose. They are not necessarily words as we know them. In the word 'plans' there are two morphemes: 'plan' and 's'. 'Plan' is a word, but 's', which serves the useful grammatical function of converting plan into the plural, is not a word as such. Prefixes, suffixes and word endings which change singular to plural or alter the tense are therefore morphemes. Linguists find morphemes much more useful than words for defining language content. Broken into morphemes, the sentence 'The girl liked to dress her dolls' would be 'The + girl + like + ed + to + dress + her + doll + s'.

The systematics of a language involves more complex combinations of symbols. Each morpheme has a particular function, and the formation of sentences by combining these morphemes so that they obey rules requires a knowledge of *grammar* (some call this *syntax*). All readers will recall having to discover the parts of speech represented by words in a sentence and making sure that they are presented in a certain order for a particular meaning. But combining morphemes in a specified order does not necessarily mean that the resulting sentence makes sense. Combining morphemes to make words and arranging them together to give meaning in a particular tongue is called *semantics*. In the sentence 'the green toes fought on the apple', the grammatical structure is correct, but the sentence is meaningless in our culture (if not most others!). The study of semantics involves the resolution of the meaning we ascribe to systems of morphemes.

# The functions of spoken language

## Egocentric and socialized speech

At the beginning of the chapter it was suggested that speech served two broad purposes, personal and social communication. These two functions are referred to as *egocentric* and *socialized* speech. Egocentric speech is characterized by the child who behaves and talks as if all points of view were his or her own. He or she seems unable to appreciate another's point of view, to conceive things from another position. The egocentric monologue is a running commentary on the child's present situation and frequently acts as a means of self-regulation and direction. At three years of age about half a child's utterances are egocentric (the rest are socialized), and this rapidly reduces to a quarter at age seven. Socialized speech has such functions as requests, persuading, providing information, and so forth. Several classifications of the functions of speech have been attempted (Hymes 1967; see also the work of Tough 1976a, mentioned later in the chapter), but for our present purposes it is sufficient to note the broad self and social functions. The child progressively recognizes the listener and tries to adapt his or her language in order to convey information which has meaning for the listener.

---

### Example

Jane was two-and-a-half and lived next door to the author. An extract from a tape-recording of her chatter while she was alone in a bedroom illustrates some features of a little one's language. She is looking out of a window and has seen a neighbour's dog, Rajah. After a lot of chatter about visiting Rajah's house, she continues the conversation, we think, with a teddy bear, or on some occasions hoping that her mother can hear. 'Look, what's that man doing? You can see. Look, he's digging the soil up. Can you see him? We have to ask mummy if we can go to Rajah's mummy's house (Rajah's mummy is the owner of the dog). We can if mummy says "yes". Can't undo this lock. Better ask mummy if we can have the paddling pool out at Rajah's mummy (thought to be the bath in which Rajah is rubbed down). Have to try and open it. Can we go to Rajah's mummy's house?'

'No. Get into bed,' says Jane's mother.

'Jane get into bed. No, I'm bright and chirpy now (a little family saying). Mummy, I'm bright and chirpy now. That sock doesn't fit me. Better see if it fits Teddy.'

The first snatch of conversation seems to be socialized speech, where Jane is trying to encourage someone else (probably her mother, who, although not there, may be thought to be within earshot) to repeat what she is doing. But then she appears to direct her conversation to something else (most likely Teddy) because she talks about her mummy as a third person. There is also evidence of monologue intended largely for self-direction. On several occasions she rehearses what she is going to say or do. 'We have to ask mummy if we can go to Rajah's mummy's house', 'I'm bright and chirpy now' and 'Better see if it fits Teddy' are three examples. Egocentric speech is not necessarily indicated by the recurrence of 'I' or 'me'. The question is for whom is the speech intended? Is it intended for self-direction or is it an attempt to communicate with others? Baron-Cohen suggests that the caring nature of the pretend conversation is an example of *empathy* prevalent in females (Baron-Cohen 2003, also see Chapter 2). The egocentric speech of a male child might be quite different.

The relative development of egocentric and socialized speech and the functions they serve was a bone of contention between Piaget and Vygotsky. The latter's position has now been accepted by most (including Piaget). Vygotsky (also see Chapter 4) supposed that all speech is social by implication, although it may not always be used as a means of communicating with others. One source of evidence for Vygotsky's belief in speech as being social in origin is that if one puts hearing children with deaf or foreign children, egocentric speech disappears (Moll 1990, Wertsch 1985). When the potential listener cannot understand, speech is no longer overt. Egocentric speech was crucial as a directive for the child's actions. It was not, as Piaget once held, a simple accompaniment to the actions with no other purpose: rather it was used by the child for laying down plans of action. Further, for Vygotsky, egocentric speech was a transitional step from outward vocal socialized speech to inner speech. Interiorization of speech means that thought processes are facilitated and self-direction follows without the attendant overt speech. (It is, none the less, difficult to determine which comes first, a thought or the speech. When Jane talks about an action she might be reminding herself of a thought.) In short, we see a change in the regulating function of speech from external sources (like mother), through egocentric speech for everyone (including self) to hear, and ultimately to speech for communication and 'internalized speech' for the regulation of behaviour and logical thinking.

# Language acquisition

How does a verbally helpless infant develop into an articulate adult? A widely held belief is that we are born with vocal equipment and a neural system which gives us the capacity to verbalize (Pinker 1994). It does not take a child very long to discover and utilize a vast range of phonemic utterances no matter which culture he or she happens to be born into. Equally, the speed with which these utterances are converted into meaningful (to both child and parent) and reproducible sounds during the first few years of life is convincing testimony to an inborn capacity. Contrast this with the slavish way in which Viki, a chimpanzee, was taught to say only four utterances in six years. Even then, there is very little evidence to lead us to suppose that the 'words' are any more than the result of conditioning. Two further capacities essential to communication are the ability to reproduce utterances *at will* when required, and the realization that one is being understood.

## The onset of language

The origins and influence of sounds heard and rehearsed by a baby and their place in language acquisition are still matters of dispute. A central point separating workers in this field is whether the baby is a passive or an active agent in the process of developing language. The acquisitive view is represented essentially by the *behaviourist* (see next chapter) school of psychology; the active, but 'hereditary', view has a wide range of adherents, including many linguists and *cognitivists* (see next chapter). Do babies start with a clean slate and build up language by imitation and reinforcement, or do they have certain inherent facilities which are activated by them or in response to stimulation?

Interesting evidence from brain studies (Kuhl 1998) tells us that those parts of the brain responsible for processing speech (mainly involving the left side of the brain – see Chapter 2) are busy from birth. Indeed, some earlier work (Mehler *et al.* 1988) suggests that the infant in the womb is already beginning to distinguish sounds specific to the mother tongue (*prosody* or *prosodic variation* where the foetus picks up variations in intonation (pitch), amplitude (loudness) and duration (length of sounds)). By one year of age, the brain appears to become unable to continue this function and second or further languages are progressively more difficult to learn.

Evidence for this critical, or sensitive, period in language acquisition, at least pronunciation, is not hard to find. Witness the difficulty a person born and bred in France has with 'th' as in 'the'. It tends to come out as a z. The Japanese have difficulty pronouncing 'r's and 'l's. English speaking people have their problems with German umlauts and French nasal sounds. Also, take it from me that as you get older it gets harder to learn a new language. Neville and Bavelier (1998) have shown how important it is to learn the pronunciation and grammar (but not necessarily vocabulary) of a second language as early as possible.

Babies make sounds from the moment of birth (possibly even before, when in the womb). These sounds accompany discomfort (cries) and pleasure (chuckles, cooing), although little is known about whether the sounds can be further differentiated in the very young baby. Starting with cooing sounds, between three and twelve months the *babbling stage* (meaningless, repetitive sounds) is reached. The sounds, which are probably inadvertent to begin with, are repeated with increasing amounts of control. With positive feedback from those around the child, the sounds develop into communication. The ability to make the sounds is inherent in the vocal system (but wouldn't it be interesting to go back 20,000 years in a time machine to a period when there was no written word in order to hear what our forebears had to say to each other!). What happens to those sounds is acquired through social contact. Deaf children between these ages do have the same basic vocalizations, but they soon become redundant as they cannot hear the repetitions from those around (Dodd 1972, Ricks 1978). Brain-scanning methods now seem to indicate that babbling is the baby's first attempts at talking. The language centres in the left side of the brain and the involvement of the right side of the mouth are clues (Holowka and Petitto 2002).

## Language learning and operant conditioning

The behaviourist position suggested by B. F. Skinner (1957) is that the babbling sounds are one starting point for conditioning the child to associate particular objects or events with particular sounds. For him, language is a skill fabricated by trial and error and reinforced by reward (or extinguished by non-reward). The reappearance of a verbal response is conditional on the receipt of a reward. Bluntly, if there is no reward when you do something, you are less likely to repeat the activity on a future occasion. In the case of language usage, the reward could be one of many possibilities. Social approval from parents or others when a child makes an utterance, such as smiles and praise, is probably the most potent in the early stage of development.

Skinner distinguishes three ways in which the repetition of speech responses may be encouraged. First, the child may use *echoic* responses. In this case, he or she imitates a sound made by others, who immediately display approval. These sounds need to be made in the presence of an object to which they may be linked. Second, we have the *mand*, a response which begins as a random sound but ends up by having meaning attached to it by others. Echoic response frequently follows a mand expression where a parent on hearing 'mama' or 'baba' uses it to form a word and encourages the child to repeat the utterance. Once the sound is firmly implanted, it gradually becomes associated with an object. Finally, there is the *tact* response (a contraction of the word contact). Where an acceptable verbal response is made, usually by imitation, in the presence of the object and the child is rewarded by approval, there is every likelihood that the response will appear again (see the Helen Keller story later (1917)). Clearly, these types of responses are closely related in the early stages of children's language formation. Note how imperative the presence of other people is. With no one around to show approval or test the accuracy of verbal utterance, they would soon be discarded.

Not all psychologists are satisfied with this paradigm of Skinner's. To begin with, verbal responses quickly take on much wider meaning, as indicated by the range of usage, than can be explained by operant conditioning. Again, there are many words which do not 'name' objects (they have no *referents*). Learning articles such as 'the' or 'a' is difficult to explain in Skinnerian terms. Add to this the phenomenal vocabulary count of young children, accumulated in a comparatively short spell, and Skinner's theory does not appear to provide the whole explanation. Noam Chomsky (Lyons 1970, Aitchison 1976) takes up a completely different position in asserting that there are common structural factors in all languages, from the simplest native tongues to the most complex in the world. Although his interests lie in theories of grammar and linguistics, he has something to say about language acquisition.

## The inheritance of linguistic competence

Chomsky could not hold with the mechanistic view of man as a computer – being fed with words (sound inputs) and reproducing them (sound outputs) in the required order from suitable programmes laid down in childhood. Apart from anything else, the actual process is far too elaborate: not even a computer could cope with a fraction of the language capacity of humans. But his theory is a difficult one and only the bare essentials are given here.

By mastering the rules governing the structure of language (syntax), a child is able to generate utterances and understand the utterances of others, even when they are completely original to the child. Language is 'open-ended', and those who can use it fluently can produce and understand sentences which they have never used or heard before. According to Chomsky, stimulus–response theories are not sufficient to account for this creative capacity in language usage or the child's ability to understand novel sentences. Further, it is assumed that children have a potential for linguistic skill which is inborn. The built-in facility is called the *language acquisition device* (LAD) – a hypothetical inner mechanism. It enables children to process incoming signals, make sense of them and produce a response. The rules of language seem to come to children quite naturally even when they are of widely differing intelligence and cultural background. The rules are obeyed (within limits) without apparent understanding. Chomsky also supports the theory that humans are unique in possessing linguistic aptitudes and can in no way be studied, by implication, using animal comparisons. Humans are qualitatively different from other animals. This view is a far cry from the developmental view of Skinner's behaviouristic outlook described above.

Note that we are back in the arena of dispute between behaviourists and cognitivists (Chapter 6). In the previous section, we observed how Skinner developed a theory of verbal behaviour without necessarily referring to any internal operations of the organism. The nearest approach to a consideration of internal processes by the behaviourists is in the mediation theory of Osgood (a 'neo-behaviourist'), whose work is considered later in the chapter. Even here, the emphasis is still on stimulus–response connections, but they have been transferred to the interior of the individual. On the other hand, the language of the cognitivists is replete with terms like 'schemata', 'styles' and 'images', and concentrates on the mental state of individuals (at a given time) in order to capture the essence of what is taking place between a human being 'receiving' and 'transmitting' information.

The evidence for the child making up his or her own rules is not hard to find. Listen to any child as he or she makes what Herriot (1971) calls 'virtuous errors' by applying standard rules to irregular cases. 'Mouses' instead of 'mice' and 'sheeps' instead of 'sheep' are common errors. Tense errors are also frequent – 'catched' rather than 'caught' and 'teached' instead of 'taught'. Without being taught, a youngster begins to create and apply rules. Through hearing a large number of examples of the regular case for the past tense of a verb where '-ed' is added, the child establishes a rule. We should not be surprised to hear 'catched', 'taked' or 'sawed'. Plurals are made by adding 's's. Most children at some time overdo it. My granddaughter, Natasha, gave the plurals of 'shoe' and 'snake' as 'shoes's' and 'snakes's'. Typically, she also had great difficulty at three years of age with personal pronouns. 'Me' was used for 'my' and 'I'. So 'my coat' and 'I go' became 'me coat' and 'me going'. 'Your shoes' became 'you shoes's'. It takes much patient repetition to teach young ones the irregular cases – not unlike the experience of learning a foreign language such as French. As we shall see later, two-thirds of seven-year-olds still have difficulty with irregular past tense endings which are other than '-ed'.

Teachers must handle these errors with care. Herriot, like many others, puts in a plea for tactful handling of mistakes in language usage arising from innocent breaking of the rules through inadequate knowledge of the exceptions. This can generally be done by repeating a *correct* version in a reply to the child without making it too obvious that you are correcting a mistake, that is, no punishments or ridicule in front of others. Some mistakes are quite hilarious, but it is often insensitive and unproductive with young children to poke fun at their language errors. At ten, my other granddaughter, Hannah, hated to be reminded of her early childhood *faux pas*. However, with her permission, I give you two examples. At seven years of age, 'synchronized' swimming became 'sink and rise' swimming – a reasonable misunderstanding. At six, she was being taught her address: Greenfield Garth, Kippax which is near Garforth. For a while, the morphemes became muddled into 'Greenfield Garforth, Pickaxe'. Also note that structure is the all-important thing in language usage (using the system with meaning), and not individual words or phrases. New concepts represented by single words or phrases must ultimately be set in a language context for an improvement in language skills.

For a summary of the debate between Chomsky and Skinner, see the paper by McLeish and Martin (1975).

## A middle way in language acquisition

Probably an answer lies somewhere between these extremes. It is hard to believe that babies do not imitate some sounds, and equally hard to believe they do not have *some* in-built facility for language acquisition (Kuhl 1998). It is most likely that they combine imitation with phonological rules, take into their systems sounds made by adults and assimilate utterances which are both phonemes and morphemes. It is at this stage that the foundations of pseudo-concepts are laid down (see Vygotsky's work in Chapter 4).

Later, children begin to accumulate more rules by which the system works. They learn regular and irregular plural endings or other morpheme combinations. Grammatical skills appear when they can put two words together (sometimes known as *telegraphic* use of words), e.g. 'cat gone', 'mamma give', and this occurs between 24 and 30 months. Herriot (1971) summarizes one point of view so:

> Children notice certain features of language behaviour, and use these features to form their own individual system of combination. However, the needs of communication, the requirement for more words and more complex ways of combining them, force them to approximate more and more to adult systems. So, of course, does the need to be understood by a variety of other people. When his only communicant is his mother or his twin, the child may be held back by baby language. But as soon as he needs to speak to other members of the community, the rules of the conventional code of language become more necessary.

It is not necessarily assumed that children are born with linguistic potential already laid down in the brain, but rather that, as the brain develops, more elaborate regulation of language behaviour becomes possible.

## Vocabulary growth

### Signs, signals and symbols

The earliest clues to the child's ability to comprehend his or her surroundings come from the use made of *signs, signals* and *symbols*. Studies using born deaf and hearing children on the question of the development of communication skills from baby movements, sounds, gestures, signs and symbols to full language usage have been informative (Volterra and Erting 1994). The newborn relies on reflex action and soon comes to depend on direct evidence which can be assimilated from his or her senses. Oral contact with objects such as a milk bottle or the mother's nipple will soon initiate sucking. Quickly the child begins to associate one aspect of the feeding ritual with the whole process. The sight of milk in the bottle or the sound of the bottle being prepared is often sufficient to set in motion anticipatory behaviour in advance of the actual feeding process.

Perception of some piece of the action, then, gives the cue for the whole action. The cue which represents part of the real thing (sight of nipple or milk, smell of milk, clank of bottle) is called a *sign*. Babies become quiet when their nappies are being removed; to a dog a lead can be a sign of the prospect of a walk; tears are a sign of joy or sorrow or something in your eye.

In the discussion of intuitive thinking in children, we showed how children are often deceived by signs. By over-generalizing they take the same sign to mean that the same event is going to take place. When mother puts her coat on it may be taken erroneously to represent a sign that she is going shopping. The important thing about a sign is that it produces behaviour characteristic of the whole response to a situation.

Certain signs become significant in the absence of the real thing. When a sign is given this special meaning in the absence of the object and it gives rise to behaviour *as if* the object were there, we call it a *signal*. Signals are often the outcome of conditioning. The hand movements, whistles and calls which send a sheep dog cavorting round a flock of sheep are signals. Likewise words take on the function of signals. To a dog the word 'sit' is a signal which has become part of the act of sitting down. Experiments with chimpanzees have shown that words are little more than signals. As we supposed above, the first child-like utterances such as 'dada' are signals acquired, possibly, through repeated association and conditioning connecting word sounds with physical objects.

When signals become endowed with meaning, which bears no resemblance to the original object, we call them *symbols*. Words in our language are obvious examples. The symbols actually represent things without looking or sounding at all like them. A symbol is sometimes referred to as a secondary signal because it is once removed from the real thing. Unlike commands to a dog or the first words of a child, the symbol becomes detached from physical events. Mead (1934) says that 'The vocal gesture becomes a significant symbol ... when it has the same effect on the individual making it that it has on the individual to whom it is addressed.' 'The same effect' is used with the reservation that no two people respond in precisely the same way.

Many stimuli not normally brought together can be represented by symbols and juxtaposed within a short time. Language results when these verbal symbols are brought together and organized into systems of meaningful patterns.

---

### Further reading

Helen Keller, in *The Story of My Life* (1917), brilliantly illustrates an unusual example of a transition from sign and signal to symbol systems. Deaf and blind from infancy, she had made little progress until, at the age of seven years, she was given a tutor, Miss Annie Sullivan. In their first days together the tutor got Helen to feel objects while they were being spelt out into the palm of her hand. Initially, there was little realization that the shapes Annie was drawing out on Helen's palm were labels for the objects she was touching. Helen, in fact, was not even detached from the signs around her. The moment of truth came when:

> We walked down the path to the well-house, attracted by the fragrance of the honeysuckle with which it was covered. Someone was drawing water and my teacher placed my hand under the spout. As the cool stream gushed over one hand she spelled into the other the word *water*, first slowly, then rapidly. I stood still, my whole attention fixed upon the motions of her fingers. Suddenly I felt a misty consciousness as of something forgotten – a thrill of returning thought, and somehow the mystery of language was revealed to me. I knew then that 'w-a-t-e-r' means the wonderful cool something that was flowing over my hand ...
>
> I left the well-house eager to learn. Everything had a name, and each name gave birth to a new thought.

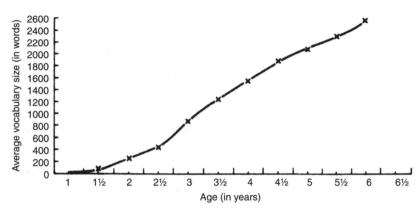

**Figure 5.1** Active vocabulary size and age. Adapted from E. H. Lenneberg in 'The natural history of language' (a chapter in *The Genesis of Language,* edited by F. Smith and G. A. Miller).

## Speed of vocabulary growth

The rate at which the child is able to use and understand words is quite slow in the early stages of language development. Note that there is a difference between the numbers of words we actually use (*active vocabulary*) and the larger number we are able to understand (*passive vocabulary*). Of course children vary enormously in their vocabulary size and usage, depending largely on intellect and linguistic opportunities. But a general picture of the average rate of vocabulary growth we can expect is shown in Figure 5.1. At one year of age the average word count is three or four. At one-and-a-half years the count is around 20 and at two years this figure rises sharply to about 200. Note how, in the Piagetian sensori-motor stage of cognitive development, progress is slow, and it is not until the transition into the stage of pre-operational thought that the child really begins to amass words. Assessing an average count is quite difficult with young children, because one is never quite sure whether all the possible utterances of which a person is capable have been spoken, or indeed if the utterances are understood. Morpheme counts are popularly used and an estimate of between 4,000 and 7,000 is thought to be the case for children just entering school (Watts 1955, Lenneberg 1966, Miller and Gildea 1987), rising to 10,000 at 14 years of age.

Growth in the acquisition of elementary meaningful forms of our language, as in the formation of plurals and tenses (morphology), has been extensively studied. Berko (1958), for example, has shown, using nonsense syllables, that at seven most children can cope with a plural formed by adding 's', but experience greater difficulty when 'es' is required. Likewise, in the formation of the past tense, 'ed' is not found to be too difficult to apply, but where a change such as 'ring–rung' is required, only a third of the seven-year-olds could manage. Grammatical skill, which is said to occur when a child can put two words together to form a meaningful expression, generally appears around two years of age.

### Sex differences in language performance

The important, detailed work of Templin (1957) set out to investigate four aspects of language amongst children of three to eight years of age. These were articulation of speech sounds, speech sound discrimination, sentence structure and vocabulary size. Of the many conclusions reached in this valuable work, perhaps the following are of particular note. In articulation skills, the three-year-old is still making, on average, 50 per cent errors, whilst at eight years he or she is accurate 90 per cent of the time. In five years the child reaches close to articulatory maturity. Boys usually take about a year longer than girls, and children from working-class homes about a year longer than those from middle-class homes. In speech sound discrimination, that is, the ability to recognize auditory differences among speech sounds, there is a consistent increase in the ability, with a gradual deceleration beyond five years of age. At the lower ages there does not appear to be any significant difference in the ability between boys and girls, but at eight years of age girls are better than boys. Sentence length and structure now appear to be longer and more complex than in previous studies (25 years earlier). No differences were detected for the boys and girls, but children from middle-class homes made longer and more complex remarks than working-class children. About half the remarks made by three-year-olds are grammatically accurate, and this improves to about three-quarters at age eight. The vocabulary count presented a lot of problems, and there seems to be little agreement between researchers about methods of finding the recognition or recall vocabulary of young children. The estimates of basic vocabulary for the six- to eight-year-olds ranged from 13,000 to 23,000 in Templin's work, although these figures seem rather high when compared with the work of Lenneberg (see Figure 5.1). The *total* vocabulary, Templin suggests, is even higher at eight, and could be as high as 28,000.

Whatever the reasons, the evidence for superior female performance in language skills is now well established (Shaywitz *et al.* (1995) and see Chapter 2). Theories abound, but one plausible biological explanation is that of Geschwind and Galaburda (1987) in which they propose that the rate of growth of brain hemispheres differs in the sexes. In males there is faster growth in the right hemisphere and this they relate to the production of testosterone and subsequently the better performance in spatial tasks in males than females (see Figure 2.3). However, this leaves females with an even distribution in the use of brain tissue as compared with males. It has even been suggested that because females use both hemispheres for language more uniformly than males, their language performance is more efficient. There is evidence to support this view (summarized in the work of Doreen Kimura, 1999). For example, when women suffer a stroke affecting the left side of the brain, they have less severe language problems, such as aphasia, than men and they recover more rapidly.

# Language and thought

It would be impossible to speak of language development without considering the possibility that it is related in some way to thinking skills. Do we need to have language in order to think, or does our cognitive equipment enable us to indulge in the use of a sophisticated language? Do language and thinking skills grow as separate entities or are they interconnected from the outset? These and many other questions continue to tax the minds of psycholinguists.

## Origins of language and thought

There is, as yet, no single, widely accepted, comprehensive account of the relationship between language and thought. We have scans of brains busy using language, but the relationship to thinking is not clear. In a most readable summary of work in this field, Cromer (1974) presents a spectrum of speculations based on research evidence. These suggest that:

(a)  language determines thought (strong form of linguistic-relativity hypothesis)
(b)  language does not determine thought but only predisposes people to think in particular ways (weak form of linguistic-relativity hypothesis)
(c)  cognition determines language acquisition (strong form of cognitive hypothesis)
(d)  cognitive abilities enable us to understand and use creatively the linguistic structures *only* when abilities are adequate (weak form of cognitive hypothesis).

These are important points for debate and the following expansions may be of help.

(a)  For some of the earliest investigators, there appeared to be no problem. Watson, an American psychologist in the behaviourist tradition, concluded that thought was language. Accordingly, thinking is manipulating words in the mind. These word-thoughts were regarded as internal speech which showed up in sub-vocal movements of the speech organs. Elaborate experiments aimed at detecting these movements while subjects were thinking out the solution to a problem were not entirely convincing. The present moderate view emphasizes the role of the CNS rather than the peripheral motor system, of which the speech organs form a part. The child quickly learns to suppress the peripheral nervous system, therefore motor action accompanying reading or thinking gradually (but not entirely) declines. The more difficult the verbal task, the more likely is sub-vocal movement. Drugs used to paralyse the larynx show that its movement is not necessary for thinking to occur. Again, the example of deaf people who can think without vocalizing at all is evidence that thought can occur without the agency of a verbal language system such as that used by hearing people. The outline of the Skinnerian hypothesis of language acquisition clearly demonstrates yet another linguistic-relativity perspective. Children accumulate language by imitation and reinforcement which, in turn, enables them to think.

Whorf and Sapir (for a summary see Slobin 1971) are most widely known for their strong contention that 'thought is relative to the language in which it is conducted'. This viewpoint is known either as the *Sapir–Whorf hypothesis* or *linguistic-relativity hypothesis*. According to Whorf (1956), 'We can cut up and organize the spread and flow of events as we do largely because, through our mother tongue, we are parties to an agreement to do so, not because nature itself is segmented in exactly that way for all to see.' Further, he believed that languages differ in the way in which they break down nature in order to make words and sentences. Thus the way we think is dependent upon the language we are using; that is, the agreed ways in which a culture has carved up its view of the world and represented it in the language. In a review of this extreme position using comparisons in concept formation between native tribes, eastern cultures and western cultures, Carroll (1964) concludes that the hypothesis has not received much convincing support: 'Our best guess at present is that the effects of language structure will be found to be *limited* and *localized*' (emphasis added).

(b) The weak form of the Sapir–Whorf hypothesis, elaborated by Brown (1973; also Sinclair-de-Zwart 1969), supposes that, rather than determining our thinking, language predisposes us to think along particular lines. This leaves open the door to an explanation of how it is that an individual can cope in several languages and also explains some notable differences in concepts between different cultures. Idiosyncrasies in languages in terms of idioms for which no translation is available in other languages will be familiar to anyone who has studied a foreign language. The terms 'gestalten' and 'déjà vu' really have no simple precise translation into English. Similarly, many of Piaget's terms in French have no equivalent translation and interpreters have had to resort to literal translation. Another much-quoted example comes from the work of Lenneberg and Roberts (see Miller and McNeill 1969) on Zuni-speaking people compared with English speakers. The Zuni speakers do not differentiate yellow and orange colours and therefore make far more mistakes when asked to distinguish between them. The Zuni/English bilinguals have less difficulty, whilst English-speaking people have none at all.

(c) The 'strong cognitive hypothesis' approach is lucidly summarized by Cromer (1974), who defines it in this way: 'We are able to use the linguistic structures that we do largely because through our cognitive abilities we are enabled to do so, not because language itself exists for all merely to imitate.' The evidence presented is of two kinds. First, Cromer attempts to show that cognition precedes language by quoting the work of, among others, Ricks (1978) on phonological rules as precursors of language acquisition rather than imitation methods (see earlier). He also examines the link between cognition and language acquisition at later ages, and he refers to Piagetian workers who maintain that language is not the origin of thinking operations. Second, Cromer emphasizes the independent development of language (1974; see also the following paragraph on Vygotsky).

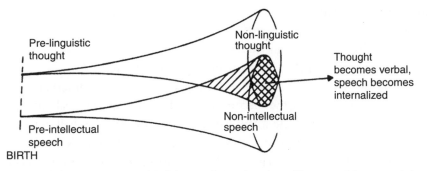

**Figure 5.2** Representative model of theory relating thought and language (after Vygotsky).

(d)  Possibly the most popular current position is the 'weak cognitive hypothesis' first formalized by Vygotsky (1962). He considers language and thought as originating from different roots. At first, there is what might be described as pre-linguistic thought and pre-intellectual speech, which gradually merge together as the child approaches the pre-operational stage. The 'fusion' of thought and speech, however, is not total, and Figure 5.2 shows a continuing independence of some aspects of language and thought. Pre-linguistic thought is very much in evidence, as we have seen, in the sensori-motor activity of infants. Beyond this stage we still employ imagery and motor skills in practical pursuits. Learning by heart without any grasp of meaning may lead to pre-intellectual speech. Jane's phrase 'bright and chirpy' (see earlier in the chapter) is probably used with little idea of what it means. Verbal strings implanted in the memory without any logical reasoning behind the content can produce non-intellectual speech.

## Cognitive growth and representation

Another approach to the study of language in the development of thinking comes from Bruner (1964). His concern is for discovering the functions of language in concept formation – the how and why of language and concepts. Piaget, as we have observed, concentrates on the description and structure of cognitive growth – the 'what happens in concept formation' approach.

How do we fix in our minds the repeated regularities of our observations? How, in other words, do we represent our experiences to ourselves? Humans, in the course of evolution, have developed systems by which they can implement their actions with increasing efficiency. First, they develop the use of tools as an extension of their *motor capacities*. A spade, for example, becomes the extension of a man's (or a woman's) hand. He makes instruments to replace his less efficient body structures. Next, he extends his *sensory capacities* by, for example, the use of signal systems. In order to enlarge on his sensory experience he builds telescopes and microscopes or uses radio to transmit sound over great distances. At the pinnacle of representational skills we find *symbol systems* for conveying experience of real (or imaginary) things in their absence. These three evolutionary changes coincide with the course of language development through *enactive, iconic* and *symbolic* representation as postulated by Bruner, and they compare closely with Piaget's theorizing.

Enactive representation, the earliest stage of development, enables us to internalize repeated motor responses so that in time they become habitual. Numerous physical activities carried out in life are habitual. Opening a familiar door, driving a cricket ball, writing, walking, etc. do not always require conscious effort in terms of directing one's muscles to do certain things. The muscles seem to behave as if the memory of familiar events had been imprinted on them without the aid of mental images. The circular reactions suggested by Piaget are the beginnings of enactive representation.

When mental images enable us to build up a picture of the environment, iconic representation is possible. We amplify sensory experiences and combine these percepts to construct images. These 'internalized imitations', as Piaget calls them, are thought by Bruner to be a composite representation of several similar events (calling up the sound of a bell would produce a combination of bell sounds heard in the past – see Chapter 4). An exception occurs in eidetic imagery, where a vivid image of a single event is recalled in great detail.

The transition from iconic to symbolic representation occurs around the age of four years, although the child begins to symbolize at about the age of two. Symbolic representation sees the use of language systems which bear no resemblance to actual objects. Symbols do more than represent reality: they enable us to transform it. This transition from iconic to symbolic representation and the central position of language are well demonstrated by an experiment of Bruner's. Children between five and seven were shown nine glasses of different sizes arranged in a pattern as shown as in Figure 5.3.

The children were asked to describe the arrangement, pointing out how the glasses were similar or different. The glasses were then dispersed and the children asked to rearrange them as nearly as possible to the original. Most children succeeded in this task. The glasses

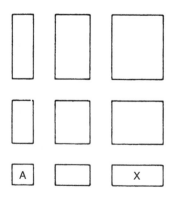

**Figure 5.3** Matrix of glasses in Bruner's transposition task. Modified from Bruner by D. G. Boyle, *A Student's Guide to Piaget*, Pergamon, London, 1969.

were dispersed again except that the glass marked A was placed in another position at X and the children asked to reconstruct the pattern with A at X. The younger children did not succeed while the seven year-olds accomplished the task.

This and other researches provide *points of value to teachers*. Children who still depend on iconic representation are dominated by the images they perceive. This is in agreement with Piaget's notions of 'centring' and 'decentring' alluded to in Chapter 4. We ought, according to Bruner, to give children every opportunity to describe events in order to encourage symbolic rather than iconic representation. This is just a high-powered way of saying that we should get our children to talk or write about experiences, to express themselves in language, as well as to do things. Frank's work, reported by Bruner (1964), used the well-known Piagetian experiment in which glass vessels containing water were hidden from view (apart from the tops of the vessels) and children were asked the typical conservation questions (see Figure 4.3 in the last chapter). It demonstrates the importance of diverting the child from visual to symbolic modes of representation and testifies convincingly to the improvement in the performance of young children when we deliberately activate symbolic reasoning. Language, then, is to be encouraged as an essential accompaniment to perceptual experience.

# Language and meaning

We are all familiar with the feelings and characteristic reactions which can be evoked when particular signs are used. Some people recoil in horror at the word 'snake' or 'spider'. Some visibly change at the sight of a baby's photograph or even the word 'baby'. Children and adults often display inappropriate or prejudiced behaviour at the sound or sight of particular words. Occasionally one meets a reception-class child or first-form secondary school pupil who has developed a distorted reaction to school (especially if the parents have said 'You wait until you get to school. They'll sort you out'). But how does meaning become attached to signs?

Of the many theories extant, Osgood's (Osgood *et al.* 1957) has received the widest currency. In a nutshell, he supposes that, in addition to receiving the direct stimulation from an adult, we regularly experience other kinds of stimulus which, by conditioning, become associated with the stimulus-object and become part of our response to the stimulus. Osgood gives an example of the spider. The hairy, long-legged body and quick movements representing the visual pattern received by our eyes may be encountered at the same time as a frightening description of its habits or when someone is leaping about in dread of the creature. With sufficient repetition of these extraneous reactions alongside the stimulus-object a complex behaviour response is established. As there are many and varied encounters with the stimulus-object, the total response pattern becomes very complicated. When the spoken word 'spider' occurs on some of these occasions, part of the total response pattern becomes linked with the word so that the sight or sound of the word 'spider' will provoke that part (or 'fraction' as it is sometimes known) of the total response. This system by which a previously neutral stimulus (a sign) involves a response (or mediates between stimulus and response) is known as a *representational mediation process*. The term 'representational' is used because the mediating response produced by the sign is only a representative portion of the whole response which would usually appear in the presence of the stimulus-object. A diagram should help to summarize the process.

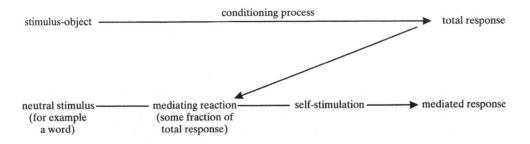

To quote from Osgood, 'Stimulus-objects elicit a complex pattern of reactions from the organism' and 'when stimuli other than the stimulus-object, but previously associated with it, are later presented without its support, they tend to elicit some reduced portion of the total behaviour elicited by the stimulus-object.'

It does not follow that direct association with the stimulus-object is necessary for mediating processes to arise. In fact we may never see an actual snake or giraffe, and yet we develop characteristic responses to signs of these animals. Photographs or verbal descriptions of the animals are sufficient to enable a response to be formulated. Where mediation responses arise from other signs rather than from the actual object we call them *assigns*, meaning assigned by association with other signs rather than the real thing.

The leap between the theoretical model of Osgood and the practical problem of how we can actually measure the meaning ascribed to a concept has been attempted in Osgood's semantic differential. In this, he tries to tap the universe of meaning built up from previous experience (as outlined above) which surrounds a given concept. This is done using a large number of rating scales consisting of bipolar adjectives (good–bad, fast–slow, active–passive). In so doing, he hopes to define the cognitive and affective meaning which the individual has grown to associate with the concept. Each scale is divided into a number of points expressing degrees of favourable or unfavourable attitude as expressed in the adjectives at each end of the scale. 'Neutral' attitude would occur at the centre of each scale. This tendency towards one end or the other is regarded as an expression of 'meaning', thus:

```
               CONCEPT
  Good    :....·....·X·....·....·....·....:   Bad
  Slow    :....·....·....·X·....·....·....:   Fast
  Active  :....·....·....·....·....·X·....:   Passive
                     ↑
                  neutral
```

By using several of these adjectival bipolar scales with each concept, it is hoped to define the semantic space, and thus to measure the 'meaning' the individual attaches to the concept. To quote from Osgood *et al.*, 1957:

> By semantic differentiation, then, we mean the successive allocation of a concept to a point in the multidimensional semantic space by selection from among a set of given, scaled semantic alternatives. Differences in the meaning between two concepts is then merely a function of the differences in their respective allocations within the same space...

Osgood's semantic differential is still a widely used technique. There are still several hundreds of citations in recent years.

In summarizing this sensitive area of the relationship between language and thought, it seems clear that there is no shortage of theory, but an embarrassing scarcity of well-founded information which can be employed by the teacher. The topic is well summarized by Greene (1987).

# Non-verbal communication

It is surprising how much information is conveyed by non-verbal means. Mime is a very common example. Friends, partners and spouses can often carry on a wordless dialogue of meaningful nods, winks and facial expressions. Stress, unhappiness or joy are frequently seen in certain faces without a word being spoken. While speaking, people use facial and body movements which become clues to the meaning of the spoken words. Females are particularly clever at reading the meanings of facial expressions and accurately evaluating the underlying emotions (Baron-Cohen 2003). In the classroom this is a particularly important skill.

*Gesture* is the commonest form of non-verbal contact. It is not just hand movements, but involves facial and body movement. A clenched fist, finger in the air, bared teeth, frowns and smiles, tongue out, stamping feet in a tantrum, voice intonation, all assist in revealing the mood of a person. Gestures frequently accompany and interplay with verbal communication, adding emphasis or purpose to what is being said. Hand movements, for instance, portray something of the speaker (see 'expressive movements' in Vernon 1953; also see Desmond Morris's *Manwatching*, 1977). Indeed, it has been argued that gestures are much more revealing in their psychological meaning than the speech which goes with them. You may have noticed on occasions that the implicit meanings of gestures are in conflict with the explicit message of a verbal communication, for example, when a person is telling a lie and you can read it in his or her face and voice. Forensic psychologists are often called on to view film footage of interviewees to see if there is any evidence of 'say one thing, but mean another'. Eyes and facial muscles are particularly revealing. Also, conversation is too obvious (governed by the social conventions of our culture) and we therefore tend to be guarded in what we say in case it lays bare our deeper thoughts and feelings. At the same time, the significance of gestures is less well understood and therefore we do not disguise them with the same subtlety as in vocalizing.

The skilful use and observation of gesture and expressive movement are assets in teaching. Skilful voice intonation, facial expression and body movement should add to what is being said. You are acting out a role. Often the best teachers are good actors. To praise or blame, you frequently have to say and portray one thing and, deep inside, think and mean another. Be careful not to give clues to these innermost feelings. Do not, for instance, prowl back and forth in front of a class like a caged tiger; don't give cues with eye movements or yawn when a pupil is trying to explain something. On the other hand, watch children's facial and body movements. These often reflect their mood and understanding.

Argyle (1983), Argyle and Trower (1979) and Desmond Morris (1977) have some useful and interesting points to make about the role of non-verbal cues for interpersonal relationships. Argyle refers, for example, to various social behaviour styles such as 'affiliative' and 'dominant' styles. Both are commonplace in the classroom. The former is exemplified by closeness, body contact, eye contact, friendly tone of voice, etc., and the latter by 'talking loud, fast and most of the time, in a confident tone of voice, interrupting others, controlling the topic of conversation, giving orders or using other kinds of influence, ignoring attempts at influence by others, adopting an attentive but unsmiling facial expression, and an erect posture with the head tilted back'. Rewards and punishments based on gestures are also common. The need for affiliation makes a reward out of smiling, agreeing, head-nodding and so on, whilst punishment is related to frowning, looking away or looking bored, disagreeing and looking impatiently at one's watch.

A particularly important application of non-verbal communication is the use made of sign language by deaf people. Many countries have developed their own sign languages. In this country, the British Sign Language (BSL) is regarded as the native language of deaf people. With the incorporation of most partially and profoundly deaf children into state schools, most teachers are likely to meet a partially deaf child in his or her class. Recent advances in making available courses and qualifications in signing have been extensive (Simpson 1998).

---

### Further reading

Several books are now available for BSL. For an introduction to the subject see Deuchar (1984) or Kyle and Woll (1985). Books and dictionaries of signs are now being published – see the *Sign and Say* series published by the Royal National Institute for the Deaf (RNID). C. Smith (1989) and Scott-Gibson (1992) have produced dictionaries of British Sign Language with its own grammar, syntax, and its own social and cultural implications (also see

$\longrightarrow$

http://www.forestbooks.com/system/index.htm). There are other signing systems such as signed English, which uses roughly the word order of the English language and the signs of BSL. Since about 1970, a philosophy has developed which encourages the use of all relevant and available means of communication. It has become known as *total communication* (Evans 1982). An appropriate combination of speech, lip speaking and reading, signing, fingerspelling, gestures, etc. form the basis of this approach, which has taken a firm hold in many countries.

On teaching practice, students will very quickly notice the reaction of a class to a lesson by watching the children's faces and interpreting the silences either as a sign that they are spellbound or, conceivably, that they have not a clue as to what the student is talking about.

# Teaching language skills – literacy

*Literacy* is 'the ability to read and write' (Oxford Dictionary). But there is far more to language usage than an ability to read and write. Naturally, a good reader is more likely to develop the broader language skills of communication and comprehension, but many teachers have become aware of the need for a systematic attack on basic language usage amongst children which has more to it than just reading. Most programme designers are generally agreed that at least three overlapping stages are required in order to assist language development. These are *reception* (listening with understanding), *internal symbolization* (interpreting, reasoning and concept-building) and *expression* (communicating by speaking or by writing). As we have suggested elsewhere, between reception and internal symbolization we require a process of *decoding* the incoming signals into a form which is readily interpreted in terms of previous traces in the brain. Similarly, the outcome of reasoning is thought to be converted or *encoded* into a form which enables individuals to communicate with their fellows.

## In the home

### Social differences

Some parents (we don't know the proportion) take delight in trying to encourage children in the art of reading. One question of interest to psychologists has been whether there is an age below which it would be a waste of time to attempt to teach reading. The concept of critical or sensitive periods mentioned earlier in the chapter is referred to as 'reading readiness', and is a matter of dispute (Clark 1994).

Having said that, home matters when it comes to children's reading skills. The longitudinal research of Douglas, Ross and Simpson (1968) and the National Children's Bureau (Essen and Wedge 1982) and the evidence collected for the Plowden Report on children and their primary schools (Peaker 1971) were consistent in pointing to certain influences linking children's educational achievement and parental attitudes and expectations (the 'educational climate' at home). The findings can be summarized as possible pieces of advice to parents, when teachers are discussing a pupil's progress.

- Become actively involved in the education of your child – visit the school when necessary, seek advice, be keen to show you want your children to attain well, obtain good exam results and, if possible, stay on at school.
- Don't hesitate to see the teacher when necessary.
- Fathers should show an interest as well as mothers.
- The time spent by mothers on educationally valuable topics seems to be proportional in some cases to the child's school performance.
- There is a link between the literacy and literary interests of parents and the success of children (books in the home, library membership).

Children can learn the language in the early stages of their development only if, and when, they hear the language spoken. Different linguistic environments have a startlingly variable effect on language usage, not just as a regional accent or dialect, but in the systematics of the language. Mother is a particularly important figure in the early language development of her children. The frequency and content of her conversation with her babies and toddlers significantly affect their progress. Mothers who provide simple explanations in answer to the many questions which children pose, lead a dialogue or describe the host of objects surrounding the child, play games involving language usage, read stories and buy toys which develop language skills are more likely to raise the linguistic standards of their children.

There may still be controversy about whether or not some linguistic structures are innate, but there is no doubt that different home environments give rise to different uses being made of language. What has given rise to disagreement is whether the distinctions observed between, for example, the language of a child from a working-class home and that of a child from a middle-class home are the result of *language deficits* or *language differences* in usage.

Of recent theories on the study of language and home background (chiefly in social-class terms), that of Bernstein (summarized in Stubbs and Hillier 1983, Lawton 1968) emphasizes the deficit model: conditions are such as to impair the progress of language growth. Bernstein's interests are essentially sociological, but his findings point to several possible implications for students of language and cognition. He believes that language is 'one of the most important means of initiating, synthesizing and *reinforcing* ways of thinking (the weak form of the Sapir–Whorf hypothesis), feeling and behaviour which are functionally related to the social group'. Children from more articulate backgrounds, generally found in middle-class homes, not only display marked differences in the vocabulary they use as contrasted with children from working-class homes, but also organize and respond to experience in more sensitive ways.

Different use of language forms does seem to relate to social class. These forms have been described by Bernstein as the *restricted code* (at one time he used the term 'public language') and the *elaborated code* (formal language). The restricted code is used by both working-class and middle-class people. The elaborated code is mostly limited to middle-class usage.

A tentative catalogue of ten basic differences between the language codes appears in a research paper by Bernstein (1971 and 1973). To illustrate some of these, the restricted-code user has short, grammatically simple, unfinished sentences with poor syntactical structure. Simple conjunctions (so, then, and) are used repeatedly. Short commands and questions are frequently used. Impersonal pronouns (e.g., one) are rarely in evidence. Terms of *sympathetic circularity* such as 'like', 'you know', 'isn't it' are often used. On the other hand, the elaborated-code user has accurate grammatical and syntactical structure, uses complex sentences containing conjunctions and relative clauses and makes discriminative use of adjectives and adverbs.

The restricted code also possesses implicit understanding through grammatically incomplete expressions (or even non-verbal communication) as well as the sympathetic circular terms and widely understood clichés. Whenever people know each other well (husband and wife, brother and sister), contracted verbal and non-verbal codes exist. An eye movement might be sufficient to replace a sentence! Note, however, the ability of those from middle-class backgrounds to use either code. Most mothers (and teachers for that matter), whether working-class or middle-class in origin, have been heard to say 'sit down and wrap up' (restricted) as an alternative to 'do sit down and make a little less noise please, darling' (elaborated).

Labov (1970) does not accept the language-deficit explanation of language differences. He declares that there is no linguistic deprivation and no lack of intelligence or linguistic thinking amongst non-standard English users. He believes that the main reason for the distinction in usage is related more to the influence of the peer group than the home for setting language-usage norms. Note how quickly the young develop and use the catchphrases of their generation. Each generation seems to create its own collection of clichés, often leaving the older generations in comparative ignorance of their meaning.

The work of Tough (1976a), for the Schools Council's Communication Skills in Early Childhood Project, provides some interesting evidence of home influences on language. Tough argues that the range of language acquired is largely a function of the range of experiences enabling language usage in the home. This is very much a 'difference' rather than a 'deficit' viewpoint, and is in the Vygotsky/Piaget tradition (see earlier in the chapter). The conclusion from the research was not that disadvantaged children had an inadequate knowledge of language (although for some this may be the case), but that they had had insufficient experiences of language being used in particular ways in the home. Her study led to several conclusions about the functions of children's use of language (see earlier section on functions). These are worth noting:

- Self-maintaining: maintaining the rights and property of the self
- Directing the child's activity and that of others (cf. egocentric speech)
- Reporting on present and past experience
- Logical reasoning
- Predicting and anticipating possibilities
- Projecting with the experiences of others
- Building up an imaginative scene for play through talk.
  (Extract from Tough, 1976b)

Using these criteria, distinctions were apparent between children from educationally advantaged homes (higher education and professional occupations) and those from disadvantaged homes (minimum period of education and unskilled or semi-skilled manual occupations), yet all the children had comparable measured intelligence. All the children used self-maintaining and reporting of present experiences; however, disadvantaged children were less likely to use language for the other purposes indicated above (Tough 1976a and b). The disadvantaged child tends not to be as explicit as the advantaged child, and tends not to be in tune with the 'communication needs' of the listener in terms of thinking about the spoken messages to give a clear indication of the meaning behind them.

This greater emphasis on the communication aspects of language and its impact on later language skills are of value to the teacher. By 'communication' is meant transmitting meanings so that the meaning intended by the sender is the one interpreted by the receiver.

The role of the family, particularly the mother, in exposing children to language usage is clear. The language skills of parents and the purposes for which language is used are dominant influences. Elaboration of the language is more likely to evolve where two-way conversation takes place, as in question-and-answer exploration, rather than one-way communication consisting essentially of instructions. Equally, opportunities for and encouragement in language usage in the home in the form of books, newspapers, games involving words ('I spy') and bedtime stories are important language contacts.

### Speech problems (also see 'Reading' in the next section)

Not all language deficits originate from environmental disadvantages. Some speech conditions with both genetic and physiological origins exist. Genetically linked problems such as dyslexia, or reading disability, will be dealt with in Chapter 11. Mild speech disorders are commonplace in young children. Examples are mild lisping (endearing for many people whilst it lasts), difficulty with 'r's (pronounced like a 'w') and 'th's (pronounced like an 'f' or 'v' – 'finking about forty farsand fevers on a frush', which translated is 'thinking about forty thousand feathers on a thrush').

Stammering or stuttering, a phonological or articulation disorder, is now thought to have a substantial genetic component (Plomin *et al.* 2001, Yairi *et al.* 1996). Part of the problem arises from poor coordination of breathing and articulation of words. The precise physiological cause has not been substantiated, but it may start as a mild physical deformity which, when aggravated by careless handling, produces emotional tension. Adult intervention (constant prompting or ridicule) does seem to make the complaint worse. It could, therefore, be a case of a mild defect being caught up in a cycle of tension and self-consciousness which becomes magnified beyond proportion.

Other physical defects of voice and articulation organs (voice box, breathing, tongue, lips or palate), giving rise to mild disorders, occur. They originate from damage to the organ, the brain or the sense of hearing. Injuries to the speech regions of the brain, producing aphasia, have a wider effect on language usage as mentioned in Chapter 2. Be on the lookout for the 'late developer' in speech. The reasons are obscure, but we do know that some children, without any apparent evidence of physical or mental defect, are very slow off the mark, only to improve quite rapidly later in their school lives.

However, when the teacher spots a voice, articulation or language problem, it is wise to seek professional advice in the first place to eliminate the possibilities of a more permanent difficulty and, if necessary, to clear the way for a programme of help for less serious cases. Where cases are thought to be more serious than a childhood developmental phase, programmes of help from language and speech therapists should be sought by parents and teachers (see Chapter 11).

## At school

Of all the areas in the school curriculum, English has produced the most imposing avalanche of books for teachers and children and within this literacy has taken the lion's share. The National Curriculum (see Chapter 15) has been a key contributor of subject matter. It is a task for the specialist tutor in this area to provide the student with suitable detailed reading lists. In this text we are concerned essentially with the psychological aspects of what is chosen and how it is delivered.

### Further reading

There are now large numbers of publications from the National Curriculum Council dealing with English. The early case was made in the National Curriculum Council, *English for Ages 5–16*, proposals of the Secretary of State for Education and Science and the Secretary of State for Wales, HMSO, June 1989. This was followed by *Aspects of English: English in the National Curriculum in Key Stages 1 to 4*, Teachers' notes, 1991 and *National Curriculum English: A Case for Revising the Order, 1992*. A revision of the attainment targets was published by HMSO, entitled *English for Ages 5–16 (1993)*, in April 1993 which gave rise to the DfE document *English in the National Curriculum*, HMSO, London, 1995.

The original documents leading to the present programmes of study and attainment targets in English make interesting reading. One in particular is the Kingman Report (1988) *Report of the Committee of Inquiry into the Teaching of English Language*. London: HMSO.

The National Curriculum Council has emphasized the importance of speaking and listening, reading, writing, spelling and handwriting and has made them the five attainment targets to be measured. Recent documents and media reports emphasize the role of English at all levels of formal schooling.

## Talking and listening

For some time now, there has been tremendous effort to encourage the three skills of reception, symbolization and expression in schools. For example, one initiative of the National Curriculum Council was the National Oracy Project 1987–93 for which several interesting *Occasional Papers* were produced (see also MacLure *et al.* 1988). The National Curriculum Council has always been concerned to develop pupils' understanding of the spoken word and to enhance their 'capacity to express themselves effectively in a variety of speaking and listening activities, matching style and response to audience and purpose' (*National Curriculum English: A Case for Revising the Order*, 1992). The psychological research in, for instance, spoken language in the early years is well documented in MacLure *et al.* (1988; also see Tough 1977, Hall and Martello 1996).

It is essential to distinguish between those programmes designed to improve the intellectual skills of the socially and culturally deprived using enrichment programmes at pre-school ages – the deficit model (e.g. *Head Start*: Pines 1966; *Talk Reform*: Gahagan and Gahagan 1970) – and those designed or adapted for normal use in primary (e.g. *Listening to Children Talking*: Tough 1976b) and secondary schools (e.g. *Language in Use*: Doughty *et al.* 1971). Tough (1976b), for example, developed a teaching scheme in the use of language with the emphasis on function rather than structure of spoken language. The scheme was designed to encourage a child to 'formulate ideas, examine relationships, reflect and reason about what he experiences, and consider the viewpoint of other people'.

Further, there is ample evidence to support pre-school provision (Sylva 1983, Schweinhart and Weikart 1980, Lazar and Darlington 1982) provided that it is not too formal or academic and exploits the enquiring, play-oriented mind at this age (Mills and Mills 1998; for a discussion of the neuro-psychological reasons, see Blakemore 2000, see website address). Government recognition of these crucial years appears in the form *of Early Learning Goals* and its successor, *The Curriculum Guidance for the Foundation Years* (QCA 2000b), although we have to guard against over-academic approaches to these early year experiences.

For a useful commentary on children's talking as a learning device, Bruner's early book, *Child's Talk* (1983) is still applicable, but also see Hall and Martello (1996).

## Reading

Reading and writing are often combined under the general heading of *literacy*. Both are so central to our way of life that it would be impossible to imagine an educational system which did not have a substantial commitment to both of them. Because of this, library shelves are groaning with literature about theories, research results and practical advice. Therefore, no attempt will be made here to advise students on the teaching of reading because it is a subject in its own right. Within psychology itself, there is a substantial literature on reading and reading development which, understandably, has blossomed in recent years. It is not possible in a few paragraphs of a general educational psychology textbook to do justice to the findings and arguments surrounding the subject. For a clear introduction and useful starting point, see Beard (1990). For recent, more advanced, thinking on the subject see Oakhill and Beard (1999) or Stainthorp and Tomlinson (2002).

The importance of literacy (and numeracy – see later section) has led successive governments to sponsor the production of reports, inquiries, guidelines and attainment targets in various shapes and sizes. For instance, the DfES produced a string of publications in 2001 relating to literacy (see publication list at the end of this paragraph). But of all publications, the Bullock Report, despite its date of 1975, has probably been one of the most influential documents produced on the teaching of English in schools. One of its statements is still a guideline for present-day practices, namely 'there is no one method, medium, approach, device, or philosophy that holds the key to the process of learning to read . . . simple endorsements of one or another nostrum are of no service to the teaching of reading'.

---

### Further reading

In the last two decades or so, we have seen the introduction of the National Curriculum and all the documents relating to it. The National Curriculum Council's attainment targets hoped to promote 'the ability to read, understand and respond to all types of writing' and 'the development of information-retrieval strategies for the purposes of study'. Here, it ought to be mentioned that the focus of attention has been on *when* and *how* to start the teaching of reading to children (excluding the somewhat specialist work of the Adult Literacy movement). Along with the literacy hour, came a wave of publications of which the National Literacy Strategy (NLS – now combined with the National Numeracy Strategy to become the Primary National Strategy) produced important sources of advice for teachers. They include an HMI Report (DfEE 1998b) and the accompanying Strategy Framework (DfEE 1998c). Commentaries by Stainthorp and others (on the NLS) can be found in *The Psychology of Education Review* (1999 and 2006). The most recent report investigating the teaching of reading comes from the House of Commons Education and Skills Committee. We shall refer later in the chapter to this report. The easiest way to see a copy on screen is to use the Internet engine, searching for 'teaching children to read education and skills'. This gives a list in which the option 'teaching children to read' appears. Click this for a copy of the report. A visit to the DfES website at http://www.standards.dfes.gov.uk/primary reveals various headings you could try, such as literacy and mathematics.

---

Converting those black marks we see on a sheet of paper (symbols) into the overt sounds we make with our voices, or converting meanings in our heads, is a miracle of human brain activity. Locating those areas of the brain responsible for various aspects of the process of speaking, reading or writing is now well established (Chapter 2). It has been said that we have to speak 'inside ourselves' before we can read or write. Discovering specific brain locations for processing of letters, words and sentences has led to several theories about how we read and what would be the best method of teaching reading (Posner *et al.* 1988). As ever in education, no one method has proved to be the only suitable method.

The symbols on the page represent letters of the alphabet to which sounds (*phonology*) have been attached. When these alphabetic symbols are combined in various ways, they give rise to words (letters and spelling – *orthography*) which have their own sounds (*phonology*). The words are then combined to give phrases and sentences (*semantics*).

For those in favour of *phonics*, the process of learning to read involves *decoding* letters by putting sounds to them, combining the sounds to make an identifiable word (*phonological recoding*), *comprehending* by giving meaning to that word, followed by stringing words together to form a progression as a *narrative*. In brief:

Letter sounds → word sounds → word meaning → sentence meaning → text meaning (full comprehension).

In learning to read, phonology, orthography and semantics are inter-related (for a commentary on the theory about their relationship (triangle model of reading), see Seidenberg and McClelland 1989 and Plaut *et al.* 1996).

Methods of teaching reading have been classified in several ways. One such is a distinction between *decoding* and *reading for meaning*. The *decoding* methods of teaching reading are based on approaches that appeal to many behaviourists. The *reading for meaning* methods are holistic approaches typified by gestalt (cognitivist) psychology.

## Decoding methods of teaching reading

*Decoding methods*, collectively known as *systematic phonics* include the *synthetic* (and *alphabetic*) *phonics* and *analytic phonics* approaches. Synthetic methods of teaching, sometimes called *structured phonics*, are carried out by first 'sound naming' the letters of the alphabet (singly or in groups) and using these sounds, *within the phonological competence of the child*, from which to build up words. Words are built up from their smallest sound units – *phonemes*. In the simplest *alphabetic method* the words 'pod' and 'tap' would first be introduced using the alphabetic sounds 'ay' 'bee' 'see', etc. Thus, 'pee-oh-dee gives pod' or 'tee-a-pee gives tap'.

But to complicate matters, the sounds of a particular letter vary in different contexts. This adds to the difficulty of both learning and teaching reading. Take the letter 'a'. A glance at the introduction to the Oxford English Dictionary, under 'pronunciation', reveals several different ways of pronouncing 'a' – ă in 'tap', ā in 'name', *a* in 'ago', ar in 'fare', ar in 'far', aw in 'paw', and so on. They all have to be memorized. When each component in a word is pronounced in succession it is sometimes called 'all-through-the-word' (see analytic methods below).

There are different methods of breaking a word down into phonemic sounds and there are also several ways of using the sounds of letters in the words (sound-letter correspondence). In the *synthetic phonic* method, words are gradually pieced together from the smallest names or sounds of letters or combinations of letters such as 'sh'. So 'pod' could be 'puh-ŏ-duh', 'puh-ŏd' or 'pŏ-duh' ('ŏ' is the phonetic symbol for 'o' as in rock); 'tap' could be 'tuh-ă-puh' or 'tuh- ăp' 'tă -puh'; 'shop' would be 'sh-ŏ-puh'. Letter recognition and the relationship between letters and their sounds in particular word contexts lie at the root of the phonic method. Its special advantage is that it can be taught systematically, starting with synthetic word building. Its problem is the huge variety of sounds associated, in particular, with vowels. The method often predates the use of books.

In the *analytic phonic* method, favoured by the National Literacy Strategy, whole or parts of words are pronounced and use is made of analogies between letters or phonemes. Ways of breaking words down are illustrated in the last two examples in 'pod' and 'tap' above. For example, the *onset-rime* method breaks words down into beginnings (onsets) and endings (rimes). The words '*p*-ot', '*p*-at', '*p*-it' show how analogies are used to demonstrate the appearance and pronunciation of 'p' at the beginning of words with various endings. For endings, similar phoneme combinations of letters which rhyme (or rime) are used, such as c-*ow*, n-*ow*, s-*ow*. But this does highlight the fact that English, having originated from several language sources such as Anglo-Saxon, Latin and French, has not only many exceptions but also several words meaning the same thing. Take 'bow' and 'row', though they could be pronounced like 'cow', they could also be pronounced like 'low'. When we get into, bough, bought, cough, dough or rough, we are into a quagmire of pronunciation. The method also involves a lot more than 50 or so phonemes. Reading material most often accompanies the teaching.

This is well and briefly summarized online at: http://www.syntheticphonics.com/links.htm, and within this click Scotland.gov.uk where there are a number of references to the comparison of synthetic and analytic phonics (e.g., Watson and Johnston 1998; Johnston and Watson 2005). They also showed that, for their age, children exposed to synthetic phonics were three and a half years ahead in reading and one year, eight months ahead in spelling at age eleven compared with those exposed to analytic phonics in the National Literacy Strategy (see Figure 5.4). This and other evidence and advice has led to a renewal of interest in synthetic phonics (for a website reference with comments about the evidence see http://www.syntheticphonics.com/links.htm and within this, click Scotland.gov.uk). But let us not forget the wise advice of the Bullock Report that 'there is no one method, medium, approach, device, or philosophy that holds the key to the process of learning to read'. For a discussion about systematic phonics see The Psychology of Education Review, vol. 30, 2, 2006.

## 'Reading for meaning' methods of teaching reading

In reading for meaning methods we find *look-and-say, whole word, whole sentence* and *whole language*. Some regard these methods as more natural than phonic methods and more akin to learning to speak by constant repetition. The principle is that children will remember the configuration or 'shape' of the whole word and associate it with a meaning – where possible, a pictorial representation. The whole-word method is frequently accompanied by pictorial aids in the first stages, while look-and-say can be applied to non-pictorial words as well. So the word 'dog', probably already in the oral vocabulary of the child, would be presented along with a picture of the object. This is good psychological thinking because we are moving from the familiar (sight of, and sound of, a familiar object) to the unfamiliar (sight of the whole word). Decoding methods, on the other hand, are said to be boring and sometimes meaningless, because the phonic-taught child can piece together long words without any idea of what the words mean. However, the 'look-and-say' child does have to wait until his or her knowledge of words is sufficient to enable unfamiliar-looking words to be deciphered. Again, the teacher's help is sought more frequently (with the consequent disadvantage of long queues waiting to be told the meanings of words). The starting vocabulary also tends to be limited because of the amount of learning required of the child. Each word is learned as an entity, although some transfer might be possible, as with phonic methods. The whole-sentence method is an extension of the look-and-say method, using sentences as the unit to be learned. Small groups of short words giving a meaningful sentence are taught along with visual props.

## The 'Searchlights Model'

Attempts at a compromise between these different approaches was incorporated into the National Literature Strategy. Figure 5.4 is a summary.

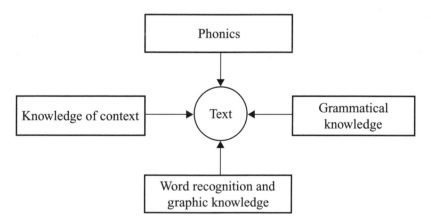

**Figure 5.4** The 'Searchlights Model', illustrated in *Teaching Children to Read*, 8th report of the Education and Skills Committee, 21 March 2005, p. 10. This parliamentary material is reproduced with permission of the Controller of HMSO on behalf of Parliament.

Presented with so many conflicting models and in the absence of firm evidence, it seemed expedient for the NLS to involve all the major approaches to the teaching of reading.

Therefore, the recommendation was to use a range of strategies as and when required. Unfortunately, using all methods has confused rather than clarified the position. Most psychologists would argue that whatever methods are used, there must be an ordered sequence in keeping with the developmental stages of the child. Research so far (Johnson and Watson 2005) suggests that, in formal education, phonics come first.

The relationships between phonics, orthographics and semantics have been explored by Snowling (2002), Plaut *et al.* (1996), in a paper on reading development, which discusses some issues which relate the sound of words (phonology), their spelling (orthography) and their meaning (semantics). These three are closely linked ('pathways') and the conclusions drawn from the research are that:

> . . . phonological skills are critical for the development of decoding skills and therefore are strong predictors of reading development in the early stages. Later on in development, language skills outside the phonological domain, particularly semantic skills, appear vital, at least for readers of English, as a foundation for the development of an efficient reading system that can deal with words that vary in regularity and in frequency. (Snowling 2002)

These conclusions will doubtless be related to brain localization research in the near future as indicated in Chapter 2.

## Reading recovery (Marie Clay)

Publicity has been given to a reading scheme devised by Marie Clay in New Zealand entitled Reading Recovery. The main purpose of the scheme, which is gaining support in the UK, is to help six-year-old children who, after one year in school, are behind in reading and writing. A diagnostic test is used by a trained teacher to detect the sources of difficulty. The sources are used as the starting point for a concentrated diet of learning sessions at the rate of one 30-minute period a day for 12 to 20 weeks. The first two weeks are spent 'roaming round the known'. The sessions are undertaken with a one-way screen behind which is a second teacher who also helps in the analysis.

The key features of the programme are that the child's existing competence is carefully analysed and used as the starting point for a concentrated remedial scheme. The sessions are well organized, intense but enjoyable. There is a one-to-one setting with each child having individual attention appropriate to the child's particular problems and in daily doses for several weeks with a second teacher in attendance. The teaching focuses on comprehension in reading and writing relevant messages using a wide range of cueing strategies such as phonic, visual, syntactic, analogy and meaning. This is a good example of Vygotsky's scaffolding technique.

With such concentrated effort, there is little wonder that the statistics of performance are impressive. Of 20 needy cases taken from every 100 pupils in school at age six, 19 will reach average reading performance in the 20-week period of the programme. What is even more significant is the follow-up three years later when these children are still performing as well as their own age group of nine years.

---

### Further reading

For an evaluation of Clay's programme in the UK, see A. Wright (1992). Two of Her Majesty's Inspectors went to New Zealand in 1992 to see Professor Dame Marie Clay's nationally adopted system at first hand. They were very impressed and their report not only summarizes the system but also gives a useful analysis of the issues. This can be found in the OFSTED report *Reading Recovery in New Zealand: A Report from the Office of HM Inspector of Schools*, HMSO, 1993a. There has also developed in this country a Reading Recovery National Network. Programmes of training, support and co-ordination for Reading Recovery are now well established in the UK. The Reading Recovery National Network is based at the Institute of Education, London University (http://www.ioe.ac.uk/readingrecovery).

---

A useful book on teaching children in difficulty has been written by Brooks *et al.* (1998). Recent research on children with reading difficulties in Britain (Sylva and Hurry 1995) has shown how effective the method can be over the medium term, but the costs, both in terms of teacher: pupil ratio (one to one) and time out for the teacher to receive specialist in-service training (at least one year) from specially trained tutors, could be prohibitive. However, with such a track record with those children far behind at age six, it is thought to be a price worth considering (OFSTED Report, 1993b).

Many publishers are now producing study schemes. The library shelves are now amply supplied. They often include helpful guides on talking, listening, reading, writing, literacy, numeracy, science and so forth.

The clear conclusion from research in this field is that reading comprehension is an essential prerequisite for later learning in school work. Even if the teacher's skills have faltered in presenting a topic, the pupil with adequate reading skills can go away and learn for him or herself.

There is now a wide range of standardized tests of reading comprehension produced by the NFER (National Foundation for Educational Research) from early years to mid-adolescence. It is certainly wise in the infant and junior years to have a clear idea of the level of competence in reading as a new class begins.

Dyslexia, that is, learning difficulties which obstruct progress in reading skills, is discussed in Chapter 11.

### *Writing*

Some believe that learning to write is harder than learning to read. With reading you have visual cues in front of you. With writing, you have to create something for yourself, except when copying. Yet, research into the national literacy programme indicates that less attention has been paid to writing than to reading (NFER Report by Sainsbury *et al.* 1998).

There can be very few days in the lives of secondary-school pupils which do not contain some kind of writing commitment. The National Curriculum target is 'to promote a growing ability to construct and convey meaning in written language matching style to audience and purpose'. The ability to spell and write clearly is also expected. The revised version of the National Curriculum in 1995 merge the three components of constructing and conveying meaning, accurate spelling and clear handwriting. Like the other areas mentioned above, to achieve this target we have to ask what should the pupils be learning and how should we be teaching it?

Beard (2000), in a thorough review of children's writing, identifies and discusses in some detail five approaches in deciding on the range of writing to offer children of various ages. They are based on five criteria of:

- *what forms* the writing should take, (concerned with the subject of the writing such as the following taken from the Key Stage 2 – poetry, narrative, report, explanation, opinion, instruction, review, commentary)
- *how* to organize writing (which concentrates on modes such as description, exposition, narrative and argument)
- *why* do we write (i.e. aims such as to be expressive (share news), transactional (inform, persuade) or poetic (entertain))
- *who* are we writing for (audiences such as self, teacher, peer group, family, friends or the public – see Britton *et al.* 1975)
- *what* are we writing *about* (content such as real life or imaginative).

A significant point is that all but the 'how' criterion emphasize products of writing rather than the processes. This is where the role of the teacher is paramount. Hillocks (1986), in a meta-analysis (Chapter 17) of teaching methods in writing, found three prevalent methods he called *presentational, natural process* and *guided.* From the discussions still to come in Chapter 14 on effective teaching, the student should be able to recognize the familiar methods of expository, discovery and guided discovery (interactional) teaching. Unlike Bennett (1976), Hillocks found presentational methods the least effective and the interactional the most effective. With the former, children's work was marked with too much emphasis on what was wrong rather than how to put things right. Children need to be given processes which help them to improve their work.

## Numeracy

The Cockcroft Report (1982) on the teaching of mathematics in schools was an important landmark. The report believed that being numerate meant two things. One was being comfortable with numbers particularly when dealing with everyday affairs; the second was understanding how numbers work. This, in effect, means confidence and competence in communicating using numbers. To achieve this, a statutory national curriculum in mathematics was created in 1989 by the DES and publications from then onwards (e.g., OFSTED 1993b and 1998; DfEE numeracy Framework and Strategy documents 1998a and 1999b; DfES 2001) have been swift to advise on content and teaching methods. It is within this context that we see several psychological principles.

For advice on the appropriateness of content, we have the seminal work on concept formation of Piaget and Vygotsky mentioned earlier in Chapter 4. The former used mathematical concepts extensively, helping to define what, in general, is attainable by children at various ages.

Coupled with content is the method of presentation – what we decide to present to children affects our methods of presentation. Vygotsky has something to say about these methods.

However, much of the debate about best practice rests on the balance between how much you need to tell children (expository) and how much you can allow them free rein in discovering things for themselves (discovery). In Chapters 12 and 14 we refer to the work of Bennett in the 1970s in which he found that children's achievements in mathematics (also reading and English) were generally better in formal, teacher-centred, subject-orientated classrooms. These findings came in the days when 'discovery methods' held sway. A similar, recent research by Askew *et al.* (1997) finds that 'connectionist' teachers produce the best results. Connectionists are those who use direct teaching, but make a point of relating different mathematical concepts, that is, connecting, say, fractions, decimals and percentages. This is the well-tried method of going from familiar to unfamiliar material (Chapter 6). It also illustrates Vygotsky's method of 'scaffolding' (Chapter 4, p. 106).

As in literacy, the stress is currently on whole class teaching which is structured, direct, expository and interactive. We shall see in Chapter 14 the major arguments in support of discovery and expository methods of teaching.

*Dyscalculia* (cf. dyslexia) involves serious learning difficulties associated with mathematics and is covered in Chapter 11.

## Summary

Readers do not have to be convinced that language is a, if not the, most important skill for human learning and communication. There are two basic requirements of a language, namely that it should be symbolic and systematic. The symbolic aspects were discussed in the form of phonemes and morphemes and the systematics in relation to grammar and semantics.

An introduction to the characteristics of spoken language (phonemes, morphemes, grammar and semantics) was followed by a section on the functions of spoken language (egocentric and social). The function of speech was the centre of controversy some years ago when Piaget and Vygotsky disagreed about the purposes served by the early speech of children. Now it is widely accepted that egocentric speech (speech intended essentially for one's own benefit) and socialized speech (for the benefit of others) are the two major functions. Egocentric speech is most often used as self-directive – giving instructions to oneself. Once this speech becomes internalized, it can regulate behaviour for both personal and social motives.

Language acquisition was then explored. At one extreme we find the behaviourist position, illustrated from the theories of Skinner, in which language is said to be acquired largely by the processes of imitation and reinforcement of acceptable sounds. On the other hand, Chomsky, whilst not rejecting the possibility of stimulus–response learning of phonemes and morphemes, nevertheless cannot accept that the highly creative nature of language is derived largely from the Skinnerian type of language conditioning. Those with some degree of fluency are well able to create and understand entirely original sentences. Human language is far more open-ended than that of other species. Although bees can communicate and even vary the intensity of their messages to give shades of meaning (variable activity amongst bees is commensurate with the distance from the hive of a supply of pollen), they cannot recombine their code to give original messages. The potency of humans' communication lies in the infinite combinations possible. New rules of language can develop, or recognized rules can be broken, especially by young children who are still in the process of learning the rules.

Efficient language acquisition is very much dependent on the linguistic environment to which children are exposed. Bernstein has shown some marked differences in the language patterns and skills deriving from different home backgrounds, and he named these patterns 'restricted' and 'elaborate' codes.

Templin's (1957) and Lenneberg's (1966) work on establishing norms of articulation, speech–sound discrimination, sentence structure and vocabulary size among children from three to eight years of age was followed by a brief introduction to some contemporary views of language acquisition.

The connection between language and thought is yet another source of disagreement among psychologists. A range of speculations is presented, from strong linguistic-relativity (Whorf and Sapir – see Slobin 1971), in which it is speculated that language determines thought, to strong forms of cognitive hypotheses (see Cromer 1974), in which it is held that we can use linguistic structures largely because of our cognitive abilities. A weak form of this latter hypothesis is proposed by Vygotsky, namely, that language and thought start from different origins at birth and gradually, but only partially, merge in the early years of life. Figure 5.2 summarizes the possibilities of pre-linguistic thought and pre-intellectual speech either fusing to become interdependent or remaining throughout life as non-linguistic thought and non-intellectual speech.

We then dealt with Bruner's work on the place of language in concept formation and the theory of Osgood, which proposes that 'meaning' is ascribed to stimuli in accordance with the actual sensations experienced at the time the stimulus is presented. The representational mediation processes suggested by Osgood are responsible for the patterns of reaction (either physical or verbal) which occur on the next presentation of a stimulus.

Non-verbal communication was also held to be important to the teacher and for the deaf community. We communicate with other human beings not only in words, but also in all our actions.

A final section on teaching literacy and numeracy skills discussed the impact of the home and school. Psychological findings relating to speaking, listening, reading, writing and numeracy are explored, particularly reading, and linked to the new arrangements of the literacy and numeracy hours in the National Curriculum.

## Tutorial enquiry and discussion

(a) Take tape-recordings of both monologue and dialogue of children at several ages (including pre-school children). Note:
- egocentric and socialized speech
- virtuous errors
- restricted and elaborated codes.

(b) Examine the methods of language teaching in schools that you visit. Bring these back to the tutorial sessions for discussion and analysis.

(c) Visit the DfES website at http://www.standards.dfes.gov.uk/primary/mathematics which has various headings dealing with the teaching of mathematics under 'Guide to Professional Development'. Note the amount of psychology in the guide.

(d) Discover what you can about non-verbal communication. Observe the non-verbal behaviour of teachers and children in the classroom and their reaction to different kinds of non-verbal activities of the teacher (also see expectations of teachers, Chapter 8, p. 260).

(e) Read your tutor's recommended texts in literacy with an eye towards the problems facing teachers who are in schools where the catchment area is largely from ethnic minorities. What problems face the teacher of immigrant children?

(f) There is now a hefty body of literature commenting on both the teaching and content of literacy and numeracy. Finding reliable criteria for sorting out the most effective texts for you and your pupils is a task worth pursuing in tutorial sessions.

(g) Examine standardized test materials in reading, comprehension and number. Also look at any available material used for SATs testing. With the tutor, explore the ways in which these are prepared, standardized, analysed and used in compiling national statistics.

## References

Aitchison, J. (1998), *The Articulate Mammal: An Introduction to Psycholinguistics* (4th edn). London: Routledge.

Argyle, M. (1983), *The Psychology of Interpersonal Behaviour* (4th edn). Harmondsworth: Penguin.

Argyle, M. and Trower, P. (1979), *Person to Person: Ways of Communicating*. London: Harper and Row.

Askew, M., Brown, M., Rhodes, V., William, D. and Johnson, D. (1997), *Effective Teachers of Numeracy: A Report of a Study Carried Out for the Teacher Training Agency*. London: King's College, University of London.

Baron-Cohen, S. (2003), *The Essential Difference: Men, Women and the Extreme Male Brain*. London: Allan Lane (and Penguin Books).

Beard, R. (1990), *Developing Reading 3–13* (2nd edn). London: Hodder and Stoughton.

Beard, R. (2000), *Developing Writing 3–13*. London: Hodder and Stoughton.

Bennett, N. (1976), *Teaching Styles and Pupil Progress*. London: Open Books.

Berko, J. (1958), 'The child's learning of English morphology', *Word*, 14, 150–77.

Bernstein, B. (1971), *Class, Codes and Control* (Vol. 1). London: Routledge and Kegan Paul.

Bernstein, B. (1973), *Class, Codes and Control* (Vol. 2). London: Routledge and Kegan Paul.

Boyle, D. G. (1969), *A Student's Guide to Piaget*. London: Pergamon.

Britton, J., Burgess, T., Martin, N., MacCleod, A. and Rosen, H. (1975), *The Development of Writing Abilities (11–18)*. London: Macmillan Education.

Brooks, G., Flanagan, N., Henkuzens, Z. and Hutchinson, D. (1998), *What Works for Slow Readers? The Effectiveness of Early Intervention Schemes*. Slough: NFER.

Brown, R. (1973), *A First Language*. Cambridge, MA: Harvard University Press.

Bruner, J. S. (1964), 'The course of cognitive growth', *American Psychologist*, 19, 1–15.

Bruner, J. S. (1983), *Child's Talk: Learning to Use Language*. Oxford: Oxford University Press.

Bullock Report (1975), *A Language for Life*. London: HMSO.

Carroll, J. B. (1964), *Language and Thought*. Englewood Cliffs, NJ: Prentice-Hall.

Clark, M. M. (1994), *Young Literacy Learners: How We Can Help Them*. Leamington Spa: Scholastic Publications.

Cockcroft Report, The (1982), *Mathematics Counts: Report of the Committee of Inquiry into the Teaching of Mathematics in Schools*. London: HMSO.

Cromer, R. F. (1974), 'The development of language and cognition: the cognition hypothesis', in B. M. Foss (ed.), *New Perspectives in Child Development*. Harmondsworth: Penguin.

Crystal, D. (1987), *Child Language, Learning and Linguistics* (2nd edn). London: Arnold.

Deuchar, M. (1984), *British Sign Language*. London: Routledge and Kegan Paul.

DfE (1995), *English in the National Curriculum*. London: HMSO.

DfEE (1998a), *The Implementation of the National Numeracy Strategy: The Final Report of the Numeracy Task Force*. London: HMSO.

DfEE (1998b), *The National Literacy Project: A Report from HMI*. London: HMSO.

DfEE (1998c), *The National Literacy Strategy Framework for Teaching*. London: HMSO.

DfEE (1999b), *The Framework for Teaching Mathematics*. London: HMSO.

DfES (2001), *The National Numeracy Strategy: Guidance to Support Pupils with Dyslexia and Dyscalculia*. London: HMSO.

Dodd, B. (1972), 'Effects of social and vocal stimulation on infant babbling', *Developmental Psychology*, 7, 80–3.

Doughty, P. S., Pearce, J. J. and Thornton, G. M. (1971), *Language in Use*. London: Arnold.

Douglas, J. W. B., Ross, J. M. and Simpson, H. R. (1968), *All our Futures: A Longitudinal Study of Secondary Education*. London: Davies.

Education and Skills Committee (2005), *Teaching Children to Read: 8th report of Session 2004–05*. London: HMSO.

Essen, J. and Wedge, P. (1982), *Continuities in Childhood Disadvantage*. London: Heinemann.

Evans, L. (1982), *Total Communication: Structure and Strategy*. Washington, DC: Gallaudet College Press.

Gahagan, D. M. and Gahagan, G. A. (1970), *Talk Reform: Explorations in Language for Infant School Children*. London: Routledge and Kegan Paul.

Gardner, R. A. and Gardner, B. T. (1969), 'Teaching sign language to a chimpanzee', *Science*, 165, 664–72.

Gardner, R. A. and Gardner, B. T. (1972), 'Two-way communication with an infant chimpanzee', in A. M. Schrier and F. Stollnitz (eds), *Behavior of Non-human Primates* (Vol. 4). New York: Academic Press.

Geschwind, N. and Galaburda, A. M. (1987). *Cerebral Lateralization*. Cambridge, MA: MIT Press.

Greene, J. (1987), *Memory, Thinking and Language. Topics in Cognitive Psychology*. London: Methuen.

Hall, N. and Martello, J. (eds) (1996), *Listening to Children Think: Exploring Talk in the Early Years*. London: Hodder and Stoughton.

Herriot, P. (1971), *Language and Teaching: A Psychological View*. London: Methuen.

Herriot, P. (1976), *An Introduction to the Psychology of Language*. London: Methuen.

Hillocks, G. (1986), 'Research on written composition'. Proceedings of a conference on research on English, reading and communication skills. Urbana, IL.

Holowka, S. and Petitto, L. A. (2002), 'Left hemisphere cerebral specialization for babies while babbling', *Science*, 297(558b), 1515.

Hymes, D. H. (1967) 'The function of speech', in J. P. De Cecco (ed.), *The Psychology of Language, Thought and Instruction*. New York: Holt, Rinehart and Winston.

Johnston, R. and Watson, J. (2005), *The Effects of Synthetic Phonics Teaching on Reading and Spelling Attainment: A Seven Year Longitudinal Study*. See website address below.

Keller, Helen (1917), *The Story of My Life*. New York: Doubleday.

Kimura, Doreen, (1999), *Sex and Cognition*. Cambridge MA: MIT Press.

Kingman Report (1988), *Report of the Committee of Inquiry into the Teaching of English Language*. London: HMSO.

Kuhl, P.K. (1998), 'The development of speech and language', in T. J. Carew, R. Menzel and C. J. Shatz (eds), *Mechanistic Relationships between Development and Learning*. New York: Wiley.

Kyle, J. G. and Woll, B. (1985), *Sign Language: The Study of Deaf People and Their Language*. Cambridge: Cambridge University Press.

Labov, W. (1970), 'The logic of non-standard English', in A. Cashdan and E. Grugeon (eds), *Language in Education*. London: Routledge and Kegan Paul.

Lawton, D. (1968), *Social Class, Language and Education*. London: Routledge and Kegan Paul.

Lazar, I. and Darlington, R. (1982), *Lasting Effects of Early Education: A Report from the Consortium for Longitudinal Studies*. Monographs of the Society for Research in Child Development, no. 195.

Lenneberg, E. H. (1966), 'The natural history of language', in F. Smith and G. A. Miller (eds), *The Genesis of Language*. Cambridge, MA: MIT Press.

Lyons, L. (1970), *Chomsky*. London: Fontana Modern Masters.

MacLure, M., Phillips, T. and Wilkinson, A. (1988), *Oracy Matters*. Milton Keynes: Open University Press.

McLeish, J. and Martin, J. (1975), 'Verbal behavior: a review and experimental analysis', *Journal of General Psychology*, 93, 3–66.

Mead, M. (1934), *Mind, Self and Society*. Chicago, IL: University of Chicago Press.

Mehler, J., Jusczyk, P., Lambertz, G., Halsted, N., Bertoncini, J. and Amiel-Tison, C. (1988), 'A precursor of language acquisition in young infants', *Cognition*, 29(2), 143–78.

Miller, G. A. and Gildea, P. M. (1987), 'How children learn words', *Scientific American*, 257, 94–9.

Miller, G. A. and McNeill, D. (1969), 'Psycholinguistics', in G. Lindzey and E. Aronson (eds), *The Handbook of Social Psychology, Vol. 3* (2nd edn). New York: Addison-Wesley.

Mills, C. and Mills, D. (1998), *Britain's Early Years*. London: Channel 4 TV.

Moll, L. C. (ed.) (1990), *Vygotsky and Education: Instructional Implications and Applications of Sociohistorical Psychology*. Cambridge: Cambridge University Press.

Morris, Desmond (1977), *Manwatching*. London: Cape.

National Curriculum Council (1989), *English for Ages 5–16*, proposals of the Secretary of State for Education and Science and the Secretary of State for Wales. London: HMSO.

National Curriculum Council (1991), *Aspects of English: English in the National Curriculum in Key Stages 1 to 4*, Teachers' notes. London: HMSO.

National Curriculum Council (1992), *National Curriculum English: A Case for Revising the Order*. London: HMSO.

National Curriculum Council (1993), *English for Ages 5–16: A Revision of the Attainment Targets*. London: HMSO.

Neville, H. J. and Bavelier, D. (1998), 'Neural organisation and plasticity of language', *Current Opinion in Neurobiology*, 8(2), 245–8.

Oakhill, J. and Beard, R. (eds) (1999), *Reading Development and the Teaching of Reading*. Oxford: Blackwell.

OFSTED (1993a), *Reading Recovery in New Zealand: A Report from the Office of HM Inspector of Schools*. London: HMSO.

OFSTED (1993b), *The Teaching and Learning of Number in Primary Schools*. London: HMSO.

OFSTED (1998), *The National Numeracy Project: An HMI Evaluation*. London: Office for Standards in Education.

Osgood, C. E., Suci, G. J. and Tannenbaum, P. (1957), *The Measurement of Meaning*. Urbana, IL: University of Illinois.

Paul, Peter V. (2001), *Language and Deafness* (3rd edn). San Diego, CA: Singular, Thompson Learning.

Peaker, G. T. (1971), *The Plowden Children: Four Years Later*. Slough: NFER.

Pines, M. (1966), *Revolution in Learning: The Years from Birth to Six. Head Start*. New York: Harper and Row.

Pinker, S. (1994), *The Language Instinct: The New Science of Language and Mind*. London: Allen Lane, Penguin Press.

Plaut, D. C., McClelland, J. L., Seidenberg, M. S. and Paterson, K. (1996), 'Understanding normal and impaired word reading: computational principles in quasi-regular domains', *Psychological Review*, 10, 56–115.

Plomin, R., DeFries, J. C., McClearn, G. E. and McGuffin, P. (2001), *Behavioral Genetics* (4th edn). New York: Worth.

Posner, M. I., Petersen, S. E., Fox, P. T. and Raichle, M. E. (1988), 'Localization of cognitive operations in the human brain', *Science*, 240, 1627–31.

Premack, D. (1971), 'Language in chimpanzees?', *Science*, 172, 808–22.

Premack, D. (1985), '"Gavani!" or the future history of the animal language controversy', *Cognition*, 19, 207–96.

QCA (2000b), *The Curriculum Guidance for the Foundation Stage*. London: QCA.

Ricks, D. M. (1978), 'The beginnings of vocal communication in infants and autistic children'. Unpublished PhD thesis, University of London.

Sainsbury, M., Schagen, I., Whetton, C., with Hagues, N. and Minnis, M. (1998), *Evaluation of the National Literacy Project: Cohort 1, 1996–98*. Slough: NFER.

Savage-Rumbaugh, E. S., Murphy, J., Sevcik, R. A., Brakke, K. E., Williams, S. L. and Rumbaugh, D. M. (1993), 'Language comprehension in ape and child', *Monographs of the Society for Research in Child Development*, 58, Serial 223.

Schweinhart, L. J. and Weikart, D. P. (1980), *Young children grow up: the effects of the Perry Preschool Program on youths through age 15*. Monographs of the High Scope Educational Research Foundation, no. 27. MI: Ypsilanti.

Scott-Gibson, E. (1992), *The Dictionary of British Sign Language*. London: Faber and Faber.

Seidenberg, M. S. and McClelland, J. L. (1989), 'A distributed, developmental model of word recognition', *Psychological Review*, 96, 523–68.

Shaywitz, B., Shaywitz, S., Pugh, K., Constables, R., Skudlarski, P., Fulbright, R., Bronen, R., Fletcher, J., Shankweiler, D., Katz, L. and Gore, J. (1995), 'Sex differences in the functional organization of the brain for language', *Nature*, 371, 607–9.

Simpson, S. (1998), 'Some advances in sign language communication with deaf people', in D. Shorrocks-Taylor (ed.), *Directions in Educational Psychology*. London: Whurr.

Sinclair-de-Zwart, H. (1969), 'Developmental linguistics', in D. Elkind and J. H. Flavell (eds), *Studies in Cognitive Development*. London: Oxford University Press.

Skinner, B. F. (1957), *Verbal Behavior*. New York: Appleton-Century-Crofts.

Slobin, D. I. (1971), *Psycholinguistics*. Glenview, IL: Scott, Foresman.

Smith, C. (1989), *Communication Link* (3rd edn). Beverley School for the Deaf, Middlesbrough. Coleford: Forest Books.

Snowling, M. J. (2002), 'Individual differences in children's reading development: sound and meaning in learning to read'. 21st Vernon-Wall Lecture, Education Section, British Psychological Society. London: BPS.

Stainthorp, R. and Tomlinson, P. (eds) (2002), 'Learning and teaching reading', *British Journal of Educational Psychology, Series II, Monograph 1, Psychological Aspects of Education – Current Trends*. London: British Psychological Society.

Stubbs, M. and Hillier, H. (eds) (1983), *Readings on Language, Schools and Classrooms*. London: Routledge, Chapman and Hall.

Sylva, K. (1983), 'Some lasting effects of pre-school provision – or the Emperor wore clothes after all', *Education Section Review*, 7, 10–16.

Sylva, K. and Hurry, J. (1995), *Early Intervention in Children with Reading Difficulties: An Evaluation of Reading Recovery and a Phonological Training*. London: Report to Schools Curriculum Assessment Authority.

Templin, M. C. (1957), *Certain Language Skills in Children*. Minneapolis: Minnesota University Press.

Tough, J. (1976a), *The Development of Meaning: A Study of Children's Use of Language*. London: Allen and Unwin.

Tough, J. (1976b), *Listening to Children Talking. Schools Council Communication Skills in Early Childhood Project*. London: Ward Lock.

Tough, J. (1977), *Talking and Listening: A Guide to Fostering Communication Skills in the Nursery and Infant School*. London: Ward Lock.

Vernon, P. E. (1953), *Personality Tests and Assessments*. London: Methuen.

Volterra, V. and Erting, C. J. (eds) (1994), *From Gesture to Language in Hearing and Deaf Children*. Washington DC: Gallaudet University Press.

Vygotsky, L. S. (1962), *Thought and Language*, (trans E. Haufmann and C. Vakar). Cambridge, MA: MIT Press.

Watson, J. E. and Johnston, R. S. (1998), *Accelerating Reading Attainment: The Effectiveness of Synthetic Phonics*. Interchange 57. Edinburgh: SOEID.

Watts, A. F. (1955), *The Language and Mental Development of Children* (reprint). London: Harrap.

Wertsch, J. V. (ed.) (1985), *Culture, Communication and Cognition: Vygotskian Perspectives*. Cambridge: Cambridge University Press.

Whorf, B. L. (1956), 'Science and linguistics', in J. B. Carroll (ed.), *Language, Thought and Reality: Selected Writings of Benjamin Lee Whorf*. Cambridge, MA: MIT Press.

Wright, A. (1992), 'Evaluation of the first British Reading Recovery Programme', *British Educational Research Journal*, 18, 351–68.

Yairi, E., Ambrose, N. and Cox, N. (1996), 'Genetics of stuttering: a critical review', *Journal of Speech, Language, and Hearing Research*, 39, 771–84.

## Further reading

Beard, R. (1990), *Developing Reading 3–13* (2nd edn). London: Hodder and Stoughton.

Beard, R. (2000), *Developing Writing 3–13*. London: Hodder and Stoughton.

Ellis, A. and Beattie, G. (1992), *The Psychology of Language and Communication*. Hove: Erlbaum.

Elkin, J., Train, B. and Denham, D. (2003), *Reading and Reader Development: The Pleasures of Reading*. London: Facet Publishing.

Koshy, V. and Murray, J. (eds) (2002), *Unlocking Numeracy: A Guide for Primary Schools*. London: David Fulton Publishers.

*Learning Support Resource Base* gives a huge list of references covering aspects of literacy and numeracy. Enter this title into the web search dialogue box.

Paul, P. V. (2001), *Language and Deafness* (3rd edn). San Diego, CA: Singular, Thompson Learning.

Stubbs, M. (1983), *Language, Schools and Classrooms* (2nd edn). London: Methuen.

## Useful websites

http://www.parliament.uk/post/home.htm. Blakemore, Sarah-Jayne (2000), *Early Learning Years*. In POST (Parliamentary Office of Science and Technology) Report 140, June. London.

http://www.forestbooks.com/system/index.htm. Dictionaries of sign language.

http://www.standards.dfes.gov.uk/primary DfES website. Can be used for information regarding literacy and mathematics.

http://www.syntheticphonics.com/links.htm. Johnston, R. and Watson, J. (2005). For a general introduction to Johnson and Watson's work and consequent opinions within this click Scotland.gov.uk.

*Learning Support Resource Base* is a large website with many references to literacy and numeracy.

http://www.ioe.ac.uk/readingrecovery. Reading Recovery National Network is based at the Institute of Education, London University website.

# Part Three
## Learning

# Learning Theory and Practice

## Chapter Outline

## Implications for teachers

- Learning is at the heart of our work as teachers. Psychologists have studied this area for years and have produced some useful information and advice.
- Many topics in other chapters of the book, such as attention, perception, memory, concept formation, motivation, intelligence and personality, are bound to influence learning, and some cross-referencing will be necessary.

> ## Implications for teachers (continued)
>
> - A study of the two broad traditions in learning theory (behaviourist and cognitivist) make a sound foundation for many explanations offered by psychologists to teachers.
> - Most classroom learning and teaching strategies are based on the two traditions.
> - Computer-based learning and teaching are now central features of educational provision.

This chapter is about general principles of learning theory, in readiness for an understanding of the many applications dotted throughout this book. A large section of Chapter 14, for example, gives practical examples of how to employ these theories in school settings.

Previous chapters have made it abundantly clear that learning is a very necessary activity for living things. Their survival depends on it. For humans, the versatility of their adaptation to diverse environments and the joys of abstraction in art and science are founded on their phenomenal learning capacity. Whilst there is no complete agreement amongst psychologists about the details of learning processes, they do accept the basic premise that learning occurs whenever one adopts new, or modifies existing, behaviour patterns in a way which has some influence on future performance or attitudes. Unless there were in fact some influence, we would not be able to detect that learning had taken place. This reasonably permanent change in behaviour must grow out of past experience and is distinguished from behaviour which results from maturation or physical deformity. This view of learning therefore excludes certain kinds of reactions which are thought to be inborn, such as reflex action or innate release mechanisms (to be mentioned in Chapter 8) where these have not undergone modification in the course of growth. But the definition includes learning which occurs without deliberate or conscious awareness, bad as well as good behaviour, and covert attitudes as well as overt performance. The importance of studying learning processes is self-evident, since one of the central purposes of the teacher's task in formal educational settings is to provide well-organized experiences so as to speed up the process of learning, thus enabling pupils to make reasoned choices in solving life's problems.

Whether we recognize it or not, every parent and teacher has a personal theory or theories about how learning best takes place. In the home, the nature and severity of punishments or rewards tell us something about parental theories of learning. In the use of corporal punishment, some believe that actions almost invariably speak louder than words, whilst others never beat their children because they believe that to apply corporal punishment to children would be to show them that violence is an acceptable way of solving problems. Most people manage to strike a balance between these extreme views of the place of physical punishment in teaching children to behave, although even here the particular occasions chosen to apply punishment reveal something of a parent's philosophy of learning.

In the classroom we constantly observe methods which depend on assumptions about the process of learning. What assumptions are made by teachers who use question-and-answer techniques, rewards (sweets, marks, class positions, etc.), 'look and say', 'phonic' or 'alphabetic' methods of teaching reading, 'Nuffield' or traditional methods of science teaching, learning tables or the alphabet to *exercise* the memory, deductive or inductive methods of teaching, the direct method of teaching in modern languages, and teaching social sciences to increase social awareness (transfer of training)?

As with so many complex issues in psychology, no one theory has provided all the answers to the kinds of questions of concern to teachers. Some theorists, as we shall see, have cornered the market in particular aspects of learning (Skinner and programmed learning, for example), but no single theory has yet been formulated which satisfactorily accounts for all the facts. Nevertheless, it is worthwhile looking at the main tenets of some theories because we must have a background against which to examine our own suppositions about learning in the light of existing experimental evidence, and to illuminate the origins and development of commonly held views about learning amongst professionals. For an excellent summary of the major theories, see Hill 2002.

# The task of learning theorists for teachers

Let us attempt to summarize the major problems of importance to teachers which any comprehensive theory of learning should be capable of answering (Hilgard and Bower 1981):

- How can we determine the limits, and influence the capacity, of learning in the individual? In this respect, what is the influence of inheritance, age, intelligence, maturational level, environmental opportunities and contexts, aptitudes, personality, motivation or practice? (See the relevant chapters.)
- What is the influence of experience, that is, the effect of early learning on later learning? How are cognitive strategies and habits assimilated and how are they affected by future experience? (This chapter.)
- There should be a place for an explanation of the complexities of symbolic learning (e.g. letters, numbers, musical notes) in humans. (See Chapter 5.)
- What is the connection between animal and human learning, and is a compromise between them possible without investing animals with human qualities, or vice versa (*anthropomorphism*)? As we shall see, Skinner has managed to build a most elaborate theory of human learning using the findings from research on animals such as rats and pigeons. (This chapter.)

- Because learning takes place as part and parcel of body mechanisms, any theory should be capable of incorporating physiological and ethological findings. (See Chapter 2.)
- Practice has a central function in learning, but we still need to know far more about the conditions which favour or adversely affect achievements after practice. Is there a threshold of practice beyond which one cannot improve? Under what circumstances is massed or distributed practice most effective (see Chapter 7.)?
- What is the place of drives, incentives, rewards and punishments in learning programmes (see Chapter 8.)?
- Is it possible to transfer learned skills from one activity to another (see 'Transfer of training' – Chapter 7)? In other words, to what extent can our learning in specific situations be generalized to similar, but not identical, situations?
- What happens when we retain or forget information (see Chapter 7.)? What part does attention or perception play in the processes of remembering and forgetting (see Chapters 3 and 7.)?
- What is the importance of 'understanding' in attempting to learn? Some things we seem able to do without any apparent 'understanding', such as physical movements of muscles in writing, and eye movements in reading, whilst to understand poetry or differential calculus requires long, sometimes arduous, mental effort involving the accumulation of simpler concepts. (This chapter.)

Most of the salient questions posed in the above list are elaborated in other chapters. In this chapter we shall deal with the rudimentary propositions of the major theories of learning. *What* happens is there for all to see; the divergence between the theories occurs in the interpretation of the causal processes which give rise to that behaviour, that is, *why* it happens. Of the many theories of learning extant, we have chosen the following because between them they form the foundation stones on which several views of teaching and learning in schools have been built. But we must hasten to add that the contribution of learning theories up to now has been only marginal to the successful formulation of educational programmes, and the questions posed above have not been satisfactorily answered by any one theory.

# Two approaches to learning

The present stances in the study of learning have their origins in the different opinions held by psychologists about how human behaviour should be studied. There are several such stances (Medcof and Roth 1991), of which two have been particularly influential. These are referred to as *behaviourist* (or *connectionist*) and *cognitivist*.

These broad traditions arise from differences in philosophical views about the way humans function and how these functions can be observed to derive generalizations about behaviour. Behaviourists have something in common with Hobbes, a seventeenth-century philosopher, who assumed that a human being could only be a material system. Therefore the task of psychology would be to discover the laws which govern the relationships between *externally* observable input and output without bothering about such inventions as 'the mind', 'purpose', 'free will', 'ability' and so on. The behaviourist similarly is chiefly concerned with stimulus (S) and response (R) connections (hence the alternative term 'connectionist'). These S–R links are of importance only when they can be manipulated and the results observed. The individual develops certain responses to given stimuli, and inferences are made by direct observation of manipulations of these in human and animal behaviour.

Most other approaches in psychology are based on the belief that inner functions of humans are also worthy of study. The brain, perception, memory, personality, motivation are but a few 'internal' structures and processes which affect human behaviour. The philosopher Kant, for example, regarded humans as free agents faced with choices and having the capacity to formulate plans of action. Therefore, to *understand* human behaviour it is necessary to know how people acquire conceptions and how these influence subsequent behaviour. The formula of S–R would need to include the organism (O) to give S–O–R, thus recognizing the importance of the organism as an interpreter of stimuli and as a wilful responder. To explore the 'O' in the above simple formula it is necessary to use *introspection* – that is, an attempt to get a person to describe internal events from which an observer would try to discover the processes of S–O–R. Something was said in Chapter 1 about introspective methods. The Cognitive School has contributed to our knowledge of learning, and subsequent sections will deal with this work.

# The behaviourists (or connectionists)

## J. B. Watson (1878–1958)

Before the nineteenth century, humans had never really been the subjects of scientific experiment. The establishment by Wundt of a psychological laboratory in Germany in 1879 saw the beginning of a more objective attack on the study of animal and human behaviour, and the impetus thus given soon created a firmer foundation for psychology. At the turn of the last century, Pavlov in Russia and Watson and Thorndike in the USA directed their attention to detailed study of *how* animals and humans *behaved* in given laboratory circumstances rather than relying on introspective beliefs or feelings. The earliest and most ardent of behaviourists was Watson (1931; Medcof and Roth 1991, Hill 2002). His fundamental conclusion from many experimental observations of animal and childhood learning was that stimulus–response (S–R) connections are more likely to be established the more *frequently* or *recently* an S–R bond occurs. A child solving a number problem might have to make many unsuccessful trials before arriving at the correct solution. Of the many responses he or she can possibly make in an effort to solve the problem, the unsuccessful ones will tend not to be repeated; thus there will be an increase in both the frequency and recency of successful responses until a correct S–R pattern appears. Trying alternative paths in the solution of problems of any kind is known as *trial-and-error* learning.

## E. L. Thorndike (1874–1949)

Thorndike (Hill 2002), working around the same time, similarly held that we *stamp in* effective S–R connections and *stamp out* those responses which are useless. Using cats, dogs and chickens, he devised experiments in which an animal was placed in a cage from which it could escape to reach food. The food was visible but not accessible from the cage, and the hungry animals soon began to seek the lure. The door of the cage could only be opened by pulling a cord hanging within reach outside the cage. In an endeavour to reach the food the animal clawed, banged and prowled around the cage, occasionally touching the release cord. In this 'trial and error' fashion some animals hit on the solution to their problem. Successive attempts by the same successful animals took shorter periods of time by cutting out the useless activities. From this work Thorndike derived several 'laws' of learning which he believed applied equally well to man as to animals.

Whereas for Watson the important thing was the simultaneous presence of stimulus and response (*contiguity* theory), Thorndike gave more weight to the end effects of the response. Satisfying and gratifying outcomes from a response are more likely to lead to that response reappearing; in other words, the S–R connection is *reinforced* whenever satisfying results are apparent. The statement that satisfaction serves to strengthen or reinforce S–R bonds is known as Thorndike's *Law of Effect*. Note also in this connection that dissatisfaction does not necessarily extinguish responses: rather, it causes the respondent to look for alternatives and seek out satisfactory solutions by trial and error. Of course, Thorndike accepted Watson's position, and it appears in the *Law of Exercise*, which states that bonds are strengthened simply by the same stimulus and response repeatedly occurring together, while a reduction in a response weakens the S–R bond to the point where it finally becomes redundant. The relevant point here is that exercise or practice alone is not enough. Knowledge of results must follow for reinforcement to take place, so the Law of Exercise is a corollary or consequence of the Law of Effect.

The particular contribution of Thorndike to learning theory and to teaching is his insistence on the use of scientific measurement as a means of examining learning skills among children and his belief in motivation through the agency of rewards rather than punishment as an efficient means of establishing good learning habits. However, punishment may have an indirect influence for the better by redirecting the attention of pupils from their existing ineffective S–R bonds to more suitable ones, and this is where the teacher can assist by providing appropriate alternative S–R routes. While the laws are somewhat rudimentary and limited in their usefulness to teachers, nevertheless they contain the germs of reinforcement theory prevalent in the work of later connectionists such as Skinner and Hull.

## I. P. Pavlov (1849–1936)

Though his major findings are of limited pragmatic value in the classroom, it would be difficult to put the present behaviourist position into perspective without reference to the physiological work of Ivan Pavlov (Smith *et al.* 2003). Like Thorndike and Watson, he viewed behaviour as responses initiated by stimuli – a reactivist. But, unlike them, his interests were strictly to do with physiological reflex actions, in particular the salivation reflex in dogs. Quite by accident he discovered (circa 1880) that dogs would salivate when some other previously neutral stimulus, besides food, was present, provided that on some previous occasions the stimulus had appeared at or just before the presentation of food. From this finding he set about intentionally teaching dogs to associate salivation with neutral stimuli, a process known as *classical conditioning*. In one such experiment, a hungry dog was placed in a harness in a soundproof room and a tuning fork was sounded. Very soon after, meat powder was presented, causing the dog to salivate. Observe that learning has already taken place, because the reflex action of salivation normally occurs initially in response to food in the mouth and not from the sight of food. However, the dog soon learns to anticipate food in its mouth and experiences anticipatory salivation from the signs (sight, smell) of the food. Pairings of the tuning fork and the presentation of meat powder ultimately led to the dog salivating at the sound of the tuning fork in the absence of the meat powder. The time lapse between the tuning fork and meat powder stimuli is critical, because the greater the time gap between the stimuli the less likely it is that the dog will connect the two events. The salivation is an *unconditioned response* (UR) innately governed and available when food, in this case meat powder, is presented as an *unconditioned stimulus* (US). The tuning fork acts as a *conditioned stimulus* (CS) giving rise to salivation as a *conditioned response* (CR). The relationship is sometimes shown diagrammatically as:

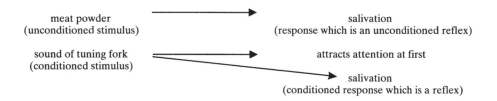

meat powder (unconditioned stimulus) → salivation (response which is an unconditioned reflex)

sound of tuning fork (conditioned stimulus) ⟹ attracts attention at first → salivation (conditioned response which is a reflex)

Whenever the tuning fork is sounded along with food, *reinforcement* takes place. But several abortive soundings of the tuning fork will lead to a lessening of the quantity of saliva and ultimately *extinction* of the conditioned S–R link.

A human condition which displays classical conditioning is a child's visit to the doctor for an injection (or to the dentist). The unconditioned situation is:

pain (US) → 'activation syndrome' (heart increases in beat along with other autonomic reactions, UR)

If the child experiences pain when doctors inject him or her, the waiting room may act as a conditioned stimulus for the activation of autonomic reactions. Where the child continues to experience pain on each visit, the conditioning is reinforced, otherwise the absence of pain will bring extinction of the fear.

doctor's surgery ⟶ general interest
(CS) ⟶ activation syndrome

Classical conditioning is rooted in the reactions of involuntary systems in the body such as the organs, emotional reactions controlled by the autonomic nervous system (see Chapter 2), and reflex actions such as salivation, eye blinking, knee-jerks and pupillary constriction in response to light intensity changes. Learning takes place by acquiring responses through conditioned ties to these reflexes. Fear has been a popular experimental condition. In the 1920s, Watson made successful attempts to condition or extinguish children's responses to fear-provoking events. By pairing pleasant and feared objects with each other or with a neutral stimulus, Watson was able to condition children. 'Little Albert' (Watson 1931) was conditioned to fear a white rat. Whenever the eleven-month-old Albert reached out to touch the rat a loud bang was created behind the child. In time, the sight of the white rat petrified Albert.

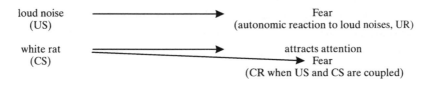

loud noise ⟶ Fear
(US) (autonomic reaction to loud noises, UR)

white rat ⟶ attracts attention
(CS) ⟶ Fear
(CR when US and CS are coupled)

Extinction of a fear or phobia can sometimes be accomplished by pairing the conditioned stimulus with a pleasurable stimulus. Albert's white rat might have been gradually introduced and brought progressively nearer at meal times. Bribes to persuade children who have built up a conditioned fear of school to go to school can be of a similar nature. The special variety of extinction is called *reciprocal inhibition*. Sometimes, programmes of therapy are employed to gradually desensitize the person having debilitating fears or anxieties. The process is known as *systematic desensitization*. This is done by getting the person into a deep state of relaxation then presenting, with increasing intensity, the cause of anxiety. This is done either verbally (*cognitive behaviour therapy*) or by using the real cause of anxiety. When the feared stimulus is presented at its full intensity, it is known as *flooding*.

In Chapter 2 we discussed the relationship between the sympathetic and parasympathetic parts of the autonomic system and it is believed that reciprocal inhibition results from the parasympathetic system (responsible for putting a brake on the energy-producing mechanisms of the body) overriding the sympathetic system (activates and excites body mechanisms which produce the symptoms of fear) and encouraging deconditioning. Sometimes a supposed extinguished conditioned response suddenly reappears after a lapse of time in which the US has not been in evidence. This is called *spontaneous recovery*.

How exact must the conditioning stimulus be each time it is presented? In fact some stimuli can have pretty wide limits within which a response is instigated and we call this *stimulus generalization*. The frequency of the tuning fork in the experiment described above does not have to be exactly the same each time; there is usually a range of effective frequencies. The animals used in the reciprocal inhibition experiments with children can vary in size and shape and still produce the desired effect. Children who fear starting school are not particular about which school. In Chapter 4 we noted that the definition of a particular concept is not easy because our generalizations require knowledge of the limits within which a classification is possible. Poodles and Irish wolf-hounds can elicit the same response 'dog' even though there are staggering differences in size, shape, colour and habits. We also met with generalization at the beginning of Chapter 3 in the discussion of encoding. In some way our reception system seems to have a built-in tolerance to divergence in percepts presented either through the various sense modalities or, as mentioned above, in the written and spoken word. There are, of course, limits to stimulus generalization and it becomes necessary to draw distinctions between similar, but non-identical, stimuli, especially when the discrimination of response is a matter of adaptive survival. This is known as *stimulus discrimination*. For a rat running a maze in order to obtain food or a child classifying the attributes of the concept of colour (refer back to Chapter 4), there has to be differentiation of superficially similar stimuli before satisfactory responses materialize.

Extinction, spontaneous recovery, stimulus discrimination and generalization emphasize the complexity of S–R connections. However, classical conditioning is limited to reflex mechanisms and in turn emotional reactions. Unfortunately the effect of, say, reward and punishment is complicated by learning processes of a higher order than a reflex. Although fear of failure and pleasure from praise might be regarded as potent unconditioned responses, they are probably the result of much more complex acquired reactions than can be explained by Pavlovian conditioning.

## C. L. Hull (1884–1952)

Clark Hull (Hill 2002) was another influential American theorist who created a complex hypothetical model of learning. He is mentioned briefly here because of his historical position in the growth of the behaviourist school. As yet, it has found little or no outlet in the day-to-day work of the teacher. But, like Freud, he has provided a theoretical conceptual framework the terms of which, for want of better, have become an inescapable part of psychology.

Like other early behaviourists (but see Skinner) Hull believed that S–R bonds depended on elicited responses and not on emitted responses to stimuli. But his major theme involved the inner states in people, for he set great store by the *intervening variables* occurring in the formation of S–R bonds in an effort to predict responses from given stimuli.

> ### Further reading
>
> In addition to the physiological internal needs which create *drives* (hunger, thirst) and provide activation for the satisfaction of these body needs, Hull postulates other intervening variables. We mentioned *excitatory potential* and *reactive inhibition* in the text. There is also *incentive* which is the strength of the reward on previous, recent occasions which is likely to intensify goal-seeking activity. *Habit strength*, the strength of the bond created between S and R, is also said to be involved and influenced by the frequency of reward.

Symbolically, his view is expressed as S–O–R to signify the importance of the intervening happenings in the organism O. We shall meet with some of these terms in his theory of *primary and secondary drives* in Chapter 8, and intervening variables of *excitatory potential* (the tendency to make a response to a stimulus) and *reactive inhibition* (the tendency not to repeat a response which has just been made) in Chapter 12. The only other term we need to mention is his theory of *need reduction*. When there is a deprivation such as food or water, or a secondary need derived from primary needs (Chapter 8), responses which lead to a reduction of the need are likely to produce an S–O–R connection. The need reduction provides the reinforcement for the connection. Learning, then, takes place as part and parcel of the process during which animal or human needs are being satisfied, which, even if we argue with the details, is not an unreasonable generalization.

## B. F. Skinner (1904–90)

Amongst recent behaviourists, the American psychologist B. F. Skinner is undoubtedly the best known. His contributions to programmed learning and behaviour therapy have been widely publicized. His main interest, like Pavlov's, was conditioning, but his special brand is termed *operant conditioning*. Initial laboratory experiments involved hungry rats placed in 'Skinner boxes', consisting of levers which, when pressed, would cause the release of food pellets. Exploratory activity of the rat in a confined space would usually end up in a chance contact with a lever. After two or three accidental lever contacts the rat would display a dramatic change in behaviour by intentionally pressing the lever, often very quickly, to obtain food. We have here another example of trial and error learning. More important is the rat's instrumental or 'operant' behaviour by which it produces its own reward or *reinforcement* by converting a productive accident into an intentional behaviour pattern. When the rat obtains a pellet of food every time it presses the bar Skinner referred to it as *continuous reinforcement*. When the rat is sometimes rewarded and sometimes not it is known as *intermittent reinforcement*. In the early stages of conditioning continuous reinforcement is needed to establish the S–R link. However, perseverance wanes when hunger is satisfied and intermittent reinforcement can then be introduced with gradually increasing intervals between each reward. In TV advertising of popular goods (soap powders, etc.), in gambling where the winnings are intermittent and in the judicious use of praise in the classroom we have examples of the powerful effects of intermittent reinforcement.

A second important series of experiments, using pigeons, will help to elucidate some of the basic principles of learning derived by Skinner. A hungry pigeon was to be taught to walk in a figure of eight. At first sight this is a difficult task because the bird must walk first in one direction and then the opposite direction in order to complete the figure. A pellet of food was given immediately the bird began to move in a clockwise direction.

Once the movement was initiated, intermittent reinforcement was used to reward extensive clockwise movements until the bird walked or ran in a clockwise circle. By carefully planning the reinforcement it was possible to introduce rewards for anticlockwise movements because on those occasions when the pigeon was not given a food pellet for a clockwise motion it would tend to explore other kinds of movement, including anticlockwise motion. Apparently it takes a surprisingly short period of time to encourage the pigeon to walk in a figure of eight, provided the pellet rewards are carefully planned; this planning of rewards by the experimenter is known as a *schedule of reinforcement*.

A modern-day equivalent is in the training of dogs and husbands. In 2005 there was a tongue-in-cheek TV programme, designed by a dog trainer, entitled *Bringing your Husband to Heel* which gave advice on how to condition these wayward creatures!

From many similar animal and human experiments, Skinner drew several valuable conclusions about learning:

- Each step in the learning process should be short and should grow out of previously learned behaviour.
- In the early stages, learning should be regularly rewarded and at all stages carefully controlled by a schedule of continuous and/or intermittent reinforcement.
- Reward should follow quickly when the correct response appears. This is referred to as *feedback* and is based on the principle that motivation is enhanced when we are informed of our progress. This is allied to the first point made above, since to ensure a high success rate the steps in the learning process must be sufficiently small and within the capacities of the learner.
- The learner should be given an opportunity to discover stimulus discriminations for the most likely path to success. In the pigeon experiment the bird has to perceive the difference between clockwise and anticlockwise motion.

Two distinctions exist between classical and operant conditioning, hinging upon the nature of the response and the source of reinforcement. In Pavlovian conditioning the response is controlled by the experimenter because he or she determines what the stimulus is and when to present it. Thus the response is *elicited* using existing reflex action either inborn or acquired. In a sense the individual's role is passive, since the response must await a particular stimulus to appear – *respondent behaviour*. On the other hand, in Skinnerian conditioning, we must wait for the desired response to appear before learning can proceed. Only when this response is *emitted* can reinforcement occur. Therefore the individual must act or operate on the environment in order to be rewarded – *operant behaviour*. The second difference is in the action of the reinforcement. In classical conditioning the unconditioned stimulus is correlated with reinforcement, so that the meat powder in Pavlov's work acts as an encourager for the repetition of behaviour. In operant conditioning the response acts as the source of reinforcement: when a reward follows a response (lever pressing in rats, or pigeon movements), the response is more likely to be repeated.

We can identify at least two kinds of reinforcement. *Differential reinforcement* occurs when only responses satisfying some specific criterion are recognized for reward. A certain pressure might have to be applied to a bar lever in the Skinner box before a food pellet is expelled. Children might have to reach a given mark in school subjects before a teacher gives praise (see *mastery learning* in Chapter 14, p. 454). Alternatively, we can condition by reinforcing each bit of behaviour which approximates to that required, a technique known as learning by *successive approximation*. The method used for teaching the pigeon to walk in a figure of eight demonstrates this technique.

Operant conditioning is far more prevalent in both animal and human learning than Pavlovian conditioning, and examples applicable in education will be discussed later in this chapter and Chapter 14. One commonplace example is animal training in circuses. Note that Skinner was not unduly concerned about knowing what happens 'inside' an organism when learning proceeds. Such intermediate or intervening variables involved in physiological or cognitive processes which might affect the nature and direction of learning are not subject to direct observation and do not figure in Skinner's psychology. For him, observable and modifiable stimuli and responses for the control and delineation of behaviour were the key variables. The stimulus may be an accident, but the overt response constitutes the means by which the organism *operates* on its *environment*. We see now the reason for regarding Skinner as a 'structuralist' or 'activist' rather than a 'reactivist' psychologist.

# The cognitive approach

One of the cardinal problems raised by the behaviourist approach is whether it is possible to evaluate total human or animal response by teasing out, observing and analysing bits and pieces of the behaviour. To what extent is it necessary to account for an organism's perception of a situation as a basis for responding to stimulation? Many have argued that human behaviour is too complex and exhibits such original pathways to the solution of problems that a simple S–R theory could not possibly explain all of it.

Wertheimer (1961), the earliest worker to attempt a cognitive interpretation, thought that breaking down behaviour into constituent parts obscured or possibly obliterated the full meaning of that behaviour. Along with Köhler and Koffka, he founded the school known as *gestalt psychology* which concentrates on a study of perception for a better understanding of learning. Some of the basic principles of this school have already been dealt with in the section on perception in Chapter 3.

In Chapters 3 and 4 we met with theories using information-processing models which base their views clearly on the belief that activities do occur in an organism between stimulus and response and that these activities are crucial to an understanding of behaviour. Words such as 'understanding', 'thinking', 'memory', 'cognitive structures' and 'cognitive processes' are characteristic of cognitive theorists. The possibility of stored information in the memory which can be retrieved and used – not just in an identical way to the initial experience, but originally – is of interest to the cognitivist.

One contribution of gestalt psychologists to learning is their study of *insight*, a term now popularly used to mean 'intuitive'. But to gestalt psychologists insightful learning is more than this. It occurs as a sudden solution to a problem in a way which can readily be repeated during a similar event in the future and which has some transfer to new situations. Köhler's first demonstrations of insightful learning took place when he was a World War 1 internee on the Canary Islands. Using chimpanzees as subjects he arranged a number of problems in which bananas were placed out of arm's reach outside the cages. The chimpanzees were provided with short sticks which, whilst not long enough to reach the bananas singly, could be made to do so when slotted together. Sometimes bananas were hung from the roof of the cage and were obtainable by piling up boxes that were strewn about the cage. In both instances *some* animals, after unproductive exploratory activity, suddenly got the 'idea' of how to solve the problem.

This sudden, immediate, repeatable and transposable behaviour he called *insight*. Trial and error might be evident in the early stages of animal exploration, but once the animal had seen the task as a whole it seemed able to restructure or reorganize the perceptual field in ways which afforded solutions to the problem.

Apart from the differences in interpretation of learning which exist between connectionist and cognitive theorists referred to above, there is a very fundamental distinction in the experimental organization. As Köhler points out, if you cage a starved rat in a puzzle box with levers, or press buttons of which it has no knowledge whatever, it is clear you will evoke trial-and-error learning. In other words, the structuring of the problem situation dictates the nature of the problem-solving. The puzzle box is so difficult for a rat that it can do little else but learn by trial and error. This is an important point in gestalt psychology, and one which is significant for teachers. In effect, Köhler is telling us that insight, problem-solving and trial-and-error learning all depend upon the context in which a problem is being solved. The stimulus for the problem-solver is not just the problem, but also its context. Illusions afford a good example of the subjectivity of perception. Also, a child presented with a problem for which it is possible to form a mental image may find a solution more readily, provided mental manipulation can be achieved. The emphasis in gestalt psychology, then, is on adaptability in the use of existing knowledge to form new insights rather than the mechanical repetition of stimulus–response bonds.

Brewer (1972) makes the further point that human conditioning may also be a measure of how much the individual being conditioned understands what is required and to what extent that individual is prepared to co-operate. In other words, conditioning makes too little of a person as a rational creature trying to discover what the experimenter is up to and, possibly, attempting to comply with (or sabotage) the proceedings of the experiment. This point of Brewer's highlights one difference between some of the classical reflexological research (eye blinking, knee jerking) in which the individual knows nothing, and the operant conditioning over which the *reasoning* individual has some control.

In this book we refer several times to the work of Piaget, in particular his theories of cognitive development (Chapter 4) and the place of language in the intellectual growth of children (Chapter 5). While his observations may not be recognized as a theory of learning, nevertheless he has quite a lot to say about the steps which lead to the acquisition of knowledge. The primary, secondary and tertiary circular reactions built onto the reflex activity of babies, the role of imitation, the internalization of actions to become thought, and the place of language as a mediator in intellectual growth and learning skills are but a few of his most important suggestions which are pointers to learning processes.

One further name of note is that of Tolman. His major work (1976, first published 1932) attempts to marry the objectivity of behaviourism to a cognition theory. For him, behaviour is purposive, that is, most of our behaviour is a striving towards a particular goal. Organisms learn to recognize *cues* or *signs* and the relationship of these cues to the satisfaction of specific goals. Rats solving a maze to reach food, or Köhler's chimpanzees, are not just connecting or associating particular responses with particular stimuli: they are assimilating signs which will lead most effectively to solving a problem (reaching a goal, in Tolman's words). These assimilated signs are known as *cognitive maps* of meanings (not movements) by which we acquire whole patterns of behaviour (*sign-gestalts*). In simple language, organisms learn from experience that purposeful behaviour based on cues and previously learned plans of action will lead to the attainment of goals. The creature acquires expectations of its environment (intervening variables again, as in Hull's case) from present and previous perceptions, and learning consists essentially of modifying these expectations in the light of new experience.

Later in this chapter, and in Chapter 14, we shall deal with the application to learning and teaching of the behaviourist and cognitivist schools.

# Learning theories and teaching children

We have made the point that no one learning theory provides us with all the answers. Furthermore, all the theories put together do not provide us with all the answers. The only course we can justifiably take is a pragmatic one, choosing from among the experimental findings the points of clear relevance to our task. In most cases, psychologists are not really arguing about the findings so much as the interpretations of those findings.

## Motivation

It would be safe to say that all theorists in the field of learning either explicitly or by implication argue that a motivated creature is more likely to learn than one which is not. The matter is so important that we devote a whole chapter to it (Chapter 8). Pavlov had to starve his dogs and Skinner his rats and pigeons to ensure they would learn. Children need to satisfy their desire to explore and manipulate their surroundings; they need the approval of others (affiliation) and to achieve; they pursue success and eschew failure. Incentives in the form of rewards (words of praise, encouragement, recognition), immediate knowledge of satisfying results (not always possible of course), co-operation and self-competition or competition with others are potent sources of motivation for learning. As we shall see elsewhere (Chapter 8), motivation, particularly achievement- and fear-generated, must not be too intense or performance suffers as a result of distracting emotional conditions such as pain, fear or anxiety. Controlled reward also appears to be a more profitable motivator than failure or punishment. Hilgard and Bower (1981) conclude from their analysis of learning theories that tolerance of failure is best realized after a history of success because it helps to compensate for the failure.

Optimum interest can be gained where information is unambiguous and the curriculum designed to engage children in pursuits that have everyday relevance. Misgivings about the raising of the school-leaving age are partly caused by our inability to motivate young people who would rather be earning than learning. 'Everyday relevance' for them is highly instrumental in terms of work when they leave school, or preparation for adulthood and leisure. Whatever designs we might have about higher-order educational objectives – enhancing intellectual skills, encouraging social awareness, preserving our habitat, using leisure time, etc. – they must be superimposed on the down-to-earth, 'bread-and-butter' outlook of our young adults.

## Habits and learning sets

A term in common usage is *habit*. Thyne (1963) defines a habit as 'an instance of learning in which a relatively simple response is made, automatically and fairly frequently, to a relatively simple kind of situation'. We talk about forming bad or good habits in many everyday activities in both social and educational contexts. We behave, by and large, in characteristic ways because we have discovered through experience that some responses are (in the short or long term) more effective than others. Therefore, we are *conditioned* to respond in these particular ways. Habits are automatic response patterns elicited by particular stimuli and are generally acquired by repeating a sequence of activities (the Law of Exercise, p. 164) until the sequence is spontaneous. Many of our daily practical routines such as dressing and eating are carried out in a regular pattern without any apparent conscious effort. Parents and teachers inevitably are concerned with encouraging children in the formation of habits – habits relating to common courtesies, habits of cleanliness and survival, habits of number and letter recognition and so on. As Thorndike has shown, the more frequently a pattern of activity is completed successfully, the more likely it is to be repeated. Repetition to the point of overlearning, that is, rehearsing a task beyond the point of successful accomplishment, as in the case of concert pianists who continue to practise familiar pieces or actors who continue to recall their lines long after they know them, not only helps to substantiate the material, but enables the performer to concentrate on the refinements of presentation.

Apart from habits of doing things, we also develop habits of thinking and characteristic ways of tackling problems (see convergent and divergent thinking, Chapter 10). Studies with human and animal subjects have revealed that an ability to learn how to solve problems of a given kind can be developed with sufficient practice on tasks of a similar nature. This ability is known as *learning set* or *learning to learn*. There is another, more limited sense in which we use the concept of transfer, known as 'transfer of training', which we shall deal with later. But this wider, more general application in the formation of learning sets is the outcome of Harlow's work with monkeys and young children (1949). He found that routines formed in the solution of certain tasks were readily adapted for use in the solution of other, similar tasks. Teaching children sets and matrices in modern mathematics syllabuses is rooted in the notion that, by establishing routines about the fundamental understanding of the nature of number, children will have a better chance of coping with more complex mathematics. Learning how to learn a subject (raised again in Chapter 7), as well as acquiring the rules to be applied to the subject matter, is a crucial classroom activity. Children's whole approach to problem-solving depends on the learning sets they bring to the solution. Their experiences at home and school, their attitudes and values all predetermine how they will characteristically organize their responses. As we saw in Chapter 3, there are also predispositions among learners for factual or conceptual styles of learning (Siegel and Siegel 1965).

## Knowledge of results

Most theorists and practitioners are agreed that favourable feedback about performance has a positive effect on subsequent performance. Skinner called it reinforcement; Thorndike called it the Law of Effect. In human terms, there must be some reassurances about levels of success and to be a really effective reinforcer in educational achievement, knowledge of results must follow quickly upon completion of a task for it to have maximum influence on future performance. School work should be dealt with and commented on as soon as possible after children have completed work; children's progress should be up to date and fed back to them while the work is still fresh in their minds and still likely to have a reinforcing effect. Skinner claimed that the steps taken in a learning programme should be sufficiently small to ensure high success rates among children (nothing succeeds like success). Knowledge of poor results for some children could be devastating, and this is why Skinner suggested that we should try to strike at the right level with each child to ensure high success rates. Nevertheless, we should avoid the fallacy of trying to pretend that a child's performance is good when it is not. As we shall see in Chapter 8 in the section on extrinsic motivation, this only leads to low personal standards being set and maintained. By insisting on realistic goals, and thus ensuring some measure of success for each child, we are increasing the likelihood of reinforcement.

## Whole or part learning

A theoretical debate surrounds the subject of whether it is better to learn by small steps (Skinner) or large chunks (gestalt psychologists). For the teacher, there is clearly a time and a place for both approaches. Later (in Chapter 7) we shall see that programmes of learning can be constructed using either technique. With some children, especially the mentally disadvantaged, small steps are useful because with a limited 'channel capacity' there is more chance that the information will be held in mind. Part learning by small steps, however, might be a disadvantage where the material is connected in some way. Poetry, theories and laws of science, for example, really need to be presented in their entirety, otherwise the relationship between the parts is lost. Learning a poem line by line was a popular compulsory pastime for school children not so long ago, and it is surprising how difficult it was to put the whole poem together without a conscious effort to establish connections between the end of one line and the beginning of the next in order to preserve the continuity. Where total context is important, 'whole' learning is an advantage because taking parts of the content out of context may lead to the material being meaningless. When to use whole or part learning is a matter which the teacher must judge from his or her experience of the content.

## Schematic versus rote learning

*Schematic learning* has been defined as using organizations of past actions which become the seed-bed for interpretation and development in future learning. Skemp (1962 and 1986) believed that the importance of schematic learning was underrated. In an intriguing experiment using a set of symbols he had invented to represent attributes capable of being combined to give more complex forms, for example, O = container, $\rightarrow$ = moves, therefore $\underset{\rightarrow}{O}$ = vehicle, he showed that schemata were absolutely essential, even in relatively straightforward learning tasks, because of the meaning they gave to the learning in hand. In any new field the schemata first formulated have a lasting consequence on future learning in that field (see learning sets, above). Therefore the first and most important task for any teacher is to discover and carefully define the elementary schemata required to enable the most productive assimilation. He or she should proceed from a familiar framework to unfamiliar knowledge. Overlapping lesson content and teaching by analogy, that is, using familiar instances to exemplify unfamiliar ones, have much to commend them. A second conclusion of Skemp's was that schematic learning could be more efficient than rote learning, in which one builds systematically on previously acquired knowledge. Rote learning in the absence of understanding precludes the logical acquisition of further meaningful knowledge.

However, this is not to imply that there is no place for *rote learning*. Some of the demands we make of children require rote learning. Any symbolic form new to the child will require rote memorization. For example, the letters of the alphabet, numbers, musical notation and chemical symbols (although there is a logic behind these once you know the chemical names) have to be learned 'by heart'. Basic mathematical or physical equations, causes and outcomes in history, structure and functions in biology, etc. require a combination of straight memorization and logical build-up from previous knowledge. Two obvious examples are provided by the illustrations in the last paragraph and in a child's first attempts at learning a language. In Skemp's experiment with the symbols, the first task in building up coherent and understood schemata was to *learn* the basic symbols. The first stages in language acquisition (see Chapter 5) involve some very straightforward stimulus–response experiences for the child, such as when a parent touches an object and says 'table'. These *tact* responses (see the section 'Language learning and operant conditioning' in Chapter 5, which also discusses echoic and mand response learning) are good examples of operant conditioning. Where the cognitivists part company is in speculating about the next stages of learning. Does a person go through life accumulating and reproducing the conditioned material, or does the person become inventive and original? (See Chomsky's work, as discussed in Chapter 5.) Is the meaning behind a newly devised sentence that has never been heard or spoken by an individual before created from more than the sum of its parts (i.e. the words)? The sentence you have just read and the one being created now are probably unique. How can this creative capacity in the use of a symbol system be explained only in terms of a stimulus–response model? 'Symbol system' is used intentionally here because it could apply to number, music, mime in drama or dance, as well as to written and spoken language.

Recent evidence using the fMRI scanning technique (see Chapter 2) points to rote learning having its own brain bases. Studies of memory show the importance of hearing the sounds of words (phonological codes) in both memorizing and storing verbal information. When rehearsing, we often repeat 'out loud' what we are trying to store. The need for verbal repetition in helping to store may arise from the fact that two locations in the brain are necessary (also see the discussion of Broca's and Wernicke's areas in Chapter 2). Scanning has shown that *rehearsing* involves the left inferior frontal cortex, while *storing* material to be recalled involves the left inferior parietal cortex (Awh *et al.* 1996, Paulesu *et al.* 1993).

## Mental exercise

If we sit and think about a physical activity, practising in our minds the various movements necessary for good performance (e.g. dance, sport, physical exercise), would it have any effect on our actual performance? Research findings (Feltz and Landers 1983) are consistent in showing that performance can be improved. The process is not unlike that described in the section on biofeedback in Chapter 2, p. 19–20.

Preparation for motor exercises, such as working in the gym, a dance sequence, using a musical instrument for a performance, rehearsing movements necessary for sports activities are important uses of this research.

Jeannerod (1994), using brain-scanning techniques, has shown that the same areas of the brain are involved in imagining a movement and actually performing that movement. Mentally practising any routine procedure, such as getting off the mark at the beginning of a race by rehearsing the 'Ready! Steady! Go!' routine in one's mind or going through safety rules in school, are examples.

# Closure

Whatever the preferred method for conducting lessons, the teacher must achieve goals, mainly predetermined, by the end of the lesson. This process of rounding off a lesson is called *closure*. Brown (1975) introduced the term as part of microteaching programmes in the 1970s. A ragged or half-finished ending to a lesson can be unproductive in terms of retention of lesson content, and ends the teacher–pupil contact in a tense rather than a relaxed fashion. These aspects of content completion and personal relationships are sometimes referred to as *cognitive* and *social closure*.

## Cognitive closure

Cognitive closure can be achieved in a variety of ways. Frequently a short written or oral test is used just to remind children of the main points. The teacher may present a summary on the blackboard or on a visual aid. Sometimes the closure is delayed for homework – 'Finish this work off in your free time'. Always give pupils an opportunity to ask any final questions. It should be common practice to hear teachers ask their children at the end of a section or lesson: 'Is there anything you did not follow? Have you any questions?'

The reasons for cognitive closure are that it (a) directs attention to the need for consolidating what has transpired in the section or lesson; (b) gives the section or lesson a coherence so that pupils can identify a relevant 'chunk' of information; (c) offers an opportunity for revision of the main points; (d) enables the teacher to appraise and reinforce work well done.

## Social closure

Social closure, as the term implies, involves the usual pleasantries of parting. Students should not need any advice on the many ways of saying goodbye! The intention is to end the lesson on a pleasant note. There is nothing worse for either teacher or children to part at the end of a lesson on a sour note. Last impressions have a habit of sticking in the mind.

## 'Insightful' learning (Roitblat 1985)

The special contribution of gestalt psychology to education is in emphasizing that we should structure our learning. Learning must involve organization of the material. The Law of Prägnanz (Chapter 3), which states that we try to impose the best possible pattern on a new perceptual experience, should be a constant source of consolation to teachers. The insightful 'penny-dropping' experience is quite common in perceptual events and has a remarkable effect in discovering meaning. An experience common to the author illustrating the sudden appearance of a solution to a perceptual problem may be familiar to other readers. The 'instant artist' in programmes such as *Vision On* (BBC TV) had an uncanny knack of being able to reach an advanced stage in a painting before it suddenly dawned on the viewer what the painting was about. When this happens, the lines, blotches and smudges miraculously become railway lines, signal boxes, signals, trains, platforms, etc. The transformation from confusion to almost complete recognition is quite startling. Structure has given meaning to parts previously incomprehensible. Those interested in the experimental work surrounding insightful learning in children should read Wertheimer's book *Productive Thinking* (1961).

## Computer-based education (Merrill *et al.* 1996)

One of the most significant academic applications of behaviour modification is computer-assisted learning and teaching.

The growth of information and communication technology (ICT) in schools has been remarkable. Such has been the advance, despite the costs, that it would be hard to find a school without some ICT facilities for administration and instructional use. Indeed, it would be hard to imagine a future without a substantial and ever-growing impact of ICT both as a subject and as a facility in the education process. The hope is to increase the efficiency of curriculum management and delivery as well as improving the quality of learning.

### Linear programs

The history of the subject stretches back to the early part of the last century when Pressey in the 1920s produced the first recognizable teaching machine. It tested previously learnt material by presenting multiple-choice answers to each question and counting the number correct. It was in the early 1950s that Skinner (1953) began to apply his principles of conditioning to produce the first *linear* teaching programs. A linear program presents information to which the pupil responds. The answer is checked by the system, marked correct or incorrect and if the latter then the respondent is given the original question to have another go. The basic requirements of a linear program are:

- Small pieces of subject matter presented in a logical sequence at such a pace pretty well guaranteeing success on the part of the pupil

- Active responses on the part of the learner – this, called 'constructed response', usually entails writing a word or phrase in answer to a question
- Immediate knowledge of the accuracy of the response, which is usually correct if the first point above is followed
- The pupils can work at their own pace; often, in formal settings, bright children can be bored and dull children left behind.

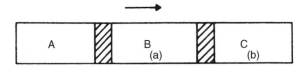

**Figure 6.1** Diagrammatic linear program (Pressey 1926).

The linear program, therefore, consists of a series of frames, each containing a small item of information to which the pupil must respond. Frames also contain the answer to the problem set on the preceding frame. There will be overlap of information from one frame to the next and revision from time to time. Diagrammatically the system can be represented as in Figure 6.1, where capital letters represent information frames and small letters the answers. Extracts from linear and branching programs are to be found in Becker (1963). A linear system might look like this:

1. If learning is defined as a change in behaviour, teaching  (Frame)
   is an interaction with the student that effects this _____  (response)
   _____  (end of frame)
             change in behaviour  (answer)
2. Teaching generally entails an _____
   with the student.

   _____

             interaction

(From J. L. Becker, *A Programed Guide to Writing Auto-instructional Programs*, RCA Service Co., NJ, 1963, p. 49.)

## Branching programs

In the 1950s, Crowder developed an alternative system called *branching programs* for the US Air Force. In these programs, a frame contains more information and is followed by questions offering several answers of which only one is correct; that is, multiple-choice responses (see Chapter 16). The alternative answers are chosen either because they are plausible (though inaccurate) or because they represent common errors. A student choosing the right answer will be passed on to the next frame of information. Inaccurate answers

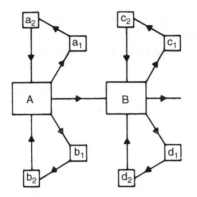

**Figure 6.2** Branching program with three alternative answers, two leading to remedial loops ($a_1$ and $b_1$), the third to the next frame B.

lead to a detour, a remedial loop, intended to show the pupil the source of the error. The pupil is then returned to the original frame to give them another opportunity to respond. This use of remedial loops is called *wash back*. A diagram of the system might be as shown in Figure 6.2.

There are, however, many ways in which branching can take place involving the remedial sub-sequences of differing length and difficulty. The following is an example of a branching system.

---

Branching can be considered a separate idiom of programing or merely a technique. This branching idiom, called intrinsic programing by Dr Norman Crowder, differs radically from linear programing. It is based on the belief that a person can learn effectively even from his or her mistakes provided they are quickly followed up by proper guidance. A high error rate is unhealthy in a linear program but not necessarily unhealthy in an intrinsic program.

In intrinsic programing much emphasis is placed on the student's covert reorganization of material. Thus, it is important to point out why the student is right and why he or she is wrong. To a linear programer, however, branching is not so much a way of teaching as it is a means of providing for individual differences. The linear idiom considers branching as:

(a) an opportunity for guidance

(b) a method of teaching

(c) a means of providing for individual differences.

(From J. L. Becker, *A Programed Guide to Writing Auto-instructional Programs*, RCA Service Co., NJ, 1963, p. 149.)

---

Apart from the obvious differences in the arrangement of frames between linear and branching techniques and the point made in the program above, there are three other distinctive features which rest on different psychological beliefs. Skinner believed that knowledge of results is central, while Crowder gave students knowledge of results incidentally. The important part for Crowder was information – information about incorrect responses as well as new matter. So there is regard for the reinforcement except that it includes information about errors as well as successes. Second, Skinner avoided error as much as possible. He made the steps small, with a gradual increase in difficulty to minimize errors. Crowder used errors as the starting point of information to the student and as an opportunity to revise the subject matter of the frame. The third distinction is the size of the information given. Skinner used small amounts of information, while Crowder programs appear to favour the gestalt view that one must see the whole context to make the parts more meaningful; therefore the frames contain much more information.

One common feature often overlooked is that the very process of answering questions and seeing the correct answers was a learning experience for the students.

## Recent developments

In 1980, R. P. Taylor suggested that we could classify the educational role of computers into three categories:

- tutor (or teacher), with computer used for

  - drill and practice
  - teaching new material
  - simulation
  - problem-solving
  - games

- tool (mechanical assistant)

- tutee (or learner).

Let us look at these in a little more detail.

*Drill and practice* devices present the student with questions and the correct responses. It is really a summative evaluation in which the student is assumed to have covered the topic beforehand. It is hoped that the student will ultimately memorize the correct responses through repeated presentations. The Pressey linear program in Figure 6.1 is an example. Many toys use this principle for learning mathematics, spelling, foreign languages, music and so on.

One ideal in teaching is for a student to have one teacher. Where outcomes can be clearly defined (Gagné *et al.* 1992), computers can, to some extent, fulfil this objective. At its most basic, the computer is programed to present pages of text followed by assessment and remedial branching (Figure 6.2). But students often find this boring. In effect, the screen replaces a book. More interest is generated when the program is written to interact with the student often by asking the student to apply the information provided. For example, after reading frames containing a lesson on pronouns, a sentence might be offered and the student asked to specify the pronoun.

> Which word is the pronoun in the following sentence:
>    Did you put a book on the desk?
>    ?

If the student types in the wrong word, the computer points out the error and usually repeats the rule by which to arrive at the correct solution. Speed through a program can either be controlled by the student or the program. The latter is regarded as better because students have difficulty in determining their own competence. Also, programs are now able to carry out an error analysis for a particular student.

*Simulation* programs attempt to imitate the 'real thing'. Models containing organs of the body, for example lungs by which to teach artificial respiration, are well known. Aircraft and car driving simulators have been in use for many years. In some programs the manager can adjust the difficulty of presentation in line with performance.

In *problem-solving* software, attempts are made to provide students with opportunities to use logic and critical thinking. Clearly the student must have some knowledge in the area before embarking on the program. Given some information, the student has to arrive at a viable solution. Problems in science, engineering and maths lend themselves to this approach.

*Computer games* have become commonplace these days, from fruit machines onwards. They are also exploited for educational purposes in the form of problem-solving adventure games which students find difficult to resist. They have found application in geography, history and drama as well as science, engineering and industry. Their great disadvantage is the trial-and-error nature of many programs which makes them time-consuming.

Note that the examples above show how many subjects in the curriculum have aspects which can be adapted for computer-based learning.

In all the above cases, the student has to do the work – answer questions, solve problems, operate a simulator and so on. The object operated on is a tool, often replacing, the teacher, for a time. As I type this sentence into the word processor (in a sluggish, two-fingered fashion!), I'm using a tool to process my thoughts through the keyboard into computer memory and on to the screen. But computers can also now draw and paint graphics, make charts and manage data (e.g. keeping records of student performance).

As an educational tool, it serves alongside chalkboards, overhead projectors, science apparatus, books and paper. Students do enjoy operating word processors and use them to write their essays, followed by spellchecks (and for sending the odd un-timetabled email!). This is one fairly painless way of learning grammar and spelling. It also enables us to manipulate our words and sentences to achieve better structure and comprehension. Editing spellings, grammatical expression and presentation are important and made easy by the use of word processors.

---

**Note**

Care is needed in spellchecking. Grammatical judgements still have to be made – is it their, they're or there? In spelling, I've seen some amusing judgements by students who need the occasional French word, as in ballet dancing. For the dancers amongst you, 'plié' and 'battement' are common words. For 'plié', if the writer does not include the acute accent over the 'e', spellchecker doesn't like it. The alternative spellings offered are headed by 'piles'. Battement is not recognized and the alternative offering is 'battlement'. Electronically typed dance essays become littered with 'piles' and 'battlements'!

---

The most recent innovations have been in *multi- and hyper-media* and *world-wide networks* (Hartley 1998). The introduction of graphics, sound, animation and videos into educational programs has revolutionized the potential for computers.

*Interactive websites* for students are now numerous and unfortunately many happy hours can be wasted 'surfing the net'. We should remember that easy access does not mean easy to learn! In response to the search instruction 'interactive websites', my computer produced many thousands of sites. Teachers and students wanting to know what their LAs are up to can search for 'interactive websites la'. Some universities now have extramural degree sites. A student learning centre with a large number of sub-sites of relevance at several levels in the educational system is available at http://slc.otago.ac.nz. There is a particularly useful section on study skills.

Treating the computer as a 'learner', so that the intelligence of the student can interact with the intelligence of the computer, is a recent innovation – the student learns through teaching. To do this, the student has to be capable of writing programs. One of the first attempts was instigated by Papert in 1980 with his creation of LOGO (also see Papert 1993 and 1999). By using the program written to solve mathematical problems it is hoped that the student will have a deeper understanding of mathematics. The importance of the multimedia and network systems is that the student can interact more effectively with the programs because they are responsive learning environments (Hartley 1998). Further, a teacher can now be at a central workstation and tap into any student's computer and carry out a discourse with that, and any other, student who happens to be on-line.

## The place of computer-based learning in schools

In a comparatively short period of time, programed learning techniques and teaching machinery have spread from the psychologist's laboratory through the business world into education. Circulars and periodicals with information relating to software and hardware now abound. In all, a formidable campaign has been launched to convince teachers that programmed teaching aids can play a major part in improving our standards of education and serve as a remedial device, while also providing the teacher with a bonus of free time for more creative activity.

Computer-based learning systems have their critics. Some would say there is inadequate software (too hard, too easy, poorly compiled, etc.), they can be boring (some people love handling books or programs are too densely written) and dehumanizing because the interaction is with a machine and not another human being. And there lurks in the minds of some teachers the feeling that a price may have to be paid (literally and metaphorically) for introducing too much inanimate machinery into the classroom. They have asked whether programed learning is the antipathy of creative thinking in not allowing the pupil sufficient opportunity for self-expression. In turn, does this mean that programing is more appropriate for subjects which are more factual in content (science, mathematics) than for subjects which are more evaluative (English literature)? The less practical teachers may not like the thought of having to watch over the machinery. Again, is the time made available for 'creative activity' going to be spent in proliferating time-consuming programs? Motivation of pupils is another source of concern, for it seems that once the novelty of the method has worn off some pupils express a feeling of boredom and monotony, especially those using linear programs. Again, when pupils can work at their own pace there is no guarantee that they are working to the best of their ability. It might be seen as an opportunity for slacking or using the machine for private purposes such as surfing the net. It may be regarded as an inefficient way of using time by endless net searching.

In its favour, computer-assisted education now provides wider access to knowledge, increased exploitation of knowledge because the programs can be professionally designed and made widely available, increased self-learning and learning efficiency, increased knowledge of one's own learning strengths and weaknesses, efficient error analysis, learning can take place at the learner's pace, programs can be tailored to adjust to the speed and competence of the learner, interest can be held by reward systems, failure is not advertised, the programs are versatile (portable so they can be used wherever there is a processor – at home as well as school, can cover a wide age range, etc.) and programs now enable students to interact intelligently with the content. Also, teachers without technical knowledge need not worry too much because many schools now employ IT specialists and technicians.

We have already pointed out some good features such as immediate knowledge of results and pupils working at their own pace and by themselves, thus avoiding the embarrassment and humiliation of displaying ignorance in front of the class. A good program becomes widely available for all to use (but so does a bad one!). In addition, the protagonists of programed instruction claim that programed learning is as effective as teaching by conventional methods, is usually faster and usually achieves better results. But there is still uncertainty as witnessed in the report of the National Council for Educational Technology (NCET 1996).

**Further reading**

*Integrated Learning Systems: A Report of Phase II of the Pilot Evaluation of ILS in the UK*, NCET, Coventry, 1996, is an evaluation sponsored by the National Council for Educational Technology; it looks at the impact of integrated learning systems (ILS) in primary and secondary schools. An ILS is 'a computer-based system that manages the delivery of curriculum materials to pupils so that they are presented with individual programs of work over a period of time'. Some were pupil driven; others were controlled by the teacher. The subjects were English and numeracy. The results were disappointing. For the pupil-driven program (SuccessMaker), those at Key Stages 2 and 3 showed significant gains over a control group. However, Key Stage 1 pupils showed no gains. With teacher-assisted programs (Global), there were no significant gains in either numeracy or reading over control groups (although this may be partly due to some system failures).

In a system which espouses discovery methods and encourages strategies which must meet the needs of individual children, one requires an army of teachers far in excess of the number likely to be appointed. Therefore we must find and exploit additional modes of communication with the children. This is particularly clear with bright pupils who outstrip their classmates and need to be given a chance of progressing faster than the rest, as well as with children in need of remedial help, where a program (provided they can read) would serve to reduce the repetitive work of the teacher. Wisely used, programed instruction should make a valuable contribution in our schools.

## Summary

In this chapter we have looked briefly at some of the major theories of learning and tried to extract from them some common ground and guidelines which might be of service to teachers. The next chapter on learning and memory continues the discussions of this chapter and further applications are to be found in Chapter 14 where we look at effective teaching.

When we face a classroom full of children, what important matters do we need to consider in order to effect behavioural changes in directions which we might prescribe? In other words, how do we encourage children to learn? In other chapters throughout the text we consider the influence of body mechanisms such as the brain and central nervous system, motivation, language, cognitive development, intelligence and personality on the learning process. Here we have tried to provide a framework of theory as a background to these other influences.

The connectionists, or behaviourists, led by Watson and Thorndike, are predominantly concerned with the relationship between stimulus (S) and response (R). Behaviour, according to them, is acquired or changed when the organism, be it a hungry rat or a child in school, builds up connections between S and R. The connections may arise because of the closeness of S and R (contiguity theory favoured by Watson), or by satisfaction which comes from giving a correct R to a given S (reinforcement theory favoured by Thorndike). Of the other behaviourists, the work of Pavlov and Skinner is outstanding. Pavlov's contribution was to show that animals and humans can be taught to respond to a stimulus, chosen by the experimenter, which may not have any apparent resemblance to the response. The well-known salivation response of dogs to the sound of a bell or tuning fork is an illustration. This is known as classical conditioning. In operant conditioning, enunciated by Skinner, a response sometimes arises spontaneously and the subsequent satisfaction will strengthen the bond between stimulus and fortuitous response. If a hungry rat accidentally touches a lever and receives a pellet of food, a connection between lever-pressing and good reception is very soon established. This latter kind of learning has been used extensively in therapy for autism and criminal deviance. Programed learning using linear techniques also owes a lot to Skinnerian theories of operant conditioning.

As connections between S and R can be forged, so can they be extinguished by removing the reward which accompanies the response. Introducing an unpleasant or a neutral response as an alternative to the rewarding response is the most common way.

Of the cognitive approaches, the best known and most useful for the teacher belong to the Gestalt School. Insightful learning occurs with a sudden, immediate, repeatable and transposable flash of inspiration. Tolman, whose stance was midway between gestalt and behaviourism, developed this view by showing that animals quickly learn to recognize cues and the link between these cues, thus giving rise to cognitive maps which assist in the solution of problems. A hungry rat running through a maze for food is thought, by Tolman, to form a pattern of clues, each one leading to the initiation of the next stage in the solution of the maze.

Summarizing some of the main conclusions arising from these theories, we find that they agree on several vital issues. Children can be encouraged to learn using intrinsic (affiliation, exploration, manipulation, achievement) and extrinsic (incentives, praise and reproof) rewards. Immediate relevance and importance have high motivational value. Habits of thinking, that is, personal and unique ways of tackling problems, are laid down in early life as learning sets (Harlow). These apply not only to cognitive habits, but also to social behaviour by imitating models of behaviour. Knowledge of results too – particularly successful results – has reinforcement value.

Whether to learn in moderate chunks or by successive, small portions depends upon the kind of material being learned. But there is support for both whole and part methods of learning. Starting from familiar, basic schemata and using analogy as a means of proceeding to the unfamiliar has much to commend it. There is also something to be said for both guided discovery and verbal reception techniques of teaching, depending on the subject matter, the previous experience of the pupils, their intelligence and the cognitive stage they have reached.

Recent developments in computer-based education with the introduction of programs for remediation, simulation, games, hyper-media, all available on interactive websites, have vastly extended the potential knowledge base for pupils, students and teachers using internet facilities.

A final section on computer-based education in schools includes a critical and detailed discussion of programed instruction using teaching machines. Consideration is given to the design of linear and branching programs and their place in the growing technology of education.

## Tutorial enquiry and discussion

(a) On teaching practice or observation, draw up a list of the factors which you consider would influence the learning habits and skills of pupils. These observations should be pooled and discussed in tutorials. To what extent have learning theories contributed to evaluating these factors?

(b) Look for examples of conditioning in everyday life, in your educational experiences and in classrooms. Teaching language and number, class control, use of rewards, punishments, ignoring bad behaviour and shaping are good starting points. Examine your findings and conclusions in tutorials.

(c) Examine the role of motivation, habit formation, learning sets and knowledge of results from both behaviourist and cognitivist positions.

(d) The group should consider in some detail the place of rote learning in classroom practices.

(e) Search the net for 'interactive websites' in your subject area, primary school subjects or in the degree subjects you are taking. Some LAs are also creating material on websites for teachers.

## References

Awh, E., Jonides, J., Smith, E. E., Schumacher, E. H., Koeppe, R. A. and Katz, S. (1996), 'Dissociation of storage and rehearsal in verbal working memory', *Psychological Science*, 7, 25–31.

Becker, J. L., (1963), *A Programed Guide to Writing Auto-instructional Programs*, RCA Service Co., NJ.

Brewer, W. F. (1972), 'There is no convincing evidence for conditioning in adult human beings'. Paper read to the Conference on Cognition and the Symbolic Processes, Pennsylvania State University.

Brown, George (1975), *Microteaching*. London: Methuen.

Feltz, D. L. and Landers, D. M. (1983), 'The effects of mental practice on motor skill learning and performance: a meta-analysis', *Journal of Sport Psychology*, 5, 27–57.

Gagné, R. M., Briggs, L. J. and Wager, W. W. (1992), *Principles of Instructional Design* (4th edn). Fort Worth, TX: Harcourt Brace Jovanovich.

Harlow, H. F. (1949), 'The formation of learning sets', *Psychological Review*, 56, 51–65.

Hartley, J. R. (1998), 'New technologies and learning', in D. Shorrocks-Taylor (ed.), *Directions in Educational Psychology*. London: Whurr.

Hill, W. F. (2002), *Learning: A Survey of Psychological Interpretations* (7th edn). New York: Longman.

Hilgard, E. R. and Bower, G. H. (1981), *Theories of Learning* (5th edn). Englewood Cliffs, NJ: Prentice-Hall.

Jeannerod, M. (1994), 'The representing brain-neural correlations of motor intention and imagery', *Behavioral and Brain Sciences*, 17, 187–202.

Medcof, J. and Roth, J. (eds) (1991, new print of 1979 edition), *Approaches to Psychology*. Milton Keynes: Open University Press.

Merrill, P. F., Hammons, K., Vincent, B. R., Reynolds, P. L., Christensen, L. and Tolman, M. N. (1996), *Computers in Education* (3rd edn). London: Allyn and Bacon.

National Council for Educational Technology (NCET) (1996), *Integrated Learning Systems: A Report of Phase II of the Pilot Evaluation of ILS in the UK*. Coventry, 1996, a recent evaluation sponsored by the National Council for Educational Technology.

Papert, S. (1999), *Mindstorms: Children, Computers and Powerful Ideas* (3rd edn). New York: Basic Books.

Papert, S. (1993), *The Children's Machine: Rethinking School in the Age of the Computer*. New York: Basic Books.

Paulesu, E., Frith, C. D. and Frackowiak, R. S. (1993), 'The neural correlates of the verbal component of working memory', *Nature*, 362, 342–4.

Roitblat, H. L. (1985), *Introduction to Comparative Cognition*. New York: Freeman.

Siegel, L. and Siegel, L. C. (1965), 'Educational set: a determinant of acquisition', *Journal of Educational Psychology*, 56, 1–12.

Skemp, R. R. (1962), 'The need for schematic learning theory', *British Journal of Educational Psychology*, 32, 133–42.

Skemp, R. R. (1986), *The Psychology of Learning Mathematics* (2nd edn). Harmondsworth: Penguin.

Skinner, B. F. (1953), *Science and Human Behavior*. New York: Macmillan.

Smith, E. E., Nolen-Hoeksema, S., Frederickson, B. L., Loftus, G. R., Bem, D. J. and Maren, S. (2003), *Atkinson and Hilgard's Introduction to Psychology* (14th edn). Belmont, CA: Wadsworth/Thomson.

Taylor, R. P. (ed.) (1980), *The Computer in the School: Tutor, Tool, Tutee*. New York: Teachers College Press.

Thyne, J. M. (1963), *The Psychology of Learning and Techniques of Teaching*. London: University of London Press.

Tolman, E. C. (reprinted 1976, first published 1932), *Purposive Behavior in Animals and Men*. New York: Appleton-Century-Crofts.

Watson, J. B. (1931), *Behaviourism*. London: Routledge and Kegan Paul.

Wertheimer, M. (1961), *Productive Thinking* (enlarged edition edited by M. Wertheimer). London: Tavistock Publications.

## Further reading

Bigge, M. L. and Sharmis, S. S. (1999), *Learning Theories for Teachers* (6th edn). New York: Addison Wesley Longman.

Hill, W.F. (2002), *Learning: A Survey of Psychological Interpretations* (7th edn). New York: Longman.

Hill, W.F. (1991), *Principles of Learning: A Handbook of Applications* (2nd edn). New York: McGraw Hill.

## Useful websites

A student learning centre with a large number of sub-sites of relevance at several levels in the educational system is available at http://slc.otago.ac.nz

# Learning and Memory

## Chapter Outline

# Implications for teachers

- The role of memory in the process of learning is central to most aspects of learning and teaching.
- The concepts of short- and long-term memory have proved useful to teachers.
- Much of our work as teachers hinges on the careful design of material to exploit short- and long-term memory.
- There is much that teachers can do to encourage the retrieval of useful information.
- Advice to pupils should include a consideration of massed and distributed practice, whole and part learning, serial learning and learning how to learn (metacognition).
- Systematic lessons for pupils on how to study, including organization, place and length of study sessions and revision techniques, are helpful to pupils

The blanket term 'memory' has often been used to describe the activities of acquiring, retaining and recalling, and at one time it was thought to be a faculty capable of being exercised, like a muscle, in order to improve the quality and quantity of what we learn. As we saw in the last chapter, rote learning is held by some to be a good method of 'flexing' their memories by sheer dogged effort. The present view is that we are endowed with a capacity for memorization and, although we can improve on our methods of assimilating information, it is possible that we have limits to our capacities. Since we probably never reach the full extent of our capacities, it should certainly be possible to improve the amount we memorize by correspondingly improving the acquisition techniques (see Gagné later). Furthermore, there may be a case for believing that several kinds of memory exist. Standard works are Baddeley 1999 and 1997; there is also a readable introduction in Smith *et al.* 2003.

How is it possible to show that learning has taken place? We have to rely on a person's ability to remember something by either mental or physical means. We refer to a hypothetical possession – the memory – which is regarded almost as a place, located in the head, where recoverable experience and knowledge are housed. When we call upon the memory, the process of recovery is called *remembering*. But this crude picture, rather like a computer bank system, is not sufficient to explain the many complex activities of which humans are capable.

Advances in recent years have been greatly aided by the scanning techniques mentioned in Chapters 2 and 3. These, and reports from brain-damaged patients, have supported the hypothesis that there are *memory stores* involving various parts of the brain. This chapter outlines recent ideas about the two major forms of short- and long-term memory, and the process of using one's memory by encoding, storage and recall. These divisions of labour in the brain have now convincing support from neuroscientists.

# Information-processing model of memory

The information-processing model of memory postulates two aspects. One relates to internal structures (mainly in the brain) and the other to the processes related to these structures (Klatzky 1980). The processes hypothesized in contemporary views about memory are *encoding, storage* and *retrieval.*

$$\text{ENCODING} \quad \rightarrow \quad \text{STORAGE} \quad \rightarrow \quad \text{RETRIEVAL}$$
(in put to memory)      (held in memory)      (taken from memory)

Encoding is the process whereby information is thought to be put into the memory; storage relates to the methods assumed to be involved in the retention of information; retrieval relates to the processes of recovery of stored information from memory.

# Encoding

The stimuli we receive from our surroundings are in the form of sight, sound, tactile (touch), taste and smell sensations. In memory research, the commonest have been sight and sound giving rise to *visual* and *phonological coding.* We certainly have memories for touch, taste and smell. Particular materials have a definite 'feel' to them which we could identify blindfolded. With our favourite foods or scents, we do not have to be told what they are. So we obviously have firmly established memories of these in our brains. But visual and auditory research is easier and researchers have tended to concentrate on them. The most popular theory is that by rehearsing the sounds (phonological code) or looking at the same scene repeatedly (visual code) we in some way implant in the brain tissue a trace (probably chemical) which when triggered will be retrieved. But we must first attend to the stimulus we want to remember. That is why we repeat things so that the trace becomes established. This is particularly effective when we use phonological coding – saying the sounds over and over again. With visual coding (remembering pictures, scenes, maps and so on), concentrating on detail of the image is important (however, see eidetic imagery in Chapter 4, p. 83).

How does the information become established in our brains? We do not know. What we do know from fMRI scanning techniques is the importance of hearing the sounds of words (phonological codes) in both memorizing and storing verbal information. We also know that encoding involves the left frontal lobe (left inferior frontal cortex), rehearing involves both left and right sides of the brain and retrieval the right frontal lobe (Shallice 1988, Shallice *et al.* 1994, Awh *et al.* 1996, Paulesu *et al.* 1993, Fletcher *et al.* 1998a and b). What we do not know is how the brain actually records these different kinds of stimulation. Encoding has also been referred to in Chapter 3.

# Storage

Figure 7.1 gives a rough idea of the storage structures hypothesized.

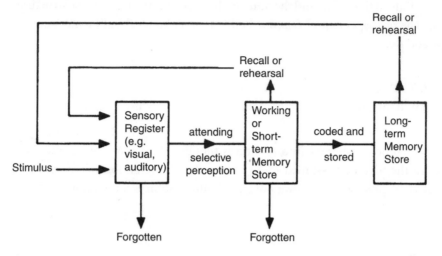

**Figure 7.1** Hypothetical structures of the information-processing model of memory storage.

## Sensory register

When our sense organs pick up a signal from the environment there is a momentary image registered (Sperling (1960) describes research into visual registry and decay). The corresponding process of attention and selective perception ensures that only particular stimulation is conveyed to the next structure, the short-term or working memory. The remaining patterns of stimulation are thought to die away from the register. The period over which the image is registered is very short (a few hundred milliseconds) before complete decay. The after-image in the eye, experienced when we look at a bright light and can detect the image for some time afterwards, is an example, although in this case the image, being so potent, tends to remain longer than a few hundred milliseconds. Three hypothesized registers are *iconic* or *visual memory*, *echoic* or *auditory* (or verbal) *memory* and *semantic memory*.

One piece of physiological evidence for a distinction between short- and long-term memory is the importance of regions in the frontal cortex for short-term and the hippocampus for long-term. Such demarcation is good evidence for the existence of the two functions.

## Short-term or working memory (STM)

Information entering the short-term memory also decays rapidly, but in seconds rather than in milliseconds as with the sensory register. If information is not selectively attended to and encoded so as to pass to the long-term store it decays. The STM is seen as a temporary store of a limited amount of information. Unattended information occurring simultaneously with that to which we are attending can be retrieved with diminishing accuracy as time goes by. Close your eyes and try to recall the objects on your desk. You should have some success in recalling peripheral images of surrounding objects which have impinged on the senses without your consciously having recorded them. Of course, the act of recalling one aspect of an event in STM interferes with the recall of remaining events.

A number of studies have suggested that the working memory has a limited capacity. For example, these are exemplified in studies of 'span of attention' or 'apprehension' where a person is required to recall a stimulus (objects on a table, dots on a sheet of paper) exposed for a brief interval. On average, people can recall between six and ten objects, numbers or letters arranged at random. So a telephone number heard or seen for a short time would be within the competence of most people. Where learning is required, teachers are well advised to note the limitations of immediate memory span.

In an amusing discussion by Miller (1956) it is suggested that our *span of absolute judgement*, which is about seven objects at once, can be improved radically by a process known as *chunking*. This consists of grouping items into chunks numbering about seven. The technique is widely used in learning subjects like Morse, typing and chemistry, where items (dots and dashes, letters or chemical symbols) are brought together and learned as groups.

Recent thinking about the working memory by Baddeley (Gathercole and Baddeley 1993; summarized in Baddeley 1999) suggests that the short-term memory, like the long-term memory, is context- and subject-specific. This whole question of context and subject specificity is crucial to our purpose in teaching. Later in the chapter we shall discuss the question of study and some implications of the influence which this specificity might have on performance.

Because the working memory has so much to deal with at any one time, Baddeley theorized that there was a *central executive* with control over satellite or *slave* subsystems, rather like an executive delegating responsibility. Two of these sub-systems he called the *phonological loop* and *visuo-spatial sketch pad*.

The phonological loop appears in several places in this book. It is our dependence on verbal repetition either sub-vocally or aloud and the involvement of the speech areas of the brain. When we read a sentence or carry out mental arithmetic a short-term memory trace is crucial. To understand a sentence we have to remember the beginning until we reach its end. To complete a mental arithmetic problem we have to carry steps in the calculation 'in our heads' before reaching a solution.

A variation on this theme was put forward by Craik and Watkins (1973). Their theory is that rehearsal takes two forms – *maintenance* and *elaborative rehearsal*. The former is empty repetition of information, often with no logical content, in order to retain it in the short-term memory for sufficient time to be of use. How many times have you chanted a number (car registration, telephone number) until it is needed, only to forget it immediately afterwards? Elaborative rehearsal should not only maintain information in the STM; it is also intended to assist in placing it in the LTM.

In the last chapter we met with recent evidence (Awh *et al.* 1996, Paulesu *et al.* 1993) using scanning techniques suggesting that rote learning has its own brain base. Hearing the sounds of words (phonological codes) in both memorizing and storing verbal information is important. Verbal repetition helps to store information because there appear to be two locations in the brain – 'rehearsal' involves the left inferior frontal cortex and 'storage' the left inferior parietal cortex.

The visuo-spatial sketch (or note) pad is hypothesized as a temporary visual image of an object for sufficient time to enable us to manipulate the image 'in our minds'. The sketch pad would be used when we are given two- (e.g. geographical) or three-dimensional re-orientation problems (rotating figures).

As mentioned previously in this chapter, memory skills appear to be task-specific. The generalizations from early research, which tended to use laboratory settings with nonsense syllables, should be regarded with some suspicion. The current view is that to discover useful and transferable information about memory, one has to get as close to the actual conditions of the situation as possible. Variations in the material, the processes and strategies used for memorizing and the skills which the person brings to the learning all play some part. Consequently, it would be very difficult to see how knowledge from learning nonsense material could be generalized to learning meaningful material in the classroom. Such factors as prior knowledge, how understandable the information being learned is to the person and the time allowed for memorization are also crucial.

As illustrated in Figure 7.1, the process of recall or rehearsal of information in the short-term store is thought to occur by passing the information through the limited-capacity channel and re-entering it in the short-term store. In other words, rehearsal is closely related to rote learning, as when we repeat a telephone number, a shopping list or historical details. The more this cycle is repeated, the more likely it is that information will pass into the long-term store. There are probably telephone numbers, car registrations and childhood incidents lurking in our long-term memory from years ago because of repeated recall.

## Long-term memory (LTM)

The information entering the long-term store, unlike that in previous stores, does not decay but seems to be permanent in most circumstances. Information flow between the three hypothetical structures is believed to be under the control of the individual.

And how is the information encoded for storage in the long-term memory? A contemporary view of Paivio (1971) has found support from physiological and psychological sources. His dual system suggests a *non-verbal imagery process* and a *verbal symbolic process*. The first process involves storage of information as a non-verbal representation – sight, sound, touch; the second involves the storage of word meanings. The first line of the poem 'The boy stood on the burning deck' may be stored and retrieved either as a visual image or as a verbal statement. One source of supporting evidence for the dual-encoding idea comes from the split-brain research mentioned in Chapter 2, where it was indicated that a differentiation exists between the left and right sides of the brain: the right hemisphere is involved in imagery processes, the left in verbal symbolic processes. The prospect of information 'reaching' the long-term memory store depends on several factors relating to the information. Four of these are the length, the content, the opportunity for initial learning and the activity taking place between successive units of information.

As every student knows, long messages are less likely to be remembered than short ones. Technical messages, the level of familiarity, the particular sense or language of a message are all significant for long-term storage. Clearly revision is going to assist pupils in transferring information from the STM to the LTM. Multiple ways of presenting the same material, permitting active recall between each unit of information and reducing the speed of presentation will help in this respect. The effect of introducing a distraction at the outset of a revision session, or producing interference (proactive and retroactive, see later) before, during or after a learning session can have a devastating effect on the amount recalled. Vocalization as a means of revision helps in the short term. Dale (1968) concludes that:

> for material to enter long-term storage it has to survive an initial period during which retention loss can be extremely rapid. In order to survive, the amount of material should be small; it should be as free as possible from inter-item acoustic confusions; it should be varied so that interference between successive messages is minimised; also an opportunity for a brief period of silent rehearsal should be provided after each component message is presented.

The storage capacity must be enormous when one considers the amount of information we use each day. Memories from long ago can be recalled, in some cases in great detail, probably through constant repetition. Whether we ever completely forget anything once it has been transferred satisfactorily to the LTM is problematic. It raises the question of whether forgetting is a complete loss from storage or an inability to retrieve what is there. Evidence from shock treatment seems to suggest that we can completely lose information (Loftus and Loftus 1980).

The theory of a two-part (or stage) memory system, sometimes called the *duplex theory*, has much to commend it. There is a degree of common sense about it and teachers will readily see from the above how it can be applied to their day-to-day classroom activities. The differences between the STM and LTM are worthy of note (see Table 7.1).

One of the problems associated with the information-processing model is the implicit assumption that the human being is essentially a passive recipient of stimulation and that processing takes place in an ordered sequence and not in any parallel sense.

**Table 7.1** Differences between the STM and LTM

| Type of memory | Capacity | Persistence | Retrieval | Input |
|---|---|---|---|---|
| Short-term | Limited | Very brief | Immediate | Very fast |
| Long-term | Practically unlimited | Practically unlimited | Depends on organization | Relatively slow |

(Adapted from F. Smith, *Comprehension and Learning: A Conceptual Framework*, Holt, Rinehart and Winston, Eastbourne, 1975.)

Some models, including psychoanalysis, behaviourism and psychometrics, tend to forget the role of that most human of activities – thinking. This, along with the influence of specific aspects of each feat of memory, has caused Morris (1988) to claim:

> the evidence suggests that there is so much variability in the type of material, the types of processes, the strategies and the processing skills upon which people can draw when they tackle memorising in different situations that the way in which information is entered into the memory will often be very different from one situation to another.

Neisser (1976) suggests that there is concurrent and interactive processing between what is referred to as 'bottom-up' and 'top-down' processes. 'Bottom-up' (or stimulus-driven) processing is said to be directly influenced by the stimulus. The stimulus is analysed into specific features, like building blocks, and assembled into a pattern which has meaning for the receiver. The written word PEAR, made up from various straight and curved lines, will stimulate the reader to interpret the information to mean a familiar fruit.

Top-down (or conceptually-driven) processing does *not* require the detailed analysis of all the data in order to make sense of it. We can use the situation to help in the interpretation of meaning. If I *said* 'Which $\frac{\text{pear}}{\text{pair}}$ would you like?' and pointed to a set of stockings, the context would quickly indicate that 'pair' was the intended meaning. Meaning is most important in ensuring long-term memory. Whilst most people may find it difficult to give the precise details of an event or give the exact words in sentences they have read, they will often be able to recall the general meaning of the event or sentence. In the main, the preferred code for long-term memory is verbal, but sensory codes such as visual scenes, smells, tastes also exist.

## Explicit (declarative) and implicit (procedural or non-declarative) memory

Much of what we do in school work is quite explicit. We work to a syllabus requiring knowledge of specified areas, we encourage pupils to acquire the knowledge and then we assess what they know. This book is mainly concerned with this kind of learning requiring *explicit memory*. It is sometimes referred to as *declarative memory* (outward declaration of what is committed to memory).

In explicit memory at least two kinds of learning have been postulated. They involve *semantic* and *episodic memory*. Semantic memory is the capacity to recall facts and knowledge about the environment established in the memory using, for example, letter, number and musical notation codes. Episodic memory, as the word implies, is the capacity to recollect past experiences in time and space – events or 'episodes' in one's life. Both require the recall of information which has meaning.

Most specialists in this field are agreed that there is another kind of memory which does not appear to depend on actively recalling earlier learning. This is called *implicit memory* (sometimes referred to as *non-declarative* or *procedural memory*). These memories require no conscious awareness. Several kinds have been postulated (Squire *et al.* 1993) of which three are of interest – *skill acquisition, verbal* and *perceptual priming* and *conditioning* (classical). Physical skill acquisition, such as playing an instrument or becoming professionally competent in football, are acquired without our seeming to 'know' how it is done. A pictorial or verbal fragment is sometimes sufficient to stimulate the recollection of the whole picture or word. We often do this with children. For instance, having given them some spellings to learn, we may test them and start them off with a few letters. We met with this phenomenon in Chapter 3 when discussing *gestalten* – perceiving incomplete patterns as wholes.

In conditioning, we respond to a stimulus without necessarily knowing why. In a classic experiment with an amnesia patient, Claparède hid a pin in his hand and shook hands so as to prick the patient. Next day the patient refused to shake hands, but was quite unable to explain why. Despite the patient's amnesia, a subconscious memory had been established.

If we are presented with the words 'RIDING A BICYCLE', both explicit and implicit memories are involved. First we have to identify those strange shapes called letters which depended upon sensory (sight in this case) examination. If I had written 'DRIGIN', you would still be able to recognize the letters, although not necessarily able to assign any meaning. The same would be true in looking at other languages where the characters could be in Greek, Russian, Arabic or Chinese. At this stage, we are operating entirely at a perceptual level. It would also be true of the skill involved in riding a bicycle. Making sense of the expression 'riding a bicycle' depends on previous learning of the meanings of the words – semantic memories. On the other hand, recognising the actual letters of the words and the skill of riding a bicycle rely on implicit memories. It's 'know how' without knowing how we know. It is extremely difficult to explain the process of riding a bicycle. Usually a parent or friend sits you on the bike and precariously hangs on to the back of the seat until you have got the idea.

### Further reading

The case for there being at least two (explicit and implicit) forms of memory has attracted considerable attention and is supported from brain-scanning research involving different parts of the brain (Squire *et al.* 1992, Gabrieli *et al.* 1998). Research involving amnesia patients has been particularly instructive. For those wanting to read some of the original work see Squire (1992), Squire, Knowlton and Musen (1993), Squire *et al.* (1990). Intriguing experiments conducted by Squire *et al.* (1992) and Gabrieli *et al.* (1998) have shown how explicit and implicit memory involves different parts of the brain. Explicit memory involves the hippocampus and damage impairs the learning of new facts (memory loss for recent events) but does not impair learning new skills. On the other hand, damage to the basal ganglia shows the reverse effect. The conclusion is that implicit and explicit learning are distinct.

The relationships between these forms of memory are:

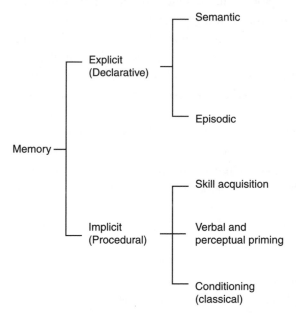

**Figure 7.2** Hypothesized forms of long-term memory.

The division of labour principle has implications for teachers. We already know, for example, that rote learning of symbols which have no inherent meaning will be inevitable. The alphabet symbols and sounds have to be learnt by heart, as do numbers. Priming, that is, providing cues (dealt with in Chapter 3), is a favoured technique for teachers. With age (Maylor 1996) and consequent failing memory, *aide-mémoire* become commonplace (strings round fingers, lists of things to be done, reminder notes in conspicuous places).

# Retrieval (recall, remembering, forgetting)

Retrieval is the process of recovering information from the memory. The term is used synonymously with recall and remembering. It is applied to either the short- or long-term memory. Retrieval from the LTM consists of returning information to the STM from the LTM store, that is, into the working memory. To initiate retrieval a cue is needed, either from an external stimulus or by a person's conscious effort to 'search' through the memory store for a link with material already in the working memory.

Three ways in which we can recover information have been described and they are *recall, recognition* and *relearning*.

Recall depends upon the active remembering of performances learned previously. Some examples are repeating a poem, a dance routine, mathematical equations and how to drive a car. We have to dig into our memories for an answer to a problem and rely entirely on our ability to recapture the relevant information. Examples of simple recall are given as part of the examination exercises mentioned in Chapter 16. This is the most difficult method of retrieving information.

In the case of recognition, we are given a clue or shown the information from which we can remember something learned on a previous occasion. To some extent multiple-choice questions, where alternative answers to a question are offered and the individual is required to select one answer, rely on recognition. However, in many instances the solution has first to be worked out and tallied with those provided, and this involves a high level of recall. We have all experienced the occasion when we see a face in the newspaper or on television and cannot put a name to it. Someone suggests a few names and the moment the correct name is mentioned we recognize it. The method is easier than recall, as can be concluded from Figure 7.3, which illustrates an experiment comparing retrieval by recognition, recall and relearning. In the latter case a pupil is asked to relearn something after a lapse of time and his or her efficiency in recall is measured by finding the time taken to relearn the task. We have all experienced the greater ease of revising something already learned.

The marked contrast between recall and recognition is worth bearing in mind, not only in the design of multiple-choice examination questions but in the prevalent method of question-and-answer teaching. Using only recall methods is exacting and fatiguing for children and should be interspersed with recognition tasks. Translation from French to English is easier for us than is translating from English to French because we can recognize the English equivalents of French words much more readily than in the reverse case. Note finally that relearning something which has been forgotten gets easier on each successive occasion, and this is why regular revision is a vital aspect of studying. Retrieval is aided where the original learning has been systematic, thorough and understood by the learner. Thus trying to recall material memorized by rote methods is more difficult than when the material is meaningful.

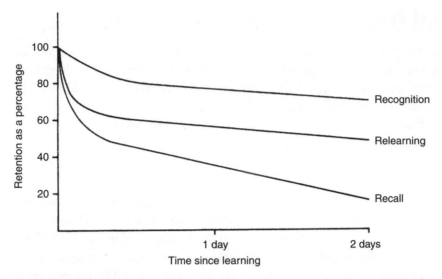

**Figure 7.3** Efficiency of three methods of retrieval. After C. W. Luh, 'The conditions of retention', *Psychol. Monogr.*, 31 (1922).

## Forgetting

*Forgetting* is the loss of ability to retrieve from either the STM or the LTM. 'Forgotten' does not necessarily mean 'gone for ever'. We have all experienced the situation where we cannot retrieve a particular memory, but it returns to us some time later. There are various theories as to why we forget and they depend on whether we are dealing with short- or long-term memory.

With the STM, three sources of forgetting have been postulated. They are *overload, trace decay* (or *atrophy*) and *displacement*. We have already referred to the capacity limitations of STM (seven plus or minus two) and it appears that beyond a certain number of units, which varies from one person to another, we can overload. How many people have tried to carry, say, a nine-digit telephone number from one place to another only to arrive at the telephone unsure of its correctness? Teachers should bear this overload possibility in mind when covering extensive topics. The careful use of chunking is important here.

Decay theory means what it says, that memories gradually disappear with time. Some physiological psychologists believe the cause is chemical. Some chemicals cause a metabolic change in the storage system bringing with it the decay and, finally, disappearance of memory traces in the nervous system.

Displacement theory assumes that if limited capacity prevails, there is a case for some information in the STM being pushed out – displaced – to make room for new inputs.

For the LTM causes of forgetting are thought to be *interference, destruction of brain tissue* and *motivated forgetting*.

Interference is thought to be the most problematic of all sources of memory loss. It arises when information being retrieved from memory has similar, but not identical, features. For example, trying to recall names or numbers which are similar can give rise to interplay and confusion both when trying to retain or recall. Some memories may not actually disappear altogether, but become obscured and overlaid with more recent memories. The sudden reappearance of long-lost memories either normally or under hypnosis is offered as evidence of interference theory.

In the short term, the recall of information can be inhibited in two ways. If we learn two lots of work, X and Y, in that order, the nature of X might influence the recall of Y, and this we call *proactive inhibition*. Underwood (1964) cites an example, well known amongst teachers, in which several lists of similar material are given to a group of people who are required to memorize them on successive days. Performance in terms of amount recalled deteriorates progressively from the first to the last list. The correct responses remembered from the preceding lists interfere with the recall of the one being learned.

When Y, the second task, inhibits the recall of X we call it *retroactive inhibition*. If the second learning task, Y, is repeated several times, each occasion makes the recall of X that much more difficult. The proactive effect of task X on Y is gradually eliminated by repeated trials of task Y, but in so doing the extinction of task X is taking place.

Experiment reveals that interference is a function of the similarity of tasks X and Y and their closeness in time. In both proactive and retroactive inhibition the subject matter is similar. Even when a task of a different nature is interposed between X and Y, recall is worse than when a complete rest is taken. Sleep between learning and recall helps retention for this very reason (also see the section on reminiscence below). In view of these findings, lessons should be interspersed with short intervals of relaxation, and the subject matter of adjoining lessons should not be similar. Learning just prior to bedtime (if one is not too tired), followed by a revision period first thing in the morning, is effective for some.

Some very helpful information about the sites in the brain responsible for memory function has been obtained from brain-damaged patients. It would appear that STM and LTM depend on several different parts of the brain. Indeed, there are cases in which damage has affected one but not the other, an observation often quoted as evidence for the dual theory of short- and long-term memory.

*Motivated forgetting* is familiar to those in psychoanalysis as *repression* (see Chapter 12) or the inaccessibility of some memories because of the (usually) unpleasant origins associated with them. Amnesia is a striking illustration in some psychopathological cases.

## A curve of forgetting

Ebbinghaus (translation of original text by Ruger and Bussenius, 1966) and his associates were amongst the first to study remembering and forgetting. His famous experiments related chiefly to the rate of forgetting with the passage of time. We are well aware that

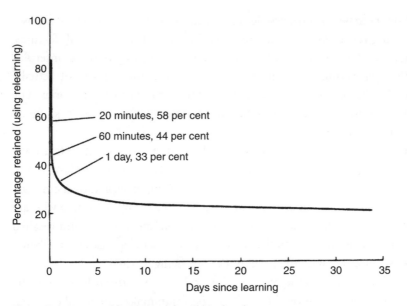

**Figure 7.4** A curve of forgetting (after Ebbinghaus).

most learned material gradually fades away, and Ebbinghaus devised experiments to see if there was any pattern to the nature of forgetting. His subjects were required to learn a list of *nonsense syllables* until they could repeat the list perfectly. A nonsense syllable consists of a three-letter arrangement of two consonants with a vowel as the centre letter. The resulting combination must not be a word in the language. Syllables such as BOL, QIS and WEJ are examples. Nonsense syllables are chosen to make sure that the learners have no prior knowledge of the task: everyone starts from scratch. The criterion of learning is the ability of the subject to repeat the list of, say, ten syllables once through completely while the task is being timed. At various intervals of time after learning, the subject endeavours to repeat the list, and if (as is usually the case) unable to repeat it he or she is timed in the relearning of the list.

The usual formula for deriving the time needed for recall is:

$$\frac{\text{original learning} - \text{relearning time}}{\text{original learning time}} \times 100$$

This gives a ratio of time saved in relearning expressed as a percentage. A typical curve of retention (or conversely forgetting) using several time intervals is shown in Figure 7.4. The higher the percentage, the more efficient recall has been. Note the rapid fall in the amount remembered and the levelling out of the curve after about five days to something like 22 per cent of the original amount retained. Later, in Figure 7.6, we shall see some marked differences in this quantity, which varies according to the kind of material being learned.

In a moment, we shall discuss how applicable Ebbinghaus's work is to learning in classrooms.

## Access and storage failure

Sometimes our failure to recall an established memory is caused by faulty retrieval and not that we have lost the information. How many times have we had that 'tip of the tongue' feeling and then recovered the information later. Facts like names and numbers can be irritatingly illusive only to be recovered later when it is no longer of use. What is usually missing is a good *retrieval cue*. Trying to pluck a memory from that huge storage in the brain needs some guidance – like looking for a book in a library. This explains why it is easier to recognize than recall information. In recognizing something, what is provided acts as a cue to finding the remaining part of the information. That is why multiple-choice questions which provide the answers are easier than essay questions where one has to recall from memory.

Interference, mentioned above, is also an example of access failure. The cue provided is sometimes a cue for more than one piece of information and the confusion interferes with retrieval of the particular information needed.

As mentioned above, there is some evidence to show that information once stored and retrieved can completely disappear (Loftus and Loftus 1980). Shock treatment which can disturb the cortex region in which long-term memories are stored can cause complete memory loss of some, but not all, information. Usually it is recent LTM memories which are destroyed.

## Reminiscence

Ballard found a curious phenomenon in 1913. Some children who had partially learned a poem were able to recall better after a period of time than immediately after the learning session. This is known as *reminiscence*. One explanation is that inhibition builds up during the task, but once the task is abandoned, dissipation of inhibition sets in and enables a better recall performance. Thus, for a short time after the learning, the dissipation might proceed at such a rate as to enable the individual to improve performance. In a research with schoolchildren the author (Child 1966) was able to show that neurotic extraverts display significantly higher reminiscence effects than stable introverts, using the inverted alphabet test. The direction of this finding is in keeping with the postulates of Eysenck regarding the levels and dissipation of inhibition in different personality types (see Chapter 12). As extraverts develop higher levels of inhibition than introverts, their performance will be poorer, relatively speaking, as the task proceeds. Consequently, after a break in which inhibition has dissipated, the performance of extraverts will appear as temporarily superior to that of introverts. Once again we see a possible connection between personality characteristics and performance which could become a valid source of information in class teaching.

## Massed and distributed practice

*Massed* practice occurs when little or no rest is permitted during a task or between tasks. When intervals during the task are allowed we have *distributed* practice. In general, massed conditions of learning are less productive than distributed conditions. A possible reason has already been broached in the discussion of interference and reminiscence, where we proposed that retention is inhibited as a task proceeds and, until there is some rest, the inhibition continues to affect performance. A rest pause enables the inhibition to dissipate. If you have ever tried 'press-ups', you will recall that a point is reached when it seems absolutely impossible to raise the body one more time. In a way, this illustrates the effects of mental inhibition, when the mind is pushed to a point where it cannot function adequately, although we rarely reach the kind of dramatic standstill experienced in physical exercise.

No satisfactory solution has been found to the questions of how long the rests should be, or how long is a reasonable stint of work in particular school subjects. The periods normally used in school are based on a rule-of-thumb and not on scientific analysis. Choosing periods of 35 minutes in primary schools, for example, is mostly experience and intuition. The idea that young children can only take about 20 minutes of narration from a teacher has very little experimental support. Nevertheless, teachers have doubtless arrived at a knowledge of timing lessons from observation and experience of handling children. The signs of fatigue or work decrement are plain to see, and inexperienced teachers would be wise to keep a wary eye open for such signs of inhibition.

## Serial learning

In a particular learning programme, the position of the material as it is presented can have a marked influence on the prospects of retention. Again, using lists of nonsense syllables which it is assumed can be generalized to meaningful material, it has been shown that the first and last few syllables are usually learned and remembered first and the central syllables last. If we plot the number of trials required to learn a syllable against its position in the list we generate a *serial position curve* (see Figure 7.5). One explanation of this phenomenon is the *primacy* and *recency* effects. The primacy effect is said to occur because we tend to remember best the first information we receive because it has the greatest effect on us. We also tend to remember better, information we have received most recently. Hence the research shows better performance at the beginning and the end. This is very useful information for the class teacher: in devising lessons some thought should be given to the order of presentation in terms of difficulty and length, and in re-ordering for revision purposes.

In a study by Murdock (1962) using English words a similar marked serial position effect was noted. Figure 7.6 illustrates the findings. These fit in remarkably well with the

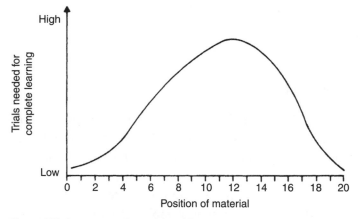

**Figure 7.5** A representative serial position curve.

duplex theory of STM and LTM. The first words to be memorized probably 'entered' a comparatively free short-term memory store and were rehearsed more frequently than the middle words. These would therefore stand a better chance of being committed to the LTM store. The middle words were entering an already 'occupied' STM store. The last words on the list would still be in the LTM when recall was required. In fact, many people give the last words first 'before I forget them'. In other words they would suffer the transient fate of STM unless they were repeated soon after being learned.

A good example of using primacy, recency and repetition is to take a list of short facts to be committed to memory, say facts A,B,C,D and E. The order of learning is A; A and B; A,B and C; A,B,C and D; A,B,C,D and E. Since primacy is not quite as good as recency, we arrange matters so that the first items are repeated more often. This is a really good technique

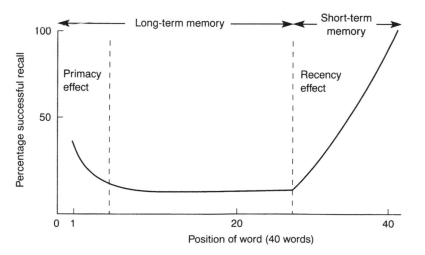

**Figure 7.6** Serial position curve for 40 words.

for learning any list. But we have to be sure that the list can ultimately be repeated in any order.

# Approaches to learning

Our main concern here will be to discuss the factors which are thought to affect the efficiency of learning for retention and recall. It is taken as self-evident that the study habits, as well as the abilities, of individuals are important in determining performance in all forms of recall, including conventional examinations. Yet research into the effect of different study habits has not given us any clear indications of the precise patterns best suited to individuals. This is not surprising when one considers the complexity of the studying task itself, quite apart from cognitive and personality factors contributing to performance.

Many factors appear to impinge on study effectiveness, most are mentioned in other chapters (motivation, intelligence, personality, knowledge of results, etc.). Texts for higher education students have been written on the subject of study since the beginning of the last century.

---

### Further reading

Student study is, and has been for almost 100 years, one of the most popular topics in education. Library shelves are groaning with the weight of books on the subject. In 1900, Hinsdale wrote a text called *The Art of Study*. One would think, and hope, that by now this nut had been cracked, but it is a very complex issue. Here is a selection which you may find helpful: Collins and Kneale (2000), Freeman and Meed (1993), Lashley (1995), Davies (1995), and one for sixth formers is by Butcher (1993).

One of many websites on student learning is http://slc.otago.ac.nz. There is a particularly useful section on study skills.

---

Many of the suggestions, such as ensuring that a suitable location or the material needed are available, are common sense and will be referred to later in this section. But most of these texts have tended to give a set of techniques and skills to be mastered without concern for individual differences or the contexts within which learning is taking place. In recent years greater emphasis has been given to the role of students in self-awareness about their learning methods and this issue will be dealt with first.

## Learning to learn (metacognition)

During the past 30 or so years, research has focused on the idea that students ought to have greater awareness of their thinking strategies. Individual students, by understanding the processes of study, their own characteristics, work conditions and subject contexts, are thought to have a better chance of improving the effectiveness of study sessions. This concept of a person self-consciously examining his or her mental processes, becoming aware of problems and adjusting accordingly in order to improve effectiveness is known as *metacognition* – learning how to learn. The term was introduced by Flavell (1976).

The study methods movement was clearly an attempt to provide a framework which students could use to examine their own methods (Nisbet and Shucksmith 1986). Unfortunately, it has not been as useful as was hoped. One serious flaw is that the recommended techniques are not always transferable from one context to another. For example, many texts on study methods give strategies for remembering lists of words, usually unconnected words. Would these strategies easily transfer to remembering laws in physics, chemical equations, poetry or music? These texts also quickly get into discussions of thinking styles. How does a teacher organize material and presentation to account for the variety of styles in a class? – a daunting task for, say, a secondary teacher of science who might see as many as 300 pupils in the course of a week. From the individual pupil's point of view, someone good at languages and poor at mathematics is not likely to adopt the same learning style in these subjects.

The study problems and strategies of students in higher education have attracted most attention from researchers and writers (see for example Collins and Kneale 2000, Lashley 1995). These problems have been exacerbated by the rapid increase in student numbers in recent years. Students are often not aware of their study shortcomings and even when they do recognize that they have problems they do not readily seek out advice. Over many years, Entwistle (1998, with Ramsden 1983) has developed a system the aim of which 'is to encourage greater awareness of the purposes in studying and to promote regular and systematic reflection on the skills and strategies adopted'. The system begins with a questionnaire for the student and this enables an analysis to be made of study strengths and weaknesses. Help is provided by the programme to meet the specific weaknesses identified, although the student can browse through other parts of the programme. Staff are also involved so that their teaching methods encourage effective study habits.

The underlying principles of much research in this aspect of higher education incorporate a view of learning expounded by Marton and Säljö (1976) which distinguishes between *surface* and *deep* approaches to study. Surface approaches focus on memorizing and reproducing information with extrinsic rewards such as a qualification, and fear of failure very much in mind. Deep approaches see the student trying to understand and extract meaning from the information with an intrinsic interest in the subject. These topics are covered in Chapter 8. Entwistle (Entwistle and Ramsden 1983) added two further approaches – *strategic* and *apathetic*. Strategic methods reflect a high need for achievement (see Chapter 8) and playing the system to obtain high marks. This kind of student likes to be noticed, hands work in on time and carefully notes the prejudices of the lecturer in order to feed them back in essays. The apathetic student has low motivation, is disorganized and has negative attitudes to work. These approaches should not be regarded as stable characteristics, but may be used by the same student for different topics.

There has been less systematic study in schools, where providing for individual variability is a very complex problem, but some attempts have been made. The Instrumental Enrichment Intervention Programme devised and used by Feuerstein (1980) for children with special needs and John Biggs's (Biggs and Collis 1982) SOLO taxonomy scheme (Structure of the Observed Learning Outcome) for evaluating the quality of learning in school and higher education are two examples. They are both orientated towards individual analysis.

The question of transferability of skills from one learning situation to another has been examined by Howe and others in a series of articles (1991). His conclusions are helpful. For transfer to be possible between two learning tasks there ought to be four different kinds of identical elements. They are (a) knowledge common to both; (b) common skills or sub-skills; (c) habits of learning (some of these are discussed below); and (d) characteristics of the learner which would generally help study (such as persistence, competitiveness, enjoyment of learning from textbooks). The first two relate to the contexts and the second two to personal differences of learners.

# Study problems

The previous section looked at the influence of particular strategies adopted by students and these have been shown to affect performance. But there are other influences relating to the circumstances in which pupils and students have to work. For a recent study guide for higher and further education students should see Northedge (2005). This was written for psychology students, but has many general points in it including some useful websites.

## Organization

There is nothing more soul-destroying than to be stumbling from one topic to another without any clear plan of action: it is uneconomic in terms of both time and effort. Gestalt psychologists have pointed out the need for an understanding of the context within which to work and for this we need to organize and order our subject matter and methods both as students and as teachers. Children quickly become confused and intolerant of situations which are unstructured and undisciplined. As students it is worth while forming some simple study routines which become habits, otherwise the many attractions of the non-academic life of a student can take over completely.

## Place of study

For concentration and learning it is necessary to have peace and quiet. A noisy classroom, television or radio in the background at home, road-works or building noises, or even the voice of others, constitute a distraction for most people. Some claim that a background of music is not a hindrance, but it does constitute a source of competition for one's attention. Technically speaking, the level of extraneous sound should not reach a level which is likely to break through the threshold of one's attention. In private study, body comfort is essential, although one must avoid sleep-inducing conditions such as easy chairs or beds or smoky atmospheres in students' rooms.

## Time of day and length of study

No hard-and-fast rule applies about the best time of day or for how long one should study at a given session. Variations between individuals make it necessary for each person to discover his or her own optimum conditions. Some individuals like to rise early in the morning and work 'whilst the mind is fresh', but few students find themselves able to take advantage of this suggestion (Child 1977). But there is reason to believe that personality is a significant variable contributing towards differential performance according to the time of day, and whether people work best individually or in a group. Using a task in which subjects were required to cancel the letter 'e' on a sheet of print, Colquhoun and Corcoran (1964) showed that in the morning or working by themselves, introverts perform better than extraverts. However, in the afternoon, or when working in a group, the performance of introverts is the same as (or even worse than) that of extraverts.

The *span of attention* (the length of time one can concentrate before distraction sets in) clearly is relevant here and probably is related to personality differences. This point will be elaborated in Chapter 12, where there is some discussion of Eysenck's theory that extraverts normally require more involuntary rest pauses than introverts in tasks requiring concentration. Some people might be unshaken by a two-hour stint of work, whilst others need more frequent rests. The build-up of inhibition to studying can be dissipated by distributing the rest and work periods. But we are not yet in a position to say with conviction how long the work or rest period should be for a given person or, for that matter, how best to use the work time. A few short breaks of about five minutes during a long study session (of about two hours) are essential, and a longer break should be taken between tasks (see proactive and retroactive inhibition in the earlier section 'Forgetting'). One thing is certain – very few children are taught how to study or how to make a self-evaluation of their study strategies to obtain maximum efficiency. In a study by the author (Child 1977), 72 per cent of a sample of university, college of education and sixth-form students claimed to have taught themselves how to study by the process of trial and error while at secondary school. Even obvious points about organization and work conditions, timetabling or avoiding fatigue are rarely mentioned by teachers.

## For parents

Students and teachers might find what follows a helpful way of approaching parents who are anxious to help their children, particularly in preparation for examinations. Most parents will have taken an exam or test at some time. Driving tests are probably the most common. Those who have taken a driving test will recall the moments of anxiety in the days before the test, those feelings of 'butterflies', while pondering about what on earth the examiner will ask from the Highway Code. Imagine that experience extended over three or four weeks with several different subjects, each demanding much more than a Highway Code, and you begin to capture the feelings children endure when preparing for and taking public examinations.

Studying for homework or an examination is hard work, if done properly. Parents cannot do the learning for their offspring, but there are several ways in which they can provide much needed understanding and support. They do not have to know anything about the subjects being studied, but what they have to do is provide the right atmosphere for study.

Teachers, when advising parents, should make the point that there are some obvious questions for parents to ask themselves. Can their sons and daughters get peace and quiet in the home when they need it? Can they provide space, reasonable comfort and warmth? Is there a reasonable table top and book space? Do they fork out when books or equipment are needed? Do they lay on the odd drink (non-alcoholic, as alcohol befuddles the mind) or snack during periods of intensive study? Are the students relieved from some routine household chores (but not all, because they should break from time to time for alternative activities)?

The important contribution of parents is really to provide support services and sympathy, *without* bringing undue pressure to bear. Many parents understandably get worried and anxious for their children's sakes, largely because parents realize the high value our society places on examination successes and the place these successes have in the career prospects of young people. Tempting though it may be to make regular enquiries about how things are going, they should try not to overdo it – they should try to avoid becoming a nagging parent. Equally, they must not ignore the activities and progress of their young. There is a responsible middle course, which is extremely difficult to steer, between the overbearing and the passive. In effect, they have to believe in their children; they must have faith in them and build up a trust in them.

Perhaps the hardest problem to deal with is the able, but lazy, son or daughter. How, for example, does a caring parent encourage an able, bone-idle youth to work without the parent 'laying on the agony'? Two major sources of trouble are lack of motivation and a troublesome personality.

To be an effective student one has to want to do well. There are so many appealing distractions for young people that the alternative of sitting for long hours poring over books or notes has to have a strong justification. The temptation to leave school for a wage is powerful, and the central discussion will doubtless be about putting off moderate, short-term satisfactions in favour of better, more rewarding and satisfying career prospects in the future. It is not easy to convince young people that longer-term rewards are worth working and waiting for. Other factors are that immediate satisfaction is usually possible when some of the subjects being studied are of genuine interest, or when they come easily to the individual. Sometimes subjects are essential for a particular career. Extrinsic rewards for success in exams can be offered – for instance, a promise of money, a bicycle, the cost of driving lessons, a holiday and so forth, as the occasion demands.

Something is said later in Chapter 12 about the possible effect of certain personality traits on study. Some people do find the act of studying for prolonged periods very tedious. They have to recognize and come to terms with this disadvantage and adjust their study plans so that the periods are interspersed. Some frank discussion between parents and offspring about these difficulties can be helpful.

Teachers should make it clear that if parents are to provide support, they need to be informed of the school's expectations. It is not a bad idea to obtain from their youngsters some outline of the homework timetable and talk through ways in which this can be achieved. Programmes for exam revision should also be shared with parents, so that they can give tactful encouragement when needed.

## For pupils – from teachers (Goacher and Reid 1983)

If you have the ability to cope with the work done during the course and you have tried to keep level with your understanding of the work, how could you possibly fail? Unfortunately, people do fail, even when they have enough ability to come to terms with the course. Why? There are several reasons, but one of the most important is that you have to be 'motivated', that is, you have to feel a need to get through the exams. If you have a definite career in mind, keep it at the focus of your thoughts. There is nothing more potent than a goal which you want to attain. If you are half-hearted and unsure if you want to go on, it will not help at all. So you must try to get in the right frame of mind. You have to be convinced about the kind of future you want and the need to pass exams as well as you can.

Think twice before giving way to temptations which will squander your time away. The hours you need to put in are different and sometimes longer than those for your friends at work; so keep a close watch on the distribution of work and leisure time. Do not misunderstand this advice. Everyone should mix pleasure with work. But *you* have to be in control. You have to judge sensibly how much time you can afford for relaxation and when it is most convenient to take it. The decisions require a pretty tough and determined person.

Thus, look for pointers which will strengthen your desire to succeed and thereby help you overcome the many alternative temptations. If you have a career in mind, work systematically towards it; where subjects interest you, work at them – almost like a hobby; take the advice of your teachers when they tell you that you have skills in certain subjects. These can all be useful motivators.

Sometimes, and in all walks of life, we become despondent, impatient and tired of the routines. Study is no exception. It is work and work can be boring at times. Some people, because of the way they react to life, find they simply cannot keep up one task for even moderate periods of time. They soon switch off, even when they are well motivated. What can be done? The first and most important thing is to recognize and face problems and try to do something about them. It is not enough to admit to oneself, and possibly others, that one cannot study for long. A regime has to be worked out which best suits one's shifts of mood.

In studying for exams, it should be emphasized that there is no one best method of studying. Broadly, there are ways and means which most people find a help or a hindrance, but in the end pupils have to try out and discover which combination of methods best suits their circumstances. Study guides are often written by those who have been successful in exams, and it becomes easy to slip into the habit of giving formulae for study which they have tried and proved effective.

Above all, pupils have to experiment and be honest with themselves. There is no future in their kidding themselves that they work brilliantly in strange places at strange times without first confirming that there is no better way. They should explore the most preferred *and* efficient techniques in preparation for and in sitting exams. Some are common sense and will be widely known, such as avoiding misreading questions or instructions, writing so badly that the examiner cannot read the script or not caring about the spelling of important concepts. Others are not so obvious, such as how should revision be spaced, judging the length of time which should be given to each subject, or whether to revise right up to the exam or not.

Pupils need to use the normal school and 'mock' examinations as a guide to the best revision strategies, and use homework as a means of discovering the most fruitful methods of study. They should treat any 'mock' exams very seriously, as if they were the real thing, and learn as much as possible about their strengths and weaknesses.

It is important to get into the right frame of mind for examinations. Others are sure to say discouraging things about their prospects (and maybe yours as well). Take no notice – unless it is advice from a teacher of course. If there are those who claim not to need to work for exams, ignore them. They are probably working harder than you think. In any case, you should know best what you could do. One has to go into this business with a positive, optimistic outlook, knowing that if one has put in the work, success can be achieved. From the point of view of the future, taking GCSEs and 'A' levels is one of the most important events in a pupil's life so far. Treat the occasion with the care it deserves.

## Personal, social and academic problems

Many students are adversely affected in their work by the existence of personal problems arising from emotional, social, academic and, for older students on grants, financial diffi- culties. Learning becomes more tedious as these influences intrude on the concentration of the learner. In both young and older pupils alike, the emotional and social 'cut and thrust' of home life and friendships probably play a significant part in learning efficiency, although the strongest evidence so far on this point comes from American research (Coleman 1961, Sanford 1962). Feelings of inadequacy are another source of trouble (see the sections on need to achieve, level of aspiration and self-fulfilling prophecy in Chapter 8). The relationship between teacher and taught is frequently held to influence the latter's attitude to learning. Where there is some good-natured friendliness with authority, derived not so much from his or her position as a teacher as from knowledge of the subject, then an atmosphere more conducive to learning seems to prevail.

One aspect of pupil–teacher relationships which has not yet been researched is the influence of characteristic teaching styles on the study habits and learning skills of children – in other words, the problem of compatibility of teaching and learning styles (Joyce and Hudson 1968).

## The peer group

Teachers probably underrate the extent to which study strategies are influenced by one's friends. American researchers (Coleman 1961, Sanford 1962) have gone some way in exploring the nature of agreements and understandings among secondary education and higher education students about their roles as students, but there is insufficient evidence for similar conclusions in Britain. The topic is concerned partly with competition and co-operation between pupils in comparing work by discussing standards, requirements and lesson content. However, it is also concerned with the motivation generated by rivalry between peers to obtain a teacher's attention, and understandings between children about what is a 'group norm' of work (and play).

## Meaningfulness of task

Grasping the meaning of a task is essential for efficient learning (see the section on 'Discovery, guided discovery and expository methods of teaching' in Chapter 14). Most of what we learn requires an understanding of the gist of an argument and not a follow-my-leader repetition of the argument. To see the logic of what is being learned greatly assists in its memorization.

It is nevertheless true that some things have to be learned by heart. There is no easy, logical way of learning letters of the alphabet or the actual symbols for the numbers 0 to 9. Formulae, scientific principles and laws, passages of prose or dates, zoological systems such as the cranial nerves often have to be learned by heart, even when one understands the meaning of the facts. Some people use props such as rhymes and mnemonics; that is, taking the initial letters of a sequence of facts and using these initial letters to make up an amusing or memorably pornographic sentence. Most students have come across these, especially in science. For example, the colours of the rainbow can be memorized using:

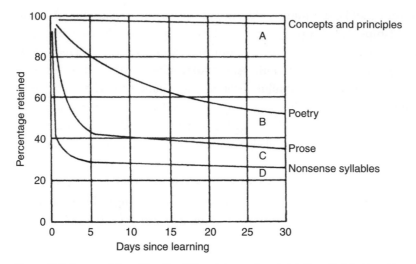

**Figure 7.7** Curves of forgetting for different types of material. From H. Maddox, *How to Study*, Pan, London, 1963.

Richard Of York Gave Battle In Vain, the initial letters of which make Red, Orange, Yellow, Green, Blue, Indigo, Violet. The rules for finding sines, cosines and tangents of angles are sometimes remembered using SOH CAH TOA (S = sine, C = cosine, T = tangent, O = opposite side, A = adjacent side, H = hypotenuse), from which we get *S*ine equals *O*pposite over *H*ypotenuse, and so on. Remembering the jingles is only half the battle because then we have to recall the facts they represent. However, their main function is to produce a link between unrelated things. Rhymes such as 'Thirty days hath September . . .' or 'Willie, Willie, Harry, Ste . . .', for the kings of England from William the Conqueror onwards, and 'i before e except after c' are also commonplace aids.

The rapidity with which we forget different kinds of material is illustrated in Figure 7.7. Note that the more meaningful topics, such as laws and concepts, are by far the best retained, whilst nonsense syllables are quickly forgotten.

## Revision

This is important because memories begin to fade with the passage of time unless we actively recall them periodically. While learning a subject it is a useful idea to set aside some time both during and after the learning session for sitting back and actively recalling or committing to paper the work covered. Some psychologists believe that we should spend at least half the study time trying to recall the work we are learning. Often the time is totally taken up in reading, without necessarily absorbing the work. Apart from anything else, it helps to vary the learning task and reduce the influence of reactive inhibition (the tendency not to repeat a response which has just been made). Active reconstruction and organization of learned material helps to fix it in one's mind.

Various suggestions have been made to help students remember material. Some have already been mentioned, such as *chunking* and the use of mnemonics or acronyms (initial letters which spell out memorable words, e.g. ASH = Action on Smoking and Health). If you are not convinced of the effectiveness of chunking, compare the difficulty you have in remembering:

EVLEWTSIEMITEHT

with the ease of remembering:

THETIMEISTWELVE

This is particularly so when you realize that the last set of letters consists of four familiar words – 'the time is twelve'. How much more quickly would you have remembered the first set of letters if you had realized they were 'the time is twelve' in reverse order?

Peg-type mnemonics are sometimes used by those who make a living from remembering vast lists of objects. The peg-word method is first to memorize a code such as one is gun, two is shoe, three is tree, four is door and so forth, then to number the objects and associate each with the peg-word; for example, if the first object is a glass, picture it stuck on the barrel end of the gun.

Linking and rhyming systems are quite common. The most famous is 'Thirty days hath September, April, June and November'.

Another system is the 'keyword' method, often used in learning foreign languages. A word in the foreign language is linked with a familiar object in one's own language. When at school I remembered words relating to silver – argentum, l'argent – by using the country name of Argentina. Greek and Latin prove to be very useful languages in deducing the meaning of English words (or vice versa). 'Epidermis' is made up from two Greek roots, *epi* – upon and *dermis* – skin, giving 'surface skin'; 'geminate' is Latin from *gemini* – twins giving 'to combine in pairs'.

In mnemonics, peg-words, rhymes, linking systems, and keywords, we are depending on familiar cues to provide the first step in the process of retrieval.

## 'Whole' and 'part' learning

The theory behind this topic was discussed in Chapter 6. Given a learning task requiring the assimilation of large slices of information, we may read through the information several times to get an overall picture of the content and to try to memorize it. On the other hand, we may break the information down into parts and learn each part first before drawing it together again. This crudely distinguishes 'whole' and 'part' learning. The pros and cons of the two approaches have been researched and debated for several years without any resulting clear-cut advice about which is the superior method. The compromise conclusion is that the nature of the material and the condition of the learner dictate the most suitable method. The holistic approach is useful where the amount of information is sufficiently small to be absorbed at one time. Also it is said to provide a better grasp of meaning and continuity between the elements of the material once the overall pattern of knowledge is understood. It is not always possible to treat chunks of information in this way, particularly if the material is difficult and unfamiliar; consequently we must resort to breaking it down into manageable portions. The central issue is understanding: provided the total context is understood, 'part' learning can be effective. Miller's $7 \pm 2$ rule also applies (see Verbal chaining, later in this chapter).

## Transfer of training

At one time the Royal Air Force had a battery of aptitude tests for those hoping to enter as aircrew. One test presented the candidate with a board full of pegs placed in square holes. One half of the top of each peg was painted white, the other black. The candidate was told to reverse as many pegs as possible with the non-preferred hand in a given time. Some had what seemed to be a natural skill at the game, but there were also those who had had previous experience as packers in industry (such as chocolate, biscuit or component packing) whose skill enabled them to perform this task with outstanding dexterity. Some of the skills they had learned in one situation were now being applied in a similar situation. This we call *transfer of training*. It is particularly apparent in physical skills and to some extent it is applicable in mental activity. Around the turn of the century there was a belief amongst psychologists and teachers that some school subjects acted as a training ground for exercising mental skills. This became known as 'the doctrine of formal training'. Mathematics was thought to develop children's powers of logic, science was seen as training children to be observant, and learning Latin and historical or geographical facts was thought to exercise the memory.

These views are no longer held by the majority of psychologists and teachers. However, there is a case for believing that some skills can be transferred and that the curriculum can play a part in this. We have seen from the researches of behaviourists that stimulus generalization occurs where animals and humans are disposed to recognize a stimulus within fairly wide limits. The dogs in Pavlov's work, whilst presumably realizing that there was a difference, were prepared to respond to a range of tuning forks or bells of slightly differing frequencies as if they were all from an identical stimulus. We also saw in concept formation that we formulate our concepts flexibly within wide limits: cats come in a variety of shapes, sizes and colours, yet we generalize our perceptions to constitute the single concept 'cat'.

A lot of research has been directed towards finding the factors most necessary for transfer (O'Connor 1968). The most significant finding is that where there are common factors in the content or in the procedures adopted in carrying out two tasks, transfer is possible.

The content of mathematics is useful in the solution of problems in physics and chemistry. Some of the procedures of mathematics are helpful in statistics. Physical skills involving similar procedures, as in the illustration at the beginning of this section, encourage transfer. Length of training also has a long-term effect, as when a person who has concentrated his or her efforts on science subjects at 'A' level and at university may find that objectivity and conciseness begin to permeate into other aspects of life requiring the assembly and dissemination of knowledge.

Three other factors which affect transfer should be mentioned. There is a better chance of transfer, assuming similarity of content and procedure, where the learner is made aware of the possibility of transfer. It was pointed out earlier in this section that transfer of training had much in common with the behaviourists' concept of stimulus generalization. Having made the point, I hoped that what the reader had gleaned about stimulus generalization would be transferred to the subject of 'transfer of training' because of content similarity. This brings us to the second influence. The more thoroughly the first task is learned, the more likely it is that transfer will occur, given the conditions in the previous paragraph. This is tantamount to saying that if one task is not learned properly it is hardly likely to have a positive influence on the performance of a similar task. Intelligence also affects transfer, because more intelligent children and adults are more likely to spot the relationship between tasks.

The instances cited above have been examples of positive transfer, but it is quite possible to have negative transfer. Where the second task possesses content or requires procedures in conflict with the first task, then negative transfer is likely. An example from sport is the hindrance experienced in trying to learn a second style of swimming after mastering one style. Negative transfer is also apparent in learning foreign languages, where the rules of grammar (adjective position, masculine–feminine rules, etc.) differ to a point which impedes transfer (see also proactive and retroactive inhibition in the section headed 'Forgetting', above).

# An overview: Gagné's conditions of learning

So much has been contributed to learning and memory that an overview which attempts to incorporate the most applicable parts is worth mentioning. Such an eclectic overview, has been proposed by Gagné (1985). He draws upon the major theories of learning mentioned in the last chapter – the fields of perception, selective attention, information-processing models of memory, concept formation and language skills – all of which are discussed in this book.

He believes that our knowledge of learning and the influence we might have upon learners is helped by identifying and elaborating three aspects of learning. These are the *conditions of learning,* the *events* or *processes of learning* and the *types of outcomes* or *capabilities displayed after learning.*

The conditions of learning are divided conveniently into *internal* and *external.* The internal conditions for learning to take place consist of the previous learning which relates to the skill and the processes which are used in order to inform the performer of the skill. External conditions include a variety of factors such as stimulation by others to recall, inform and guide the learner. A number of these factors, such as making sure the task has meaning, rehearsal techniques, transfer and motivation, are discussed earlier in this chapter.

The events or processes-of-learning model most favoured by Gagné is information-processing, discussed here and in the previous chapter. It is, of course, a postulate and not a fact, although the processes and structures are inferred from the behaviour of people as well as reflecting what we know of the action of the nervous system. Further, Gagné tries to link these processes to the outcomes of learning in the hope of providing indicators for adjusting the conditions of learning.

The outcomes of learning or the types of human capabilities learned have been classified by Gagné. To some extent this classification tries to answer some of the questions posed at the start of Chapter 6: what are the important issues which have to be explored by a learning theorist for the theory to have an impact on the work of teachers? It also draws on the work mentioned in Chapters 4 and 5. In answer to the question of what is learned, Gagné gives five categories: *intellectual skills, cognitive strategies, verbal information, motor skills* and *attitudes* (Gagné 1985, Gagné *et al.* 1992). As intellectual skills are central to the present topic more will be said about them.

A significant characteristic of intellectual skill is the dependence on previous knowledge, usually of simpler skills. This interdependence is illustrated in Figure 7.8.

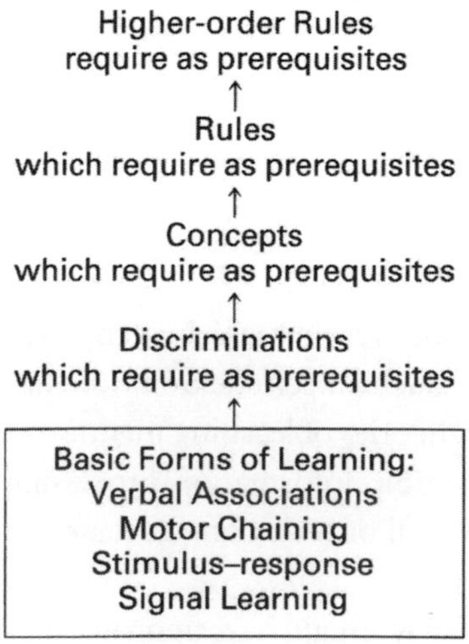

**Higher-order Rules**
**require as prerequisites**
↑
**Rules**
**which require as prerequisites**
↑
**Concepts**
**which require as prerequisites**
↑
**Discriminations**
**which require as prerequisites**
↑

**Basic Forms of Learning:**
**Verbal Associations**
**Motor Chaining**
**Stimulus–response**
**Signal Learning**

**Figure 7.8** Adapted from Gagné.

Figure 7.8 reads from bottom to top in order of complexity and dependence. *Signal learning* is exemplified by Pavlov's classical conditioning, where a signal initiates a general *involuntary* response. An example was given in Chapter 6, with the child visiting the doctor for an injection and experiencing a fear response on hearing about the visit or on sitting in the surgery. The diffuse emotion of fear is aroused by the conditional signal (sounds of words relating to visit).

*Stimulus–response learning* has also been illustrated in the work of Thorndike and Skinner (see Chapter 6), in which a particular stimulus becomes associated with a particular *voluntary* response. Examples are found most frequently in young children when they first learn words (e.g. 'echoic', 'mand' and 'tact' responses) or body responses (e.g. smiling in response to a smile).

As sensory motor behaviour and development precede verbal behaviour, the logic of Gagné's hierarchy is self-evident. An illustration of *motor chaining* is seen in the 'circular reactions' of Piaget (see Chapter 4). At a more complex level, the sequence of motor responses accompanying the throwing of a ball or using a pen demonstrates chaining. As one S–R bond is completed (reaching out) the next is set in motion (grasping the ball), and so on through the sequence.

*Verbal chaining* (or *association*) occurs when two or more established verbal S–R links are put together. Gagné uses several examples from the learning of a foreign language. For instance, we frequently use intermediate clues in translating words as in the sequence 'roi' – image of king – 'king', or 'dent' – dentist – 'tooth'. The possibility of limits to chaining are expressed in Miller's paper (1956) on the span of absolute judgement in which he regards $7 \pm 2$ as the optimum number of elements (digits, words, chemical formulae, etc.) capable of being chained and recalled comfortably for immediate memory span.

*Discrimination learning* means exactly what it says, that an individual can make different and appropriate responses to different members of a particular collection of stimuli. The process of identifying critical attributes of an object, dealt with in more detail in Chapter 4 under 'Concepts', is an illustration of discrimination learning. When a child can distinguish between numbers, objects and phonemes, he or she has accomplished the first step in concept formation. The next step, *concept learning*, requires the individual to respond to groups of objects or events. In discrimination learning the individual would respond to each object or event and distinguish it from a similar one, but to achieve concept learning, Gagné suggests, the individual must also be capable of placing an object or event into a group. He requires the skills not only of discrimination but also of identifying attributes of a single example of a concept sufficiently to be able to classify it. It is one thing to distinguish between three similar trees, but yet another to have sufficient knowledge of the concept 'tree' to be capable of deciding whether to include or exclude an object from the concept 'tree'.

*Rule learning* consists of chaining two or more concepts. Mathematical rules, for example, enable the individual to respond to a whole range of stimuli with corresponding appropriate responses: $(a + b)^2 = a^2 + 2ab + b^2$ leads to many responses, depending on the values of $a$ and $b$. What is more, several mathematical concepts are required to understand the equation.

Finally, at the pinnacle of mental activity we have *problem-solving*, which involves higher-order rules. According to Gagné, two or more rules are combined and applied to give 'higher-order' solutions, or rules. This process still requires learning. By the selective process of setting up and testing hypotheses using various strategies (see the 'formal operations' of Piaget, or Bruner's 'strategies') and different rules known to the individual, problems are attempted and sometimes solved.

Gagné concludes:

> There are several varieties of performance types that imply different categories of learned capabilities. These varieties of performance may also be differentiated in terms of the conditions for their learning. In searching for and identifying these conditions, one must look, first, at the capabilities internal to the learner and, second, at the stimulus situation outside the learner. The learning of each type of new capability starts from a different 'point' of prior learning, and is likely also to demand a different external situation. (Gagné, 1985)

The educational implications (Gagné and Medsker 1996), provided the models are acceptable and can be shown to have practical outcomes, centre on those issues which can be manipulated by the teacher. Thus the conditions of learning, particularly the external ones, can to some extent be controlled by teachers. Planning of learning and management of the learning sessions, from both the learner's and the teacher's points of view, are central to the learning of intellectual, motor, verbal and attitudinal characteristics.

## Summary

The early part of the chapter was taken up with a theoretical discussion of the recent information-processing model of memory. Other considerations included useful information on remembering and forgetting.

For the purposes of description, the overall process of remembering is divided into three stages. These are: (a) the encoding (or acquisition) stage, in which we deliberately try to memorize material; (b) storage, which is a storage stage inferred from the fact that we can reproduce information by conscious effort; and (c) the act of retrieval (recalling) information. Emphasis was also given to the context- and subject-specific nature of memory.

Effective acquisition of knowledge is aided in a number of ways. Organization of the material to be learned, careful control of working conditions, the absence of distractions (whether physical, emotional, social or academic), dealing with meaningful rather than nonsense material, and frequent revision interspersed in the learning session are all of benefit to the learner. The most significant point arising from the discussion is that there is no *one* best method of study. Each person has to discover his or her optimum conditions for effective learning. The upsurge of texts on study methods and 'learning to learn' has given new impetus to guiding students in their efforts to improve study effectiveness.

Transfer of training was seen to be possible when the tasks involved have similarities of content or procedures of learning, where the elements to be transferred are pointed out, when the first task is thoroughly mastered and when the ability of the learner is sufficient to enable him or her to see the transferable elements.

Retention has been studied using rates of forgetting of both nonsense and meaningful material. Studies have concluded that with most topics there are marked differences in the prospects of retention, which depend on the temporal position in learning of the material. Material at the start or finish of a learning session is more likely to be retained than material learned in mid-session. But this generalization applies particularly where tasks are extensive or difficult. The manner of interspersing the learning sessions and the kind of activity which precedes or follows a learning task have a significant effect on the chances of retention and retrieval. Reminiscence effects and the phenomenon of massed and distributed practice were also discussed.

Reproducing what we have retained in our memories can be achieved in at least two ways: either by recall, in which we are required to drag information from our minds without being prompted, or by recognition, in which we are presented with clues or information from which previously learned material can be recognized. One difference between unseen written examination papers and multiple-choice items is that recall is most often employed in the former and recognition in the latter.

Some aspects of the theories expanded in the last few chapters are summarized using Gagné's 'conditions of learning' theories.

## Tutorial enquiry and discussion

(a) Read the author's paper entitled 'Some aspects of study habits in higher education' (Child 1977). A list of questions appears relating to general study, study prior to examinations, the influence of the peer group and the effect of attitudes and anxiety on study. Read through this list, see how you compare with the students reported in the research and note the pattern of study habits revealed in this research. Use the most relevant questions in the list to ask children how they study.

(b) If you were helping children of a given age and ability to develop the art and science of study, what would be the main points you would stress? How do these points differ with age and ability? Use the findings for a general discussion in tutorial.

(c) Whilst on teaching practice, discover the importance attached to, and the opportunities given for, the following as aids to learning: (i) revision; (ii) 'whole' or 'part' learning; (iii) 'massed' and 'distributed' practice; (iv) different methods in the teaching of reading or number; (v) transfer of training. Discuss the findings in tutorials.

# References

Awh, E., Jonides, J., Smith, E. E., Schumacher, E. H., Koeppe, R. A. and Katz, S. (1996), 'Dissociation of storage and rehearsal in verbal working memory', *Psychological Science*, 7, 25–31.

Baddeley, A. D. (1997), *Human Memory: Theory and Practice* (revised edn). Hove, East Sussex: Psychology Press Ltd.

Baddeley, A. D. (1999), *Essentials of Human Memory*. Hove, East Sussex: Psychology Press Ltd.

Ballard, P. B. (1913), *Oblivescence and Reminiscence*. A British Journal of Psychology Monograph.

Biggs, J. B. and Collis, K. F. (1982), *Evaluating the Quality of Learning: The SOLO taxonomy*. New York: Academic Press.

Child, D. (1966), 'Reminiscence and personality – a note on the effect of different test instructions', *British Journal of Social and Clinical Psychology*, 5, 92–4.

Child, D. (1977), 'Some aspects of study habits in higher education', in D. Child, *Readings in Psychology for the Teacher*. London: Holt, Rinehart and Winston, pp. 165–75.

Coleman, J. S. (1961), *The Adolescent Society*. New York: The Free Press.

Collins, S. C. and Kneale, P. E. (2000), *Study Skills for Psychology Students: A Practical Guide*. London: Arnold.

Colquhoun W. P. and Corcoran, D. W. J. (1964), 'The effects of time of day and social isolation on the relationship between temperament and performance', *British Journal of Social and Clinical Psychology*, 3, 226–31.

Craik, F. I. M. and Watkins, M. J. (1973), 'The role of rehearsal in short-term memory', *Journal of Verbal Learning and Verbal Behavior*, 12, 599–607.

Dale, R. R. (1954), *From School to University*. London: Routledge and Kegan Paul.

Davies, Lynn (1995), *Study Skills for Teacher Training*. London: Macmillan.

Ebbinghaus, H. (1966), *Memory* (trans. by Ruger and Bussenius). New York: Dover.

Entwistle, N. J. (1998), 'Understanding academic performance at university: A research retrospective', in D. Shorrocks-Taylor (ed.), *Directions in Educational Psychology*. London: Whurr.

Entwistle, N. J. and Ramsden, P. (1983), *Understanding Student Learning*. London: Croom Helm.

Feuerstein, R. in collaboration with Rand, Ya'acov, Hoffman, M. B. and Miller, R. (1980), *Instructional Enrichment: An Intervention Program for Cognitive Modifiability*. Baltimore: University Park Press.

Flavell, J. H. (1976), 'Metacognitive aspects of problem solving', in L. B. Resnick (ed.), *The Nature of Intelligence*. Hillsdale, NJ: Erlbaum.

Fletcher, P. C., Shallice, T. and Dolan, R. J. (1998a), 'The functional roles of the prefrontal cortex in episodic memory: I. encoding', *Brain*, 121(7), 1239–48.

Fletcher, P. C., Shallice, T., Frith, C. D., Frackowiak, R. S. and Dolan, R. J. (1998b), 'The functional roles of the prefrontal cortex in episodic memory: II. retrieval', *Brain*, 121(7), 1249–56.

Freeman, R. and Meed, J. (1993), *How to Study Effectively*. London: Collins (for the National Extension College).

Gabrieli, J. D., Brewer, J. B. and Poldrack, R. A. (1998), 'Images of medial temporal lobe functions in human learning and memory', *Neurobiology of Learning and Memory*, 20, 275–83.

Gagné, R. M. (1985), *The Conditions of Learning* (4th edn). New York: Holt, Rinehart and Winston.

Gagné, R. M., Briggs, L. J. and Wager, W. W. (1992), *Principles of Instructional Design* (4th edn). Fort Worth, TX: Harcourt Brace Jovanovich.

Gagné, R. M. and Medsker, K. (1996), *The Conditions of Learning: Training Applications*. Fort Worth, TX: Harcourt Brace College Publications.

Gathercole, S. E. and Baddeley, A. D. (1993), *Working Memory and Language*. Hove: Lawrence Erlbaum.

Goacher, B. and Reid, M. I. (1983), *School Reports to Parents*. Windsor: NFER-Nelson.

Howe, M. J. A. (1991), 'A fine idea but does it work?', *Education Section Review, British Psychological Society,* 15(2), 43–6 and 54–7. Other useful papers in this volume are by N. Entwistle, G. Gibbs, P. E. Morris, J. D. Nisbet and M. Shayer.

Joyce, C. R. B. and Hudson, L. (1968), 'Student style and teaching style: an experimental study', *British Journal of Medical Education*, 2, 28–32.

Klatzky, R. L. (1980), *Human Memory: Structures and Processes* (2nd edn). San Francisco: Freeman.

Lashley, C. (1995), *Improving Study Skills: A Competence Approach*, London: Cassell.

Loftus, E. F. and Loftus, G. R. (1980), 'On the permanence of stored information in the human brain', *American Psychologist*, 35, 409–20.

Luh, C. W. (1922), 'The conditions of retention', *Psychology Monograph*, 31.

Maddox, H. (1963), *How to Study*. London: Pan.

Marton, F. and Säljö, S. (1976), 'On qualitative differences in learning 1: outcome and process', *British Journal Educational Psychology*, 46, 4–11.

Maylor, E. A. (1996), 'Older people's memory for the past and the future', *Psychologist*, 9, 456–9.

Miller, G. A. (1956), 'The magical number seven, plus or minus two: some limits in our capacity for processing information', *Psychological Review*, 63, 81–97 (or 'the $7 \pm 2$ paper').

Morris, P. E. (1988), 'Memory research: past mistakes and future prospects', in G. Claxton (ed.), *Growth Points in Cognition*. London: Routledge, pp. 91–110.

Murdock, B. B. (1962), 'The serial position effect of free recall', *Journal of Experimental Psychology*, 64, 482–8.

Neisser, U. (1976), *Cognition and Reality: Principles and Implications of Cognitive Psychology*. San Francisco: Freeman.

Nisbet, J. D. and Shucksmith, J. (1986), *Learning Strategies*. London: Routledge and Kegan Paul.

Northedge, A. (2005), *The Good Study Guide*. Milton Keynes: Open University.

O'Connor, K. (1968), *Learning: An Introduction*. London: Macmillan.

Paivio, A. (1971), *Imagery and Verbal Processes*. New York: Holt, Rinehart and Winston.

Paulesu, E., Frith, C. D. and Frackowiak, R. S. (1993), 'The neural correlates of the verbal component of working memory', *Nature*, 362, 342–4.

Sanford, N. (ed.) (1962), *The American College*. New York: Wiley.

Shallice, T. (1988), *From Neuropsychology to Mental Structure*. Cambridge: Cambridge University Press.

Shallice, T., Fletcher, P. C., Frith, C. D., Grasby, P., Frackowiak, R. S. and Dolan, R. J. (1994), 'Brain regions associated with acquisition and retrieval of verbal episodic memory', *Nature*, 368, 633–5.

Smith, E. E., Nolen-Hoeksema, S., Frederickson, B. L., Loftus, G. R., Bem, D. J. and Maren, S. (2003), *Atkinson and Hilgard's Introduction to Psychology* (14th edn). Belmont, CA: Wadsworth/Thomson.

Sperling, G. (1960), 'The information available in brief visual presentations', *Psychological Monographs*, 498.

Squire, L. R. (1992), 'Declarative and non-declarative memory: multiple brain systems supporting learning and memory', *Journal of Cognitive Neuroscience*, 4, 232–43.

Squire, L. R., Knowlton, B. and Musen, G. (1993), 'The structure and organisation of memory', *Annual Review of Psychology*, 44, 453–95.

Squire, L. R., Ojemann, J. G., Miezin, F. M., Petersen, S. E., Videen, T. O. and Raichle, M. E. (1992), 'Activation of the hippocampus in normal humans: a functional anatomical study of memory', *Proceedings of the NAS*, 89, 1837–41.

Squire, L. R., Zola-Morgan, S., Cave, C. B., Haist, F., Musen, G. and Suzuki, W. A. (1990), 'Memory: Organization of Brain Systems and Cognition' in 'A Symposium on Quantitative Biology', *The Brain*, 55, New York: Cold Spring Harbor Laboratory.

Underwood, B. J. (March 1964), *Forgetting* (reprint from Scientific American).

## Further reading

Baddeley, A. D. (1997), *Human Memory: Theory and Practice* (revised edn). Hove, East Sussex: Psychology Press Ltd.

Baddeley, A. D. (1999), *Essentials of Human Memory*. Hove, East Sussex: Psychology Press Ltd. The title was *Your Memory: A User's Guide*.

Bristow, J., Cowley, P. and Daines, B. (1999), *Memory and Learning: A Practical Guide for Teachers*. London: David Fulton Publishers.

Northedge, A. (2005), *The Good Study Guide*. Milton Keynes: Open University.

Rose, S. (1993), *The Making of Memory*. London: Bantam. Useful for the neurological advances.

## Useful websites

http://slc.otago.ac.nz. There is a particularly useful section on study skills for students.

# Human Motivation

## Chapter Outline

## Implications for teachers

- A knowledge of what motivates children to learn is crucial for a teacher.
- Critical or sensitive periods in childhood could be important in the education of young children.
- Identifying sources of difficulty in motivation when these influence performance at school is important.
- A study of children's extrinsic and intrinsic motivators is a key to unlocking the doors of successful teaching.
- Managing stress for both teachers and pupils is vital to their performance.

The increased complexity of living in our society has made it necessary to cultivate in the young the will to acquire many varied cognitive as well as physical skills. In fact, schools are created as artificial arrangements in which we require our children to carry out all kinds of activities which, for many of them, would not have been a significant part of their young lives and which would certainly not have occurred to them spontaneously. Left to themselves, the majority of children would not learn to read or pore over arithmetic problems without prompting from adults. Those teachers who have taken a bewildered group of little ones in reception class, fresh from the security of home to the uncertainty and properness of the school setting, or have taught a class of school-leavers, with their minds on worldly things, will know all about the problems of prompting the young. A study of motivation, therefore, is crucial for a teacher. Without a knowledge of the ways and means of encouraging children's learning, knowing about their 'appetites' in the widest sense of the word, being sensitive to their interests, the teacher's task would be impossible. For this purpose, most teachers place an understanding of motivation very high on their list of priorities.

A working definition of *motivation* would be that it *consists of internal processes and external incentives which spur us on to satisfy some need.* We shall return to examine some of these 'processes' and 'needs' shortly, but first it is necessary to look at some of the broader issues. In some cases we may be fully aware of a particular need and our actions will be quite deliberate in attempting to satisfy it. Hunger has fairly obvious symptoms and well-tried cures. A hungry child eats food in the full knowledge that this will relieve the feeling of hunger. On the other hand, we may be oblivious of the underlying motives when we say, undertake a course of training to enter the teaching profession. The analysis of those motives which drive us to engage in such complicated activities embodied in a course of training is very difficult. Simpler creatures with a limited span of behaviour for detecting and imbibing food or reproducing their own kind have fairly inflexible and obviously essential mechanisms for their survival. As we pass through the animal kingdom to *Homo sapiens* we find that layers of cultural influences on our behaviour obscure the origins of our motives. Satisfaction of basic body requirements such as food, air and water is still essential, but it gives way to, or is possibly built into, an intricate network of other activities designed to satisfy acquired needs within the 'rules' laid down by a society.

Incentives may have a direct effect in motivating us, as when we see or smell food. Messages are relayed to the hypothalamus and the resulting chemical changes make us 'feel' hungry. Other incentives are learnt, as we shall see presently.

The internal processes cannot be observed directly. Therefore, we guess or *infer* that they must exist from the behaviour we observe or experience. What people do can be observed; why they do it is still a matter for speculation.

# Motivation theories

Theorists in the study of motivation have generally concerned themselves with four basic questions representing stages in the processes assumed to be present in motivated behaviour. They are: what initiates action, what direction does such action take and why, how 'strong' is the action and why does action terminate? By 'action' is meant not only obvious movement, but also mental action: you can solve a problem in your head without appearing to do so. Detailed discussion of the speculations each major theorist has made in an attempt to answer these questions would not be profitable. Instead, we shall select from them those aspects which seem to hold out most hope and worth for the teacher. However, to place the development of these theories in perspective, it is worthwhile to spend a few lines indicating the most prominent views which have survived.

In trying to answer the questions posed above, several themes, which reappear throughout psychology, are in evidence (Weiner 1992). Is the *source* of action inborn (*biogenic* – having origins in inherent biological processes), acquired (*sociogenic* – having origins in social processes), a mixture of both or irrelevant (Skinner 1953, 1971)? Is the stimulus which 'taps' the source internal (*intrinsic*) and/or external (*extrinsic*)? Is all human behaviour motivated by a stimulus (humans are seen as passive agents responding to biological or social stimulation) or are some actions performed for their own sake (exploration or play, in which humans are active agents spontaneously sampling the environment)?

There have been three broad lines of development during the last century: *instinct, drive and need* and *cognitive* theories.

## Instinct theories

Prior to the eighteenth century it was generally held that humans exercised complete control over their actions. As rational creatures they had the power to direct, redirect or inhibit their passions at will. These ideas were bound up with the early philosophies relating to religion and morals. Humans were seen as pleasure-seeking, pain-avoiding creatures (*hedonistic* outlook). Animals, on the contrary, were activated by instinctive mechanisms which gave rise to fixed ways of satisfying animal needs. Darwin's *Origin of Species* (1859) thus came as a nasty shock to those who thought that humans and animals were completely unalike in their motives.

McDougall (1960, written in 1908) saw the arguments of Darwin as confirmation of his 'hormic' or *instinct theory*, which postulated that the actions of humans, as well as those of the animals to which humans are related, were the outcome of inborn *instincts* – innate, unlearned tendencies 'which are essential springs or motive power of all thought and action'. According to this theory, instincts have survival value for both the individual and the race:

# 228 Psychology and the Teacher
for example, gregariousness leads us to want to be with our own species and aggression drives us to preserve ourselves.

## Further reading

McDougall posited 14 such human instincts, some with a corresponding 'sentiment' (in brackets), which was the emotional disposition characteristic of individuals arising from their particular experience and training in coping with each instinct. Those instincts such as food-seeking and gregariousness have no obvious corresponding sentiments. Here are some: food and water seeking, gregariousness, acquisitiveness, constructive, aggression (anger), mating (sexual desire), curiosity (wonder), self-assertion (elation), maternal (tenderness), repulsion (disgust), escape (fear), self-abasement (submission).

The idea that humans, like animals, were born to fixed patterns of behaviour was widely attacked and McDougall modified his view by suggesting that humans were endowed with *propensities* rather than with animal instincts. Burt (1941) defined a propensity as a:

complex inherited tendency, common to all members of a species, impelling each individual:
(a) to perceive and pay attention to certain objects and situations; (b) to become pleasurably or unpleasurably excited about those objects whenever they are perceived; (c) thereupon to act in a way likely in the long run to preserve the individual by so acting.

## Social anthropology and instincts

The theory in its original form has very little support nowadays. Only the simplest reflexes of humans appear to be invariable in nature. Vernon (1942) was amongst many who had harsh things to say about human behaviour having its beginnings in inborn rituals of survival value. The main argument against the instinct theory was that human beings do not display stereotyped patterns of unlearned behaviour. One need only contrast the rigid antics apparent when a baby bird is being fed by its mother, or the courtship rites of many species of birds and animals, with similar events in humans to realize how unlike an instinctual drive our behaviour is.

Support for this stems from the work of social anthropologists, who claim that the supposed instincts of aggression, acquisition and sex vary considerably from tribe to tribe.

## Further reading

The much quoted work of Mead, 1935, showed major differences in child-rearing practices which led to obvious differences in the characteristics of the tribes. The Arapesh of New Guinea, we are told, were peace-loving and not particularly interested in taking on the roles of leadership.

$\longrightarrow$

Children were reared with great tenderness, given every attention and suckled at the breast for as long as the mother could hold out. The Mundugumour were aggressive, warlike and ruthless, and their babyhood likewise was made into a struggle between parent and child. Babies had to fight for the breasts for the short time they were available, and were starved of affection and handled roughly, if rarely. One is left wondering how much of the adult characteristics are the outcome of direct teaching from the parents, not so much as a baby, but later when the child could begin to understand the language and learn the tribal mores. Again, the fertility or hostility of the environment, which was easy for the Arapesh and harsh for the Mundugumour, may have determined the particular traits which would assist the tribes to survive. Thus, the question of whether we are dealing here with inherited or acquired characteristics is wide open. See also R. Benedict, *Patterns of Culture*, 1935.

Again, our motives become so overlaid with secondary and acquired desires that it makes the theory of inherited tendencies impossible to validate. Allport (1937) recognized this and coined the phrase 'functional autonomy' to describe the acquisition of new motives derived from more fundamental motives which ultimately become independent of the latter. Drug-taking, smoking or developing professional attitudes (high standards of craftsmanship) are examples of activities which continue to give satisfaction long after they have become divorced from the initial starting motive.

## Ethology – animal behaviour in natural environments

A revival of the concept of instinct as applied to humans has been brought about by the work of Lorenz and Tinbergen (for introductions, see Lorenz 1966 and 1981, Lea 1984 and Archer 1992), two famous *ethologists* (students of animal behaviour in natural surroundings). Their main contention is that humans, being biological organisms and subject to evolutionary development like the rest of the animal kingdom, are possessed of instinctive urges which, if studied, would give a sound scientific basis to human behaviour. They would argue that certain crimes, for example, are the result of individuals trying to satisfy basic needs in ways not accepted by the society in which the crimes were committed.

### Further reading

*Xenophobia*, or the hatred existing between human races, is a much-used term these days. There is a good analysis by Robert Ardrey, in *The Territorial Imperative*, 1967, as an example of an inborn biological tendency akin to the animal's desire to protect its territory against predators. We are said to dislike foreigners because they constitute a threat to survival or to our way of life.

Desmond Morris will be well known to many readers. He has written a number of popular books on the subject of human and animal behaviour from an ethological perspective. Several have appeared on TV followed by a book. He is firmly convinced that we are animals first and

$\longrightarrow$

last. He says 'we prefer to think of ourselves as fallen angels but in reality we are risen apes... Everything we do has an inborn, genetic basis and all our activities have something in common with other species.' His first successful books were *The Naked Ape* (1988), *The Human Zoo* (1971) and *Manwatching* (1977). More recently he has written *Bodywatching: A Guide to the Human Species*, 1985, *Babywatching*, 1991 and *The Human Animal: A Personal View of the Human Species*, 1994.

Two concepts central to their work are the *sign* or *environment stimulus* and the *innate release mechanism* (IRM). Largely by analogy from animal studies, Lorenz considers that humans have a parental instinct which can be released by various cues. The sight of a doll (environmental sign stimulus) elicits parental behaviour in female children (innate release mechanism). The pattern of stimulation which brings about the release of instinctive parental responses is thought by Lorenz to consist of the doll's short face, large forehead, chubby cheeks and disjunctive limb movements. This is reminiscent of Burt's definition of innate propensities mentioned earlier in the chapter. Tinbergen thinks that, at the very least, patterns of locomotion, sexual behaviour, sleep, food-seeking, care of the body surface and parenthood are instinctive in humans. Lorenz would add social and aggressive drives to this list. The IRM is seen as an innate tendency to carry through a sequence of actions triggered off by some external or internal stimulus.

The key to a creature's springs of action, according to ethologists, relates to these IRMs. The mating habits of animals have frequently been studied as illustrating IRM. Male sticklebacks have a regular cycle of behaviour consisting of territory isolation, building a nest, seeking out a mate by courting rituals, mating, fanning fresh water over the fertilized eggs in the nest and keeping watch over the territory. The satisfactory completion of one stage in the cycle seems to herald the start of the next stage and we have a hierarchy of behaviour organization in which progress through the sequence depends on ordered emergence and completion of each stage. Sticklebacks and gulls seem a far cry from human learning, but human ethologists suggest that we too have IRMs from birth. However, they differ in their greater susceptibility to change.

One further idea which may have some application in human learning is animal *imprinting and critical periods* (see later in the chapter for a discussion of critical and sensitive periods). It would seem that many animals become attached to objects other than parents soon after birth, if those objects are seen first. Birds have become attached to humans who were the only living things present at hatching. This special social attachment is termed *imprinting*, and the time at which imprinting is keenest is known as the critical period. Imprinting occurs in many species of bird and animal, including monkeys. However, imprinting from the first objects seen at birth is prevalent only in those species, such as birds, which are well developed at birth. The evidence in higher animals is less clear because of the masking effect of child-rearing processes.

Two useful concepts expounded by Tinbergen arise from his distinction between *appetitive* and *consummatory activity*. The former involves all those activities which take place in the search for a goal (food, mate) and the latter takes place when the goal is reached (eating, courting or mating).

Morris (1977) makes a powerful case for thinking that many non-verbal actions are inborn and that much information can be read into these actions. For the teacher, non-verbal cues in the classroom are an important source of ideas about children and it should pay to do further reading. The topic of non-verbal communication has been mentioned in Chapter 5.

The theory of personality expounded by Freud (1915) is referred to as a *psychoanalytical* (*depth psychology* or *psychodynamic*) theory, but it also contains references to instinctual drives. Indeed, Freud's theory is as much a theory of motivation (what drives us to behave as we do) as of personality. In Freud's later theorizing (1920) he gave these drives the striking Greek titles of Eros and Thanatos, or the *life* and *death* instincts. The life instincts include sexual instincts (*libido* instincts), required for reproducing the species, and self-preservation instincts, relating to hunger and thirst, which are required for life preservation and maintenance (*ego* instincts). Of the death instincts, only one was defined specifically by Freud – the aggressive, destructive instinct. For a fuller discussion of Freudian and similar views, the student should read the relevant part of Chapter 12 where a number of criticisms are also considered. For the moment, it is sufficient to note how Freud attempts to account for the source and direction of our motivation.

## Drive and need theories

The problem with instinct theory was that the arguments became circular and tied to inherited qualities. Anything humans did routinely was seen as a possible instinct, and the list grew to 6,000 in the 1920s. By concentrating on the innateness of instincts, psychologists created a problem when it came to connecting them with physiological functions of the body.

In the 1930s, Cannon (1932) introduced the concept of *homeostasis* (mentioned in Chapter 2) to represent the process by which the body attempts to regulate and protect the balance of physiochemistry in the tissues (food, water, oxygen, temperature of the body). Thus the body is 'driven' into action to correct any imbalance between the internal and external environment. The *drive* is seen as the source of motivation resulting from homeostatic disequilibrium. Hull (1943) in the 1940s developed the notion of psychological drives arising from basic physiological needs and equated these by the process of homeostasis. The drives are classified as *primary* and *secondary*. Primary drives are those immediately necessary for bodily survival (e.g. hunger, thirst, sexual behaviour). Secondary (or acquired) drives appear as by-products of the satisfaction of primary needs (for a clear summary see Hill 2002). Drive stimuli such as fear, money or tokens (cf. token economies in behaviour modification,

Chapter 14) are examples of secondary drives. Hull also suggested that, as drives are reduced when a goal is reached, the consequent drive reduction is said to be 'rewarding' and habits are established.

The appeal of drive theory is its obvious correlation with physiological functions of the body. In Chapter 2 we showed some recent research which strongly suggests that parts of the brain, for example the hypothalamus and the limbic system, have a crucial role in controlling the body's early warning system of chemical shortages normally found in food and water. Sections of the hypothalamus are localized into 'appestat' centres, i.e. control of the body's appetitive needs within survival limits. Centres discovered so far are hunger, thirst, sex, temperature, aggression and a 'pleasure' site.

The limbic system, located at the top of the brain stem, is one of several brain structures which form part of the reward system. The neurotransmitter (see Chapter 2) dopamine is activated by any of the satiating substances in food and drink. Interestingly, it can also be activated by a number of drugs such as opiates and alcohol. As stimulation by drugs is rewarding, humans want to repeat the process and addiction follows in some cases.

Since these early researches much time and effort has been expended in both speculating about and deriving primary and secondary drives. Murray and Cattell are amongst the most prominent to have derived models of motivational structure and deserve particular mention because their views have had some influence on psychological thinking in education.

## Physiological and social needs

Murray (1938) speculated about two broad groups of human needs, *viscerogenic* and *psychogenic*. The viscerogenic are the physiological survival needs mentioned previously. But the importance of Murray's contribution lies in the psychogenic needs (or social motives), which, as we shall see, have had a marked influence on contemporary thinking. Twenty psychogenic needs were postulated, of which the need for achievement (n Ach), the need for affiliation (n Aff), the need for aggression (n Agg) and the needs for dominance (n Dom), play (n Play) and understanding (n Und) are, perhaps, the most widely used. These needs are said to be learned and culture-specific. The term '*need*' is used by Murray in a particular way, meaning a tension or force that affects perception and action in such a way as to try to alter an existing unsatisfactory or unsatisfied situation. We are reminded here of Cannon's homeostatic imbalance.

Needs can be activated either by internal or, most commonly, by external stimuli. Arousal resulting from disequilibrium exerts a stimulating force referred to as 'press'. Thus, seeing another person being bullied is a press which brings out the need for aggression (or harm-avoidance). An attractive career may be a press for n Ach. Also, social motives are now widely accepted (e.g., n Aff, or need for nurturance (aid the helpless) or need for succurance (to seek help)). Some of the *culture-pattern* and *field* theories which have sprung into being in the past 70 years emphasize the influences of social pressures and patterns of culture on the developing child. The work of social anthropologists has already been mentioned above.

Their concern is the effect that culture patterns might have on the rearing of children and the subsequent behaviour patterns which arise from these motivational precursors.

A more recent need–drive theory involving traits was compiled by Cattell. In his seminal *dynamic trait theory of motivation*, he postulated a framework of interdependent factors called the dynamic lattice, using a technique known as factor analysis (Child 2006). Starting from a large number of measures by which human attitudes could be assessed (*devices*), he produced two basic motivational influences. One he called *ergs* – innate sources of reactivity to human needs such as food-seeking, mating, gregariousness, fear, self-assertion, narcissism (self-care), pugnacity and acquisitiveness. Note that the needs included in this list are both viscerogenic and psychogenic in Murray's terms: they go well beyond the physiological needs. The other influence he termed *sentiments* – acquired sources of reactivity to persons, objects and social institutions. Examples of sentiments already discussed are self-sentiment (the desire to maintain a favourable image in the eyes of oneself and significant others, and comparable with the 'self' concept), superego (rule-abiding and maintaining a 'moral' reputation), career, boy- or girl-friend/spouse, parental home, religion and sport. Developments in and applications to education indicate that self-sentiment, superego and a high, positive sentiment (attitude) to school correlate with achievement in school subjects (Child 1984).

---

### Further reading

To get an idea of Cattell's theory of motivation, Chapters 1 and 2 of Cattell and Child, 1975 should prove sufficient. For applications in education see Chapter 8 in the same book. For an assessment of these applications in education, see Child 1988 (pp. 81–92) and 1984.

---

## *Critical and sensitive periods – physical, psychological and social contexts*

There is evidence that animals require appropriate sensory and motor stimulation at specific times in order for the brain to develop normally. These specific times are referred to as *critical periods*. The need for sensory stimulation at particular times seems to apply to social as well as physical development.

Applied to the physical development of animals there is some support from neurological research. For example, Wiesel and Hubel (1965) covered one eye of kittens and cats so that they could not see with that eye for about three months. The kittens had permanent visual impairment; the cats did not have any impairment. It appears that whilst neural connections were being made and strengthened in the visual system of the kittens, stimulation was essential. The degree of impairment (including blindness) depended on when and for how long the deprivation occurred. With the cats the connections had already been made.

With language acquisition, the position is more complex. Children born deaf, but not identified for some time after birth, display language problems. Fortunately, if these are identified soon enough, some compensation is possible. In Chapter 5 we saw that pronunciation in the mother tongue is best established in the womb and the first year of life. Thereafter, pronunciation becomes increasingly difficult. These and other findings have led neuroscientists to prefer the term *sensitive period*. By this they wish to imply that there is flexibility in the length and timing of the period over which we need to receive sensory stimulation for normal development and that even after deprivation there can be some compensation.

Dame Marie Clay has exploited the notion of sensitive periods in language acquisition in her work on reading recovery. She believes that early detection (about six years of age) and cure of reading difficulties are essential for any lasting effects to take place (see Chapter 5 for more detail and references to Clay's work).

Sensitive periods in parental fixation at birth was illustrated earlier in the chapter from the work by ethologists such as Lorenz and Tinbergen. In social development, the researches of Harlow (Harlow and Harlow 1973) are significant. In these investigations newly born monkeys were placed with two substitute (or 'surrogate') mothers. They were not live mothers but were made of wire and cloth. One was kept as a plain wire shape with a feeding bottle protruding at the front, whilst the other was surrounded by a soft material, though without a feeder. The young ones always preferred cloth surrogate mothers and would even cling to the cloth while reaching across to the wire model for milk. When frightened, the babies would leap onto the cloth rather than the wire surrogate. This response is said to give 'contact comfort', which Harlow and his co-workers believe to be an essential basic need of young animals, including human babies. There was some evidence of a critical period between roughly the 30th and 90th days after birth, when attachment became strong and security firm. Another important observation was the distorted emotional development of monkeys raised in wire cages or with wire mothers. The monkeys tended to be: (a) lacking in affection; (b) lacking a will to cooperate; (c) aggressive; (d) deficient in sexual responses to other monkeys.

The basic idea that animal and human young need a strong association with someone, usually a parent, is a source of much research under the heading of *attachment* (originated by Bowlby, 1973). Studies with human babies show several distinct patterns of behaviour when deprived of the focus of attachment (see Ainsworth *et al.* 1978, Main and Cassidy 1988).

## Cognitive theories

The two previous groups of theories, instinct and need–drive, place considerable emphasis on human beings as passive agents, pawns in nature's grand plan for the survival of the fittest. While some theorists acknowledge the role of secondary needs, which to some extent are under the control of the individual, essentially they are regarded as linked to the primary needs, which are rarely in one's consciousness (e.g. we don't sit down to a meal concentrating on the need to nourish the body tissues).

Cognitive theorists hold that the intervention of human thinking has a substantial influence on our motivations (hence *cognitive* theories). A person's awareness of what is happening to him or her has an important effect on future behaviour in similar situations. Perceiving, interpreting, selecting, storing and using information from the environment are crucial processes which affect our present and future motivation. In fact, this view has a lot in common with the field of information processing (Johnson-Laird 1988). Thus environmental information is perceived and processed in such a way as to have an impact on future parallel events.

As an illustration of the way our reaction to an event could be tempered by previous experience and our present perceptions, take a question-and-answer session in class. A particular child's willingness to respond (stressing that humans have a choice and do not simply react mechanically) will depend on many experiential and circumstantial factors. For example, what has happened previously when answering a particular teacher, how difficult the questions are, how other children view those who are willing to answer questions, and so on. It will be observed that the influences quoted here are environmental/social.

## Social cognition

Rotter (1954 and 1966) expounded one advanced social cognitive theory. Three basic concepts are *behaviour potential, expectancy* and *reinforcement value*. Behaviour potential is the likelihood that a person will respond in a given situation in order to receive reinforcement. This likelihood of a person reacting in a given setting will depend on that person's expectation of a reward, that is, reinforcement, and the value that person places on the reward. The expectations are that certain kinds of action (*behaviours*) will give rise to corresponding outcomes which will reward (or punish). The likelihood of a pupil completing homework set in a lesson will depend, in part, on how much the pupil values the rewards which accrue from completing it, for example, mastering the work, praise from the teacher, achieving a good grade, learning for some future important exam, pleasing parents who value work at home, etc.

Another concept of *locus of control* by Rotter (1954 and 1966) has been developed in recent years. A person grows to believe that his or her own actions will bring about reinforcements he or she value most. This is referred to as *internal control*. Examples of internally controlling factors are personal competence and effort. The logic of this statement is self-evident: a person who is competent at something (e.g. mathematics) and likes doing it is most likely to succeed by his or her own efforts and be reinforced – and knows it! *External control*, that is, reinforcement which is beyond the control of an individual, is exemplified by luck or by the difficulty of the task. These are not within the control of an individual. We shall see later an illustration of how locus of control has been developed into a systematic motivational view which can be applied to educational settings (Weiner 1977).

This approach must not be confused with Skinner's behaviourist view, which also highlights the influence of the environment as a source of stimulation and reinforcement. Although Rotter uses terms familiar to behaviourists (extinction, reinforcement), the fundamental distinction between Rotter and Skinner lies in Rotter's emphasis on a situation having *meaning* for a person in order to initiate and guide subsequent behaviour, that is, he introduces elements of conscious control (see also reference to Brewer (1972) in Chapter 6). For Skinner this excursion into consciousness is irrelevant.

A line of argument presented by some cognitive psychologists suggests that activity by humans need not be the result of a stimulus (homeostatic need, pain, external incentive, etc.). Berlyne (1960) refers to *ludic* behaviour (actively seeking out particular kinds of external stimulation or images and thoughts without first having received a stimulus). Curiosity, exploratory behaviour and play have been used synonymously with the term. McV. Hunt (1960) also rejects the idea that 'all behaviour is motivated and organisms become inactive unless stimulated by homeostatic need or painful stimulation or conditional stimuli'. He prefers to think of organisms as 'open systems of energy exchange which exhibit activity intrinsically and upon which stimuli have a modulating effect, but not an initiating effect'. The evidence for this is quite convincing, and it has led several psychologists to the conclusion that, even when a person is entirely satisfied (in terms of primary and secondary needs), there is still a desire to be active and explore. Knowledge of one's environment is sought for its own sake.

## Cognitive dissonance

One further concept espoused by cognitive theorists is the notion of *cognitive imbalance* or *dissonance*. In fact, this idea of imbalance runs throughout psychology in one form or another. Earlier we discussed homeostasis (physiochemical imbalance); Piaget uses the term 'equilibration'; Bruner speaks of 'mismatch'. Cognitive dissonance, a theory developed by Festinger (1957), involves the creation of tension when we have two or more psychologically incongruous events (beliefs, attitudes, etc.). Festinger's basic theme is concerned with the motivational value of tension which accompanies 'dissonance'. Dissonance, according to Festinger, occurs when we are aware of differences between the related 'elements' in a situation. If a child who regularly does well in the school football team has a bad day, dissonance arises because of the incongruity between previous experience and present performance. The tension arising from the dissonance may be dissipated in a number of ways. If the footballer has an injury, is feeling ill or has another problem on his mind, these may be used to disperse the tension. Festinger's central hypotheses are (i) that dissonance is psychologically uncomfortable and therefore will motivate individuals to reduce the dissonance, and (ii) when dissonance is in evidence, individuals will do all they can to avoid meeting information which is likely to increase the dissonance.

## Common ground between theories

Whilst there is controversy between psychologists who have made a study of motivation, it is possible to see some common elements in their theories (Evans 1989). As a background to our understanding of a possible sequence of events which might occur when a person is motivated to action, the following simple diagram is offered which attempts to draw together the less controversial aspects of the theories:

$$
\left.\begin{array}{l}
\text{instinct} \\
\text{need} \\
\text{dissonance}
\end{array}\right\} \rightarrow \text{drive} \rightarrow \text{activity} \rightarrow \underset{\text{(or conflict)}}{\text{satisfaction}} \rightarrow \text{drive reduction}
$$

$$\longleftarrow \text{learning occurs} \longrightarrow$$

The source, whether it be called an instinct, need or whatever, is assumed to give rise to tension, which drives an organism to action in an attempt to reduce the tension. Successful tension reduction is clearly an event which is likely to be remembered, and so learning takes place.

To illustrate a successful sequence, take an example of modelling in the classroom. We all *need* to explore and manipulate our environment whether for curiosity or to satisfy some other need. Few but the senile and ill can sit motionless and uninterested for long. If you distribute modelling clay to a class of seven-year-olds there will be few who do not take up the challenge to shape the clay. Most children enjoy this kind of manipulation (for many reasons) and feel a *drive* to construction, destruction or *ludic* (i.e. play) *activity* with the material. *Satisfactions* appear when a recognizable shape emerges, when the teacher shows approval or just from the feel of the material. The challenge does not last indefinitely. The initial desire to model wanes (again for many reasons) and we might conclude that the *drive* has been *reduced*.

The likelihood of the cycle of events being repeated is high when there is success and satisfaction. Where drive is not reduced we frequently have conflict. Where a child has produced a useful, attractive or personally satisfying object, *reinforcement* of the sequence is possible, for example when the child's need for social approval is fulfilled when the teacher or the other children praise the finished article.

Successful sequences lead to learning. Manipulative and perceptual skills in this case are encouraged. But learning also occurs from unsuccessful sequences, even if one learns not to repeat the task because it gives little satisfaction. Children soon learn that some kinds of activity also lead directly to disapproval. In this event the sequence will be inhibited, a process known as *extinction*. The teacher's task is to find alternative sequences to arrive at satisfying and educative ends. Whatever the teacher's objective might be, whether it is the improvement of manipulative, perceptual or learning skills, routes must be found which offer the chance of satisfaction and need reduction in order to facilitate positive learning. Punishment, while necessary in certain circumstances, often has the effect of cutting short a sequence without replacing it with an alternative, acceptable sequence.

Activity, satisfaction and drive reduction are treated together because they are important to learning. When a sufficient level of arousal is reached, mobilization of the body or mind takes place. The resulting activity is referred to by some as *goal-seeking behaviour*. Thus the internal demands of drive states impel the individual to seek a means of gratification. The body need not move, since the arousal might be connected with the solution of a mathematical problem requiring no more than an alert mind. Reading a book to acquire knowledge is another case of covert activity. 'Goal-seeking' assumes that a direction is clearly defined by the teacher and clearly understood by the pupils. The teacher's function is to provide the direction, and much of his or her scheming in lesson preparation hinges on devising ways in which children will acquire knowledge. Badly organized goal-seeking and goal-planning might have disastrous effects on children's morale. 'Discovery' techniques, if poorly devised, can produce frustrated children with no idea of what they are intended to discover, busy pooling their combined ignorance (class participation in which the teacher plays no part) and often feeling needlessly insecure on such open-ended paths to the acquisition of knowledge. Drive reduction may, unfortunately, be attained by alternative and less acceptable forms of activity where children become desperate.

# Motivation applied in education

The relevance of most theories of motivation, especially those involving complex inherited instincts and needs, is so obscured by the detailed realities of life that it is impossible to apply them directly. A knowledge of the idea of primary needs is background, rather than foreground, information. Students of motivation have tried, with little success, to derive links between the fundamental postulated requirements necessary for survival and the day-to-day behaviour of, say, a pupil in a classroom. Therefore the trend in recent years has been to build up models of motivation which are situation-specific. Thus we now find a greater insistence on patently obvious concerns such as the prepotency of needs in creating conducive classroom learning environments, the need for achievement and affiliation among schoolchildren, success and failure and their causes as sources of motivation, and academic motivation measures.

In trying to apply the foregoing we must be careful to distinguish between those aspects of theory which provide coherent background, and within which one might try to place broader observations about human behaviour, and those other aspects of theory which start with a pupil, classroom or school as a particular case having particular motivational problems. Sufficient has been said about theories and models of motivation to convince the reader that many assumptions have to be made in attempting to give meaning to our observations in both the description and the explanation. Peters (1958), a philosopher, has little to say in favour of all-inclusive theories. Like many teachers, he feels that we should classify the *goals* of human beings if we want to make their actions intelligible. For the teacher, the external, situational and easily manipulated factors of human motivation are of primary concern. Although he lays emphasis on providing for an examination of human motivation by starting with the classification of people's observable goals and, as it were, working back, Peters does see a place for causal theories, particularly in looking at devious cases.

In the following pages we will explore some of the topics found to be of significance in classroom practice from the point of view of *outcomes* rather than their *origins*. In two practically oriented books on motivation by Pintrich and Schunk (2002), and Ball (1977), a number of the following topics are dealt with in greater depth.

## A pragmatic view of needs: Maslow's hierarchy

A model which appeals to teachers because of its common sense is that expounded by Maslow (1970). His description of human motivation derives from his own psychoanalytic research and that of others. He postulates certain *basic* human needs and arranges them in an order, a hierarchy, the needs becoming more 'human' as one proceeds through them. The hierarchy is shown in Figure 8.1 as a pyramid. Maslow distinguishes the basic needs in order of their importance and therefore prepotence, so physiological deficiencies must be satisfied before we attend to safety needs. The pyramid shape is used not only to demonstrate the hierarchical arrangement but also to show the broad base of physiological and safety factors necessary before other possible needs are likely to be considered. Progress through the hierarchy is more likely as more important needs are satisfied. Obviously, these levels are

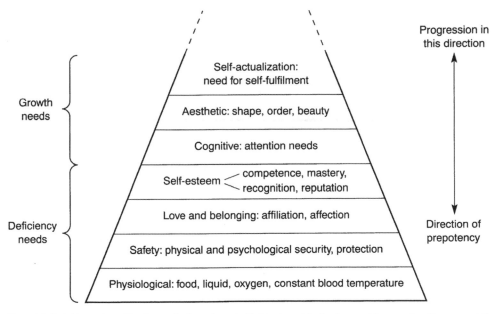

**Figure 8.1** A hierarchy of basic needs. Based on A. H. Maslow, *Motivation and Personality*, Harper and Row, New York, 1970 (2nd edn).

not exclusive. Food-seeking in primitive tribes when food is scarce would be accompanied by some regard for body safety, although probably greater risks would be taken when physiological drives were strong.

Sexual behaviour – courtship, mating, parenthood – is not classified as a physiological need because the urges do not arise from homeostatic imbalance in the same way as food or oxygen deficiency. The behaviour has more to do with species survival than with personal survival. A corollary of this is that humans in extreme hardship, for example in prisoner-of-war camps during the Second World War, experience atrophy of the sex organs and consequently have no desire for sexual or social behaviour. Healthy, hungry humans think of little else but food: all the human capacities, such as intelligence, memory and dreams, are put to work in trying to seek psychological as well as physiological comfort (Minnesota Starvation Studies, Keys, 1952).

---

### Further reading

Planarians, small, simple creatures very low in the animal kingdom absorb their reproductive organs back into the body tissue when there is no food. It almost seems as though reproduction is taken as being pointless when basic body needs cannot be satisfied. There is no purpose in bringing young into the world if they cannot be fed. But this would endow the planarian with the ability for conscious control, where in fact the absorption of the reproductive organs is entirely physiological.

Women suffering from *Anorexia nervosa*, a disease where patients develop an obsession to starve themselves in order to become slimmer, cease to menstruate. In both sexes there is increased impotence.

In the Minnesota Starvation Studies, 26 normal men were put on a six-month semi-starvation diet. In all other respects, such as living quarters, social life and exercise, their provisions were normal. All were soon preoccupied with food. A few extreme cases displayed serious mental disorders (Keys 1952).

---

Once the organic needs are satisfied, 'higher' needs emerge to be satisfied. The safety needs, that is, protection from potentially threatening objects, situations or illness, come to the fore. Children are especially susceptible to unfamiliar surroundings. They seek refuge in routines because too much open-ended and ambiguous experience may constitute a threat to their safety. Maslow suggests that one indication of children's need for safety is their preference for some kind of undisrupted routine or rhythm in life.

Tolerance to ambiguity may be an acquired characteristic depending for its quality and extent on child-rearing and childhood encounters. Inconsistency in the expectations and demands of parents and teachers can give rise to disturbing and insecure feelings among children.

The 'love and belonging' needs are clearly demonstrated in the Harlow and Harlow (1973) and Ainsworth *et al.* (1978) studies into human infant attachment, already alluded to in the section on drive and need theories. These assert themselves when physiological and safety needs are reasonably well gratified. Most humans appear to need to give and receive affection. They need the feeling of belonging, which has nothing to do with sexual desire. To some extent the feeling of belonging adds to our safety needs. Parents and teachers, inadvertently, can bring powerful pressure to bear on children who feel insecure because of lack of affection. On a wider front, 'society' can exact high levels of social control and conformity by the implicit threat of social isolation (prison, borstal, secret societies, religious sects). In the United States, those who do not successfully move to higher education are described as 'drop-outs'. Psychotherapy places great faith in the influence of thwarted love needs on the conscious life.

Maslow sees two sets of 'esteem' needs. First there is the desire for *competence*, achievement, adequacy, confidence in front of one's fellows, independence and freedom. Second, he posits the desire for *recognition*, reputation and prestige, attention, importance and appreciation by others. The first is the desire for confidence in oneself; the other is a wish for prestige and respect from others. Thwarting of opportunities for these desires to be realized is said to produce feelings of inferiority, weakness or helplessness.

The next three steps in the pyramid (*cognitive, aesthetic* and *self-actualization*) are interactive and referred to by Maslow as *growth needs*. All of us, including our pupils, want to express ourselves in a variety of ways – linguistic, artistic, musical, mathematical, bodily – kinaesthetic, etc. (Chapter 9, Gardner 1993a). We have a desire for knowledge and understanding and employ the *attention needs* of curiosity, exploration and manipulation to satisfy the desire (see the section on extrinsic motivators later in this chapter). This is so evident in the exploratory activity of children. But the accumulation of knowledge is not enough. With knowledge, humans tend to systematize, organize and analyse in a search for order and meaning in the world: they possess a desire to understand. The relevance of these cognitive needs to the basic needs is obvious when one considers the necessity of possessing the former in order actively to seek satisfaction of the latter.

The highest point on the pyramid, self-actualization, refers to the desire to fulfil one's potential. Maslow declares, 'What a man *can* be, he *must* be.' Self-actualization is also dependent on self-realization. We have to know what we can do before we know we are doing it efficiently. 'Self-actualization is growth-motivated rather than deficiency-motivated', and takes many forms, which depend upon an individual's perceived beliefs about his or her competencies.

As indicated earlier, Maslow's is a descriptive model based on observational data. Those who have applied it claim that it has face validity. Cautious analyses of its applications may prove of value. For example, there is justification for believing that hungry or frightened children are less likely to fulfil the requirements of school than well-fed and secure children.

Also, those children starved of affection at home are less likely to cope than those from emotionally well-balanced home backgrounds.

Factors often outside the control of the teacher are present. It makes sense that children who come to school hungry, tired, unwanted at home or with little desire to achieve in school (because of lack of support from parents, for example) are less likely to fulfil the goals set at school. Teachers and the school can do much in identifying these and similar sources of difficulty and, where possible, allowing for these deprivations.

Parents and teachers have a major stake in discovering, encouraging and advertising each child's capabilities for the enhancement of self-esteem and self-actualization. Teachers, too, will possess the needs speculated in Maslow's scheme. The educational system within a school, the interactions with staff and pupils, the subject(s) of interest and the status afforded by the role of teacher are vital aspects in the satisfaction of basic and cognitive needs. These are just as likely to affect work at school as unsatisfied needs of children.

## Changing emphasis from needs to goals

There are two difficulties with the Maslow theory. Whilst it has intuitive appeal, it is not based on research evidence. Like Murray's needs and McDougall's instincts, the lists are as long as you care to make them. Indeed some followers of these latter psychologists have devised lists running into hundreds of needs and instincts – too many for practical purposes and certainly not in the spirit of theorizing which should tend to reduce a model to its smallest common denominator.

The second problem is that the definitions of needs and instincts are circular. We see a child pushing a piece of wood along a surface and making a noise like a car. We define this as 'play' and conclude that as it seems to be spontaneous and universal with children the child had a 'need' to play. The problem is in deciding where the cause of the behaviour resides. Is a need to play the cause or is playing the outcome of some other need which is being satisfied by playing?

As suggested earlier (Peters 1958) there has been a shift in focus from the origins or causes of behaviour ('need' theories) to the outcomes or goals (goal orientation theories – Pintrich and Schunk 2002, Ball 1977) especially in applied fields such as education. A recent one, the Goal-setting Theory of Locke and Latham (1990; also see Bandura 1986) was devised essentially for use in occupational psychology in the study of work-based motivation, but its principles apply to educational settings. Goals, goal-setting, teacher–pupil–parent contracts to fulfil specified tasks are commonplace in schools.

For Locke and Latham (1990), a goal is something outside the individual which she or he is trying to attain. Some goals are internally derived and can be under conscious consideration such as attitudes, values, beliefs and levels of aspiration. Other goals are externally derived, that is, external to consciousness and therefore not under an individual's control, such as autonomic nervous system activity, biological needs, teacher assignments.

Two central points about goals relate to *choice* and *commitment*. With goal choice, we are concerned with the target and the level of achievement chosen by a person. A pupil may decide to go for full marks, just enough to scrape a pass, just sufficient to satisfy teachers or parents or choose a very low, failing level. Goal commitment is how strong the desire is to achieve a particular goal. Both choice and commitment can only be estimated from actual performance. It is easy to say how committed one is and yet do nothing about it. Actions speak louder than words!

What influences an individual's choice and commitment to a goal? Locke and Latham (1990) provide a familiar list of personal and environment factors (Table 8.1).

**Table 8.1** Factors influencing goal choice and commitment. Adapted from E. A. Locke and G. P. Latham, *A Theory of Goal Setting and Task Performance*, Prentice Hall, Englewood Cliffs, NJ, 1990.

| *Personal–individual* | *Social–environmental* |
| --- | --- |
| Previous performance | Group norms, goals and peers |
| Actual ability/skill | Role modelling |
| Self-efficacy | Reward structure, size and competition |
| Causal attributions | Kind of authority and goal assigner |
| Values | Nature of feedback |
| Mood | |

The personal factors of previous performance, ability, values and mood need no elaboration here. They occur frequently in this book as variables in achievement. Self-efficacy, defined by Bandura (1986) as 'people's judgements of their capabilities to organize and execute courses of action required to attain designated types of performance' and causal attributions will be dealt with later in the chapter.

Of social factors, role modelling, rewards and feedback occur in subsequent sections. Groups do have an effect on individual performance both in setting goals (which should be achievable) and in heightening commitment provided the goals are within reach of the individual. Group support and peer group pressures are other factors which affect achievement for good and ill. The way authority figures such as teachers, heads and deputy heads, handle their control over pupils has a marked influence on performance. Positive and helpful methods of feedback, supportive, trustworthy, knowledgeable, friendly but firm attitudes and atmosphere are all positive factors. Most of these topics recur several times in this book.

## Extrinsic and intrinsic motivation

A teacher, in trying to adapt the subject and the classroom setting to appeal to a child, relies broadly on two sources of satisfaction, *extrinsic* motivation and *intrinsic* motivation. No clear distinction can be made between incentives (objects external to ourselves which act as a 'pull' from without) and internal drive states (the 'push' from within, which is self-generated). The place of rewards in school – praise, grades, recognitions of progress – is crucial, and clearly they are used as incentives to encourage learning. There is no set way in which a reward is linked to the activity performed in order to obtain it (e.g. successful performance in a physical education exercise and a house point). On the other hand, as we mentioned previously in discussing the ideas of Berlyne and McV. Hunt, there is a good case for thinking that some activities, for example, exploration and play, are rewarded not by tangible things, but simply by the pleasure they give. This is regarded as intrinsic motivation. The fact that the body needs to be active and receive cues is well established (see sensory deprivation researches in Chapter 3). The step from these built-in intrinsic urges to their utilization in the classroom is a necessary one.

## Extrinsic motivators: incentives

Work in the field of extrinsic motivation owes much to endeavours in reinforcement theory, which is one of the most researched areas of psychology. In its simplest form, the theory follows from Thorndike's 'law of effect' (see Chapter 6), which tells us that, if our efforts are rewarded with something we like to receive (positive reinforcement), we are more likely to repeat our efforts, and thus habits are born.

However, the outcomes of reward systems are not as cut and dried as the Law of Effect would lead us to conclude. Research summarized in Lepper and Hodell (1989) suggests that extrinsic rewards can sometimes negate the effects of intrinsic motivation. This is referred to as *overjustification*. If a child is working well at something intrinsically interesting and receives rewards for good performance, there is a possibility that the child will begin to attach more significance to the reward than to satisfying the intrinsic interest. The child begins to complete similar tasks for the external reward and the source of motivation shifts from intrinsic to extrinsic. As Lepper and Hodell state, 'Offering people a reward to work on a task they enjoy provides more than adequate justification for (over justifies) their participation.' Harnessing intrinsic interest gets harder if other extrinsic rewards get in the way.

But frequently children are not intrinsically interested in all the school has to offer and extrinsic rewards become a necessary starting point for the growth of an interest. Whilst accepting the value of intrinsic motivation for long-term rewards, all teachers are obliged to press into service extrinsic motivating systems of immediate rewards or incentives. The knowledge that children delight in exploratory or manipulative activities and that they have a need to achieve and set themselves goals must act as a potent starting point for a teacher. Sometimes the inherent interest in some aspects of schoolwork is sufficient to arouse the children to cognitive activity, but often it will be necessary to apply external stimuli. The following are examples showing three sources of incentives, namely, knowledge of results, rewards/punishments and co-operation/competition.

**Knowledge of results:** Obtaining information about how successfully one is performing (feedback), as we have seen, has high motivational value, especially when the news is good.

Skinner, as we have seen in Chapter 6, makes much of the idea that pupils should have *immediate* knowledge of their performance for the knowledge to have any value. The longer the time between completing work and being told the verdict, particularly if it is favourable, the less chance there is of the results having a motivational impact on the pupil. This applies equally well to essays at any level of education. Skinner applied the idea in constructing the linear teaching program (see Chapter 6, p. 178), where the response given by a pupil is evaluated immediately. As we have seen, knowledge of failure, particularly if it is frequent, can be equally devastating, hence Skinner suggests that the steps taken in the programe should be short and give a slow build-up in level of difficulty to ensure a high level of success (see later under attribution theory).

**Reward and punishment:** In a classic experiment by Hurlock (1925), ten-year-olds were given practice in a series of addition tests, all of equal difficulty. Four groups were formed: (a) a *control* group given no special motivation and kept separate from the other groups; (b) a *praised* group who were complimented on the preceding day's work irrespective of the level of performance; (c) a *reproved* group who were chided for poor work, careless mistakes or lack of improvement – in fact, any pretext by which to chastise individuals; and (d) an *ignored* group who were neither praised nor reproved but were present in the same room with the praised and reproved groups so that they could hear comments made to other children. Figure 8.2 displays some clear differences in the performances of the groups over the five days of the research.

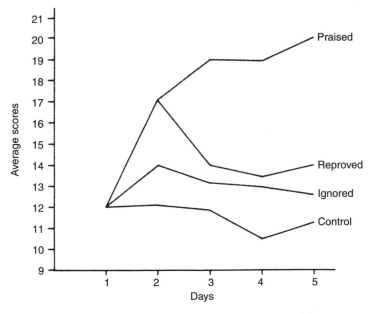

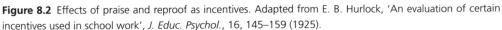

**Figure 8.2** Effects of praise and reproof as incentives. Adapted from E. B. Hurlock, 'An evaluation of certain incentives used in school work', *J. Educ. Psychol.*, 16, 145–159 (1925).

The conclusion is that, while the performances of the pupils on the first day were the same, the praised group outstripped all the others in subsequent performance. The reproved group improved in the short term, but continued harassment tended to have a deleterious influence. It may be that where standards are too exacting, where teachers are perfectionists, study and performance suffer because the pupils, unable to live up to the impossibly high standards, just capitulate. The complacency of the ignored and control groups is worth noting. Schmidt (1941) repeated this research with rather less success. This was because the variations in settings, in which praise or reproof can occur, also have a marked effect on the extent to which they influence performance as well as on the level of anxiety experienced by the pupil (see later section on drive and performance).

Brophy (1981) has also pursued the question of teacher praise and found that it does not always work positively, particularly if it is not immediate. He concludes from the research that praise does not correlate highly with achievements and in some circumstances may have a negative correlation (Dunkin and Biddle 1974). As a reinforcer, praise becomes less and less effective as one proceeds from primary to secondary school. Also, too much praise for almost anything might give pupils the idea that low standards are acceptable. The individual does not get a clear idea of his or her competence. Brophy gives some guidelines for the use of praise which are helpful. Praise should be simple, direct, unambiguous and put over in a natural way (not as if you were praising a dog for good behaviour). Short, straightforward, varied expressions are best. Indicate what in particular is being praised and look for effort, carefulness and persistence. Couple verbal and non-verbal responses when giving praise. Sometimes the praise should be given to a person in confidence and not in front of the class; it depends on the pupil concerned, but some are embarrassed by it and may even get teased. Praise should really be for learning well done and not compliance. This question of the effects of reward and punishment was considered in Chapter 6 in the discussion of behaviour modification.

The misfortune is that we tend to dichotomize reward and punishment. There is doubtless a continuum of feedback mechanisms employed between teacher and taught (from high praise through mild words of caution to much more serious rebuking on the punishment side) which induces a whole spectrum of pupil reaction (Johannesson 1962). Also, what is rewarding for some may be punishment for others (and vice versa). Given the limitation of Hurlock's work, it does support the contention that both praise and reproof are more effective in their different ways than is a neutral setting. Operational conclusions also arising from this work are that the balance along the continuum of reward and punishment should be tipped in favour of reward. The problem with punishment is in its effects, which tend to be less predictable than those of rewards.

Some punishments are actually enjoyed by pupils and therefore are more likely to reinforce than extinguish misbehaviour. Temporary suspension from school may be welcomed by pupils who regularly 'bunk off' because, in any case, they don't like school and see no purpose in it. Staying on after school may free a pupil from household chores. Punishment tends to indicate what *not* to do: some idea of what ought to be done does not always accompany punishment. Unfortunately, some teachers treat necessary day-to-day class activities as if they were punishments: doing extra mathematics or essays as a punishment could turn some children off these activities.

A summary of the effects of physical punishment can be found in Walters and Grusec (1977), who, in general, conclude that there is a place for punishment in the socialization process, given careful consideration of the intensity, duration and timing (the punishment should not take place too long after the misdemeanour).

Errors need to be pointed out, and misbehaviour which is antisocial should be corrected, but the teacher should always attempt to ascertain the reasons for failure or blatant misconduct before applying punitive methods. Personal problems, home circumstances, misjudgements in the standard of work being given to a child (either too hard or too easy) and many other causes may be at the roots of underachievement (performance below that expected from previous performance or standardized tests). Therefore, one should not be too hasty in applying pressure until valid, reasonable causes have been eliminated.

**Co-operation and competition:** Research into the relative merits of co-operative and competitive methods in class has not been particularly illuminating. To begin with, we have the dilemma of encouraging both co-operation and competition within the same teaching systems. The only generalization which emerges from a mass of research is that in none of the studies does competition yield more effective learning than cooperation (Stendler *et al.* 1951). Nevertheless, the one thing that seems certain is that both devices are valid motivators.

Provided the level of competitive antagonism is not too high, performance appears to be improved (Stendler *et al.* 1951). Where the stakes are very high, children opt out or resort to cheating. Self-competition has already been alluded to as an effective means in our discussion of n Ach and levels of aspiration. The matter of social motives such as dependence, affiliation and desire for approval also have a great deal to do with encouraging children to participate in co-operative ventures.

### *Intrinsic motivators: challenge, curiosity, control and fantasy*
Summarizing the research into intrinsic motivation, Lepper and Hodell (1989) postulate four key sources – challenge, curiosity, control and fantasy.

*Challenge*, as the name implies, involves finding activities which challenge the student's interests and capabilities. The challenges should be of intermediate difficulty. If the work is too hard it discourages progress; if it is too easy, boredom and loss of interest set in. Having a clear idea of a pupil's competence is the starting point for any task analysis to ensure that he/she is pushed just enough to maintain interest and encourage learning.

*Curiosity* is probably a natural propensity in human beings. Creating situations which make pupils curious to know the answer is a sure way of catching their attention. Presenting ideas which are discrepant with the existing knowledge of the student is one way of stimulating curiosity.

Much has been written about curiosity. Collectively the activities of exploration, manipulation and curiosity (Berlyne 1960, McV. Hunt 1960) are known as *attention needs*. They depend for detection or satisfaction on the senses and the extent to which we pay attention to our surroundings. The McGill experiment referred to in Chapter 2, indicated that almost total inaction has serious disorientating effects on the mind. Even before this stage is reached, people subjected to prolonged inaction become extremely frustrated. Belief in these as components of human behaviour reflects an active rather than a passive view of life, with humans as goal-orientated animals actively engaged in exploring their environment. Children, once they can move, do not lie or sit around waiting for information to wash over them: they actively seek out and manipulate. Mothers and teachers in primary schools are fully alive to this. The idea of an active, experience-seeking child is prominent in Piaget's theory of cognitive growth (see Chapter 4).

*Control* is an important motivator. Providing opportunities for pupils to take some control over their academic lives enhances intrinsic motivation. The key is involvement – pupils have an interest in those things over which they have some control. Allowing carefully planned exploration in a topic or letting the pupil choose amongst a number of learning options are two ways of giving some responsibility.

*Fantasy* seems an unlikely candidate for a list of intrinsic motivators, but a little consideration shows that many classroom events involve make-believe, simulation and games (Bateson 1955). Several computer programs are written with an element of fantasy to maintain student stimulation. The teacher has, nevertheless, to guard against turning the situation into play without productivity.

### Play (Saracho and Spodek 2003)

It is noteworthy that all four intrinsic motivators of challenge, curiosity, control and fantasy are present in *play*. It is a universally spontaneous activity, especially among the young of most higher animals. Many theories have arisen to explain the urge which makes all young things want to play. We saw in Murray's needs an 'n play' (need to relax and seek fun) and most theories of child development find a place for it (Bruner *et al.* 1976, Moyles 1989 and 2005, Saracho and Spodek 2003, Hughes 1999); but uncertainty still surrounds its biological origins. In one sense, it may not matter so long as we can exploit it for educational purposes.

But let us first deal with developmental views about play. Regardless of theory, play is, first and foremost, enjoyable. It can be of significance in the intellectual, physical, social and moral development of children (Bee and Boyd 2004) and can be directed to therapeutic and educational ends. Mental development and body tone (muscles, organs, circulation) are kept in trim by the activities in play. Co-operation and competition provide an opportunity for social development.

Four stages of development were identified by Parten (1932). In early childhood, children appear to prefer *solitary play* or, a little later, playing side by side without sharing toys (*parallel play*). Later they engage in *associative play* with sharing and taking turns. Subsequently, *co-operative play* appears in which the rules of procedure and co-existence with others are gradually observed or taken into account, and all this in the first few years of life. To this could be added a further stage of *competitive play* where not only rules apply, but there are winners and losers. Thus play also gives children the chance to develop moral judgements, as Piaget has shown (Kay 1968, and Kohlberg and Lickona 1986 met with in Chapter 4). Play also opens up the opportunity for children to manipulate the materials of their environment, to discern shape, texture, size, weight, etc., and assists them in differentiating the real from the imaginary.

The social, developmental 'how' of play as outlined above is there for us to observe. The biological 'why' of play is more difficult to explain. Among the theories we find:

Classical theories of play $\longrightarrow$
$\begin{cases} \text{Surplus energy} \\ \text{Recreative} \\ \text{Preparatory} \\ \text{Achievement and mastery} \\ \text{Recapitulation} \end{cases}$

The 'surplus energy' theory regards play as the inevitable outlet for the abundant energy of youth made available for the survival of the species. Once the business of survival has been catered for, the surplus is used in exploratory activities. 'Recreative' theories emphasize the therapeutic, hedonistic aspects of play. We play for pure joy, pleasure and relaxation. In a sense, it is the opposite of the surplus energy theory in that play is used to replenish rather than use up energy.

Play has also been thought of as a preparation and rehearsal for adult roles where grown-ups are imitated and life is played out in miniature. These views are sometimes referred to as 'practice' or 'pre-exercise' theories.

'Achievement-mastery' and a desire to have physical mastery over the environment have also been seen as having some bearing on the motivation to play. 'Rough and tumble' play, usually males, is a possible manifestation of mastery in order to establish pecking orders so important in the animal kingdom. Finally, a view, which now has few supporters, is the 'recapitulation' theory. This supposes that play follows a series of stages similar to the evolution of the species; thus the behaviour of young children is reminiscent of the early stages in human development.

Most developmental theorists have found a place for play in their schemes of things. In our discussions elsewhere in the book, particularly approaches to learning, motivation and personality, various ideas about play have been incorporated. Current theories which include play are *psychoanalytic theory* (Freud, above and Chapter 12), *attention needs* (*arousal theory*, Berlyne), *cognitive theories* (Piaget and Vygotsky) and *metacommunicative theory* (Bateson 1955).

In *psychoanalytic theory* (Freud, above and in Chapter 12) early childhood experiences are paramount in later personality development. In play, one can pretend to fulfil wishes, relieve tensions and resolve problems. Indeed, play therapy is about relieving emotional problems in children by drawing them out during play sessions. With arousal and cognitive theories, Berlyne is mentioned earlier in this chapter and both Piaget and Vygotsky have been covered in some detail in Chapter 4. Bateson's metacommunicative view is that children operate at two levels. One is fantasy or make-believe and the other is real. Play enables a connection to be made between fantasy and reality.

Two lines of contemporary research are the role of *pretence* (Lillard 2001) and *cultural (or social) contexts* in play. Pretence is, apparently, a skill. Some children really get into the role they are pretending to be. Individual differences have been identified in representational competence and problem solving. One wonders if actors are high on this skill.

### Play and socio-cultural interaction (Roopnarine, Lasker, Sacks and Stores 1998)

Social and cultural influences are certainly candidates as factors affecting play activity. Materials to hand, physical space and conditions, weather, parental choice of toys (if available), parental encouragement of play, educational opportunities and teacher preferences for play are some of the factors affecting a child's play. Not a lot of imagination is needed to compare the opportunities of, on the one hand, a child exposed to play materials and methods when reared in poverty in a third world country with those, on the other, of a child in an industrialized and wealthy country. Differences in the range and variety of materials, living conditions, parental education, educational opportunities, etc. within which playful expression takes place are not hard to deduce. These issues, particularly as they affect child development, are the focus of feverish research effort at present.

### Play and formal education

The importance of studying play has increased in intensity during the past decade. More parents are in paid employment than ever before and seek care for their children. Consequently, the government has encouraged nursery and pre-school educational programmes for three- to five-year-olds. These programmes are becoming increasingly academic and 'syllabus bound' in readiness for state education at five. In the midst of this, exploiting play as an educational tool has become a crucial vehicle. The difficulty comes when play has to be focused towards specific needs in basic skills such as reading, writing and number work. So as not to kill the enjoyment experienced by the children, finding a balance between personal enjoyment and rote learning is a vital challenge.

One central question is whether the play should be structured, semi-structured or unstructured. The deliberate use of unstructured play in education is sometimes referred to as *free play* (or the *playway*). Apart from being based on the belief that all children want to play, it assumes that learning will occur at the same time, as a bonus in a sense. It is achieved by devising suitable situations in which children can both play and learn without interference. By shaping the order and nature of the methods, materials and environment, as well as having a keen sense of the things which children enjoy doing, play is pressed into productive service in the process of learning without destroying the pleasure of play.

A sizeable literature has accumulated about the arguments for and against free play (Lillemyr 2003). The heart of it is that if there are objectives to be met (social and intellectual), as in formal educational settings, you cannot guarantee they will be realized during free play. The dilemma facing teachers is how to introduce useful skills during intellectual and social development in free play without losing the sense of enjoyment. Bennett *et al.* (1997) found that teachers in their sample appreciated this, but did not practise what they believed to be true. Teachers appreciated the value of encouraging social skills and giving choice, but neither was in evidence in the play areas.

Conversely, there is a case for some structuring of the play sessions. One way of turning children off is by having endless unstructured, unguided, 'free for all' play activities in the nursery or classroom. They can be wasteful, frustrating and unnecessary. The gravest disservice to our young would be to transmit, by default, the idea that learning does not require reality and personal effort. The whole of Part Three on learning has emphasized that most learning requires effort. As students know, learning has its enjoyment, but, to do it well, it demands hard work.

## Achievement motivation

### *Need to achieve*

The motive to achieve, whilst having no well-established origins in primary needs, is nevertheless a useful concept which has some face validity in the classroom. Ausubel (Ausubel and Robinson 1969) perceives at least three components in achievement motivation. They are: (a) *cognitive drive*, which is *task-oriented* in the sense that the enquirer is attempting to satisfy the need to know and understand (see Maslow above), and the reward of discovering new knowledge resides in the carrying out of the task; (b) *self-enhancement*, which is *ego-oriented* or *self-oriented* and represents a desire for increased prestige and status gained by doing well scholastically, and which leads to feelings of adequacy and self-esteem; and (c) a broader motive of *affiliation*, which is a dependence on others for approval. Satisfaction comes from such approval irrespective of the cause, so the individual uses academic success simply as a means of recognition by those on whom he or she depends for assurances.

Parents play an active part in the young child's affiliation needs. Later the teacher often becomes another source of affiliation satisfaction.

Earlier we mentioned the views of Murray, who postulated a number of needs. McClelland, greatly influenced by Murray, developed the need for achievement aspect (n Ach).

---

### Further reading

An enormous volume of research has sprung from D. C. McClelland's use of Murray's concept of n Ach. Some of this is summarized in the former's books (1955 and 1987). The most detailed statement of his view is to be found in McClelland, Atkinson, Clark and Lowell, *The Achievement Motive* (1976). See also Atkinson and Raynor (1974). For more information about McClelland's use of TAT (Thematic Apperception Test), see McClelland's 1972 reference. For advice to teachers see his paper, 'Towards a theory of motivation acquisition' in *American Psychologist* (1965).

---

The persistence of both children and adults to master objects and ideas suggests that they have a strong desire to achieve. Whatever the cause, its presence is a constant source of hope and encouragement to teachers. McClelland adopted 'projection' techniques (Chapter 12) to differentiate the levels of need to achieve following a variety of experimental conditions. In one research there were two stages to the experiment: the first stage consisted of seven pencil-and-paper verbal and motor tests; the second stage followed with a test of 'creative imagination', in which the subjects had to write stories about several pictures (projecting their achievement motive) from which a measure of achievement motivation was taken. Six experimental conditions were chosen:

- Relaxed: the students were told that the research had been devised to improve the quality of the tests; in other words, the tests and not the students were being tested.
- Neutral: again, the tasks were oriented towards the tests rather than the students, but in this instance they were asked to take the tests seriously and to do their best.
- Success: the first of the seven tests was first completed and scored as a carefully timed exercise. Students were then asked about their individual class marks and positions, IQ and a personal estimate of their ability. They were also told that the present series of tests were measures of intelligence in which students at a rival institution had excelled. After these false statements the students were given some inverted 'norms' for the first test, making it look as though most had done well. Similarly, results of the next six tests were announced to maintain the impression that the group had been successful.
- Achievement oriented: instructions were the same for this group as for the 'success' group, except that no norms were given.

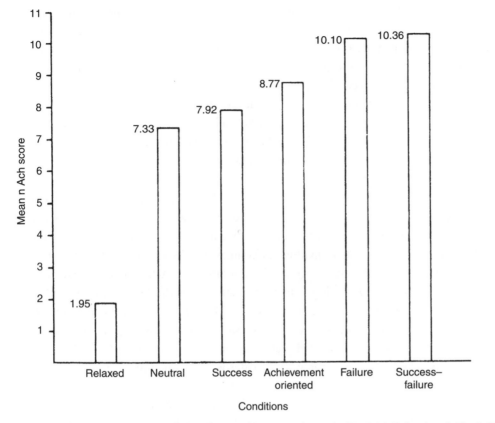

**Figure 8.3** Need achievement in different circumstances. From the work of D. C. McClelland *et al.*, *The Achievement Motive*, Irvington Publishers, New York, 1976.

- Failure: similar instructions to those given to the 'success' group were used, except that the invented norms after the first and the next six tests were so high as to make it appear as though most of the group had failed.
- Success–failure: the norms announced after the first test were low, so that almost everyone was successful, while very high norms followed the six tests.

The results are expressed diagrammatically in Figure 8.3. The order in which the conditions appear bears some profitable information for the teacher. Note the relative position of 'relaxed' and the other forms of motivation. The results seem to show that the difference between the 'success' and the 'success–failure' groups is statistically significant.

A direct outcome of McClelland's work is the development of training programmes aimed at encouraging achievement motivation in students of all ages. The argument used is that if we can specify the characteristics of the high achiever, some of these might be stimulated in less achievement-oriented individuals, using tailor-made programmes of training. The ultimate aim would be to improve the performance of students. The findings so far summarized by McClelland (see above) are encouraging, in showing that some students display significant improvement. He recommends a number of ideas for teachers to achieve this. Some of the important ones are (a) give the learner sound, believable reasons for needing to succeed; (b) give knowledge as to how need for achievement works; (c) encourage positive attitudes to learning the motive to achieve; (d) be systematic in noting what succeeds (or fails). Research undertaken by McClelland and his associates has shown promising results, and that it is possible to create classroom environments in which the need for achievement in academic studies is raised.

This field is still an active source of research (summarized in Covington 1992, and Smith 1992). Atkinson (1964), using n Ach concepts, has developed McClelland's ideas into a theory of behaviour which has some relevance to teaching. For him, three factors were important in determining the level of arousal and likelihood of actually carrying out a task. These he regarded as the stable individual differences and dispositions. The first, *motives*, incorporated two aspects of seeking success (the now familiar n Ach) and fear of failure (FF). These two aspects were gauged using different tests: the Thematic Apperception Test (TAT) for n Ach and the Test Anxiety Questionnaire (TAQ) for FF. The other two factors were the person's expectation of success (*probability of success*) and the strength of the incentive following a successful outcome on completion of the task (*incentive value*). These are all positive factors. The higher each one is, the greater is the probability of action to achieve the task.

Further, Atkinson regarded the two motives of n Ach and FF as independent influences, the FF dimension having the same three factors of the motive to avoid failure, the likelihood of failure and the strength of the incentive for failure (Mahone 1960, Birney *et al.* 1969). If the product of the positive factors is greater than that of the negative factors, there is an overall positive achievement motivation – the stronger, the better. The reverse applies if the negative factors are greater.

Covington (1992) has developed an interesting 2-by-2 model (Figure 8.4) in which the n Ach motive is contrasted with the fear of failure.

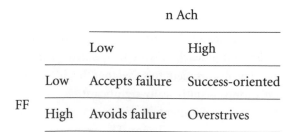

**Figure 8.4** A summary of Covington's interactive model of need for achievement and fear of failure (Covington 1992).

The *overstrivers*, whilst they thirst for success, are so fearful of failure they overwork – pulled up by high n Ach and pushed up by high fear of failure. One wonders if this is related to the 'type A' personality described in Chapter 12. Teachers and students have met pupils who work hard, but anxiously need feedback about their performance and progress.

The *success-oriented* students do not have hang-ups about some degree of failure. Their need for achievement sees them through. Teachers will also recognize those who accept failure ( *failure acceptors*) and can live with their lack of success. The reasons are many, but principally they may be indifferent to success, may not like the subject of study, may have no respect for the teacher or may not have the ability to cope with the set work. Finally, there are those who, though having low need for achievement, fear failure. A common reason is undue pressure from parents or teachers. They are frequently masters of the art of designing excuses for failure or avoiding work.

There are other interesting implications of use to teachers in this theory. Research comparing those high on n Ach and low on FF with those low on n Ach and high on FF have shown the former to be more realistic in decision-making which involves achievement (Atkinson and Litwin 1960). With high motivation to achieve, the former do not take the risk of choosing very difficult tasks, nor are they interested in easy tasks because the incentive will be too small. With those having high FF, moderately difficult tasks create the greatest anxiety. With easy tasks there would be no problem; with difficult tasks there are similarly no perceived problems because the *negative* incentive of failing is small. Mahone (1960) has found that those higher on n Ach are more realistic in career choices than those high on FF.

Birney (Birney *et al.* 1969) has also looked at fear of failure. He points to the paradox in our society, with its overriding respect for those who strive and succeed, that an advance towards achievement is also a retreat from the fear of failure (Gjesme 1971). Notice that in McClelland's work the highest levels of n Ach are obtained by those who think they have failed, especially those who have tasted success. As Birney observes, 'success and failure can best be understood *only in an interpersonal context*... In an achieving society, success is highly instrumental in gathering esteem and respect, while failure is a standard way of losing esteem.' Fear of failure may have many causes, but three important ones are lessening of self-esteem, lowering of public image and the loss of rewards accompanying poor attainment. Where self-ratings on a questionnaire are used to show differences in expressed attitudes towards achievement motivation and actual performance, those with high achievement professed to be self-confident, diligent, serious, single-minded and conformist.

Children need to succeed. In catering for this we have to keep a close watch on their abilities and potential when devising their classroom work. Herein lies one of the important reasons for individual attention of children: that we can set goals for each child in accordance with what the teacher sees as being within the capabilities of that child, thus ensuring that the child tastes success in preference to failure.

A learner's need to achieve fluctuates tremendously from time to time and topic to topic. Without a need to achieve by the pupil in those subjects prescribed in school, the teacher is presented with a tremendous task trying to find ways of rekindling the interest. The later years of secondary schooling are especially problematic – pupils frequently complain that what they are taught is not of immediate interest or relevance to them as potential post-school citizens and workers.

## Level of aspiration

In the light of experience and advice, we all set ourselves standards of achievement. These can be referred to as *levels of aspiration*. Plainly the level at which we set our sights has an important bearing on our levels of performance. Children without a challenge are less likely to improve their skills than those who are encouraged to strive for better performance. This topic is summarized in Weiner (1992).

In a well-known study by Sears (1940), fourth-grade, fifth-grade and sixth-grade children (ten- to twelve-year-olds) were divided into three groups of those who had been successful, unsuccessful and 'differentially' successful in school subjects, including arithmetic and reading. The differential group had succeeded in reading, but had done badly in arithmetic. Under familiar, normal classroom conditions the children were given several tasks in arithmetic and reading. After a task each child was asked to give an estimate of how long it would take to carry out the next task; this was taken as a measure of the level of aspiration. Discrepancies between actual time taken and estimated time needed were used to compare groups. Three particularly interesting findings were: (a) children with a background of success set themselves realistic levels of aspiration; (b) those with a background of failure tended to set unrealistic levels of either overestimates or underestimates; (c) the differential group was realistic in reading, that is, its normally successful subject. In a continuation experiment in which each group was divided randomly into two, one half was told falsely that it had done well. Self-estimates of the time needed to complete the tasks were again requested of the pupils. In this case, Sears was interested in the short-term effects of success and failure for those who usually experience long-term effects. The results showed that (a) the short-term success group tended to set realistic levels of aspiration; and (b) short-term failure had little effect, particularly for those in the group normally experiencing long-term success.

Several helpful pointers gleaned from this and other evidence are:

- repeated failure does not enable children to make a reasonable estimate of their capabilities; naturally, if children have no idea what they can do successfully they cannot possibly be in a position to set themselves realistic goals
- the effects of intermittent failure are more varied than those of success
- unexpected failure gives lowered levels of aspiration
- continued failure produces a decline in levels of aspiration; nothing enhances failure better than failure

- a combination of failure and success (see McClelland's work, referred to earlier in the chapter) raises levels of aspiration and the need to achieve
- where there is knowledge that a goal has been achieved, children will often be inspired to set their sights higher on the next occasion; their levels of aspiration are raised
- the greater the success of a child, the stronger is the tendency to raise levels of aspiration
- where success and praise come too easily or too frequently, levels are generally lowered (see Brophy 1981)
- highly cherished goals may be reflected in lowered levels of aspiration to ensure some success
- unexpected success often leads to raised levels of aspiration.

In conclusion, the judicious use of success and, to a limited extent, failure must form an important element in classroom practice. Children need help in discovering their capacities and setting realistic goals for themselves.

## Expectancy

The *expectancy process* has become a most important development in social cognitive theory applied to education. As stated when discussing various motivation theories, the cognitive approach has *expectancy* as one of its central constructs. How a person responds in a given setting will, to some extent, depend on that person's expectations of reward and the value of the reward (internal as well as external). This distinguishes the cognitivist from the behaviourist positions. As 'cognitive' implies, the individual 'thinks' about the consequences of behaviour in the light of previous experience and responds accordingly.

We have met several examples of expectancy theory already. The level of aspiration concept, referred to by Sears (1940) in the previous section as the goal or target aimed for, is dependent on a person's expectations about the chances of success, the level having been set as a result of previous experience. Atkinson's analysis of n Ach involving motives, probability of success and incentive value are clearly criteria by which an individual arrives at a reasoned judgement about expectations of success.

Pintrich and Schunk (2002) identify three recent advances in expectancy research of value to teachers. The first, led by Eccles (1983) and Wigfield (Wigfield and Eccles 1992), is called the *expectancy-value model* (the probability of success and incentive value in Atkinson's theory mentioned above). Their main concern has been to look at students' expectancy of success and how they perceive their ability to cope with academic tasks. With large-scale samples and classroom-based tasks, they regularly found that both expectancy and perceived ability are highly related to classroom achievement and standardized test scores.

The second recent line of approach owes much to Harter (1982, last up-date of perceived competence scale was 1998) on children's perceptions of their own competence (*self-perception of ability*). Two important conclusions are that self-perception of competence is specific to a subject rather than global. How specific one can be about a 'subject' is still debatable, but Harter suggests that conventional school subjects (e.g. maths, English, history, chemistry) are sufficiently specific. The majority of pupils are fairly accurate in their self-estimates of ability in specific subjects. Where error does occur, it seems to be in the direction of overestimate.

The third, *self-efficacy* (Bandura 1986), has been alluded to above in the section on goal-orientation. Put simply, self-efficacy is how well people judge their competence in doing a task in order to achieve a desired goal. Again, self-efficacy correlates well with school achievement and standardized tests.

## Attribution theory and expectation

The three elements of expectancy – expectancy-value, perceptions of competence and self-efficacy – are criteria by which an individual arrives at a perception of how she or he will perform. They help to define the motivational intensity and hence the likelihood of a task being undertaken and achieved at a particular level. For example, if you do not think you are any good at maths, you will drop the subject as soon as you can and avoid it whenever possible. But these are consequences. What incidents along the way lead to them? How do we arrive at self-perceptions? This is the province of *attribution theory* – to what do we attribute our success or failure? But first let us explore an overall picture of how attribution affects performance.

Weiner (1992) developed a model which started with *antecedent conditions* – what a person brings to a specific event. Examples of antecedents are listed under 'student pre-dispositions' in Figure 14.1. Weiner, in fact, defined the list in terms of environmental and personal factors. The *perceived causes* are of special interest and we shall return to them presently. They include such factors as aptitude, effort, chance, mood, fatigue, health, teaching methods, the teacher and so on. These occur along at least two *causal dimensions* of stable–unstable and internal–external causes or locus of control (see earlier in the chapter). The next postulated stage of the process, consequences, are the now familiar expectancy, self-efficacy and perception of competence discussed in the last section. The final stage is the action taken by an individual such as choosing one course of action in preference to another, persisting, aiming at a certain level of achievement, avoiding some activities.

Of Weiner's (1992) model, the perceived causes are central to attribution. Some causes were regarded as being within the control of an individual (internal), while others were not (external). Weiner (1977 and 1992) developed this further by suggesting that individuals tend to *attribute* their success or failure to either internal or external causes, and this in turn affects their perception of a similar task undertaken in the future. The causes of success and failure are classified by Weiner in two ways: the *locus of control* mentioned earlier in the

**Table 8.2** To what do we attribute success and failure?

|  | Locus of control | |
|---|---|---|
|  | External | Internal |
| Stable | Objective task characteristics | Aptitude Long-term effort |
| Unstable | Chance | Skills/knowledge Temporary effort |

chapter (Rotter 1954) and *stability*. Four main locus-of-control attributions are *aptitude* and *skill* or *knowledge* (internal, because a person already possesses aptitude and can be personally responsible for the amount of effort required to acquire skill or knowledge), *objective task characteristics* and *chance* (external, because a person does not feel responsible for either task difficulty or unpredictability, for example unlucky in the questions revised for an exam). On the other hand, aptitude and task difficulty are reasonably stable, in that they do not vary all that much from occasion to occasion when the same task is undertaken. Skill or knowledge and luck, however, are unstable, because they can vary from one time to the next. Table 8.2 illustrates this.

Those students who read the literature on Weiner's model may find the attributions differently worded from the above. In the early 1990s he changed the terms because the earlier ones were misleading. 'Ability' has become 'aptitude (long-term effort)', 'effort' has become 'skill/knowledge (temporary effort)', 'task difficulty' has become 'objective task characteristics' and 'luck' has become 'chance'.

A person reacts with pride or shame depending upon his or her perceived source of success and failure. This also affects future attempts. For internal locus of control, there is a maximum pride with success and maximum shame with failure. There are also greater expectations of success with stable than with unstable causes.

The crux of attribution theory is *causal perception*, that is, to what an individual attributes the cause of his or her success or failure, and the influence this has on perceptions of future performance. Pupils who attribute their failure to stable causes (lack of aptitude) generally do not persist when they fail ('if ability is fixed there's not much I can do about it'). Pupils who believe their failure is brought about by unstable or internal causes, for example lack of effort, tend to persist in the face of failure ('I'm just not trying hard enough').

The link between this and McClelland's n Ach is most instructive (Weiner 1992). It seems that pupils with a high need to achieve attribute their success to internal causes of aptitude and effort and their failure to lack of effort, while low need achievers attribute their failure to external factors (and in some cases to lack of ability). This knowledge, alongside the training programmes developed by McClelland (1972) and his associates, has been used with some success.

## Self-concept and achievement: expectations of pupils

A theme running through the researches mentioned in the last few pages is the importance attached to how we rate our competence in a particular task. The image we create of ourselves and the self-value or esteem generated from this image are going to affect our approach and level of performance in solving life's problems. These conceptions which we hold of ourselves as a result of interaction with significant others and which influence our behaviour are known collectively as the *self-concept*. The topic will be considered in Chapter 12 and see Burns (1976), but the motivational aspects are of interest here.

In Maslow's theory, a prominent position was given to self-esteem and self-actualization in the hierarchy of human needs. Confidence in oneself and the need for respect from others were felt to be crucial in providing a base for intellectual pursuits. Ausubel suggested the importance of self-enhancement and affiliation, that is, the prestige we gain by doing well in school or college and the dependence we have on others' recognition and approval of our academic prowess. McClelland's n Ach researches clearly highlight the importance of differing effects of failure-oriented and success-oriented feedback in the enhancement of achievement motivation. Fear of failure, says Birney (Birney *et al.* 1969), drives the student towards trying to be successful because to be a failure is a damaging image (failure repels, success attracts). Of course, persistent failure, or continually telling a child he or she is stupid, is like the Chinese water torture: one ultimately capitulates to the belief that one is a failure or stupid, and a depressing self-concept is formed. As Rosenthal and Jacobson (1968, 1992) found, children fulfil the prophecy they think others expect of them. In the work of Cattell (mentioned above), well-designed motivation tests used with both adult and school samples gave support to the high position of self-concept in relation to achievement. The picture emerging with high and low achievers is consistent (Child 1984, 1988) and underlines the importance to high achievement of the esteem one has been led to have of oneself (self-sentiment), of a sense of duty, conscientiousness and acceptance of authority (superego), of curiosity, of fear of insecurity (cf. Birney) and of positive attitudes to school.

A useful point is made by Brookover *et al.* (1967) who distinguish *self-concept* of academic ability as one of a number of possible self-concepts. This distinction has enabled him to concentrate on those aspects of school life which impinge directly on self-concept and academic achievement. The results from his and similar studies (Barker Lunn 1970) show a positive relationship over time: the better the self-concept of academic ability, the higher achievement, and changes in self-concept correspond with changes in achievement. Teachers have an important part to play in establishing positive but realistic self-concepts in their children. Bloom (1976) concludes that 'academic self-concept is the strongest of the affect measures in predicting school achievement'.

## The self-fulfilling prophecy: expectations of teachers

Once we have made up our minds about the capabilities of each child, to what extent does this decision adversely influence our treatment of the child? Do children perform in the way we expect them to perform? In a survey of the literature and research by Rosenthal and Jacobson (1968), it emerges that performance and attainment in school subjects were significantly improved where improvement was anticipated. They go on to speculate that:

> by what she said, by how and when she said it, by her facial expressions, postures, and perhaps by her touch, the teacher may have communicated to the children of the experimental group that she expected improved intellectual performance. Such communications together with possible changes in teaching techniques may have helped the child learn by changing his self-concept, his expectations of his own behaviour, and his motivation, as well as his cognitive style and skills.

This is an illustration of the process of a *self-fulfilling prophecy*.

Rogers (1982, Burns 1982, Satterly and Hill 1983) identifies four stages whereby teachers' expectations might influence pupils' performance: (a) teachers form impressions of pupils, and on the basis of these they derive expectations of the pupils' performance; (b) consciously or otherwise the behaviour of teachers must be affected by these expectations; (c) the pupils must, whether they are consciously aware of it or not, recognize the teacher's expectations through the latter's behaviour; (d) the pupils respond to the teacher's behaviour in a manner which more closely matches the teacher's expectations.

Another key influence involves the pressures bearing on teachers as a result of the circumstances in which they have to work. These help to form and shape expectations. The more a system conspires to distance the teacher from pupils, the more likely it is that teacher-expectancy effects will play a part in influencing pupil performance. Rogers lists a number of factors that create differential pressures on teachers and that, in turn, creates different sorts of 'distancing' between teacher and taught. Examples of such factors are type of school (urban/rural; inner city/middle-class suburban), resource levels, pupil–teacher ratios, degree of support from the local community, status of teachers in society (and the effect this has on morale) and inter-staff relationships in the school.

The opportunities for these unintentional influences abound in every classroom. Presumably the reverse effect of inadvertently depressing a child's performance by setting goals which are too low is yet another possibility. In many ways, the self-fulfilling prophecy can be used to advantage by adopting an optimistic attitude towards the performance of children in the hope that they will learn more than was deemed possible at first sight.

## Further reading

It must be said that several pointed criticisms of this and similar research have been published and should be consulted. Critical writings about *Pygmalion in the Classroom* (Rosenthal and Jacobson 1968 and 1992) soon followed its publication. One was *Pygmalion Reconsidered* by Elashoff and Snow (in Davies and Warren 1973). There is an excellent summary of the research on self-fulfilling prophecy by Braun (1976).

Rogers (1982) gives a good, balanced critical view of the field and offers a word of caution. From his review of the research he concludes that

> teacher expectancy effects are more likely to occur (but certainly not exclusively so) when younger pupils are involved, when teachers have formed social expectations for their pupils under conditions likely to lead to the establishment of relatively distant teacher–pupil relationships and under conditions (as yet largely unspecified) where the actions and expressed attitudes of the teacher are most likely to affect pupils' level of tuition and self-concepts.

For a recent summary of contemporary research interests in teacher expectancy see Rogers (1998).

# Drive and performance

Throughout this chapter several terms have been used which suggest that motivation involves some kind of tension state. We talk of 'fear of failure', anxiety and drive states, conflict, frustration or emotional tension, all implying some kind of disturbance or dissonance. What we have not discussed is the connection between the 'amount' of drive present and the nature and extent of the ensuing activity. Is there a straightforward link between drive and performance such that an increase in one gives rise to a corresponding increase in the other? Or are there times when a maximum level of performance is reached beyond which no amount of drive will increase output? Will highly motivated (or highly anxious) performers invariably do better than moderately motivated ones?

The answers to these questions are not simple. The factors involved are many and of devious influence. But two factors of primary importance which have been examined are the *level of motivation* or *arousal* and the *difficulty*, of the task. As long ago as 1908, Yerkes and Dodson found from their work with rats that, as the level of motivation is increased for a given task, an optimum is reached beyond which performance increasingly deteriorates.

Figure 8.5 is a theoretical graph of this statement. As we pass from one kind of task to another, the difficulty of each task also affects the optimum level of arousal at which learning and performance are adversely influenced. A general statement of this finding is that, as the difficulty of tasks increases, the optimum motivation for learning or performance decreases. This became known as the Yerkes–Dodson Law. The law is beautifully demonstrated by Broadhurst (1957), using three levels of difficulty for tasks performed by rats as shown in Figure 8.6.

Everyday examples of achievement being influenced by the level of difficulty are not hard to find. Very simple tasks (shelling peas) are not likely to cause us concern even under stressful circumstances, whereas highly provoking tasks where emotional arousal is in evidence (e.g. sitting an examination or taking a driving test) do not need to become

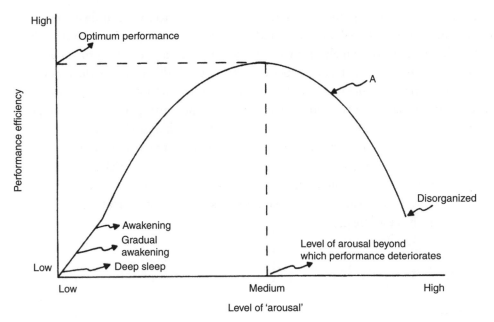

**Figure 8.5** Hypothetical relationship between arousal and performance efficiency (after Hebb).

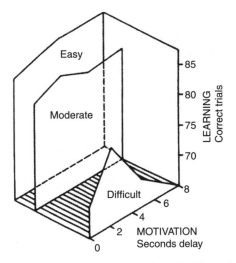

**Figure 8.6** A three-dimensional graph of the Yerkes–Dodson Law. Reprinted from P. L. Broadhurst, 'Emotionality and the Yerkes–Dodson Law', *J. Exp. Psychol.*, 54, 348 (1957) with the permission of the American Psychological Association.

too complex before we begin to make silly mistakes. However, there are dangers in drawing direct analogies between the moderately simple activities required of rats in maze-running or food-seeking problems and the highly intricate tasks required of children or students. The relationship could not be as clean-cut as the Yerkes–Dodson effect. The curvilinearity (the inverted U-shape of Figure 8.5) applies to rat performance. What little evidence we have for complicated tasks will be considered in more detail in Chapter 12, but we have cause to believe that those in highly provoking situations, or high-anxiety-prone people as measured in tests of neuroticism, may experience disruptive influences from the very outset of task performance. In other words, as the stress in a situation mounts, our performance deteriorates immediately. Representing this graphically, the starting point of our graph in Figure 8.5 would be around point A, which is beyond the peak of performance.

It would be premature to draw generalizations about class practices from the evidence presented above. A little tension or 'dissonance' might well be essential for arousal and learning. What we do not know is the limit of the tension which can be tolerated by individuals in given circumstances. The main point is to be wary of creating a classroom atmosphere which is too stressful.

# Stress

## Definition

Much of this book is devoted to children and their problems. But teachers too have problems, not least of which is the growing volume of demands which have been placed on their shoulders by changes in the education system. Teaching has always presented stresses and strains, but there can be little doubt that today's teachers are high amongst over-stressed professionals (Travers and Cooper 1996). The introduction of so many innovations into school life, such as the National Curriculum, more detailed and time-consuming methods of assessment, more administration and committee meetings within the school, fewer sanctions which teachers can apply for misbehaviour, changing attitudes of children to schoolwork, etc., have all conspired to increase the tension in teaching. The topic straddles a number of chapters in this book, but there is logic in including stress in a chapter on motivation since this is one of the first things to be affected by stress.

When specifically applied to teacher stress, Kyriacou and Sutcliffe (1979) have provided a thorough definition:

> a response syndrome of negative affect (such as anger and depression), usually accompanied by potentially pathogenic physiological changes (such as increased heart rate), resulting from aspects of the teacher's job and mediated by the perception that the demands made upon the teacher constitutes a threat to his (or her) self-esteem or well-being and by coping mechanisms activated to reduce the threat.

We saw in Chapter 2 that threatening stimulation can provoke emotional states and chemical changes in our bodies, giving rise to emotional responses. The 'drive' harnessed from these emotional states affects performance, as indicated in the previous section. The scientists amongst readers will recognize that stress and strain are physical terms and the analogy is useful. Stress, for the physicist, is the external pressure (force) applied to an object such as a length of wire. Strain is the result of applying that pressure. A sufficiently heavy weight hung on the end of a dangling wire could cause it to stretch. The weight is the stress. The greater it is, the more likely that stretching will take place. With lower weights, the wire returns to its original length when the weight is removed. With heavier weights, the lengthening (deformation) is permanent. With even greater pressure, the wire snaps. Different materials have different flexibilities and strengths. With humans, stress can be regarded as the pressures in an environment which are brought to bear on an individual. Strains are the outcome of how the individual perceives these pressures. Textbooks sometimes use stress to cover both terms (i.e. the whole process) or just strain (i.e. the effects of stress). In what follows, we shall use the 'whole process' definition. Figure 8.7 illustrates one interpretation of this process.

Demands are made of an individual by his or her environment. At best, if these demands are perceived as manageable, even exciting, performance is enhanced. If the demands are perceived as threatening or intolerable, then we are likely to exhibit symptoms of strain. These cover a range of physical, behavioural, mental and emotional reactions. These are discussed in more detail in the next sections.

## Stress in teachers

The general process outlined in Figure 8.7 will now be applied to the specific case of problems encountered by teachers. Some expansion of the sources (stressors), (including individual characteristics and symptoms and effects on performance) and some suggestions for managing stress are outlined below. Several good articles on stress in teachers have appeared in the last decade (Travers and Cooper 1998, Kyriacou 1987).

### Stressors: the sources of stress

External sources of stress are numerous. But there are some basic ingredients which many researchers have identified in the workplace. Travers and Cooper (1996) give a useful summary of occupational stressors such as:

- those *intrinsic to the job* (poor physical conditions, work overload, time pressures)
- one's *role in the organization* (role ambiguity and conflict, self-image in the job)
- *career development* (over- or under-promotion, lack of job security)
- *relationships at work* (with headteacher, head of department, colleagues, pupils)
- *organizational structure and modus operandi* (little participation, rule bound, poor channels for consultation)
- *home–work interface* (arising from the mismatch between the demands of work and the demands of home life)
- *threat of redundancy*.

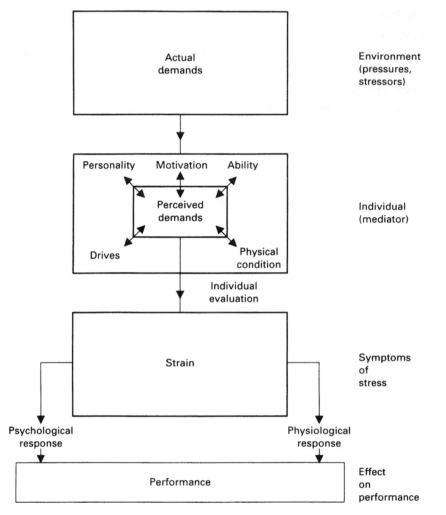

**Figure 8.7** Simplified model of stress process.

In a study by Travers and Cooper (1996), a questionnaire given to a large sample of teachers showed convincingly that the main stressors in order of significance were:

- *pupil–teacher interaction* (e.g. verbal and physical aggression from pupils, dealing constantly with behavioural problems and lack of parental back-up about discipline)
- *management and structure of the school* (e.g. too little influence and responsibility in the school, low status and conflict between colleagues)
- *working conditions* (e.g. particularly large class sizes and lack of resources)
- *rapid and extensive changes taking place in education*
- *appraisal of teachers* (e.g. high demands from parents, official appraisals)
- *low status* (e.g. being a good teacher does not necessarily lead to promotion, public image worsening, lack of support from government).

This list is very close to a study reported by Kyriacou in 1989. It is important to reiterate that individuals react to different stressors to different extents. For some, the cut and thrust of classroom life is exciting. For others, it proceeds to cumulative despair.

A teacher has responsibilities laid down in the job description. These duties interact with the occupational expectations, desires, abilities and personality of the individual. Conflict comes when the perceived demands of the workplace, that is, demands by the regime (resources, local rules) and the pupils (unwilling workers, indiscipline) are not matched by the competences *as perceived by the individual*. If the duties, desires and capabilities required of the task of teaching are greater than the demands, the energies of stress can be used to advantage. If the demands created by the above sources are greater than the duties, expectations and capacities required of the job, as anticipated by the teacher, then we have the potential for overload and stress.

The characteristics of the teacher which are invoked by stressors will be the subject of later chapters in the book. Motivation and emotional reaction have been dealt with already, and here it was argued that individual differences occur in levels of physiological reaction, aggression or fear. Ability to cope with the school subjects being taught and with the relationships in the classroom are significant. Personality, particularly Type A (Strube 1991) is important. Type A behaviour is exhibited by people who are driven, impatient, over-workers, overactive, ambitious, impatient with those who get left behind and so on. Type A teachers tend to be early victims of strain. Anxiety, neuroticism and difficulty in coping with ambiguity can also heighten strain. (See Chapter 12 on personality for more details of Type A characteristics.)

## The symptoms

The symptoms exhibited by stressed people vary enormously. Broadly, the reactions can be divided into physical and psychological (mental, emotional, behavioural).

The *physical* reactions of the body help to mobilize energy used to support body functions, concentrate effort and increase the defensive functions. When present in temperate quantities all are advantageous, but excesses can lead to abnormal functioning. For example, the release of chemicals into the bloodstream (e.g. hormones, see Chapter 2) increases heart rate, sugar production and metabolic rate. An excess and prolonged secretion of these chemicals can lead to heart attack, strokes, high blood pressure, kidney damage, exhaustion, skin irritations, weight loss, ulcers, digestion problems, slowing down of mental and sensory functioning and sexual impotence.

*In extremis*, we have a condition known as *learned helplessness*. Research using dogs (Seligman 1975, Overmeier and Seligman 1967, Maier and Seligman 1976) exposed to a mild electric shock from which there was no escape, showed that in time they would not even attempt to escape even when there was an opportunity. They seemed to have given up all hope. Some humans when exposed to prolonged stress are also thought to display learned helplessness. One example often quoted is persistent and threatening abuse (physical, mental and sexual) leading to withdrawal and silence (e.g., battered wives, excessive verbal bullying and child abuse). Another is the outcome of persistent torture (concentration camps in WW2). One wonders if, to a lesser extent, those pupils given low self-esteem through constant and inaccurate criticism of their academic competence fall victim to feelings of helplessness.

*Psychological* reactions can take many forms. Mental or cognitive problems include decline in memory and attention, thus errors increase. Delusions are possible in extreme cases. *Emotional* reactions involve increased tension (can't relax), personality changes or exaggerations (tidy people become sloppy, anxious people get progressively worse), depression sets in and feelings of worthlessness appear (can't face a class). Also stress-related psychosomatic disorders appear, such as high blood pressure, colitis and ulcers, caused by emotional pressures rather than physical damage. *Psychosomatic* disorder is when physical symptoms, like those just described, appear having their origins in distressed mental states. They are just as real and potent as conditions and complaints arising from physical causes.

*Uncharacteristic behaviour* intrudes. Leisure pursuits are dropped ('can't be bothered doing anything these days') and absenteeism appears. Escapist drinking and drug-taking might start. Sleep patterns are affected. Job dissatisfaction and exhaustion is expressed in several ways such as doing the absolute minimum, passing the buck to others, adopting a laid-back and negligent style and losing the ambition to progress. In extreme cases, there may be suicide threats.

A prolonged period of stress with its progression of physical and mental ill-health culminates in *teacher burn-out*. This is a collective term for those symptoms appearing in an overstretched individual which affect his or her performance as a classroom teacher. Burn-out is most often associated with the behavioural attitudes described in the previous paragraph.

### Managing stress

Prevention is always better than cure and most of the strategies to be described can be used as interventions before stress becomes debilitating. De Frank and Cooper (1987) suggest three focal points at which intervention or help can be offered to teachers: the individual, the individual–school interface and educational organizations. They are inter-related sources, but are here separated for ease of description. Using these foci, Travers and Cooper (1996) give a most useful summary of what teachers see as most helpful.

Individuals can help themselves in the prevention of stress. But for those in the grip of stress-related symptoms, help from outside is necessary. It is not only crucial for them to come to terms with stress but to share the problems with understanding and trusted people – spouses, partners, relatives, friends, experienced counsellors.

Of those things which teachers can do for themselves – exercise, relaxation training, biofeedback (see Chapter 2), cognitive coping strategies, time management – all these have been found helpful. The effects of body chemistry and reduction of anxiety brought about by exercise are well documented. Breathing exercises, muscle relaxation, meditation have all been found useful. The voluntary control of the autonomic system – heart rate, muscle tension, blood pressure – assist in reducing tension, headaches, anxiety and Type A personality symptoms. Time management is one of the most difficult to achieve. Making time for one's family, recreation, having a short breathing space at work or winding down from time to time eludes some people, particularly the Type A personality with high ambitions. But these have to be planned to avoid stress and strain. Expert guidance is most often needed in carrying out the above suggestions.

When things get too serious, teachers need a counselling service, usually provided either at school or local authority level. They need to feel that their employing authority is supportive in providing adequate resources, staffing and work conditions. Sensible régimes of contact time, time out and administrative duties are essential. Teachers feel that regulations prevent them from applying discipline in the classroom and that stronger measures must be made available to counteract disruptive behaviour, one critical cause of stress. Management in schools has to be professional. Amateur, all-powerful, weak or autocratic heads of sections, departments or schools are likely to generate tension *as well as being the victims of stress.*

Educational organizations have a responsibility to provide a work environment which is as stress free and supportive as realistically possible. Apart from this obligation to protect the health of employees, it serves the interests of efficiency. Fairness and effectiveness in teacher and in-service training, promotion prospects, support in and out of school, financial incentives and doing everything to heighten the professional image of teachers are all seen by teachers as necessary to reduce stress.

## Stress in pupils

Young people in educational settings have their problems too, sometimes of sufficient intensity for them to end up in serious physical or mental states. Extreme cases, fortunately few in number, reach suicidal proportions and there are also on record students who have developed ME (myalgic encephalomyelitis). The causes are varied and range from parental pressure to do well at school or university, feelings of inadequacy (often ill-founded), to bullying. Broadly, these reasons group into *academic* and *interpersonal* pressures.

Most schools, universities and colleges have counselling and personal tutorial systems designed to give students a contact who might act as a mentor in academic work or in a pastoral role. This is more characteristic of further and higher education, but it has been introduced in recent years in some secondary schools. This topic is dealt with later in Chapter 15. In this section we shall concentrate on a particular non-academic stress which affects the motivation and performance of schoolchildren – bullying.

### Bullying

One particularly nasty source of stress in pupils is bullying, usually from one or more pupils in the same school. The systematic study of the topic by psychologists has intensified in recent years. It tends to have been ignored in the past, because 'it's all in the process of growing up'.

*Bullying* is aggressive behaviour, usually persistent, arising from the deliberate intent to cause physical or psychological distress in others. It takes many forms, but generally consists of direct physical action (e.g. hitting, tripping, pushing, nipping, stealing belongings), direct verbal abuse (e.g. aggressively demanding something, name calling, incessantly taunting and poking fun) and indirect verbal abuse (e.g. spreading rumours, 'sending to Coventry'). Direct methods tend to be used by boys and indirect by girls (Ahmad and Smith 1994).

The extent of bullying has been researched, but it is difficult to be certain that every child admits to being a victim. It is certain that more takes place than is reported (Randall 1996) and parents of both bully and victim are shocked to discover their children's involvement. A research into the bullying of girls (for the NSPCC and a teenager magazine, *Sugar*, press report, September 2005) claims that two-thirds of their sample (nearly 1,000) said they were bullied at some time. Whatever else, it is widespread (Smith 2002).

In a thorough research in Sheffield, Smith and his team (Smith and Sharp 1994) found differences between early and later schooling. In junior/middle schools, 27 per cent of pupils admitted to being either frequently or sometimes bullied, and of these 10 per cent were bullied once a week or more frequently. In secondary schools, 10 per cent admitted to being frequently or sometimes bullied of which 4 per cent occurred once or more than once a week. The figures also showed a steady decline with age and a greater prevalence amongst boys than girls. The commonest places are in the playground or in the classroom between members of the same class (Whitney and Smith 1993).

What are the effects of bullying on the hapless victims? Bullying can be very hurtful to the recipient and the degree of hurt often not realized by those doing the bullying or by teachers who have not experienced bullying as a child. The range of effects stretch from loneliness, unhappiness and misery, depression and other emotional disorders, low self-esteem, truancy, sleep and eating disturbances, long-term effects on social relationships and suicide (Randall 1996). A research into bullying of girls mentioned above (for the NSPCC and *Sugar*, press report, September 2005) discovered that 25 per cent of bullied girls felt suicidal. Victims are often milder persons and find assertive reaction difficult.

How is the problem of bullying being tackled? Awareness has been heightened in the last two decades and many schools now have a policy to counteract bullying. However, at one extreme we still find schools where bullying is ignored. Where this happens, it is sometimes the case that heads and teachers who have never experienced bullying are reluctant to accept that it occurs. Those who know it occurs, but do nothing, often have a philosophy that children should be able to take the knocks of life without being 'overprotected', otherwise they will not learn how to cope in adult life. One grave concern about this view, as mentioned above, is the lasting and often disastrous effect which bullying has on victims. The sooner the problem is identified, corrected and counselled, the better.

School policies in vogue cover a wide range of actions, most of which are described by Sharp and Smith in Sharp *et al.* (1994). One dimension concerns the *degree* of involvement of agencies, running from teacher/class to local community and LA. Another is the *nature* of the involvement from assertive methods to 'no blame' approaches.

The degree of involvement may see the headteacher or a nominated teacher dealing with both the victim and the bully or bullies if they are in the same class, which is often the case; there may be a support group, class or school council of pupils (*'bully' courts* – Elliott (2002) at *Kidscape*; also see 'young-voice' website, www.young-voice.org); there may be specialist advisers (psychologists, teachers trained in counselling); there may be a *whole school policy* (Smith and Sharp 1994); the net may be even wider and include the LA or a community approach (Randall 1996, in which Appendix A gives references to literature, curriculum and resource materials).

The methods adopted involve 'straight talk' and even aggressiveness towards the bully and sympathy for the victim. This approach to the bully is not liked by many specialists in the field because it teaches the bully that aggressive behaviour is an acceptable way of dealing with others – just what the bully has been up to. The school curriculum can be a powerful way of showing the agonies of the victim and more socially desirable behaviour. Literature, role play, videos and drama are all playing a part in the re-education process. The use of victim support groups (Arora 1989) and *assertiveness training* (Elliott 2002), that is, learning how to stand up for one's rights and firmly stating these to the bullies in a clear, honest and direct way, are also favoured by many teachers.

Two further methods, related but not identical, are the *common concern* method (Pikas, 1989) and the *no blame approach* (Maines and Robinson 1998). In the no blame approach, the central argument is that punishment is not the most effective way of putting a stop to bullying. Maines and Robinson offer a seven-step plan:

1   Interview the person being bullied. The emphasis of the interview is on the feelings of the victim rather than who did it, when and how.
2   Bring together the people responsible. This group could include bystanders. A group of six to eight is found to be a good number.
3   Explain the problem by telling the group of the feeling experienced by the victim using any verbal, written or drawn material. No specific blame is directed at anyone in the group.
4   Share the attribution of blame by saying that they are all responsible in some way.
5   Get each member of the group to suggest ways in which the victim could be helped to feel happier. The teacher might contribute some positive ideas, but no 'contract' is drawn up. The ideas need to be listed and agreed by those present.
6   Leave it to the group to solve the problem and arrange to meet the group at some later date for a progress report.
7   Meet the victim and individual members of the group about a week after the first meeting to see how things have progressed.

Prevention, of course, is better than cure and most of the above kinds of involvement can be introduced to reduce the prospect of bullying in schools. It has been, and probably always will be, a feature of school life. We now need to *anticipate* its onset rather than have to mediate in its effects.

## Summary

Children abound with vitality and an urge to satisfy many kinds of human needs. Armed with this knowledge, teachers are able to make the formal setting of school into an environment in which children can learn and develop efficiently. The process of motivation sees the release of energy which can be utilized for, and directed towards, educational objectives. Where children are physiologically satisfied, where they feel secure and wanted and where they have the opportunity to grow in confidence, independence and self-esteem through achievement, there is every likelihood that they will go on to seek the intellectual satisfactions provided at school.

For our purposes, the important emphasis is in the testable outcomes of our methods in the classroom, rather than in seeking the elusive origins of human needs. For example, we know that young children become puzzled by their surroundings; they poke around, question and show inquisitiveness; they manipulate and inspect most things that come within reach. The classroom, therefore, should be designed to take advantage of these ready-made characteristics. Children also strive to succeed or achieve in their attempt to master environmental obstacles (material, social or intellectual). We would not have survived if this had not been so. Of course, the conditions for achievement are varied, and research shows that a skilful combination of success and failure is more favourable for stimulating positive achievement than a distant or 'neutral' atmosphere. Children tasting success and failure – in that order – are most likely to continue the struggle to achieve. They also set themselves goals, and teachers must ensure that these goals are adequate and realistic for each child. The teacher must beware, however, of prejudging the capabilities of a child to the point where the teacher consistently underestimates or overestimates them. It is so easy to 'give a dog a bad name'.

Extrinsic motivators in the form of incentives are a very necessary part of a teacher's life. Children, like adults, want to know how they are faring in relation to their own previous performance and the performance of others. Research tells us that the sooner people know the outcome of their work the more likely it is that they will be reinforced to continue learning – always provided they meet with sufficient success, because knowledge of repeated failure is not likely to stimulate further activity. As we observed above, positive achievement must be part of the teacher's design. Praise and reproof from a respected teacher are powerful incentives. Younger children delight in approval in the presence of their peers.

Knowledge of childhood motives is one of the essentials of teaching skill. When children are pursuing purposeful activities in class because they feel the need and want to learn, their teacher is clearly well on the way to an understanding of these motives.

Stress in the workplace, arising from increasing demands made on an individual's physical and mental resources, has become a real problem for the teaching profession. Performance in various aspects of a teacher's life suffers as a consequence. Awareness of what the stressors are and what might be done to overcome them goes some way towards alleviating the stressful symptoms. Stress in children caused by bullying has also received increasing attention by psychologists in recent years.

## Tutorial enquiry and discussion

(a) In tutorials, examine Maslow's theory for its possible applications in education. Using the theory as a possible framework, consider the varied conditions of home and school likely to affect the highest desire of humans to satisfy their need for knowledge and understanding.

(b) On school observation, carefully note those activities which children in particular age groups most enjoy. Can these be turned to good effect in class? What criteria have you used for detecting interest and enthusiasm amongst children? Discuss with your tutors whether these are valid criteria.

(c) Observe children at play and note the differences according to age. Is playing a 'natural' educator? How can interest in play be canalized to good effect in schoolwork? Where should teachers draw the line between 'play' and 'work'?

(d) Colin Roger's book, *A Social Psychology of Schooling*, raises a number of issues about expectancy. Look particularly at those relating to teacher and pupil expectations, self-concept and self-esteem, attribution of success and failure. It gives a reasoned argument for and against the generalizations arising from the research in this area. With the tutor, read and examine the relevant parts of this book with an eye on those points which can be of immediate value in classrooms. Are there differences arising from age, sex or ability?

(e) Examine the possibility that the performance of girls in science and maths in primary schools, is partly a product of self-fulfilling prophecies. What can a teacher do to avoid the self-fulfilment of adverse prophecies?

(f) Note the use made by teachers of incentives. Compare the relative merits of incentives in particular age groups and, where possible, with different ability ranges.

(g) After reading the recommended literature on stress, discuss the issues in tutorials and in school to discover which are the important stressors. How do pupils and teachers cope with stress?

(h) Examine the 'fight against bullying' policy in schools you have visited. Pool these in tutorial and discuss their effectiveness.

## References

Ahmad, Y. and Smith, P. K. (1994), 'Bullying in schools and the issue of sex differences', in J. Archer (ed.), *Male Violence*. London: Routledge.

Ainsworth, M. D. S., Blehar, M. C., Waters, E. and Wall, S. (1978), *Patterns of Attachment: A Psychological Study of the Strange Situation*. Hillsdale, NJ: Erlbaum.

Allport, G. W. (1937), *Personality*. New York: Holt.

Archer, J. (1992), *Ethology and Human Development*. Hemel Hempstead: Harvester Wheatsheaf (Simon & Schuster).

Ardrey, R. (1967), *The Territorial Imperative*. London: Collins.

Arora, T. (1989), 'The use of victim support groups', in P.K. Smith and D. Thompson (eds), *Practical Approaches to Bullying*. London: Fulton.

Atkinson, J. W. (1964), *An Introduction to Motivation*. Princeton, NJ: Van Nostrand.

Atkinson, J. W. and Litwin, G. H. (1960), 'Achievement motive and test anxiety as motives to approach success and avoid failure', *Journal of Abnormal and Social Psychology*, 60, 52–63.

Atkinson, J. W. and Raynor, J. O. (eds) (1974), *Motivation and Achievement*. Washington, DC: Winston & Sons.

Ausubel, D. P. and Robinson, F. G. (1969), *School Learning: An Introduction to Educational Psychology*. New York: Holt, Rinehart and Winston.

Ball, S. (ed.) (1977), *Motivation in Education*. New York: Academic Press.

Bandura, A. (1986), *Social Foundations of Thought and Action: A Social Cognitive Theory.* Englewood Cliffs, NJ: Prentice Hall.

Barker Lunn, J. C. (1970), *Streaming in the Primary School*. Slough: NFER.

Bateson, G. (1955), 'A theory of play and fantasy', *Psychological Abstracts Research Report,* 2, 39–51.

Bee, H. and Boyd, D. (2004), *The Developing Child* (10th edn). Boston, MA: Pearson and AB.

Benedict, R. (1935), *Patterns of Culture*. London: Routledge and Kegan Paul.

Bennett, N., Wood, E. and Rogers, S. (1997), *Teaching Through Play: Teachers Thinking and Classroom Practice*. Buckingham: Open University Press.

Berlyne, D. E. (1960), *Conflict, Arousal and Curiosity*. New York: McGraw-Hill.

Birney, R. C. Burdick, H. and Teevan, R C. (1969), *Fear of Failure*. Princeton, NJ: Van Nostrand.

Bloom, B. S. (1976), *Human Characteristics and School Learning*. New York: McGraw-Hill.

Bowlby, J. (1973), *Attachment and Loss: Separation, Anxiety and Anger*. London: Hogarth Press.

Braun, C. (1976), 'Teacher expectation: sociopsychological dynamics', *Review of Educational Research*, 46, 185–213.

Brewer, W. F. (1972), 'There is no convincing evidence for conditioning in adult human beings' paper read to the Conference on Cognition and the Symbolic Processes, Pennsylvania State University.

Broadhurst, P. L. (1957), 'Emotionality and the Yerkes–Dodson Law', *Journal of Experimental Psychology*, 54, 345–52.

Brookover, W. B., Erikson, E. L. and Joiner, L. M. (1967), *Self-concept of Ability and School Achievement III: Final report on Cooperative Research Project No. 2831*. East Lansing: Michigan State University.

Brophy, J. (1981), 'Teacher praise: a functional analysis', *Review of Educational Research*, 51, 5–32.

Bruner, J. S., Jolly, A. and Sylva, K. (1976), *Play: Its Role in Development and Evolution*. London: Pelican Books.

Burns, R. B. (1976), 'The self-concept and its relevance to academic achievement', in D. Child (ed.), *Readings in Psychology for the Teacher*. London: Holt, Rinehart and Winston.

Burns, R. B. (1982), *Self-Concept Development and Education*. Eastbourne: Holt, Rinehart and Winston.

Burt, C. (1941), 'Is the doctrine of instincts dead? A symposium. I – The case for human instincts', *British Journal of Educational Psychology*, 11, 155–72.

Cannon, W. B. (1932), *The Wisdom of the Body*. London: Norton.

Cattell, R. B. and Child, D. (1975), *Motivation and Dynamic Structure*. London: Holt, Rinehart and Winston.

Child, D. (1984), 'Motivation and the Dynamic Calculus – a teacher's view', *Multivariate Behavioral Research*, 19, 288–98.

Child, D. (1988), 'Recent developments of MAT and SMAT', in K. M. Miller (ed.), *The Analysis of Personality in Research and Assessment*. London: Independent Assessment and Research Centre, pp. 81–92.

Child, D. (2006), *The Essentials of Factor Analysis* (3rd edn). London: Continuum.

Covington, M. V. (1992), *Making the Grade: a Self-worth Perspective on Motivation and School Reform*. New York: Cambridge University Press.

De Frank, R. S. and Cooper, C. L. (1987), 'Worksite stress management interventions: their effectiveness and conceptualisation', *Journal of Managerial Psychology*, 2, 4–10.

Dunkin, M. J. and Biddle, B. J. (1974), *The Study of Teaching*. New York: Holt, Rinehart and Winston.

Eccles, J. (1983), 'Expectancies, values and academic behaviors', in J. T. Spence (ed.), *Achievement and Achievement Motives*. San Francisco: Freeman.

Elashoff, J. D. and Snow, R. E. (1973), 'Pygmalion Reconsidered', in G. A. Davies and T. F. Warren, *Psychology of Education: New Looks*. New York: Heath.

Elliott, M. (2002), 'Bully "courts"', in M. Elliott (ed.), *Bullying: A Practical Guide to Coping for Schools* (3rd edn). London: Pitman. Also see website reference.

Evans, P. (1989), *Motivation and Emotion*. London: Routledge.

Festinger, L. (1957), *A Theory of Cognitive Dissonance*. Evanston, IL: Row Peterson.

Freud, S. (1915), 'Instincts and their vicissitudes', in *A Collection of Papers of Sigmund Freud* (Vol. I), (trans. by Riviere, 1949). London: Hogarth.

Freud, S. (1920), 'Beyond the pleasure principle', in J. Strachey (ed.), (1955) *The Standard Edition of the Complete Psychological Works of Sigmund Freud* (Vol. 22). London: Hogarth.

Gardner, H. (1993a), *Frames of Mind: The Theory of Multiple Intelligences* (10th anniversary edn). London: Heinemann.

Gjesme, T. (1971), 'Motive to achieve success and motive to avoid failure in relation to school performance for pupils of different ability levels', *Scandinavian Journal of Educational Research*, 15, 81–99.

Harlow, H. F. and Harlow, M. K. (1973), 'Effects of various mother–infant relationships on rhesus monkey behaviors', in B. M. Foss (ed.), *Determinants of Infant Behavior* (Vol. 4). London: Methuen.

Harter, S. (1982), 'The Perceived Competence Scale for Children', *Child Development*, 53, 87–97.

Hill, W. F. (2002), *Learning: A Survey of Psychological Interpretations* (7th edn). New York: Longman.

Hughes, F. P. (1999), *Children, Play and Development* (3rd edn). Boston, MA: Allyn and Bacon.

Hull, C. L. (1943), *Principles of Behavior*. New York: Appleton-Century-Crofts.

Hunt, J. McV. (1960), 'Experience and the development of motivation: some reinterpretations', *Child Development*, 31, 489–504.

Hurlock, E. B. (1925), 'An evaluation of certain incentives used in school work', *Journal of Educational Psychology*, 16, 145–59.

Johannesson, I. (1962), 'Effects of praise and blame upon achievement and attitudes in school children', in I. Johannesson, *Child and Education*. Copenhagen: Munksgaard.

Johnson-Laird, P. N. (1988), *The Computer and the Mind*. London: Fontana.

Kay, W. (1968), *Moral Development: A Psychological Study of Moral Growth from Childhood to Adolescence*. London: Allen and Unwin.

Keys, A. (1952), 'Experimental introduction of psychoneuroses by starvation', *The Biology of Mental Health and Disease*, 27th Annual Conference: New York: Millbank Memorial Fund, Harper and Row.

Kohlberg, L. and Lickona, T. (1986), *The Stages of Ethical Development: From Childhood through Old Age*. New York: Harper and Row.

Kyriacou, C. (1987), 'Teacher stress and burnout: an international review', *Educational Research*, 29(2), 146–52.

Kyriacou, C. (1989), 'The nature and prevalence of teacher stress', in M. Cole and S. Walker (eds), *Teaching and Stress*. Milton Keynes: Open University Press, pp. 27–34.

Kyriacou, C. and Sutcliffe, J. (1979), 'Teacher stress and satisfaction', *Educational Research*, 21, 89–96.

Lea, S. E. G. (1984), *Instinct, Environment and Behaviour*. London: Methuen.

Locke, E. A. and Latham, G. P., (1990), *A Theory of Goal Setting and Task Performance*. Englewood Cliffs, NJ: Prentice Hall.

Lepper, M. R. and Hodell, M. (1989), 'Intrinsic motivation in the classroom', in C. Ames and R. Ames (eds), *Research in Motivation in Education*. San Diego, CA: Academic Press, pp. 73–105.

Lillard, A. (2001), 'Pretending, understanding pretence, and understanding minds', *Play and Culture Studies*, 3, 233–54.

Lillemyr, O. F. (2003), 'Play in school – the teacher's role: reforms and recent research', in O. N. Saracho and B. Spodek (eds), *Contemporary Perspectives on Play in Early Childhood Education*. Greenwich, CON: Information age Publishing.

Lorenz, K. (1966), *On Aggression*. London: Methuen.

Lorenz, K. (1981), *The Foundations of Ethology*. New York: Springer-Verlag.

Mahone, C. (1960), 'Fear of failure in unrealistic vocational aspirations', *Journal of Abnormal and Social Psychology*, 60, 253–61.

Maier, S. F. and Seligman, M. E. P. (1976), 'Learned helplessness: theory and evidence', *Journal of Experimental Psychology (General)*, 105, 3–46.

Main, M. and Cassidy, J. (1988), 'Categories of response to reunion with parents at age 6: predictable from infant attachment classi?cations and stable over a 1-month period', *Developmental Psychology*, 24, 415–26.

Maines, B. and Robinson, G. (1998), 'The no blame approach to bullying', in D. Shorrocks-Taylor (ed.), *Directions in Educational Psychology*. London: Whurr.

Maslow, A. H. (1970), *Motivation and Personality* (2nd edn). New York: Harper and Row.

McClelland, D. C. (1955), *Studies in Motivation*. New York: Appleton-Century-Crofts.

McClelland, D. C. (1965), 'Towards a theory of motivation acquisition', *American Psychologist*, 20, 321–33.

McClelland, D. C. (1972), 'What is the effect of achievement motivation training in the schools?', *Teachers College Record*, 74, 129–45.

McClelland, D. C. (1987), *Human Motivation*. New York: Cambridge University Press.

McClelland, D. C., Atkinson, J. W., Clark, R. A. and Lowell, E. L. (1976), *The Achievement Motive*. New York: Irvington Publishers.

McDougall, W. (1960), *An Introduction to Social Psychology*. New York: Barnes and Noble (original: Methuen, London, 1908).

Mead, M. (1935), *Sex and Temperament*. London: Routledge.

Morris, Desmond (1971), *The Human Zoo*. London: Corgi.

Morris, Desmond (1977), *Manwatching*. London: Cape.

Morris, Desmond (1985), *Bodywatching: A Guide to the Human Species*. London: Cape.

Morris, Desmond (1988), *The Naked Ape*. London: Corgi.

Morris, Desmond (1991), *Babywatching*. London: Cape.

Morris, Desmond (1994), *The Human Animal: A Personal View of the Human Species*. London: BBC Books.

Moyles, J. R. (1989), *Just Playing? The Role and Status of Play in Early Childhood*. Buckingham: Open University Press.

Moyles, J. R. (ed.) (2005), *The Excellence of Play* (2nd edn.). Buckingham: Open University Press.

Murray, H. A. (1938), *Explorations in Personality*. Oxford: Oxford University Press.

Overmeier, J. R. and Seligman, M. E. P. (1967), 'Effects of inescapable shock upon subsequent escape and avoidance responding', *Journal of Comparative and Physiological Psychology*, 63, 28–33.

Parten, M. (1932), 'Social participation among preschool children', *Journal of Abnormal and Social Psychology*, 27, 243–69.

Peters, R. S. (1958), *The Concept of Motivation*. London: Routledge and Kegan Paul.

Pikas, A. (1989), 'The common concern method for the treatment of mobbing', in E. Roland and E. Munthe (eds), *Bullying: An International Perspective*. London: David Fulton Publishers.

Pintrich, P. R. and Schunk, D. H. (2002), *Motivation in Education: Theory, Research and Applications* (2nd edn). Upper Saddle River: Merrill.

Randall, P. (1996), *A Community Approach to Bullying*. Stoke-on-Trent: Trentham Books.

Rogers, C. (1982), *A Social Psychology of Schooling: The Expectancy Process*. London: Routledge and Kegan Paul.

Rogers, C. (1998), 'Teacher expectations: implications for school improvement', in D. Shorrocks-Taylor (ed.), *Directions in Educational Psychology*. London: Whurr.

Roopnarine, J. L., Lasker, J., Sacks, M. and Stores, M. (1998), 'The cultural contents of children's play', in O. N. Saracho and B. Spodek (eds), *Multiple Perspectives on Play in Early Childhood Education*. New York: Suny Press.

Rosenthal, R. and Jacobson, L. (1968), *Pygmalion in the Classroom*. New York: Holt, Rinehart and Winston.

Rosenthal, R. and Jacobson, L. (1992), *Pygmalion in the Classroom: Teacher Expectation and Pupils' Intellectual Development* (new edn). New York: Irvington.

Rotter, J. B. (1954), *Social Learning and Clinical Psychology*. Englewood Cliffs, NJ: Prentice-Hall.

Rotter, J. B. (1966), 'Generalized expectancies of internal versus external control of reinforcement', *Psychological Monographs*, 80, 1.

Saracho, O. N. and Spodek, B. (eds) (2003), *Contemporary Perspectives on Play in Early Childhood Education*. Greenwich, CON: Information age Publishing.

Satterly, D. and Hill, J. (1983), 'Personality differences and the effects of success and failure on causal attributions and expectancies of primary school children', *Educational Psychology*, 3, 245–58.

Schmidt, H. O. (1941), 'The effect of praise and blame on incentives to learning', *Psychological Monographs*, 53, 240.

Sears, P. S. (1940), 'Levels of aspiration in academically successful and unsuccessful children', *Journal of Abnormal and Social Psychology*, 35, 498–536.

Seligman, M. E. P. (1975), *Helplessness*. San Francisco: Freeman.

Sharp, S., Cowie, H. and Smith, P. K. (1994), 'Responding to bullying behaviour', in S. Sharp and P. K. Smith (eds), *Tackling Bullying in Your School: A Practical Handbook for Teachers*. London: Routledge.

Skinner, B. F. (1953), *Science and Human Behavior*. New York: Macmillan.

Skinner, B. F. (1971), *Beyond Freedom and Dignity*. New York: Knopf.

Smith, C. P. (1992), *Motivation and Personality: Handbook of Thematic Content and Analysis*. New York: Cambridge University Press.

Smith, P. K. and Sharp, S. (1994), *School Bullying: Insights and Perspectives*. London: Routledge.

Smith, P. K. (ed.) (2002), *Violence in Schools: The Response in Europe*. London: Routledge.

Stendler, C.B., Damrin, D. and Haines, A.C. (1951), 'Studies in cooperation and competition: I: the effects of working for group and individual rewards on the social climate of children's groups', *Journal of Genetic Psychology*, 79, 173–97.

Strube, M. J. (ed.) (1991), *Type A Behavior*. Beverly Hills, CA: Sage.

Travers, C. J. and Cooper, C. L. (1996), *Teachers Under Pressure: Stress in the Teaching Profession*. London: Routledge.

Travers, C. J. and Cooper, C. L. (1998), 'Stress in teaching', in D. Shorrocks-Taylor (ed.), *Directions in Educational Psychology*. London: Whurr.

Vernon, P. E. (1942), 'Is the doctrine of instincts dead? A symposium. II – Some objections to the theory of instincts', *British Journal of Educational Psychology*, 12, 1–10.

Walters, G. C. and Grusec, J. E. (1977), *Punishment*. San Francisco: Freeman.

Weiner, B. J. (1977), 'An attributional approach for educational psychology', in L. Shulman (ed.), *Review of Research in Education*. Itasca, IL: Peacock.

Weiner, B. J. (1992), *Human Motivation: Metaphors, Theories and Research*. London: Sage.

Wiesel, T. N. and Hubel, D. H. (1965), 'Extent of recovery from the effects of visual deprivation of kittens', *Journal of Neurophysiology*, 28, 1060–72.

Whitney, I. and Smith, P. K. (1993), 'A survey of the nature and extent of bully/victim problems in junior/middle and secondary schools', *Educational Research*, 35, 3–25.

Wigfield, A. and Eccles, J. (1992), 'The development of achievement task values: a theoretical analysis', *Developmental Review*, 12, 265–310.

Yerkes, R. M. and Dodson, J. D. (1908), 'The relation of strength of stimulus to rapidity of habit-formation', *Journal of Comparative Neurological Psychology*, 18, 459–82.

## Further reading

Alderman, M. K. (1999), *Motivation for Achievement: Possibilities for Teaching and Learning*. London: Lawrence Erlbaum.

Fitzgerald, D. (1999), *Bullying in our Schools – Understanding and Tackling Bullying: A Guide for Schools*. Dublin: Blackhall. Easy to read.

Glover, D., Cartwright, N. with Gleeson, D. (1998), *Towards Bully-free Schools: Interventions in Action*. Buckingham: Open University Press. A research-based book, but plenty of important issues are examined.

Pintrich, P. R. and Schunk, D. H. (2002), *Motivation in Education: Theory, Research and Applications* (2nd edn). Upper Saddle River: Merrill. Employs an updated cognitive approach with many useful ideas for teachers.

Saracho, O. N. and Spodek, B. (eds) (2003), *Contemporary Perspectives on Play in Early Childhood Education*. Greenwich, CON: Information age Publishing.

Weiner, B. J. (1992), *Human Motivation: Metaphors, Theories and Research* (2nd edn). San Francisco: Sage. A cognitive psychology text written by a leading authority.

## Useful websites

http://www.young-voice.org/documents/camdenbullyfree.pdf
Young Voice

# Part Four
## Individual Differences

# Human Intelligence

---

# Implications for teachers

- Children's intellectual abilities vary considerably. Whatever the source of this variability, teachers have to assume that they can influence the achievement of their children.

- Suspicions of underperformance of a child have to be explored. Intelligence testing by the Psychological Service of an LA or by teachers qualified to use standardized test materials is an important contribution to defining the nature of the problems.

- Intelligence tests are capable of diagnosing specific intellectual problems relevant to schoolwork.

- Given the wide variety of school subjects, including dance, drama, music, physical education, religious and social studies, there is a case for considering the concept of multiple intelligences (Gardner 1999).

- Knowledge of intelligence test design can only help a teacher in making decisions about appropriate courses of action for a particular pupil.

- The continued use of IQ tests in grammar schools and occupational selection makes knowledge of the area important.

- The debate about the relative contribution of inherited and acquired intellectual characteristics is important for teachers.

# General cognitive ability (intelligence)

Few topics in psychology can have attracted more widespread attention than *intelligence* or *general cognitive ability*. The reasons are not hard to find. Until recently, everyone's educational and some career prospects hung almost entirely on standardized tests of number, verbal or general ability with assessments by teachers in selection for secondary schooling. Some education authorities still use them for this purpose. The confirmation of children with special needs (SEN) for purposes of providing special educational facilities has been based on IQ (Intelligence Quotient) tests. The civil service, armed forces, industry, some professions such as nursing and some universities include an IQ test in their selection procedures. In America, preparatory schools, secondary schools, universities, medical, law and business schools use a variety of selection devises closely related to intelligence tests. The subject is also a tender spot for many social scientists, who see it as having a divisive effect in social and ethnic matters, and it must be admitted that intelligence measurement had, in the past, a decisive influence on the educational and occupational life-chances of many people.

Nevertheless, the existence of differences in the distribution of human abilities is well established and the measures amongst the most reliable and valid in human behaviour measurements (Neisser *et al.* 1996, Mackintosh 1998). Exploration of human ability is inevitable. It is almost a platitude to say that as intelligent creatures we will question the nature of our intelligence. If we abandoned the concept of intelligence today, we would re-invent it tomorrow.

The detection and measurement of differences are important for the teacher. It would be disastrous for children if we did not quickly recognize their cognitive strengths and weaknesses, because the intellectually dull cannot, in general, cope with the same cognitive tasks as the intellectually bright of the same age, although they may possess special skills in particular abilities. In some cases it is difficult to discover the scholastic potential of a child by observing school work and we need to resort to standardized tests of general cognitive ability. This chapter, therefore, will be concerned with a discussion of how far we have got in defining the nature of intelligence, in assessing intelligent behaviour and in elaborating models of the intellect.

# Defining intelligent behaviour

The concept of intelligence is complex and there is no single, one sentence definition. It is said that if you ask a dozen psychologists to define intelligence, you will get a dozen definitions. Even the word 'intelligence' has developed some unfortunate implicit meanings over the years. In common parlance it has erroneously come to mean a possession, something one has in a fixed quantity, and probably located in one's head! The concept of the intelligence quotient (IQ) is probably responsible for conveying this impression of intelligence as a fixed quantity. But there is more to human intelligence than is captured using IQ tests. Therefore, it is important to remember in much of what follows that intelligence tests do not define human intelligence; they only sample it.

The habit of looking on intelligence as a possession of precise dimensions (known as *reification*) was discussed by Miles (1957). He recommended that we abandon the term 'intelligence' and replace it with the less ambiguous term 'intelligent behaviour'. In so doing we lay stress on the activity of a person exposed to certain kinds of experience and how he or she would respond. We can then define this behaviour as more or less intelligent. Of course, this still leaves undefined the vital question of what intelligent behaviour is. Nevertheless, having noted Miles's cautionary comments and the dangers of misusing the term 'intelligence', we shall continue to apply it in the text synonymously with 'intelligent behaviour', 'general cognitive ability' and 'psychometric intelligence'. The latter term exists because the most widely used measures of intelligence are standardized psychometric tests from which much of the research in this area has been derived.

Vernon (1979), in an address to the British Psychological Society, perceived three broad inter-related categories for defining human intelligence. These were biological, psychological and operational. Biological definitions emphasize the individual's capacity to adjust or adapt to environmental stimuli. 'Adaptation' here refers to modifying behaviour either overtly or covertly as a result of experience. Heim's (1970) definition of intelligent activity as consisting of 'grasping the essentials in a given situation and responding appropriately to them' comes close to a biological one. There is something of this definition in the work of Piaget in Chapter 4. Hebb (1966) has also maintained that adaptation depends on the quality of neurological connections in the brain and CNS: high intelligence for him is founded on having a 'good' brain and CNS. Humans have certainly outstripped the animals in their gift as adaptors of, and to, environments, essentially by virtue of their more advanced neural endowment in the form of a large neocortex (see Chapter 2).

A problem in studying biological adaptation as a definition of cognitive ability is the masking effect of our self-made systems which overgrow and obscure our adaptive qualities from the hard biological facts of life. However, from animal, brain damage, neuro-genetic and twin study research (Plomin *et al.* 2001) there is now little doubt that intelligence as we currently define it has a gene-based component, related to both cognitive ability and disability. For example, genes appear to be associated with reading disability and dementia (Plomin, *et al.* 2001) and the next step is to identify those linked to specific abilities. Equally, it cannot be regarded as immutable since both environmental factors and personal qualities will also affect behaviour (Howe 1998). We shall look again at the genetic and social influences later in the chapter.

Psychological definitions stress *mental efficiency* and the capacity for abstract reasoning which requires the use of symbolic language. Spearman's famous formulation of intelligent behaviour as 'the eduction of relations and correlates' is an example of a psychological definition. This approach accounts much more for the higher abstract conceptualization prevalent in humans. There is more recognition of verbal, numerical and spatial skills. Taking a common example from an intelligence test to illustrate Spearman's definition, find the missing word:

Hand is to arm as foot is to . . .

There are two statements here:

hand is to arm     (A)
foot is to          (B)

The relationship we *educe* (infer) from statement (A) is based on our knowledge of limb attachments. Using this fact, we attempt to *correlate* the first part of the statement (B) with the second part, in this case 'leg'.

Operational definitions involve making detailed specifications of intelligent behaviour and then finding measures of these specifications. Intelligent behaviour thus becomes expressed in terms of these measures. As Miles (1957) so aptly puts it:

psychologists have desired standardized tests – it is the items in these tests which are regarded as exemplars of the word intelligent (exemplars = actual or possible manifestations of behaviour which are claimed to be intelligent). Correct responses to these items shall be deemed to constitute acts of intelligent behaviour.

*Psychometric intelligence* extracted from standardized tests is the outcome of these operational definitions. The expression 'intelligence is what intelligence tests measure' is often used to describe the operational definition, although, as we shall see presently, it is not really as superficial as this statement would suggest.

## Intelligence A, B and C

The prevailing view of intelligent behaviour brings out the dynamic interplay between inborn potential and circumstances. One particularly instructive approach was elaborated by Hebb (1966). He distinguishes between *Intelligence A* and *Intelligence B*, which we can identify with the genotype and phenotype, respectively, of intelligence. For Hebb, Intelligence A represents an innate potential which depends entirely on neurological facilities and signifies the capacity of an individual to develop intelligent responses. Whether the individual realizes this capacity or not depends on his or her life-chances. Thus, Intelligence B represents a hypothetical level of development which has resulted from the interaction of Intelligence A and environmental influences.

Neither Intelligence A nor Intelligence B can be measured directly. As we have suggested above, Intelligence A is masked by the immediate impact of experience. In the case of Intelligence B, we would have to devise a vast array of measures in order to sample the numerous aspects of human ability. Note that we would be *sampling* intelligence, not measuring it directly. Intelligence B is not fixed because changes of environment produce variations during its emergence particularly in childhood and adolescence. Consequently we must expect to find anomalies in the sampling of Intelligence B between cultures or sub-cultures arising partly from major differences in child-rearing habits which encourage or inhibit mental development, partly because there will be natural variation in the genotypic distribution of general cognitive ability between cultures (as one finds giants and pygmies), and partly because the sampling measures may favour some cultures more than others (verbal skills are often at a premium in some cultures).

Vernon (1979) introduced the term *Intelligence C* (synonymous with *psychometric intelligence*) to describe the sampling of Intelligence B using standardized tests. This is a very useful concept because IQ scores are often misguidedly taken as direct measures of Intelligence A or B, whereas they result from a sampling only of the latter. Much of the subsequent discussion will rest on evidence gathered using measures of Intelligence C. It is essential, therefore, to be aware of the special relationship between it and the other hypothesized origins of intelligence. The connection between Intelligence A and Intelligence C is, by definition, only fragmentary. As C samples B, and B is derived from A, we can assume a link between C and A. But it is virtually impossible to be certain of the precise relationship. Therefore we cannot regard an IQ score as a measure of innate capacity any more than we would regard it as an accurate measure of Intelligence B.

We shall return to psychometric test design shortly but first we should mention two recent developments suggesting that Intelligence C should be much wider in sampling intelligent human behaviour.

## Information processing and intelligence

The last 20 years or so have seen a shift in the approach of some psychologists towards information-processing explanations of intelligent behaviour. Psychometric test scores indicate *how much* of the quality we define as intelligence is exposed by the person doing the test but they tell us little about *how* the individual arrives at the solution to questions in the test. What is happening inside the person?

Information-processing (Sternberg 2000, but see the end of this section for further references to his work) is one approach and interested psychologists would ask such questions as what rules govern the systematics of how a person arrives at a solution to a problem? With a given knowledge base, what processing routines does a person use to arrive at a solution? What parts do efficiency in speed and accuracy (power) of processing play? And what aspects of the foregoing would be measured by conventional IQ tests? The aim of this approach is to examine how a person processes information to arrive at a solution and not just to look at the end product (the IQ score).

There are several kinds of process that could be examined. Amongst them are *chronometric measures* of cognition (how quickly do people respond to cognitive stimuli), for example, speed of reaction to and solution of various visual problems. The assumption is not unlike Hebb's brain/CNS efficiency hypothesis (see Neisser 1996 for references). Other researches have involved EEG (electroencephalograms, see Chapter 2) and power tests (Stein 1994 for EEG; Eysenck 1987 for reaction time and power tests). These have all been shown to correlate with IQ scores but the results are marginal. Indeed, the search for correlates has now got down to the nerve fibre level in the form of *nerve conduction velocity* (Reed and Jensen 1992). With corrections, the value of the correlation is about $+0.4$, which means that only 16 per cent of the variance is accounted for (0.4 squared and converted to a percentage of one). Put another way, 84 per cent of the variance in IQ scores depend on other, unidentified variables.

Another approach, postulated by Sternberg (1985a), is called the *triarchic theory*. It postulates three aspects of intelligence, namely, *analytic, creative* and *practical*. Only the first of these is tapped by intelligence tests. Creativity is dealt with in the next chapter. Practical intelligence is characterised by problems which are poorly defined, need a search for information, have several feasible solutions, require past experience, motivation and personal enthusiasm.

---

### Further reading

For an original view which espouses the information processing model, see Sternberg, *Beyond IQ: A Triarchic Theory of Human Intelligence* (1985a) and *Human Abilities: An Information-Processing Approach* (1985b). A recent relevant book by him is *In Search of Mind* (1995). His edited text, another *Handbook of Intelligence* (2000), is a very useful general sourcebook as well as giving his most recent thinking.

---

## Multiple intelligences (Gardner 1999)

Deciding on the specifications of intelligent behaviour has been quite a problem. Many people are still not convinced that we have succeeded in tapping anything like all abilities. Presently we shall look at some typical intelligence-test items which exemplify the kinds of specifications already widely accepted as demonstrating verbal, non-verbal and spatial reasoning. Reasoning tests containing analogies, synonyms, memory items and word and number series are very common, but there may be talents which are not yet entirely susceptible to testing in the conventional ways dictated by intelligence-test design. Creative thinking and writing (Chapter 10), music or art, business acumen and cognitive development in the Piagetian tradition have not all been convincingly measured, although recently some have been incorporated into the British Ability Scale (see 'Criterion-referenced testing', this chapter). These activities seem, at a common-sense level, to require higher mental processes. Also, at present we know more about *what* children can do in specified circumstances than *how* they do it. This intractable problem of defining our terms of reference arises because effects are more readily observed than causes; hence we have concentrated deliberately on measuring the outward manifestations of intelligent behaviour using test materials.

In a proposal by Gardner (1993a and b; Gardner *et al.* 1996) a case was made for there being six independent kinds of intelligent human behaviour. These are *linguistic, logical–mathematical, spatial, musical, bodily–kinaesthetic* and *personal.* Since then, the number has increased to ten with the separation of *personal* into *interpersonal* and *intrapersonal* and the inclusion of *naturalist, spiritual and existential* (Gardner 1999). The first three are familiar in contemporary test design as we have seen from the Vernon definitions, but the last seven of his ten intelligences have not been researched as thoroughly and are more contentious. One source of contention is that some of Gardner's proposed 'intelligences' (e.g., music, emotional sensitivity, spiritual and existential personal relations) do not correlate with general human ability.

What evidence did Gardner use to isolate these intelligences? He looked at those activities which (a) were affected by brain damage in different locations of the brain; (b) were represented by exceptional people; (c) had unique core skills; (d) had distinct developmental histories; (e) were plausible on historical and evolutionary grounds; and (f) had support from psychological research.

Musical ability incorporates pitch and rhythm applied to performing and composing music. In fact, Gardner appears to define music as 'sounds emitted at certain auditory frequencies and grouped according to a prescribed system'. Kinaesthetic ability has to do with body motion and manipulation, including manual control. In addition to dancers and gymnasts, one might also include surgeons and sports players. Personal intelligence includes *interpersonal* (that is understanding the moods and needs of others in such a way as to be capable of predicting how others would behave in similar future circumstances) and *intrapersonal* – the ability to understand one's own emotions and to harness them appropriately in one's actions. A few people do one or more of these intelligent activities superlatively; others seem quite unable. Gardner would maintain that there does not seem to be a correlation between the last three or with conventional measures of intelligence. *Naturalist, spiritual* and *existential* intelligences are in the process of clarification and definition.

The next stage in the development of this theory is to show how these intelligences can be assessed and subsequently to verify if there is or is not a relationship between them and with general ability. It should also be noticed that most of Gardner's abilities correlate with other human attributes such as personality, physical skill and so forth. Gardner's views are mentioned again in Chapter 10. One source of concern in Gardner's work is likely to be the confusion between intellectual, physical, personal and social skills all counting as 'intelligence' (i.e. general cognitive ability).

# Intelligence testing

## The work of Binet

Although the earliest tests are no longer used, the following section is a brief history of their origins.

At the turn of the last century, Alfred Binet suggested that the French Ministry of Public Instruction support him in devising a series of tests designed to pick out the mentally defective and retarded children in state schools who were unlikely to benefit from the normal school system. The idea was to segregate these children and provide them with special education more in keeping with their inabilities. This principle is still in operation today, although to a lesser extent. Binet's aim was to derive a scale of items answerable by about 75 per cent of children at given age intervals. The figure of 75 per cent was chosen because it was thought that the 'middle' 50 per cent (in ability) of an age group should be capable of solving the problems. Naturally the top 25 per cent should also have the ability, thus making 75 per cent in all. The performance of individual children was then compared with the expected performance of other age groups. If a child could answer questions for all age groups up to, say, nine years, the child's *mental age* was said to be nine years, irrespective of the actual (*chronological*) age. Sub-tests enabled the mental age to be assessed in two-monthly intervals from three years to about 13 years of age.

How did Binet decide on the sort of questions to ask the children? In the first place he used hunches from his observations of children in a variety of practical and theoretical tasks which appeared, at a common-sense level, to discriminate between their abilities. Items included naming or pointing to parts of the body, repeating digits or sentences, counting, producing rhymes for given words and defining familiar objects. For the most part the items were verbally biased. On referring back to his sample of scholastically bright, moderate and inadequate children he was able to choose items possessing the highest level of discrimination.

The concept of mental age is most useful when we express it in terms of the chronological age of the child. Stern introduced the idea of *mental ratio*, which he derived by dividing the child's mental age by the actual age. The resulting ratio was thought by Stern to be constant for a given child. We now know that mental age, and in consequence the mental ratio, may have an erratic history.

The small number obtained for the mental ratio is awkward. Terman proposed, therefore, that the ratio be multiplied by 100 to give a more convenient range of numbers. The final figure obtained is known as an *intelligence quotient*, or IQ for short. If a child of 5 years 0 months has a mental age of 6 years 0 months (i.e. can answer items normally answered by six-year-olds), the mental ratio would be:

$$\text{mental ratio} = \frac{\text{mental age}}{\text{chronological age}} = \frac{6}{5} = 1.20$$

The intelligence quotient or IQ $= 1.20 \times 100 = 120$. A child of six with a mental age of five would have an IQ of 83.33 recurring. Actually, we express IQs to the nearest whole number, in this case 83.

Binet's method is satisfactory only as long as we can produce cumulative norms for each age group. But as mental development beyond 15 or 16 years is irregular and sometimes non-existent, it is not possible to establish a continuous yardstick for comparison in the manner of Binet. Sooner or later age-related mental development as measured by conventional tests tails off.

---

### Further reading

Binet's original test has since undergone several revisions and translations from the French and appeared as the Binet–Simon Test, the Stanford–Binet (sometimes referred to as the Terman–

$\longrightarrow$

Merrill version). The fifth revision (by Gale H. Roid) is now being used for ages ranging from two years to 85+. There are five factors of *fluid reasoning, knowledge, quantitative reasoning, visual-spatial* and *working memory* (see http://www.nfer-nelson.co.uk/catalogue/catalogue.asp and enter 'binet' into the catalogue search box for more details).

## Modern test design

### Norm-referenced testing

The method now used extensively for calculating IQ scores, seen, for example, in the first Stanford–Binet norm-referenced tests mentioned above, employs the distribution of scores for each age group using representative samples, and they are then rescaled using a convenient mean and standard deviation (see Chapter 18). It compares the performance of an individual with that of a representative group from which 'norms' of performance have been derived. Usually the mean, no matter what value it may have in the first place, is made equal to 100. The distribution of the scores on each side of the mean is then usually manipulated so that about 70 per cent of the scores fall within the range from 85 to 115 (i.e. 15 points, or one standard deviation, on either side of the newly created mean). For this method to work properly, the distribution has to be 'normal' or very near to normal (see Figure 9.1). That means the distribution of scores on either side of the mean will tail off in a regular and symmetrical fashion. If this distribution does not appear, the test is modified

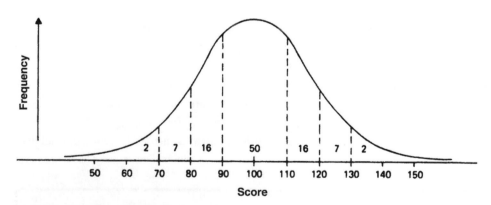

**Figure 9.1** Approximate normal distribution of people using a mean of 100 and standard deviation of 15. The figures under the curve represent the percentage of people falling within the limits indicated by the broken lines. Thus, 50 per cent fall between the scores of 90 and 110, 16 per cent between 80 and 90, or between 110 and 120, etc.

until it does. In other words, the normal distribution of IQ scores is not necessarily a fact of life but a feature of IQ test design. What is more, there is no direct evidence to suppose that 'intelligence' is normally distributed in society. So many factors of upbringing, inadequate sampling of intellectual skills, etc., already mentioned above, conspire against an accurate knowledge of IQ distributions. But their design is such as to impose the spread shown in the accompanying figure.

Figure 9.1 is based on the distribution with a mean of 100 and a standard deviation of 15 IQ points. There are, of course, an infinite number of means and standard deviations which could be used, but generally for IQ scales we adopt a mean of 100 and a standard deviation of 15, with a few using 10 or 20 points. These possible options in the standard deviation provide the reason why we have to state the name of a test when quoting an IQ because, unless the norms are the same, the scores from different tests will not correspond. If we were comparing IQs from tests both with a mean of 100, but having, say, standard deviations of 10 and 20, an IQ of 120 on the first would be equivalent to an IQ of 140 on the second. For those baffled by the calculations needed to produce Figure 9.1, there is an example on page 570–2, Chapter 18.

The important feature of norm-referencing, as the term implies, is the use of the performance of others who have taken the test under controlled conditions in order to make an assessment of an individual's performance in relation to those others – how 'normal' is the individual's score compared with others. Fundamentally, norm-referencing has to do with discriminating between individuals in a group by comparing all their scores.

At one time, these discriminations were converted into words and phrases along a rough scale, from very poor, poor, average, good, very good, excellent, or synonyms for these. It is very tempting and not unreasonable for teachers to compare the standing of a child with that of others in the same age and/or abilities range.

## Further reading

Years ago, it was common to find verbal descriptions associated with IQ ranges. For instance, those obtaining IQs greater than 140 were referred to as 'very superior' and those below an IQ of 70 (both on a scale having a mean of 100 and SD 15) as mentally deficient. In the UK these labels fell out of use long ago. Later the term 'ESN' (educationally sub-normal) was used to refer to pupils who, because of mental disadvantage, were not able to benefit from conventional forms of education. The IQ of these children was used as one criterion amongst others, and a value of around 70 was regarded as critical. In the 11+ examination, a figure of 115 was often quoted as the cut-off point above which pupils were deemed suitable for a grammar school education. This amounted to roughly 16 per cent of an age group (see Figure 9.1).

Perhaps the best-known norm-referenced test was designed by David Wechsler. Around 1939, he created the Wechsler–Bellevue tests of adult intelligence which went some way towards a scale suitable for testing beyond 15 years of age. He designed sections on performance and verbal reasoning. The tests have been standardized for adults in the UK and the most recent version for children was 1992. Standardized scores can be obtained for performance and verbal reasoning or as an overall IQ score.

Some examples of norm-referencing in schools will be recognized by the reader. Some schools have a policy of converting marks to percentages and banding these, sometimes as literal grades A to E or F, sometimes as standard comments which reflect performance above, at or below average. Public examinations such as 'O' and 'A' levels are based on trends in performance from year to year by large numbers of pupils. Primary and middle schools often give children reading tests from which a 'reading age' is obtained. This age is worked out using the performance statistics of many youngsters of a similar age. Competence is expressed in terms of the age-level at which the child is performing. This may then be compared with the child's chronological age. If Jane is 8 years and 3 months and her reading age is 10 years and 1 month, then she is a bright, exceptionally good reader. Intelligence tests are also based on norms derived from sampling and comparing large numbers of people.

### Criterion-referenced testing

The comparison of a person's performance on any standardized test with that of others serves as an indicator of relative capacity and can be one of several clues in the diagnosis of, for example, actual or potential school performance. However, norm-referenced tests are not really designed to answer questions about a child's level of performance in a particular task or to help in the diagnosis of performance. To do this one would need to establish a series of criteria – hurdles which need to be cleared – in order to be able to judge whether a level or stage had been reached by an individual. In other words, we decide on criteria which we judge should have been achieved by an individual. There is no halfway house: the person either does or does not achieve a predetermined level of performance. An example from arithmetic might be to ask whether a child can subtract single digits. The criterion for successful achievement might be reached when a child can answer, say, ten consecutive problems correctly or can achieve eight correct answers in ten problems. Note that the criterion is not necessarily based on age norms or sample norms, although teachers do operate on notional expectations of the kinds of problems suitable for particular age groups.

There are several useful basic principles applied in the design of criterion-referenced tests (Gronlund 1973). First, the task or tasks to be achieved must be clearly defined at the outset. This is really an exercise in curriculum planning and analysis (see Chapter 15). Second, the purposes of the tasks must be clearly understood. For example, what is to be achieved in fulfilling a task (to identify, to describe, to calculate)? Third, the standard required from the pupils must be decided beforehand. It may be that the teacher requires answers to be 100 per cent correct (in a small, comparatively undemanding task), or some lower level of performance may be regarded as satisfactory (for example 80 per cent correct). *Mastery testing* is sometimes an alternative term for this criterion; that is, the criterion set is regarded as sufficient to conclude that, if it is reached, the individual can be said to have mastered the task. Fourth, each topic tested should be adequately sampled. One or two problems, for instance, in number or spelling may not be sufficient to test out mastery. Fifth, there must be an adequate scoring and feedback system which describes the learning tasks of the pupil.

One advantage of this approach is that judgements about progress are made in terms of a child's personal progress. Monitoring is very much geared to the differences between children, and therefore to the needs and pace of the individual child. The method is also helpful in profiling where it is required to plot the progress of a pupil. Nevertheless, there is bound to be some norm-referencing involved. Decisions about what topics to choose, at what level to pitch the difficulty and the definition of satisfactory mastery criteria are largely based on a teacher's knowledge of what can be expected of a child at a given age or standard – and this is in a sense relying on norms built up during teaching experience.

Sometimes a teacher might want to give children an enjoyable educational experience to stimulate interest. There is frequently a learning objective behind the experience, but the primary object is to capture the imagination and motivation of the child. Illustrations of this are field trips, films and dramatic experiences in or outside the school (e.g. inviting a group of professional artists, singers or dancers to talk to a group of children). The ideas of interest-based planning are often generated by the children – crafty teachers gain a lot from informal discussions about things which might excite the educational interests of pupils.

The act of making explicit what you hope to achieve and how this is to be done is an exacting and necessary process, but a fundamental question is how much detail is needed? Several curriculum developers in the USA (e.g. Mager 1962, Gronlund 1978) are highly specific and very detailed, so much so that each statement could be converted into a set of questions for evaluation of the lesson (questions for the pupils). In fact, Gronlund's intention was to tabulate the objectives so that they would possess the necessary content for a criterion-referenced test. An example of this detailed analysis follows. It is taken from a set of classroom instruction texts designed in the USA (Gronlund 1973) and intended to illustrate criterion-referencing. It is part of a programme for teaching the science of weather. The objectives are broken down into four major areas, and within each one there are several subsidiary objectives. The four major ones are given below, with the first expanded to illustrate the amount of detail required in a behavioural analysis of objectives. The pupil should:

1   *Know* basic terms:
    *   *write* a definition of each term
    *   *identify* the term that represents each weather element
    *   *identify* the term that best fits a given weather description
    *   *match* the term to a picture of the concept
    *   *distinguish* between correct and incorrect uses of the terms
2   *Know* map symbols
3   *Know* specific facts
4   *Interpret* weather maps.

Notice three points about this kind of detailed analysis. First, every possibility is covered by the objectives. Second, the teaching purpose is made quite clear in terms of the learning outcomes. Third, the verbs depicting what is to happen are unambiguous.

The most recent and widely used criterion-referenced test for cognitive evaluation, called the 'British Ability Scales: Second Edition (BAS II)', has been devised and revised by Elliott and co-workers (Elliott 1996; originally Warburton 1966 and Elliott 1975). The scales are usable in the age range 2 years 6 months to 17 years 11 months. Table 9.1 gives an indication of the tests available and the ages for which they have been designed. For example, the *speed of information processing* test uses a simple number exercise to measure the speed rather than the power (number correct) of a child's problem-solving ability. *Immediate and delayed recall of objects* tests involve showing a child a card containing, say, 20 objects and asking him or her to recall as many as possible immediately and then after, say, 20 minutes. These give rise to the two sets of scores for immediate and delayed recall. Matrices, a very popular device for non-verbal reasoning, might involve discovering a pattern from given figures and producing the next pattern in line.

Combinations of the Core Scales are used to derive *General Conceptual Ability* scores (GCA) which provide a general measure of intelligence. These are age-related so that the first four Core Scales are used to give a GCA score for $2\frac{1}{2}$- to 3-year-olds. The Core Scales 2 to 7 inclusive combine to give a GCA for $3\frac{1}{2}$- to 6-year-olds, whilst 7 to 12 inclusive gives the GCA score for 6- to 18-year-olds. Notice that the six scales for the last two age groups contain two verbal, two pictorial and two spatial tests. Table 9.2 is an example from the 2 to 7 Core Scales.

The Diagnostic Scales are used to probe the functioning in specific areas and can be compared with GCA scores. The Achievement Scales are for use in school in number, spelling and word reading. The versatility of the BAS II makes it a very useful tool for educational psychologists.

Readers may see other terms in use (particularly in the US) as alternatives to criterion-referenced, such as *domain-referenced*, *competency-based* or *mastery* tests, but we shall stick to the term 'criterion-referenced tests'. The use of this method has become widespread in this country with the introduction of the national system of assessment and the issue will be taken up in Chapter 16.

**Table 9.1** The British Ability Scales Second Edition (BAS II) (from the promotion pamphlet, NFER-Nelson, 1996).

| Scales | Standardization age | | |
|---|---|---|---|
| | Early years | | School age |
| *Core Scales* | | | |
| 1. Block Building | $2^1/_2$–7 | | |
| 2. Verbal Comprehension | $2^1/_2$–7 | | |
| 3. Picture Similarities | $2^1/_2$–7 | | |
| 4. Naming Vocabulary | $2^1/_2$–7 | | |
| 5. Early Number Concepts | $2^1/_2$–7 | | |
| 6. Copying | $3^1/_2$–7 | | |
| 7. Pattern Construction | 3 | – | 18 |
| 8. Recall of Design | | | 5–18 |
| 9. Word Definitions | | | 5–18 |
| 10. Matrices | | | 5–18 |
| 11. Verbal Similarities | | | 5–18 |
| 12. Quantative Reasoning | | | 5–18 |
| *Diagnostic Scales* | | | |
| Matching Letter-like Forms | 4–8 | | |
| Recall of Digits Forwards | $2^1/_2$ | – | 18 |
| Recall of Digits Backwards | | | 5–18 |
| Recall of Objects Immediate | 4 | – | 18 |
| Recall of Objects Delayed | 4 | – | 18 |
| Recognition of Pictures | $2^1/_2$ | | 18 |
| Speed of Information Processing | | | 5–18 |
| *Achievement Scales* | | | |
| Number Skills | | | 5–18 |
| Spelling | | | 5–18 |
| Word Reading | | | 5–18 |

The age 18 in the Table represents an actual age of 17 years 11 months

**Table 9.2** Core Scales used in deriving General Conceptual Ability scores (GCA) for $3^1/_2$- to 6-year-olds (from the promotion pamphlet, NFER-Nelson, 1996).

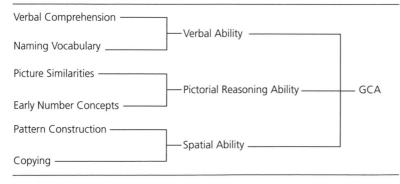

## Intelligence test items

Over the years since Binet's earliest work, we have amassed many items thought to reflect cognitive ability. Let us look at some of the commonest kinds of item.

> There are many group tests on the market. Most can be obtained from NFER-Nelson. But there are restrictions imposed on test users to safeguard the reliability of the tests and their correct usage. NFER-Nelson supplies catalogues of the tests in its stock (Educational and Specialist Assessments). Non-verbal tests such as Raven's Progressive Matrices are also obtainable from this source. The website is http://www.nfer-nelson.ac.uk/catalogue/catalogue.asp

They have been specially compiled for the text and are not taken from existing IQ tests. It will be clear to students that we cannot use standardized items from tests as examples because they are 'closed', that is, their content is subject to restrictions of both publication and circulation. Answers appear at the end of the chapter.

### *Analogies* (see end of chapter for answers)
An example has already been provided to demonstrate Spearman's 'eduction of relations and correlates'. Here are a few more.
Choose the correct alternative:

1 Rein is to rain as stem is to (a) item (b) twig (c) seem (d) reign
2 Male is to female as dog is to (a) cat (b) vixen (c) canine (d) bitch
3 AUTHOR is to WORDS as (CONDUCTOR, COMPOSER, PLAYER) is to (MUSIC, NOTES, ORCHESTRA).

### *Synonyms*
Choose one term in the bracket which means nearly the same as:

1 SLAKE (GROW, DRINK, QUENCH, POUR, LOOSE)
2 PREEN (TEACH, GLAND, BE ANNOYED, TRIM FEATHERS).

### *Antonyms*
Choose one word in the first bracket which means the opposite of one word in the second bracket:

1 (TAP, TUP, TOP) (EWE, EYE, EVE)

Which one of the four words on the right bears a similar relationship to each of the words on the left?:

2 EASY, SOFT (PUTTY, HARD, SIMPLE, BRITTLE).

$\longrightarrow$

## Memory

The subject is given digits orally and is asked to repeat them. Most adults can manage to repeat around seven (telephone numbers and car registrations are about the limit). In young children, short sentences are sometimes given (Binet tests, for example).

## Number and letter series (induction tests)

Fill in the missing number or letter:

1   60, 12, 3, 1, –, –
2   JFMAM –, –
3   2, 6, 12, 20, –, –.

## Ordering and classification

Arrange the following in descending order of complexity:

1   carnivore, vertebrate, animal, domestic cats, feline animals

Which word does not belong in the list?:

2   riot, subversion, turmoil, meeting, rebellion
3   bit, piece, fraction, portion, a half.

## Examples of non-verbal items

1   Find the patterns for the four missing pieces:

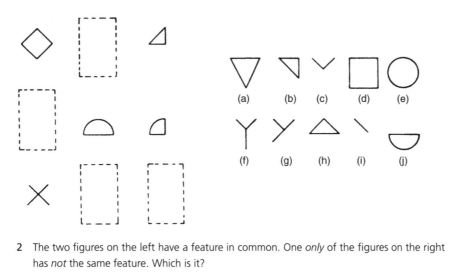

2   The two figures on the left have a feature in common. One *only* of the figures on the right has *not* the same feature. Which is it?

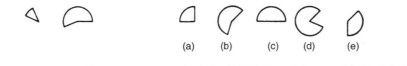

$\longrightarrow$

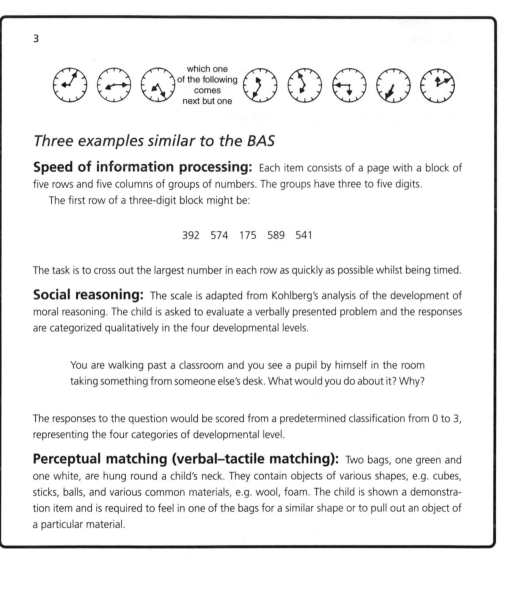

### Three examples similar to the BAS

**Speed of information processing:** Each item consists of a page with a block of five rows and five columns of groups of numbers. The groups have three to five digits.

The first row of a three-digit block might be:

392  574  175  589  541

The task is to cross out the largest number in each row as quickly as possible whilst being timed.

**Social reasoning:** The scale is adapted from Kohlberg's analysis of the development of moral reasoning. The child is asked to evaluate a verbally presented problem and the responses are categorized qualitatively in the four developmental levels.

> You are walking past a classroom and you see a pupil by himself in the room taking something from someone else's desk. What would you do about it? Why?

The responses to the question would be scored from a predetermined classification from 0 to 3, representing the four categories of developmental level.

**Perceptual matching (verbal–tactile matching):** Two bags, one green and one white, are hung round a child's neck. They contain objects of various shapes, e.g. cubes, sticks, balls, and various common materials, e.g. wool, foam. The child is shown a demonstration item and is required to feel in one of the bags for a similar shape or to pull out an object of a particular material.

# Some uses of intelligence tests

There are several ways of classifying intelligence tests. We can think of them in terms of:

- the group for whom they were intended (children or adults, low or high levels of intellect, culture fair – that is, 'free' from cultural bias which might depress or elevate scores unfairly)
- whether they are for individual or group administration

- as a diagnostic tool of general or special skills of those tested (verbal, spatial, performance, memory, numerical, etc.).

When we talk of intelligence tests it is important to know and to specify which combination of these special features applies. It is also essential to note that intelligence test administration and interpretation is a skilled affair. Therefore testers require tuition and training in order to get reliable and valid results. For examples of available tests, see http://www.nfer-nelson.co.uk/catalogue/catalogue.asp

## Verbal group tests

Tests designed specifically for use with large numbers of children or adults have been widely used since their introduction as a grammar-school selection device. Their advantages are that large samples can be reliably tested in a relatively short time in the same conditions. They are particularly reliable for groups of older children and adults where it is clear that written instructions are understood and motivation is likely to be maintained throughout the testing period. Where they do not prove reliable is in testing those at the extremes of the distribution. Also, with dull children the opportunity for personal contact and for elaborating on the test instructions is vital. It is also helpful to construct separate tests of high level intelligence to obtain a greater degree of refinement and discrimination in the score range. This follows because, where a test is intended to cover the whole range, the scores at the tail ends of the distribution cannot be sufficiently widespread to give a distinctive spectrum of scores.

## Non-verbal group tests

Tests such as Raven's Progressive Matrices and Cattell's Culture-free Scales have been used as a supplementary and alternative measure in secondary schools. They are *not* strictly culture fair, but they do provide additional evidence of mental competence where, for some reason, verbal opportunities in our culture have not been satisfactory. Specific group tests of number, mechanical and spatial skills are also available.

## Individual tests

These are most helpful as diagnostic tools with pre-school children, infant-school children and children with special needs, where written communication, reading skills, motivation and concentration are among the particular problems which preclude group testing. The preamble to many group tests attempts to encourage continued participation (BAS II is a good example) during the testing session. Often the tests begin with a warm-up period to ensure that test instructions are fully understood. But even this care would not be adequate for young children. The administration of individual tests is a highly skilled and time-consuming job needing patience and a knowledge of how to extract the best from young people. They form a crucial part of the diagnostic service provided by the local authority's psychological service, and student teachers should familiarize themselves with the functions of this service in relation to schoolchildren.

Individually administered measures of intelligence are used as one criterion for *giftedness*; this complex subject is taken up in Chapter 10.

## Selection tests

In the early part of the twentieth century, Godfrey Thomson became the first of several people designing group IQ tests for selecting grammar school pupils in the 10- to 11-year age group. Sir Cyril Burt followed soon after. They were both experts in test design and wrote leading texts on the subject. In 1925 Thomson became the Director of Moray House, Edinburgh, which, in his time there, produced many standardized IQ tests, including some 11+ selection tests. In fact, the IQ results from these early days (1930s) have been used in recent research on IQ and mortality (summarized in Deary 2005).

Thomson also worked at Newcastle University prior to Moray House and paved the way for the development of annual tests to help in the selection of 10- to 11-year-olds for education in grammar schools in Northumberland. Like so many at the time, he was conscious of the fact that many bright boys and girls from poor and socially deprived homes were not able to pay for grammar school education. The Northumberland tests were designed to overcome this problem. Children at 10 and 11 years of age from deprived backgrounds who passed the IQ test were offered free places by the local education authority (LEA). The idea developed into the 11+ selection system, which is still used in about 160 schools in Britain. These tests now contain verbal, non-verbal, numerical and spatial items as well as a test of English language.

In America, selection throughout school and university is partly based on cognitive ability test scores. The equivalent of Britain's primary and secondary schools use standardized tests. Entry to university is also based on ability scores with specialist testing in such areas as medicine, law and business.

Occupational selection procedures sometimes include IQ tests. For example, the standard entry requirement to nurse training is five GCSE passes, usually in any subject. Those who have not got five GCSEs could either take an alternative test or enter an access course of one or more years. Until recently, the alternative test was the DC test (Child and Borrill 1990). It consisted of verbal, non-verbal, spatial, numerical and graphical items as well as tabular and English comprehension tests. The civil service, armed forces and some industries use psychometric intelligence test scores for selection purposes.

A note of caution needs to be sounded about the use of conventional IQ tests as measures of potential in educational achievement. There is circularity in the use of verbal and numerical items. Many depend on the literacy and numeracy of those taking the test. These latter are taught in schools. Therefore some variation in the scores is a function of the educational opportunities of those tested as well as their innate capacities. This point is taken up again below in the section on coaching.

## Tests for babies

Tests for babies from the prenatal stage onwards have been the focus of several researches. The earliest established test battery in the UK was compiled by Griffiths (1954), who derived an intelligence score from five major indices of infant behaviour skills. They are:

- locomotor (body movement, sitting, walking)
- personal–social (reaction to other humans)
- hearing and speech (response to aural stimuli, vocalization skills)
- eye and hand (response to visual stimuli, hand–eye co-ordination, use of hands)
- performance (broadly reaction and manipulative skills in situations conjured up by the experimenter – for example, if a baby is holding wooden blocks in both hands what will it do if a third block is presented?).

The norms were obtained by observing many babies and noting the average achievement for each age in the five ways mentioned above. The reliability of the scores (how similar the performance is in several testings of the same child or group of children), particularly below two years of age, is not very high. Progress in the first year is so rapid and erratic that precise measurements are not really feasible. However, as descriptive norms for use in diagnostic cases, these measurements have proved to be of immense value.

Since the early test of Griffiths, there have been several more. The *Bayley Scales of Infant Development* (Bayley 1969), still available, were produced in the 1960s. The *McCarthy Scales of Children's Abilities* (1972) were designed to cover the age range of $2^1/_2$ to $8^1/_2$ years, giving a diagnostic profile in verbal, non-verbal, spatial, memory and motor skills. Lynch *et al.* (1982) have compiled a British version.

Actually, these tests of ability for babies are not particularly good indicators of later psychometric intelligence. The most reliable test to correlate with later IQ scores is the *habituation* test (Columbo 1993, Rose and Feldman 1995).

# Factors influencing measured general cognitive ability

## Brain size and other biological factors

In this age of brain scanning, we are now able to measure the size of a person's brain with a high degree of accuracy. We can also measure a person's psychometric intelligence. Several studies by Vernon *et al.* (reported in Sternberg 2000), using more recent sophisticated scanning methods, have been put together to create a meta-analysis (Chapter 17). They showed a statistically significant overall correlation of +0.4. Deary says that this is a moderate effect size: not a huge association, but large enough to state securely that people who score better on mental tests do tend to have bigger brains.

This finding generates a number of interesting questions. Why should size make a difference? Women are, on average, smaller than men and, proportionally, their brain sizes are smaller. Even when body size is taken into account, men have larger and heavier brains (Ankney 1992, Pakkenberg and Gundersen 1997); but their *overall* intelligence, on average, is the same as men (Neisser *et al.* 1996). How is this explained? The brain is not a functional unity. It consists of many components serving different functions. Are there some components closely related to psychometric measures where size would have a significant effect?

Answers to these questions are still in the melting pot. Speculations abound. For example, we know that larger means more nerve cells (neurons), therefore greater capacity for detail (males and uni-tasking?), but less capacity for an overall picture (females and multi-tasking?); thicker layers of fat surrounding the nerve fibres (myelin sheaths) having no intellectual function at all. Therefore, is the density of brain tissue rather than size more important? What is the significance of females having a larger number of inter-connecting fibres between the frontal lobes of the brain than males, and so on?

Several other biological factors have been explored. Of particular interest to teachers is the effect of nutritional variations in the eating habits of children upon intelligence. Prominence has been given in recent years to companies claiming to have found a substance which will increase intelligence. Discovering certain food substances which could hold the key to increased problem-solving ability is likely to be a preoccupation of parents, teachers and pharmaceutical companies alike – all for completely different reasons.

However, the research is far from conclusive and a series of papers in *The Psychologist* (1992), Eysenck and Schoenthaler (1997) and Neisser *et al.* (1996) show the state of progress so far. The most optimistic conclusions by Eysenck are that:

> (1) Fluid IQ can be increased significantly by dietary supplementation; (2) Crystallized IQ cannot be so; (3) Both conclusions may apply to certain types, amounts and times of supplementation, and should not be generalized beyond these limits; (4) Duration and amount of supplementation multiply to give predicted increases; (5) Increases in fluid IQ are most likely to occur in subsamples suffering from insufficient intake of vitamins and minerals . . . (6) RDAs (Recommended Dietary Allowances) for vitamins and minerals (even American ones) may be too low and should be set at a higher level; (7) Improvement of diet is the most obvious choice for producing IQ increases, but chemical supplementation is another, if inferior, choice. (*The Psychologist*, 1992, p. 411)

The topic is going to be a focal point in the coming years. The summary at present is that the effect of physical and nutritional factors such as these is present, is small and needs to be the subject of long-term, follow-up studies.

Other biological factors (Neisser *et al.* 1996) include gene anomalies (e.g., Down's syndrome and some cases of ADHD – see Chapter 11), the prenatal period (alcohol, drug and tobacco intake) and perinatal exposure to toxins during early development (e.g., lead).

## Age

We have already remarked on the complications of measuring adult intelligence. This is caused partly by the irregular development of mental ability and partly by the decline in mental ability beyond adolescence. Let's face it, brain tissues, like all other body tissues, deteriorate with time. In general, physical and cognitive development for an individual increase in proportion with chronological age up to 14 or 15 years of age. Once in school, children's knowledge base, language, reasoning, social skills, etc. begin to increase. Plainly, there are exceptions and irregularities in the course of individual development, but in the main the ratio of mental to chronological age is stable to mid-adolescence, when a slow decline in mental development sets in during the rest of life (Dixon *et al.* 1985). If mental age is decreasing as chronological age increases, the mental ratio will gradually decline; that is why we cannot use the method adopted by Binet and his associates for ascertaining the intelligence of adults.

In summary, an individual's score on comparable tests from early childhood to adolescence would progress, but in comparison with other people of the same age, the scores from a valid and reliable test would be stable.

However, Salthouse (1996a and b) has some interesting observations about the relationship between age and IQ. Because our bodies are slowing down in their rate of functioning (nerve conduction and so forth), the speed of information processing is correspondingly slowed. This has the effect of reducing scores in some of the specific abilities which make up the complex of general ability (e.g. those depending on memory).

There are several limitations to be borne in mind when we are considering the results of research in this field. The particular methods and test materials we use to measure the ability of five-year-olds are conspicuously different from those for 15-year-olds or adults.

The earliest research, dating back to the First World War, used cross-sectional methods, that is, testing a wide age range at one time and comparing the results for various smaller age ranges within this. This contrasts with longitudinal studies which follow a cohort of people and test them at intervals throughout their lives. Overall, cross-sectional studies show a plateau between early and mid-adulthood followed by gradual decline in measured intelligence. The decline was more rapid in non-verbal than in verbal test scores and Botwinick (1977) referred to this as the *classic intellectual aging pattern*.

The most systematic longitudinal study is being conducted by Schaie in the Seattle study. It started in 1956 (for a summary see Schaie, 1983 and for later work, Hertzog and Schaie, 1986 and 1988) and continues (for updates, see Schaie 1996 and Birren and Schaie 2001). The findings suggest that the decline up to age 50 in the cross-sectional method might be due to *cohort effects*, that is, differences in test score means between different cohorts

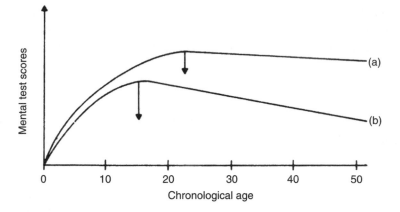

**Figure 9.2** A representative graph of mental development with chronological age. (a) Continued intellectual stimulus beyond mid-adolescence can lead to prolonged development and slower decline. Also more likely to be those of higher intelligence who avail themselves of the opportunity for continued intellectual work. (b) Those who do not continue with intellectual pursuits beyond mid-adolescence experience an earlier and more rapid decline than those in (a) above.

may be a function of educational, social and cultural experiences and not biological. For example, if today we tested a group of 20-, 40- and 60-year-old people, any differences may be due to the changing pattern of education in the years between the groups. Schaie finds the 'decrements in the 50s are small enough to be of little practical importance, whereas the decrements observed in old age (60–80) are of considerable salience'.

However, the present consensus of evidence (Figure 9.2) points to a slow decline which varies with the mental stimulation experienced by the individual. Those who continue to be mentally active after mid-adolescent schooling are more likely to have continued growth in verbal ability than others (Burns 1966, Horn 1967, Cattell 1982). This fact has special significance at a time when more young people are staying in education, one consequence of which will be prolonged contact with verbal learning.

The main arguments seem to hinge on what declines and when. One thread of evidence for the decline is found in the researches of Horn (1967), who was investigating the growth of *fluid* and *crystallized* intelligence (see Cattell's theory later in the chapter). For technical detail and possible formulae for the variation of fluid and crystallized intelligence with age, see Cattell (1982). Horn was able to show that fluid intelligence, believed to be correlated with biological factors, deteriorates along with the normal physical decline of the body, and therefore rises up to early adulthood, and declines steadily thereafter (have pity on me, all you young readers!). But crystallized intelligence, associated with the accumulation of 'wisdom' and experience, rises steadily throughout life particularly if verbal experience is continued. Therefore, in measured intelligence, believed by Horn to be proportional to the sum of fluid and crystallized intelligence, there is a steady rise in performance up to middle age, followed by an steady decline thereafter.

As I walk across campus in my advancing years, I cannot help noticing that the height and width of students is increasing as time goes by (unless I'm getting shorter and thinner!). This is supported by statistical evidence – young people now are, on average, taller than their parents. A similar increase in psychometric intelligence test scores has been noted. This is known as the *Flynn effect* (Flynn 1984, 1987). This states that the increase in IQ score is 3 points per decade (mean 100, SD 15). The outcome is that psychometric tests must be re-standardized regularly in order to make scores from decade to decade comparable. The reasons for the increase have not been settled to everyone's satisfaction. So far, three have been postulated. First, with the increase in information flow (TV and other technological devices), lengthening of schooling (IQ and school performance are highly correlated as we shall see) and increased complexity of life, our knowledge base has, on average, increased. But this does not explain the corresponding increase in non-verbal measures. Second, nutrition has improved for everyone, witness in the increase in average height and width of people. An equivalent increase in brain size and efficiency of brain functioning is postulated (Lynn 1990). However, the nutritional link has not been firmly established (Neisser 1996). Thirdly, Flynn himself (1987) does not accept that 'real' intelligence can be changed and thinks that some smaller component such as advances in 'abstract problem solving ability' are the cause.

## Sex and gender differences in psychometric intelligence

A sensitive question these days is whether there are any sex or gender differences in psychometric (measured) intelligence. If there are, we as teachers ought to know about it, be honest, recognize them and ensure that our curricula and teaching techniques compensate for these differences when necessary and as far as we can. The important thing is equal opportunity, despite the differences. Unfortunately, 'differences' have often been confused with 'difficulties' or 'disadvantages', even 'discriminations'; also, the differences have been exaggerated. It has been suggested that a negative stereotype of a particular group can lead to underperformance of that group (Steele 1997). This is called *Stereotype Threat Theory* (STT).

Recent meta-analyses by Lynn and Irwing (2004, Irwing and Lynn 2005, but see shortcomings of meta-analysis in Chapter 17) using Raven's Progressive Matrices show a small, but significant, difference in performance on this non-verbal test with males over 16 years-of-age getting slightly higher scores, on average, than females. This does not apply to those younger than 16 years. The theory is that girls' intellectual development is faster than boys up to 16 years when boys catch up and overtake.

But the overall conclusion of psychologists, despite Lynn and Irwing 2004 and Irwing and Lynn 2005, is that:

> Most standard tests of intelligence have been constructed so that there are no overall score differences between females and males. Some recent studies do report sex differences in (*overall*) IQ, but the direction is variable and the effects are small (Lynn 1994). This overall

equivalence does not imply equal performance on every individual ability. While some tasks show no sex differences, there are others where small differences appear and a few where they are large and consistent. (Neisser *et al.* 1996, p. 91)

Here, we shall concentrate on the 'large and consistent' differences. Significant differences favouring males occur in visual-spatial and some quantitative tasks. Above, we gave examples in non-verbal items which involve rotation of two and three dimensional figures. In tasks involving spatial relations such as aiming, throwing, tracking and orientation in space, males, on average, achieve higher scores than females. These differences are carried through in academic performance in scholastic aptitude tests and some areas of mathematics (see Chapter 16). We are reminded of Baron-Cohen's (2003) hard-wiring of males in Chapter 2 – 'systemizing' and 'the drive to analyse, explore and construct a system'.

Females are better, on average, than males in some verbal and numerical abilities. These, such as verbal fluency, reading, spelling and verbal memory tasks, help in performance in academic subjects such as language, literature and essay-based topics. Baron-Cohen's hard-wiring for females is 'the drive to identify another person's emotions and thoughts and to respond to them with an appropriate emotion'. For this, one needs caring and communication skills (also see Chapter 12 on personality).

These differences are bound to affect academic performance and the implications are discussed in Chapter 16. Also, there is persuasive evidence that these differences arise from biological rather than social sources (Baron-Cohen 2003). In other words they are prevalently sex, rather than gender, related. At first sight, it might be thought that as girls are given 'caring' toys (e.g., dolls, nursing sets) and boys 'practical' toys (e.g., construction kits such as Meccano and Lego sets, pretend weapons), our culture predetermines our children's preferences. But cross-cultural studies confirm the strength of their different drives and interests despite child-rearing practices. In fact, the differences have been of benefit in the survival of our species. With females who are built for caring and efficient communication, and males who are spatially adept as dwelling-builders and hunters, it is not surprising that our species has survived. And these differences must surely have existed before we had toys. In effect, we are reinforcing rather than creating our sex-based differences.

## Practice and coaching

Research into the effects of practice and coaching on ability test scores is extensive and the findings quite well established (Vernon 1960 and 1979). There is usually an overall improvement in scores as a result of coaching or practice.

We first need to distinguish between practice and coaching. *Practice* involves taking the same or parallel tests at intervals *without* any special instructions or rehearsal in the interval. *Coaching* involves teaching a testee (including self-help) the 'tricks' of how to take a test, of how to analyse and become familiar with the test instructions and types of items, of how to use time effectively, of working through trial items similar to those in the test to be taken and of overcoming anxiety by building confidence.

If a person sits the same test fairly soon after the first attempt, a practice effect is possible. The maximum gains are likely within a few weeks of the first test. Gains average about 5 IQ points. Gains are also possible if parallel forms are taken within a few weeks of each other. After several retakes, the scores level out – provided that the testee does not have any coaching. The score tends to level out after about five or six retakes. Practice effects are quite lasting. Gains have been recorded as long as a year after the first test. The effect is greatest when there is a wide variety of test items. The smallest gains come from verbal and comprehension tests, the largest from non-verbal and numerical tests. There appears to be little or no practice effect when there is a short practice session at the beginning of the test. For those who have never taken a test before, the practice effects are greatest.

Coaching without any practice in doing similar items to the final test is ineffective. It is usually the case that all coaching is accompanied by practice sessions. The typical gain after several hours of coaching is about 9 IQ points. In other words, coaching adds about another 4 points to practice effects. With several resits, the gains can be as much as 12 points on average. The effects of coaching reach a peak after a few hours. Further coaching leads to little improvement. Coaching gains, like practice gains, are smallest for verbal and comprehension tests and largest for non-verbal and numerical items. The effects of coaching decline more rapidly than is the case with practice.

## Race, home and school

There are striking differences in the way people from different cultures resolve their problems. Many may rarely, if ever, have used a symbolic code to solve abstract problems, as in verbal reasoning. Indeed, Sternberg (1985a) suggests a 'practical intelligence' in his triarchic theory (see earlier in the chapter). In any case, what use would the solution of abstract problems be to a tribesman or woman living in a hostile environment of long heat and short rain periods?

The perceptual emphases of a culture must also have an influence on the solution of spatial tasks. For example, there is less preoccupation with linearity in some African cultures than in some western cultures, consequently the latter are more susceptible to vertical and horizontal line arrangements and to illusions (Biesheuvel 1949, Gregory 1998). It is hardly surprising, then, to find anomalies in the IQ measures of western and non-western cultures. The art of devising intelligence tests which are reliable and valid for all cultures has never been accomplished satisfactorily, mainly because they were devised in western cultures. Some psychologists (Cattell, see later) claim to have found *culture-fair* or *culture-free* items, but the overwhelming opinion from the evidence is that there is no such thing as a culture-fair test. Whichever medium we try to communicate in – verbal, spatial, pictorial, etc. – it is evident that cultural differences produce variations in test results. Vernon (1969) concludes that:

> while western tests often worked well in other cultural groups especially when slightly adapted to increase their intelligibility and acceptability, it is generally preferable to devise new ones locally to suit the modes of perception, the language background and concepts of the particular culture.

What happens when we compare the IQs of sub-cultures (e.g., home and social class) in one society? As early as the 1960s, several large-scale researches in Britain (Wiseman 1964, Douglas 1964 and Douglas *et al.* 1968) were concluding that there were differences in the IQs of children from different social backgrounds. Moreover, the differences widened as the children grew older. But, there is a real problem here because we have to disentangle the inherited ability from the acquired – separating out what a child brings to this world 'in the genes' from the developmental opportunities presented in the home and at school. These can represent a double dose of the same medicine – inheritance reinforced by one's biological parents. But we take up this issue in the next section. Influences such as family size (Nisbet 1953), language opportunities in the home (Lawton 1968) and resources in the family home (Gottfried 1984) may make a difference. But the positive impact of the broader issue of family environment on intelligence, investigated, for example, by Harris (1998 and website), has been seriously questioned. Neisser *et al.* (1996) conclude that:

> These findings suggest that differences in the life styles of families – whatever their importance may be for many aspects of children's lives – make little long-term difference for the skills measured by intelligence tests. We should note, however, that low-income and non-White families are poorly represented in existing adoption studies as well as in most twin samples.

Some intelligence test questions depend for their solution on knowledge (see analogies, synonyms, antonyms, ordering and classification in the IQ items above) and much of this is imparted in schools, some homes and TV. We should, therefore, not be surprised to see a correlation between attainment in school and psychometric intelligence scores. There is clearly an interaction between these two influences. Therefore, attempting to partial out the contribution of school on the interaction of achievement and ability is not easy. In the next section, we shall look at ways of solving this problem. Acceleration and deprivation studies have also figured (Jensen 1971 and 1977 (*cumulative deficit*), Head Start (Chapter 5), summarized in Ceci 1991). But heat rather than light has so far been generated by the arguments. For example, see the responses to Jensen's 1971 article by Burt, Butcher, Eysenck, Nisbet and Vernon in the same journal (Eysenck *et al.* 1972), especially where the discussion involves the differences between ethnic or social groups (Kamin 1974, Eysenck and Kamin 1981, Stott 1983).

Jensen (1967) also makes the interesting proposal that environmental influences obey a 'threshold' effect. That is, below a certain range of intelligence (not specified precisely) the influence of the environment is of paramount importance, while above the range it becomes progressively less influential. The principle is said to work in the same way as the vitamin supply to the body. The latter can only assimilate so much (up to a certain threshold) beyond which further quantities are eliminated and serve no useful nutritional purposes. Also, the very bright are proportionately more able to cope with environmental disadvantages. In the next chapter we shall meet an added complication that among the highly intelligent it becomes difficult to distinguish the more creative minds. Further, personality may play a vital role in the expression of intelligent behaviour.

## Comparing genetic and cultural influences – heredity and environment

Much of the foregoing debate focuses on arguments about inherited and acquired characteristics. What do we bring to this world and to what extent does our environment contribute in shaping what we are? Following many years of research (e.g., bright and dull maze running rats, MZ and DZ twin studies, adoption studies, gene location (Human Genome Project, http://www.genome.gov/10001772), there can be no doubt remaining that general human ability, defined and measured using psychometric tests, has a significant genetic and a lesser environmental component.

It is newsworthy, so the popular press and other mass media often get embroiled in the 'nature/nurture' controversy surrounding the subject of intelligence. The dispute centres on the dilemma of how our inherited qualities and developmental prospects interact to affect intelligent activity. The disputants seek an answer to the question 'What is the relative influence and importance of inherited and constitutional characteristics in the growth of human ability?' Some, like Burt (1955), were defining intelligence as 'innate general cognitive ability'. Others, like UNESCO (1951), were asking whether human beings were 'born equally endowed and therefore entirely at the mercy of the environment in creating variations in measured intelligence, or in any case is interaction of endowment and environment such that we cannot extricate their relative influence?'

Research has come a long way since those mid-twentieth-century days. From the biological and twin study evidence (behavioural genetics) there can be little doubt about the reality of inherited intellectual capacities. Equally, from social psychological studies, coaching and practice research, studies of home and school influences, nutrition, etc., there can be no doubt about the influence of environmental factors on improving the performance in psychometric intelligence tests. Nevertheless, there is debate about the extent of the contribution of these two factors (Plomin *et al.* 2001).

The refined mathematical and methodological 'nit-picking' which the problem has generated would probably leave most students cold, and would be of little benefit in its detail. We shall, therefore, tread a middle way in looking briefly at the broad issues.

'Proof' that a particular proportion of measured intelligence is due to heredity or environment is not possible, and can only be estimated indirectly, since the two influences are interactive from the moment of conception (see Chapter 2). Teasing out the threads which are 'purely' innate or 'purely' environmental is not, as yet, within the capabilities of behavioural scientists. The main indirect lines of evidence have come from the study of intellectual genealogies, twin studies, studies of relatives reared together and apart, gene studies and neuroscience (Chapter 2).

### Further reading

The earliest serious study was done by Galton (1892) who looked at eminent people. He showed that eminence seemed to be prevalent in some families more than in others – evidence of selective breeding in much the same way as producing fine racehorses. The study, unfortunately, did overlook the possibility that the home of an eminent person might have a marked effect on the children in terms of encouragement, availability of literature, the presence of a wide and varied collection of objects – enriched 'environment', 'intelligent' games and rituals, etc. At the other extreme we find the Kallikak family reported by Goddard (1921). A certain Martin Kallikak (false name) had children by two women, one feeble-minded, the other of normal intelligence. The feeble-minded mother gave rise to a high proportion of feeble-minded descendants, while the mother with normal intelligence had no feeble-minded children at all. At a pinch, we could argue that the living conditions of the feeble-minded parent would be most likely to foster dull children, although the contrast in the two sets of data is rather striking.

Studies of twins reared together and apart form the most common line of investigation. Monozygotic twins (MZ) – that is, two youngsters created from one fertilized egg which has accidentally broken apart early in conception and given two identical eggs – have precisely the same genetic endowment. Dizygotic twins (DZ) occur when two separate eggs are fertilized at roughly the same time and grow in the womb side by side. They have genetic relationships similar to those we might find among brothers and sisters (*siblings*). A meta-analysis of the research literature on the correlations between the intelligence of people of varying degrees of family relationship reared together and apart was conducted by Erlenmeyer-Kimling and Jarvik (1963) and subsequently by Bouchard and McGue (1981). These, plus evidence since then, are summarised in Plomin *et al.* 2001 (p. 168) and adapted in Table 9.3.

It shows an impressive picture of orderly decreases in the values of correlations from high for monozygotic twins reared together to no correlation for a random selection of unrelated children reared apart. The gradations between these extremes have a convincing logic which provides a place for both genetic and environmental influences. Plomin concludes, after careful heritability calculations that:

Family, twin, and adoption studies converge on the conclusion that about half of the total variance of measures of general cognitive ability can be accounted for by genetic factors . . . About half of the environmental variance appears to be accounted for by shared environmental factors.

**Table 9.3** Correlations between IQ scores for pairs of individuals having varying degrees of familial relationship, reared either together or apart (based on data in Plomin *et al.* (2001).

| Relationship | How reared | Correlation between IQ scores |
| --- | --- | --- |
| Identical twins (MZ) | together | 0.86 |
| Identical twins (adopted) | apart | 0.78 |
| Non-identical twins (DZ) | together | 0.60 |
| Siblings | together | 0.47 |
| Unrelated (adopted) | together | 0.32 |
| Siblings (adopted) | apart | 0.24 |
| Unrelated (random) | apart | 0.00 (theoretically) |

This leaves a quarter of the variance not accounted for and these comparative variances are shown diagrammatically in Figure 9.3. Some will be error of various kinds (measurement errors, etc.). But a portion will relate to learning activities outside the home environment such as school, TV and peers and have nothing to do with direct parental influence.

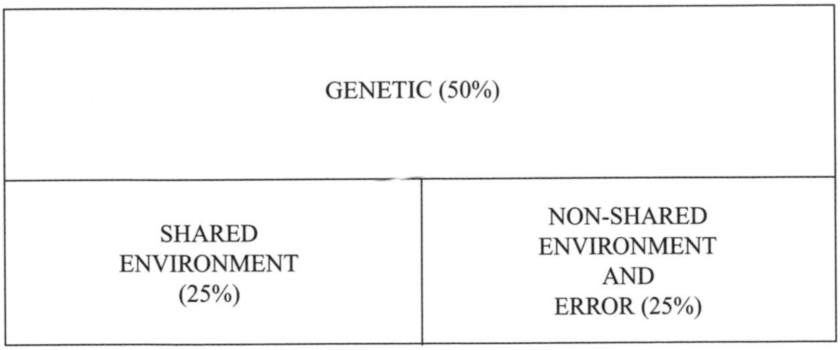

| GENETIC (50%) | |
| --- | --- |
| SHARED ENVIRONMENT (25%) | NON-SHARED ENVIRONMENT AND ERROR (25%) |

**Figure 9.3** Approximate proportions of variance attributed to genetic, environmental and error variance (based on data provided in Plomin *et al.* (2001).

Debate about the relative influence of nature and nurture raged in the latter half of the last century. But more sophisticated technology and mathematics have helped to resolve some of the issues. The contenders both accept the roles of genetic and environmental influences, but disagree about the extent of the influence of these two factors. Some, such as Eysenck (in Eysenck and Kamin 1981), claimed that approximately 80 per cent of the variability in individual measures of intelligence can be explained by genetic factors. Others, such as Kamin (1974; Eysenck and Kamin 1981), whilst not denying the influence of genetic factors, believe that their influence is very much less than 80 per cent. The arguments are clearly and concisely set out in a short pamphlet by Stott (1983) who concludes that 'the interaction between heredity and environment is so continuous, intricate, variable, cumulative and specific that no general statement can be made about their relative contributions'.

As regards the tests of intelligence, Vernon (1979) has also written an extensive book in which he concludes that:

> there is no clear verdict in either direction. Genetic and environmental factors are always both involved . . . Despite current attacks on tests in general (as well as on genetic explanations), they have much to contribute to the diagnosis of the type of education best suited to a child's needs and potentialities.

Plomin, amongst others, observes that these proportions vary dramatically during childhood development; for parents and teachers alike, this is a very important issue of prime significance and, consequently, the subject of contemporary research. As far back as 1988, Locurto, in a stimulating article, makes the suggestion that perhaps our efforts should shift in emphasis from that part of the equation dealing with genetics to the other parts dealing with shared and non-shared environments and more likely to be susceptible to educational processes. As indicated in Figure 9.3, we are talking about 20 to 30 per cent of the variance. In other words, we should be looking at the *malleability* of IQ – that is, what and how we can manipulate the environment so as to gain the maximum intellectual potential from each person. Evidence from pre-school intervention programmes, adopted siblings and within-family influences lend support to this view. It should also be good news for teachers if, using suitable school curricula, they can enhance the intellectual prowess of children. A note of caution is necessary. The lack of lasting effects of such intervention programmes has been discouraging.

The importance of monitoring intelligence with brain development, both pre- and postnatal, has been highlighted in the recent work of neuroscientists (see Chapter 2). The location and extent of neuron connections, the speed of processing information and brain metabolism are some of the topics under examination.

# The structure of abilities

This section is technical, but important if you need to know something about how intelligence tests were first designed. If nothing else, have a look at the figures in the section to get the feel of how intelligence tests were built up and developed. It also answers a number of questions about the differences between British and American approaches to structure and philosophy regarding psychometric intelligence.

A common theme throughout the study of intelligence is the possibility that we possess a fundamental general ability which we bring to bear on all problems – a kind of general level of mental efficiency which we all possess in some degree. In the discussions above we met several kinds of items, all purporting to measure some aspect of this general intelligence. Verbal, numerical, spatial and mechanical skills were mentioned which, while displaying individual variations, nevertheless may be subsumed to give a level of ability we call 'g', general ability.

The question was first examined around the turn of the last century, when Spearman introduced a mathematical technique called *factor analysis*. He endeavoured to determine the extent to which all the various kinds of problems thought to reflect intelligence really did possess something in common. It is not an easy subject and the interested reader is advised to look at a basic text (Child 2006) for an understanding of the principles on which the method is based. For our present purpose, we will mention only enough to give the reader an idea of how the important models of the structure of human ability have appeared.

For now, let us look at a thumb-nail sketch of correlation. When two variables, for example, size of house and the income of the occupant, alter together, we say they are correlated (see Chapter 17). With the variables we have chosen, it would be safe to conclude that the larger a person's income, the more likely it is that he or she will own a larger house. This relationship would give a positive, but not a perfect, correlation (some people run the risk and buy a house they cannot afford). Where an increase in one variable is accompanied by a decrease in a second (intelligence and family size), we have a negative correlation. Two unrelated variables (intelligence and eye colour) show zero correlation. If we obtain a systematic change in several variables it could well be that there is some common causal factor. For example, in the illustration using a person's income, we would probably find many other related variables, especially in material possessions (size of house, car, furniture, etc.), the common denominator being the person's salary. Applying this to human ability, suppose the scores on several tests purporting to identify intelligent behaviour were all positively intercorrelated. It could be concluded that there is a basic factor underpinning this common relationship. The mathematical procedure of factor analysis seeks to identify and isolate these common factors by using the correlations between the variables.

Spearman, using a prototype factor analysis, formulated his *Two-factor Theory* (1904). His view was rooted in the assumption that general ability, 'g', accounted in substantial measure for differences in human performance. You will remember his belief that intelligence consisted of 'the eduction of relations and correlates'. Further, each test was thought to require a specific ability, 's', unique to each test. Specific abilities accounted for the unevenness in an individual's score from one kind of test to another over and above minimum competence in all the tests (g). A child with high general ability, therefore, would be expected to perform well in most aspects of an intelligence test, while at the same time displaying variations in test scores arising from his or her special talents. Spearman's 'two factors', then, consisted of g-type and s-type factors.

Figure 9.4(a) shows that all the tests deemed to measure intelligence are sufficiently intercorrelated for them to appear together as factor I. Then follows a separate column for

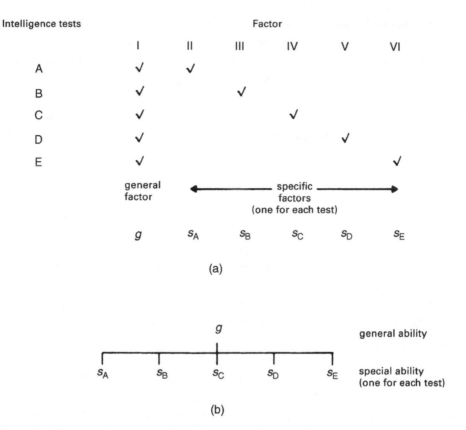

**Figure 9.4** Diagrammatic representation of Spearman's Two-factor Theory.

each test to indicate that certain variations in the test scores are due to the specific and unique demands made by each. A simpler diagrammatic view is given in Figure 9.4(b).

This over-simplified theory was soon superseded by the work of Sir Cyril Burt, who proposed the *Hierarchical Group-factor Theory*, widely supported in Great Britain. Spearman's choice of test material was restricted and insufficient to allow for the existence of groups of tests which reflected common skills. Many tests, for instance, require verbal ability in addition to a specific ability. Therefore Burt suggested 'group' factors as well as $g$ and $s$. Group factors are illustrated in Figure 9.5, which also attempts to show the tree-like connections postulated in the hierarchical theory of Burt and developed by Vernon (1969).

During the twentieth century, there were many factorial studies of the structure of ability. An American psychologist, John Carroll, decided to re-analyse about 400 sets of these data from as many studies as he could find which were reliable and compatible (Carroll 1993). His conclusion was very similar to the three stratum version shown in Figure 9.5 of $g$, group factors (visual perception, auditory perception, retrieval ability, cognitive speediness, processing speed, general memory and learning, crystallized intelligence and fluid intelligence), and specific abilities subsumed in the individual tests. One crucial factor related to aging

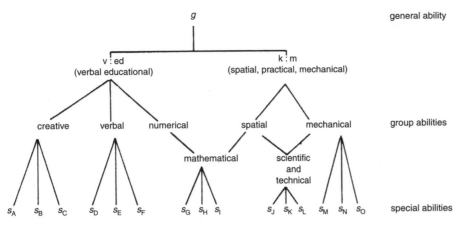

**Figure 9.5** Diagrammatic model of the hierarchical group-factor theory. These include some of the main group factors underlying tests relevant to educational and vocational achievements. Adapted from P. E. Vernon, *Intelligence and Cultural Environment*, p. 22, Methuen, London, 1969.

is processing speed. Once the effects of speed are removed from consideration in the aging process, intelligence test scores tend to be stable. Tests relying on verbal ability tend not to decline to any extent (for a summary, see Deary 2001).

Thurstone, an American psychologist, was not satisfied with the all-inclusive measure *g* because it revealed so little of the special talents of each person. In the 1930s he employed another factor-analytical procedure which compounded *g* and *s* to give several factors referred to as *primary mental abilities*. Examples of these are verbal comprehension (V), number ability (N), word fluency (W), perceptual flexibility and speed, inductive reasoning, rote memory (M) and deductive reasoning. They are sometimes denoted by initial letters as shown in some cases above. Thurstone, it should be noted, did not deny the possibility of a general factor, but his factor approach enabled him to isolate independent mental abilities which he regarded as more productive when applied to educational or vocational guidance. For him, it was more revealing to have a broad profile of an individual's mental abilities than one overall measure.

Finally, we turn briefly to two sophisticated models of human ability expounded by Cattell and Guilford. To understand the implications of these theories the reader would need to refer to more advanced texts, but the following very simple outline should serve as an introduction. Cattell (1963 and 1967) has advanced a theory in which two general factors are postulated, namely fluid ($g_f$) and crystallized ($g_c$) general ability. In discussing age and intelligence earlier in this chapter, we met up with this concept (see Horn 1967). $g_f$ is regarded as a measure of the influence of biological factors on intellectual development and thought to be comparable to inherited ability. $g_c$ represents the outcome of cultural experiences such as parental and educational contacts. Clearly $g_f$ and $g_c$ are not directly related to Hebb's Intelligence A and B respectively because, as we have already noted, the latter cannot be assessed directly, whereas Cattell has claimed to have measured both $g_f$ and $g_c$.

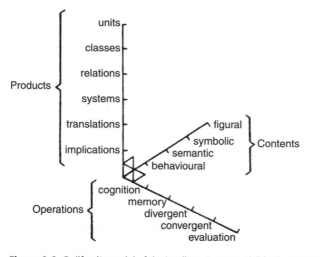

**Figure 9.6** Guilford's model of the intellect. From D. Child, *The Essentials of Factor Analysis*, Continuum, London, 2006 (3rd edn).

Guilford's model of the intellect (1968) was first proposed in the early 1950s (see Figure 9.6). This ambitious model postulates no fewer than 120 mental factors, of which he claims to have isolated about 80. He derives the mental factors from three independent dimensions which he calls *operations*, *contents* and *products*; that is, each intelligent act requires the individual to carry out various thinking 'operations' (such as memory, convergent thinking, divergent thinking) using 'content' media (such as symbols, figures or semantics) in order to 'produce' such things as classes, relations or implications. With this three-dimensional arrangement, 5 operations × 4 contents × 6 products, we get 120 possibilities for intellectual factors.

Both theories are speculative and are the subject of criticism and controversy. Their value lies in the options which they offer in a field where there is still plenty of scope for hypothesis and experimentation. Two operations mentioned by Guilford will be central to our discussion of creative thinking in the next chapter. They are convergent and divergent thinking.

## Summary

The concepts of intelligence and psychometric intelligence testing have been with us for some time and are probably going to stay for a good while longer. Whilst intelligence tests are by no means perfect, they are certainly amongst the most reliable of tests so far constructed. Educators and psychologists have used them extensively and with sufficient success for us to feel justified in noting their application with children.

We started the chapter on a cautious note by defining intelligent behaviour instead of intelligence. This was done to set the record straight about intelligence not being a fixed quantity, and to show that our concern should be for the quality rather than the quantity of human behaviour. Definitions incorporate biological, psychological and operational approaches to the study of intelligent behaviour.

Inborn intellectual potential cannot be assessed directly. Similarly, the influence of the environment cannot readily be estimated. Indirect sampling of some aspects of intelligent behaviour by the use of standardized tests is the nearest we have come to judging the intellectual ability and potential of individuals. The mathematical technique of factor analysis has been used to show a differentiation between the verbal, numerical, mechanical and spatial abilities of humans. These abilities have, in turn, formed the nucleus of numerous standardized tests used with both primary and secondary schoolchildren as prognostic and diagnostic tools.

But intelligence test scores are not fixed for each person (see Locurto 1988, on malleability). There are many reasons for fluctuations in an individual's IQ score. The age of a person, whether he or she is coached, and the ethnic and cultural experiences of social background all contribute in differing degrees to the variability of test scores. Early childhood experiences also seem to have a marked effect on the extent to which intellectual ability finally emerges. The near abandonment of 11+ selection was partly the result of anomalous IQ measures as, for example, occurred when retesting of the same children occasionally produced conflicting scores or when a child's mental age developed more rapidly than his or her chronological age, especially in early adolescence (sometimes known as *late development*).

The unresolved nature/nurture controversy is likewise a dispute about the extent of their influences. What children bring with them into the world and the effect which particular home, community and school provisions can have upon their intellectual development is one major concern. At present, most psychologists have tentatively settled for a middle-of-the-road policy in recognizing that interactive effects between inborn potential and environmental pressures exist and the extent is a matter for further research. Twin studies and neuroscience have gone some way to resolving the question of quantifying the impact of inheritance and environmental inputs to intellectual development. In the meantime, and in the face of mounting evidence (Jensen 1971), teachers must continue to be optimistic about the role of the school in developing intellectual skills.

Most educators are dedicated to the task of accommodating the individual differences displayed by children. The teacher, in the face of large classes, is set an almost impossible task not only of distinguishing the individual characteristics of the children but also of providing appropriate individual tuition to suit these characteristics. At the very least, the study and judicious application of intelligence and intelligence tests has something of value in it for teachers who wish to discover some background information about their children. IQs are not sufficient to direct the educational patterns adopted by teachers. They must be used along with other measures of scholastic variability such as the attitudes of children to work, school and teachers, motives, interests, achievement in specific subject areas and personality.

In these days of a growing conscience about the provision for the educationally underprivileged, the gifted and the backward, and the increased use of unstreamed classes, the teacher needs every available test he or she can depend on. Intelligence tests, if administered satisfactorily, should provide the teacher with one of a number of valuable pieces of supplementary evidence in deciding a child's educational programme.

## Tutorial enquiry and discussion

(a) Using whichever sources and resources are available (college or department libraries, school, tutors, etc.), discover as much as you can about the range and use of intelligence tests. It might prove helpful to invite guest speakers from the Local Authority Child Guidance Service to talk about psychological testing, especially about the use made of intelligence tests.

(b) Discuss with the group tutor the problems of testing a group of children (or an individual) with widely available (*open*) intelligence tests. Inspect a range of test materials for this purpose and note carefully the manual of instructions and the kind of items used. Include a consideration of:
  - the age of the children
  - the tests most appropriate for your purposes
  - where one can obtain the tests and their price
  - administration and scoring procedures
  - how to interpret the scores and relate them to school work
  - other possible achievement tests.

(c) In tutorial groups examine the possible reasons for:
  - the problem of defining the nature of intelligence
  - the negative correlation between family size and IQ
  - the decline of mental age with age (are there compensatory gains?)
  - the effects of coaching and practice
  - the difficulty of producing a culture-free test of intelligence
  - ethnic differences in measured IQ
  - the difficulty of measuring the ability of babies
  - the relative influence of genetic and environmental factors
  - the order of magnitude of correlations in Table 9.3 and variance in Figure 9.4.

(d) What are the strengths and weaknesses of streaming according to ability? Consider the position of the mentally gifted and mentally disadvantaged in your consideration of streaming.

(e) Examine the research literature with respect to the relationship between intelligence and academic achievement in one of the following sectors of education (you may also need to consult Chapter 16):
  - primary schools
  - secondary schools
  - some field of higher education.

## References

Ankney, H. (1992), 'Sex differences in relative brain size: the mismeasure of woman too?' *Intelligence* 16, 329–36.

Baron-Cohen, S. (2003), *The Essential Difference: Men, Women and the Extreme Male Brain*. London: Allan Lane (and Penguin Books).

Bayley, N. (1969), *Manual of the Bayley Scales of Infant Development*. New York: Psychological Corporation.

Biesheuvel, S. (1949), *Psychological Tests and their Application to non-European Peoples. Yearbook of Education*. London: Evans.

Birren, J. E. and Schaie, K. W. (2001), *Handbook of Psychology of Aging* (5th edn). London: Academic Press.

Botwinick, J. (1977), 'Intellectual abilities', in J. E. Birren and K. W. Schaie (eds), *Handbook of the Psychology of Aging*. New York: Van Nostrand Reinhold.

Bouchard, T. J. (jnr) and McGue, M. (1981), 'Familial studies of intelligence: A review'. *Science*, 212, 1055–9.

Burns, R. B. (1966), 'Age and mental ability: re-testing with thirty-three years' interval', *British Journal of Educational Psychology*, 36, 116.

Burt, C. (1955), 'The evidence for the concept of intelligence', *British Journal of Educational Psychology*, 25, 158–77.

Carroll, J. B. (1993), *Human Cognitive Abilities: a Survey of Factor Analytic Studies*. Cambridge: Cambridge University Press.

Cattell, R. B. (1963), 'Theory of fluid and crystallized intelligence: a critical experiment', *Journal of Educational Psychology*, 54, 1–22.

Cattell, R. B. (1967), 'The theory of fluid and crystallized intelligence checked at the 5–6-year-old level', *British Journal of Educational Psychology*, 37, 209–24.

Cattell, R. B. (1982), *The Inheritance of Personality and Ability: Research Methods and Findings*. New York: Academic Press.

Ceci, S. J. (1991), 'How much does schooling influence general intelligence and its cognitive components? A reassessment of the evidence'. *Developmental Psychology*, 27, 703–22.

Child, D. (2006) (3rd edn), *The Essentials of Factor Analysis*. London: Continuum.

Child, D. and Borrill, C. (1990), *Taking the DC Test: a Guide for Candidates*. Nurse Selection Project, Leeds: University of Leeds.

Columbo, J. (1993), *Infant Cognition: Predicting Later Intellectual Functioning*. Newbury Park, CA: Sage.

Deary, I. J. (2001), *Intelligence: a Very Short Introduction*. Oxford: Oxford University Press.

Deary, I. J. (2005), 'Intelligence, health and death'. *The Psychologist*, 18, 10, 610–13.

Dixon, R. A., Kramer, D. A. and Baltes, P. B. (1985), 'Intelligence: a life-span developmental perspective', in B. B. Wolman (ed.), *Handbook of Intelligence: Theories, Measurements and Applications*. New York: Wiley.

Douglas, J. W. B. (1964), *The Home and the School*. London: MacGibbon and Kee.

Douglas, J. W. B., Ross, J. M. and Simpson, H. R. (1968), *All our Future: A Longitudinal Study of Secondary Education*. London:

Elliott, C. D. (1975), 'British intelligence scale takes shape', *Education*, 25, 460–1.

Elliott, C. D., leading author (1996), *British Ability Scales Second Edition (BAS II)*. Windsor: NFER-Nelson.

Erlenmeyer-Kimling, L. and Jarvik, L.F. (1963), 'Genetics and intelligence', *Science*, 142, 1477–9.

Eysenck, H.J. (1987), 'Speed of information processing, reaction time and the theory of intelligence', in P. A. Vernon (ed.), *Speed of Information Processing and Intelligence*. New York: Ablex.

Eysenck, H. J. and Kamin, L. J. (1981), *Intelligence: The Battle for the Mind*. London: Pan Books.

Eysenck, H. J. *et al.* (1972), Responses to Jensen's article (see Jensen, A. R., 1971 for list of contributors), *Educational Research*, 14, 87–100.

Eysenck, H. J. and Schoenthaler, J. J. (1997), 'Raising IQ levels by vitamin and mineral supplementation', in R. J. Sternberg and E. Grigorenko, *Intelligence, Heredity and Environment*. Cambridge: Cambridge University Press.

Flynn, J. R. (1984), 'The mean IQ of Americans: massive gains 1932 to 1978', *Psychological Bulletin*, 95, 29–51.

Flynn, J. R. (1987), 'Massive IQ gains in 14 nations: What IQ tests really measure', *Psychological Bulletin*, 101, 171–91.

Galton, F. (1892), *Hereditary Genius: An Enquiry into its Laws and Consequences* (2nd edn). New York: Horizon.

Gardner, H. (1993a), *Frames of Mind: The Theory of Multiple Intelligences* (10th anniversary edn). London: Heinemann.

Gardner, H. (1993b), *Multiple Intelligences: Theory and Practice*. Basic Books: New York.

Gardner, H. (1999), *Intelligence Reframed: Multiple Intelligences for the 21st century*. New York: Basic Books.

Gardner, H., Kornhaber, M. L. and Wake, W. K. (1996), *Intelligence: Multiple Perspectives*. Fort Worth: Harcourt Brace.

Goddard, H. H. (1921), *The Kallikak Family*. New York: Macmillan.

Gottfried, A. W. (ed.) (1984), *Home Environment and Early Cognitive Development: Longitudinal Research*. New York Academic Press.

Gregory, R. L. (1998), *Eye and Brain: The Psychology of Seeing* (5th edn). Oxford: Oxford University Press.

Griffiths, R. (1954), *The Ability of Babies*. London: University of London Press.

Gronlund, N. E. (1973), *Preparing Criterion-Referenced Tests for Classroom Instruction*. New York: Macmillan.

Gronlund, N. E. (1978), *Stating Objectives for Classroom Instruction*. London: Macmillan.

Guilford, J. P. (1968), 'The structure of intelligence', in D. K. Whitla (ed.), *Handbook of Measurement and Assessment in the Behavioral Sciences*. Reading, MA: Addison-Wesley.

Harris, J. R. (1998), *The Nurture Assumption: Why Children Turn Out The Way They Do*. New York: Free Press.

Hebb, D. O. (1966), *A Textbook of Psychology* (2nd edn). Philadelphia: Saunders.

Heim, A. W. (1970), *The Appraisal of Intelligence*. Slough: NFER.

Hertzog, C. and Schaie, K. W. (1986), 'Stability and change in adult intelligence: 1. Analysis of the longitudinal covariance structures', *Psychology and Aging*, 1, 159–71.

Hertzog, C. and Schaie, K. W. (1988), 'Stability and change in adult intelligence: 2. Simultaneous analysis of longitudinal means and covariance structures', *Psychology and Aging*, 3, 122–30.

Horn, J.L. (1967), 'Intelligence – why it grows, why it declines', *Trans-action*, 5, 23–31.

Howe, M. J. A. (1998), 'Intelligence theory and young people's mental abilities (with peer review of the articles)', *The Psychology of Education Review*, 22(2), 3–19.

Irwing, P. and Lynn, R. (2005), 'Sex differences in means and variability on the progressive matrices in university students: A meta-analysis', *British Journal of Psychology*, 96, 4, 505–24.

Jensen, A. R. (1967), 'The culturally disadvantaged: psychological and educational aspects', *Educational Research*, 10, 4–20.

Jensen, A. R. (1971), 'Do schools cheat minority children?', *Educational Research*, 14, 3–28. For responses by Sir Cyril Burt, H. J. Butcher, H. J. Eysenck, J. Nisbet and P. E. Vernon, see (1972) *Educational Research*, 14, 87–100.

Jensen, A. R. (1977), 'Cumulative deficit in IQ of Blacks in the rural South', *Developmental Psychology*, 13, 184–91.

Kamin, L. J. (1974), *The Science and Politics of IQ*. Harmondsworth: Penguin.

Lawton, D. (1968), *Social Class, Language and Education*. London: Routledge and Kegan Paul.

Locurto, C. (1988), 'On the malleability of IQ', *The Psychologist*, 11, 431–5.

Lynch, A., Mitchell, L. B., Vincent, E. M., Trueman, M. and Macdonald, L. M. (1982), 'The McCarthy Scales of Children's Abilities: a normative study on English 4-year-olds', *British Journal of Educational Psychology*, 52, 133–43.

Lynn, R. (1990), 'The role of nutrition in secular increases in intelligence', *Personality and Individual Differences*, 11, 273–85.

Lynn, R. (1994), 'Sex differences in brain size and intelligence: a paradox resolved', *Personality and Individual Differences*, 17, 257–71.

Lynn, R. and Irwing, P. (2004), 'Sex differences on the progressive matrices: A meta-analysis', *Intelligence*, 32, 481–98.

Mackintosh, N. J. (1998), *IQ and Human Intelligence*. Oxford: Oxford University Press.

Mager, R. R. (1962), *Preparing Instructional Objectives*. Belmont, CA: Fearon.

McCarthy, D. (1972), *The McCarthy Scales of Children's Abilities*. New York: Psychological Corporation.

Miles, T.R. (1957), 'Symposium: Contributions to intelligence testing and the theory of intelligence', *British Journal of Educational Psychology*, 27, 153–210.

Neisser, U., Boodoo, G., Bouchard, T. J. (jnr), Boykin, A. W., Brody, N., Ceci, S. J., Halpern, D. F., Loehlin, J. C., Perloff, R., Sternberg, R. J. and Urbina, S. (1996), 'Intelligence: knowns and unknowns', *American Psychologist*, 51, 77–101.

Nisbet, J. D. (1953), *Family Environment*. London: Cassell.

Pakkenberg, B. and Gundersen, H. J. G. (1997), 'Neurocortical neuron number in humans: effect of sex and age', *Journal of Comparative Neurology*, 384, 312–20.

Plomin, R., DeFries, J. C., McClearn, G. E. and McGuffin, P. (2001), *Behavioral Genetics* (4th edn). New York: Worth.

*Psychologist, The*, (1992), a series of articles on nutrition and IQ, 15(9), 399–413.

Reed, T. E. and Jensen, A. R. (1992), 'Conduction velocity in a brain nerve pathway of normal adults correlates with intelligence level', *Intelligence*, 16, 259–72.

Rose, S. A. and Feldman, J. (1995), 'The prediction of IQ and specific cognitive abilities at 11 years from infancy measures', *Developmental Psychology*, 31, 685–96.

Salthouse, T. A. (1996a), 'Constraints on theories of cognitive ageing', *Psychonomic Bulletin and Review*, 3, 287–99.

Salthouse, T. A. (1996b), 'The processing-speed theory of adult age differences in cognition', *Psychological Review*, 103, 403–28.

Schaie, K. W. (1983), 'The Seattle longitudinal study: a 21-year exploration of psychometric intelligence in adulthood', in K. W. Schaie, *Longitudinal Studies of Adult Psychological Development*. New York: Freeman.

Schaie, K. W. (1996), *Intellectual Development in Adulthood*. Cambridge: Cambridge University Press.

Spearman, C. (1904), 'General intelligence objectively determined and measured', *American Journal of Psychology*, 15, 202–93.

Steele, C. M. (1997), 'A threat in the air: how stereotypes shape intellectual identity and performance', *American Psychologist*, 52, 6, 613–29.

Stein, J. F. (1994), *Introduction to Neurophysiology* (2nd ed). Oxford: Blackwell.

Sternberg, R. J. (1985a), *Beyond IQ: A Triarchic Theory of Human Intelligence*. Cambridge: Cambridge University Press.

Sternberg, R. J. (1985b), *Human Abilities: An Information-Processing Approach*. New York: Freeman.

Sternberg, R. J. (1993), 'Procedures for identifying intellectual potential in the gifted: a perspective on alternative "Metaphors of Mind"', in K. H. Heller, F. J. Mönks and A. H. Passow, *International Handbook of Research and Development of Giftedness and Talent*. Oxford: Pergamon.

Sternberg, R. J. (1995), *In Search of Mind*. Fort Worth: Harcourt Brace.

Sternberg, R. J. (ed.) (2000), *Handbook of Intelligence*. Cambridge: Cambridge University Press.

Stott, D. H. (1983), *Issues in the Intelligence Debate*. Windsor: NFER-Nelson.

Vernon, P.A., Wickett, J. C., Bazana, P. G. and Stelmack, R. M. (2000), 'The neuropsychology and psychophysiology of human intelligences' in R. J. Sternberg (ed.), *Handbook of Intelligence*. Cambridge: Cambridge University Press.

Vernon, P. E. (1960), *Intelligence and Attainment Tests*. London: University of London Press.

Vernon, P. E. (1969), *Intelligence and Cultural Environment*. London: Methuen.

Vernon, P. E. (1979), *Intelligence: Heredity and Environment*. San Francisco: Freeman.

Warburton, F. W. (1966), 'Construction of the new British Intelligence Scale', *Bulletin of the British Psychological Society*, 19, 68–70.

Wiseman, S. (1964), *Education and Environment*. Manchester: Manchester University Press.

## Further reading

Child, D. (2006), *The Essentials of Factor Analysis* (3rd edn). London: Continuum. One of the few introductory texts for those with little knowledge of statistics.

Deary, I. J. (2001), *Intelligence: A Very Short Introduction*. Oxford: Oxford University Press. This should be read before getting into the more technical presentations in the other recommended texts.

Harris, J. R. (1998), *The Nurture Assumption: Why Children Turn Out the Way They Do*. London: Bloomsbury and the website listed below.

Kline, P. (1991), *Intelligence: The Psychometric View*. London: Routledge. Technical, but a sound introduction to the problems of defining and measuring intelligence.

Kline, P. (1999), *The Handbook of Psychological Testing* (2nd edn). London: Routledge.

Mackintosh, N. J. (1998), *IQ and Human Intelligence*. Oxford: Oxford University Press.

Plomin, R., DeFries, J. C., McClearn, G. E. and McGuffin, P. (2001), *Behavioral Genetics* (4th edn). New York: Worth.

Sternberg, R. J. (ed.) (2000), *Handbook of Intelligence*. Cambridge: Cambridge University Press.

## Useful websites

http://home.att.net/~xcher/tna/
J. R. Harris website containing several references to the nurture assumption at.
http://www.genome.gov/10001772
Human Genome Project
http://www.nfer-nelson.ac.uk/catalogue/catalogue.asp
NFER-Nelson publishers have a useful website catalogue of tests.

### Answers to intelligence test items

## Analogies

1  (c) seem (first one and last two letters common to both).
2  (d) bitch.
3  COMPOSER is to NOTES.

## Synonyms

1  Slake – quench.
2  Preen – trim feathers.

$\longrightarrow$

## Antonyms

1  Tup – ewe.
2  Easy, soft – hard.

## Number and letter series

1  1/2, 1/2. Starting with 1/2 at the left-hand side, multiply it by 1, then multiply this answer by 2, and the next answer by 3, and so on.
2  JJ (months of the year).
3  30, 42 (1 × 2, 2 × 3, 3 × 4, etc.).

## Ordering and classification

1  Animal, vertebrate, carnivore, feline animals, domestic cats.
2  Meeting.
3  A half (word signifying a precise quantity).

## Find the patterns

1

2  (c): the others are three-sided figures.
3  A quarter to six (next but one!).

# 10 The Gifted and Talented

## Chapter Outline

## Implications for teachers

- Most teachers have gifted and talented children in their classrooms.
- Every child has 'special needs', not least those who are gifted and talented.
- Teachers must not think that the gifted and talented can 'fend for themselves'. They need special attention suited to their abilities.
- Once gifted and talented children have been identified, the school authorities should be informed.
- Support is now available from various sources to enhance the teacher's role in providing for such children.

There can be few students who have not encountered the concepts of 'giftedness', 'the talented' or 'creative thinking', or failed to detect the upsurge of interest in recent years. At a national level, we are told that advanced industrial societies cannot survive, develop or compete without the continued emergence of highly able people in ever-increasing numbers in political, social and scientific pursuits. This has prompted many governments (HMI

1992, Freeman 1998) to sponsor research dedicated to the task of identifying, measuring, cultivating and exploiting the potential of highly able and creative children.

A second reason for the upsurge in enthusiasm for creative thinking is the knowledge explosion which has tended to render conventional modes of learning and teaching of limited efficiency. The teaching of science, especially in preparation for examinable subjects, has frequently taken the form of 'here are the facts; now use them'. This is not to deny the central importance of fact assimilation and recall (even the most gifted must have a knowledge base), but where the psychologist's interests lie is in the strategies of learning and reasoning which the situation imposes on the child, and the lasting influence these might have on the way that the child tackles problems. Heim's definition of intelligence in the previous chapter – the grasping of essentials in a situation and responding appropriately – goes only part of the way to an understanding of creative human behaviour because there is also the important preliminary step of exploring the situation and deciding on those essentials. Learning tactical skills of approaching a task in an open-minded fashion and selecting the important aspects in arriving at solutions may well be enhanced or inhibited by the learning methods we encourage in the classroom.

Third, we have long been interested in the interaction between cognitive and non-cognitive variables. Undoubtedly, there are personal aspects such as motivation, personality (e.g. determination), attitudes and intellectual style (i.e. qualities other than purely cognitive ones) as well as situational variables such as opportunities at the 'right time' which are involved in releasing and making the best use of creative talent. Once giftedness has been identified it is important to ensure that other influential factors are taken into account (Freeman 2000).

Fourth, every child has special needs. This includes the gifted and talented and our education system should reflect this. Unfortunately, there is still the lingering fallacy that bright children can take care of themselves and do not need any special attention. Consequently, recent governments have been made aware of the need to include concentrated provision for gifted children.

The majority of the highly able, as Terman showed in his monumental longitudinal study of over 1000 gifted people from childhood over a 40-year period (Terman 1925, Oden 1968), do not become highly creative or well-known figures. Nevertheless, many do lead productive lives in some useful human endeavour. Therefore, we shall treat productive creativity as a special case of giftedness.

American and British psychologists use a variety of terms such as 'creative', 'gifted', 'talented', 'imaginative', 'original', 'inventive', 'divergent thinker', 'exploratory' to mean much the same. Of these, creative, gifted, talented and divergent thinking have developed special meanings which we shall discuss. For example, *talent* has become associated with exceptional creativity in a specific field of human endeavour such as art, dance, drama, science, mathematics, writing and music.

# Processes leading to exceptional ability

As suggested above, the process by which a new-born develops into a highly able adult is guided by several major influences – inherent abilities, personal attributes, personal environmental circumstances and learning experiences. For any individual, the unique interaction of these factors *may* give rise to a creative person in some particular field of study. For psychologists, these four factors have been the core of research in giftedness and creative thinking.

Inherent human abilities and the problems of assessing intelligence have been a source of concern as we saw in Chapter 9. Some argue that there is one important general measure, *g*; others have multi-variable models. Gardner (1999), for example, proposes ten abilities: linguistic, logico–mathematical, spatial, musical, bodily-kinaesthetic, interpersonal, intrapersonal, naturalistic, spiritual and existential. Gagné (1993) hypothesizes five 'aptitudes' or 'natural human abilities': intellectual, creative, socio-affective, sensori-motor and 'others' to allow for hidden talents not yet defined. Some of these are similar to Gardner's. Some models (Renzulli 1986, Sternberg and Lubart 1992, Cropley 1994) put creativity as central to all giftedness, whereas Gagné does not see creativity as a necessary ingredient of performance in some areas (e.g. athletics, music, teaching), although there are creative people in these activities.

But, can conventional IQ tests detect a potentially brilliant musician or ballet dancer? Again, do they convincingly distinguish the creative from the not so creative? Teachers, incidentally, have suspected for a long time that they do not and the point was made in Chapter 9 that Intelligence C is but a sampling of human ability. It is just possible that the kind of items we find in IQ tests demand a particular kind of thinking strategy which may not entirely tap the creative capacities of those tested. We shall return to this point later. As Liam Hudson observes in his book *Contrary Imaginations* (1966), when you look at a class of bright boys and girls with high measures of intelligence it is virtually impossible to pick out those who will go on to be creative people from those who will not. Thus, whilst it remains true that creative individuals are amongst those with high intelligence, the relationship between creative capacity and IQ is not straightforward.

At least three elements make up the personal attributes. These are preferred processing methods, namely, *intellectual style, motivation* and *personality*. To some extent, intellectual style overlaps or interacts with inherent abilities. Aspects such as memory or how much knowledge a person has to bring to a problem are related to intelligence. Other style factors are speed and accuracy, metacognitive skills, flexibility, originality. Unmotivated, a person is hardly likely to display abilities. Without a burning desire to achieve and be task-orientated, it would be difficult to show one's high ability or creativeness. Later in Chapter 12 we shall explore the role of personality in academic achievement.

Environmental circumstances will include encouragement from family, school and peer group and opportunities being offered at the right time. These, along with intellectual style,

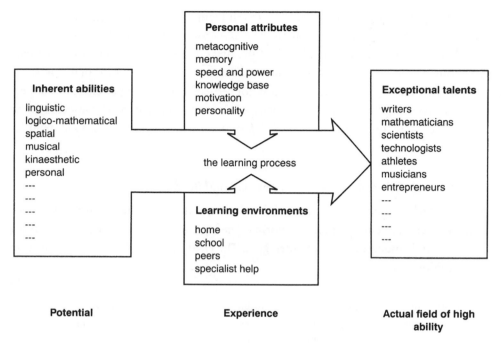

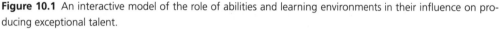

**Figure 10.1** An interactive model of the role of abilities and learning environments in their influence on producing exceptional talent.

all contribute to the progress of an individual's learning experiences. Figure 10.1 is a simple diagram of the process outlined above.

If a person is lucky enough to be born with a superb ability, there is no guarantee that she or he will end up as a superb performer. Progress through early life at home, in school, with specialist teachers, along with other personal qualities, such as motivation, persistence, a will to succeed, a love of one's special gift, a good memory, a knowledge of one's subject, and one's learning strengths and weaknesses, are important prerequisites. Not all of these attributes need be present at once, but there must be some combination which will lead to success. Figure 10.1 represents an interactive model. There is no linear path through life, but a series of interactions of inborn qualities and external supports and pressures which give the blend necessary for exceptional performance.

# Defining and assessing the qualities of giftedness

There is no single, widely accepted definition of giftedness. In the end, what defines the concept is determined by the measures psychologists choose to investigate it. There are broadly four approaches and these are reflected in Figure 10.1. The longest tradition is to look at those with exceptionally *high measures of human abilities, an ability* or *talent(s)*. The 'potential' attributes in the left-hand part of the diagram represent these. *High creativity* using various tests is the second. It combines the inherent abilities with some of the personal attributes. *High talent* in a particular field is concerned with looking at exceptional performance, often using biographical and interview information. This aspect appears at the right-hand side of Figure 10.1. Finally, *high information processing ability* looks at qualities in both the inherent and personal attributes.

## Performance on ability tests (see Chapter 9)

A popular criterion for selecting gifted children has been how well they perform in intelligence tests in relation to the population norms. The logic of this is that the gifted are most likely to be found amongst the highly intelligent. The HMI Report (1992) on the education of gifted children says:

> the majority of educationalists working in this field accept criteria which include general intellectual ability, specific aptitude in one or more subjects, creative or productive thinking, leadership qualities, ability in creative or performing arts and psychomotor ability. The term 'very able' is intended to refer broadly to the top 5 per cent of the ability range in any of these areas, while the term 'exceptionally able' refers to that tiny minority . . . functioning several years beyond their age group.

The 'very able' in the above quotation are sometimes defined as the highest 1 per cent.

### Longitudinal research: Terman

The 11+ examination was based on the assumption that the top 15 per cent or so in IQ distribution would be those most able to benefit from the fast track in grammar schools. Many research studies also use this starting point. One of the earliest and certainly the most extensive studies is that of Terman (1925), whose famous longitudinal study of gifted American children is an outstanding masterpiece. 'Gifted' in this case is defined as having an IQ greater than 140 on the Terman–Merrill Intelligence Test. In seeking out those with the highest IQs, Terman clearly believed in a linear connection between IQ and creative talent.

However, his, and subsequent, work is especially interesting for the light it sheds on the personality characteristics of highly intelligent and creative people. This group was revisited periodically from the early 1920s up to 1968 when Oden (1968) retested a portion of the group. She compared the childhood of the top and bottom 100 men selected by compounding professional productivity, the extent of responsibility, influence and authority over others, honours and income. In other words, the status afforded by society to its most highly productive members was used to distinguish two groups for the research. A detailed interview with each individual revealed that the top group had less illness and greater stability in the home during childhood. Many more of the top group came from professional homes where parents had well-defined attitudes about education and gave positive encouragement to the children to do well at school. Learning tended to be valued for its own sake by their parents. There was also in the top group a higher need to achieve during early childhood.

For other examples of small-scale longitudinal studies see Subotnik and Arnold (1993).

## Current achievements of children

Many researchers begin by looking at the current performance in school or as assessed by parents. Actually, Terman's first move was to find children who were doing very well at school; he then gave them IQ tests and chose those (approximately 1500) with the highest IQ scores.

In a study by Freeman (1979, 1991, 2001), the sample was chosen from those whose parents had joined the National Association for Gifted Children (NAGC). The views of parents in this case were used as the yardstick. They believed their children were unusually gifted in a variety of subjects – maths, music, creative arts and so on. The number in the sample was 70, spread over almost as many schools. All children in the selected child's class were given Raven's Progressive Matrices to obtain a culture-fair measure. A second child in the same class was chosen who had the same score on the Raven's test and a third child was chosen at random. This gave three samples with 70 in each – a target sample, a matching control sample and a random control sample. All the children were then tested using intelligence, personality, creativity and music ability tests; they were interviewed, as were their parents.

The findings were intriguing. One hundred and forty-five were above IQ 121 of which 82 fell in the top 1 per cent of the population (IQ 141–70). This, to some extent, confirmed the parents' belief in their children's exceptional talent. More importantly, those with identical scores on the Raven's test had significantly different scores on the general test of ability which in turn was related to their home and school backgrounds. Freeman concludes that:

> the brighter the children, the more they had taken in from their surroundings . . . This study which had taken home and school into account, had demonstrated that a bright child living in an educationally poor environment could score the same IQ as a child of more modest abilities in a really good educational environment.

In other words, the Raven Matrices type of test is closer to an aptitude measure, whereas a general IQ test is closer to an achievement test – the scores having been affected by educational provision at home and school (see Chapter 16 for a discussion of aptitude and achievement test scores).

Freeman concludes that the selection of gifted children using only general IQ measures would miss those gifted children from poor educational environments. Another conclusion of interest to teachers is that if the educational environment is so influential, it is imperative to have special educational provision.

Mothers of the target children tended to have reached higher-level occupations and took more responsibility for their children's education than the fathers. Both target parents put greater pressure on their children than the control group. They complained more about, and at, school and they thought of their children as more 'difficult'. Freeman showed that these difficulties were not related to IQ, but to other environmental factors. There seemed to be no differences between the groups on physical and emotional development or personality profiles (using Cattell's HSPQ, see Chapter 12) other than there being more extravert children amongst the musically talented. The brightest children were often early developers in reading, writing and talking. They also had much greater powers of concentration and much better memories.

The importance of home comes through clearly in the study. Both material provision (books, games, instruments, etc.) and positive parental involvement (doing things together, being taken to galleries, live performance, etc.) were found to be crucial. In addition to the intellectual ability displayed by the children, the role of environmental influences as displayed in Figure 10.1 comes through strongly in this study. The children in the original study have now been tracked down and studied in adulthood (Freeman 2001).

So far, the methods have involved intelligence test scores either as a starting point or as confirmation. Latterly, some authorities and researchers have taken to using *checklists* containing central characteristics of gifted children. For example, Montgomery (1991, 1998) lists 18 criteria in her study of learning difficulties. Many have been confirmed in other studies, such as the Freeman research above. 'Keen powers of observation, unusual imagination and plenty of ideas, a good memory, may develop special interests in music, arts, sports out of school' are a few. The more criteria which apply, the more likely it is that the child is gifted.

Unfortunately, the range and depth of ability can become so much a matter of subjective judgement that selection and discrimination are very difficult to justify. The descriptions which arise from the profiles are often so all-inclusive as to apply to almost any child. Some checklists also contain criteria which have been shown not to apply. For example, 'sleeplessness', 'always asking questions', 'emotionally unstable' or 'difficult' are often found in checklists, yet there is little scientific justification for their inclusion. It still remains true that what is useful on checklists can, in the main, be tested with some degree of objectivity.

The exploration of a single ability or talent has also developed in the last century. In Chapter 4, we gave some examples of researchers who were attempting to develop tests in order to examine cognitive development in various subject areas including mathematics, history (concepts of time), music and science. These were sometimes used to choose talented youngsters. Gardner's work on multiple intelligences (Chapter 9) is another potential source for defining and testing specific talents. Recently, the *World Class Tests* (for a useful introduction see QCA (2002) compiled and edited by Carolyn Richardson) have been designed to select the most talented in mathematics and problem-solving. The items are for 9- and 13-year-olds and have been trialled in the USA, Australia and Hong Kong as well as the UK. Amongst other things, the intention is to produce an international benchmark, identify the top 10 per cent in mathematics and problem-solving and ultimately to encourage teachers to give them special provision in keeping with their talents (http://www.worldclassarena.org).

## Trait creativity – using divergent thinking tests

Creativity has been used in two senses. One identifies it as a broad trait or cognitive ability tested using such devices as divergent thinking tests. Eysenck (1993a and b) refers to this as *trait creativity*. The second use relates to highly creative people and the exploration of their characteristics. We shall call this *talent*, that is, exceptional creativity in a particular field of human endeavour such as art, science, mathematics, writing or music. The people involved would be a tiny proportion of the population and their names would be known, certainly within their fields of interest. There is no evidence, as yet, to show a link between high trait scores and exceptional talent. The only evidence so far shows that highly talented people tend to have high measures of intelligence, indicating they may have been most capable in whatever they had tackled. Sternberg and Lubart (1992) refer to this distinction as *reproductive* and *productive* (or *creative*) giftedness. In this section we shall concentrate on divergent thinking, or trait creativity, and return to talent on p. 337.

The criteria for judging an eminent person's competence in a special field are fairly obvious: he or she must create original ideas which can be clearly recognized as pushing forward the frontiers of knowledge in a chosen field. But can we devise objective tests which would predict this creative talent?

One approach to the problem was opened by Guilford in the early 1950s, when he introduced his 'model of the intellect' (see previous chapter). He postulated several cognitive operations, amongst which he included *convergent* and *divergent thinking*. The convergent thinker is distinguished by an ability to deal with problems requiring one conventional correct solution clearly obtainable from the information available. Problems of this kind can be found in all intelligence tests and in many 'objective-type' questions, in which a problem is presented with several solutions, only one of which is correct. We saw in the last chapter several examples of intelligence test items which require the testee to focus attention and reasoning to provide a single correct solution. No opportunity is given for productive thinking beyond the information supplied; in fact, items with more than one solution are discarded as unsatisfactory.

The divergent thinker, on the other hand, is adept in problems requiring the generation of several equally acceptable solutions, where the emphasis is on the quantity, variety and originality of responses. Guilford's two categories attempt to discriminate between the styles of problem-solving behaviour adopted in closed and open-ended problems. Although these are not exclusive processes (solving convergent problems might require a great deal of 'diverging' before a solution presents itself), in general the items of convergent and divergent thinking tests do encourage different approaches, and it is this aspect which has led some psychologists to correlate divergent thinking with creative thinking. As yet, the relationship has still to be verified convincingly (Subotnik and Arnold 1993).

Guilford (1959) has defined numerous kinds of divergent test items. Although this unwieldy number has been abandoned, there is mounting evidence to support the view (Nuttall 1973) of there being distinct *verbal* and *non-verbal* (or *figural*) factors in ideational fluency. Of the verbal kind, the 'uses of objects' test, 'consequences' test and the 'S' test are three of many in common usage. Here are some examples.

### Uses of objects test:

Write down as many *different uses* as you can for a BUCKET. Work as quickly as possible and remember that points will be given for answers which are unusual.

### Consequences test:

Below is given a change in the way we live. It is not likely to happen, but you are asked to pretend that it really does happen. Write down as many different results of the change as you can invent. Your score will depend on how many different and unusual ideas as well as the number of ideas you can write.

The change is: we all have four fingers and no thumb on each hand.

### 'S' test:

Write as many different five-letter words as you can beginning with S.

### Number test:

An example of a number test is: Given the numbers 2, 3, 4, 5 and 6, construct as many different equations as you can using only these numbers (e.g. $5 - 4 + 2 + 3 = 6$).

### Circles, squares and parallel lines:

Of the many non-verbal tests, the commonest in Great Britain have been the 'circles', the 'squares' and the 'parallel lines' tests. A page of circles (or squares) is presented to the subject, who is told to add lines to the circles (squares) to complete a recognizable drawing. Lines can be inside the circle, outside the circle or both inside and outside the circle. The score depends on the number of objects, their variety and their originality. The 'parallel lines' test has a similar format.

**Further reading**

A detailed analysis of test materials is given by E. P. Torrance in *Guiding Creative Talent*, Prentice-Hall, Englewood Cliffs, NJ, 1962. He has also produced a standardized test battery of items known as the *Torrance Tests of Creative Thinking*, Personnel Press, Princeton, NJ, 1966. Torrance's tests are also summarized in Goldman, R. J. (1964)

The scoring techniques tell us quite a bit about the aims of the tests. There are three basic types of score obtainable. The first is a *fluency* score obtained by counting the number of responses given (but excluding those which are nonsensical or which do not answer the question as posed). In effect it is a measure of the speed with which the individual can summon up ideas. A second score can be obtained by grouping responses into categories. This score is known as *flexibility*, and in effect measures the variety of responses given. The scorer's subjectivity enters into decisions about the groupings, but this can be partly offset by assembling the opinions of several judges and using the majority consensus. In Figure 10.2 five possible responses to the 'squares' test are shown. The fluency score is five, but as the first and fourth responses fall into the same category of 'letters of the alphabet', the flexibility score is four. A third measure is *originality* and is derived from the most infrequent responses. By counting the number of times a response occurs within the group under test, it is possible to arrive at a frequency distribution for each response and to allot scores for the least frequent. As these types of score (i.e. fluency, flexibility and originality) are based on the same responses, it is not surprising to find high correlations between them.

In terms of the requirements for an act of originality, the divergent thinking tests leave a lot to be desired. The underlying assumption that divergent thinking scores correlate with future originality has yet to be established experimentally. Moreover, the responses are at a lower level of originality than would be required for, say, a new invention. The responses frequently serve no useful purpose and often display flights of fancy bordering

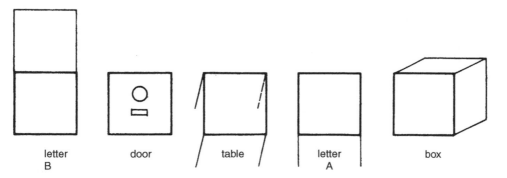

**Figure 10.2** Examples of answers to the 'squares' test of divergent thinking.

on the grotesque, sadistic and trivial. What we have are two operational definitions of short-term thinking styles: one, the divergent kind, relying on ideational fluency in open-ended problems; the other, convergent thinking, favouring those who like homing in on one solution. Much of the research on creativity has employed divergent thinking tests and we should bear in mind when reading the results of these researches the tenuous assumption that they give some clue to the creative ability or potential of individuals.

As we shall be referring to research in which divergent thinking scores have been used extensively, it would be valuable to look at other examples of their shortcomings. Perhaps their most obvious drawback lies in the administration and scoring of the tests. They are usually timed and presented as a *test*, whereas a creative act may be time-consuming and require a relaxed atmosphere. Ideas frequently need to be chewed over before enlightenment occurs. The tension of a test situation may also militate against creative output. Wallach and Kogan (1965), using untimed procedures in a playful atmosphere, produced divergent thinking scores which were more unrelated to IQ scores than had been obtained hitherto. Scoring the tests requires more subjective evaluation than does the scoring of standardized tests of intelligence. We saw the difficulty posed in arriving at a flexibility score, and a similar problem arises when we have to decide on the level to be chosen in awarding a score for originality using the least frequent responses. Wallach and Kogan used only unique responses (occurring only once in their sample), but others, such as Torrance, have accepted frequencies occurring in up to 15 per cent of their samples.

As we saw above, the scoring depends to some extent on the subjective judgements of the scorers and there is doubtful uniformity amongst these about what is an acceptable response and what is not. The existence of correlation between the scoring strategies also tends to lead to unwarranted conclusions about the nature of divergent thinking in relation to convergent thinking.

It should be noted that not all novel responses reflect creative talent. False answers are novel so are the bizarre statements and actions of the mentally ill; but we could hardly classify these as creative in the cognitive sense. Originality, then, is not enough. There must be a measure of relevance to the solution of a problem as well. Usefulness is not quite so obvious because in science we often find that an original idea has no immediate application and must wait for advances in other fields before it becomes useful.

## Divergent thinking and intelligence

Following the appearance of Guilford's model of the intellect (see Chapter 9) and his views on creativity (1950 and 1956), several researchers have attempted to confirm the independence of his convergent and divergent intellectual operations, the former being measures using IQ tests, the latter being taken as a measure of creativity. The earliest and most widely known research is that of Getzels and Jackson (1962), in which 12- to 16-year-olds in an American high school were given intelligence and divergent thinking tests. The scores were used to select two groups: one, the 'high creative', having high divergent and low IQ scores, and the other, the 'high IQ', having the reverse of this arrangement of scores. These groups had similar achievement levels, but they differed in several other important respects. 'High creatives' were less conformist, tended to overachieve and possessed a lively sense of humour when compared with the high IQ group. But the overall principal finding that IQ and divergent thinking scores were not significantly correlated, and therefore should be treated as separate entities, has been hotly contested largely on the grounds that Getzels and Jackson's methods of analysis left much to be desired. Moreover, the sample chosen by them was restricted to the upper ranges of intelligence (average IQ score for the sample was 132), thus rendering the results untypical of the population.

Subsequent studies have tended to use more representative samples than Getzels and Jackson. The findings, in the main, have managed to show some degree of positive relationship between divergent thinking and IQ scores. Hasan and Butcher (1966) carried out a close repetition of the American study using Scottish schoolchildren, but with a much wider and more characteristic range of IQ scores. The correlations between divergent thinking and IQ scores were all positive and significant, with some as high as +0.7. In the few researches where no relationship has been found, the samples tend to be drawn from the upper end of the IQ range (Hudson 1966, using public-school boys; Child and Smithers 1971, using university students).

The case for or against the distinction between divergent thinking and intelligence is a difficult one to answer. Advanced mathematical procedures, such as factor analysis and careful monitoring of test materials and their administration, do tend to show a measure of separate identity, especially where the test materials involve 'ideational fluency', that is, items designed and scored to show how quickly people can produce verbal or non-verbal responses. In the United Kingdom, Sultan (1962) was able to show a measure of independence using divergent tests which encouraged verbal ideational fluency. We have already mentioned the carefully constructed work of Wallach and Kogan (1965), in which, it will be remembered, a completely tension-free and friendly atmosphere was created, no time limit was imposed, each child was questioned individually and scoring for original responses was confined to unique answers.

Some evidence (Yamamoto 1965, Ginsburg and Whittemore 1968, Child and Croucher 1977) points to a differentiation in the relationship between divergent test scores and IQ which depends on the level of IQ being considered. At low and moderate levels of IQ a linear relationship holds. Beyond a broad *threshold* somewhere in the region of 110–20 IQ in tests with a standard deviation of 15, the relationship of intelligence and divergent scores appears to become increasingly random; in other words, the highly intelligent are less predictable in their divergent thinking ability. This tallies with Hudson's observation that, in a class of bright children, it is difficult, if not impossible, to pick out those who will be exceptionally creative. The basic question of whether intelligence tests and divergent thinking tests are measuring different, partially related or the same human attributes is still a matter for psychological research.

In the present state of research the safest conclusion is that divergent thinking is partially dependent on intelligence and partially a function of other personality characteristics. The predictive validity of Torrance's Tests of Creative Thinking for future creative achievements is still a matter of dispute (Subotnik and Arnold 1993).

## Divergent thinking and subject bias

A recurring theme in the study of convergent and divergent thinking is the possible connection between performance on the tests and arts/science bias. Hudson (1966 and 1968, Hudson and Jacot 1986) has been most prolific in this field. He defined a *converger* as one who obtains a relatively high score on an IQ test and at the same time a relatively low score on a divergent thinking test compared with others in the test sample. The reverse definition was used for the *diverger*. He was able to show that science students (particularly those studying physics) tend to be convergers. Divergers, on the other hand, tend to be students of English literature, history and modern languages. The emphasis has shifted from regarding the divergent thinking tests as measures of creativity to one of looking upon them as reflecting a preferred thinking style. Hence IQ and divergent tests are more likely to distinguish science from arts specialists than to distinguish the creative from the not so creative. However, the weight of evidence from other experiments in this area (Nuttall 1973, Child 1969, Child and Smithers 1971) so far favours the convergent test as a more consistent discriminator of the science specialist, with much less support for the arts–diverger connection.

The fact that science specialists do comparatively well in convergent (IQ) tests may reflect the kind of thinking strategies in which they excel. As we have indicated above, IQ items require people to take information as given and use it to arrive at a single correct answer, a procedure not unlike the traditional demands made in science lessons.

In looking for origins, Hudson (1966) sees the home (cf. the findings of Roe (1953) later in the chapter) as the most probable source of inspiration. He says:

> The convergent parent . . . is probably the one who shies away from all expression of strong feeling, affectionate or otherwise. If the child demands affection, the parents do their best to provide it, but fail. In this case, either of two things may happen. The parents may guide their child into less embarrassing spheres by offering approval whenever he masters some safe, impersonal skill. Or, as a reaction to the embarrassment the child has caused them (out of shame or irritation or both), they become critical. Either way, the child realizes that security lies both in choosing an impersonal field within which to work, and in being right. Furthermore, the child latches on both to his parents' distaste for 'gush', and to their relief when the mood is once more safe . . . In every sense, therefore, impersonal work and interests become a haven: from embarrassment, from criticism, and from emotions which are disruptive and inexplicable.
>
> The diverger's mother, on the other hand, is one who binds her child to her by disregarding his practical, logical accomplishments (or even ridiculing them) and by holding out a promise of love which she may or may not be able to fulfil. The child grows up addicted to people.

Notice the importance ascribed to personality development as a feature of cognitive processes (Hudson 1966 and 1968) (Figure 10.1).

## Talent

The term *talent* is used in various ways, but the commonest and the one adopted here refers to exceptional performance in a specific field of human endeavour. Great artists, athletes, scientists, musicians, dancers, writers or engineers, for example, would fall into this definition. By examining the intellectual and personality profiles of living or past talented people, several psychologists have tried to build up a stereotype of characteristics typical of the talented.

### *Biographical details from investigations*

Two studies conducted by Roe (1953) and MacKinnon (1961) in the United States predicted a number of the qualities found by Oden (1968). They used short-term, intensive interviews of eminent and widely accepted experts from certain professions. MacKinnon, in fact, invited his subjects to a weekend gathering at which personal, social and biographical information was compiled. Biographical similarities in most enquiries in this area, particularly those of home background, are quite striking. For some professional groups, for instance psychologists, architects, biologists and anthropologists, it seems that a permissive, settled, middle-class home with loose emotional ties is the prerequisite for creative thinkers. MacKinnon (1961) remarks that the parents of creative architects, for example, had an 'extraordinary respect for the child and confidence in his ability to do what was appropriate'. Roe's method was to take a detailed life history from each individual in her sample, including present work, an interview, projection and IQ tests. One exception is the scientists in Roe's work, particularly physicists and mathematicians, who seem to have had the lion's share of distress in childhood. Separation of the parents, strict and conventional upbringing (MacKinnon 1962) and illness were the commonest sources of distress. Roe's explanation is that scientists might be seeking to compensate for their earlier insecurity by choosing occupations which, superficially at least, involve convergent and clear-cut procedures leading to well-defined goals. However, this provides a reason for subject choice rather than for creative talent.

Cattell (1963), using a combination of detailed literature search of biographies and measures of personality from living eminent researchers, was able to show surprising uniformity in the profiles. The tendencies, and they are only tendencies, since not all eminent scientists possess exactly the following profile, are for the researchers to be more reserved, intelligent, dominant, serious, emotionally sensitive, radical and self-sufficient than the population at large. Some of these qualities add up to an introverted personality. Other generalizations about the personal qualities of creative men and women from these and other studies depict them as single-minded, stubborn, non-conformist and persistent in tasks which engage their imaginations. Tolerance to ambiguity (Snyder 1967) is high (they are not perturbed when a problem has a number of plausible solutions); they may even enjoy dilemmas and searching out problems which have diverse possibilities. Risk-taking and venturesomeness with ideals appeal to the creative mind. What we are not clear about is the evidence for distinctive qualities in the thinking styles adopted by creative people when they solve problems. The work of Harvey *et al.* (1961) and his colleagues on patterns of concept formation goes some way towards drawing attention to the relationship between the levels of abstraction attainable by individuals and their likelihood of producing original concepts. As one might have guessed, in general the higher the level of abstraction attainable by an individual, the more creative are his or her concepts.

## Biographical details from introspection

Searching through autobiographies, letters, papers and diaries of famous people from the past or closely questioning living creative people have been used to see if there is a particular *process of creativity*. Vernon, in his book *Creativity* (1970 and recommended for further reading), brings together some fascinating extracts from the work of famous people. Several attempts have been made to formulate the stages perceived to take place when creating great musical works, theories, books or works of art. Graham Wallas (1926) was one such researcher. After studying Helmholtz and Poincaré, he recognized four stages in the creative cycle, namely preparation, incubation, inspiration (or illumination) and verification.

**Preparation:** The forerunner of the preparatory stage is the ability to spot a problem. The existence of a problem often excites and obsesses the creative mind so much that it becomes restless and disturbed. Preparation then takes place and involves a detailed investigation of all the possibilities surrounding the problem from reading, discussing and questioning to making notes and trying out solutions.

**Incubation:** Following a period of deliberate activity in search of evidence and solutions comes a time when no conscious effort is made. This incubation period may be short or very extensive. Some authors in both arts and science have remarked on the time it sometimes takes for the germ of an idea to take shape. We have no idea what goes on during this period, but speculation has it that ideas are 'worked on' at a subconscious level to re-form and evolve new combinations of ideas.

**Inspiration:** This is a sudden flash of insight, that penny-dropping sensation we all experience when a confusion of ideas suddenly takes shape. Sometimes it happens after sleep, during a walk or in the bath (Archimedes). Tchaikovsky, in a letter to his patron, Mme Von Meck, describes his fourth symphony and makes a general comment about creative inspiration: 'As a rule the germ of a new work appears suddenly and unexpectedly. If the soul is fertile – that is to say, if the composer is suitably disposed – the seed takes root, rapidly shooting up stem, leaves and finally blossom.' We have here a classical example of the inspiration stage.

**Verification:** Having bright ideas is one thing; they then require confirmation. Often the creator is fairly convinced of the veracity of the solution long before he or she puts it to the test. But there follows a stage of active revision, expansion and correction.

We see from this creative cycle that creativity is rarely, if ever, an event which happens over coffee. There is usually a time-consuming, tenacious and detailed period of mental activity. The inescapable conclusion from Wallas's work (1926) is that creative output needs time and effort. As Edison (one of the inventors of filament lamps) proclaimed, genius is 1 per cent inspiration and 99 per cent perspiration.

# Recent developments

## Neurophysiology

Interest has shifted somewhat in recent years from 'how much' to 'how' and 'why' creative activity takes place. As we saw in Chapter 2, neuropsychologists are taking much more interest in 'how' the brain operates during problem-solving. But, as Eysenck and Barrett (1993) conclude:

> The whole area promises to give us many answers to causal questions raised by the problems associated with giftedness (but so far) much of the work done . . . is of inferior quality . . . The next few years will see a marked increase in the number and quality of papers devoted to this topic.

## Information processing

Another 'how' type approach is that of psychologists interested in information processing. Novelty is not enough to define creative activity. It has been used in the foregoing discussion of divergent thinking as combining or rearranging established patterns of knowledge in unique fashions; of course, this can happen at many different levels, as when children constantly create new ideas which, for them, are completely original, but which within their culture are quite familiar. Originality at the highest level would have to occur in the much wider context of the world of knowledge. Nevertheless, many studies are based on the assumption that fluency, variety and novelty of ideas contrived by young people, using familiar material, signify a potentially creative mind. Perhaps one important consideration of a novel response, at present impossible to gauge with certainty, is the *quality of the process* which produced it. Even in scientific discovery where the claim is made that it has come about by serendipity, a great deal of spadework has almost invariably preceded it.

The kinds of measures used to determine the quality of processing are meant to find answers to such questions as 'what route has a person taken in order to solve problems', 'how long has been spent on the process', 'how susceptible is the person to errors' and so on (Sternberg 1993). Tests involve reaction time, speed of task, accurate performance, memory-scanning tasks and speed in conventional IQ test items such as analogies, series completion, classification and syllogisms. This work is still developing.

## Why are we creative?

Ethologists have had something to say about why humans engage in creative work. Amongst them, Desmond Morris (1994) has been foremost in speculating on the reasons. The life of animals in the wild is filled with activity almost entirely to do with survival – hunting, eating, drinking, watching, waiting, reproducing, resting. Only the young animals have time for playing because the adults provide them with the means for survival. For humans, Morris suggests that intelligence enables us to become efficient hunters using brain not brawn to survive and creating lots of spare time. Moreover, the intelligent brain also needs and wants to keep active. Consequently, 'instead of ceasing to play when they become adults, humans retained that childlike playfulness and extended it . . . to adult forms of play . . . such as art, poetry, literature, music, dance, theatre, cinema, philosophy, science and sport'. We engage in them also as a means of survival by proxy because they earn money. Some are also built into our survival kit (e.g. science's contribution to technology).

## How are gifted children different?

Gathering the generalizations from all the quoted researches mentioned above gives a formidable, if not too-good-to-be-true, profile of the creative person. Personal qualities include higher intelligence (convergent thinking), higher divergent thinking ability, earlier development in reading, writing and talking, good memory and consequent good knowledge base, greater speed of problem-solving, enjoyment of complexity, tolerance of ambiguity, persistence in tasks of interest with high powers of concentration and so on. Environmentally, they benefit from having parents with well-defined attitudes to education, who are positive in their encouragement of children to do well at school, who are positive in their involvement ('doing things together'), who are prepared to support with material help (books, instruments), etc.

Shore and Kanevsky (1993) from a review of the research settled on seven distinctive qualities of gifted learners. These were:

- *Memory and the knowledge base*: Nickerson *et al.* (1985), speaking about 'experts', say that they 'not only know more, they know they know more, they know better how to use what they know. What they know is better organized and more readily accessible and they know better how to know more still.'
- *Metacognition* (see Chapter 7): gifted people are able to monitor their own thinking strategies and adjust them whilst engaged on a task.
- *Speed*: the issues of speed and power were raised in the chapter on intelligence. IQ tests measure power, but they can be used to measure the rapidity with which individuals can arrive at correct solutions, as in the work of Sternberg (1993). Gifted children work at great speed on a task, but spend longer in planning, i.e. metacognition.

- *Problem representation and categorization*: the gifted go beyond the information given to identify missing data whilst excluding irrelevant information. They also grasp the essentials more readily than others do (compare the definition of intelligence by Heim, Chapter 9, p. 284).
- *Procedural knowledge*: how to use one's knowledge effectively and switch around as necessary in the methods of solution is procedural knowledge, as distinct from routine solution methods.
- *Flexibility*: this is a characteristic of divergent thinkers; it is akin to lateral thinking where one shifts the focus of problem-solving.
- *Preference for complexity*: as a better challenge to their intellect, gifted people tend to favour more intricate or complex problems often created out of existing problems.

# Educating gifted and talented children

At the beginning of the chapter, several reasons were given for the increase of interest in giftedness. With this has come the conclusion that gifted and talented children should be given special consideration in the school system.

Several methods of helping the gifted have been tried, with varying degrees of success. The commonest, often in combination, are acceleration, enrichment and segregation, that is, separating and grouping within the classroom. Much has been written on the subject, but a detailed summary can be found in Southern *et al.* (in Heller, Mönks and Passow 1993).

- *Acceleration* occurs when a pupil is allowed to pass through the standard curriculum faster than his or her own age group and to undertake work appropriate for older children. This assumes higher and faster rates of achievement. Southern *et al.* (see also Rogers and Span, in Heller *et al.* 1993) list a large number of ways in which this can happen. At its simplest, a child is allowed to enter school a bit earlier than age would normally allow. Sometimes children can miss a grade or attend a higher class in a particular subject (often mathematics or science). A subject may be telescoped so as to cover the syllabus in a shorter time. Outside school a child might join organizations – such as the National Association for Gifted Children summer schools. Occasionally a mentor, quite often a parent, accelerates the child through a curriculum. Ruth Lawrence obtained the necessary A Levels in maths to enter St Hugh's, Oxford at the ripe old age of 12 and received her BA two years later. She became Dr Lawrence at 17. Now that age is not a bar to taking GCSE exams, August each year finds newspapers keen to publicize the results of very young children obtaining high GCSE marks, particularly in maths and computer studies.

  An important point is that there is little evidence to show that such a course of action is harmful to the development of children (Southern *et al.* 1993). Indeed, the common practice of streaming is a tried method of accelerating the progress of groups of brighter children.

- *Enrichment* involves giving gifted children an extended, modified curriculum both in content and presentation. It had its origins in the US when enrichment programmes were introduced into the state education systems. The children were not separated from their age group, but given specially designed teaching programmes. The enrichment may range from a special corner with advanced books and materials to a full programme of lessons, projects and visits designed to stimulate intellectual interest. Passow, as far back as 1958, set out four principles of enrichment programmes – modifications in breadth of approach, pace of presentation, content of material and teaching process skills such as critical thinking, problem-solving, communication and social skills.

- *Segregation* (sometimes referred to as *differentiation*), as the term implies, involves teaching the gifted (or children with learning difficulties) as a separate group, but in the same classroom with their peers. Integration takes place whenever possible. The technique is essentially a British phenomenon introduced after the Warnock Report relating to children with special needs. The gifted children are given different tasks at varying levels of difficulty (differentiation by 'inputs') and/or required to give more advanced responses than their peers (differentiation by 'outputs').

Montgomery (1996) gives a useful discussion and analysis of these three approaches as applied in the UK. (Shore and Kanevsky (1993) do the same for the American scene.) Montgomery also looks at a variety of methods now employed in the teaching of gifted children in the UK. These include the deliberate teaching of cognitive processes (referred to in a previous chapter as part of metacognition), investigation and problem-solving experiences, self-directed learning, games and simulations and experiential and collaborative learning (which includes 'brainstorming').

Regarding *brainstorming*, there is a view which maintains that, as our minds become cluttered with ideas, so we become inhibited in the way we re-express them. Ideas are censored and we prejudge their value before expressing them. Osborn (1957; see also Torrance and Myers 1970) suggests that there is a greater chance of producing original ideas when the mind is allowed to run riot in attempting to solve a problem. The ideas must come freely and without regard for their feasibility. In other words, think now, evaluate later. A technique since developed by Parnes (1963 and 1977) uses a group of people who concentrate on a problem, producing as many hypotheses as possible without bothering to evaluate them. The interplay of ideas apparently sparks off far more good ideas than conventional, problem-solving techniques.

The idea has been tried with children of primary-school age in America, by assembling them around a table, presenting an open-ended problem and tape-recording the ideas, which are allowed to flow uninterrupted by the teacher. At the end of the session the ideas are discussed for their feasibility. The point is to encourage ideational fluency without fear of intervention or ridicule from teachers or peers. A major task in using the method with children is the preparation needed to assemble the facts as a prerequisite to innovation. What is more revealing in brainstorming sessions with children is the knowledge teachers can gain about the paths a child's roving mind will take. The central aim of the method is to produce some lasting habits of ideational fluency in the children, though this aim has never been validated. The method certainly improves the self-confidence of children in the presence of others, for they can express views without fear of rebuke or derision, but a possible limitation is that it may induce non-critical, non-factual rambling in place of reasoned judgement.

Another approach to the problem of thinking strategies has been enunciated by Edward de Bono (1969, 1976, 1990) at Cambridge. Using his collection of parlour games, he argued that logical or longitudinal reasoning is not always the most effective way of arriving at a solution. Indeed, a cold, calculating, stepwise approach to problem-solving may distract a person from experimenting and may thus obscure more fruitful routes leading to a solution. How many times do we let our minds fixate on a certain way of solving a problem, convinced that we are on the right track, only to discover after much trial and error that we could never have solved the problem in that way? This process of constantly returning to 'square one' and trying a new line of approach de Bono calls *lateral thinking*. In other words, our minds should not pursue one line of thinking (longitudinal thinking) to the exclusion of all others, but should frequently return to the information provided and try another approach. The idea of the mind flirting with ideas is also embodied in brainstorming and synectics. One practical outcome is a website with several courses and publications – http://www.edwarddebono.com/products.php

There is much controversy over the effectiveness of 'programmes' for the very able. Shore and Kanevsky (1993) conclude that in training thinking processes there are many models that attempt to describe what is going on and insufficient applied programmes for the highly able with convincing results. This stricture also applies to underachieving able pupils. Freeman (1998), in a recent report for OFSTED (Office for Standards in Education) on educating very able pupils, is critical of the many amateur individuals and groups claiming to provide guidance who have little professional knowledge of giftedness. Clearly there is much to be done to help teachers in their task of providing suitable programmes for gifted children in the normal school setting.

## Summary

Detecting gifted and talented children, creating learning environments to encourage creative thinking and ensuring that potentially gifted and talented people are given every opportunity to fulfil their potential are ambitions for most advanced education systems. But how well do we do it? The annals of psychology are rich in attempts to discover what makes a gifted person, from the early efforts of Galton looking at 'genius' (see Chapter 9 on intelligence), Terman's longitudinal studies, biographical scrutiny to the use of divergent thinking tests.

Concern for the gifted amongst teachers is still not universal. Some believe that the bright ones can look after themselves.

Despite years of effort, psychologists are not yet united about the nature of creative thinking, how to assess it and what can be done to stimulate it. Conventional ability tests are still in the forefront of detecting potential and most studies start with them. Unfortunately, apart from the non-verbal tests, they are subject to environmental influences (Freeman (1979, 1991, 2001) gives good examples). Divergent thinking tests have also been used to measure ideational fluency, flexibility and originality. Apart from their possible relationship to IQ, they are not clearly related to future creativity. Psychologists have looked at biographical data and questioned eminent people to try to analyse the creative process. But none of these methods has so far provided us with incontrovertible evidence of value to teachers.

One important benefit we have reaped from the study of creative thinking is the challenge it has offered to teachers to examine the learning environments they provide in school. Do rote methods of teaching produce different styles of problem-solving in children than discovery methods? What is the relative efficiency of directed learning and discovery methods? Does our educational system tend to produce convergers who are looking always for one right answer, and can the system produce divergers who are just as happy with open-ended or ambiguous problems? If children are always told how to solve problems, will they be less able to meet new problems?

To develop an atmosphere within which children feel sufficiently free to explore and make discoveries while being given guidance is a difficult balance for a teacher to obtain. Too much freedom might encourage anarchy; too much guidance might produce sterile conformity. Moreover, when we encourage children to be active participants in their own learning through such media as clay, bricks, paints, musical instruments, body movement, words and number symbols in speech and writing, drama, handicraft and science, we are hopefully trying to assist them in finding their particular modes of communication, and this requires concentration and self-discipline.

## Tutorial enquiry and discussion

(a) In your observation of children, attempt to determine those behaviours which you consider to be 'creative'. What methods are used by the teacher to create the 'right' atmosphere?

(b) In tutorials, discuss what is understood by 'discovery methods'. Are they the same for all subjects? Are there differences between primary school and secondary school methods in guided discovery?

(c) Organize a 'brainstorming' session with a small group of children by tape-recording their spontaneous responses to an open-ended problem.

(d) The role of parents in creating suitable environments for gifted and able children is crucial. Examine this issue in relation to how teachers can help. Don't forget to consider such subjects as music, dance, drama and sport.

(e) Examine the various programmes for stimulating creative thinking (e.g. de Bono). Is there a place for World Class testing in order to identify the gifted and talented? What should teachers do with the information that some of their pupils are 'World Class' (http://www.worldclassarena.org)?

## References

Cattell, R. B. (1963), 'The personality and motivation of the researcher from measurement of contemporaries in and from biography', in C. W. Taylor and F. Barron (eds), *Scientific Creativity*. New York: Wiley.

Child, D. (1969), 'A comparative study of personality, intelligence and social class in a technological university', *British Journal of Educational Psychology*, 39, 40–6.

Child, D. and Croucher, A. (1977), 'Divergent thinking and ability: is there a threshold?', *Educational Studies*, 3, 101–10.

Child, D. and Smithers, A. (1971), 'Some cognitive and affective factors in subject choice', *Research in Education*, 5, 1–9.

Cropley, A. J. (1994), 'Creative intelligence: a concept of true giftedness', *European Journal of High Ability*, 5, 16–23.

de Bono, E. (1969), *The Mechanism of Mind*. London: Cape.

de Bono, E. (1976), *Teaching Thinking*. London: Temple Smith.

de Bono, E. (1990), *Lateral Thinking: A Textbook of Creativity*. Harmondsworth: Pelican.

Eysenck, H. J. (1993a), 'Creativity and personality: an attempt to bridge the divergent traditions', *Psychological Inquiry*, 4, 238–46.

Eysenck, H. J. (1993b), 'Creativity and personality: suggestions for a theory', *Psychological Inquiry*, 4, 147–78.

Eysenck, H. J. and Barrett, P. T. (1993), 'Brain research related to giftedness', in K. H. Heller, F. J. Mönks and A. H. Passow (eds), *International Handbook of Research and Development of Giftedness and Talent*. Oxford: Pergamon.

Freeman, J. (1979), *Gifted Children: Their Identification and Development in a Social Context*. Lancaster: MTP Press.

Freeman, J. (1991), *Gifted Children Growing Up*. London and Portsmouth: Cassell and Heinemann.

Freeman, J. (1998), *The Education of the Very Able: Current International Research*. Report to OFSTED. London: HMSO.

Freeman, J. (2000), 'Gifted children: the evidence', *The Psychology of Education Review*, 24(1), 35– 40.

Freeman, J. (2001), *Gifted Children Grown Up*. London: Fulton.

Gagné, F. (1993), 'Constructs and models pertaining to exceptional human abilities', in K. H. Heller, F. J. Mönks and A. H. Passow, *International Handbook of Research and Development of Giftedness and Talent*. Oxford: Pergamon.

Gardner, H. (1999), *Intelligence Reframed: Multiple Intelligences for the 21st Century*. New York: Basic Books.

Getzels, J. W. and Jackson, P. W. (1962), *Creativity and Intelligence*. New York: Wiley.

Ginsburg, G. P. and Whittemore, R. G. (1968), 'Creativity and verbal ability: a direct examination of their relationship', *British Journal of Educational Psychology*, 38, 133–9.

Goldman, R. J., (1964), The Minnesota Tests of Creativity. *Educational Research*, 7, 3–14.

Guilford, J. P. (1950), 'Creativity', *American Psychologist*, 5, 444–54.

Guilford, J. P. (1956), 'The structure of the intellect', *Psychological Bulletin*, 53, 267–93.

Guilford, J. P. (1959), *Personality*. New York: McGraw-Hill.

Harvey, O. J., Hunt, D. E. and Schroder, H. M. (1961), *Conceptual Systems and Personality Organization*. New York: Wiley.

Hasan, P. and Butcher, H. J. (1966), 'Creativity and intelligence: a partial replication with Scottish children of Getzels and Jackson's study', *British Journal of Psychology*, 57, 129–35.

Hudson, L. (1966), *Contrary Imaginations*. London: Methuen.

Hudson, L. (1968), *Frames of Mind*. London: Methuen.

Hudson, L. and Jacot, B. (1986), 'The outsider in science: a selective review of evidence, with special reference to the Nobel Prize', in C. Bagley and G. K. Verma (eds), *Personality, Cognition and Values*, pp. 3–23. London: Macmillan.

HMI (1992), *The Education of Very Able Children in Maintained Schools*. London: HMSO.

MacKinnon, D. W. (1961), 'Characteristics of the creative person: implications for the teaching-learning process', in *Current Issues in Higher Education*, pp. 89–92. Washington, DC: National Education Association.

MacKinnon, D. W. (1962), 'The nature and nurture of creative talent', *American Psychologist*, 17, 484–95.

Montgomery, D. (1991), *The Special Needs of Able Pupils in the Ordinary Classroom* (revised version). Maldon: Learning Difficulties Research Project.

Montgomery, D. (1996), *Educating the Able* (3rd edn). London: Cassell.

Montgomery, D. (1998), 'Gifted education: education of the highly gifted', in D. Shorrocks-Taylor (ed.), *Directions in Educational Psychology*. London: Whurr.

Morris, Desmond (1994), *The Human Animal: A Personal View of the Human Species*. London: BBC Books.

Nickerson, R. S., Perkins, D. N. and Smith, E. E. (1985), *The Teaching of Thinking*. Hillsdale, NJ: Erlbaum.

Nuttall, D. L. (1973), 'Convergent and divergent thinking', in H. J. Butcher and H. B. Pont (eds) *Educational Research in Britain* (Vol. 3). London: University of London Press.

Oden, M. H. (1968), 'The fulfilment of promise: 40-year follow-up of the Terman gifted group', *Genetic Psychology Monograph*, 77, 3–93.

Osborn, A. F. (1957), *Applied Imagination*. New York: Scribners.

Parnes, S. J. and Meadow, A. (1963), Chapter 25, in C. W. Taylor and F. Barron (eds), *Scientific Creativity: Its Recognition and Development*. New York: Wiley.

Parnes, S. J., Noller, R. B. and Biondi, A. M. (1977), *Guide to Creative Action*. New York: Scribner.

Passow, A. H. (1958), 'Enrichment of education for the gifted', in N. B. Henry (ed.), *Education for the Gifted: Fifty-seventh Yearbook of the National Society for the Study of Education, Part I*. Chicago, IL: University of Chicago Press.

QCA (2002), (compiled and edited by Carolyn Richardson) *Assessing Gifted and Talented Children*. London: QCA.

Renzulli, J. S. (1986), 'The three-ring conception of giftedness: a developmental model for creative productivity', in R. J. Sternberg and J. E. Davidson (eds), *Conceptions of Giftedness*. New York: Cambridge University Press.

Roe, A. (1953), 'A psychological study of eminent psychologists and anthropologists and a comparison with biological and physical scientists', *Psychological Monographs*, 67(2).

Rogers, K. S. and Span, P. (1993), 'Ability grouping with gifted and talented students: research guidelines', in K. H. Heller, F. J. Mönks and A. H. Passow (eds), *International Handbook of Research and Development of Giftedness and Talent*. Oxford: Pergamon.

Shore, B. M. and Kanevsky, L. S. (1993), 'Thinking processes: being and becoming gifted', in K. H. Heller, F. J. Mönks and A. H. Passow (eds), *International Handbook of Research and Development of Giftedness and Talent*. Oxford: Pergamon.

Snyder, B. (1967), 'Creative students in science and engineering', *Universities Quarterly*, 21, 205–18.

Southern, W. T., Jones, E. D. and Stanley, J. C. (1993), 'Acceleration and enrichment: the context and development of program options', in K. H. Heller, F. J. Mönks and A. H. Passow (eds), *International Handbook of Research and Development of Giftedness and Talent*. Oxford: Pergamon.

Sternberg, R. J. (1993), 'Procedures for identifying intellectual potential in the gifted: a perspective on alternative "Metaphors of Mind"', in K. H. Heller, F. J. Mönks and A. H. Passow (eds), *International Handbook of Research and Development of Giftedness and Talent*. Oxford: Pergamon.

Sternberg, R. J. and Lubart, T. L. (1992), 'Creative giftedness in children', in P. S. Klein and A. J. Tannenbaum (eds), *To Be Young and Gifted*. Norwood, NJ: Ablex.

Subotnik, R. F. and Arnold, K. D. (1993), 'Investigating the fulfilment of promise', in K. H. Heller, F. J. Mönks and A. H. Passow (eds), *International Handbook of Research and Development of Giftedness and Talent*. Oxford: Pergamon.

Sultan, E. E. (1962), 'A factorial study in the domain of creative thinking', *British Journal of Educational Psychology*, 32, 78–82.

Terman, L. M. (1925), *Genetic Studies of Genius, Volume 1: Mental and Physical Traits of a Thousand Gifted Children*. Stanford, CA: Stanford University Press.

Torrance, E. P. (1962), *Guiding Creative Talent*. Englewood Cliffs, NJ: Prentice-Hall.

Torrance, E. P (1966), *Torrance Tests of Creative Thinking*. Princeton, NJ: Personnel Press.

Torrance, E. P. and Myers, R. E. (1970), *Creative Learning and Teaching*. New York: Dodd, Mead.

Vernon, P. E. (ed.) (1970), *Creativity*. Harmondsworth: Penguin.

Wallach, M. A. and Kogan, N. (1965), *Modes of Thinking in Young Children*. New York: Holt, Rinehart and Winston.

Wallas, G. (1926), *The Art of Thought*. New York: Harcourt, Brace and World.

Yamamoto, K. (1965), 'Effects of restriction of range and test reliability on correlation between measures of intelligence and creative thinking', *British Journal of Educational Psychology*, 35, 300–5.

## Further reading

Alban Metcalfe, R. J. (1983), *Creativity*. Rediguide 17. Oxford: TRC-Rediguides.

Freeman, J. (1998), *The Education of the Very Able: Current International Research*. London: OFSTED, HMSO.

Heller, K. H., Mönks F. J. and Passow, A. H. (eds) (1993), *International Handbook of Research and Development of Giftedness and Talent*. Oxford: Pergamon. This is one of the most comprehensive texts on the subject of giftedness. Every important issue is covered by a specialist.

HMI (1992), *The Education of Very Able Children in Maintained Schools*. London: HMSO.

Montgomery, D. (1996), *Educating the Able*. London: Cassell. A contemporary source book which also fits the education of highly able children into the context of special educational provision.

Vernon, P. E. (ed.) (1970), *Creativity*. Harmondsworth: Penguin.

## Useful websites

Work relating to de Bono.
  http://www.edwarddebono.com/products.php
For talented young people in mathematics.
  http://www.worldclassarena.org

# 11 Special Educational Needs

## Implications for teachers

- Provision for children with special educational needs is part of the daily work of most teachers. Therefore, knowledge of this area is crucial.
- Most teachers will have children in their classes with SEN. To ensure best practice in providing for them, the SENCO in the school should be an early source of information.
- School Action, School Action Plus and Individual Education Plans will be part of most teachers' administrative responsibility.

- In the early years, any signs of decline in achievement should be monitored with an eye to some causes requiring special provision, informing the SENCO and, if necessary, seeking the advice of professionals (e.g. psychologists, language and speech specialists, etc.).

In the 30 or so years since this book first appeared, our attitudes to, and methods in, the education of children experiencing difficulties at school have changed. The language has correspondingly changed largely because it tended to create a stigma, even to the point of abuse, and in some cases it exaggerated the downside of problems. Expressions used as technical terms at one time, such as idiot, moron, educationally sub-normal, mentally deficient and dull, have all but disappeared. Even the replacement terms such as 'special' and 'needs' are regarded by some as discriminatory. In American and European literature, the term 'mentally retarded' is still used for the narrower concept of cognitive disabilities. Both the American Psychiatric Association and the International Classification of Diseases (World Health Organization used widely in Europe) have similar codes for defining levels of cognitive retardation assessed using IQ measures (see Chapter 9 and later in this chapter). Whatever educational problems are called, we as teachers have a responsibility to find ways of identifying and dealing with them effectively and sensitively.

The *Education Act* of 1981, formally introduced in 1983 and based very much on certain recommendations made in the Warnock Report (1978), introduced a much broader concept of *special educational needs* (SEN) involving some 20 per cent of the compulsory education population. This was in stark contrast to the 2 per cent of 'handicapped' children already receiving some degree of specialist educational provision. The broader term incorporated an additional 18 per cent of the school population and recognized that there were many pupils requiring other than conventional classroom practices. It now included children with varying degrees of difficulty in learning which had previously prevented them from using all the normal educational facilities provided in schools. The important thing is that the change in terminology was intended to shift the emphasis from the disability of the child to the particular educational provision needed. Nevertheless, it was recognized that the disabilities have to be identified and these now tend to be grouped in terms of general areas of development. They include physical, motor, cognitive, language, social, behavioural and emotional development exemplified by such problems as hearing and visual impairment, learning difficulties, autism, emotional and behavioural difficulties (EBDs) and dyslexia.

It is important to point out early in the chapter that *special educational needs* is a much narrower concept than *mental health* (Atkinson and Hornby 2002). Mental health includes such problems as eating and anxiety disorders, substance abuse, depression, suicidal tendencies, psychotic conditions, attention deficit hyperactivity disorder (ADHD), physical impairment (e.g., deaf, blind, thalidomide injury) and autism. These are often so serious as to make state school provision unequal to the highly specialist physical and mental tasks involved in care and education. Individual attention is needed to have any effect on the children's development. Therefore, special and separate educational provision becomes necessary. However, where it is possible for a child to attend state mainstream schools (*inclusiveness*), the teacher must know something of the special needs of that child.

It is also important to mention at this early stage that *special educational needs* is a much broader concept than cognitive disability. The latter is defined using IQ tests (see Chapter 9). However, the terms used to describe levels of cognitive disability and SEN are the same and confusion can occur.

Since the 1981 Act, which incorporated many recommendations from the Warnock Report, a succession of Education Acts (1988, 1993 (Part 3) and 1996 (Part 4)) have been published. As a result of the 1993 Act, the most significant document on special educational needs to come out of the DfE was the Code of Practice on the Identification and Assessment of Special Educational Needs (DfE 1994 and and DfE Circular 6/94). This was revised in 2001 (DfES 2001b). It covers much more ground than we can encompass in a book about psychological issues in education, but we shall return to the Code for a brief summary.

---

### Further reading

There are many Government publications which would require endless time to read. You have to be selective. If you put 'special educational needs code practice' into an Internet search engine, you will recover a large number of sources of information. Some important ones are the Education Acts of 1981, 1988, 1993 (Part 3), 1996 (Part 4) and 2001. Others of value are the DfE (1994) *Code of Practice on the Identification and Assessment of Special Educational Needs*, HMSO, London; *Circular 6/94: The Organisation of Special Education Provision*, HMSO, London; and the revision of the 1994 Code, *Special Educational Needs Code of Practice*, DfES, 2001b. Many Circulars associated with the Code of Practice followed its publication and cover 'The Organisation of Special Education Provision' (Circular 6/94); 'Pupil Behaviour and Discipline' (Circular 8/94); DfE Circular 9/94, *The Education of Children with Emotional and Behavioural Difficulties*, HMSO, London, 1994; 'Exclusions from School' (Circular 10/94); 'The Education of Sick Children' (Circular 12/94); 'The Education of Children being looked after by Local Authorities' (Circular 13/94).

---

None of us, of course, is completely equipped for all eventualities in life, yet most of us manage to survive either because some of our assets can be used to compensate for our inabilities or because we are able to avoid situations in which our weaknesses are exposed. Of the 20 per cent, there is likely to be around 2 per cent of children whose disabilities are so extreme that they are unable to benefit from our normal state educational facilities alone and therefore must receive special provision (referred to as *statementing* – see later).

The new Acts also endeavour to place the remaining 18 per cent of children with special educational needs in the ordinary primary and secondary system. It will thus be impossible to go through one's professional life without meeting several children with serious learning difficulties. With these percentages, in every classroom of 30 children, a teacher could have as many as six children with special needs at any one time. This does place a significant burden on the shoulders of teachers having to deal with a widely diverse class of children.

# The Warnock Report

Probably the most influential report on special education has been the Warnock Report (1978) on children with special educational needs. Several of its conclusions were incorporated into the *1981 Education Act*. A summary of the important conclusions follows. The central aims of special education should be to help children towards understanding and independence within the limits of their capacities. The reader will recognize these aims as the same as those of education in general. The Committee abandoned the notion of a distinct definition of handicapped and non-handicapped and preferred the idea of a continuum of severity, the most serious of which would require a particular form of educational provision (possibly 2 per cent of school-aged children), but included in the brief of the Committee would be a further 18 per cent or so requiring special provision in normal schools.

> The form of the child's need is not necessarily determined by the nature of his disability or disorder. At present children are categorized according to their disabilities and *not* according to their educational needs. But the Committee recommended that *statutory categorization of handicapped pupils should be abolished*. The basis for this decision about the type of educational provision required should not be a single label, but rather a detailed description of the special need in question. (*DES, Meeting Special Educational Needs*, DfE 1979)

However, they agreed that in the case of severe, complex or long-term disabilities there would have to be special provision. It was important to start special education as early as possible and finish late. The under-5s and over-16s were coped with least satisfactorily.

Thus special schools would still be needed for severe cases, but integration was crucial wherever feasible. This process of *inclusiveness* (Ainscow 1999) in the state system has been recognized in recent Government publications such as the National Curriculum Inclusion Statement (QCA 1999 and 2000a). With the passing of the category approach to special education, the method of assessment required rethinking. Teachers in the normal state system had to be able to recognize children in special need, learn about special educational provision and keep clear records of assessment and progress.

This report has had a substantial impact on the view taken of special educational provision. An increase in the training of specialists by means of in-service courses, attempts at improving the resources necessary if normal schools are to cope, the introduction of some elements on the teaching of children with special needs in courses of initial teacher-training and a revised system of assessment are just some of the directions it is now taking.

# Code of Practice (DfES 2001b)

As Warnock (1978) pointed out, the 18 per cent have always been there in the state system. What has not been there is a conscious effort to integrate and provide for these children within the system. In the years between the Warnock Report and the present, legislation has gradually appeared. Now there are legal requirements which oblige schools to provide for children with learning difficulties. The first Code of Practice, produced in 1994, was the result and this was revised in 2001.

Several definitions are needed. To quote from the 1993 Act, 'a child has *special educational needs* if he or she has a learning difficulty which calls for special educational provision'. A child has *learning difficulty* if he or she has 'a significantly greater difficulty in learning than the majority of children of the same age' or 'has a disability which either prevents or hinders the child from making use of educational facilities of a kind provided for children of the same age in school within the area of the local educational authority'. These definitions apply to children from under five years of age to school leaving at 16.

The new Code (DfES 2001b) came into force on 1 January 2002 and its contents can now be obtained widely. A good source and summary are available from the British Dyslexia Association (website http://www.bda-dyslexia.org.uk/ main/information/parents). Its predecessor of 1994, which provided the blueprint for the 2001 Code, came hard on the heels of the *1993 Education Act* (especially Part 3 which deals with SEN), and the Education (Special Educational Needs) Regulations 1994. As a result, all schools are obliged to publish their SEN policies and have a named person, the SEN coordinator or SENCO (normally a member of staff) designated as responsible for coordinating SEN provision in the school and keeping records for each SEN pupil. In small schools, this might fall to the Head or Deputy Head. In large schools, it might require a small team. Books advising on the implementation of the Code and SENCOs abound, but some readable ones are Smith (1996), Goddard and Tester (1996), the DfES *SEN Toolkit* (2001a) and Ramjhun (2002).

Other changes introduced by the Code include a shift in responsibility for SEN children. The 18 per cent are now firmly the responsibility of the school governors and teachers and not, as previously, the LA. The latter is still responsible for the 2 per cent requiring 'statements' (see pp. 357–9) and the process of 'statementing' has to take place in a given time (not to exceed 26 weeks). Greater collaboration is required between the school, parents, children and all the services (education, medical, psychological, social). Schools now have to report to parents annually about the SEN policy in the school as well as their children's progress.

Parents and SEN pupils (Wolfendale 1997, Beveridge 1998) are much more involved both in discussions with the school and, if necessary, in deciding on a special school.

The 1994 Code had five stages through which schoolchildren suspected of having learning difficulties might pass. These have now been replaced by *School Action* (replacing the first three stages) and *School Action Plus* (replacing the last two stages) procedures. For pre-primary school provision these are known as Early Years Action and Early Years Action Plus. School Action is essentially school-assessment and provision, although specialists are not excluded from this stage. School Action Plus is intended for more serious cases involving statutory assessments and statements.

In School Action there is a build-up of assessment and provision starting with class or subject teachers identifying a child's special educational problems and, after consulting the school's SENCO, taking action. If this is not sufficient, the SENCO takes lead responsibility for gathering information and for coordinating the child's special education provision, working with the child's teachers. At this stage it may be necessary for the SENCO to seek some support from specialists outside the school.

The Code of Practice uses separate sections to deal with pre-statutory (early education), primary and secondary schooling, but they are all concerned with similar issues. One of these is the provision of *Educational Development Plans* (EDPs) which should reflect all aspects of schooling which is *additional to* or *different from* normal curricular provision.

School Action Plan Plus involves the LA, parents and outside agencies such as psychological, social and medical services. They consider the need for a statutory assessment and, if appropriate, make a multidisciplinary assessment. If appropriate, the LA considers the need for a '*statement of special educational needs*' (see p. 357) and arranges, monitors and reviews the required provision.

Within these stages there is a role for either standardized tests and/or the help of an LA educational psychologist. The 2 per cent referred to above would only appear in the Action Plan Plus group and generally receive most of their education in special schools provided by the LA.

# SEN in state schools

All teachers are concerned with the academic progress of children by promoting intellectual skills in the acquisition of knowledge. Further, they attempt to encourage individual children in their efforts to adjust both personally, in preparation for adult life, and socially, as a member of a community. The same aims are true of special educational provision, except that the order of priority must take into account the exceptional disadvantages of each child. The key to special educational provision is to help each needy child to adjust and compensate for his or her disability as well as to fulfil the broader aims suggested above. The mentally retarded will grow up, find work, run a home and have many exacting responsibilities for which they must be prepared. Work that is other than skilled is becoming harder to find and the business of budgeting for a family taxes the ingenuity of most people, let alone those with learning difficulties. Sometimes the physically disabled are prone to emotional and social side-effects because they have difficulty in coming to terms with the inadequacies they feel in comparison with others. Problems of this kind require different emphases and careful handling which only special, individual education can provide.

In the school-based School Action Plan stage, identifying and making reliable assessments of the nature and extent of learning difficulties require some knowledge of testing procedures. We have discussed several standardized testing methods in Chapters 9 and 10, along with norm- and criterion-referencing. Later, we shall look at profiles and checklists, all of which can be helpful in the assessment process. It is important that several sources of evidence are used – classroom teacher, parents, previous teachers, any outside agencies such as psychologists and social workers, as well as the results of attainment and aptitude test scores. When all this information is put together in a systematic analysis, it is referred to as *screening*. The earlier such identification takes place, the better. Indeed, there are now fairly extensive provisions in the Education Acts and the Code for the under fives.

Several screening systems exist. Most LAs and schools have devised their own. For an example of a screening system, see the document produced by Visser (1994) for the National Association for Special Needs (NASEN). It contains a very useful grid table with levels of disability against seven kinds of disability. Levels 1 to 4 are from severe to average difficulties and 5 is above average. The seven areas of difficulty chosen are Health/physical, Emotional maturity, Social, Motivation and, say, three areas of mathematics. These last three could be any number of basic subject areas. Other, less formal schemes are presented in NASEN publications and Ramjhun (2002, pp. 16–19).

Once the range and depth of the problems have been recognized, the teacher, with the help of the SENCO, is required to design an *Individual Education Plan* (IEP) for each SEN child (*SEN Code of Practice* 2001, Ramjhun 2002). This IEP has to be widely available in the school and to parents.

It is important to notice that classifications of children with special needs are avoided in an effort to prevent stereotyping and labelling. Over the years, several terms have been used to describe the degrees of learning difficulty, placing emphasis on curricula and organizational problems as much as the child's difficulties. The 1994 Code, the American Psychiatric Association and the World Health Organization use the following categories: *mild, moderate, severe, profound* and *specific learning difficulties.*

Children with mild learning difficulties would tend to be in the School Action procedures and would receive mainstream teaching with support from ancillary helpers and special facilities in the normal classroom. The children would have the normal curriculum with some additional help. Those children with moderate learning difficulties require a 'modified curriculum similar to that provided in ordinary schools but, while not restricted in its expectations, has objectives more appropriate to children with moderate learning difficulties'. This is a somewhat circular definition, but in practice most children would find themselves in a mixture of mainstream classes doing SATs and in specialist classes or individual tuition to fit the particular needs. Mild and moderate difficulties account for the 18 per cent of the school population referred to above.

Children with severe and specific learning difficulties require individually worked out curricula with 'a range of educational experience but more selectively and sharply focused on the development of personal autonomy and social skills'. Many of these children are multiply handicapped and will require special educational and physical resources. They will constitute the 2 per cent referred to above and often, but not invariably, require a statement of SEN.

Another shift in emphasis is from child-focused assessments to a curriculum focus. Traditionally, the approach has been child-focused, which places importance upon identifying the intellectual deficiencies of a child using norm-referenced tests such as ability (Chapter 9) or personality (Chapter 12) tests. These are still needed to show the potential of a child and in some cases the root problem in specific difficulties, but they are insufficient in providing details for Individual Education Plans. Sometimes this trend is described in terms of psychological shifts of emphasis (Sugden 1998). In the 1960s, 'ability training' was popular. Tests were given to discover physical or intellectual problems (e.g. visual discrimination, perceptual motor skills) and training programmes were designed to correct these. In the early 1980s attention turned to 'behaviourist' methods (Chapter 6). Both these methods are child-centred.

At about the same time, the 'cognitive' approach was applied – an interactive model of the child's resources, the task to be learned and the context of the task.

These three (ability testing, behaviourist and cognitive approaches) are still the subject of contentious debate (Sugden 1998).

# Statutory assessment of, and statement for, SEN

Sometimes, despite the best efforts of teachers in mainstream education, a child does not appear to benefit from the special provisions in School Action and School Action Plus. In a few cases, the learning difficulties are so great that an assessment is made before, or very early in, the child's school life. For example, in profound sensory or physical conditions, children may need to be referred at an early age, through the LA, to the agencies for assessment. Whatever the route, an officer of the LA is named and he or she is the major point of contact between the authority, parents and other agencies.

However, before a statement (see later) is made about a child's needs, several preliminary steps are required. Procedures have to be followed, the first of which is to inform the parents (i) that an assessment is to be made, (ii) of the procedures to be followed in making the assessment and (iii) of the rights of the parents. After a fixed period of time (a few weeks) in which an appeal and further evidence can be presented, the LA can begin the assessment.

## Psychologists in the service of education

One of the most important contributions in the assessment and statementing of children in special educational need is made by professionally trained psychologists. The two significant branches are educational and clinical psychology (see Chapter 1). To become an educational psychologist, a person would need a first degree in psychology, obtain a PGCE teachers' qualification, teach for two years and then obtain a master's degree in educational psychology (usually one year of full-time study) before being allowed to practise (seven years of study in all). Before being employed, the person must be registered with the British Psychological Society. This qualification enables him or her to deal with students from pre- to post-school (Lindsay and Miller 1991) and to make assessments in learning difficulties, behavioural and social skills. This is followed by recommendations about the most suitable educational programmes. There are about 2000 in the UK and they are employed by the LAs.

## Assessment

The SENCO, through the school, informs the LA about each child exhibiting serious educational difficulties. The LA, in turn, has a statutory obligation to identify and make an assessment of the child. The purpose is still to find the best solution for the learning difficulties experienced by the child. This is the point at which the LA draws together all the sources of evidence and advice from the school and outside agencies likely to be of help in arriving at a reliable assessment. The main outside sources are parental, educational, psychological, social and medical.

The sources of advice are of significance. The help of teachers is sought for educational advice – usually all those who have taught the child and the headteachers of the schools attended by the child. It is also possible to bring in persons who are qualified to teach children with special needs, including specialists in the education of deaf and blind people.

Medical advice is obtained from a medical practitioner chosen by the district health authority. Social workers may also be involved.

Psychological advice is obtained from a qualified educational psychologist appointed by the LA. Either one or both school-based curriculum assessment and standardized tests of the kind described in Chapters 16 and 18 can be used to make the psychological assessment.

In making an assessment, the LA uses four *areas of need* to define the problems and possible provisions necessary should a statement be required. The areas are:

- communication and interaction
- cognition and learning
- behaviour, social and emotional development
- sensory and/or physical needs.

Overlap between these is recognized. These four are looked at in more detail below. The outcome of assessment will be to define the next steps to be taken. In some cases, the child remains at the mainstream school with specialist teaching and provision. In most cases, the child proceeds to statementing and specialist school provision.

## Statements of special educational need (statementing)

The *Special Educational Needs Code of Practice* (DfES 2001b) gives advice on the form which a statement should take when submitting comments about a child's problems and the proposed special educational provision most suitable for that child. At the end of the *Code of Practice* are the *Regulations* which give the advice referred to. Schedule 2 at the end of the Code of Practice contains several headings under which the LA is required to set out the special needs and corresponding *provision* and *placement* required, any additional non-school provision and the various reports and advice given by the educational, medical, social and psychological specialists involved as well as the parents' view. Although dated, a useful source is DES Circular 22/89 (1989) which gives a checklist of points which specialists are advised to consider when assessing a child. This is shown in Table 11.1. Discussion about a number of elements in the list will be found in other chapters of this book (e.g. emotional states, cognitive functioning, educational attainments).

After the assessment and statement a decision has to be made as to the *placement*, that is the most appropriate school or schools for the child and in which the parents have a say. The child may continue in a mainstream school, have a dual attendance with a special unit or school or attend a special unit/school full-time.

In the period from 1990 to 2000, the percentage of statemented children in England, for example, has risen from approximately 2 to 3 per cent of the total school population. The number of children requiring statements in, for example, 2000 was around 253,000 which was just over 3 per cent of the total school population (8,345,815). However, the percentage of children in some form of special school or dually registered (that is, in both a state day school and a special unit or school) has declined over the same period from about 1.5 to 1.35 per cent of the school population, supporting the policy for greater inclusiveness (DfES 2001c, *Statistics of Education: Schools in England*, contains a table covering the period 1996–2001).

**Table 11.1** Advice on special educational needs: suggested checklist.

(a) DESCRIPTION OF THE CHILD'S FUNCTIONING
1. *Description of the child's strengths and weaknesses*
   Physical state and functioning
   (physical health, developmental function, mobility, hearing, vision)
   Emotional state
   (link between stress, emotions and physical state)
   Cognitive functioning
   Communication skills
   (verbal comprehension, expressive language, speech)
   Perceptual and motor skills
   Adaptive skills
   Personal and social skills
   Approaches and attitudes to learning
   Educational attainments
   Self-image and interests
   Behaviour
2. *Factors in the child's environment which lessen or contribute to his or her needs*
   In the home and family, and including the language of the home
   At school
   Elsewhere
3. *Relevant aspects of the child's history*
   Personal
   Medical
   Educational

(b) AIMS OF PROVISION
1. *General areas of development (reference should be made to the relevant attainment targets of the National Curriculum where possible)*
   Physical development
   (e.g. to develop self-care skills)
   Motor development
   (e.g. to improve co-ordination of hand and fingers, to achieve hand-eye co-ordination)
   Cognitive development
   (e.g. to develop the ability to classify)
   Language development
   (e.g. to improve expressive language skills)
   Social development
   (e.g. to stimulate social contact with peers)
2. *Any specific areas of weakness or gaps in skills acquisition which impede the child's progress*
   (e.g. short-term memory deficits)
3. *Suggested methods and approaches*
   Implications of the child's medical condition
   (e.g. advice on the side-effects of medication for epilepsy)
   Teaching and learning approaches
   (e.g. teaching methods for the blind or deaf, or teaching through other specialized methods)
   Emotional climate and social regime
   (e.g. type of regime, size of class or school, need for individual attention)

*(cont.)*

**Table 11.1** (*Continued*)

---

(c) FACILITIES AND RESOURCES

1. *Special equipment*
   (e.g. physical aids, auditory aids, visual aids)
2. *Specialist facilities*
   (e.g. for incontinence, for medical examination, treatment and drug administration)
3. *Special educational resources*
   (e.g. specialist equipment for teaching children with physical or sensory disabilities, non-teaching aids)
4. *Other specialist resources*
   (e.g. Nursing, Social Work and Welfare Support, Speech Therapy, Occupational Therapy, Physiotherapy, Psychotherapy, Audiology, Orthoptics)
5. *Physical environment*
   (e.g. access and facilities for non-ambulant pupils, attention to lighting environment, attention to acoustic environment, attention to thermal environment, health care accommodation, privacy of continence care)
6. *School organization and attendance*
   (e.g. day attendance, weekly boarding, termly boarding, relief hostel accommodation)
7. *Transport*

---

*Source*: Annex 1 of DES Circular 22/89.

# Communication and interaction

As mentioned above, in assessing and arriving at a statement, the LAs look at four areas of *communication and interaction, cognition and learning, behaviour, social and emotional development* and *sensory and/or physical* need which we now look at in more detail.

Fundamental to almost all learning is the need for language and communication. This need not necessarily be the written and spoken word. Musical notes, Braille and sign language are examples of alternatives. But in acquiring the knowledge offered in school subjects, an ability to use a language and communicate is essential.

Many of the cognitive, behavioural and sensory dysfunctions mentioned in the other three areas are also responsible for difficulties experienced in language and communication. All degrees of learning difficulty or sensory problems such as profound deafness or aphasia (see Chapter 5) or conditions such as dyslexia (reading), dyspraxia (speech) and dysgraphia (writing) or autism (discussed below) present problems which may contribute to language and communication difficulties.

The role of the speech and language therapist is vital in the educational process. Although the therapists are employed by the health authority, they are now more readily available for treating children with language disorders.

As an example of special needs education in language and communication, see the section on deaf pupils in Chapter 5.

# Cognition and learning

The terminology used by the American Psychiatric Association and the World Health Organization to describe IQ ranges is mild (70–50), moderate (50–35), severe (35–20) and profound (below 20). Many children with mild, moderate and even severe measures of IQ fall into this section on cognition and are found in mainstream schools.

It should be made clear from the outset that these IQ scores are only part of the story. Although there are still institutions where specialist attention is provided (schools for profound educational difficulties, partially sighted, profoundly deaf, etc.), they all recognize that a stereotyped pattern of educational facilities would be totally inadequate for the range of problems one can find within each kind of institution. Frequently those with one major disability suffer in other ways. A physically disabled child may also be mentally disadvantaged, have language difficulties or suffer from emotional and social problems; the emotionally disturbed, in addition to faltering in their school work, sometimes display socially deviant behaviour.

## Mild and moderate learning difficulties

Most of the cases we are likely to consider here, whether the children are physically disabled, emotionally disturbed or culturally deprived, exhibit some degree of intellectual or mental disability where scholastic performance is below the average expected of a child's age group. Most teachers who deal with average and below-average pupils, especially in infant and primary schools, meet children who do not seem to profit from the usual educational methods and content provided. Intellectual disability in the present context is being reserved for those who are *slow learners*. Where children are not coping with the work normally expected of their age group, they are said to be slow learners.

To assess the gap between a child's intellectual ability and that normally expected of his or her age group, intelligence tests are used. The British Ability Scales and the Wechsler Intelligence Scale for Children are now widely used (see Chapter 9). We saw in Chapter 9 that IQs are distributed 'normally' in the population. There are a few very bright and a few who, for various reasons, get very low scores; the rest are distributed around the average. There are also a few for whom intelligence testing would be a nonsense because of their inability to cope. When a mean of 100 and standard deviation of 15 have been used in test design, something approaching 70 per cent of the population would obtain an IQ between 85 and 115 (standard deviation is dealt in Chapter 18, Figure 18.4 and distribution of IQ scores in Chapter 9, Figure 9.1). Those with cognitive problems tend to fall in the range below 70. This is about 2 per cent of the population (Figure 9.1). Children whose intellectual development has been environmentally retarded may, in fact, be quite bright (see the next section on 'Learners who are retarded').

The majority of those with mild and moderate learning difficulties find their way into the School Action and School Action Plus in primary and non-selective secondary schools. They are part of the 18 per cent of schoolchildren mentioned above by Warnock and consequently demand a substantial investment of teachers' time and effort. The Individual Education Plans (IEPs) offered endeavour to find and provide ways by which the children can fulfil whatever potential they possess. Sometimes they are placed in a separate group or class, but it is often the case, especially in unstreamed class groups, to find them with brighter children. Provided the class is small enough, individual help from a sympathetic and adequately trained teacher can be effective in unstreamed classes. Where circumstances permit or when class sizes are too large, remedial education using part-time or visiting teachers often becomes an additional source of educational provision. Involvement in the normal school setting of those with mild and moderate learning difficulties is to be encouraged. Most of them grow up to be useful members of the community consisting of people from all walks of life and of varying intellectual skills; therefore segregation early in life could militate against the slow learner's taking a responsible part in the community.

Children with learning difficulties need tactful, resourceful and skilful teaching of basic language and number skills. Their IEPs require programmes of *activities*, with the emphasis on children doing things in craft, art, drama, movement and communication. The curriculum is very much concerned with the concrete and practical aspects of scholastic work rather than with abstract thinking. Both from our definitions of intelligent behaviour and from Piaget's view of concept formation it follows that those with cognitive difficulties are not likely to cope with abstract thinking. Indeed, research outlined in Chapter 4 suggests that some children may rarely, if ever, operate abstractly in the sense used by Piaget in concept formation. Nevertheless, they still have to grow to adulthood, facing similar problems of earning a living, providing for a family and taking leisure. Clearly the examination system is quite unsuited to the needs and abilities of these pupils.

Teachers have, understandably, been worried about their abilities to cope with any form of special need as their training and experience have largely been devoted to normal school settings. Despite this, the evidence shows that children do benefit from integration.

### Further reading

A considerable amount has been written in support of greater integration in mainstream schools of pupils with varying degrees of learning difficulties. Hegarty *et al.*, *Educating Pupils with Special Needs in the Ordinary School*, 1981, and *Integration in Action*, 1982 are both published by NFER-Nelson, Windsor. The National Association for Special Education Needs (website http://www.nasen.org.uk/publications.asp), based at Tamworth in Staffordshire, and David Fulton Publishers, London, have produced many recent texts on special needs. NASEN (published at Tamworth, 1996) has produced a 'Spotlight on' series of texts about *Hearing Impairment* (L.

$\longrightarrow$

Watson), *Physical Disabilities* (H. Kenwood), *Specific Learning Difficulties* (D. Smith), *Learning Difficulties* (S. Beveridge), *Speech and Language* (B. Daines, P. Fleming and C. Miller) and *Visual Impairment* (H. L. Mason).

Warnock (1978) drew an interesting distinction between *social* integration (children mixing for leisure), *locational* integration (where a special unit or separate building is incorporated on a normal school site) and *functional* integration (where children are mixed socially and intellectually).

### Learners who are retarded

Some children are behind in school work not because they lack intellectual ability, but because their school achievement has been depressed by some environmental cause (see sections in Chapter 9 relating to environmental influences on psychometric test results). These children are most likely to be found in mild and moderate cases of learning difficulty. Implicit in remedial education is the notion that there is going to be an improvement after a short- or medium-term remedial programme intended to remove or counteract the source of trouble and recover lost ground in the scholastic attainment of the child to a point more in keeping with his or her potential ability. It is quite possible to find children with IQs of well over 100 in need of remedial teaching.

The conditions which accompany retardation tend to resolve into physical–personal, environmental and emotional difficulties, all of which appear in the other areas proposed in the Code of Practice. Personal factors include long illness or absence from school, undetected physical defects such as partial sight and hearing and mild aphasias (see Chapter 2); environmental variables range from poor home facilities for learning speech and reading skills, low quality and quantity of food, shortage of sleep and adverse parental attitudes towards education, to poor or inappropriate opportunities at school, such as large classes, poor teaching of basic skills (going too quickly or too slowly, choosing inadequate or advanced material), incompatibility between home and school, repeated changes of school and consequent changes in teaching styles and content (e.g. changing from one reading system to another or from 'new maths' to conventional number teaching). Emotional states will be dealt with later, but here we should mention dislike of teacher through clashes of personality, negative parental attitudes to school, creating in the child similar adverse attitudes, failure in school, snowballing into feelings of inadequacy and subsequently depressing the child's confidence and need to achieve, and extreme timidity and anxiety, giving rise to poor levels of attainment.

## Severe, profound and specific learning difficulties

Starting as far back as Circular 276 of the Department of Education and Science (1954), which said that 'no handicapped child should be sent to a special school who can be satisfactorily educated in an ordinary school', educationists agree that the policy of integration is a good one. But it is sometimes in the best interests of the severely incapable child to attend a special school which can cater for individual needs. These frequently require skilled and specially trained educational, medical, psychological and welfare staff and low staff: pupil ratios, which few state schools are able to provide at the moment. Where possible, children with severe learning difficulties attend a day special school, but when:

- home conditions adversely affect the child's development
- special services such as medical or psychological treatment are necessary
- rural children have no local day special facilities
- there are emotional complications aggravated by home circumstances

the children are sent to a residential special school (also see Atkinson and Hornby 2002).

These children cannot fully profit from the same educational provision found in classes in normal schools. Small classes (ideally containing no more than 12 pupils) are in evidence and the school size is rarely more than 200. The curriculum is less verbal and more practical. The three Rs are taught with a view to helping children in the difficult task of adjusting to a normal life in society. Special facilities are provided for the physically disabled.

Those not capable of taking advantage of mainstream schooling are now under the jurisdiction of the Department for Education and Skills through the local authority. The special schools, along with hospitals for the disadvantaged (children with physical complications as well, who cannot care for themselves), cater for children who would get no benefit from academic kinds of schooling.

Until recently these children were considered to be ineducable, but it has been shown that some can learn simple reading and writing skills. The priority is to help them in motor, perceptual and simple language skills so that they can gain some personal competence in looking after themselves (feeding, dressing, toilet, homely routines), social competence in communicating with others and possibly engaging in some kind of manual work. There are some unfortunates who are hospitalized and never attain even these basic human competencies, and who must depend on others for their daily routines.

A large number of pupils in special schools are Down's syndrome children (also incorrectly called Mongolism). This is a chromosomal abnormality (see Chapter 2) and most of the children have IQ measures below 80. There are other organic disorders which sometimes lead to low mental competence. During pregnancy the brain may be damaged, or diseases of either mother or foetus can lead to degeneration of brain tissues. These are congenital disorders of mental functioning. Injury during birth is also a possible, but a comparatively rare, cause nowadays. These give spastic and cerebral palsied conditions. Diseases in early childhood can leave a permanent mental scar if they are serious and remain untreated (measles, scarlet fever and several others).

## Dyslexia, dyscalculia and autism

Two particular disorders which have attracted the attention of psychologists in special needs are dyslexia and autism. Children have widely varying degrees of learning difficulty as a result of these and can be found in both mainstream and special schools.

### Dyslexia and dyscalculia

Confusingly, dyslexia is sometimes called *specific learning difficulty*. As we have seen above, the term 'specific learning difficulty' is now used in government documents to represent a much wider range of specific problems. In the population, the estimate of those with dyslexia is 5 per cent (three million). This is an alarmingly high percentage of the population. It is believed by some that this high number comes from confusion between those having learning difficulties in reading and the set of symptoms called *dyslexia*. There are others who prefer not to use the label 'dyslexia' and believe the common understanding of the 'condition' is a myth (see articles by Nicholson and Elliott (November and December issues of *The Psychologist*, 2005)).

The Dyslexia Institute defines dyslexia as 'a specific learning difficulty that hinders the learning of literacy skills' (Townend and Turner 2001). By literacy skills is meant reading, spelling and writing. Literally, the word means difficulty (dys) with words (lexia). It is also believed to be neurologically based and to run in families. Other symbol systems can be affected such as musical notation and number – sometimes called *dyscalculia* (difficulty (dys) with calculations (calculia)). Chinn (2004) defines the subject and offers a practical guide to teaching learners with numeracy problems (also see a chapter on dyscalculia in Townend and Turner, 2001). Measured intelligence of dyslexics is widely dispersed and most cases are found in mainstream schools. But as some intelligence test items are verbal, there is certain to be some disadvantage in this kind of problem.

One neurological base is thought to be a weakness in the processing of speech sounds, or phonological difficulties (see Chapter 5 for more about phonology) and the involvement of the cerebellum. As we saw in Chapter 2, the cerebellum coordinates fine movement of the body and it collaborates with the frontal lobes in language and reasoning. There is a genetic link from evidence that chromosomes 6 and 15 may be involved in transmitting dyslexic conditions to the next generation.

Signs of dyslexia vary from one child to the next (for a discussion, see Miles and Miles, 1999), but generally dyslexic children display the following:

- marked contrast between their oral and writing skills such as confusing written letters ('b' and 'd') and letter order inversions
- suffer short-term memory and concentration problems such as memorizing multiplication tables

- have difficulty in right–left orientation
- problems in repeating tongue-twisters like 'preliminary' and 'statistical'.

A useful way of thinking about dyslexia has been suggested by Frith (1997). She prefers to consider the impact of developmental disorders such as dyslexia at three levels, namely, biological, cognitive and behavioural. There are biological abnormalities such as cerebellar deficiencies or the question of a genetic link which affect the next level of cognitive functioning. The latter is displayed in phonological difficulties which in turn affects a person's output or 'behaviour' in reading, spelling and number. But, behaviour is context specific and the outcome of a dyslexic condition depends on the life experiences of the person involved. For instance, recognition and support from parents and school play a crucial role in the progress of a dyslexic person.

The fact that the majority of dyslexic children are to be found in state schools means that most teachers will meet them. Townend and Turner (2001) have several chapters on ways in which teachers might approach their work with dyslexic children. Whatever else, it is important to remember that, intellectually and physically and with the right guidance from teachers, there is no reason why dyslexic children should not be capable of experiencing fulfilling lives.

## Autism

Autism is from the Greek word *autos* which means *self*. This characteristic of looking inwards, rather than outwards, is deduced from the poorly developed social and communication skills. Autistic people also have strong obsessional interests.

Its frequency is a matter for debate. If we adopt the view that autism covers a spectrum of characteristics, then something like one in 200 children has autism (Baron-Cohen 2003). The most recent report puts the figure at 1 in 100 (*Lancet*, 2006). Also, four times as many boys as girls display it. The range, collectively referred to as *Autistic Spectrum Disorders* (ASPs) has at least three points of interest. These are the well-established (i) severe form of autism, (ii) high-functioning autism and (iii) Asperger's syndrome.

The severe, traditional form has been the basis for defining autism (Atkinson and Hornby 2002). The symptoms include silence or poor language usage and below-average IQ scores (see Chapter 9). They have obsessions and live in their own world, sometimes referred to as 'in a bubble'.

But a small proportion of about 25 per cent displaying autistic symptoms, including delay in language development and obsessional behaviour, have average or above average intelligence. This is referred to as *high-functioning autism*. These individuals are a fascination to observers, including TV programmes, because they have specific abilities such as remembering football tables, being able to calculate the day of the week of any date, doing lightning mathematical calculations involving multiplication and so on. Parrot-fashion learning is also displayed by some who can learn a foreign language without being able to use it in conversation with a native of the language. So limited social and communication skills do not prevent some individuals from highly competent performance in remembering tables, mathematics, chess and other rule-based topics (requiring almost computer-like recording and reproduction of data).

The most advanced point in the autism spectrum is Asperger's syndrome (AS). Again, social and communication problems exist alongside obsessional behaviour, but there is no delay in language or cognitive development. Some achieve high status in occupations not requiring social skills.

---

### Further reading

Several informative books have been written about autism. Try C. Travarthen, *Children with Autism: Diagnosis and Interventions to Meet Their Needs*, Jessica Kingsley, London, 1996 and R. C. Koegel and L. K. Koegel, *Teaching Children with Autism: Strategies for Initiating Positive Interactions and Improving Learning Opportunities*, Brookes Books, London, 1995. Also try R. P. Hobson, *Autism and the Division of Mind*, Erlbaum, Hove, 1993. As a starting point for the autism spectrum, see Baron-Cohen (2003).

---

To an outsider the most conspicuous symptom of classic autism is the lack of contact, either with eyes or in speech, between the child and others (even parents). Speech, where it appears, is grossly retarded and unusual (e.g. *echolalia*, where the child repeats something which has just been said). Excessive and persistent movement such as rocking in a chair and banging the head against the back of it or flapping hands with or without a piece of string or paper are characteristic. Some perceptual experiences are ignored (sights and sounds and even heat and pain) whilst other perceptual experiences seem to become hypnotic (music and regular beats).

The special provision for autistic children has not been clear-cut. The numbers involved are not clear if we include the full spectrum of autism. The classic, but severe, cases receive attention in specialist hospitals and schools with a few in mainstream schools. Those in mainstream schools are essentially the high-functioning and Asperger's cases.

# Behaviour, social and emotional development

The Code of Practice (DfES 2001b) defines 'children and young people who demonstrate features of emotional and behavioural difficulties' as those 'who are withdrawn and isolated, disruptive and disturbing, hyperactive and lacking concentration'. They also include 'those with immature social skills and those who present challenging behaviours arising from other complex special needs'. Anxious and depressed children would be found amongst those with emotional difficulties. In the 1994 Code, this area was referred to as EBDs (emotional and behavioural difficulties) and this term is still widely used in the literature.

Emotional disturbance is commonplace. All of us at some time have experienced symptoms of emotional stress and disturbance without their unduly affecting our daily lives. Temporary effects such as lack of concentration, quick arousal to anger or tears, temperamental fickleness or fecklessness are soon overcome. There is a small, but significant, group of children and adults who are unable to overcome their emotional problems. In a submission from the Plowden Committee (1967) it seems that more than 15 per cent (cf. Coopers and Lyband 1996) of schoolchildren in primary schools experience strong debilitating influences from their emotional stresses.

When emotional handicaps reach the stage of being so grave as to affect social development leading to behaviour disorders (and frequently influencing schoolwork), special courses of action are required. Such problems as fears and anxiety, marked solitariness and timidity appear. Habit disorders such as speech defects and stammering (other than those caused by physical defect), excessive day-dreaming, sleeplessness and nightmares, facial and body tics, nail-biting, rocking, bedwetting and general incontinence and physical symptoms such as asthma and allergies are in evidence. Other behaviour problems are temper tantrums, destructive, defiant or cruel actions, stealing, lying, truancy and sex aberrations.

The appearance of any of these symptoms does not of itself signify EBD. Nor are these symptoms necessarily permanent. They range from mild to severe, and many cases can be dealt with in the normal school setting by teachers aware of the problems and possible solutions. Many people have an eye or facial twitch, bite their nails or have sleep problems. But when these symptoms accumulate we usually have a special case on our hands.

It might be, as we will note in Chapter 12, that some individuals are predisposed to personality disorders given the right conditions. Consequently, it is important to examine the environment in which these behaviours are exhibited. Home and school, therefore, could present problematic situations which might provoke emotional discord. Frustration and strained relationships between parents, parent and child, teacher and child or between the children will influence some children more than others. Withholding affection or generating feelings of insecurity are likely to precipitate maladjustment in some children. Inability to cope with schoolwork or teachers whose approach is too demanding or intimidating are also likely causes.

EBDs are frequently dealt with while the child is attending a primary or secondary school (Chazan *et al.* 1991). Close liaison between the school and home to discover the background to the child's problems and the involvement of social psychiatric workers, psychiatrists and psychologists from the School Psychological Service are necessary in determining possible causes and, in some cases, preventing the situation from worsening. School attainment often shows a marked improvement as a consequence of detecting and tackling the cause. This is sometimes accomplished by visits to the home and school from the School Psychological

Service and social workers. At school or the clinic the child receives lessons and treatment in keeping with the causes. Where the home is clearly not suitable in its influence on the emotional development of the child, the child is sent to a special residential school designed to provide a safe and supportive environment.

Many of the methods used in dealing with EBDs have been alluded to in Chapter 6. Circular 9/94 which accompanied the Code of Practice deals with the topic of EBDs (see also McNamara and Moreton 2001).

# Sensory and physical needs

## Sensory difficulties

Sensory problems are largely hearing and visual difficulties. Both *hearing* and *visual* losses can range from profound and permanent levels of loss, through partial permanent loss to temporary conditions. Indeed, upwards of 20 per cent of primary school children may experience some degree of temporary hearing impairment. But many have moderate or profound problems which are either congenital (present at birth) or adventitious (happened through accident or illness after birth).

Often, deafness is not spotted by parents until several months after birth. As with all problems which get in the way of learning, the earlier deafness is recognized, the better. With severe and profound hearing loss, communication difficulties are likely. Signing, lip-speaking and lip-reading are very important at any early stage.

Many special schools or units within state schools now encourage British Sign Language as well as English. The two languages are not the same – they have different grammatical and syntactic rules. Such abilities in signing and lip-reading are now an important communication vehicle in higher education. In the USA, for example, there are institutions (Gallaudet University and Rochester National Institute for the Deaf) which specialize in education for all levels of deafness through to degree standard. The advances made in deaf education and the integration of the profoundly deaf into society is progressing remarkably because of these institutions. Several universities in the UK now have facilities for deaf students (see the section on non-verbal communication in Chapter 5).

Special units or schools are needed to help blind children with the particular facilities they require and to learn Braille (Best 1992). With the use of high-powered magnification and suitable seating in the classroom, many partially sighted children can be found in state day schools.

## Physical difficulties

There are many forms of physical disability which may be congenital or the result of illness or injury. Some overlap considerably with other areas such as the aphasias (communication and outlined in Chapters 2 and 5). But this area relates to children whose condition arises from physical, neurological or metabolic causes. The ability range is wide because there are many cases of physical disability not accompanied by any mental difficulties.

Examples of conditions are loss of limb functioning, in many cases causing pupils to be chair- or bed-bound, muscular dystrophy, spasticism, spina bifida, polio, cerebral palsy, arthritis and delicacy. Generally, these conditions require pupils to attend special schools which can provide custom-made facilities and cater medically whilst offering normal educational services. There are cases, and we have probably all met some, of children with physical handicaps who are quite able to attend normal day school, but these cases are rare. Special schools account for 1.4 per cent of the total school population between 5 and 16 years of age. Now, many more children are within or attached to normal schools in special units with about 2.6 per cent statemented.

Teamwork in special schools is necessary. The paramedical staff (nurses, physiotherapists, occupational and speech therapists) work alongside the teaching staff to give individual help to the child. Where children are able to go on to more academic work every encouragement is given. The greater use of information technology in schools and universities has been a tremendous advantage for certain kinds of physical problems where a keyboard or other input format can be used. Many universities are now offering facilities for sensory and physically disabled students, including a counselling service.

## Medical conditions

The distinction between a physical and a medical condition is not always clear. One might argue that all the physical problems mentioned in the last section require medical monitoring. In general, though, medical problems in SEN relate to those which require regular, ongoing treatment. The physical conditions include epilepsy, asthma, cystic fibrosis, haemophilia, sickle cell anaemia, congenital heart disease, diabetes, renal failure, eczema, rheumatoid disorders and leukaemia and childhood cancers which present particular problems for the state system unless adequate medical, psychological and social support are provided.

There are also mental health problems (Atkinson and Hornby 2002) such as eating disorders, substance abuse, neurotic (depression and obsession, suicidal behaviour, excitability – apathy, hysteria and amnesia, phobias) and psychotic disorders (hallucinations, schizophrenia, delusions, bizarre behaviour) which are few and far between. Some symptoms, such as psychotic and organic disorders, are quite chronic in their effects and can only be dealt with by psychiatrists, clinical psychologists and nurses in special establishments.

## Summary

There is now a substantial investment of time and effort in our educational system devoted to the task of providing for those with special needs. Strictly speaking, children who, by virtue of physical, mental, emotional or behavioural difficulties, are not always fully able to benefit from conventional mainstream day schools are included in the official definition of children with educational difficulties. They amount to 20 per cent of the age range 5 to 16. We meet about 18 per cent of these children in need of special education in our daily work. This arises from a policy of *inclusiveness* in education where it is believed that most can benefit more from companionship in both work and play, despite learning difficulties. With this percentage across the school system, we will all at some time have to deal with children having special educational needs.

The Warnock Report (1978) and subsequent Education Acts (1981, 1988, 1993, 1996, 2001) have had a marked influence on the direction of special education in the UK. The main reason is a change of philosophy regarding the recognition and assessment of children with special needs and the strategies recommended for suitable educational programmes. To assist in the process, the Government produced a Code of Practice (1994, 2001b) on the Identification and Assessment of Special Educational Needs along with Regulations and several circulars about specific aspects of special needs.

Categorization has been replaced with less formal descriptions. These rely more on the degree of learning difficulty than the source of the difficulty. *Mild, moderate, severe* and *specific* learning difficulties are identified. This, in turn, has led to greater focus on pupils being educated in mainstream school settings and to revisions in the content, resources and delivery of the curriculum for the 18 per cent of children mentioned above.

Those SEN children who remain in the general school system are integrated as far as possible. A person, the Special Educational Needs Coordinator (SENCO), is chosen to oversee provision for their educational needs. For mild and moderate cases of learning difficulty, it is generally sufficient to have a School Action plan. With more severe cases, a School Action Plus plan is frequently needed. These are called Early Years School Action and Early Years School Action Plus for children aged three to five years. The SENCO is responsible for seeing that an Individual Education Plan (IEP) is devised and in place for the benefit of all those involved in the educational progress of the child.

Procedures for an *assessment* of the most severe cases were introduced in 1983 and monitored in Codes of Practice up to the last in 2001. These involve an assessment based on advice from educational, medical, social, psychological and other relevant specialists.

The Code of Practice (2001b) sets out in some detail the sources and kinds of evidence needed for the assessment. Areas of need are defined as: (i) *communication and interaction*, (ii) *cognition and learning*, (iii) *behaviour, emotional and social development* and (iv) *sensory and/or physical*. These are discussed above in some detail.

The assessment enables an education authority to recommend to the parents and school the most appropriate provision for the child's particular educational needs. Some will be *statemented* and receive special educational provision in a mainstream school or special unit/school, or both. The placement must have the consent of the parents. Special units and schools are noted for their small class sizes (about ten per teacher) and specialist helpers.

The number of children being assessed and consequently statemented has risen in the last ten years. At the same time, the number of children transferred to dual schooling (part mainstream, part special unit or school) or entirely special units and schools has fallen. This is in keeping with the introduction of an *inclusiveness policy* over the same period.

## Tutorial enquiry and discussion

(a) Invite a SENCO and a psychologist to speak to your tutorial group. This would be an effective way of getting introduced to School Action, School Action Plus, IEPs and the role of the SENCO and psychologist in the assessment and statementing process.

(b) School visits and teaching should also offer opportunities to see the SENCO and SEN provision in operation. If possible, discuss the issues and use the Code of Practice, 2001, as a guide.

(c) For statemented children, it will be necessary to visit the special unit or school or invite speakers who can give specialist information about the identification, assessment and statementing process. Try to observe a range of learning difficulties originating from medical, physical and sensory disabilities.

(d) Discuss the strengths and weaknesses in the present system of inclusiveness.

## References

Ainscow, M. (1999), *Understanding the Development of Inclusive Schools*. London: Hodder and Stoughton.

Atkinson, M. and Hornby, G. (2002), *Mental Health Handbook for Schools*. London: Routledge Falmer.

Baron-Cohen, S. (2003), *The Essential Difference: Men, Women and the Extreme Male Brain*. London: Allan Lane (and Penguin Books).

Best, A. (1992), *Teaching Children with Visual Impairment*. Milton Keynes: Open University Press.

Beveridge, S. (1998), 'Parent–professional partnerships in provision for children with special educational needs', in D. Shorrocks-Taylor (ed.), *Directions in Educational Psychology*. London: Whurr.

Chazan, M., Laing, A. F. and Davies, D. (1991), *Helping Five- to Eight-Year-Olds with Special Educational Needs*, in the series 'Theory and Practice in Education' (General Editor D. Child). Oxford: Blackwell.

Chinn, S. (2004), *The Trouble with Maths: A Practical Guide to Helping Learners with Numeracy Difficulties*. London: Routledge Falmer.

Coopers and Lybrand (1996), *The SEN Initiative: Management Budgets for Pupils with Special Needs*. London: Coopers and Lybrand.

DES (1979), *Meeting Special Educational Needs*, London: HMSO.

DES Circular 22/89 (1989), *Assessments and Statements of Special Needs*. London: HMSO.

DfE (1994), *Code of Practice on the Identification and Assessment of Special Educational Needs*. London: HMSO.

DfE Circular 6/94 (1994), *The Organisation of Special Educational Provision*. London: HMSO. (This was revised in 2001 DfES 2001b).

DfE Circular 8/94 (1994), *Pupil Behaviour and Discipline*. London: HMSO.

DfE Circular 9/94 (1994), *The Education of Children with Emotional and Behavioural Difficulties*. London: HMSO.

DfE Circular 10/94 (1994), *Exclusions from School*. London: HMSO.

DfE Circular 12/94 (1994), *The Education of Sick Children*. London: HMSO.

DfE Circular 13/94 (1994), *The Education of Children being looked after by Local Authorities*. London: HMSO.

DfES (2001a), *SEN Toolkit*. London: HMSO.

DfES (2001b), *Special Educational Needs Code of Practice*. London: HMSO.

DfES (2001c), *Statistics of Education: Schools in England*. Covering the period 1996–2001. London: HMSO.

Elliott, J. (2005), 'The Dyslexia debate continues', *The Psychologist*, 18, 12, 728–9.

Frith, U. (1997), 'Brain, mind and behaviour in dyslexia', in C. Hulme and M. Snowling (eds), *Dyslexia: Biology, Cognition and Intervention*. London: Whurr.

Goddard, C. and Tester, G. (1996,) *Managing the Code of Practice: A Whole-School Approach*. London: David Fulton Publishers.

Hegarty, S., Pocklington, K. and Lucas, D. (1981), *Educating Pupils with Special Needs in the Ordinary School*. Windsor: NFER-Nelson.

Hegarty, S., Pocklington, K. and Lucas, D. (1982), *Integration in Action*. Windsor: NFER-Nelson.

Hobson, R. P. (1993), *Autism and the Division of Mind*. Hove: Erlbaum.

Koegel, R. C. and Koegel, L. K. (eds) (1995), *Teaching Children with Autism: Strategies for Initiating Positive Interactions and Improving Learning Opportunities*. London: Brookes Books.

Lindsay, G. and Miller, A. (1991), *Psychological Services for Primary Schools*. London: Longman.

McNamara, S. and Moreton, G. (2001), *Changing Behaviour: Teaching Children with Emotional and Behavioural Difficulties in Primary and Secondary Classrooms* (2nd ed). London: David Fulton Publishers.

Miles, T.R. and Miles, E. (1999), *Dyslexia – a Hundred Years On*. Buckingham: Open University Press.

NASEN (1996), has produced a 'Spotlight on' series of texts about: *Hearing Impairment* (L. Watson), *Physical Disabilities* (H. Kenwood), *Specific Learning Difficulties* (D. Smith), *Learning Difficulties* (S. Beveridge), *Speech and Language* (B. Daines, P. Fleming and C. Miller) and *Visual Impairment* (H. L. Mason). Tamworth, Staffs: NASEN.

Nicholson, R. (2005), 'Dyslexia: beyond the myth'. *The Psychologist*, 18, 11, 658–9

Plowden Report, The (1967), *Children and their Primary Schools*, Vol. 1. London: HMSO.

Ramjhun, A. F. (2002), *Implementing the Code of Practice for Children with Special Educational Needs: A Practical Guide*. London: David Fulton Publishers.

Smith, H. (1996), *Procedures, Practice and Guidance for SENCOs*. Tamworth, Staffs: NASEN.

Sugden, D. (1998), 'Helping children with learning difficulties', in D. Shorrocks-Taylor (ed.), *Directions in Educational Psychology*. London: Whurr.

Townend, J. and Turner, M. (eds) (2001), *Dyslexia in Practice: A Guide for Teachers*. London: Kluwer Academic/Plenum Publishers.

Travarthen, C. (1996), *Children with Autism: Diagnosis and Interventions to Meet their Needs*. London: Jessica Kingsley.

Visser, J. (ed.) (1994), *A Guide to the 1994 Code of Practice, OFSTED Inspections and Related Documents*. Tamworth, Staffs: NASEN.

Warnock Report, The (1978), *Special Educational Needs*. London: HMSO, Cmnd 7212.

Wolfendale, S. (ed.) (1997), *Working with Parents of SEN Children after the Code of Practice*. London: David Fulton Publishers.

## Further reading

Alcot, M. (1997), *An Introduction to Children with Special Needs*. London: Hodder and Stoughton.

Atkinson, M. and Hornby, G. (2002), *Mental Health Handbook for Schools*. London: Routledge Falmer.

Chazan, M., Laing, A. F. and Davies, D. (1991), *Helping Five- to Eight-Year-Olds with Special Educational Needs*. In the series 'Theory and Practice in Education' (General Editor D. Child). Oxford: Blackwell. It is easy to read. Though it deals with younger children, the information is widely applicable.

DfES (2001), *Special Education Needs: Code of Practice*. London: HMSO and on the British Dyslexia Association website below.

Farrell, M. (1997), *The Special Education Handbook*. London: David Fulton Publishers.

Goddard, C. and Tester, G. (1996), *Managing the Code of Practice: A Whole-School Approach*. London: David Fulton Publishers.

Stakes, R. and Hornby, G. (2000), *Meeting Special Needs in Mainstream Schools* (2nd edn). London: David Fulton Publishers.

## Useful websites

British Dyslexia Association website:

http://www.bda-dyslexia.org.uk/main/information/parents

National Association for Special Education Needs website:

http://www.nasen.org.uk. For publications by this organization, see http://www.nasen.org.uk/publications.asp

Elliott and Nicholson in *Psychologist*, 2005, 10, 11 and 12. The latter contains several website references to the views of Elliott).

# 12 Personality, Learning and Teaching Styles

# Implications for teachers

- Many of our judgements as teachers relate to personality. It is therefore sensible to study this aspect of psychology.
- The various theories of personality provide a framework within which we can attempt to define personality and relate it to our work as teachers.
- Relationships have been found between personality factors and school performance.

> # Implications for teachers (continued)
>
> - What you believe about yourself (self-concept) can affect your performance.
> - Not only what we teach, but also the way that we teach it, may have a significant effect on what students learn and the way that they learn it.

Why is it necessary for teachers to make a study of human personality? One reason is that we are daily making judgements about the affective qualities of ourselves, our pupils and our colleagues. We should, therefore, be fully conversant with the extent to which we can form a reliable assessment of personality using these judgements. Personality factors also affect learning and performance and, although we have no formula that we can apply for guiding children with diverse personal attributes, nevertheless we should recognize that the differences which exist in their scholastic performance may be as much a function of their personalities as their intellects. Recognition of the mentally disturbed and immediate recourse to professional help, especially in the earliest stages as signified in Chapter 11 on special needs, can prevent eleventh-hour therapy. Again, our work as teachers consists of influencing attitudes and the more we know about attitude formation and change, the better are our chances of influencing others.

Most of the time we casually observe the way people move, talk or react on different occasions. We watch their faces for clues to their attitudes and we listen to their prejudices; we find ourselves changing to suit the circumstances, so when people are amongst friends they are usually not the same as when being interviewed for a job. Baron-Cohen (2003) has shown that females, on average, identify other people's emotions and thoughts more readily than males – they are more empathic (see Chapter 2). But the superficial observation of how others behave in particular circumstances and its use as a means of describing personality has serious drawbacks, as we shall see. The popular view of personality, where we typify others in such vague terms as 'generous', 'bad-tempered', 'morbid', 'aloof', etc., without regard for the many other qualities which go to make up an individual's overall profile, has been unfortunate. Psychologists, on the other hand, have been more concerned with a description of the total organization of a person's behaviour, and this chapter will be devoted to a discussion of some of these approaches.

The task of describing and defining the total organization of humans is very complex. Whilst we do not find any generally agreed definition of personality amongst psychologists, one which is sufficiently comprehensive for our purposes is 'the more or less stable and enduring organization of a person's character, temperament, intellect and physique which determines his unique adjustment to the environment' (Eysenck 1953, Smith *et al.* 2003). Note that the definition carefully distinguishes such attributes as temperament and character (as well as intelligence and physique) because, as we shall show next, these terms have rather special meanings in psychology.

*Temperament* is a quality we reserve to describe the inherent disposition underlying personality (Eysenck 1990). Physiological factors there from birth, such as variations in endocrine gland secretions in response to different environmental settings, distinguish our excitability, instability or placidity, so that temperament is closely allied to emotional dispositions which even at a common-sense level are seen to vary enormously from person to person. The evidence for inherited temperamental traits, as in our consideration of intelligence, is indirect. Like intelligence, temperament cannot be observed directly because the influence of environmental factors is immediate, but the study of twins, brothers and sisters and family trees gives us a clue to hereditary influence. When we compare the response patterns exhibited by new-born babies from different families, it soon becomes obvious that even in the same situation their responses are dissimilar. In research where babies' toes were dipped into icy water a whole range of responses ensued. Some babies took the whole sordid affair in their stride and placidly withdrew their limbs; at the other extreme, some screamed blue murder; others showed fear, horror and recoil (Thomas *et al.* 1964). In this textbook, the term 'temperament' is used synonymously with 'personality'.

*Character*, on the other hand, is an evaluative term referring to such traits as honesty, self-control, persistence and sense of justice. It relates to qualities which we can define as socially acceptable or objectionable and incorporates the development of attitudes and values. Environmental constraints accompany the expression of inherited temperamental qualities and lead to character development. The relationship between temperament and character described here is not unlike that between Intelligence A and B described in Chapter 9. Having certain temperamental potentialities at birth gives a blueprint for the development of character which to some extent depends on the processes of socialization to which the child is exposed. The guidelines laid down in a permissive or an authoritarian home are thought to determine the social and moral life styles (values and attitudes to race, religion, morals, etc.) within the context of the child's temperamental possibilities.

Since our definition of personality deals with 'adjustment to the environment' it is clear that intelligence must play a role in personality. Mention was made of this in Chapters 9 and 10. Intelligence is likely to affect the way we adjust to our environments. For example, there may be a correlation between the level of abstraction people can reach and their preferred methods of solving life's problems. *Physique* and personality will be dealt with later in the chapter.

# Theories of personality

Interest in personality has a very long history. As far back as the second century AD, Galen proposed a typology of personality based on the distribution of the 'body fluids' or 'humours' first suggested by Hippocrates (Greece, fifth century BC). The personality types

**Table 12.1**

| Humour | Personality type | Characteristic behaviour |
|---|---|---|
| Black bile | Melancholic | Pessimistic, suspicious, depressed |
| Blood | Sanguine | Optimistic, sociable, easy-going |
| Phlegm | Phlegmatic | Calm, controlled, lethargic |
| Yellow bile | Choleric | Active, irritable, egocentric |

were called the *melancholic, sanguine, phlegmatic* and *choleric*. The corresponding 'humours' and characteristics are drawn-up in Table 12.1. Notice that melancholics are opposite in nature to sanguines and phlegmatics opposite to cholerics. This particular fourfold scheme of personality types survives in a modified form in several contemporary theories (see, for example, Eysenck's work later in the chapter).

Modern theories of personality structure are many and diverse. To contain them, modern specialist texts on personality (e.g. Mischel 2003, 'Further reading') now classify the theories into four major approaches: *Humanist* (or *Phenomenologist*), *Psychoanalytic*, *Social Learning* (or *Behaviourist*) and *Trait Theories* (or *Psychometrics*). To these may be added the *Naïve* approach which will be dealt with first. Readers should note the overlap between aspects of this chapter and Chapter 8 on motivation.

## Naïve approaches to personality

Naïve interpretations are based essentially on superficial, face-value observations and interpretations of overt behaviour without the use of norm-referencing. What we see in other people is conditioned by our own dispositions, attitudes, motives, biases and interests, and we build up a rule of thumb about human nature on the grounds of previous anecdotal experience. Some have suggested that what we perceive in another person depends entirely on the intention we ascribe to that person; in other words, we project our own interpretations of behaviour to explain the intentions of others. It is very easy, for example, to invent malicious motives for the behaviour of children, which might provide one reason for child battering and abuse, when their actions are playfully and innocently disobedient. In this case we are investing their immature actions with adult motives.

There are many behavioural cues which affect people's judgement. Two important ones are *physical characteristics* and *social response* factors. Likely physical features include facial expressions, body movements, clothes, handwriting and speech. Social response factors indicate our actual or perceived social role. We try to adopt modes of behaviour and social postures in keeping with what we think are characteristic of the circumstances. Goffman (1956) thinks that, even in trivial contacts, individuals try to impersonate the image they think will fit the event and possibly satisfy the expectations of others. The implication of this kind of theorizing is that there are stereotypes which we use as models for our aspirations. The doctor or headteacher might have an image of the 'typical' doctor or headteacher which he or she attempts to emulate. Children may use their fathers and mothers as models of parenthood in their approach to other people, or in solving life's problems. In short, we learn about the various roles in life by observing the important people (sometimes) already established in these roles – called *role models*.

## Interviews

Perhaps the most extensive use made of superficial criteria for evaluating personality is in the interview. Interviews are held by some to be a reliable method for assessing personality. Most serious research by psychologists directed towards assessing the reliability and validity of the interview as a selection procedure has been discouraging. They now accept that general, unstructured ('let's have a chat') interviews, which are neither fact-finding nor job-related, are not reliable in predicting performance. Volumes have been written about the effectiveness of interviews in the selection process (for summaries see Cook 1993a, and Anderson and Herriot 1994). There has been much more success in structured interviewing especially when this involves questions derived from detailed job analysis.

Vernon (1953) and Cook (1993b) quote a lot of evidence against the use of interviews for selection and Vernon concludes that oral questioning and the interview are useless for assessing ability or the results of teaching. He also maintains that:

> While there is much else to be said later [in his book], particularly about clinical and counselling interviews, it may be stated here that the selection interview is at its best when it is used: (a) for expanding, checking and probing the information previously provided by paper qualifications and biographical data; (b) for assessing particular qualities, mainly physical, social and intellectual, that have a good chance of expression during the interview situation. It is at its worst when it is conceived as a means for the interviewer: (a) to intuit or infer fundamental qualities of personality and character; (b) to weigh up and synthesize the evidence from diverse sources and reach a decision in the light of his 'experience' and judgement of job requirements. (Vernon, 1969, pp. 70–1)

The comments were made as a result of synthesizing research findings, and they raise many doubts about traditional interview methods of selection. For example, career and job selection from age 16 onwards nearly always uses a conventional interview. In a research by the author (Child *et al.* 1988) into nurse selection, the interview was an integral part of selection procedures for admission to nurse training. However, in keeping with the findings from many similar researches, the methods used at interview were questionable. The findings showed that schools and colleges of nursing rarely had clearly stated criteria for interviews in order to make judgements about suitability. Even those criteria specified like 'has a caring attitude' or 'had understanding' were not clearly defined. Indeed, some expressions were very difficult to define. One method of improving the validity of the interview was for interviewers to have a checklist of clearly definable criteria and to pose questions from this list in such a way as to expose the extent to which the interviewee met the criteria.

## Inadequacies of the naïve approach

Naïve interpretations of personality are doomed to failure for several reasons. These interpretations tend towards an over-simplified view of human nature, aggravated by the fact that most people create masks in order to disguise or create particular qualities at will and according to circumstances. They tend to employ stereotypes, which are frequently based on limited and biased experience, to describe the behaviour observed. Naïve impressions of others are very much bound up with the interaction occurring between people. This interaction often rests on superficial contact in highly specific incidents. An added complication results from the *role play* of individuals when they are trying to put over a particular image. There is also a temptation for interviewers to observe the irregular, because idiosyncratic behaviour is more conspicuous. Eccentricities such as voice intonation, twitches or an aggressive approach can disturb a balanced judgement. We also tend to undervalue those with a different point of view from our own. All in all, these shallow attempts at personality analysis are not likely to give us a stable, comprehensive picture of another's personality. In judging children it could, if carried too far, lead to quite distorted views about their actual or potential aptitudes (see the section on expectancy in Chapter 8).

## The humanist approaches to personality

There has undoubtedly been an upsurge of interest in humanistic psychology since the 1960s (the Association of Humanistic Psychology was founded in 1962) which has emphasized both the importance of the *whole being*, the person, as the centre of personality study (and not particular parts of an individual's behaviour) and the inevitable tendency of human beings to desire and actively seek to achieve life goals. These are strongly reflected in the humanists' avoidance of 'data' collection and analysis of groups to form generalizations, and their preference for whole-life case studies of individuals. The ideas of looking at the 'experiencing' person from his or her point of view and the importance attached to self-determinism of human beings are not new, for these notions come over strongly in earlier gestalt writings.

Basically what humanists are saying is that we react to the world as we believe it to be and not as it really is. My wife and I are sitting in a room; she tells me she is freezing and I feel comfortable. She believes it is cold and I believe it is warm. What is it 'really'? 'We see things not as they are but as we are' (Kant).

The names most often associated with the humanist tradition are Lewin, Rogers, Maslow (1968) and Kelly. Lewin (1936) was a *field* theorist. The term 'field' has a similar meaning to the magnetic field around a magnet. Interaction of all the factors of the present environment, including personality characteristics, is stressed as the dominant criterion governing behaviour (like a piece of iron in a magnetic field). Lewin (1936) thinks that 'the behaviour of a person or group is due to the distribution of forces in the social situation *as a whole*, rather than the intrinsic properties of the individual'. Thus the dynamic aspects of our present experience are the all-important things. However, it has to be said that this approach leaves the teacher somewhat empty-handed when he or she wants to use knowledge of social and individual differences in order to determine the factors which may assist in motivating children.

One of the first and widely acknowledged humanist theories of personality was expounded by Maslow (1968 and 1970). His hierarchy of needs appears in Chapter 8, and it forms the basis of his views on personality. The personality is shaped by the individual's reactions along the paths taken while the needs are in the process of being satisfied. As we saw in Chapter 8, the order in which the individual satisfies the needs is fundamental and those needs higher on the scale of things are more typical of adults than of children. Where deprivation occurs at a point in the hierarchy, 'stunting' of personal development involving those needs above that point occurs. Thus, if the esteem needs are deprived, development of self-actualization and cognitive understanding are distorted. Unfortunately, Maslow's work has never been thoroughly researched, largely because the concepts are very difficult to operationalize (i.e. it is hard to make and test hypotheses relating to the theory). Therefore his work has tended to remain as a descriptive rationalization of children's behaviour.

Carl Rogers (1970) takes Maslow's view a stage further by suggesting that human beings perceive their experiences as reality and respond in a way which helps the individual to 'self-actualization'. This term is used in the same way as in Maslow's theory (see Chapter 8) and is the central motivational concept for Rogers. The young child, for instance, behaves as an organized whole (cf. Gestalt Theory) and is regulated in the direction of his or her behaviour by the organism's *valuing* process; that is, a process enabling the individual to evaluate the worth of experiences which might maintain and enhance the physical and social self. Hence, Rogers is referred to as a *phenomenologist* because he believes the person places emphasis on what he or she *thinks* is happening and not on what *is* happening. This is closely tied to the *self-concept*, which is, for Rogers, that part of the individual's *awareness of himself or herself* using all the perceptual means at his or her disposal. The awareness acts as a frame of reference by which an individual makes judgements about his or her well-being in relation to physical and social preservation in an effort to achieve self-actualization. We shall deal later in the chapter with self-concept.

### Kelly's personal construct theory and repertory grid

One attempt at a *rapprochement* between the humanist, psychoanalytic and psychometric traditions come in the work of Kelly (Bannister and Mair 1968). A basic premise is that the theories we have regarding the world about us form the basis from which we perpetually seek to 'guess' what will happen next. In this manner we construe or reconstrue our world of experience. 'A person's processes are psychologically channelized by the ways in which he anticipates events' (Bannister and Fransella 1971). This view is in marked contrast to that of the inferential theorists, because Kelly's fundamental belief is that human behaviour is anticipatory rather than reactive. Thus, we react *not* to a stimulus but to what we interpret the stimulus to be. If someone digs a piece of metal out of the ground he or she may construe it as a 'thing', as a lump of metal, as a coin, as a Roman coin or as a coin of particular value from the reign of Constantine the Great, depending on his or her personal constructs. Each person's reaction to the find is different, even though the superficial sensory stimulation is the same.

The technique developed by Kelly (Bannister and Bolt 1973) for comparing our reactions to people who are significant in our lives is referred to as the *repertory grid method*. One popular method for initiating the grid is to ask a person to name several people known to him or her (six in the grid below). These are known as *elements* in the grid and could be objects or concepts, besides people. Next, the person is asked to group the elements into three (the *triad* method) from the list of significant others (which might consist of mother, father, sister, brother, work friend, boss, neighbour, etc.) in such a way that two are alike but at the same time dissimilar to the third person in some specified way. The 'specified ways' are called *constructs* and are commonly expressed in bipolar form such as powerful–weak, cruel–kind, mature–immature, generous–stingy, intelligent–stupid. If the subject is now asked to place each person at one or other end of each pole (x = one end of pole, blank = the other), a grid can be constructed thus:

| *Constructs* | | *Elements* | | | | | |
|---|---|---|---|---|---|---|---|
| | | 1 | 2 | 3 | 4 | 5 | 6 |
| A | powerful–weak | x | x | x | | | x |
| B | cruel–kind | x | | | x | x | |
| C | mature–immature | | x | | | x | |

---

### Further reading

The Repertory Grid continues to have many users. Look to website http://eric.ed.gov and enter 'repertory grid' as keywords in the search dialogue box. Many recent researches, including several in education, are available. ERIC, Education Resources Information Center, is a most fruitful source of information regarding recent research in a wide variety of educational topics.

---

From the grid, many kinds of information are possible. By looking along each row in turn we have an idea of the individual's definition of each construct in terms of the person's acquaintances; from each column we have a personality profile of each acquaintance in terms of the constructs chosen by the individual; a 'matching score' can be obtained by counting the number of compatible elements for each pair of constructs and taking this figure from the number of pairs expected by chance. Consequently, for the constructs A and B, there is one matching pair (the first element); by chance there would be three matching pairs, and so the matching score will be $1 - 3 = -2$. For A and C the matching score is $2 - 3 = -1$, and for B and C it is $3 - 3 = 0$. These scores are the basis of statistical procedures too complex for our needs, but by which a construct universe can be designed for an individual which Kelly claims will define the major personality variables of that individual (Bannister and Bolt 1973). Hence we see the clinical technique involving a description of *individual* personalities, referred to earlier as the *idiographic* approach to personality, as compared with the *nomothetic* approach which endeavours to portray human behaviour in terms of 'average' tendencies or norms, as in the work of Eysenck and Cattell (see later). The method has been used extensively in educational research.

## Psychoanalytic theories of personality

Theories under this heading are referred to by Vernon (1969) as 'intuitive' because the psychologists, usually those who adopt a clinical approach to their study of human personality, believe in an 'unlearned capacity for understanding others'. Clinical studies frequently depend on exploration of motivations and needs which cannot be directly observed.

Surely the most famous psychologist of all time is Sigmund Freud (1856–1939), the father of *depth psychology* (also known as *psychodynamics* or *clinical psychology*). The theory is extensive and has had a substantial following both as an instrument of research and as the basis for therapy among the mentally ill. But at present much of his theorizing has limited practical value to the teacher. For those who wish to dig deeper see Mitchell and Black, 1995. In this chapter we shall restrict ourselves to a consideration of the basic aspects of his theory which illustrate the 'intuitive' approach to personality; 'intuitive' is also used here to emphasize the subjective, and assumed unlearned, understanding of human conduct forming the basis of Freudian psychology.

Some psychologists have little time for the theories of Freud and his followers (Crews 1998). They claim that his view is based largely on supposition and limited experimental evidence; an 'unsinkable theory', according to Hudson (1966), which can be adjusted whenever conflicting evidence is found; his methods are said to be unscientific and employed biased samples of middle-class Viennese women with sexual problems; the proportion of 'cures' of the mentally ill brought about by psychoanalysis is little better than chance, and in any case Freud exaggerated much of what he did find. These are harsh comments for a theory which has given both the layman and the psychological world a seminal framework of personality composition along with a voluminous rag-bag of terms which permeate our language (repression, ego, Oedipus complex, etc.). More important, Freud's methods have opened up new approaches to the study of human beings (for instance, Piaget used techniques of a clinical kind in his earliest work) and have given a terrific stimulus to other fields of psychology such as motivation and development. Freud's gifts to psychologists and teachers were in drawing their attention to another way of looking at childhood, to the child's affiliative relationships with parents, brothers and sisters, to the existence and potency of infantile sexuality, to the possible unconscious nature of a great deal of human motivation, to the continuum between normal and neurotic behaviour, to the ambivalence of early child–parent relationships (Oedipus and Electra complexes) and to the enduring effects of many early childhood experiences.

## Some basic principles relating to Freud's work

Amongst other things, Freud's theory stresses these points:

- There are *life* and *death* instincts. The life instincts include sexual instincts (*libidinal* instincts), required for reproducing the species, and self-preservation instincts, relating to hunger and thirst, which are required for life preservation and maintenance (*ego* instincts). Of the death instincts, only one was defined specifically by Freud – the aggressive and destructive instinct.
- The behaviour exhibited by mentally ill people arises from the same motives as the mentally healthy.
- In addition to a *conscious* level of mental operations, where we are fully aware of mental events, there is also the *unconscious mind* (mental traces of past experiences which were once at a conscious level). Unconscious traces can affect our behaviour without our being aware of the source. Freud considered that the unconscious was a repository consisting of *repressed*, unpleasant experiences ('repression' in this context means exclusion from the conscious level, but see later), which could not be entertained at the conscious level. A *sub-conscious* or *pre-conscious* level was also postulated, consisting of traces which, though not in the conscious mind, nevertheless can be brought there by active recall of past experiences.
- Unconscious motives arise from *defence mechanisms*. These we shall elaborate shortly, but they are ways of behaving which enable us to protect ourselves from conflicting and intolerable situations.
- Early childhood experience is the key to later behaviour patterns. For Freud, the unfolding of sexual behaviour in childhood had much to do with later motivation and personality formation.

Freud believed the life and death instincts to be present at birth as a 'cauldron' of instinctual energy referred to as the *id*. The constraints placed on the expression of these basic desires by conscious effort on the part of individuals or as a result of social pressures, chiefly parental influences, lead to repression of the desires. The 'taming of the passions' of the id is made possible by the ego, such that many *defence mechanisms* replace the immediate gratification of basic desires and the motive energy is used in more socially acceptable ways. Exclusion from the conscious mind of less desirable solutions to instinctive cravings does not mean that they have disappeared altogether. Freud creates the *unconscious* mind, which contains the traces of unpleasant and repressed memories. Later behaviour is influenced whenever circumstances similar to the original experiences occur, but the individual is not aware of the source of his or her behaviour. The root causes of motives will break through only in special circumstances such as hypnosis, dreams and drugs or in a psychotherapeutic session when the defences are down.

We have already said, in Chapter 8, something of Freud's views on the basic motivating forces of human action. Briefly, we noted that at the heart of our driving force are the *libidinal* (sexual) and *ego* (biological) instincts. These natural forces he referred to as the *id*. Unleashed and uncontrolled, they would give rise to animal behaviour in violation of the cultural taboos of the child's society. Parental and societal pressures and constraints create in the developing child a conscience known as the *superego*, brought about by absorbing the mores of society (*introjection*). There is also a part of the personality in contact with the id, superego and the realities of the outside world. This is the *ego*, which acts as an adjuster between the raw requirements of the id and the censure of the superego.

To bring about a resolution to the demands of the id and the constraints of the superego, the ego resorts to *defence mechanisms*; these act as a shield against the otherwise intolerable conflicts between the naked demands of the human as an animal and the acquired conscience built up in childhood from the rules of society. The behaviour ensuing from defence mechanisms is, then, largely unconsciously motivated. Freud believed that simple slips of the tongue, pen or memory (Freud 1914), serious mental disarray, dreams and fantasies in waking and sleeping are all rooted in unconscious processes. Information about these processes can be teased out by devious means such as psychoanalysis, hypnosis or the use of drugs.

Let us look at a few simple illustrations of defence mechanisms which we might find in normal life:

**Compensation:** When an individual replaces one means of expressing a motive by some other, less direct means, compensation occurs. Couples who are childless, or couples whose children have grown up and left home, may treat a dog as if it were a child; parents who have missed a chance in their own education may make sacrifices to ensure success for their children.

**Identification:** When a person is moved to regard himself or herself as another, admired person, the result is called identification. Films or television programmes give opportunities for some to identify themselves with the people on the screen. Sometimes children try to imitate their parents as authority figures in an effort to get their own way.

**Regression:** Regression is said to have occurred when an individual utilizes behaviour more characteristic of an earlier stage in life. Even amongst adults it is possible to find those who occasionally resort to stamping, weeping, overt aggression and 'going home to mother' behaviour in an effort to get their own way. The logic of this is that as children they may sometimes have been successful in getting what they wanted by stamping or weeping. As adults they regress to this earlier tactic.

**Sublimation:** When an original desire is unfulfilled, sublimation is the redirection of one's activities into similar activity. For example, when students who want to become doctors are unsuccessful, they often sublimate their enthusiasm in other paramedical fields (nursing, physiotherapy, pharmacy, medical social work).

**Projection:** When there is a tendency to project one's faults or wishes into others, projection occurs. Occasionally an adolescent girl may claim that she is constantly being watched by boys – more a wishful thought than a statement of fact. Countries often accuse each other of stockpiling troops and armaments on each other's borders whilst in fact doing it themselves.

We shall see in a moment that projection is one method used by psychotherapists and depth psychologists as a means of exposing hidden motives.

**Rationalization:** Also called the 'sour-grapes syndrome', rationalization is really an example of self-deception where we try to find excuses for our shortcomings – too much study ruins your eyes, if you are not fond of reading!

**Repression:** This is the final example – the deliberate thrusting aside, because of social inhibitions, of the libidinal forces which are striving for expression. The repressed drives do not disappear; instead, they remain as traces in the unconscious and influence the actions of individuals when similar unpleasant situations arise.

All these defensive methods occur, according to Freud, as perfectly normal reactions. Where they get out of proportion *neuroses* develop as mental conditions such as anxiety states, phobias, obsessions or hysteria. Neuroses are the outcome of an inability to find recognized ways of adjusting to life's problems. The disorders which result affect emotional and intellectual functioning, although the neurotic patient is not deprived of contact with reality. In the most serious mental illnesses, known as *psychoses* (manic-depressive conditions involving delusions and hallucinations, or schizophrenia), the sufferer is completely dissociated from reality. The neurotic, on the other hand, has the problem of living in a real world and knowing it; the psychotic lives in quite a different mental world and dissociation from the real world does not worry that person.

Freud's theory did not stand still. His two closest disciples, Adler and Jung, stressed different sources of man's motivation, such as striving for self-fulfilment and superiority (the *mastery drive* of Adler) or the desire to belong (Jung). More recently, insecurity in childhood (Horney, Fromm), social interpersonal relations (Sullivan) and creativity have attracted the attention of the 'new' or neo-Freudians.

In addition to the criticisms raised at the start of this section, we should also note the difficulty of verifying the views of depth psychologists. Attempts to survey the research in support of Freud's theory were made by Kline (1982, 2nd edn; 1972, first edn). Kline's supporting evidence was criticized by Eysenck and Wilson (1973).

There is also too little consideration given to human adaptability; instead, we are led to believe that our basic personalities are founded in the first few years of life and that we must live with this for the remainder of our lives. Curiously, Freud places great emphasis on the impact of the family environment, yet neglects the impact of genetic factors and wider social influences. Only recently have neo-Freudians paid attention to the impact of social phenomena as a source of motivation. Later in the chapter we shall refer to some of the methods of depth psychology.

## Social learning theories

The main tenets involved in this section have already been mentioned earlier in the book. The subject is well covered in Mischel (2003) in 'Further reading'. All that remains is to draw them together and refer readers to the relevant sections.

Social learning theories are based on the behaviourist model. Personality development is a matter of learning from one's social environment. As we saw in Chapter 6, Skinner avoids referring to internal 'motives' and concentrates on observable and controllable behaviour. When social behaviour is rewarded and rewarding, it is repeated. 'Bundles' of habits are thus formed and these bundles, unique for any one person, define the personality of that person. Two points arise from this. One is that habits change and therefore the personality will change accordingly. This point is disputed by those (e.g. Eysenck – see later in the chapter for the evidence) who believe in the heritability of personality. Relating to this is the crucial importance of other people in the development of personality.

Rotter (covered in Chapter 8) took the basic Skinnerian view a stage further by insisting that people were not passive receptacles, but had expectations about the outcome of a course of action (expectancy theory), and this would influence their behaviour. In other words, they thought about the consequences of their actions. They were *aware* of what was going on and not merely passive recipients.

Further advances in the theories were proposed by Bandura (Chapter 6) including the concept of 'efficacy' (a special form of expectancy) in which people hold beliefs about their effectiveness, and 'modelling' (copying other people's behaviour). There is a difficulty in deciding whether the social learning theories are more concerned with motivation than personality.

# Trait theories of personality

The most influential paradigm has been *trait* or *inferential* theories of personality. They depend on scientific, objective analysis and are the province of the *psychometrician* (Kline 1993, 1999). The psychometric movement has its origins in the belief that our behavioural tendencies can be classified as *traits* or *factors* measurable using tests and evaluated chiefly by the use of factor analysis (Child 2006). The idea that humans possess personality traits is not a new one. We saw Galen's typology based on the body humours; also, Jung's extraversion–introversion typology arises from his conviction that there are stable patterns of personality characteristics. For the extravert the outer world is most important; the extravert is active rather than passive; he or she is given more to subjective feelings than to objective thoughts. Introverts resort more to the inner, personal world and are given to introspection rather than action. This is not a complete description, but it will suffice to show how Jung first conceived the concepts of introversion and extraversion. The same terms have been adopted by later psychologists, notably Eysenck, who, as we shall see, defines the traits more extensively.

## *Eysenck's work*

In a very long list of books (Eysenck 1947, 1952, 1967, Cook 1993a), H. J. Eysenck (1916–97) elaborated a most comprehensive objective approach to the study of personality. His theories have grown out of research with psychiatric patients at the Maudsley Hospital in London. Like the British school of thought regarding the structure of intelligence (see Chapter 9), Eysenck holds a hierarchical view of personality. At the highest point we find personality *types*, and in fact Eysenck expresses personality organization in terms of three basic types, *neuroticism–stability* (neuroticism in short), *extraversion–introversion* (sometimes contracted to extraversion for convenience), and *psychoticism–normality* (psychoticism in short).

---

### Further reading

In Eysenck and Eysenck (1976) and Eysenck (1970, 3rd edn) there are outlines of a revised approach which overlaps and partly supersedes his previous view in which Hull's theory of learning played a large part. Because this latter theory still appears in the literature and still finds a place in contemporary educational journals, it is briefly mentioned here. There are two basic postulates which involve the use of the concepts of *excitatory potential* (that is, the tendency to make a response to a given stimulus) and *reactive inhibition* (that is, the tendency not to repeat a response which has just been made). The two postulates are:

(a) Human beings differ in the speed and strength with which excitation and inhibition are produced and the speed with which inhibition is dissipated.

$\longrightarrow$

(b)   Individuals in whom excitatory potential is generated slowly and relatively weakly and in whom reactive inhibition is developed quickly and strongly, but dissipated slowly, are thereby predisposed to extravert patterns of behaviour. The reverse is true of the introvert.

The notion expressed in (a), that we are aroused to different levels by similar events, is widely accepted. Some people become much more excited by certain pleasant or unpleasant events than others. Similarly, some people take longer to 'cool off' after arousal than others. What Eysenck has done in (b) is to relate these differential levels of excitation and inhibition to the extravert and introvert personality. The extravert experiences far more involuntary rest pauses than the introvert. Because excitatory potential is generated slowly and weakly while inhibition is quick and strong, the actual excitation will not be high unless the driving force which is motivating the activity is very high. The important point to remember from Eysenck's work is that extraverts possess high levels of reactive inhibition, and this tends to make them less able to concentrate for any length of time on tasks requiring prolonged concentration. They require more lapses, or *involuntary rest pauses*, in carrying out a task, although these breaks are fractions of a second. The longer the task, the greater is the inhibition which accumulates.

By a similar argument, introverts are more readily conditioned than extraverts. The reason is that the involuntary rest pauses which extraverts experience more frequently than introverts interfere with the concentration necessary for conditioning to occur.

Eysenck also believes that intelligence is a fourth dimension. But these dimensions are thought to be normally distributed in the population, so the majority of people possess an admixture of the qualities underlying the types and therefore would obtain scores around the mid-point of each dimension. In fact, Eysenck's starting point was the mentally ill, that is, the extremes of the dimensions, and from these extremes he devised tests and questions which defined the dimensions. He is at great pains, nevertheless, to remind us that dimensionality implies a continuum of personality possibilities and not categorical definitions. Unfortunately, the use of such black and white terms as 'introvert' and 'neurotic' give the erroneous impression that people are either one thing or the other.

Figure 12.1 illustrates the interdependence of personality characteristics and the way in which Eysenck envisages a connection between the levels of personality organization which underpin the fundamental type. Qualities which characterize the introvert, such as persistence, rigidity, subjectivity, shyness and irritability, are known as *traits*. These in turn are associated with *habitual* ways of responding in similar conditions, so that in problem-solving or in mechanical tasks requiring vigilance we might expect the introvert to be, in general, persistent. In particular circumstances requiring vigilance we might find variations in the degree of vigilance displayed, but we would expect an introvert to be vigilant in most of his or her specific responses.

**Extraversion–introversion:** Extraverts, in Eysenckian terms, are outgoing, relatively uninhibited, fond of activities which bring them into contact with other people, not attracted

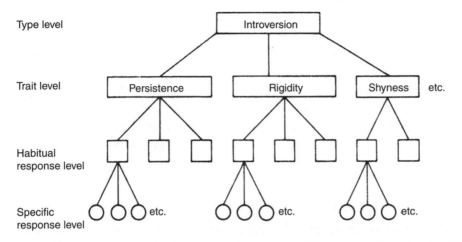

**Figure 12.1** From H. J. Eysenck, *The Structure of Human Personality*, p. 13, Methuen, London, 1953.

by solitary pursuits such as study, cravers after excitement, aggressive, unreliable, easy-going and optimistic. Introverts tend to possess the opposite of these qualities. Most of us, mercifully, possess most of these qualities to some degree – ambiverts. But this has been a particularly interesting personality dimension for educational psychologists. A glance at the list of traits just mentioned will soon reveal that they bear directly on a number of qualities of advantage in traditional educational settings. However, before we deal with this matter there are one or two theoretical issues to consider.

A theory posited by Eysenck (1970) attempts to provide causal connections between physiological brain mechanisms and the personality dimensions of extraversion and neuroticism. In Chapter 2 we mentioned the ascending reticular activating system (ARAS) as the seat of arousal in response to external stimuli. Eysenck proposes that there are individual differences in the extent of arousal which can be related to extraversion–introversion. 'Arousal under identical stimulating conditions is higher in introverts than in extraverts.' The differences, therefore, can be related directly to inherited qualities in brain structure. Another part of the brain, the *visceral brain*, is thought to be responsible for individual differences in emotionality as measured using the neuroticism dimension.

The theory leads to a number of propositions. The notion that we are aroused to different levels by similar events is not new. Some people become much more 'aware' of stimulation than others. Similarly, some people take longer to 'cool off' after excitation. If Eysenck's arousal proposition is valid, introverts, by implication from our knowledge of brain functioning, are less likely to develop inhibition in a task than extraverts. Thus introverts are more likely to be able to concentrate for longer periods of time in tasks requiring vigilance, i.e. they have longer spans of attention. We shall apply this later.

Again, introverts are more susceptible to conditioning than are extraverts. This could be a decided advantage in some formal educational settings, and may mean that the introvert is likely to be more readily socialized in childhood. We must not forget, however, that in using concepts such as 'introvert' and 'extravert' we are dealing with extreme cases. Most individuals are ambivert in their behaviour. For this reason, the findings we shall refer to later, in the absence of more refined measures, relate mainly to those with more extreme personality manifestations. Another complication in dealing with extraversion and neuroticism is the possibility of excessive visceral brain activity affecting the arousal mechanisms of the ARAS as well. In other words, those with high neuroticism scores are often in a state of arousal, and thus we have an interaction effect between extraversion and neuroticism.

### R. B. Cattell (1973, Kline 1993)

Another psychologist who has successfully applied psychometric methods (chiefly factor analysis) to explore personality, intelligence and motivation is British-born Raymond B. Cattell (1905–98), working in the United States. Using a different factor analytic approach (Child 2006) to Eysenck, he obtained 16 factors for adults (14 for high school pupils and the same for children) after many years of exploration. The 16PF, an inventory designed from these factors, has recently been revised as the 16PF Fifth Edition (Conn and Rieke 1994) referred to as 16PF5. The 16 *Primary Factors* (also known as *first order factors*) are shown in Figure 12.2.

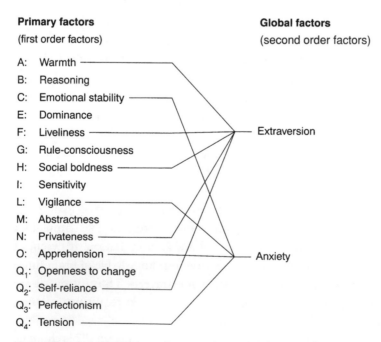

**Figure 12.2** Cattell's 16 Primary Factors and two Global Factors of Extraversion and Anxiety.

Because of the way Cattell analyses his data, it is possible to carry out a second factor analysis using the 16 Primary Factors as a new starting point. This gives several *Global Factors* (also known as *second order factors*), which are linked to the 16 Primary Factors. The two better-known ones are Exvia–Invia (which we met in Eysenck's analysis as Extraversion–Introversion) and Anxiety, which has common components but is not identical to Eysenck's Neuroticism. Three other Global Factors commonly identified are *Tough-mindedness, Independence* and *Self-control.*

This relationship needs some explanation. Cattell distinguishes between what he calls *source traits*, which are at the root of observed behaviour and believed to be the basic ingredients of personality structure, and *surface traits*, which are superficial, broad and detectable patterns of behaviour having their origins in source traits (Kline 1993).

An analogy may help. Surface traits have many underlying influences, some of which are source traits. A physician looks for symptoms (some are at the source trait level such as temperature, pain in a specific region, etc.). On putting these symptoms together, the patient might come up with an illness ('flu, heart condition) which is at the surface trait level. Neuroticism as defined by Eysenck would be a surface trait for Cattell, and the qualities which go to make up neuroticism (emotional instability, tenseness, timidity, etc.) would be source traits. Figure 12.3 demonstrates the connection between the two points of view. There are matters of detail in which the two would differ, for not all the 16 factors of Cattell will 'compress' to give the E and N dimensions of Eysenck. Nevertheless, there is a large measure of agreement between these two.

In Chapter 2 we outlined a proposal summarized by Baron-Cohen (2003) suggesting that females are more empathic than males. Research using Cattell's inventory lends strong support to this view. Smith, 1994, standardized the most recent version of 16PF5 for use in the UK. She found that females were significantly 'warmer' (Factor A) and more sensitive (Factor I) than males (see Figure 12.2 above). Both of these characteristics are found in empathic people.

## The 'Big Five': Costa and McCrae

For several years now Costa and McCrae (1992) have been working on a personality test which has five major factors and has thus become known as the 'Big Five'. Because of the all-inclusive nature of the concept and its brevity, it has become popular. The five dimensions which, like Eysenck's, are designed to be unrelated, are Neuroticism–Emotional Stability, Introversion–Extraversion, Openness–Covergence, Agreeableness–Antagonism and Conscientiousness–Undirectedness. But to achieve the level of predictive validity, clarity of the five factors and sufficient coverage of the personality domain, the 'Big five' have a long way to go (Child 1998b).

The approach of these and other psychometricians is not without its critics. The primary source of information for the detection of the dimensions is the pencil-and-paper test (see later in the chapter), which raises several questions. Do people tend to give socially desirable

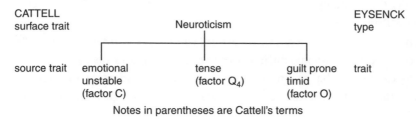

CATTELL surface trait — Neuroticism — EYSENCK type

source trait — emotional unstable (factor C) — tense (factor Q₄) — guilt prone timid (factor O) — trait

Notes in parentheses are Cattell's terms

**Figure 12.3** The relationship between the terminology of Cattell and Eysenck. Taken from D. Child, The *Essentials of Factor Analysis*, Continuum, London, 2006 (3rd edn).

responses to these tests and are there universal 'yes' or 'no' responders? How total is the profile of human personality; in other words, have all the relevant questions been posed on these pencil-and-paper inventories? How stable are the factors across different groups of people or for the same person, and where variations in the scores occur are they due to unreliable test material or to genuine changes in personality from one test to the next? Trait theory tells us something about personality structure, but what does it tell us about how human personality functions? These and many other questions are levelled at inferential personality approaches.

### The inheritance of personality traits

Trait theorists, in general, certainly Eysenck and Cattell, lend unequivocal support to the inheritance of personality characteristics. The reason is that evidence for the inheritance of personality components derived from self-report questionnaires is now overwhelming (Plomin *et al.* 2001; for a useful, broad discussion, see Bee and Boyd 2004; early work is reviewed by Cattell 1982 and Loehlin 1992).

Similar techniques to the study of intelligence were used. As readers will recall, this involved twin studies, neurophysiology and genetics (e.g., brain damage, genetic coding, psychopathology). Plomin *et al.* (2001) conclude that the 'basic message is quite simple: genes make a major contribution to individual differences in personality when assessed by self-report questionnaire'.

The evidence, and the debate surrounding this issue, also takes on a similar form to that dealt with in intelligence (Chapter 9). Results from twin studies (summarized in Loehlin 1992) show high correlations in adulthood using the extraversion (+0.51) and neuroticism scales (+0.46). Studies of the consistency in the personality profiles of babies lend further support (see the discussion of temperament at the beginning of the chapter; Eysenck 1990; Thomas *et al.* 1964). A thorough review of the research on genetic and environmental factors relating to personality traits is given in Loehlin, 1992 (see Plomin *et al.* 2001 for summaries). His total sample involved several studies in a meta-analysis (see Chapter 17) generating a massive sample of twins and other relationships (24,000). His evidence points to genetic factors accounting for 40 per cent of the 'variance' and environmental factors, the remaining 60 per cent. What does seem important is that the environmental factors are *non-shared.* This means the influential environmental factors are experienced by the twins independently of each other.

In exciting new research, links have been found between particular genes and personality factors (Plomin *et al.* 2001, Chapter 12). It is now clear that neurotransmitters (see Chapter 2) play an important part in the expression of personality, particularly dopamine and serotonin. Changes in personality accompany the taking of certain drugs. Serotonin levels, for instance, are raised by the drug Prozac. This has the effect of relaxing individuals and reducing their levels of stress and worry. The drug alters the functioning of the neurotransmitters which, in turn, alters personality.

**Neuroticism–stability:** The term *neurosis* was first used to describe a collection of abnormal mental conditions including anxiety, obsessions and hysteria. Thus, in hysterical cases physical symptoms sometimes accompanied a mental condition (sometimes referred to as *psychosomatic* disorder). Sickness and nausea caused by apprehension before such anxiety-provoking events as examinations or interviews may be physical manifestations of a mental condition. However, the term has developed a more particular meaning in Eysenck's model because we all possess some measure of neuroticism, ranging from stability to high anxiety, worrying unduly, panicking under stress and being over-emotional.

We have already seen that anxiety, a major correlate of neuroticism, has a physiological basis. The hypothalamus was noted as the centre of control for the autonomic nervous system and endocrine secretions via the pituitary gland (Chapter 2). The extent of hypothalamic reaction depends on many factors, not least of which are inherited autonomic functioning and the extent of the crisis which initiates anxiety. We have also mentioned how severing the frontal-lobe connections of the brain has the effect of reducing the level of anxiety displayed by individuals (frontal leucotomy). Arousal has also been referred to in connection with motivation. Here we saw that, in difficult tasks, high levels of anxiety could adversely affect performance, and we shall say more later about a possible application of measures of neuroticism to performance in academic work.

# The assessment of personality

The approaches to the study of personality at which we have been looking have generated many methods of assessing personality and our purpose here will be to give a summary account of the better-known methods. The task facing the psychologist concerned with personality study is very complex. As we saw from the definition above, the terms of reference are broad and the intrusion of intervening variables, both personal and social, makes analysis very difficult. One of the clearest expositions of the task facing the student of personality is given by Vernon (1953; dated, but still applicable). In this section we shall look at physique and temperament, experimental and physical measures which relate to personality, ratings made by self or others, attitude and interest inventories and the better-known methods of depth psychology, such as projection techniques.

**Table 12.2** Correspondence between physique and temperament

| Body type | Temperamental traits |
|---|---|
| Endomorph (round, fat, soft) | Viscerotonia (sociable, affectionate, lover of comfort) |
| Mesomorph (hard, muscular) | Somatotonia (aggressive, assertive, energetic) |
| Ectomorph (fragile, 'linear' physique) | Cerebrotonia (withdrawn, lover of privacy and mental activity) |

## Sheldon's typology of physique and personality

Galen's body humours mentioned earlier constitute one of the first attempts to link physiological characteristics with personality types. Kretschmer (1925) drew up a body typology which was developed and refined by Sheldon and Stevens (1942). The latter postulated three basic body builds having corresponding temperamental traits. The three basic body-build types are: *endomorphs*, who are round, fat and soft; *mesomorphs*, who have hard, muscular bodies; and *ectomorphs*, with a delicate, lean, linear physique. The biologists among our readers will recognize that Sheldon has taken the embryonic layers of endoderm (responsible for laying down the digestive system), mesoderm (lays down muscle, bone, heart and blood system) and ectoderm (lays down the surface structures such as the skin and sense organs, and the nervous system including the brain) as the predominant systems characterizing, respectively, the body-build types of endomorph, mesomorph and ectomorph. Each body-type dimension was rated by Sheldon using a seven-point scale. Therefore, a person with a normal physique would be rated 4 on each dimension, giving a profile of 4–4–4.

Sheldon claimed a close correspondence between these threefold measures of physique and the temperaments of an individual. Using nude photographs and detailed analytical interviews of individuals he concluded that it is possible to obtain a correspondence between physique and temperaments as portrayed in Table 12.2.

Although Sheldon has obtained some convincing correlations between physique and temperament, his work has found critics who have questioned the methods and statistics he uses. Also, there does not appear to be a satisfactory explanation for the changes in physique which often occur with age and which are not accompanied by a corresponding change in temperament.

## Physical experiments and personality (Mangan 1982)

Eysenck (1952) has been particularly active in finding a series of physical tests which appear to have personality correlates. The *pursuit rotor*, which is said to discriminate between introverts and extraverts, is one such device. A disc like a CD, with a metal stud near the edge, is set in motion on a turntable. The idea is to keep a metal probe, like a pencil, held in contact with the stud for as long as possible while the disc is spinning. Concentration and persistence are obvious qualities for this task, and those in whom reactive inhibition (see *Eysenck's work* above) is high will be at a distinct disadvantage. Thus the extravert is rendered less efficient at this game than the introvert, so an electrical timing mechanism which can measure accurately the contact time over a given test period will show introverts as having longer contact time than extraverts. Many other experimental ploys have been used to assess persistence, dark-adaptation, reminiscence, condition-ability, etc.

Cattell and Warburton (1967) compiled an astonishing compendium of hundreds of tests in existence up to the late 1960s and it is doubtful whether many additional ones have been added since then. The list includes projection tests and several of interest to information-processing models (see Chapters 9 and 10). However, there has not been any great advance in their use to date. They are untried, generally time-consuming to administer, taking longer than pencil and paper tests.

## Self-rating inventories of personality (psychometrics)

Certainly the most popular means of measuring such dimensions as neuroticism–stability, introversion–extraversion, tender-minded–tough-minded, apprehensive–placid, self-concept and the like is by the use of questionnaires. These contain items by which the individual can rate himself or herself, usually by agreeing or disagreeing with the items. The following are typical examples from personality inventories:

---

### Example

After each item is a space for answering 'YES' or 'NO'. Answer each item by putting a tick in the appropriate space provided at the end of each item which best expresses the way you usually act or feel.

           YES    NO

1  Are you a nervy person?
2  Do you like playing practical jokes?
3  Are you frequently moody?
4  As a child were you afraid of the dark?
5  I would rather work with things than with people.
6  I enjoy closely reasoned argument.

---

In some inventories, a separate answer sheet is completed using pencil marks in the chosen answer box, often one of three. Scoring can now be done using scanning techniques. An example might be:

---

**Example**

Wealth cannot bring happiness
**(a) true (b) in between (c) false**
I am quickly roused to anger
**(a) yes (b) in between (c) no**

---

Using factor analysis (Child 2006) a pool of items which measure the same dimension are assembled. In the examples above, the items have been chosen to represent different personality dimensions, but normally one would find several items in an inventory which are typical of each dimension being measured. In the self-concept field many devices have appeared (Cohen 1976), consisting mainly of self-appraisal scales. Test administration and interpretation require skill and training, so it would not be possible for all and sundry to obtain copies of these tests.

Much of the research to be discussed under the heading of 'traits and school achievement' has been carried out using personality inventories of the kind described above. Students should take the opportunity to look at test materials provided by their college and explore the kinds of questions which psychologists use for assessing personality types. Despite new developments, the four most used personality tests in English speaking countries are the:

- EPS (Eysenck Personality Scales)
- 16PF5 (Fifth Edition, Cattell's 16 Personality Factors)
- MMPI-2 (Minnesota Multiphasic Personality Inventory)
- NEO PI-R (Neuroticism, Extraversion, Openness: Personality Inventory – Revised).

The reliability obtained from testing and retesting the same group with the same or a parallel form of inventory has been encouragingly high. The closer the testing sessions in time, the higher is the reliability. Our reservations about such inventories include the problem of knowing whether changes in the score from one occasion to the next are due to the unreliability of the test material or are an accurate measure of personality change (or both). Moreover, we cannot be certain that *all* dimensions of personality have been catered for in the selection of items on existing inventories, a problem similar to that met in our discussion of intelligent behaviour.

## Attitude and interest inventories

In a sense, a personality questionnaire of the kind described above is an attitude scale. However, the term 'attitude' is generally reserved for an opinion which represents a person's overall inclination towards an object, idea or institution. Interests differ from attitudes in at least three important ways:

(i)   Interests are always positive, whereas attitudes can be positive, negative or neutral.
(ii)  Interests are always active, while attitudes can be dormant.
(iii) Interests are specific and functioning here and now, while attitudes are more generalized and may not function at all.

Attitude measurement has very wide currency, particularly in social psychology. Scales have been created for attitudes to almost every aspect of our lives from soap powders to school subjects. Measures attempt to detect one of three kinds: the cognitive attitude, which is what we actually *know* about an object or event; the affective attitude, which is what we *feel* about an object or event; and the behavioural attitude, indicating how we *behave* towards an object or event. Several techniques exist (Oppenheim 1966, Krebs and Schmidt 1993), of which the *Likert scale* is now the most used. It consists of an attitudinal statement followed by a scale running from one extreme of opinion to the other. Between these extremes, the respondent is given a number of points which express shades of opinion. For example, here are a few statements taken from an attitude-to-school questionnaire. The respondent indicates the degree of importance he or she attaches to each attitude by using the five-point scale of numbers after each statement:

1 –   absolutely essential
2 –   important but not essential
3 –   of only moderate importance
4 –   of very little importance
5 –   of no importance at all.

A typical item for, say, choosing the qualities of an 'ideal' school might be:

(a)  plenty of opportunity for sports and athletics
(b)  informal relations with staff
(c)  has social as well as academic activities
(d)  separates the sixth formers from the rest
(e)  is concerned with preparing students for future work.

Although five points have been used along the scale, it is quite possible to have seven, nine or eleven; odd numbers are chosen so that it is possible to give a central neutral response.

Interest inventories have taken four basic forms (Super 1957b). *Expressed interests* consist of extracting a direct statement of a person's liking or disliking for something. The answers tend to be very unstable, and subject to the transient moods of individuals. If you ask someone 'Do you like science?', the answer could vary from one day to the next. *Manifest interest* is shown by an individual's participation in an activity. But this could be misleading, e.g. when one participates in an action for other motives, such as companionship. *Tested interest*, not often used today, is ascertained using objective measures of the information known by a person. Interest in a particular field is assumed to lead to an increase in the information known in that field. Thus some believe that a measure of acquired knowledge is a partial indicator of interest (Cattell's motivation scales provide examples; see Cattell and Child 1975). Two sample questions of the kind used in general information tests are:

---

### Example

1   Here are the titles of five books. Underline the one written by Robert Louis Stevenson:
    Robinson Crusoe; Dog Crusoe; Coral Island; Treasure Island; Jungle Book.

2   Which of the following is true of a penguin?
    A penguin is (a) a mammal, (b) a bird, (c) a fish, (d) an insect.

---

*Inventoried tests* of interest are usually constructed for the purpose of choosing occupational preferences (see later, Chapter 13). The earliest kinds required respondents to place school subjects or occupations either in rank order or as *paired comparisons* (Chapter 13).

Research into the subject interests of children using the instruments mentioned has shown in general that their choices are not particularly reliable in terms of the subjects which they choose later when specialization is possible, in vocational choice or when interest is correlated with attainment. Correlations of interest with school subjects are low and add very little in the way of predicting success at school.

## Projection techniques

One of the sharp dividing lines between depth psychologists and psychometricians is in the techniques they employ in studying human personality.

The anti-depth psychology lobby, championed by Eysenck (Eysenck and Wilson 1973), feels that psychoanalytical sessions give an opportunity for the mind of the analyst to run riot in seeking to make sense out of the mumbo-jumbo of semi-consciousness. Jensen (1958) found little by way of validation for projection techniques and Eysenck doubts whether they are any better than chance in helping to cure the mentally ill. Crews (1998) also finds little time for the methods.

Nevertheless, the data generated from psychoanalytic studies are worthy of exploration and explanation. The clinical orientation of depth psychologists involves them in intuitive and subjective encounters with, in the main, mental patients. The purpose of these psycho-analytical techniques is to reach the recesses of the unconscious mind in an effort to expose inner, hidden motives which are said to be the cause of overt behaviour. Consequently, part of the secret is to disguise the purpose of these techniques from the patient by using indirect and veiled methods in the kind of questioning used. Then follows an interpretive session when the depth psychologist attempts to read into the findings the hidden causes of the patient's actions either with or without the presence of the patient. The psychoanalyst, therefore, is trying to break through the patient's defence mechanisms and discover their origins.

---

### Further reading

There are several projection techniques, of which *association* has proved to be an attractive one. Free word association requires a quick pairing of words from a given one; for example, given 'knife', what would its pair be? Most people would answer 'fork' to this stimulus word, but occasionally people give unusual and bizarre replies such as 'cell' or 'murder' which are thought to have hidden meaning. Continuous association requires a string of words from a given stimulus word. Incomplete sentences such as 'Other people . . . ' or 'My father . . . ' are also used, and the subject is required to finish the sentence. Whatever associations transpire are thought to arise from deep motives unrealized by the respondent.

*Story telling* is a method in which a person is asked to write a pen-picture of him or herself or an invented person in the hope that an individual will expose deeper motives about him or herself in the story. A third technique, *thematic apperception tests* (or TATs), has arisen from these. TATs demonstrate a projection device, in that they require an individual to make up a story from a picture he or she is shown and to say what might have led up to the scene in the picture, what is happening currently and what might happen in the future. By doing so one is thought to project one's own problems into the characters portrayed in the story. For a clear and readable account of an application of TATs see McClelland's work (McClelland and Steele 1972).

The *Rorschach ink blot test* is very well known. Again, a set of figures, originally made from symmetrical ink blots by inking a piece of paper and folding it down the middle to give a symmetrical pattern, is presented to a subject, who is asked to report on what he or she sees in the figures. The subject's responses are then analysed for deeper motives which underlie the choices. Those who favour the method have devised an extensive classification of replies from large numbers of people.

---

The interest of these tests to the teacher is academic, but for those interested in further examples, see Kline (1982). Should a child ever need the help of a psychiatrist, the teacher should immediately see that this help is given. Professional psychoanalysis has its limitations, let alone amateur psychoanalysis which could well aggravate rather than alleviate a mental condition; thus teachers should seek professional advice if they suspect that they have a mentally sick child on their hands.

# Self-concept

Self-concept has already been alluded to in Chapter 8 as an important element in motivation. In fact, the term 'self-concept' (and synonyms such as 'self', 'self-image', 'self-esteem') is a twentieth-century one. The roots of our present study of self-concept go back to William James at the turn of the century who raised the question of the difference between 'I' and 'me' – 'I' is what does the thinking and 'me' is what 'I' am thinking about! The concept appears in some shape or form in all the personality approaches mentioned above.

> ### Further reading
> The study of self-concept has grown massively in the past 70 years. For comprehensive coverage by one author see Hattie (1992), *Self-Concept*. For specific areas written by specialists see Bracken (1996), *Handbook of Self-Concept: Developmental, Social, and Clinical Considerations*. For a good introduction to the subject relating specifically to educational issues, see Colin Rogers (1982) *A Social Psychology of Schooling*.

Self-concept has been variously defined, but perhaps the definition offered by Burns is sufficient for our needs here. He suggests (Burns 1976) that self-concept 'is the individual's percepts, concepts and evaluations about himself, including the image he feels others have of him and of the person he would like to be, nourished by a diet of personally evaluated environmental experience'. He distinguishes between self-concept and self-esteem which he takes to be the outcome of the processes of self-evaluation and self-worth. It is a 'conscious judgement regarding the significance and importance of oneself or of facets of oneself'. As Colin (not Carl) Rogers (1982, Chapter 7) remarks, 'the self-concept is what we are like, while self-esteem is the degree to which we like what we think'.

There are many and diverse influences which will tend to shape the self-concept. The greatest impact is undoubtedly from parents, both in terms of inborn characteristics (tendencies towards being reserved, conscientious, tough-minded, self-sufficient) which might predispose us to determine, interpret and *react* to events, and in terms of the impact of external events in child-rearing patterns. Children watch and assimilate the methods parents use in solving day-to-day problems (calmly, systematically, impatiently), which helps to create the structures of the self-concept valuing processes. Added to this is the vastly important regard which the individual builds up about his or her own competence to solve these problems as a result of interaction with significant others (whether they give one confidence, how they react to one's solutions, etc.).

Until the mid-1970s, *the* self-concept was treated as unidimensional. Following a seminal paper by Shavelson *et al.* in 1976, researchers began to single out several dimensions. Their theory postulated both a hierarchical and a multidimensional model. The highest point was *general self-concept* which broke down into *academic, social, emotional* and *physical self-concepts*. These, in turn, broke down to sub-areas, for example, in academic self-concept, several school subjects appeared (English, history, maths and science). Physical self-concept divided into physical ability and physical appearance. This idea of subject-specific concepts is of particular significance to teachers (for recent refinements, see Marsh and Hattie 1996). One's self-image and self-esteem are also likely to be raised in subjects that one can do well.

Two important questions for teachers are:

**(a)** What is the relationship between a pupil's self-concept and his or her academic performance?

**(b)** Can modifications of pupil self-concepts be made and, if so, will they have any effect on academic performance?

In answer to (a), earlier studies – up to 1980 – showed zero to modest correlations between *general* measures of self-concept and academic performance. A meta-analysis (Hattie 1992, and see Chapter 17 for a definition of meta-analysis) puts the average at +0.20, which is not so good. Reasons for this low value were thought to be over-generalization of the self-concept measure and excessive use of standardized tests. The general measure would mask differences in self-concept between, say, maths and English. Also the standardized tests are only modestly correlated with school achievement. Since the early 1980s, new tests have been developed (Byrne 1996) which take into account the Shavelson model, and the results have been better. The correlations between maths self-concept and maths achievement (and the same for English) range between +0.45 and +0.70.

To answer (b) we have to decide on the causal direction – does increase in self-concept change (raise/lower) school achievement or do increases in achievement change (raise/lower) self-concept? The balance of evidence (Byrne 1996) gives the direction from academic self-concept to academic achievement. Thus, a change in academic self-concept can affect academic achievement provided the latter is measured using school marks and not standardized test results. There is also a link between this section and need for achievement (n Ach) discussed in Chapter 8.

Controversial research findings surround the question of school organization and its influence on children's self-concepts (Rutter *et al.* 1979). Certain school and class arrangements, such as streaming, special education, grammar, secondary modern, comprehensive, single-sex or mixed, have all been investigated inconclusively. Given the constraining effects of institutional settings, perhaps the strongest influence is related to attitudes, values and expectations of those who operate within the organization.

# Personality and school achievement

## Traits and school achievement

The definitions of neuroticism and extraversion given above have some clear implications for educational performance, especially in a system where long periods of study and concentration, both in general work and in preparation for examinations, are at a premium. Personality, then, plays an important part in learning and attainment, as well as the more obvious factors of intelligence, motivation and cognitive development. However, the *orectic* variables (variables other than the purely cognitive), especially personality, have, until recently, taken a subsidiary place in education thinking. Yet it would be surprising if temperament and drive were not intimately involved in performance. Common experience teaches us that fear and high anxiety can play havoc with the efficiency of performance.

In Chapter 8 we mentioned that drive and performance were connected, and the Yerkes–Dodson Law was one expression of this relationship. Evidence is accumulating to show that anxiety and drive are closely related. This being the case it is tempting to arrive at a picture something like this:

> low anxiety → low drive → poor performance
> moderate anxiety → healthy drive → good performance
> high anxiety → high drive → disrupted, poor performance

However, research (e.g., Child 1976 and 1980) shows neither a clear, curvilinear effect nor a correlation with the level in the educational system. Anxiety is so situation-specific and the tasks we ask of students so complex that it should not surprise the reader to see no consistent pattern emerging from the research.

The case for a positive correlation between introversion as measured by trait psychologists and secondary school or college attainment is substantial. When we look at the characteristics of the extravert in the definition earlier, it is not difficult to imagine why he or she is at a disadvantage in academic pursuits. If reactive inhibition is high, then concentration in studious tasks will be marred by involuntary rest periods, and vigilance must suffer. During examination revision the extravert will have difficulty in maintaining interest in what can be a boring task. Amongst primary school children (Entwistle and Cunningham 1968), introversion is not of as much advantage for girls as it appears to be for boys. But in secondary education (Callard and Goodfellow 1962) and university education (Child 1976, Child and Smithers 1971) the connection has been established. Using Cattell's personality scales, there is a tendency for academic success to be linked by age to certain introversion–extraversion traits. Younger students, while showing social interests (participating and friendly), have also introvert qualities of conformity, seriousness and self-sufficiency. Older students show all the introvert traits except aggressiveness and competitiveness. This age inversion between personality and achievement at around 12 to 15 years is discussed in more detail in Child, 1976 and 1980. Thus we find a tendency for those in higher education to be more neurotic and introverted than the population at large. By definition, the introvert avoids personal situations and enjoys bookish and conceptual pursuits, all of which are rewarded by the present educational selection system. Given students with sufficient intelligence to cope with the demands of higher education, the examination system itself selects not only by ability, but also by personality; it filters out the neurotic introverts. Moreover, amongst university students it appears that the science specialists are even more introverted and less neurotic than the arts specialists (Child and Smithers 1971).

In the present state of research in this field it would be wise not to make too much of the connections indicated above, especially at primary school level. More helpfully, it is important to be aware that personality characteristics play a significant role both in the act of learning and in attitudes towards the act of learning. Variations in performance are not entirely a question of intellect, motivation or thinking skills, but may depend on the personal attributes which can enhance or inhibit the quality of that performance. This fact alone is sufficient to justify continued research in this field.

## Type A behaviour (personality)

Type A behaviour was first identified and defined by two American heart specialists, Friedman and Rosenman (1974), who started their studies in the late 1950s. They noticed that a larger than average number of young heart attack victims possessed particular constellations of personality characteristics. They referred to those displaying the characteristics as *Type A* personalities. It is interesting to note that some of these appear in most people, but it must not be assumed that the possession of a few of the characteristics necessarily means that the individual is a Type A personality. There must be a regular, persistent appearance of the bulk of the defining features.

The following is a list of the main characteristics. For a fuller list, the reader is advised to look at the source book by the doctors (Friedman and Rosenman 1974).

1 Tries to do or think of two or more things at once
2 Cannot sit doing nothing – feels guilty when not working
3 Develops ticks, facial movements (eyebrow raising)
4 Has a 'thing' about punctuality
5 Gets impatient watching others doing a job he or she thinks can be done better
6 Plays to win – even when playing with children

7 Drums fingers impatiently
8 Does lots of arm waving when talking
9 Hurries others along who are speaking
10 Tries to steer conversation to her or his own interests
11 Tries to pack a lot of work into a little time
12 Shows no interest in aesthetic aspects of surroundings
13 Gets very cross in queues
14 Has the motto 'if you want something doing properly, do it yourself'
15 Pushes other people hard at work.

Since the early days of their theory, much research has been done with varying degrees of success in verifying their original speculations. A book edited by Strube entitled *Type A Behavior* (1991) contains many reports of recent research including one using meta-analysis (Chapter 17). These are in general supportive. The hard core of findings is that Type A behaviour is characterized by ambitiousness, aggressiveness, competitiveness and impatience. The overt signs are often muscle tenseness, quick-fire speaking style, abruptness and alertness, irritation, hostility and a penchant for anger.

Given this combination of behaviours, it is not difficult to speculate that Type A persons are not suitable as teachers and make very difficult students. They come across as impatient, intolerant, aggressive, 'no nonsense' and fidgety. They are frequently ambitious people who are 'pushy', have a lot of self-confidence and believe in the hard work ethic (fine, if it does not become obsessional). The price they sometimes pay is heart-related complaints, chief amongst which is stress (Chapter 8).

# Learning and teaching styles

The concept of *learning style* in education is important because it incorporates all those human attributes which help to determine and characterize a person's preferred approach to problem-solving. The Oxford Dictionary tells us that style is the *manner* of doing something as opposed to the *matter* with which a person is working. Therefore style has to do with personality and motivation, as well as the thinking tactics used for tackling problems. To misquote a dated, popular song, 'it's not only what you do, but the way that you do it'. But it has to be admitted that 'style' in educational psychology has become a much used and abused concept. There are many style theorists and we can only look at the most significant of these.

Successful patterns of behaviour most suited to our personal make-up and external constraints become established as habits of responding. These 'response sets', as they are called, become the bricks from which our personal lifestyles are built, and it is within this area that we might look for useful generalizations about achievement styles. Two crucial aspects of style are of particular concern. These are 'cognitive' and 'affective' style.

## Cognitive style

*Cognitive style* involves those characteristic patterns of perceiving and thinking which an individual exhibits in problem-solving. Sometimes the patterns are referred to as 'learning' and 'thinking' styles. Cognitive (or 'thinking' style) has been defined by Messick as:

> consistent individual differences in . . . ways of organizing and processing information and experience . . . These styles represent consistencies in the manner or form of cognition, as distinct from the content of cognition or the level of skill displayed in the cognitive performance. They are conceptualized as *stable attitudes, preferences or habitual strategies determining a person's typical modes of perceiving, remembering, thinking and problem solving.* (Messick 1976)

A lot of speculative work has concentrated on cognitive styles and we have space only to draw attention to a few important ones. Some have already been considered, as in the case of *convergence* and *divergence*, or Bruner's strategies of thinking, *focusing* and *scanning* in Chapter 7. Three others, which to some extent overlap, owe their origins to:

- Witkin – *field dependence* and *field independence*
- Kagan – *impulsive* and *reflective*
- Pask – *holist* and *serialist.*

In Witkin's theory (see Chapter 3), the difference established between field dependence and field independence arose from perceptual experiments. The central question 'are people able to keep the centre of interest separate from the background?' (see gestalt work on figure and ground in Chapter 3 under the heading of 'The nature of perception') led to the conclusion that some people are given to observe their surroundings *in toto* (field-dependent perceivers), whilst others are able to separate the figure from the ground (field independent). The act of faith needed here is to believe that perceptual differences will also reflect the same intellectual differences, that is children who perceive their environments in a field-dependent way will think this way as well. Vernon (1969) draws together some findings relating field-independent characteristics to other attributes. Field-independent people tend to be better at spatial tasks and mathematical and scientific studies, have self-sufficiency, are assertive and encourage independence of thought. It is important, however, to keep in mind the essentially perceptual nature of Witkin's work and resist, in the absence of firm evidence, the 'halo' effect of ascribing personality characteristics as well.

Kagan's concept of impulsive–reflective (Kogan 1994) is more concerned with decision-making in problem-solving. The child who makes an impulsive, off-the-cuff response is contrasted with the child who is prepared to pause and reflect on the nature of a question and the accuracy of the answer. The latter has been associated with a more analytical style of problem-solving, and Kagan's findings show that reflective children make fewer errors.

The third approach is that of Pask (Entwistle 1978), who distinguishes between those who are good at 'seeing things as parts of a whole' (holists) and those who are good at 'stringing sub-problems into sequences' (serialists). The distinction is seen clearly in people's preferences when studying new material. Some people like to get the feel of a new area of study and skip over the whole field before embarking on the details, whilst others prefer to pursue several lines of detail before trying to form a picture.

The common element in all these styles is the *way* people perceive problems and the effect this might have on the paths taken to a solution. So far, these theories have only pointed in directions with which we might experiment in the classroom. Certainly the direction of research in classrooms will be towards obtaining more detailed knowledge of the strategies children adopt in problem-solving.

For a tutorial on styles, see the work of Cornelius and Higginson on the following website: http://www.otis.scotcit.ac.uk/onlinebook/otisT1cs.htm

### Affective style

The second aspect of style – affective processes – involves those motivational and tempera-mental characteristics which influence an individual in problem-solving. The examples of cognitive style given in the previous section all correlate with measures of intelligence and problem-solving skills. The convergent/divergent thinking tests mentioned in Chapter 10 also correlate with conventional ability measures. However, a good measure of affective style should not be related to intelligence.

Kirton (1976) introduced a dimension, *adaptors* and *innovators*, which he and others have shown to be unrelated to intelligence and yet to give some additional information about a person's preferred affective style in terms of the criteria set out in Table 12.3. He draws a clear distinction between preferred style of problem-solving and capacity or ability in problem-solving (Kirton 1989). Adapting or innovating is the 'preferred mode of tackling problems at all stages. It is presumed to be unrelated to level or capacity, such as IQ, level of cognitive complexity or management competency.' Kirton believes the dimension is closely related to personality and should be regarded as an affective style.

The scale has been used largely in studies of organizational management, but on reading the list of characteristics in Table 12.3 it seems reasonable to assume some relevance to learning and teaching in schools.

## Styles and pupil performance

Under this broad heading we need to look at teaching styles, pupil styles and the effects of the interaction of these on achievement. In recent years, the study of 'styles' has become cautious and waned. The issue is well summarized by Galton *et al.* (1999) in their re-run

**Table 12.3** Characteristics of adaptors and innovators (after Kirton)

| The adaptor | The innovator |
| --- | --- |
| Characterized by precision, reliability, efficiency, methodicalness, prudence, discipline, conformity. | Seen as undisciplined, thinking tangentially, approaching tasks from unsuspected angles. |
| Concerned with resolving residual problems thrown up by the current paradigm. | Could be said to search for problems and alternative avenues of solution, cutting across current paradigms. |
| Seeks solutions to problems in tried and understood ways. | Queries problems' concomitant assumptions: manipulates problems. |
| Reduces problems by improvement and greater efficiency, with maximum of continuity and stability. | Is catalyst to settled groups, irreverent of their consensual views; seen as abrasive, creating dissonance. |
| Seen as sound, conforming, safe, dependable. | Seen as unsound, impractical; often shocks his opposite. |
| Liable to make goals of means. | In pursuit of goals treats accepted mean with little regard. |
| Seems impervious to boredom, seems able to maintain high accuracy in long spells of detailed work. | Capable of detailed routine (system-maintenance) only works for short bursts. |
| Is an authority within given structures. | Tends to take control in unstructured situations. |
| Challenges rules rarely, cautiously, when assured of strong support. | Often challenges rules, has little respect for past custom. |
| Tends to high self-doubt. Reacts to criticism by closer outward conformity. Vulnerable to social pressure and authority; complaint. | Appears to have low self-doubt when generating ideas, not needing consensus to maintain certitude in face of opposition. |
| Is essential to the functioning of the institution all the time, but occasionally needs to be 'dug out' of his system. | In the institution is ideal in unscheduled crises, or better still to help avoid them, if he can be controlled. |

of the ORACLE project (see later in the chapter) in which they say that 'Where ... the concept of teaching style can be helpful is in showing that certain patterns of classroom organization tend to enhance or reduce the capacity to engage in certain kinds of teacher–pupil interactions and that further, certain interactions show small but positive correlations with pupils' test scores.'

Style is a vaguer concept than personality. Consequently, the correlations with achievement are harder to track down. Indeed, some authors (Child 1985, Mortimore *et al.* 1988, Bennett 1988) have been sceptical of the applications of 'style' to education. Four questions have been raised which should occupy researchers in this field:

1   What is the relationship between the styles, and can they be rationalized in any way?
2   Are cognitive style characteristics stable or capable of modification in the student or the teacher? Can students or teachers readily adapt styles, or are they too well established to alter?

3  How important are *contexts* in discussing the appearance of style characteristics in teachers or students? Have we a clear idea of learning contexts? If it is reasonable to suppose there are different contexts, do they bring out of the student a range of styles?

4  How can a study of individual differences in cognitive styles be made so that the findings are helpful to teachers, especially in an increasingly technological era?

In considering teacher styles we would be interested in the contribution of cognitive and affective characteristics of the teacher in classroom tactics and their relationship to the achievement of the pupils. The interaction of cognitive styles of students and teachers has been looked at by Joyce and Hudson (1968) in research using medical students. From the results, they felt there were some indications 'that teachers and students having similar styles [convergent and divergent, in this research] formed the most successful combination' in terms of examination results. It would not be surprising if the style adopted by teachers did not have some effect on the learning of individuals with compatible styles, but the evidence from a large volume of American literature is not wholeheartedly supportive.

At the grosser level of classroom organization (also confusingly referred to as 'style'), Bennett (1976; Aitkin *et al.* 1981) has shown that children's achievement in reading, mathematics and English is generally higher in the more formal, teacher-centred, subject-orientated atmosphere, than in an informal, child-centred, discovery-orientated one. When personality is considered, the insecure and less stable child appears to work harder and more successfully in a formal class setting. In writing an imaginative story no difference could be detected in 'creative' output of children in the formal or informal settings. Changes in educational practice over the years since the Bennett study in the 1970s have been in the direction of more formal classroom arrangements.

One important conclusion from Bennett's work was the significance of *structure* – whether the atmosphere in a classroom is formal or informal. There are dangers in unstructured, free-for-all episodes. Children whose interests have not been roused can, and do, idle away their time on projects which are not demanding. To keep things stirring in this kind of class is exhausting and requires a vigilant, grasshopper-like creature who flits from child to child probing and directing their energies. Learning will not take place *in vacuo* and we cannot expect children to rediscover from scratch the wealth of knowledge, already assimilated by our culture. No matter how subtle we try to make the teaching–learning–thinking processes, well-founded knowledge must be transmitted so that new experiences can be built on a foundation of knowledge already amassed.

Therefore some structure is inevitable, and it is within this structure that we establish learning strategies. If the teacher chooses 'free discovery' sessions for his or her pupils, the sessions require careful planning to ensure that children's private enterprise ends up in productive assimilation of useful knowledge.

Another important piece of research looking at the styles adopted by teachers in classroom organizational strategies is known as the ORACLE project (Observational Research and Classroom Learning Evaluation) and was conducted at Leicester University (Galton *et al.* 1980, Galton and Simon 1980). It defined four types or styles, one of which had three manifestations giving six in all. The four styles, briefly, were:

1   *Individual monitors* – characterized by the low level of questioning and the high level of non-verbal interaction, consisting largely of monitoring the individual pupil's work (marking). The teacher using this style engages in the highest number of interactions concerned with telling pupils what to do, and to a lesser extent with marking work.

2   *Class enquirers* – place great emphasis on questioning. Most learning is teacher-managed. They begin new topics with a class, progress using the question and answer technique and walk amongst the children asking and answering questions.

3   *Group instructors*, whom the ORACLE team regards as one of the most interesting groups of teachers, tend to give a large number of factual statements compared with the number of ideas. They prefer carefully structured group work before engaging in discussion (hence the high level of information transference).

4   *Style changers* – come in three forms, that is *infrequent changers, rotating changers* and *habitual changers*. The ORACLE team found that 50 per cent of all the teachers they looked at fell into this category: 'They ask the highest number of questions relating to task supervision, make more statements of critical control and spend more time hearing pupils read than do teachers using other styles.' *Infrequent changers* were prepared, very occasionally, to change their teaching tactics to suit a change of circumstance. *Rotating changers* had groups of children working at tasks with one particular part of the syllabus being studied at any one table. The pupil groups rotated, passing from one curriculum interest to another with the whole class moving round at the same time. *Habitual changers* made frequent changes between class and individual instruction. There did not seem to be any plan to the changes.

Unlike the Bennett study, no overall best style emerged, although class enquirers' pupils were most successful in mathematics and language skills and those of infrequent changers made the greatest progress in reading. On the other hand, the style chosen by rotating changers was the least successful.

Galton and Simon (1980) finish with a discussion of leadership and management styles in the classroom, using some recent researches in this area, with a final consideration of the learning and teaching styles of children and teachers and their relevance to performance, particularly in the primary school.

The ORACLE research was repeated 20 years on and reported in 1996 (Galton *et al.* 1999). The '*style changer*' has disappeared. Probably because of the shift to a National Curriculum in the interim, the *rotating* and *habitual changers* were not identifiable in 1996. In turn, this has led to more direct instruction and less time spent on individual children's needs. Also as a result of the change to more whole-class teaching the *infrequent changers* style has also disappeared from the analysis.

The 1976 ORACLE team also identified three self-evident pupil strategic styles of *intermittent worker*, *solitary worker* and *attention seekers*. In the 1996 repeat, the first two categories reappeared, but instead of *attention seekers* two other categories surfaced. They were *eager participants* and *easy riders* (an inconspicuous, solitary pupil who likes to be seen on task, but works as slowly as circumstances allow).

## Summary

If the definition of personality involves a knowledge of the total organization of humans, then most avenues of educational psychology lead ultimately towards a greater understanding of personality. A classroom is not just a cognitive habitat, but consists of intricate personal interactions which deeply affect the learning and teaching processes. The pity is that psychologists are only scratching the surface of this very complex mesh of characteristic temperamental, intellectual and physical determinants of each person's adjustment and their relationship to scholastic achievement.

In this chapter we noted a distinction between temperament (which refers to inherent dispositions) and character (which is an evaluative term associated with social behaviour: honesty, cruelty, self-control).

Five broad approaches to the study of personality are the naïve, humanist, psychoanalytic, social learning and trait theories. The first kind of approach relies essentially on superficial observations of other people's behaviour. All the idiosyncratic, as well as the 'normal', experiences in our lives are compounded to give us thumbnail sketches of how people 'tick', and from these we establish a theory of human personality. The humanist emphasizes the whole being striving towards self-fulfilment. Psychoanalytic or intuitive theories, 'intuitive' because they are dependent on subjective assessments of human conduct, are led by the psychoanalytical school of psychology. Freud and his followers constitute the mainstay of this movement. Although psychoanalytical theories were outlined, it was suggested that there were few direct applications in classroom practice. Nevertheless, the particular contribution of this line of thinking was to increase our awareness of the importance to be attached to the lasting influences of childhood experiences as a source of adult motivation.

Social learning theories, based initially on behaviourist teachings, emphasize the central importance of learning from one's environment. The conditions accompanying development are crucial; role models such as parents, grandparents, teachers and friends are influential. Expectation of the outcome of a course of action is also valued by contemporary social learning theorists.

Trait theories were illustrated using the psychometric analyses of Eysenck, Cattell and the 'Big Five' theory of Costa and McCrae. In particular, the dimensions of extraversion–introversion and neuroticism–stability described by Eysenck were discussed in some detail and their bearing on academic achievement explored. The idea was mooted of a connection between the emphases and appeal of particular educational methods and corresponding personality characteristics. Introverts, for instance, tend to prefer their own company and tend not to be as inhibited by routine tasks (study, for example) as extraverts. Clearly, these are advantageous qualities for students.

The possibility of inheriting personality traits was discussed. The research is convincing and there seems little doubt that we do inherit certain characteristics measured using self-report inventories.

The problem facing psychologists who attempt to quantify personality characteristics was put into perspective by describing some of the assessment methods now in use. These included Sheldon's typology of physique, physical experiments, rating scales and inventories and projection techniques.

Self-concept, leadership and classroom organization are considered. Finally, cognitive and affective styles and pupil performance by reference to several recent researches are dealt with. In the latter, the most important issue is the interaction between the styles of pupils and teachers and the impact this has on academic achievement.

## Tutorial enquiry and discussion

(a) Gather the following information for tutorial discussion. Look at pupil record cards, reports, etc. and decide on the validity and reliability of any personality characteristics described. While observing children, which personality qualities would you consider to be really important ones from the point of view of both learning behaviour and conduct in class? What dangers exist in this kind of observation?

(b) Get your tutor to show the group some sample personality questionnaires, including projection tests. Inspect these in terms of:
  (i) the traits they purport to measure
  (ii) their fallibility – whether the responses are superficial, whether the respondent can falsify answers, how these problems have been countered by the test designer (lie detection, duplication of items, parallel forms of the tests, etc.)
  (iii) their particular use (age range, intelligence, verbal skills)
  (iv) the use to which teachers can put the results of such tests when applied to children.

(c) In tutorials, debate the various roles of leadership by teachers in the classroom and their possible impact on the pupils.

(d) Using the research from Bennett (1976) and the ORACLE project (Galton et al. 1980 and 1999), examine the critical aspects of styles which teachers appear to adopt in primary classrooms. Are they likely to be the same in secondary schools? Does the adaptor/innovator theory of Kirton add anything to our knowledge of affective styles?

## References

Aitkin, M., Bennett, N. and Hesketh, J. (1981), 'Teaching styles and pupil progress: a re-analysis', *British Journal of Educational Psychology*, 51, 170–86.

Anderson, N. and Herriot, P. (eds) (1994), *Selection and Assessment in Organisations* (up-date and supplements). Wiley: Chichester.

Bannister, D. and Bolt, M. (1973), 'Evaluating the person', in P. Kline (ed.), *New Approaches in Psychological Measurement*. London: Wiley.

Bannister, D. and Fransella, F. (1971), *Inquiring Man: The Theory of Personal Constructs*. Harmondsworth: Penguin.

Bannister, D. and Mair, J. M. M. (1968), *The Evaluation of Personal Constructs*. London: Academic Press.

Baron-Cohen, S. (2003), *The Essential Difference: Men, Women and the Extreme Male Brain*. London: Allan Lane (and Penguin Books).

Bee, H. and Boyd, D. (2004), *The Developing Child* (10th edn). Boston, MA: Pearson and AB.

Bennett, N. (1976), *Teaching Styles and Pupil Progress*. London: Open Books.

Bennett, N. (1988), 'The effective primary school teacher: the search for a theory of pedagogy', *Teaching and Teacher Education*, 4(1), 19–30.

Bracken, B. A. (1996) (ed.), *Handbook of Self-Concept: Developmental, Social, and Clinical Considerations*. New York: Wiley.

Burns, R. B. (1976), 'The self-concept and its relevance to academic achievement', in D. Child (ed.), *Readings in Psychology for the Teacher*. London: Holt, Rinehart and Winston.

Byrne, B. M. (1996), 'Academic self-concept: its structure, measurement, and relation to academic achievement', in B. A. Bracken (ed.), *Handbook of Self-Concept: Developmental, Social and Clinical Considerations*. New York: Wiley.

Callard, M. P. and Goodfellow, C. I. (1962), 'Neuroticism and extraversion in school children as measured by the Junior Maudsley Personality Inventory', *British Journal of Educational Psychology*, 32, 241–250.

Cattell, R. B. (1973), *Personality by Mood and Questionnaire*. San Francisco: Jossey-Bass.

Cattell, R. B. (1982), *The Inheritance of Personality and Ability: Research Methods and Findings*. New York: Academic Press.

Cattell, R. B. and Child, D. (1975), *Motivation and Dynamic Structure*. London: Holt, Rinehart and Winston.

Cattell, R. B. and Warburton, F. W. (1967), *Objective Personality and Motivation Tests: A Theoretical Introduction and Practical Compendium*. Champaign, IL: University of Illinois Press.

Child, D. (1976), 'Personality and achievement', in D. Child (ed.), *Readings in Psychology for the Teacher*. London: Holt, Rinehart and Winston.

Child, D. (1980), 'Affective influences on academic performance', in P. Gordon (ed.), *The Study of Education* (Vol. 2). London: Woburn Press.

Child, D. (1985), 'Cognitive styles: some recent ideas of relevance to teachers', in C. Bagley and G. K. Verma, *Personality, Cognition and Values*. London: Macmillan.

Child, D. (1998b), 'Some technical problems in the use of personality measures in occupational settings illustrated using the "Big Five"', in D. Shorrocks-Taylor (ed.), *Directions in Educational Psychology*. London: Whurr.

Child, D. (2006), *The Essentials of Factor Analysis* (3rd edn). London: Continuum.

Child, D. and Smithers, A. (1971), 'Some cognitive and affective factors in subject choice', *Research in Education*, 5, 1–9.

Child, D., Borrill, C., Boydon Jagger, J. and Bygrave, D. (1988), *Selection for Nurse Training: Making Decisions*, Nurse Selection Project. Leeds: University of Leeds.

Cohen, L. (1976), *Educational Research in Classrooms and Schools: A Manual of Materials and Methods*. London: Harper and Row.

Conn, S. R. and Rieke, M. L. (1994), *The 16PF Fifth Edition Technical Manual*. Champaign, IL: Institute for Personality and Ability Testing (IPAT).

Cook, M. (1993a), *Levels of Personality* (2nd edn). London: Cassell.

Cook, M. (1993b), *Personnel Selection and Productivity* (2nd edn). Chichester: Wiley.

Costa, P. T. and McCrae, R. R. (1992), *NEO PI-R Professional Manual*. Odessa, FL: Psychological Assessment Resources.

Crews, F. C. (ed.) (1998), *Unauthorized Freud: Doubters Confront a Legend*. New York: Viking.

Entwistle, N. J. (1978), 'Knowledge structures and styles of learning: a summary of Pask's recent research', *British Journal of Educational Psychology*, 48, 255–65.

Entwistle, N. J. and Cunningham, S. (1968), 'Neuroticism and school attainment – a linear relationship?', *British Journal of Educational Psychology*, 38, 123–32.

Eysenck, H. J. (1947), *The Dimensions of Personality*. London: Routledge and Kegan Paul.

Eysenck, H. J. (1952), *The Scientific Study of Personality*. London: Routledge and Kegan Paul.

Eysenck, H. J. (1953), *The Structure of Personality*. London: Methuen.

Eysenck, H. J. (1967), *The Biological Basis of Personality*. Springfield, IL: Thomas.

Eysenck, H. J. (1970), *The Structure of Human Personality* (3rd edn). London: Methuen.

Eysenck, H. J. (1990), 'Biological dimensions of personality', in L. A. Pervin (ed.), *Handbook of Personality: Theory and Research*. New York: Guilford Press.

Eysenck, H. J. and Eysenck, S. B. G. (1976), *Psychoticism as a Dimension of Personality*. London: Routledge and Kegan Paul.

Eysenck, H. J. and Wilson, G. D. (1973), *The Experimental Study of Freudian Theories*. London: Methuen.

Freud, S. (1914), *The Psychopathology of Everyday Life*. London: Penguin.

Friedman, M. and Rosenman, R. H. (1974), *Type A Behavior and Your Heart*. New York: Knopf.

Galton, M. J. and Simon, B. (eds) (1980), *Progress and Performance in the Primary Classroom*. London: Routledge & Kegan Paul.

Galton, M. J., Simon, B. and Croll, P. (1980), *Inside the Primary Classroom*. London: Routledge and Kegan Paul.

Galton, M. J., Hargreaves, L., Comber, C. and Wall, D. with Pell, S. (1999), *Inside the Primary Classroom: 20 Years On*. London: Routledge.

Goffman, E. (1956), *The Presentation of Self in Everyday Life, Monograph 2*. University of Edinburgh: Social Science Research Centre.

Hattie, J. (1992), *Self-Concept*. Hillsdale, NJ: Erlbaum.

Hudson, L. (1966), *Contrary Imaginations*. London: Methuen.

Jensen, A. R. (1958), 'Personality', *Annual Review of Psychology*, 9, 295–322.

Joyce, C. R. B. and Hudson, L. (1968), 'Student style and teaching style: an experimental study', *British Journal of Medical Education*, 2, 28–32.

Kirton, M. J. (1976), 'Adaptors and innovators: a description and measure', *Journal of Applied Psychology*, 61(5), 622–9.

Kirton, M. J. (ed.) (1989), *Adaptors and Innovators: Styles of Creativity and Problem-Solving*. London: Routledge.

Kline, P. (1982), *Fact and Fantasy in Freudian Theory* (2nd edn). London: Methuen.

Kline, P. (1993), *Personality: The Psychometric View*. London: Routledge.

Kline, P. (1999), *The Handbook of Psychological Testing* (2nd edn). London: Routledge.

Kogan, N. (1994), 'Cognitive styles', in R. J. Sternberg (ed), *Encyclopedia of Human Intelligence*. London: Macmillan.

Krebs, D. and Schmidt, P. (1993), *New Directions in Attitude Measurement*. New York: W. de Gruyter.

Kretschmer, E. (1925), *Physique and Character*. New York: Harcourt Brace.

Lewin, K. (1936), *Principles of Topological Psychology*. New York: McGraw-Hill.

Loehlin, J. C. (1992), *Genes and Environment in Personality Development*. Newbury Park: Sage.

Mangan, G. L. (1982), *The Biology of Human Conduct*. Oxford: Pergamon.

Marsh, H. W. and Hattie, J. (1996), 'Theoretical perspectives on the structure of self-concept', in B. A. Bracken (ed.), *Handbook of Self-Concept:*

Maslow, A. H. (1968), *Toward a Psychology of Being* (2nd edn). Princeton, NJ: Van Nostrand.

Maslow, A. H. (1970), *Motivation and Personality* (2nd edn). New York: Harper and Row.

McClelland, D. C. and Steele, R. S. (1972), *Motivation Workshops: A Student's Workbook for Experimental Learning in Human Motivation*. New York: General Learning Corporation.

Messick, S. and associates (1976), *Individuality in Learning*. San Francisco: Jossey-Bass.

Mitchell, S. A. and Black, M. J. (1995), *Freud and Beyond: A History of Modern Psychoanalytic Thought*. New York: Basic Books.

Mortimore, P., Sammons, P., Stoll, L., Lewis, D. and Ecob, R. (1988), *School Matters: The Junior Years*. Wells: Open Books.

Oppenheim, A. N. (1966), *Questionnaire Design and Attitude Measurement*. London: Heinemann.

Plomin, R., DeFries, J. C., McClearn, G. E. and McGuffin, P. (2001), *Behavioral Genetics* (4th edn). New York: Freeman.

Rogers, Carl R. (1970), *On Becoming a Person: A Therapist's View of Psychotherapy*. Boston, MA: Houghton Mifflin.

Rogers, Colin (1982), *A Social Psychology of Schooling*. London: Routledge and Kegan Paul.

Rutter, M., Maughan, B., Mortimore, P. and Ouston, J. (1979), *Fifteen Thousand Hours*. London: Open Books.

Shavelson, R. J., Hubner, J. J. and Stanton, G. C. (1976), 'Self-concept: validation of construct interpretations', *Review of Educational Research*, 46, 407–41.

Sheldon, W. H. and Stevens, S. S. (1942), *The Varieties of Temperament: A Psychology of Constitutional Differences*. New York: Harper.

Smith, E. E., Nolen-Hoeksema, S., Frederickson, B. L., Loftus, G. R., Bem, D. J. and Maren, S. (2003), *Atkinson and Hilgard's Introduction to Psychology* (14th edn). Belmont, CA: Wadsworth/Thomson.

Smith, P. (1994), *The UK Standardization of the 16PF5: A Supplement of norms and Technical Data*, IPAT. Test distributed in the UK by OPP, Oxford.

Strube, M. J. (ed.) (1991), *Type A Behavior*. Beverly Hills, CA: Sage.

Super, D. E. (1957b), *The Psychology of Careers: An Introduction to Vocational Development*. New York: Harper.

Thomas, A., Chess, S., Birch, H. G., Hertzig, M. E. and Korn, S. (1964), *Behaviour Individuality in Early Childhood*. London: University of London Press.

Vernon, P. E. (1953), *Personality Tests and Assessments*. London: Methuen.

Vernon, P. E. (1969), *Intelligence and Cultural Environment*. London: Methuen.

## Further reading

Bracken, B. A. (1996), *Handbook of Self-Concept: Developmental, Social and Clinical Considerations*. New York: Wiley. This recent text is the most comprehensive and even-handed book available.

Burns, R. B. (1982), *Self-Concept Development and Education*. London: Holt, Rinehart and Winston. Despite its age, the book is useful in its orientation to teachers and teaching.

Cook, M. (1993a), *Levels of Personality* (2nd edn). London: Cassell. Despite the off-putting chapter titles, it is easy on the eye, and has an up-to-date introduction.

Kline, P. (1983), *Personality: Measurement and Theory*. London: Hutchinson.

Kline, P. (1993), *Personality: The Psychometric View*. London: Routledge.

Kline, P. (1999), *The Handbook of Psychological Testing* (2nd edn). London: Routledge. Technical, but full of useful detail for those wanting to research the area.

Mischel, W. (2003), *Introduction to Personality: Towards an Integration* (7th edn). Chichester: Wiley. A standard text for psychology students.

## Useful websites

For a tutorial on cognitive styles, see the work of Cornelius and Higginson on the following website:
http://www.otis.scotcit.ac.uk/onlinebook/otisT1cs.htm.

The ERIC (Education Resources Information Center) website is:
http://eric.ed.gov

# Psychology and Career Choice

## Implications for teachers

- An important contemporary offering in secondary education is to give young people the opportunity to realize a stable, satisfying and rewarding career.
- All kinds of work are important to an economy and young people can get satisfaction from a wide range of choices.
- Various psychological theories of occupational preferences give only a sketch of the problems encountered by teachers.
- An efficient school career guidance and counselling system is crucial in secondary, further and higher education.

We cannot survive without working and education is the most important means by which we make ourselves marketable in the workplace. For most, this happens immediately after secondary, further or higher education. Sometimes we end up in jobs we never dreamt we would. Others have little choice because they have to stay local and take whatever jobs are available. Most of us have really no idea what a job entails until we are actually doing it. Some occupations are fortunate in having a training period when people can discover what a job is about, such as school practice in preparation for teaching. But most employment starts with 'suck it and see'!

# Background to the present position

Since this book first appeared in the 1970s, the prospects and nature of careers have changed dramatically. For example, in the 1950s, less than 10 per cent of school leavers went to university. Now, the figure is over 40 per cent and rising to a target of 50 per cent by 2010. Skilled workers in, for instance, the construction industry (such as building, plumbing, decorating, carpentry), clerical, service industries and nursing, utility specialists (electricity, gas and water), the motor vehicle industry, IT specialists (TV, telephone and computing) are becoming a precious commodity. In fact, some manufacturing of clothes and household hardware is not done in this country. Pressures from home and school, transparently encouraged by the Government, have placed tremendous importance on achieving broadly academic qualifications. Unfortunately, this has shifted the focus of young people's ambitions from skill-based careers to academic ones with, in some cases, little hope of realizing a satisfying career. Targets in English, maths, science and ICT have only a limited relevance to the 20 per cent of school leavers at 16 years who want trade skills. In addition, many who go on to further education leave early to take up work. Changes in attitudes towards female employment have occurred, although equality of opportunity and pay are still contentious issues.

The important role of our educational system in forming and directing occupational preferences has not, until recently, been fully appreciated in Great Britain. The many psychological and sociological influences brought to bear on young people by the family, peers, school and government in shaping career life-chances tend, in the past, to have been ignored in our educational arrangements. In the USA, career and personal counselling are well established as necessary elements in the educational system, and there is no doubt that their value has at last been recognized in this country.

In the 1990s there were several government initiatives to encourage careers education and guidance. Initiatives like the introduction of careers education and guidance as one of five cross-curricular themes in the National Curriculum, the introduction of Training Credits, more systematic resources and information about careers in schools through the Training and Enterprise Council (TEC), the development of vocational qualifications (VQs of various kinds), the creation of a Learning and Skills Council (LSC), more funding from the DfES specifically to the Careers Service to provide more guidance support in schools, and the involvement of the School Curriculum and Assessment Authority and its successor body the Qualifications and Curriculum Authority (QCA) have all happened in the last ten years. Despite scepticism about the implementation and effects of career guidance initiatives (Cleaton 1993; also http://www.guidancecouncil.com), the coming years will see a growth in career education and guidance in our schools. Specialist teachers will play an ever increasing and significant coordinating role within schools and with the Career Services, using, in part, psychological material and its evaluation.

Perhaps the most striking feature of getting a job was, and to some extent still is, the apparently haphazard or coincidental way in which young people end up in work. Talent-matching, either cognitive or affective, between individuals and the work they undertook was more a matter of chance than choice. Work choice was, and still is to some extent, governed far more by availability in circumstances such as geographical distribution of industries (Raby and Walford 1981), regional manpower needs or the financial position of the family and its willingness to be mobile in pursuit of work than by medium-term or long-term analysis of talent (Early Leaving Report 1954, Crowther Report 1959). The emergence of guidance and counselling in our schools is, of course, in response to a great many related factors. Change in political ideology towards an egalitarian system, which attempts to provide for the underprivileged and adds a measure of security in employment, is one reason. Again, the growth of our economy requires employees who are more adaptable to work situations and more highly, and differently, skilled than previous generations. With fewer unskilled and semi-skilled jobs available, it becomes ever more important to seek out the talents of people to avoid wastage and disappointment. But the really crucial point is for individuals to find work which is personally satisfying whilst being useful to the community.

Despite this gloomy picture, psychologists have shown that there is a relationship between intellectual and personality characteristics and the demands of certain occupations as well as the sex of workers. This chapter can do no more than introduce students to some elementary theories having a bearing on careers education and guidance in schools. In addition, we shall look at the systematic attempts to discover useful psychological factors in vocational choice.

# Theories of careers development

Prior to the 1950s, no thoroughgoing theory describing careers development had been formulated. No one had drawn together the rapidly accumulating results of research, chiefly in the USA, to provide a working model. Indeed, up to then, three broad approaches had been suggested, based more on speculation than on empirical research. These early speculations about occupational choice are known as:

- Accident
- Impulse
- Talent-matching.

Some people are convinced that their entry into a career arises from some unexpected incident thought to be beyond their control. 'I was watching my teacher one day and suddenly thought that I wanted to do a similar job.' This accident hypothesis takes no account of personal and social factors which in unperceived ways might have rendered one range of jobs more appealing than others.

Impulse theories stress the unconscious drives laid down in childhood and their pervading influence on the pattern of occupational choice. In later life, particular occupations will gratify particular personality needs. Galinski (1962; Vachmann 1960) was able to show that discipline in the early lives of physicists was rigid, stressed obedience and was consistent and predictable while, for clinical psychologists, childhood discipline had been flexible, unpredictable and appealed more to 'feelings'. Impulse theory shifts the emphasis to internal factors and early influences. Both this and the accident viewpoint place the individual in a somewhat passive role, helplessly drifting in the currents of chance or irrevocable influence of infantile experience.

The third approach, talent-matching, attempted to fit a person's expressed occupational interests with previously determined interest profiles of people already established in occupations. Strong (1948), who produced a vocational-interest questionnaire, was a pioneer in this field. The weakness of these questionnaires is the limited information they afford. It is not possible to evaluate from the responses why or how a person arrives at a choice of job, so vital when we want to know the effect of educational or home circumstances. The information they provide is very much 'after the fact'. Again, interests tend to be unstable in early life, hence one cannot be certain about the lasting appeal of a choice. However, interest inventories certainly have a place as part of the picture we build up about an individual's occupational possibilities.

Attempting to classify the ideas of theorists in vocational development and guidance is difficult. Whatever else, psychology has played a significant part (for a summary see Watts *et al.* 1996). One analysis is:

- *Person-environment fit* (*trait-and-factor* and *talent matching* (mentioned above) are examples)
- *Developmental* (following the study of career development theories)
- *Personal-centred* (client-centred approaches)
- *Goal-centred* (social learning theory which also overlaps with the self-concept theory mentioned in Chapter 12).

These will be developed in the following sections.

It is significant that these orientations closely relate to the four approaches to the study of personality discussed in Chapter 12. Person-environment fit is based on the trait or psychometric view; the developmental theories bear a remarkable resemblance to Freudian theory; person-centred approaches are based on the humanist tradition; goal-centred theories are based on social learning or the behaviourist tradition. It is not a surprise to find career specialists basing their client contact on personality theories.

Others (Law 1996) also include a dimension involving social psychologists' approaches. The psychological approaches above concentrate on the impact of individual differences and self-concept in occupational selection. Social psychologists are also concerned with environmental impact. Here we have *opportunity-structure* and *community-interaction* theories which place greater emphasis on factors outside the person as chiefly responsible for work opportunities. With the former, a person's social position is regarded as important in job opportunities. Individuals become trapped because they lack either support or opportunity. Family traditions of work, peers and neighbourhood are central influences which define the criteria with which a person identifies. Breaking out of the mould does happen. Many teachers, for example, come from humbler backgrounds than the 'semi-professional' group to which they belong as teachers. Community interaction is what it says – we are influenced by our encounters with others. This figures in the goal-centred theory above (social learning theory) and will be elaborated later.

# Trait-and-factor theories

As we saw in Chapter 12, trait theories are based on the premise that all human beings have stable characteristics which can be measured. Second, the abilities and personal qualities relating to particular occupations are also determined using standardized tests on those already successful in those occupations, giving profiles assumed to be needed in that work environment. The personal and work environment characteristics are then compared for congruence – the closer, the better. A good example is found in the work of Cattell who provides personality *specification equations* for a variety of occupations (Cattell *et al.* 1970). Selection of this kind is intended to choose those better adapted and probably having a preference for the occupations coming closest to their profiles.

In this approach, congruence or talent-matching is looked for between the characteristics and interests of the person and the demands of the work environment. Hence these are also referred to as 'person-environment fit' theories.

## Rodger's Seven Point Plan

We owe the earliest attempt at matching to Rodger (1970) and his *Seven Point Plan*. He devised a systematic exploration of a client's potentialities. Below, we look in detail at the seven points, not so much to promote Rodger's plan, but because they act as a very useful starting point for exploring an individual's profile – necessary information no matter what approach is used.

The resulting profile can be matched against the profiles of people already in work and against the special intellectual, physical or social challenges of the work itself. This is not the only format, but it is sufficiently comprehensive to overlap with all the others. Its particular merit is in directing our attention to some really essential factors which affect occupational choice and performance. Rodger's seven points, although examined separately, should ultimately be considered together. The results also represent a poorly focused snapshot in the life of the client at a time when, as Ginzberg observed (see later), the choices are still only tentative and partially informed. Let us look at Rodger's seven points – physical make-up, attainments, general ability, special aptitudes, interests, disposition and circumstances – in some detail. A book by Kline (1975) gives further helpful information on exploring these determinants.

### Physical make-up

It is self-evident that certain physical attributes are essential for some jobs. Small stature bars a man or woman from entering some police forces, although a person must be small in order to work as a jockey! Physical handicaps place limitations on the kind of work people can attempt. The loss of limbs or senses imposes some restrictions. Physical stamina obviously plays a part in fitting boys or girls for jobs requiring tough constitutions. Knowledge of physical prowess is more likely to operate in a negative sense in excluding people with deficiencies or disabilities from certain jobs rather than in deeming them suitable. Physical or personal attractiveness and an ability to handle people are useful qualities for work involving contact with others, as in the case of shop assistants and social work.

### Attainments

Bearing in mind the limitations referred to in Chapter 16, scholastic achievement is one source of information. To begin with, the level of education and success at school are widely used by employers as measures of potential competence. Certification, amount and quality of schooling and progress through the school are most commonly used as evidence for suitability and entry level to industry or higher education. Whatever might be said about the unreliability of public examinations as an indicator of occupational competence, employers continue to use exam results, such as the GCSE 'O' and 'A' level and degree classifications, as one of the first criteria for reducing the application list. This is particularly true in times of massive unemployment when there may be many applicants for few jobs. Often the first sifting of application forms consists of selecting those with the highest formal qualifications.

The vocational counsellor needs a well-documented record card of clients' achievements, together with background information from teachers and parents. Knowledge of weaknesses is just as valuable as knowledge of strengths: clients who have great difficulty with, say, number skills might be discouraged from entering certain occupations such as accountancy.

### General cognitive ability

Our educational system has for many years used general ability as one of several criteria, for choosing children for, or excluding them from, certain kinds of educational opportunity, at least in the early stages of secondary education. An up-to-date assessment of a client's *general* level of ability can give a clue to broad occupational horizons which may satisfy his or her intellectual powers. Obviously a pupil with low general ability would never obtain the level of attainment needed for a career in medicine. A bright boy or girl *might* be dissatisfied with a job requiring little use of the intellect, particularly if it involved routine concrete operations.

There are many reasons which have nothing to do with intelligence for under-performance in public examinations. A pupil may dislike a subject or the teacher. There may be no motivation to perform well or little encouragement from home. A pupil may have been tempted to leave school at 16 in order to earn money rather than staying on at school or college for several years with little more than a grant. Intelligence tests can often give a more objective estimate of a person's abilities than school marks, exam results or teachers' estimates.

Examples of occupations requiring applicants to undergo testing are the police and nursing. In the latter case, the author designed a test, the *DC test* (Child and Borrill 1990) for applicants to nursing who had not obtained the statutory entry requirement of at least five passes in 'O' level or GCSE as part of the selection process for entry to nurse training. There were many keen applicants of all ages who would have liked to have entered nursing but had not managed to achieve five passes. The DC test was designed to overcome this problem for those with the necessary ability. About a third of those who took or retook a parallel version of the test succeeded, thus increasing the potential entrants to nursing.

### Special aptitudes

As we saw in the chapter on human ability, there are a number of specific capacities, such as memory, spatial perception, number manipulation, manual dexterity, artistic ability, music and verbal fluency, which may be present to a greater or lesser extent in individuals in spite of a modest overall general intelligence. Combinations of these aptitudes can give composites such as clerical and musical talent. Possession of a special aptitude can compensate to some extent for a deficiency in general intelligence, provided, of course, that the deficiency is not marked. The aptitude may be pressed into service in certain kinds of work (Vernon 1950). For example, even moderate intellectual power together with numerical aptitude can be an advantage in work requiring manipulation of numbers, as in accountancy, but not necessarily in higher mathematics, which requires a high general intelligence.

*Interests*

The exploration of occupational interests and dispositions (see the next section) has become an important industrial enterprise (Williams 1994). A number of companies now offer expertise in job selection, evaluation of employees and training in the use of psychometric tests. These tests consist of ability, aptitude and interest inventories, personality tests and occupational inventories.

The design of occupational inventories remains a matter for research and their administration and interpretation are the subject of several courses. Super (1957a and b) has given a handy classification of interests in terms of the methods applied to their assessment. He suggests four categories: expressed, inventoried, tested and manifest interest. Of these, we are concerned with inventoried interest tests.

---

### Further reading

The growth of psychological testing in interest and personality inventories has been almost exponential over the past 40 years. R. S. Williams has done a survey of test usage for selection in the UK. His findings are reported in *The Psychologist* (1994). At the last count (1994) there were well over 500 companies dealing with various aspects of occupational selection. Research producing such inventories continues unabated. The older ones, such as the Strong Vocational Interest Blank, the Kuder Preference Record and the Thurstone Interest Schedule in the USA, and the Rothwell-Miller Interest Blank, the Connolly Occupational Interests Questionnaire, the Factual Interest Blank and the APU Occupational Interests Guide developed by the Applied Psychology Unit, University of Edinburgh in this country, are rarely used now, although the recent ones have built on the shoulders of the earlier versions. They have been replaced by those produced by, for example, the JIIG-CAL system mentioned above, the SHL occupational interest inventories or Team Focus's Office Systems Battery to measure the skills required within an office environment. In addition to these outlets, the Careers Research and Advisory Centre in Cambridge (CRAC) and the Careers and Occupational Information Centre in Sheffield (COIC) are active in producing courses and information about tests in use.

Super (1957a and b) devised the following. 'Expressed' interests are disclosed by asking a person to name his or her choice directly. In younger children these choices are subject to change and therefore are not reliable, although exceptions exist where, for example, family pressure leaves little to chance in career expectations for the children. Ranking and rating methods fall into this category; in these, pupils are presented with a list of school subjects or occupations and are asked to reassemble them in order of preference. 'Inventoried' interests are examined using questionnaires endeavouring to discover preferences by objective methods. The vocational-interest inventories of Strong, Kuder and Thurstone are based on this principle and make the assumption that a person with interest patterns similar to those of people already committed to, and successful in, an occupation is most likely to follow that occupation. 'Tested' interest relies on the assumption that an interested person will learn more about a topic than one who is not motivated. By sampling a person's knowledge it may be possible to assess the ultimate

$\longrightarrow$

preference. 'Information' and 'culture' tests are examples which seek to discover the level of accumulated knowledge as a measure of interest. Finally 'manifest' interest is revealed by a person's strength of participation in activities, such as an interest in sport which leads a child to playing that sport. But this method of assessment can be highly unreliable, in that the centres of this kind of interest often show marked changes.

Commonly, the client is required to make a choice between two or three occupations or activities involved in an occupation, over a wide range of vocations (sometimes known as the method of *paired comparisons* for two-way choices). The same occupation turns up in combination with all the others so that an order of preference can be obtained.

As a sample of how *paired comparisons* works, let us imagine that we give a client three occupations in every possible combination of pairs presented in the following way:

Place a tick against the one of each pair of occupations you would probably prefer:

| | | | | | |
|---|---|---|---|---|---|
| doctor | ☐ | bricklayer | ☐ | commercial traveller | ☑ |
| commercial traveller | ☑ | doctor | ☑ | bricklayer | ☐ |

Preferences fall into an order, with commercial traveller = 2, doctor = 1, bricklayer = 0. Straightforward counts of the number of times each activity is given preference are used for a profile. Note that calculating such quantities as a mean is pointless where the scores obtained are inter-related. Apart from anything else, the scores are *relative* to each other: as 'commercial traveller' has two endorsements, it would be impossible for either 'doctor' or 'bricklayer' to have the maximum of two. Therefore the profile must be viewed as a whole and not in isolated parts.

The most comprehensive inventory is found in Miller's work (1968), consisting of twelve 'stereotype categories and representative occupations'. Examples are given below. In this inventory a ranking method is used between the twelve categories.

## Further reading

The *Manual of the Rothwell-Miller Interest Blank* (Miller 1968) has some useful examples of occupational categories. Illustrations from this inventory are given here to demonstrate these categories. The twelve categories are: 'outdoor' (e.g. farmer, surveyor, physical education teacher); mechanical (civil engineer, motor mechanic, weaver); computational (auditor, cashier, income tax clerk); scientific (industrial chemist, laboratory assistant, geologist); persuasive (sales manager, insurance salesman, radio announcer); aesthetic (artist, photographer, window-dresser); literary (journalist, librarian, book reviewer); musical (music teacher, pianist, music-shop assistant); social service (teacher (primary), social worker, missionary, overseas aid worker); clerical

$\longrightarrow$

(bank manager, office worker, town clerk); practical (carpenter, house decorator, cook); medical (doctor, physiotherapist, pharmacist).

The evidence for a marked positive connection between success in an occupational pursuit and a stated interest, using an inventory, is by no means conclusive. In general, it seems that interest patterns of young people of 14 years are beginning to look like those of adults (compare Ginzberg *et al.* 1951, in the 'Developmental theories' section below). Thus the inventories can be used to identify the general direction of vocational aspiration (and assumed concomitant success). In addition, the inventory profile points to wider occupational horizons than would be the case if the client simply stated a job preference.

## Disposition

The use of well-designed personality inventories as part of the occupational selection and monitoring process has become widespread (Mabey 1989, 1992, Williams 1994). The most frequently used is Cattell's 16PF (16 personality factors – Cattell *et al.* 1970). There are versions for primary age (CPQ – Children's Personality Questionnaire) and secondary age (HSPQ – High School Personality Questionnaire). The scores from these tests have been used as the basis for occupational profiles relating to specific jobs. Some technical problems in using these tests are discussed in Child (1998b).

### Further reading

For details of occupational profiles from the 16PF, see Cattell, Eber and Tatsuoka, 1970 edition (1988 reprint). Interpretation of 16PF profiles is a skilled and technical task. Krug (1981), in *Interpreting 16PF Profile Patterns*, gives a good introduction. Two other books giving details of profiles for various activities and clinical cases are H. Birkett Cattell (1989) and S. Karson and J. W. O'Dell (1976). The manual for the most recent version of the 16PF, the 16PF5, is full of useful definitions and information about the scientific nature of the test (see Conn and Rieke 1994).

Tests of general and occupational values have been devised. Rosenberg (1957), using a large sample of American College students, found three major value orientations. First, he found a 'people-oriented' value complex preferred by those who view work in terms of pleasure derived from personal contacts. Ideally, they like a job which offers an opportunity to work with, and be helpful to, other people. The second is an 'extrinsic reward-oriented' value complex appealing to those who emphasize rewards obtained for work done. They prefer a job to offer a chance to earn a lot of money and to give prestige and status. The third value complex Rosenberg called 'intrinsic reward-oriented'. Those responding to this value viewed work as an opportunity to be creative and self-expressive. They looked upon work as a chance to permit them to use special abilities and be original.

Clearly, the direction of a client's values and beliefs in terms of social and personal relationships, need for status, leadership, scholarship, aesthetic experience or autonomy is central to an understanding of the kind of work which might appeal to the client.

### Circumstances

The home background of a client is a most important determinant in career choices. The ambitions, values and actual employment of parents will have had some effect on the client. The economic position of the family, whether they are willing to forgo another wage packet and encourage their children are important considerations. As Rodger (1970) declares, it is only by looking at the social and economic conditions in which a client has been raised that we can evaluate past performance and forecast his or her future prospects.

## Holland's theory

A further sophistication was introduced by Holland (1959 and 1985a). His model, like most congruence models, is based on the assumption that people choose work environments where there are people like themselves. But the model also demonstrates a convenient link between the theoretical formulations already described and the practical issues of defining occupational interest profiles for the benefit of counsellors. His theory:

> assumes that at the time of vocational choice the person is the product of the interaction of his particular heredity with a variety of cultural and personal forces including peers, parents and significant adults, his social class, American culture, and the physical environment. (Holland 1959)

Holland postulates six *occupational environments* (Table 13.1) or major kinds of work situations typical of western cultures. Others have attempted to define occupational categories, and some will be discussed later in the chapter.

**Table 13.1** Holland's occupational environments (1985a).

| Environment | Illustrative occupation |
| --- | --- |
| Realistic | Labourer, machine operator, truck driver |
| Investigative | Physicist, anthropologist, biologist |
| Artistic | Musician, poet, writer, photographer |
| Social | Social worker, teacher, vocational counsellor |
| Conventional | Secretary, book-keeper, clerk |
| Enterprising | Salesman, politician, publicity officer |

Each person has a lifestyle compounded from values, interests, aptitudes, personality factors, intelligence and self-concept which helps to orientate him or her in differing degrees towards the six occupational environments. In fact, for everyone, we can arrive at a rank order of these orientations by using measures of occupational interests, personality, values, needs, etc. The orientations are given the same names as the occupational environments and the rank order of these orientations is referred to as the *developmental hierarchy*.

With each of the six occupational environments is an associated personality profile. For example, a person in the 'Realistic' category is said to be shy, genuine, persistent, stable, conforming and practical. Those in the 'Investigative' category are analytical, original, curious and independent. The 'Artistic' group tends to be imaginative, disorderly, idealistic, emotional and impractical. In the 'Social' category, a person is sociable, friendly, co-operative and understanding. If the six are arranged in a hexagon in the order they appear in Table 13.1, adjacent categories are related whilst those directly opposite are highly dissimilar. From the descriptions above, it can be seen that 'Realistic' and 'Investigative' (adjacent) are close, but 'Realistic' and 'Social' (opposite) are dissimilar. Holland's theories have culminated in a series of inventories known as the Vocational Preference Inventory and the Self-Directed Search (1985b).

# Developmental theories

There are several approaches which have two ideas in common. First, a career is a lifelong process of development and second, the development takes place in stages. The two most outstanding contributors from the 1950s and 1960s are Ginzberg and Super. Their pioneer work has been the basis of many theories since then and some space is devoted to these theories for those who wish to study them. These periods occur largely during the school-life of young people and it should certainly be of interest to most teachers.

## Ginzberg's theory

It is to Ginzberg and his associates (Ginzberg *et al.* 1951) that we owe the earliest detailed formulations. Their main interest was to elucidate a sequence of developmental stages leading to entry into an occupation. The model was based on three postulates which they regarded as basic conditions in the process of vocational choice. These were: occupational choice is a development process consisting of three periods covering 15 or so years from early childhood; the process is largely irreversible; compromise is an essential aspect of every choice.

### Occupational choice as a developmental process
Occupational choice as a developmental process is seen to last from four or five years of age to early adulthood. This time span embodies three periods:

- *fantasy choices* (thought to coincide with the Freudian latency period from 6 to 11 years of age)
- *tentative choices* (between 11 and 17 years of age)
  - (i) interest
  - (ii) capacity
  - (iii) values
  - (iv) transition
- *realistic choices* (between 17 and the early 20s)
  - (i) exploration
  - (ii) crystallization
  - (iii) specification

The timing of these periods depends to some extent upon other aspects of development (e.g. intellectual), cultural variations such as school-leaving age and the availability and complexity of work, to mention but a few.

During the period of *fantasy choices* children believe that they can become anything they desire. If you ask children what they want to be when they grow up, the answer will probably be based on recent experience of watching someone at work or hearing a description of work, and the preference will have no regard for the skills or qualifications necessary. The child can think itself into any role without having to bother about such grown-up complications as training or physical strength. The dream world of play does much to obscure the realities of working life. Frank and Hetzer (in Ginzberg *et al.* 1951) discerned two stages of this period. Young children are more concerned with satisfying some specific pleasure they might experience in a job. Bricklaying might appeal because of the enjoyment the child can have in mixing up and splashing around in the cement and water and sticking the bricks together; shopkeeping might appeal because the child could rifle sweets or cakes at will. Frank and Hetzer referred to this earliest kind of motivation as 'functional pleasure' and noted that pleasure was based on superficial observation of the enjoyable aspects of work. The later stage was thought to be motivated by more socially orientated notions of doing work which gave self-satisfaction derived from helping or pleasing others. Nursing would enable the child to help other people (notably parents) back to health; bus drivers could carry people where they wanted to go without having to walk.

The essential features of this period are the lack of regard for medium-term or long-term outcomes of the choices made and an almost complete disregard for the skills or qualifications required. There is no connection in the child's mind between means and ends. Often children centre on pleasant or simple, beneficial aspects of a job while being able to ignore the less pleasant, complicated or routine nature of the work. The child fantasizes about work in the same way as any other activity he or she sees taking place.

The period of *tentative choices* coincides roughly with the period of adolescence from 11 to 17 years of age. The onset of a transition from the fantasy period varies according to the experiences and personal maturity of the individual. It is characterized, like many other features of adolescent life, by uncertainty, exploration and self-conscious analysis. Wisely, the young adolescent makes few firm commitments about occupational choices, although exceptionally one meets a very determined youngster who has an occupation in mind, often conditioned by parents, and sticks to it. The period sees the gradual awareness of the need for criteria by which the adolescent can make reasoned choices. It is, nevertheless, a most difficult time because often many decisions have to be made from the flimsiest evidence; our educational provisions demand it. Secondary school pupils often have to choose between several subjects at 13 or 14; they may have to decide whether to stay on at school and take certificate examinations or whether to make an early start in an apprenticeship. Directions chosen at this time feel as though they are irrevocable in a system which values the specialist, although career change is much easier these days.

Ginzberg divides the period into four stages: interest, capacity, values and transition. Taking them in order, at the *interest* stage, around 11 and 12 years of age, children begin to realize that they will be required to make a decision about their future jobs. Their outlook is not too serious and their choices are based primarily on interests and hobbies. New subjects at school often act as a temporary spur to choosing a job; starting technical drawing or science usually produces a short-term rash of potential draughtsmen and scientists. Parents' occupations also intrude at this age, and the influence of parents' suggestions about future employment is beginning to take effect.

Soon the adolescent realizes that interest is not enough. Enthusiasm for an interest or hobby does not guarantee success. Consequently what we see of the skills required in occupations directs our attention to our own *capacities* and a career pattern becomes oriented towards those things we are good at. Teachers, as well as parents, now become influential, because they are the means by which we can discover our capabilities, chiefly from feedback in school subjects. The adolescent also begins to recognize more clearly that education has a role to play in helping future career decisions.

At the *values* stage, around 15 to 16 years, the adolescent begins to relate capacities and skills to the satisfaction that might be realized from the range of occupations suited to his or her abilities. Value complexes, which have built up in childhood and adolescence from personal and social influences, make their appearance and help to guide the adolescent in choosing which capacities and skills to apply. Such questions as the personal satisfaction offered, prospects (in very sketchy terms), income and scientific orientation become important. However, questions of status or leadership opportunities do not appear voluntarily at this stage. The need for indirect satisfaction is also in evidence. The desire to be a doctor for its own sake becomes an intrinsic desire, thought by Ginzberg to satisfy an emotional need and a desire to do something constructive. This is in contrast with earlier stages of development where a boy or girl might say, 'I want to do so-and-so because I am interested in (or good at) it.' Now he or she would say, 'I want to do so-and-so because I think I might like to do it – it has value for me and others.'

The final stage in the tentative period of occupational choices is known as the *transition* stage because it is at this time that the realities of impending work prospects, opportunities and demands begin to assert themselves. A consideration of values, interests and capabilities alongside the hard facts of work conditions tends to complicate rather than simplify the decision-making process; a period of consolidation and adjustment is therefore needed. The age at which transition occurs is determined largely by the school-leaving age. Ginzberg's analysis was carried out using evidence from the USA, where large numbers of 17-year-olds are still at school and many will move on to some form of higher education. The transition stage, whenever it might appear, is clearly a time in which realistic goal-setting in relation to achievement becomes increasingly important. At the same time, these older and more stable adolescents have to realize that they will have to wait until they have sampled work before an intelligent decision can be made. For those leaving for work there is a pre-occupation with what is in store. Likewise, those going into higher education are waiting in anticipation, having made a tentative choice to enter on a degree or profession. Ginzberg calls this a time of 'restrained suspense about the future'. Concern about work conditions, length and nature of preparation and the financial returns are uppermost in their minds. In a word, youth becomes more 'instrumental' in outlook.

The stages briefly outlined above are cumulative and not mutually exclusive. The point has been made of a gradual build-up in the realization of personal strengths and limitations and a growth of self-knowledge, all of which help the adolescent in occupational decision-making. A burning interest in an occupational task at 12 soon begins to die when the child realizes that certain abilities are required to carry out the task adequately. Also, the ability to perform a task is no guarantee that the child would want to do it for the rest of his or her life. Routine work probably would not appeal to most bright adolescents. They are likely to aspire to more mentally exacting work for personal satisfaction and reward. Here we see values operating. We can readily discern how home and school play a critical part in the development of values. Contrast the short-term hedonistic philosophy in some working-class homes with the long-term, cold, calculating, almost ruthless view of occupational preparation prevalent in middle-class homes (Raby and Walford 1981). This has often been demonstrated in the past by the early school-leavers who are disproportionately represented from working-class backgrounds, while many who stay on from middle-class homes, a number with modest intellectual means, succeed and go to college or university. The way in which a boy or a girl handles occupational choice is a measure of his or her level of maturity; Super called it *vocational maturity* (Super 1955).

The period of *realistic choices* during early adulthood marks the final stage in Ginzberg's developmental hypotheses. It is important to note that he derived these later stages using students in higher education, and this accounts, in part, for the examples he chooses. The period is divided into three stages: exploration, crystallization and specification.

The individual passes from the uncertainty inherent in the transition stage, while changing from school to work or to another educational institution, through an experimental stage in which a person explores in some detail the occupational horizons open to him or her. During the *exploration* stage, the individual gains experience by looking closely at the intellectual or physical requirements within the band of jobs available. The focus has narrowed because one has chosen a job or subject area with specific demands. But one will still search within the narrow band of possibilities for those aspects which are likely to give greatest satisfaction and prospects.

When the individual becomes increasingly conscious of the attractions of particular aspects or studies he or she is said to have reached the stage of *crystallization*. For students in higher education, Ginzberg found this stage at around 20 to 22 years of age. It may happen at a different, and probably earlier, time for school-leavers. It is a time when, rightly or wrongly, an individual feels in possession of sufficient information about his or her potentialities to make a firm decision about entering a career. The distinguishing feature from earlier stages is the firm commitment, a series of compromises having culminated in an unswerving choice.

Having crystallized their views in broad terms, the individuals in Ginzberg's sample now select a *specific* occupation which calls for particular requirements. Having settled for history, they might choose to teach the subject or enter politics or become an archaeologist. The characteristics of this last stage are a willingness to state a speciality and to possess a determined dedication to the idea of a specific occupation. Obviously many students are still in need of guidance, which in Great Britain is conducted by appointments services within the universities. Appointments officers are kept busy with clients who need help in finding work in keeping with their specific aspirations. Some clients may not have reached the stage of crystallization, while others may even want to change direction. Moreover, Ginzberg observed a greater degree or variation in the *pattern* of development during the period of realistic choices than in other periods.

It appears (Ginzberg *et al.* 1951, pp. 133–59) that a similar pattern existed in the tentative period for young people who were not going into higher education. However, there were fundamental differences in the expectations and values held by school-leavers. They tended to be looking for work which offered more money than their fathers were earning, steady employment, skilled work so that in time they could become their own bosses and a job free from serious accident risk. Ginzberg says little of the realistic period for normal school-leavers.

As with most developmental theories, it is not claimed that these periods and stages are rigid in their emergence. We only need recall our own experience in occupational terms to be aware that variations and omissions in the pattern outlined above are quite feasible. Ginzberg showed a number of variations in his own researches. Some young people had a clear idea of the work they wanted to do from an early age, and not only stuck to it but reached a high level of accomplishment. Others with special aptitudes, such as musical, mathematical or mechanical skills, also displayed single-mindedness in their desire to achieve an occupational aim once they had recognized their talents. For teachers, a major concern must be vocational *immaturity*; that is, where young people have arrested or omitted essential stages in occupational development, giving rise to inappropriate choices later on. A person who 'gels' at an early stage in development or who is inadequately informed about aptitudes or work availability is at a serious disadvantage. As Super suggests, work is a way of life, and if one has to live with it for so many years it is imperative to have made a decision which is likely to give some lasting satisfaction.

## The irreversibility of occupational choice

This is a second postulate of Ginzberg. The longer one is engaged in the preparation or execution of a career, the harder it is to change track and find another job with different demands. The dilemma of a three-year college of education student in training as a teacher affords a good illustration of this statement. Having entered college by the conventional academic route of GCSE and 'A' level successes and having discovered that teaching is not what had been anticipated, what can a student do? Or what should a person do who has spent many years in industry and administration suddenly wanting to be a teacher? It becomes increasingly difficult to reverse the investment in time and effort as one continues along a given occupational route. Psychologically, feelings of failure can have a devastating effect on self-esteem and security. Also salary could well reduce appreciably for those who have already got a fair way up one ladder and then decide to climb another one!

Ginzberg was researching at a time (1950s) when many people stayed in one occupation for life. Nowadays, this is only true of occupations where specialization is at a premium, particularly in the long-term training professions such as medicine and dentistry. But in most walks of life, changing is not the trauma it used to be. There is much freer movement between jobs nowadays and changing is becoming the rule rather than the exception. Indeed, some industries prefer employees with width rather than depth of experience, and versatility rather than speciality.

Industry often looks for these qualities because many of the specifics of the workplace are better learnt in that workplace. Degrees are more widely marketable than they were and industry is often more interested in employees using their ingenuity and learning skills – qualities which a degree might indicate. The more we can do to help schoolchildren in becoming informed about their potentials, intellectual, practical and occupational, the better. As we shall see later in the chapter, the work of vocational counsellors involves this kind of service.

## Occupational choice: the outcome of compromise

The main point here is that the vast majority of young people are engaged in decision-making and risk-taking as a product of assembling what information they can muster. Each step usually requires a compromise between two or more possibilities, as when interests have to be balanced against talents, or later, when one must contemplate the subjects needed in order to enter a profession, even though it may involve one in the study of subjects not necessarily to one's liking. Medical students need to have sciences other than the biological sciences. The greater an individual's vocational maturity in terms of using the information available, the more enlightened the compromise decision is likely to be.

## Super's view of occupational development

One of the best-known names in the field of occupational choice is that of Super (1953, 1957a and b). His researches have partly been incorporated in the theory proposed by Ginzberg, although he makes several points of criticism. He felt that the Ginzberg theory did not take into account all the relevant research which had preceded it, particularly in the use and value of occupational interest inventories. The use and interpretation of the word 'choice' left much to be desired. In some cases it was used to signify *preference* for an occupation in the absence of any urgency to enter that occupation, as when a 12-year-old boy says he would like to be a plumber without having the obligation to stand by his decision. This hypothetical kind of choice has a different implication and meaning from that made by someone seeking a job who, having made a choice, must act on it and *enter* a career. Another drawback of Ginzberg's formulation was the absence of a detailed analysis of the compromise process. For the purposes of guidance and counselling, Super rightly claims that we need an elaboration of the variables and the routes by which people arrive at, and enter, an occupation.

Super was also responsible for a life-stages model of occupational development, details of which can be found in the references (Super 1953, 1957a and b). The time spans are compared with Ginzberg's in Figure 13.1. Super regards the whole of life in five major states: growth, exploration, establishment, maintenance and decline of occupational choice. Further, he makes ten propositions which he feels are central to any enlightened theory of vocational development. They are considered here very briefly. Students will notice that they are incorporated in one form or another into later models.

(a)  Individual differences such as abilities (both general and specific), interests and personality should be considered.

(b)  There exists in all of us 'multipotentiality' by which the attributes mentioned in (a) above qualify us for a number of occupations by which we can succeed and gain satisfaction. These can be discerned using occupational-interest inventories.

(c)  Occupational ability patterns are present in us all. A characteristic pattern of abilities, interests and personality is more appropriate for some occupations than for others.

(d)  Vocational preferences and competencies change with time and experience, thus making choice and adjustment a *continuous* process.

(e)  This process can be expressed as a series of life stages, outlined in Figure 13.1.

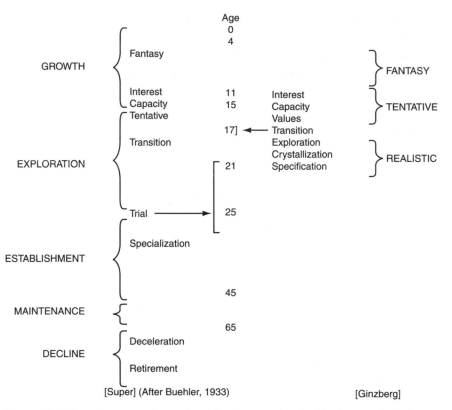

**Figure 13.1** The main stages of voccational development described by Super and Ginzberg. Reprinted with permission from B. Hopson and J. Hayes, *The Theory and Practice of Vocational Guidance*, Pergamon, Oxford, 1968.

(f)   A career pattern, that is, the level, sequence, frequency and duration of trial and stable jobs, is determined by external factors such as socioeconomic background and work opportunities, and internal factors such as mental abilities, achievements and personality.

(g)   Progress through life stages can be guided by counselling in which self-knowledge of abilities and interests, aptitudes and career prospects is encouraged.

(h)   The process of vocational development is essentially that of developing and implementing a self-concept; it is a compromise process in which the self-concept is a product of interaction of inherited aptitudes, neural and endocrine make-up, opportunity to play various roles and evaluations of the extent to which the results of role playing meet with the approval of superiors and fellows.

(i)   The role-playing suggested in (h) above is a process of compromise between one's self-concept and the realities of external social affairs.

(j)   Work is a way of life. Adequate vocational and personal adjustment are most likely when both the nature of work and the way of life that goes with it are congenial to the aptitudes, interests and values of an individual.

Super stresses the interaction effects of personal and social factors and the part they play in forming a self-concept. The latter has a crucial influence on the choice of, entry into, maintenance of and satisfaction gained from work. Another point is his emphasis on development as a continuous process following a sequence of characteristic stages only loosely connected with chronological age. For the counsellor, awareness of the level of developmental maturity attained by a client is important, for it is only when the client's vocational maturity is known that steps can be taken to decide on a course of guidance.

# Person-centred approaches

Far less has been done in applying person- and goal-centred theories to career education and counselling. They differ in the practical strategies used to help individuals in realizing career ambitions. In person-centred approaches, individuals are encouraged to discover for themselves what is a realistic career prospect. Goal-centred approaches have their origins in social learning theory (a variant of behaviourist theory) discussed in Chapters 6 and 12. Setting realistic goals and planning the route to achieving the goal is a major concern in this approach.

Person-centred means that the focal point for guidance is the client and the method is associated with humanists such as Rogers and Kelly, both of whom are mentioned in Chapter 12, although neither of these psychologists applied their ideas to career education and guidance. When applied, the aim is to help clients to be more aware of their own potential and to see how this awareness can be used in the process of finding a satisfying career. Clients are encouraged to express attitudes and feelings which lead to decisions about appropriate careers.

In the UK, the foremost exponent of applying Kelly's Personal Construct Theory to careers is Offer (1995 and 1993). In addition, he has mapped this approach onto a model proposed by Law and Watts (1977) called DOTS, also very much in the humanist tradition. These are the initial letters of four broad aims of any career guidance, though the aims do not necessarily occur in the order of the letters.

- 'D' is for *Decision-learning*. The client has now to face what would be involved in making the career choice and is helped to make a decision.
- 'O' is for *Opportunity awareness*. This involves helping a person to discover what work is available and to whom, and what the work offers in terms of interest, satisfaction, rewards, incentives, demands, etc.

- 'T' is for *Transition learning* which involves an individual in discovering how to make the decisions a reality as, for example, in trying to find a suitable job.
- 'S' is for *Self-awareness.* This involves helping a person to realize his or her abilities, motives, potential, strengths and weaknesses. This amounts to a self-analysis of what a person wants from work and how it can be achieved.

Offer (1993) sees the DOTS learning scheme as a cycle of experience for the client – passing from self-awareness about one's view of work life, what is available in the job market, using these two starting points for making decisions about what is feasible, and then seeking work. If this is an experience cycle, then the client will always be returning to review these four steps.

# Goal-centred approaches

Goal-directed approaches are about social learning and how our experiences help to build values and beliefs about work. The name of Krumboltz (1979, 1981, 1994) is most often associated with this approach. As readers would expect with a behavioural approach, the emphasis is upon how we arrive at our present beliefs about the world of work through instrumental learning. Our parents, teachers, friends, the media – all regularly mention aspects of employment and it would be difficult to deny that, as we grow up in a world so preoccupied by earning a living, we become conditioned to certain views about most aspects of work. Determining how accurate and useful this bombardment has been would be part of the process of goal-orientation.

Krumboltz used the behaviourist terms *instrumental* and *associative learning experiences* to define the ways in which we arrive at a knowledge of work (see Bandura in Chapters 6 and 12). In a nutshell, work preferences are a process of learning. Instrumental learning occurs when our work-related activities are rewarding (or disappointing) and this reinforces our interest in that work. Preference and performance become linked. Associative learning happens when we see *others* who are role models being rewarded or disenchanted with the work they do. This leads to self-analysis (*self-observation generalizations*, to quote Krumboltz) and decision-making, work habits and feelings about the work (*task-approach skills*).

At a practical level, the task of the counsellor is to discover what has been learnt by the client, how accurate it is and what plans can be laid for cognitive restructuring of belief systems and decision-making using time-honoured conditioning procedures.

# Careers education and guidance in schools

The last 40 years have seen a marked advance in the importance attributed to careers education and guidance in local authorities and schools. This applies to primary as well as secondary education. Government education and training initiatives, such as the Technical and Vocational Education Initiative (TVEI), appeared alongside publications from the DES/DoE. These included *Working Together – Education and Training* (1986), *Working Together for a Better Future* (1987) and *Careers Education and Guidance from 5 to 16* (1988). More recently, the Department for Education (1995a and b) circulated documentation about career guidance syllabuses in an attempt to ensure that this topic permeates the curriculum of state schools.

Recent initiatives have helped to raise to consciousness the importance of career education and guidance in the state system of education. The involvement of the School Curriculum and Assessment Authority (SCAA) and its successor, the QCA, in pressing for some work to be done in primary schools, suggesting a curriculum, requesting audit, planning, implementing and evaluating should be productive. Unfortunately, these ideas are not yet mandatory and in the light of other pressing demands on teachers' time and energy, career education has tended to be in the afterthought region.

Despite this stimulus, the presence of pressure groups such as the National Advisory Council for Careers and Education Guidance, sources of help and information such as the Institute of Careers Guidance, the National Institute for Careers Education and Counselling (to mention a few), the army of careers officers in the Authority Career Services and Career Coordinators in schools, we are still a long way from an effective, efficient, statutory system of career education and guidance in state schools.

Well-meaning teachers with full teaching programmes take on additional career advice duties and are approached by pupils and parents bewildered by the job market. Therefore, greater emphasis is now placed on the training of teachers willing to become specialist careers teachers and coordinators.

## Government guidance

The curriculum guidance documents from the National Curriculum Council (1990) and DfE (1995a and b) set out in some detail the contemporary thinking. There are several psychological principles elaborated in the recommendations. Broadly, career education should help pupils to get to know themselves better, become aware of the training and career opportunities available, be capable of making reasoned choices about further education, training and career pathways and to be capable of making the transition into new work roles and situations. These aims are thought to be met by assisting pupils in five areas of concern. These are:

- *self* (knowledge of self – qualities, attitudes, values, abilities, strengths, limitations, potential and needs)
- *roles* (position and expectations in relation to family, community and employment)
- *work* (application of productive effort, including paid employment and unpaid work in the community and at home)
- *career* (sequence of roles undertaken through life and the personal success, rewards and enjoyment it brings)

- *transition* (development of qualities and skills which enable pupils to adjust to and cope with change, e.g. self-reliance, adaptability, flexibility, decision-making, problem-solving) (National Curriculum Council 1990; DfE 1995a and b).

An important aspect of the curriculum planning is that the aims should run through subject areas and ages from 5 to 16.

## Career, sex and gender issues

The theorists mentioned above are cautious in their comments about links between particular occupations and the sex of the workers. But they all seem to conclude that certain occupations have a very long history of being sex-linked – not exactly a startling or original observation. For example, nursing, junior school teaching, shop assistants and clerical work have traditionally attracted predominantly more females than males; building, farming, weapon making, mechanical engineering (cars, buildings, etc.) seem to appeal to males more than females. It will not have escaped readers that the former are to some extent 'empathic occupations' requiring skills of identifying and responding to the thoughts and emotions of others. On the other hand, the latter are construction or 'systemizing' occupations and as Baron-Cohen (2003) observes:

> Some occupations are almost entirely male. Take, for example, the fields of metalworking, weapon-making or crafting musical instruments. Or the construction industries, such as boat-building. These occupations are almost always carried out by men, and this sex difference is seen universally, not just in the Western world. This sex difference does not reflect the greater physical strength in males since, in many of these occupations... strength is not the key factor. The focus of these occupations is on constructing systems'... and 'of 122 societies studied, weapon-making (a clear example of a systematizing skill) is an exclusively male activity in 121 of these'. (Pp. 71 and 79).

Research results from studies in motivation (Chapter 8), cognitive ability (Chapter 9), personality (Chapter 12) and interest profiles from such tests as Rodger's Seven Point Plan (interests) all point in the same direction – some occupations are preferred by either males or females. However, the majority of occupations offer satisfying prospects for both sexes, and the likelihood is that they gain satisfaction from different aspects of the same occupation.

As we shall see presently, part of the skill when guiding pupils is to allow for their different preferences, not based on gender biases, but on genuine personal desires and competencies. Careers teachers, our next port of call, are careful to ensure that a student, no matter which sex, is given every opportunity and guidance in selecting a career likely to give job satisfaction.

# Careers teachers/co-ordinators

Planning for a career is now seen as a long-term and wide-reaching function of schools from reception onwards. But specialist input from a teacher is generally left to the secondary stage. As we saw in the formulations of Ginzberg and Super, vocational development and choice are cumulative processes and these require regular tracking and guidance.

Careers teachers have an exacting responsibility for which specialist training is imperative. Initial teacher-training courses do not, at present, guarantee to provide this specialist training. On entering school, teachers sometimes find themselves teaching personal and social education of which 'careers' forms a small part. To obtain a specialist qualification in careers education and guidance, there are part-time courses in further education and higher education institutions, and distance learning packages (Law 1995).

Careers teachers should at least have a knowledge of occupational development and guidance theory and be capable of relating this knowledge to the practical needs of adolescents. As their planning runs across the curriculum, they will have to know which aspects of the curriculum are related to working life and opportunities. To ensure coordination requires skilful negotiation between staff and careers teachers. They will also have to acquire skills in careers counselling and have a wide and detailed knowledge of the educational, employment and training opportunities available in the area. Knowledge of statutory requirements and the laws and regulations relating to employment are also of importance.

There is now a wealth of information aimed specifically at the secondary-age group about work chances. Several have been computerized, of which CASCAID and JIIG–CAL are best known (Watts 1996). But the teacher also needs to have a firm idea about economic and occupational trends and how these relate to local circumstances.

---

## Further reading

Computer-based job information, analysis of a pupil's occupational interests, guidance on suitable job areas and subjects to take at school for particular occupations are now widely available. The key words 'career choice' in the web 'search' dialogue box will produce a rash of sites of interest. Some examples of computer aids are JIIG-CAL (Jobs Ideas and Information Generator-Computer Assisted Learning, based at Edinburgh University), CASCAID (Careers Advisory Service Computer Aid) and JOBWISE. These systems are for adult as well as young clients.

For example, the JIIG-CAL system claims to be the most comprehensive careers guidance system in the UK, providing job ideas, careers education, career plans, job information, subject choice advice and adult guidance. It is suitable for all ages from school pupils through further and higher students to adults. It consists of a three-year programme offering career work materials, computing facilities and career support for classrooms. The programme is administered by those trained in the use of JIIG-CAL materials. Many local education authorities are registered users.

The DOTS model has been mapped on to computer-aided career systems. Under self-awareness there are available self-assessment profile forms and various psychometric tests. Opportunity awareness is enabled using information retrieval systems which give details of job descriptions and availability. There are computerized decision aids and finally job-search instructional programmes.

Links with important outside agencies are essential. The Careers Service, employers and parents are part of this network, and understanding how the Service and industry operate is necessary. Experience of work and the workplace is essential. Arranging visits by pupils to local workplaces, work and interview simulations, projects about industrial problems and the community give some idea of what might be achieved. However, many school-aged young people have part-time jobs. This has led to a greater knowledge for them of working for an income, having to keep time and cover certain tasks as required by the employer, and so on.

The Careers Service is a crucial part of the partnership with schools. Careers officers need to be involved with schools in their area in order to help in planning those parts of the curriculum relevant to occupational interests. They should contribute to the school programme and keep the careers teachers informed of job opportunities in the locality. They will also be knowledgeable about guidance and the use of computers in providing job information checklists. Careers officers also have strong links with industry and this should be used by the schools.

The National Curriculum Council (1990) places great importance on career guidance and it concludes that:

> Careers education and guidance is an essential part of every pupil's curriculum. In promoting self-awareness, it is a prerequisite to pupils making well-informed educational, vocational and training choices and to managing the transition from education to new roles, including employment. . . This process of personal and social development begins in the home and continues through adult life.

## Summary

If we took work and leisure away from adult life there would not be much left. Our life-chances are so closely tied to the nature and demands of our work that we cannot escape from the need to consider, as scientifically as we can, the adequacy and influence of our educational provisions on career choice. Whilst many teachers may feel that their influence on, and opportunity to assist, children in selecting a career is marginal, an awareness of the effects of school life and schoolwork on career choice is most important. This is not to suppose that each teacher should feel obliged to act in the capacity of a citizens' advice bureau, but one must at least be alive to the relevance of one's contribution in the career structure of one's children. There is no doubt about the increasing importance which will become attached to those aspects of the curriculum dealing with career prospects in these days of prolonged schooling at adolescence.

We have seen in this chapter some of the important psychological and social factors which profoundly influence, or which are profoundly influenced by, the work we choose. Ginzberg and his colleagues pointed to some valuable conditions present in the process of vocational development and choice which have since been elaborated by Super. Basically, occupational choice is preceded by a gradual developmental process from childhood through adolescence. The process is largely irreversible and the final choice is essentially a compromise between several possibilities available at the moment of choice. As well as having an understanding of the part played by home and school, we need to know something about individual abilities, interests, personality, occupational interests, self-concepts and self-knowledge in order to ascertain whether a choice is realistic and appropriate for a particular person. The question of irreversibility is a constant source of concern to most people. Because work possesses our lives so substantially, it might make better sense if we reorganized the time devoted to educational and career matters so that we dispersed them during a lifetime, rather than having a 'grand slam' of education in childhood, thus having to commit ourselves so early in life. With the system as it exists at present, Ginzberg and Super have provided a theoretical framework which must be set against a background of such practical problems as manpower demands, geographical distribution of work, guidance facilities available and other external agencies. Recent trends in person- and goal-centred approaches based on well-established psychological principles have led to some practical suggestions.

Counselling in schools can take many forms. We pass from the informal, 'over coffee' chat to a full-blooded analysis of educational and occupational potential. Where counselling is taken seriously, it appears to have at least six objectives. Counselling is a long-term and continuous process from primary school onwards; it is wide in its concern about social as well as personal characteristics; it is the pupil who must ultimately make the decision and must, therefore, be led to a position of independence in order to make such a decision adequately; counsellors should be specialists and not necessarily teachers; there should be no room for last-minute decisions; counsellors should be able to call on all the resources of the school and community in helping each child. It must be remembered that counselling school-leavers is a very small part of the task: the work extends well beyond the boundaries of finding jobs for the boys and girls. Advice on curriculum choice, achievement and motivation are but a few additional concerns of the educational and vocational counsellor. There are also behaviour problems and anxieties which require specialist therapeutic counsellors who have undergone training in psychology. Behaviour deviance in the delinquent, minor neurotic or anxiety states prior to examinations or as a result of social relationships in class, truancy and underachievement are the kinds of difficulties with which a therapeutic counsellor might be faced.

There is still much to be done in this complex area of vocational guidance and counselling before we can place it on a firm scientific footing. We have at our disposal a number of psychological tools which can give us information about physical make-up, attainment, intelligence, special aptitudes, interests, temperamental and cognitive dispositions. The coming years should see an increase in the refinement and use of these instruments.

## Tutorial enquiry and discussion

(a) By using visits and/or inviting speakers, become familiar with the structure and functions of:
   (i) any local and national careers services
   (ii) JIIG-CAL and/or CASCAID (or other local computer-based service)
   (iii) the Child Care and Probationary Service.
     What links are usually forged between these services and the schools?

(b) Discuss the possible terms of reference of a careers education and guidance service within the school framework (include work experience, industrial visits, social studies about the trade union movement, work communities, the EU, economic issues), particularly in the light of Government, SCAA and QCA initiatives.

(c) Investigate:
   (i) occupational interest inventories and their uses
   (ii) the idea that personality characteristics are associated with particular occupational groups (see the Cattell references)
   (iii) the use of DOTS in career guidance.

(d) As a group, discuss how each of you came to decide on your present career choice. You will probably have some difficulty recalling the precise details or the precise moment of decision, but try to discover *who* or *what* influenced you most in arriving at the decision. Now that you are 'on course', what information would you have liked prior to coming on a course of teacher-training? How might this information have been conveyed to you while in the sixth form (or whenever you had to make the decision)?

## References

Baron-Cohen, S. (2003), *The Essential Difference: Men, Women and the Extreme Male Brain*. London: Allan Lane (and Penguin Books).

Cattell, R. B., Eber, H. W. and Tatsuoka, M. M. (1970, reprint 1988), *Handbook for the Sixteen Personality Factor Questionnaire (16PF)*. Champaign, IL: Institute of Personality and Ability Testing (IPAT).

Cattell, H. Birkett (1989), *The 16PF: Personality in Depth*. Champaign, IL: Institute for Personality and Ability Testing (IPAT).

Child, D. (1998b), 'Some technical problems in the use of personality measures in occupational settings illustrated using the "Big Five"', in D. Shorrocks-Taylor (ed.), *Directions in Educational Psychology*. London: Whurr.

Child, D. and Borrill, C. (1990), *Taking the DC Test: A Guide for Candidates*, Nurse Selection Project. Leeds: University of Leeds.

Cleaton, D. (1993), *Careers Education and Guidance: A Survey, on behalf of the Institute of Careers Guidance (ICG) and the National Association of Careers and Guidance Teachers (NACGT)*. Stourbridge: ICG.

Conn, S. R. and Rieke, M. L. (1994), *The 16PF Fifth Edition Technical Manual*. Champaign, IL: Institute for Personality and Ability Testing (IPAT).

Crowther Report, The (1959), *15 to 18*. Central Advisory Council for Education. London: HMSO.

DES/DoE (1986), *Working Together – Education and Training*. London: HMSO.

DES/DoE (1987), *Working Together for a Better Future*. London: HMSO.

DES/DoE (1988), *Careers Education and Guidance from 5 to 16*. London: HMSO.

DfE (1995a), *Better Choices – The Principles*. London: HMSO.

DfE (1995b), *Better Choices: From Principles to Practice*. London: HMSO.

*Early Leaving Report, The* (1954) Central Advisory Council for Education. London: HMSO.

Ginzberg, E., Ginsburg, S. W., Axelrad, S. and Herma, J. L. (1951), *Occupational Choice: An Approach to a General Theory*. New York: Columbia University Press.

Galinski, M. D. (1962), 'Personality development and vocational choice of clinical psychologists and physicists', *Journal of Counseling Psychology*, 9, 229–305.

Holland, J. L. (1959), 'A theory of vocational choice', *Journal of Counseling Psychology*, 6, 35–43.

Holland, J. L. (1985a), *Making Vocational Choices: A Theory of Vocational Personalities and Work Environments* (2nd edn). Englewood Cliffs, NJ: Prentice-Hall.

Holland, J. L. (1985b), *The Self-Directed Search: Professional Manual and the Manual for the VPI*. Odessa, FL: Psychological Assessment Resources.

Hopson, B. and Hayes, J. (1968), *The Theory and Practice of Vocational Guidance*. Oxford: Pergamon.

Karson, S. and O'Dell, J. W. (1976), *A Guide to the Clinical Use of the 16PF*. Champaign, IL: IPAT.

Kline, P. (1975), *Psychology of Vocational Guidance*. London: Batsford.

Krug, S. E. (1981), *Interpreting 16PF Profile Patterns*. Champaign, IL: IPAT.

Krumboltz, J. D. (1979), 'A social learning theory of decision making', in A. Mitchell, G. Jones and J. D. Krumboltz (eds), *Social Learning and Career Decision Making*. Cranston, RI: Carroll Press.

Krumboltz, J.D. (1981), 'A social learning theory of decision making – a revision', in A. Mitchell, G. Jones and J. D. Krumboltz (eds), *Career Development in the 1980s: Theory and Practice*. Springfield, IL: Thomas.

Krumboltz, J. D. (1994), 'Improving career development theory from a social learning perspective', in M. L. Savickas and R. W. Lent (eds), *Convergence in Career Development Theories*. Palo Alto, CA: Consulting Psychologists Press.

Law, B. (1995), 'Pilgrim's progress: encounters in staff development for careers work', in D. Frost, A. Edwards and H. Reynolds (eds), *Careers Education and Guidance*. London: Kogan Page.

Law, B. (1996), 'A career-learning theory', in A. G. Watts, B. Law, J. Killeen, J. M. Kidd and R. Hawthorn, *Rethinking Careers Education and Guidance: Theory, Policy and Practice*. London: Routledge.

Law, B. and Watts, A. G. (1977), *Schools, Career and Community*. London: Church Information Office.

Mabey, B. (1989), 'The majority of large companies use psychological tests', *Guidance and Assessment Review*, 5(3), 1–4.

Mabey, B. (1992), 'The growth of test use', *Selection and Development Review*, 8(3), 6–8.

Miller, K. M. (1968), *Manual of the Rothwell-Miller Interest Blank*. Slough: NFER.

National Curriculum Council (1990), *Careers Education and Guidance. Curriculum Guidance Pamphlet, No. 6*. London: HMSO.

Offer, M. (1993), *The usefulness of the psychology of personal constructs to occupational choice theory and the theory of vocational guidance*. National Institute for Careers Education and Counselling.

Offer, M. (1995), 'Personal Construct Theory: a complete programme for careers education and guidance?', *Careers Education and Guidance*, October, 21–4.

Raby, L. and Walford, G. (1981), 'Job status aspirations and their determinants for middle and lower stream pupils in an urban, multi-racial comprehensive school', *British Educational Research Journal*, 7, 173–81.

Rodger, A. (1970), *The Seven Point Plan, Paper No. 1* (3rd edn). London: National Institute of Industrial Psychology.

Rosenberg, M. (1957), *Occupations and Values*. Glencoe, IL: The Free Press.

Strong, E.K. (1948), *Vocational Interests in Men and Women*. Stanford, CA: Stanford University Press.

Super, D. E. (1953), 'A theory of vocational development', *American Psychology*, 8, 185–90.

Super, D. E. (1955), 'Dimensions and measurement of vocational maturity', *Teachers College Record*, 57, 151–63.

Super, D. E. (1957a), *Vocational Development: A Framework for Research*. New York: Teachers College Press, Columbia University.

Super, D. E. (1957b), *The Psychology of Careers: An Introduction to Vocational Development*. New York: Harper.

Vachmann, B. (1960), 'Childhood experiences in vocational choice in law, dentistry and social work', *Journal of Counseling Psychology*, 7, 243–50.

Vernon, P. E. (1950), *The Structure of Human Abilities*. London: Methuen.

Watts, A. G. (1996), 'Computers in guidance', in A. G. Watts, B. Law, J. Killeen, J. M. Kidd and R. Hawthorn, *Rethinking Careers Education and Guidance: Theory, Policy and Practice*. London: Routledge.

Watts, A. G., Law, B., Killeen, J., Kidd, J. M. and Hawthorn, R. (1996), *Rethinking Careers Education and Guidance: Theory, Policy and Practice*. London: Routledge.

Williams, R. S. (1994), 'Occupational testing: contemporary British practice', *The Psychologist*, 7(1), 11–13.

## Further reading

Ball, B. (1984), *Careers Counselling in Practice*. Basingstoke: Falmer.

*Careers Education and Guidance*, National Curriculum Council, Curriculum Guidance Pamphlet No. 6, 1990.

Department for Education has produced two interesting documents: *Better Choices: The Principles* and *Better Choices: From Principles to Practice*, ED/DfE, HMSO, London, 1995.

Frost, D., Edwards, A. and Reynolds, H. (eds) (1995), *Careers Education and Guidance*. London: Kogan Page. A teacher-oriented text which is an easy-to-read, practical guide.

Kline, P. (1975), *Psychology of Vocational Guidance*. London: Batsford. A standard text on the psychometric approach to career guidance.

Watts, A. G., Law, B., Killeen, J., Kidd, J. M. and Hawthorn, R. (1996), *Rethinking Careers Education and Guidance: Theory, Policy and Practice*. London: Routledge.

## Useful websites

For career guidance see: http://www.guidancecouncil.com

# Part Five
## Classroom and Curriculum Management and Assessment

# Effective Classroom Strategies

## Chapter Outline

## Implications for teachers

- Learning and teaching in schools are not random activities, but depend, at least, on factors relating to the pupil, the teacher and the syllabus.
- Psychologists from both the behaviourist and cognitive traditions have had much to say of value to teachers for both discovery and expository methods of teaching.

> ## Implications for teachers (continued)
>
> - Useful models of instruction, particularly one devised by Bloom (1976), provide a helpful starting point for student-teachers.
> - Effective class management is essential for the learning and teaching processes.
> - Leadership and exercising control in the classroom can be acquired by a student.

It would be wonderful if I could set out for you a strategy which would make your classroom life trouble-free and solve all the problems you are likely to encounter. Unfortunately I cannot. The best I can hope for is to offer the equivalent of a 'menu' of options from which you could trial those which seem to be to your taste. In any case, there is no single way of solving classroom problems. Each class has its own particular problems and some trial and error is inevitable.

All chapters in this book contribute to the menu. For instance, motivation, learning strategies, level of concept development, ability, personality, self-concept or the examination system are some of the psychological influences affecting conduct in the classroom. They all have a bearing on activities in the classroom. Who – that is the characteristics of teachers and pupils and their interaction, what – the curriculum, how – the methods employed in teaching, and where – the arrangement of pupils in the classroom, constitute the main concerns. They interrelate and the following sections reflect these factors.

Learning is at the heart of classroom life whether it be academic, social or moral. The effectiveness of whatever the teacher is trying to transmit and share with pupils relies on many factors, some mentioned in the last paragraph. The strategies to be considered below apply to learning and classroom control. There are several approaches suggested by psychologists broadly relating to behaviourist and cognitivist philosophies. But first, we turn to an overall proposal by Bloom (1976) which sets the scene.

# Cognitive psychology – models of instruction (teaching)

One outcome of developments in cognitive psychology has been the elaboration of 'models' of instruction or teaching. Of these, the most useful and widely used has been Bloom's (1976). He suggests that there are six major specifications necessary to any theory of instruction, all of which are sensitive to individual differences. The six specifications are:

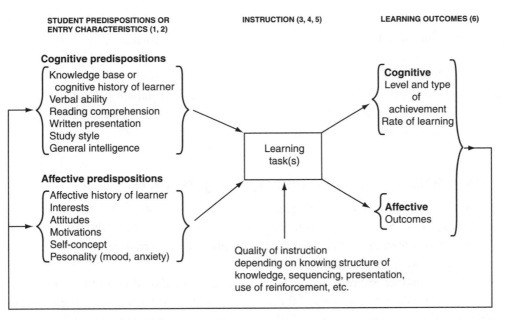

STUDENT PREDISPOSITIONS OR ENTRY CHARACTERISTICS (1, 2)     INSTRUCTION (3, 4, 5)     LEARNING OUTCOMES (6)

**Cognitive predispositions**
Knowledge base or
  cognitive history of learner
Verbal ability
Reading comprehension
Written presentation
Study style
General intelligence

**Affective predispositions**
Affective history of learner
Interests
Attitudes
Motivations
Self-concept
Pesonality (mood, anxiety)

Learning task(s)

Quality of instruction depending on knowing structure of knowledge, sequencing, presentation, use of reinforcement, etc.

**Cognitive**
Level and type of achievement
Rate of learning

**Affective**
Outcomes

**Figure 14.1** The instructional process (adapted from B. S. Bloom, *Human Characteristics and School Learning*, McGraw-Hill, New York, 1976).

1 the cognitive predispositions of the learner – that is, the knowledge, skills and abilities which a learner brings to a task and which would influence performance
2 the affective predispositions of the learner – that is, the interests, attitudes and self-concept brought to a task
3 how a body of knowledge needs to be structured in order for efficient and effective learning by individuals to take place
4 the sequencing and best methods of presenting that body of knowledge
5 the reinforcement mechanisms necessary to ensure continued interest such as rewards, incentives, feedback
6 evaluation of pupil performance and of the system used.

To help in summarizing the advances which might be generated from these specifications, Figure 14.1 is a cannibalized diagram from Bloom (1976; also look at Child 1998a).

Note that Bloom is mainly concerned with what the pupil's qualities are and the role of teacher as 'manager' of learning. Understandably, he says little about the curriculum (see Chapter 15) or the 'where' of teaching, that is, how children could be arranged in the teaching space available (see the ORACLE Project in Chapter 12).

Points (1) and (2) above represent what are called 'student entry characteristics' or 'predispositions'. In plain language they are concerned with how the history of the learner, prior to the task in hand, will affect performance of the present task. The third, fourth and fifth points are about structuring of knowledge, sequencing of presentation and reinforcement mechanisms, and are incorporated into the central part of the diagram under 'instruction'. The last column (6) is about learning outcomes, that is the effects of learning, and they involve both assessment and evaluation of some kind. Note also that the 'learning outcomes' become part of the history of the learner. That is why there is an arrow at the end of the model pointing back to the beginning.

## Entry predispositions ((1) and (2) in Figure 14.1)

Entry variables, such as general intelligence (Chapter 9) and personality (Chapter 10), give useful background knowledge, which can help a teacher in detecting whether a pupil is achieving in line with his or her capabilities, and provide some background explanations of uncharacteristic performance.

But these qualities are regarded as fairly stable and we should concentrate on other predispositions which can be utilized for the benefit of the learner. The numerical, verbal, reading, writing and communication skills of the young (Chapters 4 and 5) are inescapable and profoundly affected by child-rearing practices. We have a lot to learn about early home and school influences, and about discovering ways of improving these skills by capitalizing on this critical early period (Chapter 8). Studies in paediatrics and the physiology of early child development (Chapters 2, 7 and 8) have made significant contributions to educational psychology.

We have only a hazy idea of how a child assimilates and organizes knowledge and how this process in turn will affect decision-making and problem-solving. How do previous experiences, and the generalizations formulated from them, impinge upon new experience? Driver (1983, see Chapter 4) looked at the ways in which children develop specific ideas and concepts in science and how these compete with accepted scientific generalizations. Whether we like it or not, children, it seems, formulate their own laws of nature from their experiences and these may be in conflict with those presented by the science teacher. This illustrates very clearly the importance of studying the entry characteristics of pupils from their learning history and of finding ways of unravelling false notions and replacing them with methods for finding those which are more acceptable.

'Study style' is listed on the diagram (Chapters 7 and 12). By this is meant the characteristic and unique ways in which an individual tries to cope with the learning process. We all have our own favoured tactics and strategies which we bring to study. How efficient are they? Could they be improved? Is the teaching we receive compatible with our favoured strategies? Most of the research in this field has been concerned with secondary and higher education (Chapter 7), giving useful descriptive glimpses of student methods or characteristics. The study methods of students in higher education are probably well established on reaching university, and support systems (Entwistle at Edinburgh, for example, 1998) have to be well managed to be effective. Yet at the other important end of the system, in primary schools, we almost completely ignore training in study methods. We wrongly assume that effective methods of study are automatically picked up as children progress through the system. We need detailed researches of how study skills grow and how to teach them to the individual's best advantage.

One need hardly remind the reader of the central importance of interest and motivation to pupil or student performance (Chapter 8). Yet we have a long way to go in trying to comprehend and do something about the credibility gap which exists between pupils, teachers, parents and society as to the place of a formal system of education in the life-chances of an individual. Selling the system gets harder as one reaches the final two years of secondary school life, especially to those with little hope of obtaining good GCSEs. There will have to be a considerable shift in syllabus content and design as changing patterns of work and leisure, individuals' expectations and technological advances bite deeper and deeper into our present way of life. Unfortunately, society inadvertently generates in the young expectations which the educational system can rarely fulfil.

## Instruction or teaching process ((3), (4) and (5) in Figure 14.1)

The central portion of Figure 14.1, instruction or teaching process, places great demands on the teacher as a manager of learning and this is addressed later in the chapter. The aspiration of teachers should be to lead learners to a point where they, the pupils, can help themselves. This is becoming increasingly more important as our knowledge base rapidly increases. Information retrieval and self-help are growing in significance. The cheap miniaturization of equipment suitable in educational settings will have a marked effect on educational provision in both the curriculum and teaching arrangements in some subjects. The design of software requires a deep knowledge of the structure of a subject, and teachers will need to know more about how to unwrap their areas of knowledge for presentation in a variety of ways.

The simulation of human thinking and action in the form of artificially intelligent systems may have something to offer to teachers. Our inventions are often extensions of ourselves. Telescopes and microscopes are extensions of our eyes, amplifiers of our ears, tools and vehicles of our limbs. Robotics combines some of these senses and is taking the routine out of some manufacturing industries. Apart from the obvious impact this will have on our work and leisure activities in the future, the study of artificial intelligence must in time have some bearing on the analysis and presentation of subject matter, and knowledge about the human being as a learner.

To enhance the quality of instruction a number of innovations are finding their way into the system. A few examples from courses provided for trainee teachers are (a) flexiprogrammes and adaptive tutoring which are designed to be adjusted to the needs of particular children by using either reproduced materials, video or microprocessors; (b) courses for students on instructional craft knowledge; (c) the use of simulation exercises using closed-circuit or recorded television programmes; (d) the more extensive use of recorded teaching episodes – sometimes called micro-teaching; or (e) courses in diagnostic techniques and social skills.

For children, technology has added considerably to their knowledge base. Apart from programmes at school, there are many learning sources available on the Internet.

## Learning outcomes

In a sense, learning outcomes need to be considered alongside entry predispositions, because one needs to know the destination before being able to choose an appropriate route. Assessment (see Chapters 16 and 18) is an essential part of the process of learning. Indeed, that is life! The development of skills and tools which enable teachers to evaluate (make accurate diagnoses and treat individual children's problems competently) is crucial and badly in need of research.

# Discovery, guided discovery and expository methods of teaching

Two significant contributions by psychologists to instructional ideas are found in the work of Bruner (1966) and Ausubel (Ausubel and Robinson 1969; for a detailed analysis, see Lefrançois 2000). They are similar in many of their views, both having a cognitive outlook and rejecting behaviourism.

Bruner emphasizes active restructuring of knowledge through experience with the environment. Learners should organize knowledge for themselves, for example by using discovery methods, rather than having material pre-packaged by the teacher. He has been a most prolific writer; in this book we refer to him several times on concept development, perception, the origins of speech, play and symbol systems. Unfortunately Bruner has not yet brought his many ideas together in a coherent overview. Nevertheless, he does believe that learning is most effectively achieved when children are encouraged to engage in guided discovery (see the example from geography later in this chapter).

His train of thought for the purposes of deriving a method *or* methods of instruction runs like this: starting with the categorization of our environment (see Chapter 4), in an attempt to reduce its complexity, we develop coding systems which are hierarchies of categories. To assist this process, education should be concerned with the analysis of areas of knowledge so as to ensure that the most fundamental aspects are presented first, i.e. there is an ordering in the exposure we give an area of knowledge based on the levels of complexity of the categories involved. To ensure that children 'crack' the codes, they should be encouraged to explore for themselves at an appropriate level of presentation (see symbolic systems in Chapter 4) using a *spiral curriculum*. This latter involves the exposure of children to subject matter in such a way as to ensure both overlap with previous material (repetition and revision) and a steady progression in the complexity of the material – hence a spiral effect.

The processes of learning by discovery have been interpreted and applied in many ways and research findings have been the centre of controversy for many years (Rowell *et al.* 1969). For an excellent discussion of the dilemmas thrown up by this subject, students should read Shulman and Keislar (1965) in which several famous American psychologists conferred and debated the numerous issues involved. The process of learning by discovery involves (a) *induction* (taking particular instances and using them to devise a general case) with the minimum of instruction; and (b) *'errorful' learning* employing trial-and-error strategies in which there is a high probability of errors and mistakes before an acceptable generalization is possible.

Bruner cites some useful illustrations (1961 and 1977) which demonstrate both these activities. One describes a class of fifth-graders (ten to twelve years of age) who were handed charts of north Central America containing nothing but the major rivers, lakes and natural resources. The pupils were asked to indicate where they thought we might find the principal cities, the railways and the major roads. The children were not allowed to use other maps or source books. Naturally, the children were not starting from scratch because they would have some prior knowledge of geography, but this knowledge now had to be pooled in an effort to find the answer to the question. In the discussion which followed, the children had to justify their choices. By piecing together the particulars they had accumulated from previous geography lessons, the children formed for themselves generalizations from which to locate the positions (both induction and deduction). When the actual chart was exposed at the end of the exercise, the children discovered their mistakes, and in so doing they learned, by induction, that cities arise where there are water and other natural resources, where materials can be shipped and where climatic conditions and land shape are congenial.

Ausubel emphasizes the role of *expository* or *reception learning* and is quite critical of some aspects of discovery learning. At the heart of Ausubel's ideas are the concepts of *meaningful verbal learning* and *advance organizers*. To be meaningful, new material must be related to existing knowledge. The teacher therefore has to find ways of associating the new material with ideas or objects with which the pupils are familiar. This, according to Ausubel, is most efficiently done by straightforward explanation and exposition rather than by time-consuming pupil-generated discovery methods. To help in this process, Ausubel recommends the use of *advance organizers*, which he defines in two forms – *expository* and *comparative organizers*. An advance organizer is introductory subject matter presented before a lesson begins in order to put it into the context of the pupil's existing knowledge. With completely new material expository organizers are used. They present a simplified outline of ideas and/or concepts of the new learning. Where the material overlaps with the previous knowledge of the pupils, comparative organizers can be employed. As the term implies, comparisons are drawn between the existing and the new subject matter.

One further concept, *mastery learning*, needs to be mentioned here. The concept was first elaborated by Carroll (1963) and its effectiveness discussed by Bloom (1976). An argument within education which is fundamental to the instructional procedures used relates to whether anything could be taught to anyone, given the right approach and plenty of time. Bloom summarizes the 'mastery learning' position by claiming that 'what any person in the world can learn, almost all persons can learn if provided with appropriate prior and current conditions of learning'. The essential characteristics of mastery learning are that the appropriate method of presentation has to be carefully worked out to meet the abilities and needs of a child; as much time as is necessary must be provided for the child to achieve a pre-determined level of accomplishment (or mastery) – this is often in the region of 80 per cent correct response rate along with ample cues, pupil participation, feedback (reinforcement) and the tactful correction of errors. One of the confusions presented by the term 'learning by discovery' is whether it is intended to imply the means – to give practice at discovery in order to acquire knowledge – or to imply the end product – to develop the ability to discover. Indeed, do the programmes of 'free' or 'guided' discovery embarked on in schools produce an *ability to learn in particular ways* as well as enabling an accumulation of knowledge (quality of learning as well as quantity of learning)? One needs to discern what a teacher can do to encourage the process, what the pupil must do in discovery learning and what is achieved by the procedures encouraged and adopted. These variables are still the focus of research work. In research by Rowell *et al.* (1969), the relative effectiveness of discovery and verbal reception programmes was tested using the kind of material adopted by Skemp (see Chapter 6).

In common with several other researchers, Rowell and his associates found that verbal instruction had significant merit, more so than is often given credit for by those who take up an extreme 'discovery method' position. Further, the verbal reception technique produced relatively superior results, both in the short and long term, to the discovery approach when used with students who had reached the formal operational stage of Piaget's theory of mental growth. One possible explanation offered was that:

> discovery learning, even guided discovery, requires that the student first discover and organize any new subject matter before internalization in schematic form is possible. For verbal reception learning, however, the student has only a minimum of reorganization of the material before he can internalize the schema, provided that the material has been carefully structured to meet his requirements. (Rowell *et al.* 1969, p. 242)

The findings, of course, are limited to particular forms of schemata with students who have reached mental maturity in an educational system which is essentially oriented to verbal reception techniques. The students, in effect, are more familiar with, and probably better at, verbal reception than any other strategy of learning.

Ideally, teachers who favour learning by discovery hope to produce problem-solving skills, especially those involving inductive reasoning; they assume that discovery learning is intrinsically more satisfying and therefore of greater motivational value than rote learning; they hope that pupils will learn the art of modifying generalizations in the light of new evidence, that is, that pupils will not accept propositions without examining them; they expect that their pupils will become more self-sufficient and resourceful and will not have to rely too much on the transfer of ready-made solutions from others; they anticipate that discovery learning helps in rule-finding at a time when knowledge is expanding at a phenomenal rate, and thus, by learning the rationale of a subject, knowledge acquisition is made easier. But these aspirations remain as intuitions and speculations in need of investigation using meaningful material from current curricula.

## Impact of these methods on British education

The influence of these broad approaches on the British educational system has been profound.

Active participation, enquiry and discovery methods have a long and distinguished tradition throughout the world. In formal educational settings it is associated with the names of Pestalozzi (1746–1827), and in the nineteenth century, Froebel, Montessori and Dewey. But the general trend, particularly in late primary and secondary schools, has been subject-based.

As a consequence of the Plowden Report (1967) on primary education in Britain, a wave of enthusiasm for child-centred education swept the country. Plowden wanted to see:

- less subject orientation because the boundaries between them were thought to be artificial and knowledge should be holistic
- better stimulation of children's intrinsic motivation by topic approaches in which the children would be active participants (doing, making, problem-solving)
- small group work being encouraged because it was natural to the social and co-operative learning development of children.

Subsequent HMI reports from the 1980s onwards painted a disappointing picture. Many teachers had difficulty in handling the techniques of the enquiry method and the basic subjects such as English and mathematics were suffering. Hence the onset of the National Curriculum requiring specified levels of attainment in basic subjects. The methods used are still in the hands of teachers, but most use a combination of enquiry and formal 'tell it' delivery methods (Bennett 1976, Galton *et al.* 1980, Galton and Simon 1980, Branwhite 1983, Galton *et al.* 1999).

The pendulum is at the expository end of its swing with the Government's contemporary policy and directives on minimum compulsory whole-class teaching in maths and English. This subject has attracted government funding in recent years (Alexander *et al.* 1992, Bennett

1987, Campbell 1993). Another example is the debate about declining standards in primary schools and their causes (Hayes 2003, Richards 1997).

The role of pupil participation in the learning process and the place of the teacher in this process have been recurring issues in this book. There are times when children want and need to sit back and listen; there are times when they need actively to explore for themselves. Piaget (see Chapter 4) has suggested that active involvement helps to lay down schemata. Model making, visits and well-organized project work plainly encourage the child to participate in learning. Most teachers now use a combination of methods to suit the curriculum.

## Individual learning and diagnosis

The most successful techniques in education seem to be those involving one-to-one methods between teacher and pupil. Programmes for children with special needs (Chapter 11), teaching exceptional children (Chapters 9 and 11), methods used for teaching musical instruments or practical work or the New Zealand Reading Recovery scheme (Clay's work, discussed in Chapters 5 and 7) are largely dependent on individual teaching schemes. Were it not for the economic prohibitions which face education at present, there could well have been more facilities for individual tuition. As computers, word processors and their successors become cheaper, we shall see more use made of them in our homes and classrooms (*electronic learning*) (Hartley 1998). It is already possible to use the Internet for several curriculum topics and as a source of information, much the same as using a book except that the information can be available at home and can be made interactive with the pupil.

Most theories applied to educational problems tend to *describe* rather than *assist* learning and intellectual development. The reason is that the former is much easier than the latter; also, description is easier to live with than prescription, especially when one is dealing with the future of someone else's child. Nevertheless, this is the direction in which the subject is heading. Teaching is becoming more diagnostic. Learning is becoming more clearly directed towards greater self-sufficiency in the learner. The history of the learner, such as home influences, early schooling, life experiences, is more and more the subject of intense inspection by researchers for its impact on later learning. Syllabuses, subjects and exams are being dismantled and scrutinized for improved methods and sequences of presentation. Indeed, assessment is now obligatory at particular ages in the school system.

# Behaviour modification: social and academic learning

The term *behaviour modification* involves the systematic application of learning theories (particularly those of Skinner and his operant conditioning) to bring about a desired change in patterns of behaviour. Its relevance to the classroom is obvious, because the major function of any teacher is to change 'for the better' the academic, social and moral behaviour of children. The technique of reinforcement, already mentioned above, is used. Positive reinforcers are intended to maintain or increase the observed behaviour. Encouraging comments about work, and rewards of various kinds, are examples. A negative reinforcer is intended to reduce and even eliminate an observed behaviour. Shouting for silence, punishments, etc. are negative reinforcers. Unfortunately, some of these reinforcement schedules have a nasty habit of working in unforeseen directions. Attention-seeking children are often prepared to put up with the milder negative reinforcers because of the attention which they receive as a result of trying to apply the schedule. These and other strategic ploys are described in readable detail in Poteet (1973).

One of the first direct applications of laboratory psychology has come largely from the work of Skinner (1953), using his techniques of operant conditioning schedules of reinforcement for controlling and shaping human behaviour. The system has been used to reshape the behaviour of children and adults in the usual classroom settings from mild misbehaviour to serious SEN conditions (Chapter 11). A few examples are:

- fear and anxiety of various aspects of school life – even going to school is fearful for some pupils, particularly those being bullied
- gross misbehaviour in class, thereby in need of some special educational programme
- wetting and soiling clothing or substance abuse
- serious conditions of children included in state classrooms with learning, communication and behavioural difficulties, e.g., dyslexia, autism, attention deficit, eating disorders (anorexia, bulimia), to obsessive/compulsive disorder
- criminal and delinquent activity.

The range of behaviour modification techniques includes rewarding and/or ignoring behaviour, modelling, shaping, token economies. We defined some of these in Chapter 6 (pp. 164–70) where 'little Albert' was given as an early example of *systematic desensitization* – gradual introduction of the feared stimulus in the presence of a pleasant stimulus.

## Reinforcement – rewarding and/or ignoring behaviour

Wheldall and Glynn (1989; Wheldall and Beaman 1998) give an instantly recognizable example of a harassed teacher trying to settle a class down, more in the nature of a noise abatement officer. 'Right, that's enough . . . settle down . . . I said "settle down" and I mean what I say, SETTLE DOWN. Now yesterday we were looking at . . . John! Stop pulling Janet's hair and turn this way . . . etc.' Often these outbursts are negative (*don't* do this) and confrontational. They found that two behaviour problems – talking out of turn (TOOT) and hindering other children (HOC) – were by far the most frequent in both primary and secondary schools. Physical aggression was rare. TOOT and HOC do not sound serious, but irritating, time-wasting and persistent occurrences, like the Chinese water torture, can wear teachers down and contribute to exhaustion and stress.

At the very least, there are three critical steps needed before running any behaviour modification programme. We have to decide in detail:

- what behaviour(s) we do not accept and/or want to change
- what behaviour(s) we accept instead
- the strategy to be used to modify the behaviour.

TOOT and HOC behaviour is not tolerated by most teachers. But we have to pinpoint the specific activities we will not tolerate, such as getting out of a seat and wandering round unnecessarily or shouting out answers to questions put to another pupil. The desired behaviours in these instances are fairly obvious; in short, sit down and shut up! The hardest part is to decide which strategy will redirect the pupil in the desired direction. There are several possibilities discussed in the next few pages.

From a research in the US (1968) Madsen *et al.* concluded that the technique of 'rules, praise and ignoring' (RPI) was effective. This involves first establishing rules of conduct in the class such as 'We try to work quietly and put up our hands when we need help or want to answer a question', 'We listen carefully to instructions and read the board', 'We try not to interrupt either the teacher or other pupils.' These derive from a careful analysis of unacceptable behaviour and substituting with rules.

Next, the teacher praises when the rules are kept and ignores the breaking of rules. 'Ignoring' by itself (i.e. without having rules or praising) has been shown to be quite ineffective. The essential part, once rules have been established, is praise. Research shows that reinforcing desired behaviour of rule-keeping and on-task behaviour with praise leads to an increase in desired behaviour. Equally, increasing the number of commands against undesirable behaviour such as 'sit down' *increases* out-of-seat behaviour. Basically, teachers have to be shrewd rather than crude in their methods.

Praise or reward mechanisms can take many forms such as verbal ('well done!' 'good work'), non-verbal (nods, smiles, facial and body gestures), token (marks, stars, points) and back-up (so many tokens, stars, points can be used for a more substantial reward, such as feeding the animals in the classroom (primary), or receiving some extra privilege – free time in school).

To increase a teacher's range of reinforcers one has to look for those aspects of classroom life that children find rewarding, many of which are the rewards in life itself, no matter where a person is, but some are specific to classroom life. Whatever else, the rewards must have meaning, otherwise they will not survive. There are many to choose from, and a little thought should produce quite a formidable list ranging from intrinsic rewards which are difficult to objectivize (feelings of satisfaction, joy) to extrinsic rewards (the verbal, non-verbal, token rewards mentioned in the last paragraph). Of these, we can only make guesses about the intrinsic ones from what children say. Extrinsic factors are observable and, to the advantage of the teacher, manipulable. The introduction of this method does not necessarily bring change right away. It has to be worked at systematically.

A rewarding activity can be used as 'bait' for a less rewarding one, for example, 'If you eat your tea, you can go out to play', 'The first to put books away and clear their desktops can feed the rabbits' – the *Premack Principle.*

The ground rules enunciated by Skinner and his associates need to be borne in mind when applying reward systems. These are:

- make sure the learner knows exactly why he or she is being rewarded
- reward should quickly follow the required behaviour (correct answer to oral question, good essay)
- there should be consistency in the reward system. Irregular, patchy, uneven systems which the children cannot fathom are obviously not going to be recognized and utilized by them
- frequent reward should be applied in the early stages (continuous reinforcement) and gradually reduced as circumstances permit (intermittent reinforcement). But it is unwise to overdo the frequency of rewards if it is not necessary (learners become immune – see Brophy 1981). Also, do not give rewards which are disproportionate to the deed – let the reward fit the deed in form and magnitude
- situations should be created to enable all those in the class to be rewarded appropriately at some time.

But there is another input which is crucial (the subject of Chapter 8). The pupils have to be interested and well motivated. Interested minds tend not to be disruptive. Nevertheless, there are always the few pupils who are impervious to RPI and sanctions become necessary. Telling off, *time-out*, going to the headteacher, detention, writing to parents and ultimately exclusion from the school are the usual sanctions. Time-out usually consists of removing someone from a place they like to be to a place they definitely do not like to be, usually exposed to prowling head or senior teachers on empty school corridors during lessons. A common one is to stand outside the classroom or the headteacher's room for 15 to 20 minutes. It's equivalent to showing a footballer the red card and being sent off!

A government report on expulsions from schools (DfEE and OFSTED report, 1996) highlights the points made in the previous two paragraphs. The inspectors from OFSTED found that the schools which were effective in dealing with problem children shared certain features:

- good, interesting teaching so the pupils were not bored
- clearly stated boundaries of behaviour
- policies for rewards and sanctions.

Though expulsion or exclusion from school may be thought of by some as the ultimate sanction, others on the receiving end may regard it as the ultimate prize. Some of the older pupils in the fourth and fifth secondary forms cannot wait to leave school and thus regard exclusion as a reward rather than a punishment – unless parents become involved.

## Modelling

The study of motivation and learning as a consequence of social interaction and imitation has become a fruitful area of investigation within social cognitive theory. Bandura and his co-workers set out to define the modelling process (Bandura and Walters 1963) and develop a social cognitive theory around the findings (Bandura 1986). The theory is based on three assumptions:

- there is triangular interaction between stimulus, person and response (not linear S–O–R as in behaviourist theory)
- people only demonstrate what they have learnt by imitation when they are motivated to do so
- there are two kinds of learning – *enactive* and *vicarious*.

Enactive learning occurs by doing and then experiencing the consequences of one's action. Successful actions are likely to be repeated; unsuccessful actions are likely to be discarded, much as in the behaviourist tradition. Vicarious learning occurs when a person observes living or symbolic (e.g. books, TV, films, cartoons) models without overtly doing anything. In effect, it is the difference between active and passive learning. In active learning, the individual is personally exploring and being influenced by his or her own success or failure. In passive learning, the person is motivated by observing the success (or failure) of the model.

*Modelling* occurs when an individual's behaviour changes as a result of observing another person's behaviour. Children frequently try to imitate adults, peers and characters they read about or see on TV. For instance, the evidence for the influence of TV in providing role models is now overwhelming.

### Further reading

The influence of TV on children's behaviour is a controversial area. TV, the window on the world, is here to stay. It has many useful applications, but the impact of aggressive, violent and depraved programmes is a matter for concern. In the 1960s, Bandura *et al.* started the ball rolling with their paper, 'Imitation of film-mediated aggressive models' (1963). For a readable, recent, summary of the uses and abuses of TV have a look at Gunter and McAleer, *Children and Television: The One Eyed Monster?* (1990).

There are, according to Bandura, at least three effects of exposure to *models* (parents, teachers, friends, famous people) which give rise to behavioural change. First, children may copy an entirely new response pattern not in their behaviour repertoire. This is called the *modelling effect*. The unit of behaviour is frequently complete at an early stage of imitation and seems to bear little resemblance to the trial-and-error or successive approximations of stimulus–response theory. A now famous piece of research by Bandura, Ross and Ross (1963) presented several children with a film showing aggressive adults. Without prompting or reinforcement of any kind, the children quickly began to display similar aggressive behaviour.

Second, observation of behaviour of a model may lead children to alter their own established responses by strengthening or inhibiting the responses. In this way children adjust the 'limits' of their behaviour as they discover, through watching others, the tolerance levels in particular situations. For example, if children see a certain kind of behaviour go unpunished which they previously regarded as punishable, they are less likely to inhibit their behaviour on subsequent similar occasions. These are called *inhibitory* or *disinhibitory* effects.

The third behavioural change arises from what Bandura calls the *response facilitation effect* (sometimes known as the *eliciting effect*). Behaviour is sometimes initiated in an observer by the cues given to that person from a model. The process has much in common with the ethologist's explanation of innate release mechanisms (see Chapter 8) except that the patterns of social behaviour are not regarded by Bandura as inborn. The child matches the behaviour observed in others with behaviour already in the repertoire. It appears as if the behaviour of the model acts as a releaser for parallel behaviour in the observer. For example, if a child notices someone helping a distressed person and voluntarily goes to add assistance, it would be a case of elicited response. Another example, illustrated in many TV programmes using behavioural techniques to change child behaviour in a problem family, is that often one or both parents exhibit the behaviour to be extinguished from the child. Argumentativeness and spiteful behaviour are two common examples.

What are the characteristics of effective models? We do not automatically copy others and would need to be motivated to do so. Models are most effective when they:

- show competence
- are perceived by the observer to have similarities between him or herself and the model
- have credibility, that is, models who practise what they preach
- show enthusiasm – models who glow with interest in what they are doing or saying are more likely to influence observers.

All these features are clearly useful for teachers who are acting as role models. The distinctive styles of the teacher as a model of social behaviour, that is, his or her aggressiveness, friendliness, aloofness, co-operativeness, calmness, etc. will act as the initiators of novel behaviour changes in the child or will modify or trigger off existing patterns. The teacher is clearly a potent figure in the social behaviour modifications of children. Once language has been acquired, the models need not be real, but can be pictorial or verbal. The acquisition of certain kinds of language usage and meaning are thought by Bandura to be partly the result of modelling from adult conversation (see the work of Bernstein in Chapter 5). Some children from working-class backgrounds have difficulty in compromising between their home models and those of their middle-class teachers. Another point worth considering is the extent to which the student-teacher's style is modelled on others he or she has seen as teachers.

The holistic rather than the 'bit-by-bit' approach to social learning is emphasized by Bandura (1970), who concludes:

> It is evident from informal observation that vicarious learning experience and response guidance procedures involving both symbolic and live models are utilized extensively in social learning to short-circuit the acquisition process. Indeed, it would be difficult to imagine a culture in which the language, mores, vocational and avocational patterns, familial customs, and educational, social, and political practices were shaped in each new member through the gradual process of differential reinforcement without the response guidance of models who exemplify the accumulated cultural repertoires in their own behaviour. In social learning under naturalistic conditions responses are typically acquired through modelling in large segments or *in toto* rather than in a piecemeal, trial-and-error fashion.

How often do we say to pupils 'stop and think about what you are doing'? *Cognitive behaviour therapy* is about altering people's behaviour by talking to them and offering alternatives. It is an attempt to modify the behaviour of others by getting them to think differently about their actions. The process is to get people to express their thoughts, feelings and subsequent actions, and replace these with other, more desirable thoughts feelings and actions. It is a close relative of modelling. Persuasion usually takes the form of talking matters through and, where possible, demonstrating the effects of the alternative actions.

It is often used by psychologists (Atkinson and Hornby 2002) in cases of conduct disorder, ADHD (attention deficit hyperactivity disorder), eating disorders, obsessive-compulsive disorder and post traumatic stress.

## Shaping methods in the classroom

*Shaping* is the technique of reinforcing successive bits of desired behaviour in order to build up an acceptable pattern of action. This is a very familiar procedure in many behaviour-therapy schedules. Lovaas (1967, 1987, 1993) in a long and well-documented research with autistic children under four years of age, produced lasting improvements in their behaviour and language performance. The characteristic signs of autism (Chapter 11, pp. 365–6) include an inability on the part of the child to communicate or socially interact with others.

He or she finds even looking at another person very difficult. To improve this condition, Lovaas (1967) used a schedule involving food, drink and praise as rewards. A therapist is seated opposite the autistic child, who is rewarded with a spoonful of food or a drink each time he or she attempts to look in the direction of the therapist. Next, the therapist concentrates on rewarding sounds or lip movements, then words and finally sentences. By a process of rewarding small improvements in desired behaviour, the child develops social and language skills. To be realistic, we must point out that this was a most intense project involving not only therapists but also parents and teachers applying the technique over a long period. Follow-up studies (McEachin, Smith and Lovaas 1993) show that the improvement was lasting.

The technique has much in common with the experiment described in Chapter 6 where a pigeon was taught to walk in a figure of eight. Note the need in both schedules to use a step-wise reward system until the total behaviour required has been pieced together. The method works, although its critics feel it to be an inhuman way of dealing with children, particularly when the long-term effects are not completely known, even if, in many cases, it does work better than other methods. The behaviourist techniques used here are also an example of *differential reinforcement* because only certain parts of the behaviour are rewarded.

## Token economies

The use of tangible reinforcers such as stars, prizes, money or gifts is not new. Indeed, it is why we go out to work! But the systematic application of a reinforcement schedule of tokens is quite recent. In fact, the rapid growth of *token economy* methods with humans has taken place over the past 20 years or so, from the earlier work of such people as Tyler and Brown (1968) (academic performance of delinquent boys) to the original and stimulating work of Hoghughi (1979 – token treatment methods for gravely disturbed adolescents in residential care) (see also Hoghughi 1988 and Kazdin 1977). In normal classrooms the idea of using extrinsic rewards which might be expensive is prohibitive. Therefore several programmes have been devised which start with external rewards of one kind or another (prizes, etc.) and become transferred to inexpensive reinforcers (free time, enjoyed activities).

Work with a group of delinquents in a Washington reform school provides an example. Forty young criminals, including murderers, rapists and other serious offenders, were submitted to a schedule involving their living conditions. Leisure activities, food and living quarters were used as incentives for improving their behaviour and learning a trade. At worst, the offender could sit around doing little of interest, live on a boring frugal diet and sleep in a dormitory. Good behaviour and learning using teaching machines, however, were rewarded by better food, private quarters, colour television and a free day out. By the time they were due out, many had learned useful skills from the programmed learning texts – a feat they had abandoned at school. Normally, most delinquents are in trouble within three years of leaving a reform school in America. In Skinner's sample only 45 per cent were in trouble within three years.

## Applied behavioural methods in classroom management

Behaviour modification programmes applied in normal school settings to change disruptive and antisocial behaviour have been especially prominent in the American and Australian educational systems (Whitman and Whitman 1971, Poteet 1985, Sparzo and Poteet 1989). In Britain there is still a reluctance to apply what appear to some to be mechanical strategies in such an essentially varied habitat as the classroom. However, there has been an upsurge of interest arising from the work of Wheldall and associates at Birmingham and in Australia (Wheldall and Merrett 1985a and b). As the term 'behaviour modification' has had some unfortunate associations, they prefer to use the expression 'applied behavioural analysis' to the techniques used.

The behavioural approach to teaching is based on conventional Skinnerian traditions:

- the concern of the psychology of teaching is with the observable, that is, what a child actually does rather than speculations about the underlying processes
- for all practical purposes behaviour can be regarded as learned, that is, what a person does depends on his or her learning from interaction with the environment and is not innate
- learning means change of observable behaviour, that is, the only way one can know that learning has taken place is by a change in behaviour
- learning is governed principally by the 'law of effect', that is, behaviour which has led to a desirable or rewarding outcome tends to be repeated, whereas aversive or punishing outcomes of behaviour tend not to be repeated
- learning is also governed by the context in which it occurs, that is, certain kinds of behaviour are more appropriate in some situations than others and we quickly learn to recognize this and act accordingly.

The principle is that a desirable or rewarding outcome tends to be repeated, whereas aversive or punishing outcomes of behaviour tend not to be repeated. A useful table summarizing a pattern of teacher behaviour designed to change, appropriately, learner behaviour is adapted from Skinner (Table 14.1).

With these lines established, Wheldall and Merrett (1985a and b) have designed a behavioural approach to classroom management for the in-service training of teachers called the BATPACK (Behavioural Approach to Teaching Package). The idea is to provide a method for training primary and middle school teachers in some key behavioural skills. It is skill-based and aims to change teachers' methods towards more positive teaching, e.g. effective use of praise, positive rule-setting, pinpointing behaviours. It is carried out in groups rather than by individuals and is therefore of more value in a school setting where several teachers

**Table 14.1** Techniques for changing behaviour (after Skinner)

|  | *To increase behaviour(s)* | *To decrease behaviour(s)* |
|---|---|---|
| Delivery of | 'Good things', i.e. rewarding with smiles, sweets, toys, praise, etc. | 'Bad things', i.e. punishing with smacks, frowns, reprimands, etc. |
|  | Technical term: | Technical term: |
|  | Positive Reinforcement | Punishment |
| Removal of | 'Bad things', i.e. allowing escape from pain, noise, nagging, threats, etc. | 'Good things', i.e. losing privileges, house points, money, opportunities to earn, 'good things', etc. |
|  | Technical term: | Technical term: |
|  | Negative Reinforcement | Response Cost |

are working on the BATPACK together. It is run after school, on school premises if possible, by a tutor who is trained in its use. The BATPACK course consists of six one-hour sessions taught weekly. The units are:

**Unit 1:** Identifying troublesome behaviour
Take-home 1: The five principles of the behavioural approach to teaching
**Unit 2:** Focusing on desirable behaviour
Take-home 2: The behavioural teacher's ABC
**Unit 3:** Eliminating (or, at least, reducing) the negative
Take-home 3: Negative consequences
**Unit 4:** Accentuating the positive
Take-home 4: Using positive reinforcement effectively
**Unit 5:** Getting the classroom setting right
Take-home 5: Antecedents – settings for behaviour
**Unit 6:** Where do we go from here?
Take-home 6: Behavioural charter and evaluation.

The take-home material is more theoretical and intended to reinforce the sessions.

> The method concentrates on improving the teacher's ability to manage the classroom situation as a whole rather than the behavioural/learning problems of particular children. It attempts to do this by helping teachers to define clearly the commonest classroom behaviour problems and to observe them carefully, whilst concentrating upon positive measures to bring about change. . . . The contingent use of praise is particularly emphasized. Teachers are taught praising skills alongside related skills such as 'rule setting' and deliberate 'ignoring'. (Wheldall and Merrett 1985b)

Wheldall is now able to claim that it is possible to modify teacher behaviour to benefit classroom behaviour.

# Class management strategies

## Leadership

Wherever a group is formed, either formally or informally, leaders emerge. In the classroom, the teacher has a formal commitment to take the role of leader, although some activities result from democratic and shared decision-making. Leaders are those who have power to influence others. This power may be given to a person – when it goes with the job, such as service officer or foreman in industry – or it may be earned through respect from the rest of the group. Several researches have attempted to discover the characteristics of the effective leader, but no reliable generalizations have resulted from them (Schmuck and Schmuck 1971).

Several kinds of leadership descriptions have been proposed. Generally, they reduce to the twofold Model A and Model B of Hoyle (1975). These idealized models, to which a third, *laissez-faire*, has been added, are:

- Model A – *a bureaucracy* with a clearly defined hierarchy, authority being vested in a chosen person, that is, an authoritarian system.
- Model B – *a human relations* model where decision-making is shared and authority spread widely, that is, a democratic system.
- *Laissez-faire* (defined in the next paragraph).

These three were used in one of the earliest researches on leadership patterns and their effect on performance. Lippitt and White (1970) set out to describe the leadership styles of youth club leaders. The effectiveness of the various styles was assessed using the criteria of productivity and enjoyment of the activity for members of the group (i.e. enjoyment of the relationships). The *authoritarian* system was a teacher-centred one highlighting formality, teacher-directed communication and dominance, competition and punishment. In the *democratic* system, the stress was on learner participation in decisions, on co-operation and open-ended structures in human relationships. The *laissez-faire* system was one in which the leader or teacher gave complete freedom to the group to make decisions and offered the minimum of guidance. The effectiveness of these styles was quite enlightening. The authoritarian-led group produced more in less time, but relationships were not good. The *laissez-faire* group displayed both poor productivity and inter-relationships. The democratic group was a little less productive than the authoritarian group, but their relationships were the best.

In the classroom, the style of leadership will need to change with the circumstances. A lot depends on the organizational demands of a particular lesson. It is therefore not wise to limit one's leadership stance to any one of the above. Thinking of the variety of situations in a typical classroom, it seems that all three will find a place at some time in the organizational management. However, leaderless children (the *laissez-faire* régime) will quickly find their own, usually very inadequate, substitute leaders (intuitively and cleverly portrayed in William Golding's book *Lord of the Flies*). They create their own standards of performance (not strenuously high) and discipline is hard to keep.

## Leadership and exercising control

How do teachers attempt to achieve the leader role? The three broad leadership types of authoritarian, democratic and *laissez-faire* described in the last section can be seen in action in the variety of techniques noted by Woods (1979) in a descriptive study of secondary school pupils. It is instructive to look at the important and useful techniques he describes. These are *socialization, occupational therapy, domination, negotiation, fraternization* and *ritual and routine.* Most of these methods are used by most teachers, in moderation, and can be employed to good effect, provided they are not carried to extremes. Woods' descriptions are exemplified by extreme cases, but modest and caring use are effective.

The process of *socialization* at home and school is essential. There are rules to every well-organized system, and living in harmony with others in a culture similarly must have its dos and don'ts. Schools, in effect mini-societies, are obvious places for teaching those rules. Some rules are clearly stated, such as the laws of the land or matters of common courtesy and decency. Schools develop guidelines such as knowing about the school, classroom conduct and what some describe as the Puritan or Protestant ethic of 'hard work, sober living and good manners'. Actually, if one condoned the opposite of these – laziness, intemperance and bad manners – life would be intolerable for teachers. Students and beginning teachers need to familiarize themselves with the school traditions and help to apply them. Classroom codes are partly laid down by the school, but are mainly left to the teacher. Have a clear idea of your own codes of practice, your expectations of pupils' behaviour and strive to ensure that the class follows them.

The term *occupational therapy* is used by Woods as a somewhat derisory way of describing the use of practical sessions as a means of killing time with dulling, but acceptable (to the pupils), activities – more in the nature of play than work. Practical work in science, housecraft, wood or metal work, drawing maps, patterns and so forth are patently part of the essentials of these practical subjects. Students must guard against the use of practical sessions as a means of occupying the class. There must be an expectation of useful outcomes. This also applies to 'duties' handed out to pupils. This is a very acceptable process of involving children in the life of the classroom. The important distinction between occupational therapy as a playway and as a practical learning device is *educational purposefulness*. There has to be a clear, but defined learning outcome, where children can still enjoy the practical work.

*Domination*, if it means crude physical punishments such as lifting children by their ears or hair or rapping knuckles with a block of wood, is a totally unacceptable and an outlawed way of exercising authority. On the other hand, domination, if it means the forceful, but compassionate, application of authority (such as verbal control done sensibly and not abusively), is inevitable. Later we shall take up the question of discipline in the classroom, but, for the moment, this extract from a practising headteacher summarizes a sensible middle road:

> You have to be able to dominate the group. Obviously this is an ability that has to be used tactfully and sensitively – but it must be possible. It is pointless to be afraid of 'dominating' the pupils, whether for the sake of creating good relationships or from a wish to allow individualists to flourish.
>
> There is amongst many young teachers a diffidence that makes them pull back from imposing their will: the result, too often, is that a clique of pupils in the class imposes its will instead. This is resented by other pupils, and the resentment sours those pupils' relationship with the teacher. Diffidence is a virtue in many circumstances, but it is dangerous in the classroom: it often allows those who are not diffident – and there are likely to be a few in every group – to dominate. (Marland 1993)

Related to the domination issue is the place of *negotiation* in applying codes of practice. About some issues in the classroom (e.g. discourtesy, excessive noise, violence, crudeness), there can be no compromise. They should not be allowed to persist. Other issues can be negotiated. Agreements about classroom behaviour are frequently mapped out by discussion between teacher and pupils. Indeed, pupils who move from teacher to teacher, as in the secondary school, experience almost as many régimes as there are teachers, each one having worked out a set of ground rules.

*Fraternization* or 'if you can't beat them, join them', if used sensibly, can help to bridge the generation gap by skilful identification of common interests. For example, sport (particularly football and less so cricket, tennis, hockey, self-defence), physical fitness, hobbies, music ('pop' or otherwise), drama, TV are sources of common interest. What the student or beginning teacher must avoid is adopting the role of an adolescent – or even worse a young child. An embarrassing situation can easily be provoked in schools by a middle-aged 'trendy' attempting to emulate an adolescent in word and deed. Respect should be earned through having something worth looking up to, not by lowering one's sights in order to gain favour.

The human race survives by *ritual* and *routine*. Random and constant change would be both exhausting and destructive in the end. We saw earlier that life in the classroom for a teacher becomes tolerable when some decision-making, probably most of it, is routine. In fact, Woods (1979) showed that routine systems of regulated activity tended to give fewer management problems than self-paced activities.

All these devices for survival are described by Woods in a somewhat exaggerated way. There is, however, real value in subtle and thoughtful appreciation by teachers of all the above tactics. All are aimed at establishing the teacher as leader in the exercise of control.

# Group management strategies

Good group management starts at the top and works downwards. Looking back at your own educational experiences should soon reveal that the quality of the education you received had something to do with the headteacher's attitudes. Without a clear lead from the head, teachers are often placed in a vacuum. As we saw above, children need to know the boundaries within which they are required to operate in a school. The head, along with the cooperation of staff, set these boundaries, support each other in making sure the rules are applied and should feel confident that the head will support the staff in applying them.

In the classroom, one of the earliest and most influential pieces of research was undertaken by Kounin and associates (Kounin 1970), who used classroom observation techniques including videotapes. Kounin observed teachers' group-management techniques, choosing extremes of successful and unsuccessful managers in an effort to tease out those qualities which distinguished them. Intriguingly, Kounin did not manage to isolate a single *consistent* variable that characterized successful or unsuccessful teachers although they all dealt with behaviour problems in very much the same fashion. Detailed study of the tapes, however, did reveal some useful positive points worthy of note which are associated with reasonably well-controlled classes.

## *Anticipation*

Anticipation of possible sources of trouble is an asset. 'Prevention is better than cure' works especially well and seems to be the order of the day with successful teachers. The teacher who can 'suss out' a possible centre of deviant behaviour and nip it in the bud before it escalates has a better chance of surviving than one who allows matters to reach a point where disciplinary action has to be taken.

## *'Withitness'*

This ability to anticipate sources of trouble Kounin called 'withitness'. It is the teacher with eyes at the back of the head, omnipresent (who always seems to be on the spot and does not miss a trick), one who has the whole class in the sights by effective scanning. It is almost tantamount to a sixth sense about the origins of children's disruptive tactics. The secrets seem to be *timing, targeting* and *temperate reaction*. One has to judge the right moment to intrude in the appearance of misbehaviour; some jump in too soon and have a repeat performance on their hands a little later. To aim at the wrong target can be disastrous. Miscreants get great pleasure from seeing others blamed for their transgressions, and the innocent, quite rightly, find it very hard to forgive the injustices of being falsely accused and condemned. Temperate reaction is needed, not overreaction. Overreaction can be fatal. Judging the level of reaction to particular situations is most important. Avoid overdoing the reaction to the point of loud, hysterical shouting. Move in long before this point. Tantrums from a teacher are not exactly the model one wishes to convey to pupils. The failing student is often the one who is swamped by the situation. He or she tends to concentrate on the detail of a child's problems and loses sight of the rest of the class.

### Smoothness

Smoothness in keeping children at work is important. Avoid: (a) intruding when there is useful, business-like activity; (b) starting a new activity abruptly before the present one has been finished; and (c) chopping and changing activities by starting and finishing abruptly (Kounin refers to this as 'flip-flops').

### Do not stay on a topic too long

Do not remain on a topic too long and avoid organizational arrangements which will slow the majority down to a pace below their competence. Flow and continuity – keeping children busy with what they see as interesting material – is effective ('they don't have time to misbehave').

### Overlapping

Overlapping, or the ability to do more than one thing at once, is a useful strategy. The idea is that no child should feel able to go unobserved or unnoticed for any length of time. While helping one child, it should be possible to cast eyes around the class for disruptive behaviour or those needing help, and make sure the children know you're looking.

One aspect of Kounin's work which is useful to know is that a correlation exists between successful instructional management and behavioural classroom management. In plain terms, those who have their material well prepared, who organize and present activities in tight, interesting ways tend to have fewer behavioural problems.

Another key to success found by Kounin (and confirmed in much recent research, including Wragg 1996) is the extent of *teacher and pupil* involvement in lessons. There is a significant relationship between high involvement and low deviancy (the more the pupils are involved, the less time they have to be disruptive).

There are age-related differences in the above strategies. The socialization process for the little ones forms a major part of a reception teacher's day – innocent high spirits sometimes appear. In primary school, vigilance is not such a severe problem as in the secondary age-range of 12–15 years. A host of factors – changing motivation patterns, puberty, change of teaching system, striking out for independence, teachers are not in contact for as long as in the primary school, and so on – give rise to changing attitudes and interactions between teachers and pupils. The observations of Kounin are particularly relevant to this latter age group.

Several books have appeared on class and individual behaviour control. A recent one by Cowley (2003, with an interesting title) summarizes in practical ways the findings of research outlined in the above sections.

## Teacher's clarity of exposition

Success in the classroom is not just a matter of how well children can learn to communicate. The teacher also has a responsibility to develop skills of clear presentation. The starting point for any explanation is the pool of knowledge and experience which the teacher and learners bring, and the wider fund of knowledge obtainable from the literature, samples, experiment, etc. These resolve into verbal presentation or demonstration and the use of aids of all kinds, using where possible the learners' knowledge and experience.

A number of guidelines are listed below, some from research into verbal style of presentation (Hargie *et al.* 1994). They are guidelines, *not* rules. Their main concerns are for brevity, simplicity appropriate to the level of the learners, order, fluency and use of language.

- Use grammatically simple presentation and make points quite explicit.
- Use appropriate language understandable by the age group being taught; define all technical terms and never try to blind youngsters with science.
- Do not use vague or 'padding' language.
- Use brevity, appeal and coverage. A learner's day is packed full of different new ideas; if every description consisted of weaving webs of words around learners, they could end up paralyzed and mentally inactive.
- Put in the main points early on, unless it is a gradual build-up lesson.
- Use analogy and metaphor: analogies from familiar experience or graphic metaphors help to implant ideas.
- Repeat ideas, when possible in a different way or by using analogies.
- Keep up fluency and continuity. A hesitant style can be off-putting, and darting about in the content whenever the mood takes you can be fatal if you want the pupils to remember anything.
- Emphasize and pause for effect.

These guidelines contain a number of criteria which students can observe for themselves. Discovering the most useful attributes for one's particular approach to teaching is an essential part of school practice.

## Summary

Having a firm grip on both the academic and behavioural processes in a classroom is the bread and butter of a teacher's life.

Frameworks or *models* supporting the academic presentation of the syllabus include a comprehensive proposal by Bloom (1976) and this is elaborated. Three major sections in the model spread out to other chapters of the book. They are the characteristics which each pupil brings to learning, the *modus operandi* of teaching (American authors have no difficulty with the word 'instruction') and learning outcomes which include assessment results. These are dealt with in some detail.

A great debate of our time is the relative merits of 'discovery' and 'expository' methods. Should children be allowed free rein in coming to terms with knowledge about their environments? Should they be given a few clues and left to find the rest for themselves? Should they be told what we know so far and encouraged to learn it? The answer probably lies somewhere between all these and most teachers use a combination of the methods. Children need to know how to access knowledge and to think clearly for themselves. But in a world where knowledge is expanding exponentially, trying to discover entirely from scratch, or to learn most of what is known about a topic, is totally unnecessary and unrealistic. Knowing how to access knowledge when required is far more important.

But learning the basics of any subject is important in order to enable a student both to build a knowledge base and search for more advanced material. Indeed, some foundation stones of knowledge have no logic and require rote learning. For instance, symbols such as numbers, letters and musical notation have to be learned by heart. Also, scientific and mathematical laws, events and dates in history, geographical facts, conventional steps in dancing or moves in karate are usually committed to memory.

The Behaviourist School has made a particularly significant contribution in both academic and social learning. Methods to help rote learning, assist in motivating pupils and class control are examples. Encouraging desired behaviour and extinguishing undesired behaviour are helped using modelling, shaping, token economies and reinforcing programmes. These are now available for teachers in the BATPACK (Wheldall and Merrett 1985a and b).

Leadership and exercising class control are central features in class management for academic, social and behavioural reasons. Several examples of the issues and strategies are provided.

## Tutorial enquiry and discussion

(a) Examine the work of Bruner, Ausubel, Bloom and Gagné (references in 'Further reading') and their contributions in the light of the model of instruction, Figure 14.1. How firm is the evidence for the comparable effects of discovery learning and expository learning? Are there situations when one method is more suitable than the other?

(b) Try to get hold of the BATPACK (Wheldall and Merrett 1985a and b) and explore with tutors the value of this procedure in classroom management. Try to observe it in action in a school.

(c) What do children find rewarding in classroom life?
   (i) What influences self-concept and self-esteem?
   (ii) Look for verbal and non-verbal responses from the teacher which might be rewarding.
   (iii) What token systems are possible in primary and/or secondary schools?
   (iv) What effect does age or ability have on the nature of rewards?

(d) Look for examples of 'modelling' among children, that is, the imitation of novel chunks of behaviour *in toto*. Compare and contrast the technique needed for teaching behaviours using modelling or operant conditioning.

(e) Examine your personal leadership preferences (authoritarian ('strict and scary'), democratic ('firm but fun') or *laissez-faire*).

(f) Explore which of Woods' (1979) techniques (*socialization, occupational therapy, domination, negotiation, fraternization* and *ritual and routine*) you use and in what circumstances.

(g) Couple (e) and (f) with Cowley's text on *Getting the Buggers to Behave* (2006).

(h) Look at Kounin's (1970) group-management techniques (anticipation, 'withitness', smoothness, overlapping) and compare them with your own.

## References

Alexander, R., Rose, J. and Woodhead, C. (1992), *Curriculum Organisation and Classroom Practice in Primary Schools: A Discussion Paper*. DES. London: HMSO.

Atkinson, M. and Hornby, G. (2002), *Mental Health Handbook for Schools*. London: Routledge Falmer.

Ausubel, D. P. and Robinson, F. G. (1969), *School Learning: An Introduction to Educational Psychology*. New York: Holt, Rinehart and Winston.

Bandura, A. (1970), *Principles of Behavior Modification*. London: Holt, Rinehart and Winston.

Bandura, A. (1986), *Social Foundations of Thought and Action: A Social Cognitive Theory.* Englewood Cliffs, NJ: Prentice Hall.

Bandura, A., Ross, D. and Ross, S. A. (1963), Imitation of film-mediated aggressive models. *Journal of Abnormal and Social Psychology*, 66, 3–11.

Bandura, A. and Walters, R. H. (1963), *Social Learning and Personality Development*. London: Holt, Rinehart and Winston.

Bennett, N. (1976), *Teaching Styles and Pupil Progress*. London: Open Books.

Bennett, N. (1987), 'Changing perspectives on teaching-learning processes in the post-Plowden era', *Oxford Review in Education*, 13(1), 67–79.

Bloom, B. S. (1976), *Human Characteristics and School Learning*. New York: McGraw-Hill.

Branwhite, A. B. (1983), 'Boosting reading skills by direct instruction', *British Journal of Educational Psychology*, 53, 291–8.

Brophy, J. (1981), 'Teacher praise: a functional analysis', *Review of Educational Research*, 51, 5–32.

Bruner, J. S. (1961), 'The act of discovery', *Harvard Educational Review*, 31, 21–31.

Bruner, J. S. (1966), *Towards a Theory of Instruction*. New York: Norton.

Bruner, J. S. (1977), *The Process of Education*. Cambridge, MA: Harvard University Press.

Campbell, R. J. (ed.) (1993), *Breadth and Balance in the Primary Curriculum*. Basingstoke: Falmer.

Carroll, J. B. (1963), 'A model of school learning', *Teachers College Record*, 64, 723–33.

Child, D. (1998a), 'Psychology in the service of education: a review', inaugural lecture, University of Leeds, 1983, in D. Shorrocks-Taylor (ed.), *Directions in Educational Psychology*, pp. xxi–xxxvi. London: Whurr.

Cowley, S. (2003), *Getting the Buggers to Behave* (2nd edn). London: Continuum.

DfEE and OFSTED report (1996), *Exclusions from Secondary Schools*. London: HMSO.

Driver, R. (1983), *The Pupil as Scientist?* Milton Keynes: Open University.

Entwistle, N. J. (1998), 'Understanding academic performance at university: a research retrospective', in D. Shorrocks-Taylor (ed.), *Directions in Educational Psychology*. London: Whurr.

Galton, M. J. and Simon, B. (eds) (1980), *Progress and Performance in the Primary Classroom*. London: Routledge and Kegan Paul.

Galton, M. J., Simon, B. and Croll, P. (1980), *Inside the Primary Classroom*. London: Routledge and Kegan Paul.

Galton, M. J., Hargreaves, L., Comber, C. and Wall, D. with Pell, S. (1999), *Inside the Primary Classroom: 20 Years On*. London: Routledge.

Gunter, B. and McAleer, J. L. (1990), *Children and Television: The One Eyed Monster?* London: Routledge.

Hargie, O., Saunders, C. and Dickson, D. (1994), *Social Skills in Interpersonal Communication* (3rd edn). London: Routledge.

Hartley, J. R. (1998), 'New technologies and learning', in D. Shorrocks-Taylor (ed.), *Directions in Educational Psychology*. London: Whurr.

Hayes, D. (2003), *Planning, Teaching and Class Management in Primary Schools: Meeting the Standards* (2nd edn). London: David Fulton Publishers.

Hoghughi, M. (1979), 'The Aycliffe token economy', *British Journal of Criminality*, 384–99.

Hoghughi, M. (1988), *Treating Problem Children: Issues, Methods and Practice*. London: Sage.

Hoyle, E. (1975), 'Leadership and decision-making in education', in M. G. Hughes (ed.), *Administering Education: The International Challenge*. London: Athlone Press.

Kazdin, A. E. (2001), *Behaviour Modification in Applied Settings* (6th edn). Belmont, CA: Wadsworth.

Kazdin, A. E. (1977), *The Token Economy*. New York: Plenum.

Kounin, J. S. (1970), *Discipline and Group Management in Classrooms*. New York: Holt, Rinehart and Winston.

Lefrançois, G. R. (2000), *Psychology for Teaching* (10th edn). Belmont, CA: Wadsworth.

Lippitt, R. and White, R. K. (1970), 'An experimental study of leadership and group life', in E. E. Maccoby, T. M. Newcomb and E. E. Hartley, *Readings in Social Psychology*. New York: Holt, Rinehart and Winston.

Lovaas, O. I. (1967), 'A behavior therapy approach to the treatment of childhood schizophrenia', in J. P. Hill (ed.), *Minnesota Symposium on Child Psychology*. Minneapolis: University of Minnesota Press.

Lovaas, O. I. (1987), 'Behavioral treatment and normal educational/intellectual functioning in young autistic children', *Journal of Consulting and Clinical Psychology*, 55, 3–9.

Lovaas, O. I. (1993), 'The development of a treatment-research project for developmentally disable and autistic children', *Journal of Applied Behavior Analysis*, 26, 617–30.

Madsen, C. H., Becker, W. C. and Thomas, D. R. (1968), 'Rules, praise and ignoring: elements of elementary class control', *Journal of Applied Behavior Analysis*, 1, 139–50.

Marland, M. (1993), *The Craft of the Classroom: A Survival Guide* (2nd edn). London: Heinemann Educational. A third edition appeared in 2002.

McEachin, J. J., Smith, T. and Lovaas, O. I. (1993), 'Outcome in adolescence of autistic children receiving early intensive behaviour treatment', *American Journal of Mental Retardation*, 97, 359–72.

Plowden Report, The (1967), *Children and Their Primary Schools*. Vol. 1. London: HMSO.

Poteet, J. A. (1973), *Behaviour Modification: A Practical Guide for Teachers*. University of London: Unibooks.

Poteet, J. A. (1985), *Changing Behavior: A Practical Guide for Teachers and Parents*. Phi Delta Kappa.

Richards, C. (1997), *Primary Education, Standards and OFSTED: Towards a more Authentic Conversation*. Warwick: CREPE.

Rowell, J. A., Simon, J. and Wiseman, R. (1969), 'Verbal reception, guided discovery and the learning of schemata', *British Journal of Educational Psychology*, 39, 235–44.

Schmuck, R. A. and Schmuck, P. A. (1971), *Group Processes in the Classroom*. Dubuque, IA: Brown.

Shulman, L. S. and Keislar, E. R. (eds) (1965), *Learning by Discovery: A Critical Appraisal*. Chicago: Rand McNally.

Skinner, B. F. (1953), *Science and Human Behavior*. New York: Macmillan.

Sparzo, F. J. and Poteet, J. A. (1989), *Classroom Behavior: Detecting and Correcting Special Problems*. Newton, MA: Allyn and Bacon.

Tyler, V. O. Jnr, and Brown, G. D. (1968), 'Token reinforcement of academic performance with institutionalized delinquent boys', *Journal of Educational Psychology*, 59, 164–8.

Wheldall, K. and Beaman, R. (1998), 'Helping children with behaviour problems', in D. Shorrocks-Taylor (ed.), *Directions in Educational Psychology*. London: Whurr.

Wheldall, K. and Glynn, T. (1989), *Effective Classroom Learning: A Behavioural Interactionist Approach to Teaching* (in the series edited by D. Child, Theory and Practice in Education). Oxford: Blackwell.

Wheldall, K. and Merrett, F. (1985a), *The Behavioural Approach to Teaching Package*. Birmingham: Positive Products.

Wheldall, K. and Merrett, F. (1985b), 'BATPACK: Evolution and evaluation', *Behaviour Change*, 2, 21–32.

Whitman, M. and Whitman, J. (1971), 'Behaviour modification in the classroom', *Psychology in the Schools*, 8, 176–86.

Woods, P. (1979), *The Divided School*. London: Routledge and Kegan Paul.

Wragg, E. C. (ed.) (1996), *Classroom Teaching Skills*. The Research Findings of the Teacher Education Project. London: Routledge.

## Further reading

Wheldall, K. and Glynn, T. (1989), *Effective Classroom Learning: A Behavioural Interactionist Approach to Teaching*. In the series *Theory and Practice in Education*, D. Child (ed.), Oxford: Blackwell. This is a readable, introductory text on the applications of behaviour modification in educational settings.

Four books containing independent views about the nature and role of instruction at school which should be of interest are:

Ausubel, D. P. and Robinson, F. G. (1969), *School Learning: An Introduction to Educational Psychology*. New York: Holt, Rinehart and Winston.

Bloom, B. S. (1976), *Human Characteristics and School Learning*. New York: McGraw-Hill.

Bruner, J. S. (1966), *Towards a Theory of Instruction*. New York: Norton.

Gagné, R.M., Briggs, L. J. and Wager, W. W. (1992), *Principles of Instructional Design* (4th edn). Fort Worth: Harcourt Brace Jovanovich.

The following are books about leadership and management practices in classrooms:

Hargie, O., Saunders, C. and Dickson, D. (1994), *Social Skills in interpersonal Communication* (3rd edn). London: Routledge.

Hayes, D. (2003), *Planning, Teaching and Class Management in Primary Schools: Meeting the Standards* (2nd edn). London: David Fulton Publishers.

Kounin, J. S. (1970), *Discipline and Group Management in Classrooms*. New York: Holt, Rinehart and Winston.

Marland, M. (2002), *The Craft of the Classroom: A Survival Guide* (3rd edn). Oxford: Heinemann Educational.

Woods, P. (1979), *The Divided School*. London: Routledge and Kegan Paul.

Wragg, E.C. (ed.) (1996), *Classroom Teaching Skills*. The Research Findings of the Teacher Education Project. London: Routledge.

# The Curriculum Process

## Implications for teachers

- The curriculum process is an essential part of a teacher's work.
- It involves teachers in planning what to teach, how to teach it and how to evaluate the outcome of teaching.
- In some subject areas, the Government has defined the content and method of presentation.
- Taxonomies of educational objectives can be restricting. Use them with care.
- To plan curriculum processes, the teacher's knowledge base has to be sound.
- Keeping up-to-date with curriculum modifications is crucial. The Sweetman reference in 'Further reading' is very helpful in this respect.

The word 'curriculum' is on everyone's lips these days. The creation of the National Curriculum (Barber 1996) which affects every pupil, teacher and parent in the UK has seen to that. In Great Britain, a tradition evolved in which teachers in both primary and secondary schools, with the exception of public examination classes (GCSE and A levels), were in control of their own curricula. They had considerable freedom in what was taught, how it was taught and how achievement was gauged. This persisted until the early 1980s. But a number of factors accumulated to change the situation.

A belief that (a) child-centred education had failed many children (post Newsom and Plowden) gave birth to the 'back to basics' movement; (b) industry-related subjects were being neglected (science, technology, problem-solving approaches, information technology, a greater need for industry to concern itself with the curriculum of schools – which can be traced back to Prime Minister Callaghan's speech at Ruskin College in 1976); and (c) market forces should apply equally well in education as elsewhere in the economy – all of these have contributed to a shift in responsibility for curricula.

One of the first government bodies to be formed was the Schools Council in the 1960s. Their brief was advisory and certainly not prescriptive. The first signs of government intervention in the curriculum came with the demise of the Schools Council and its rebirth in 1983 as twins in the form of the School Curriculum Development Council (SCDC) and Secondary Examination Council (SEC). Since then, there have been two further transitions, all having slightly more power than its predecessor. In 1988 the SCDC became the National Curriculum Council (NCC) and the SEC became the School Examination and Assessment Council (SEAC). In 1993, the twins again became one by the formation of the School Curriculum and Assessment Authority (SCAA) and now renamed the Qualifications and Curriculum Authority (QCA). In this period, the responsibility for specifying the curriculum and assessing the outcomes of teaching it have been transferred from the teacher (SEAC) to the SCAA and the QCA (reflected in the change of title from 'Council' to 'Authority'). In effect, the input and output is decided. Not much is left to chance, though in getting from input to output the teacher still has responsibility provided that specified periods in basic subjects are taught to the whole class.

As public interest in education increases, as qualifications become ever more important as a passport to work, as our mode of living increases in complexity and the knowledge explosion imposes increases in both the quantity and levels of abstraction, we must recognize the need for a systematic appraisal of school curricula. Assumptions about what is worth teaching, priorities in subject matter, order of presentation, how a subject might be presented, what forms the evaluation of learning experiences for the children or teaching methods of the teachers might take are but a few major considerations. It should come as no surprise to student teachers that this book includes a chapter on some factors bearing on curriculum development. One of the first and inescapable jobs of a teacher is to design or work to a curriculum and psychologists have made a significant contribution here (Taylor 1968, onwards). Some of the references look dated, but do not be put off by this. Emphases in delivery and content might have shifted, but the psychological principles involved in curriculum design have not.

Often the term 'curriculum' is associated with 'syllabus'. It is more than that, as we shall demonstrate in the next section. To emphasize the more complex meaning, we use the term 'curriculum process' synonymously with 'curriculum'.

# The meaning of curriculum process

What do we mean by curriculum process? Is it that timetable pinned to the staffroom notice-board or in the back of the diary, looking for all the world like a bookmaker's price list of runners in a horse-race with the times of races? Is it the syllabus or the lesson notes? In fact, the curriculum is more than these. Neagley and Evans (1967) propose that the curriculum process is *all of the planned experiences provided by the school to assist pupils in attaining the designated learning outcomes to the best of their abilities.* Hirst (1968) puts it another way: programmes of activities designed so that pupils will attain, so far as possible, educational ends or objectives. This conscious, planned aspect of the curriculum process is sometimes referred to as the *intentional* curriculum, but we need to bear in mind that some of our influences are not planned and are by-products of the main purposes. These are *unintentional* curriculum processes (Hirst 1968), or the *hidden curriculum.*

Implicit in most definitions of the curriculum process are at least four important elements. The order is not fortuitous, although, as we shall see, there is a very necessary interplay between the elements in the construction of a curriculum. Tyler (1949) expresses these elements in the form of questions:

- What educational purposes should the school seek to attain?
- What educational experiences can be provided which are likely to attain these purposes?
- How can these educational experiences be effectively organized?
- How can we determine whether these purposes are being attained?

These four questions often appear in contracted form as:

objectives → course content → methods → evaluation

Note that Tyler prefers to talk about 'educational experiences' in preference to course content, because experience involves not only the substance of what is taught but also the processes by which the pupil learns. In other words, educational experience involves content *and* what the pupil does.

As was hinted above, before deciding what to teach, we have to settle the matter of the reasons for its being taught in the first place and the outcomes we anticipate. Why teach

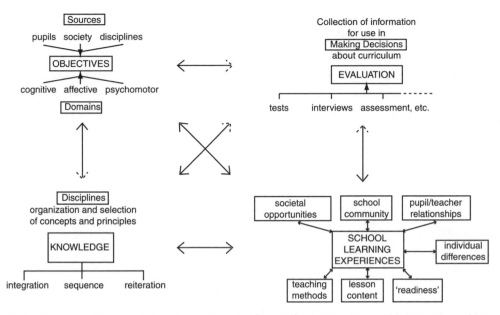

**Figure 15.1** A model for curriculum theory. Reprinted from Professor Kerr's inaugural lecture, 'The problem of curriculum reform', University of Leicester, 1967, with kind permission of the author. (Broken arrows represent connections not always observed.)

reading to children? What should an 8-year-old of average ability be capable of achieving in maths or English? What purposes are served by studying art in secondary schools? It is also necessary to make a regular appraisal of whether the purposes of a curriculum are being fulfilled.

The linear representation of Tyler's questions gives an over-simplified view of the inter-action of these components of curriculum design. It gives the impression that evaluation is the end of the line, but as Richmond (1971) remarks, 'Death is the only terminal behaviour'! It also makes the assumption that each element is regarded as of equal importance. As we shall see in the next section, the history of curriculum theory shows changing emphases over the years. A more comprehensive and dynamic demonstration of curriculum theory can be gained from Kerr's model (1968), containing components similar to Tyler's but presented in a cyclical pattern. This is shown in Figure 15.1. Note the inter-relationships between the components demonstrated by the arrows. Another variation on the theme is the *spiral* curriculum model, proposed by Bruner (1966 and 1971), where the four stages in Figure 15.1 are returned to at progressively more advanced levels of knowledge. There are, of course, dangers in selecting just one model *if* we forget that it is only representative of complex processes. Also, we get no idea from the model of the relative importance attached to each component.

The impact of psychology on curriculum processes has been significant. Considerations such as Piaget's scheme of cognitive development (especially influential in the junior-school curriculum), the concept of readiness, learning theory (for example, activity rather than passivity programmes, aids in mathematics teaching, programmed learning in the broadest sense), language and concept formation, studies in skills, aptitudes, attitudes and values and the contribution of psychologists to the question of evaluation in education are just a sample of psychological influences on curriculum processes. This contribution has been well summarized by Taylor (1980) who sees psychology as having been used for three purposes:

- as a guide to the structuring of the subject matter for learning and teaching
- as a source of empirical methodologies for studying how the curricular materials are transacted in teaching
- similarly, as a source of methodologies, of instrumentation for the evaluation of outcomes.

# Curriculum interpretation

All curriculum theorists see four elements in Tyler's or Kerr's model – content, methods of exposure (or learning experiences), objectives and evaluation – occur in the process of formal education; they will be dealt with in greater detail presently. Where the differences between theorists lie is in which is chosen as the starting point and the emphasis given to each element. Kelly (1999) makes a useful distinction between, on the one hand, the purposes of the education being provided and, on the other, the curriculum necessary to achieve those educational purposes.

Three major theoretical positions predominate. They have been variously defined. One possible classification is *content-based* (in Kelly's terms 'curriculum as content, education as transmission'), *process-based* ('curriculum as process, education as development') and *product-based* ('curriculum as product, education as instrumental').

## Content-based curriculum

The longest and most pervasive tradition is to regard the organized knowledge in the disciplines as the basis for the curriculum (sometimes known as the liberal-humanist tradition). The typical school subject areas tend to be defined as sciences, arts, philosophy, culture, etc. The objectives would therefore be to teach others the knowledge and characteristics of the discipline. The central function of this kind of education is the transmission of the knowledge. GCSE, 'A' levels and university degree courses are typical examples. The important point is that the content of the discipline sets the scene for methods, objectives and evaluation. Teaching is most often didactic and evaluation is generally by some form of examination.

The choice of particular disciplines was also justified in the nineteenth century because it was thought to be a means of training certain mental capacities. For example, learning Latin was said to improve memory; science developed powers of observation; maths developed logical thinking. No evidence has ever been assembled to show this to be true.

This tradition would also include those who believe that passing on the common cultural heritage of our society from generation to generation should be a major, if not the central, subject of the curriculum (sometimes called the cultural-analysis tradition, Lawton 1973, 1975). The syllabus would include 'the best' in art and literature, the habits and beliefs of the culture, the finest achievements (both artistic and scientific) of the society.

The National Curriculum now in place is a good example of a content-based model. More will be said later in the chapter about how the system works, but there are ten *foundation subjects* of which three are called *core* foundation subjects. The core subjects are English, mathematics and science. The foundation subjects are history, geography, technology, music, art, physical education and modern languages. Content and outcomes in the form of standard assessments are controlled by SCAA, but:

> how and in what depth to teach the material contained in the subject Orders is for schools to decide. No priority or methodology is implied in the Orders. Decisions on the depth of treatment of aspects of subjects are for the professional judgement of teachers. The Orders should not be over-interpreted as requiring teaching to the same degree of detail in all aspects. (SCAA, *Revised National Curriculum*, 1995)

## Process-based curriculum

In this tradition, which also has a long and distinguished history, the focal point is the child and his or her intellectual development. 'Child-centred education' and 'progressive movement' are alternative names applied to this tradition. Learning should be an active process based on the interests and unfolding mental development of each child. For this to happen, the child should be offered a range of experiences and opportunities to discover the world.

Froebel and Montessori in the nineteenth century, following in the footsteps of the philosopher Rousseau, became well-known educators using these principles and methods. In the last century, Piaget and Bruner (both of whom have been considered in earlier chapters) are developmental psychologists, and have been major contributors. The Plowden Report recommendations were very much in the spirit of this movement.

The fundamentals – that syllabus content is determined by a child's experiential needs, that understanding and encouraging the cognitive processes are most helpful in development and are more important than specifying objectives – are views still held by a few in primary school teaching, but recent research has shown that they are not prevalent. The pros and cons of 'discovery' and 'guided discovery' methods have been discussed in Chapter 14 (see also Bennett *et al.* 1984).

## Product-based curriculum

Here, the end product of education is first clearly defined and cast as 'objectives' to be attained. The teacher then works back from these objectives to decide on content and methods which would achieve the objectives. This is also called the 'technocratic' or the 'objectives' tradition. The evaluation consists entirely of testing to see if the student has reached the objectives.

The system has the flavour of behaviourist principles where goals are set and the best routes to achieving the goals are discovered. American psychologists have been particularly attracted to this method. Famous names already met with in this text, such as Bloom (see Chapter 14 and below) and Tyler (1949) favour the approach. It should also be noted that in this country developments in the Technical and Vocational Educational Initiative (TVEI) and more recently National General Vocational Qualifications (NVQs and GNVQs) require specified levels of competence (objectives) which have to be attained for the awards.

All three waves of fashion influence our present arrangements in primary, secondary and tertiary education. The next sections will look in general terms at the four key elements of objectives, content, learning experiences and evaluation. The last three will consist of a gathering of material already referred to in the text, but more space will need to be given to objectives.

# Objectives

When we specify the behavioural changes we anticipate as a result of learning experiences, the specifications are said to be *objectives*. They usually begin with a verb, thus emphasizing that certain behaviours are hoped for; 'to recognize...', 'to acquire...', 'to apply...', 'to understand...' are examples. Returning to a question posed in the previous section: What are the objectives of teaching children to read? There are several possible objectives; for example, children learn to read to gain knowledge and understanding, to reap satisfaction from being able to read, to assist their work and leisure and so on. Some activities are more specific, as when we teach Newton's laws of motion to help in an understanding of the generalizations applying to bodies which move on earth with low or moderate velocities. There could be other objectives subsumed under the ones suggested above and applying to each of Newton's three laws of motion. But, clearly, defining objectives is a skilled occupation requiring a careful consideration of the knowledge we wish to transmit to our children and the impact this knowledge will have on them.

The term 'aim' is sometimes used as an alternative to objective. However, it is more accurate to distinguish between the two. Aims are much more general and frequently refer to philosophical issues in the wider context of education. They also tend to refer to the end-product of the system. We might find expressions of the aims of a course couched in more general terms such as 'to produce technologists' or 'to educate for leisure'. Objectives relate to the route as well as the goal, whereas aims usually relate only to the goal.

## Bloom's taxonomy (1956, 1964 and 1976)

Nowadays it would not be possible to write about objectives without making some reference to the major psychological contribution to curriculum development of Bloom and his associates on a taxonomy of education objectives and their influence on examining techniques. Broadly, he classified objectives into three major domains: (a) *cognitive objectives*, placing the greatest emphasis on remembering, reasoning, concept formation and creative thinking; (b) *affective objectives*, emphasizing emotive qualities expressed in attitudes, interests, values and emotional biases; (c) *the psychomotor objectives*, emphasizing muscle and motor skills and manipulation in all kinds of activities such as handwriting, speech, physical education, etc. A brief gallop through the full list of objectives in the cognitive or affective domain would do very little to assist the student in understanding Bloom's intentions. The only way of really getting to grips with his views would be to refer to his books. However, one illustration will be given to show how the taxonomy operates.

Bloom and his associates organized their taxonomy (or classification) of cognitive factors under six major headings. The six are arranged hierarchically to demonstrate that the objectives are cumulative, so higher classes are built on the skills involved in lower classes. Briefly, the six classes involve *knowledge* which emphasizes those processes which require recall of such things as specific facts, terminology, conventions and generalizations. Clearly, if one has no fund of knowledge, one cannot operate cognitively. *Comprehension* represents a low level of understanding sufficient to grasp the translation and meaning of mathematical or verbal material for the purposes of interpretation or extrapolation. *Application* employs remembering and combining material to give generalizations for use in concrete situations. *Analysis* means the breakdown of material into its constituents in order to find the relationship between them. Note that all the previous classes are required before analysis is possible. *Synthesis* necessitates the putting together of the constituents by rearranging and combining them to give an arrangement not apparent before. Lastly, *evaluation* requires value judgements about materials, ideas, methods, etc. All the skills of knowledge, comprehension, application, analysis and synthesis are necessary to perform this operation satisfactorily and for a valid judgement to be made possible.

## Task analysis

In Chapter 7 we met with the theories of Gagné (1985 and *et al.* 1992), which provide an alternative approach to objective-based curricula. In his book on the conditions of learning he postulates that when a learning task is decided upon in order to arrive at a particular learning outcome, it should be possible to construct a *learning task analysis*. It is clearly a behaviourist approach which relies on a carefully planned sequence of steps drawn up as a flow chart of activities necessary for the satisfactory completion of the learning event. In Chapter 7 we referred briefly to learning outcomes or 'human capabilities', as Gagné calls them. A corresponding verb is used to signify unambiguously the type of task implied in the learning outcome. Table 15.1 illustrates how his human capabilities can be phased.

**Table 15.1** Illustrations from some of Gagné's learning outcomes with corresponding verbs and examples.

| Capability | Verb | Example |
|---|---|---|
| *Intellectual skill* | | |
| Discrimination | Discriminates | Discriminates, by comparing outlines, the difference between oak and chestnut leaves |
| Concrete concept | Identifies | Identifies, by pointing, named countries on a map |
| Defined concept | Classifies | Classifies, by writing lists, the phyla of a given number of animal species |
| Rule | Demonstrates | Demonstrates, by writing down the arrangement of 'i' and 'e' after 'c' |
| Higher-order rule (problem-solving) | Generates | Generates, by building up the steps in the arrangement, the solution to a quadratic problem |
| *Motor skill* | Executes | Executes a handstand |
| *Attitude* | Chooses | Chooses, on leaving school, a job which does not involve manual labour |

Examples are also included. Once a task has been categorized using the table, Gagné then proposes a task analysis of prerequisites for the achievement of the learning. Put simply, each step in a learning event requires some previous kind of accomplishment. Successful task analysis consists of accurate judgements of the size and hierarchical arrangement of the steps.

The flow chart created by such hierarchical choices looks something like the example shown in Figure 15.2 (White and Gagné 1978). This is a much more detailed and painstaking approach than the one suggested by Bloom. It has a salutary effect on the person planning the lesson. The detailed knowledge required of a teacher to make this kind of analysis is quite appreciable. In addition the teacher must have a sound knowledge of the logical sequence and developmental capabilities of pupils in an age group. Such cold-blooded, detailed tactics are very time-consuming, but repay dividends, especially where the teacher is dealing with a topic for the first time.

## Defining objectives

Several authors have laid down guidelines which will assist curriculum planners during their attempts to establish curriculum objectives (Taba 1962, Wiseman and Pidgeon 1970). When we are planning a course, the objectives must be:

(a) Realistic, appropriate and capable of being translated into learning experiences in the classroom. Plans are laid after we have borne in mind the limitations imposed by, for example, the intellectual development of children, their home circumstances and school background. There is no point in specifying objectives which cannot be defined operationally. For instance, the term 'creativity' is sometimes used in

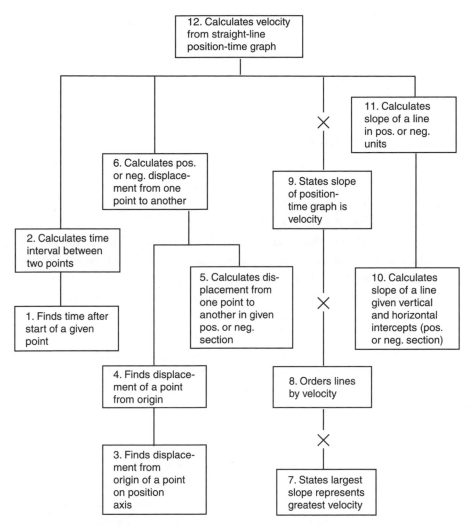

**Figure 15.2** A learning hierarchy showing relationships of prerequisite skills to the task: calculating velocity from a straight-line graph of position (vertical axis) and time (horizontal axis). X = relationships found invalid. (Based on a description in R. T. White and R. M. Gagné, 'Formative evaluation applied to a learning hierarchy', *Cont. Educ. Psychol.* (1978), 3, 87–94.)

primary and secondary curricula without any clear indication of its meaning in this context, or of the processes by which it can be achieved, or for that matter precisely how or when it *has* been achieved.

(b) Specified in terms of behaviour which is recognizable. Aims as we have defined them above are often not capable of being recognized in the short term. 'To educate a child so as to enable him or her to play a useful part in a community' would require some very careful defining of terms such as 'useful' and 'community' so that we could pin down the learning experiences necessary in the curriculum. Bloom's taxonomy of educational objectives is useful in providing recognizable behaviours.

(c) Capable of being evaluated. Needless to say, if it is intended to bring about behavioural change in learners, we ought to be able to assess the quality and quantity of this change.

## Criticisms of behavioural objectives

There have been several critics of the rigid, detailed approach to lesson planning. Nobody would argue against planning lessons, but some people consider very detailed planning of the kind required by the Bloom taxonomy (1956 and 1964) as not always helpful (Kelly 1999).

The critics argue that broad criteria are sometimes more helpful than narrow ones. Narrow criteria seem to relate to simple factual recall, and do not allow for the broader aims of the teacher, such as 'understanding'. Teachers often have these broader goals for which the short, step-by-step breakdown of behavioural objectives is not appropriate; they also require a lot of time. Eisner (1969; see also Stenhouse 1975 and Barnes 1982) reckons that the number of objectives for a primary curriculum is well over 25,000. In some cases this preoccupation with behavioural objectives could well mean an uneconomic use of a teacher's time. Where a pupil's contribution, particularly in exploratory activity, is extensive, behavioural objectives are difficult to define precisely. Some of the outcomes of exploratory learning are not always predictable and many teachers use incidental findings by children as a source of material for their lessons. Rigid objectives seem more suited to knowledge which is to be recollected (i.e. straight learning), and this does not necessarily mean that the learner 'understands' what has been assimilated. Methods of learning vary according to the aspects of knowledge or experience being dealt with. It is necessary for the teacher to match his or her teaching with what the children are expected to be doing, for example, creative and expressive activities, and this frequently extends beyond the narrow confines of the acceptable behavioural terms found in, for example, Bloom's taxonomy.

Other critics argue that an 'objectives' approach assumes that human behaviour can ultimately be analysed and modified with the same precision and beneficial effects as with the inanimate objects of science. The pupil is seen as having too passive a role in learning and as the subject of too much instruction and training.

# Knowledge or subject content

Deciding what to select from the whole spectrum of content in a discipline in order to achieve our stated objectives is the central concern in this stage of curriculum planning. But what do we hope will be the essential influence of the content? Taba (1962) supposes there are two schools of thought which we might term *structure-oriented* and *task-oriented*. There are those who see each subject as having its own brand of mental discipline quite apart from the teaching methods employed. Physics, for example, demands a different mental attitude and cognitive style from literary criticism. Expectations in art are not the same as those in history. With this in mind, the proponents of structure orientation tend to concentrate on the theoretical aspects of the subject to illustrate the characteristic way of thinking afforded by the nature of the subject itself.

Task-oriented teachers view the subject matter as a means of acquiring learning skills such as memorizing (e.g. historical dates, chemical formulae, poems) or developing manual skills (play with material which is manipulated, physical education, handicraft). There is a good deal of faith placed in the concept of transfer of training.

However, most curriculum planners steer a course between these extremes, allowing that some subjects demand specialized cognitive strategies while recognizing certain similar cognitive demands which cut across subject disciplines. In fact there is a decided move towards more integrated syllabuses, although there is little research of any kind to show the advantages or disadvantages of combined courses. Teaching number skills to a junior class, quite apart from the basic numeracy of the children or their developmental level, presents special problems which contrast sharply with, say, the teaching of reading. Yet both these subjects involve memorization or relational thinking.

Decisions about the content of the school curriculum are as much a matter of philosophical and political debate as psychological. Views have focused on seven or eight areas (historically accumulated 'forms' of knowledge – Hirst (1974), a selection from the 'culture' – Lawton (1975)).

These are not necessarily equivalent.

---

**Hirst**

1 Mathematics knowledge
2 Empirical knowledge in the physical and social sciences
3 Aesthetic knowledge
4 Moral knowledge
5 Mental and personal knowledge involving explanations of human behaviour
6 Religious knowledge.
7 Philosophical knowledge

**Lawton**

1 Mathematics
2 The physical and biological sciences
3 The expressive and creative arts
4 Moral education
5 Humanities and social sciences (including explanations of human behaviour, history, geography, classical studies, literature, film, TV, religious studies)
6 Interdisciplinary work

(See Barnes (1982) for a discussion of these points.)

A document from the DES (1981) roots the curriculum in educational aims and suggests the following as desirable:

- to help pupils to develop lively, enquiring minds, the ability to question and argue rationally and to apply themselves to tasks and physical skills
- to help pupils to acquire knowledge and skills relevant to adult life and employment in a fast-changing world
- to help pupils to use language and number effectively
- to instil respect for religious and moral values, and tolerance of other races, religions and ways of life
- to help pupils to understand the world in which they live, and the interdependence of individuals, groups and nations
- to help pupils to appreciate human achievements and aspirations.

There is some interesting discussion in the DES document about how these aims might be achieved in terms of the subjects in primary and secondary curricula.

# Learning experiences

Few would now deny the importance of purposeful activity by the learner as an aid to learning. We pay a good deal of attention to methods of presenting material, so much so that we often forgo the content. Vast methodological researches and school programmes have been mounted – Nuffield Science, integrated day methods, 'free activity' methods – all testifying to the enthusiasm generated. Less emphasis is now placed on transmission of knowledge and more on the processes of assimilation by developing skills in understanding.

Psychology has much to offer in this respect. Considerations of learning, individual capacities, motivation, personality, the growth of skills and 'readiness' are all major issues in devising learning experiences for pupils. In one sense this aspect of curriculum planning draws together many threads in the syllabus of educational psychology.

Our view of childhood has altered and has in turn affected the teacher's approach to structuring learning situations in the classroom. A greater recognition of individual worth and differences has brought a corresponding recognition that individual help is a vital additive to class teaching. Our knowledge of child development and our changed attitudes towards the young have revitalized learning procedures. They have converted us from regarding the child as a passive receptacle to seeing him or her as an active participant in learning.

The return of expository methods of instruction, explored in Chapter 14, arises because of pressure for 'prescriptions' of learning and teaching rather than the 'descriptions' so prevalent in learning theories. Bruner (1966) pays attention to the most effective 'sequence' in which materials should be presented and goes on to argue that optimal sequences need to be judged in terms of an individual's speed and power to learn, transfer possibilities, economy of learning in keeping with the 'cognitive strain' imposed and the ability of the material thus learned to help in generating new ideas.

The impact of social psychology has rapidly made us aware that children's learning processes are markedly influenced by social factors and group dynamics. Studies of home background, the school community and teacher–pupil interaction are leaving their mark on the methods we are adopting. Experiments with open-plan schools, unstreamed classes, sixth-form colleges and schools where the local community is being drawn into the life of the school are but a few recent examples.

# Evaluation

Curriculum evaluation is the servant by which we clarify and substantiate the effectiveness of our objectives, learning experiences and content. The idea of evaluation as an ongoing process is conveyed in Kerr's model (Figure 15.1) by the dotted arrows pointing to the evaluation component from all the other components. Evaluations should be seen as a tool to assist in refining learning processes as well as in measuring the acquisition of knowledge.

Thus evaluative techniques should do more than examine a pupil's knowledge. They should also help in locating the factors which influence performance, such as the conditions and procedures in the classroom. Two kinds of evaluation which draw attention to this dual function have been defined (Wiseman and Pidgeon 1970). *Formative evaluation* takes place during the developmental stages of a curriculum and is seen as a continuous process, whilst *summative evaluation* occurs when the curriculum is established and we are measuring the achievement of those on the course as well as the effectiveness of the course. Even with established courses, formative evaluation would still be an essential aspect for reappraising the curriculum.

Mention will be made of evaluation techniques in Chapters 16 and 18. In most instances teachers have to devise their own instruments. There are standardized tests in mathematics, English, reading and spelling for a wide age range (NFER, http://www.nfer-nelson.co.uk/catalogue/catalogue.asp), but these have a special function and, like all standardized material, require very careful handling. There are now Standard Assessment Tests (SATs) at 7, 11, 14 and 16 years.

A necessary first step in evaluation is to prepare a test blueprint (see Chapter 18). This is a carefully designed breakdown plan of the content areas and objectives showing their relative importance in terms of hours (or units of time) allotted to each section. A blueprint should be assembled *before* the course commences. As we shall see in Chapter 16, multiple-choice items are particularly favoured for evaluation, although orals, written essays and practical work may be used provided they can be validated and made reliable. Other forms of evaluation have been tried with limited success; custom-made attitude and interest scales and interviews are amongst those currently being tried.

It is important to remember that our primary aim in using evaluative methods is concerned with the value of the course using group performance of the pupils in knowing, understanding and applying the skills specified. We would not necessarily be concerned with diagnosing pupils for selection or with finding their rank order of achievement.

## Curriculum planning and the teacher

Establishing a new curriculum is really a combined effort requiring expert advice in the aspects we have discussed above. However, there is also the task of keeping a close watch on our existing programmes and modifying or changing parts of them as the need arises. In the light of what has been said above, we might apply one method suggested by Taylor (1970) who recommends that the teacher should keep a double-page 'ledger' account of the syllabus topics with a column for answers to each of the following questions:

- What am I expected to teach, and in what order? (CONTENT)
- What educational purposes is my teaching to serve? (AIMS)
- What teaching methods are known to achieve these purposes? (METHODS)
- What standard of achievement am I expected to aim at? (OBJECTIVES)
- How will I discover whether the course I've been teaching has been successful or not? (EVALUATION)
- What can I usefully be told about the abilities, interests and attitudes of the pupils I am to teach? (PUPILS)
- COMMENTS about alternative possibilities.

As Taylor comments, the purpose of the ledger is 'to help the teacher understand the nature and purpose of the course, not to determine the form and style of his teaching'.

## Curriculum trends

The present state of affairs in curriculum design is part of a chain of events in the development of educational practices in this country. Looking back over the history of our present curriculum, there seem to be at least two major strands in the development of educational practices in Great Britain. One strand arises from the public-school system of the past, which permeated the grammar-school system. The other strand arises from legislation relating to the elementary-school system of education for all.

The classical tradition of Latin and Greek, with a little geography, history and mathematics, prevailed through many centuries. Latin, in the first instance, was very important because most of the literature, including law, medicine and theology, was written in that language. In time, however, it became symbolic of a particular way of life serving to distinguish the gentry, leaders with 'cultivated' minds, from the 'serving classes'. Where the latter were able to receive an education it consisted of an iron ration of the three Rs, just sufficient to enable children to serve God and the factory owners. Later, the 1902 Act insisted that children should be fitted to meet the practical as well as the basic intellectual demands of a working life. In the last century we saw rapid and extensive changes in elementary education, emerging as the present-day primary and secondary systems.

A long train of Education Acts and government reports (Plowden and Newsom, for example) have had a marked effect on the direction of curriculum designs. Consider the effect of the Spens and Norwood Reports on the 1944 Act. The Reports saw children as falling into three categories, academic, technical and practical, for which the secondary-grammar, secondary-technical and secondary-modern schools were created. Curriculum designers attempted to build into their schemes a style of teaching and a special emphasis on content design to satisfy the supposed characteristics of 'academic', 'technical' and 'practical' children.

During the past 25 or so years we have experienced a phenomenal period of experimentation without finding, regrettably, a corresponding rigour in the evaluation of these innovations. In the content areas, we have seen 'modern' maths, French and science (other than 'nature study') in the junior schools, together with Nuffield, the Schools Council programmes, STEP (Science Teacher Education Project) and so on at all ages. Greater and diverse use of technological aids have been evident (TV, radio, programmed learning, computer-assisted learning, microprocessors, etc.). On the other hand, there has been a decline in, for example, cultural pursuits such as music, drama, dance. Many schools are hard-pressed to find a member of staff capable of playing a piano. Classroom organization now includes informal arrangements, vertical grouping, team teaching, open plan, mixed-ability grouping and the integrated day.

Since the 1944 Act we have seen the gradual evolution of a system dedicated to giving pupils an equal chance to benefit from whatever education would be satisfying and serviceable. Theoretically, there also seems to be a strong desire to extend the syllabus to give more attention to moral and social education: the behavioural sciences at secondary level (psychology, sociology and anthropology) and what might be termed the 'survival sciences', such as demography, pollution and conservation, race relations, peace studies, contraception, sexually transmitted diseases and health studies. In practice, the emphasis, as seen by teachers, has been largely on intellectual and moral development. Musgrove and Taylor (1965) asked primary, secondary modern and grammar school teachers to rate the relative educational relevance of moral training, social training, intellectual training (instruction in subjects), education for family life, social advancement and education for citizenship. Grammar school teachers had a more confined outlook than secondary modern teachers and viewed their role as limited to intellectual and moral education ('character training'), with indifferent regard for social training. Surprisingly, primary school teachers likewise seemed to place less emphasis on social than on intellectual and moral training.

Parents of university students also have some clear ideas about the roles which universities should serve through their curricula. Child *et al.* (1971) showed three aspects of university life which were uppermost in the minds of parents: (a) students should be worked hard in a few specialized subjects with a supporting cast of academic counsellors; (b) the university should be primarily concerned with preparing and guiding students for a career; (c) the university should help in developing students' skills in dealing with other people. The study of knowledge 'for its own sake' and without regard for its practical application was placed right at the bottom of the list of priorities. Here we see an important dilemma between the teachers' cognitive outlook and the parents' highly businesslike vocational and instrumental order of priorities.

# The National Curriculum (Moon 2001)

As mentioned earlier in the chapter, one of the most persistent criticisms of curriculum planning in schools has been aimed at the vagueness with which the content and evaluation have been handled, apparently sometimes without regard as to whether the content is justified and relevant. An attempt to give purpose as well as direction to school curricula has been enshrined in the new National Curriculum which came into force in England and Wales in 1989. The *Education Reform Act* of 1988 stated that the National Curriculum was to give a 'balanced and broadly based curriculum which ... promotes the spiritual, moral, cultural, mental and physical development of pupils at school and of society and prepares pupils for the opportunities and experiences of adult life'. For recent developments in the National Curriculum, have a look at http://www.standards.dfes.gov.uk, click 'pick an area' or type 'national curriculum' into the search dialogue box.

There are three *core foundation subjects*, namely, mathematics, English and science (plus Welsh in schools where it is the language of instruction). Religious education must also be provided, but the curriculum and assessment, if required, are decided at local authority rather than national level. There are seven other *foundation subjects* consisting of history, geography, technology (including design), ICT (Information and Computer Technology), music, art, PE and modern foreign languages (including Welsh).

Four landmarks in a pupil's school life are defined as *Key Stages* with a *Foundation Stage* prior to compulsory education at 5 years of age. The Foundation Stage covers 3–5 years which are nursery and reception classes. Sometimes they are found on mainstream sites. Compulsory school age from 5 to 16 is broken into ranges. These are shown in Table 15.2.

As we shall see in Chapter 16 attainment targets have been set to occur at the end of each Key Stage.

**Table 15.2** Ages and stages of the National Curriculum (England and Wales).

| Age | Key stage | Year number | Type of school |
|-----|-----------|-------------|----------------|
| 3–5 | Foundation | | Nursery and Reception |
| 5–7 | 1 | 1 and 2 | Infant or Primary |
| 7–11 | 2 | 3 to 6 | Primary (or Junior) |
| 11–14 | 3 | 7 to 9 | Secondary |
| 14–16 | 4 | 10 and 11 | Secondary |

In each subject, there is a *Programme of Study* (PoS) founded by the SCAA, succeeded by the QCA, and containing the contents and methods of approach. *Attainment Targets* (ATs) are set at every stage which indicate the standard expected of each age group. Each Attainment Target is divided into eight *Levels* (except for art, music and PE). Level 1 is what you would expect of a child just starting school. Level 8 is the standard expected at age 14. Children will obviously progress at different rates and this would be reflected in the Level reached by an individual. As a general rule, most children should have reached Level 3 during Key Stage 1 (5–7 years), Levels 5 or 6 at the end of Key Stage 2 (8–11 years) and Levels 7 or 8 by Key Stage 3 (12–14 years).

*Statements of attainment* (Chapter 17) are detailed objectives to be achieved for a particular age group and performance level. Assessments, both internal and national, are derived and used to judge the quality of the child, the teacher and the school. Attainment targets are clearly defined for all the core and foundation subjects mentioned above. The national assessment aspect referred to above, the standard assessment tasks (SATs), is used alongside the internal assessment to give the level of attainment. From these are obtained the *profiles of attainment* and *records* for the benefit of other teachers, parents and employers.

All schools are provided with detailed information about the National Curriculum and the methods of assessment to be used. HMSO documents are available. Reports, 'coloured' papers, acts are pouring out from government bodies (e.g. DfES, OFSTED, QCA). For hard-pressed students and teachers, there is a most useful annual summary of curriculum and other educational changes occurring between each issue called *Curriculum Confidential* by Sweetman (2003/4, 12th issue).

## Summary

One of the most important jobs for any teacher is to plan what to teach, how to teach it and how to evaluate the outcome of teaching. But it is no accident that a chapter on the curriculum appears near the end rather than at the beginning of the book. Curriculum design is a difficult task requiring a profound knowledge of psychological principles apart from content knowledge. So, although it is one of the first things to confront a student on school practice or fresh out of training, curriculum planning is most effectively done as a consequence of accumulated information and skills in handling children and the subject area.

The curriculum is erroneously thought of by many as the subject matter of a course. This is a very limited view. In fact, the curriculum represents the interaction of all the activities aimed at assisting pupils in reaching specified educational objectives. In short, curriculum planning involves specifying objectives, devising appropriate content, arranging educational experiences for presenting the content and evaluating the processes of learning which have taken place, along with testing the suitability of the content in relation to the stated objectives.

This is a tall order. To begin with, we have to know a lot about children in terms of their interests, motives, intellectual competence or what they have done already in school in addition to making judgements about what is most suited to their skills and needs at a particular stage in their development. Hence it is clear that objectives can be specified only against this background of information in order to make them realistic, appropriate and capable of being expressed in terms which can be transposed into learning behaviour. Vague, all-inclusive statements are not appropriate when they cannot be converted into activities. Again, objectives must ultimately be put to the test: they must be capable of evaluation because all educational objectives lead to learning, and we must be in a position to assess whether learning has taken place.

Evaluation is an ongoing process. It enables us to review the objectives and modify them if they prove to be inappropriate. Mention will made of methods of evaluation in Chapter 16. Selecting content demands both a knowledge of particular cognitive structures inherent in a subject area and a knowledge of general learning tactics common to all disciplines.

Needless to say, much of the earlier part of the book concentrated on the individual qualities and learning habits of children most likely to influence learning. Such factors as motivation, attention, retention, recall, language skills, cognitive developmental stage, intellectual abilities and personality are frequently the source of variability and interaction in the learning experiences of the individual child.

The coming years will see greater demands being made of teachers in the application of the school curricula provided by government bodies. Innovation is now almost a routine in education and teachers should be in a strong position to examine the worth of the many new ideas which will flood into their working lives.

## Tutorial enquiry and discussion

(a) Take a close look at the topics you teach in terms of objectives, content, methods of teaching and evaluation. Use the tutorials to explore age, primary/secondary and subject differences.

(b) What do you consider to be the important criteria when deciding on the methods or 'educational experiences' you would offer a specified group of children in a given topic? (You may have to think out a solution to this problem for a mixed-ability group or in an integrated subject area.)

(c) Government documents appear at regular intervals. Examine the psychological assumptions implicitly or explicitly connected with recommendations in these publications.

(d) Read *Curriculum Confidential 2003/4* by Sweetman and discuss in group tutorials the implications in terms of classroom practice.

## References

Barber, M. (ed.) (1996), *The National Curriculum: A Study in Policy*. Keele: Keele University Press.

Barnes, D. (1982), *Practical Curriculum Study*. London: Routledge and Kegan Paul.

Bennett, N., Desforges, C., Cockburn, C. and Wilkinson, E. (1984), *The Quality of Pupil Learning Experiences*. London: Erlbaum.

Bloom, B. S. (ed.) (1956), *Taxonomy of Educational Objectives. Handbook I: Cognitive Domain*. London: Longman.

Bloom, B. S. (1964), *Taxonomy of Educational Objectives. Handbook II: Affective Domain*. London: Longman.

Bloom, B. S. (1976), *Human Characteristics and School Learning*. New York: McGraw-Hill.

Bruner, J. S. (1966), *Towards a Theory of Instruction*. New York: Norton.

Bruner, J. S. (1971) *The Relevance of Education*. New York: Norton.

Child, D., Cooper, H. J., Hussell, C. G. I. and Webb, F. (1971), 'Parents' expectations of a university', *Universities Quarterly*, 25, 484–90.

DES (1981), *The School Curriculum*. London: HMSO.

Eisner, E. W. (1969), 'Instructional and expressive educational objectives: their formulation and use in curriculum', in W. J. Popham *et al.*, *Instructional Objectives*. Chicago: Rand McNally.

Gagné, R. M. (1985), *The Conditions of Learning* (4th edn). New York: Holt, Rinehart and Winston.

Gagné, R. M., Briggs, L. J. and Wager, W. W. (1992), *Principles of Instructional Design* (4th edn). Fort Worth: Harcourt Brace Jovanovich.

Hirst, P. H. (1968), 'The contribution of philosophy to the study of the curriculum', in J. F. Kerr (ed.), *Changing the Curriculum*. London: University of London Press.

Hirst, P. H. (1974), *Knowledge and the Curriculum*. London: Routledge and Kegan Paul.

Kelly, A. V. (1999), *The Curriculum: Theory and Practice* (4th edn). London: Chapman.

Kerr, J. F. (1968), 'The problem of curriculum reform', in J. F. Kerr (ed.), *Changing the Curriculum*. London: University of London Press.

Lawton, D. (1973), *Social Change, Educational Theory and Curriculum Planning*. London: University of London Press.

Lawton, D. (1975), *Class, Culture and the Curriculum*. London: Routledge and Kegan.

Moon, R. (2001), *A Guide to the National Curriculum: Essential Reading for Parents and Teachers* (4th edn). Oxford: Oxford University Press.

Musgrove, F. and Taylor, P. H. (1965), 'Teachers' and parents' conception of the teacher's role', *British Journal of Educational Psychology*, 35, 171–9.

Neagley, R. L. and Evans, N. D. (1967), *Handbook for Effective Curriculum Development*. Englewood Cliffs, NJ: Prentice-Hall.

Richmond, W. K. (1971), *The School Curriculum*. London: Methuen.

SCAA (1995), *Revised National Curriculum*. London: HMSO.

Stenhouse, L. (1975), *An Introduction to Curriculum Research and Development*. London: Heinemann.

Sweetman, J. (latest 2003/4) *Curriculum Confidential 2003/4: The Complete Guide to Education and the National Curriculum*. Westley, Suffolk: Courseware Publications.

Taba, H. (1962), *Curriculum Development: Theory and Practice*. New York: Harcourt.

Taylor, P. H. (1968), 'The contribution of psychology to the study of the curriculum', in J. F. Kerr (ed.), *Changing the Curriculum*. London: University of London Press.

Taylor, P. H. (1980), 'Purpose and structure in the curriculum', in P. Gordon (ed.), *The Study of Education* (Vol. 2). London: Woburn.

Tyler, R. W. (1949), *Basic Principles of Curriculum and Instruction*. Chicago: University of Chicago Press.

White, R. T. and Gagné, R. M. (1978), 'Formative evaluation applied to a learning hierarchy', *Journal of Continuing Education and Psychology*, 3, 87–94.

Wiseman, S. and Pidgeon, D. A. (1970), *Curriculum Evaluation*. Slough: NFER.

## Further reading

Barber, M. (ed.) (1996), *The National Curriculum: A Study in Policy*, Keele: Keele University Press. This gives a brief, readable introduction to some aspects of the political background of the present National Curriculum.

Barnes, D. (1982), *Practical Curriculum Study*. London: Routledge and Kegan Paul. A thoughtful and full text giving all the basics.

Kelly, A. V. (1999), *The Curriculum: Theory and Practice* (4th edn). London: Chapman. This is a wordy book, but contains some useful critical material about curriculum theory and practice.

Moon, R. (2001), *A Guide to the National Curriculum: Essential Reading for Parents and Teachers*. Oxford: Oxford University Press – a short, non-technical, easily read and assimilated book.

Sweetman, J. *Curriculum Confidential 2003/4: The Complete Guide to Education and the National Curriculum*. Westley, Suffolk: Courseware Publications. This gives a most readable and helpful guide to changes in the curriculum over the period between each issue.

## Useful websites

Many useful publications about the National Curriculum have been produced by the National Curriculum Council, the School Curriculum and Assessment Authority and the Qualifications and Curriculum Authority, published by HMSO. For example, see: http://www.curriculumonline.gov.uk and http://www.standards.dfes.gov.uk (click 'pick an area' or type 'national curriculum' into the 'search' dialogue box).

NFER, http://www.nfer-nelson.co.uk/catalogue/catalogue.asp

# Educational Assessment

## Chapter Outline (continued)

## Implications for teachers

- Assessment is so crucial in our educational system that all teachers need to know the range of methods available and their limitations.
- Recording and presenting assessments of pupils to those who require them is a skilled and difficult task. Present systems need to be studied.
- The psychological effects of assessment, both for the student and the teacher, are important areas of study.

Attempting to assess the quality and quantity of learning has been, and probably always will be, a regular feature of classroom practice. While experts argue the toss about the efficiency or desirability of examinations, teachers will continue in their own way to establish whether their pupils have been learning. There are many ways in which teachers might try to assess progress, ranging from simple observation or conversation to standardized testing. It will not be possible to touch on the multitude of methods which could be adopted. Instead, this chapter will tend to draw on the more acknowledged methods of assessment employed by examining bodies and teachers, although many of the arguments can be applied equally well to less formal classroom procedures.

The size of the assessment problem grows by the hour. Formal assessments taking place at the *Key Stages*, such as *Standard Assessment Tasks* (SATs) and numbers for examinations such as NVQs, GCSE and GCE 'AS' and 'A' Level continue to occupy much of a teacher's time. In the 1960s, we had the 11+, 'O' and 'A' Levels at (usually) 16 and 18 years and degree exams for about 7 per cent of the 21 years of age group. Now, in the twenty-first century, we have an avalanche of tests in the national system of SATs for 7, 11, 14 and 16-year-olds, GCSE and GCE for 16, 17 and 18 year-olds and degree exams for about 35 (rising fast to 40) per cent of the 21+ year age group. The number taking SATs in any one year is about two-and-a-half million. In England, the number of 'A' levels successfully passed (A to E grades) by students of 17+ years-of-age rose from 620,164 in 1996 through 672,362 in 2000 to 691,389 in 2005, partly reflecting increased numbers of students. In 1995/6, 594,035 pupils were entered for one or more GCSE 'O' levels. By 2004/5, this figure had risen to 636,796. Statutory assessment was also with us from 1997 in the form of Stage 9 assessments in core subjects. With statistics such as these, the importance of having a good knowledge of educational assessment is overwhelming.

If you are having difficulty getting to sleep, try the DfES website containing government statistics (see the end of the chapter for the address).

# Classroom assessment practices

Teachers view assessment as an important part of their work. They need to know something about pupils' attainment because parents, other teachers, governors, other schools, local authorities, employers and other institutions of further and higher education want to know. And teachers want to know if their teaching is effective.

The pupils also like to know how they are progressing. Diagnosis of difficulties or consistent errors, the evaluation of standards or content (e.g. national surveys, NFER tests, assessment of performance in various school subjects – see Chapter 18), and both formative and summative feedback are not possible without some form of assessment.

The form (the *how*) of assessment varies considerably according to circumstances, but Satterly (1989) gives a useful summary adapted in Figure 16.1. The vertical line labelled 'Instrument' relates to the particular form of presentation used, whether it be a published standardized test, home-made teacher test through to simple checklists (e.g. list of spellings, ten snappy arithmetic questions with simple answers). Teachers will recognize all these methods. The second, horizontal dimension distinguishes informal–formal assessments. Teachers very frequently make informal assessments, particularly in formative judgements during normal class learning. On the other hand, formal judgements tend to be made at times set aside specifically for the purpose of testing (e.g. examinations).

Figure 16.1 covers most of the methods used by teachers in their day-to-day work in the classroom. More will be said later about the various methods.

## Distinction between assessment and evaluation

A distinction needs to be drawn between the terms *assessment* and *evaluation*. They are often used interchangeably, but this is not an accurate or useful way of applying the terms. Satterly (1989) distinguishes clearly between them. *Assessment* is 'an omnibus term which includes all the processes and products which describe the nature and extent of children's learning,

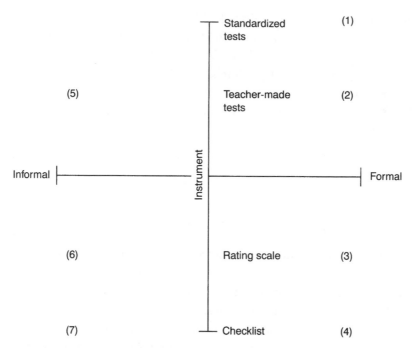

**Figure 16.1** A classification of classroom assessment practices, adapted from D. Satterly, *Assessment in Schools*, Blackwell, 1989 (2nd edn).
(1) Standardized tests (see Chapter 9) and the SATs tests at 7, 11, 14 and 16; (2) Carefully made teacher tests for examinations; (3) using, say, a 5-point scale to assess a pupil; (4) ticking off a list of requirements in, for example, a practical examination; (5), (6) and (7) are teacher-made tests, rating scales and checklists used in a classroom without any attempt at a formal assessment, i.e. impression marks.

its degree of correspondence with the aims and objectives of teaching and its relationship with the environments which are designed to facilitate learning'. *Evaluation* is what follows once an assessment has been made. It involves judgements about the effectiveness and worth of something for which the assessment has already been made – usually a teaching objective. One would assess the level of performance of a child in a given topic, but these results would be used to examine the suitability of the material for that child – that is, evaluation.

# Purposes of assessment in schools

What are the main purposes for which assessments are made? For whom are they made? The list below gives a pen-picture of the range and purposes for which assessment takes place:

| Type of assessment | Purpose |
|---|---|
| 1. Pretask | To discover the knowledge and skills possessed by someone before embarking on a learning task. |
| 2. Formative | To assess the progress and development of knowledge and skills during the process of learning. |
| 3. Diagnostic/remedial | To locate particular difficulties in the acquisition or application of knowledge and skills. |
| 4. Summative | To measure the outcomes of learning. |

Those who are most interested in the information provided by assessments are the learners, the teachers and others outside the classroom who need to know the competence or progress of the pupils. The pupils probably gain most from formative and diagnostic analysis, because these assessments are built in such a way as to be valuable for feedback to the pupils. Summative assessment, most frequently applied at the end of a topic or course, is not usually analysed for feedback, but used as an estimate of knowledge and skills learned in readiness for further applications. Clearly this kind of information is useful for parents, employers, other institutions (next school, university) or teachers (next class). Teachers make use of all four types of assessment. In this section we shall look a little more closely at these purposes, and in the next section we shall combine the sections dealt with so far in looking at some examples of classroom assessment.

In *pretask assessment* the teacher is concerned to discover the knowledge base from which subsequent lessons can take off. Students just beginning their teaching practice with unknown pupils are rightly worried about the level at which to pitch the lesson topics allocated. In most cases they are advised by the teacher who normally takes the classes. Occasionally it is necessary to devise a pretest. A new class at the beginning of the school year is sometimes questioned before the serious business of planning begins. Experienced teachers who are familiar with the age groups they inherit tend not to need to be cold blooded in their pursuit of this information; they have seen it all before! But it is wise for the inexperienced to build up firm knowledge of each child's incoming competence.

The methods used range from informal, almost casual, to standardized tests (see the 'instrument' dimension of Figure 16.1). A few question-and-answer sessions at the beginning of the academic year with those pupils not seen before is often used. As well as oral questioning, the early work of new pupils is examined for consistent errors or omissions. Teachers' home-made tests are sometimes used, often designed from previous experience, to find the range of talent amongst the pupils. Less frequently, standardized tests are employed; reading and number tests, for example (details from the National Foundation for Education Research at http://www.nfer-nelson.co.uk/catalogue/catalogue.asp), are sometimes given to new entrants to lower primary school or as part of SEN policy. At transfer to middle or, more particularly, secondary school, standardized ability tests in general intelligence, number and English are sometimes used. Some authorities still retain the 11+

entry examination as a 'pretask' mechanism by which to predict the most advantageous educational provision according to ability.

*Formative assessment* (also referred to as formative evaluation, but it is frequently employed as an assessment) takes place during the process of instruction and is used to guide, evaluate, feed back information to pupils and estimate the effectiveness of teaching. Most of the teacher's assessment effort is taken up in this way. Again, a whole range of instruments from informal checklists to standardized diagnostic tests are used for this purpose. Of all the forms of assessment referred to above, children are supposed to benefit from the most formative methods. The intention is to optimize feedback to pupils, pointing out strengths and weaknesses, and guiding their subsequent work. This strategy, however, equally applies to the teacher. His or her schemes are subject to modification in the light of lessons learned from pupil responses. The essential idea of formative assessment is to obtain information by which to modify and improve a programme of work.

*Diagnostic assessment* is crucial when you wish to provide help and guidance to individual pupils who have difficulty with particular aspects of work. It arises with the formative assessment period, when children are displaying problems. Again, the range of methods used stretches from informal analysis to standardized methods using specific tools designed to pinpoint the sources of difficulty.

Finally, *summative assessment* takes place at the end of the process of instruction and is used to discover the effectiveness of learning. It is rarely used to analyse difficulties (although one might learn from the mistakes in readiness for a repeat assessment, if this is available). A driving test, SATs, GCSE, GCE, 'O', 'AS' and 'A' Levels, end-of-term examinations in primary and secondary schools are examples. The outcome of these assessments is most often used by those outside the classroom. As is well known to the readers, GCSE results are used not only as measures of learning achieved, but also as predictors of future performance (not always in comparable situations, such as industry and university). End-of-term exams are one well-used means of summarizing the competence of pupils, although reports these days also contain other kinds of evaluation of work during the year.

## Evaluating teaching

As an example of diagnostic and summative assessment, we reproduce here two schedules from a teacher-training course in order to inform the student of the kind of activities about which he or she must make personal judgements. It is not only a diagnostic tool, but also a statement of the requirements of a student on school practice and is thereby a clear indication of what a student should be proficient at when he or she leaves the professional training course. In the student's teaching-practice file, there should be a section for personal evaluation. Some of the criteria in Figure 16.2 should appear in the student's statements about his or her competence.

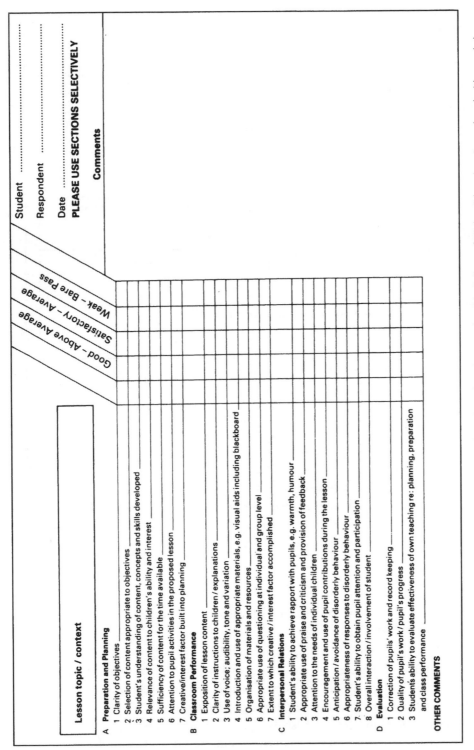

Lesson topic / context

Good – Above Average
Satisfactory – Average
Weak – Bare pass

Student  ..............
Respondent  ..............
Date  ..............

**PLEASE USE SECTIONS SELECTIVELY**

Comments

**A  Preparation and Planning**
1  Clarity of objectives
2  Selection of content appropriate to objectives
3  Student's understanding of content, concepts and skills developed
4  Relevance of content to children's ability and interest
5  Sufficiency of content for the time available
6  Attention to pupil activities in the proposed lesson
7  Creative/interest factor built into planning

**B  Classroom Performance**
1  Exposition of lesson content
2  Clarity of instructions to children / explanations
3  Use of voice: audibility, tone and variation
4  Introduction and use of appropriate materials, e.g. visual aids including blackboard
5  Organisation of materials and resources
6  Appropriate use of questioning at individual and group level
7  Extent to which creative / interest factor accomplished

**C  Interpersonal Relations**
1  Student's ability to achieve rapport with pupils, e.g. warmth, humour
2  Appropriate use of praise and criticism and provision of feedback
3  Attention to the needs of individual children
4  Encouragement and use of pupil contributions during the lesson
5  Anticipation / avoidance of disorderly behaviour
6  Appropriateness of responses to disorderly behaviour
7  Student's ability to obtain pupil attention and participation
8  Overall interaction / involvement of student

**D  Evaluation**
1  Correction of pupils' work and record keeping
2  Quality of pupil's work / pupil's progress
3  Students ability to evaluate effectiveness of own teaching re: planning, preparation and class performance

**OTHER COMMENTS**

**Figure 16.2** Diagnostic assessment of observed lesson. © School of Teacher Education, Humberside College of Higher Education. Reproduced with permission.

| Overall assessment of school placement | _____ First / Second | File Copy |
| --- | --- | --- |
| | _____ Final | |

Student _____  School _____

Respondent _____  Age range taught _____

Date _____  Type of organisation _____

| Good – Above Average | Satisfactory – Average – Pass | Fail | Grades are composite / summative ones based on diagnostic / formative **lesson schedules** and **general impressions** gained over the whole serial / block period. |
| --- | --- | --- | --- |
| | | | **Preparation and Planning** including File / Scheme / Lesson plans |
| | | | **Classroom Performance** including displays |
| | | | **Interpersonal Relations** |
| | | | **Evaluation** including recording of pupil's work / progress / adequacy and regularity of marking |
| | | | **Professional**<br>1 Relations with school staff ...............................................<br>2 Willingness to teach across a reasonable range ...........................<br>3 Interest and involvement across the life of the school ...........................<br>4 Willingness to accept responsibility for pupil's learning ...........................|

**Further Comment**

**Figure 16.3** Summative assessment. © School of Teacher Education, Humberside College of Higher Education. Reproduced with permission.

The assessment in Figure 16.3 is a summative assessment of student performance. It is the basis upon which a final assessment of teaching competence is made. It is compiled from several sources, including tutors from the training institutions, teachers in the school on which teaching practice has taken place and who have seen the student teaching or in other roles important to the assessment and the external examiner in some cases.

It is a compressed version of Figure 16.2. I hope these examples of evaluation schedules will serve both students and tutors as a source of information about some of the important aspects of practical teaching which should appear as part of the teacher-training course.

# Major reasons for assessment

A system which is used so extensively should have substantial justification. Let us look, therefore, at the arguments put by the protagonists of conventional assessments (discussed in Satterly 1989). Later it will be necessary to re-examine some of these points to assess the extent to which these purposes are achieved. By assessment we include any method used by a teacher or examining body to arrive at a measure of achievement of pupils. As we shall see, some measures are more reliable than others.

## Attainment (achievement)

One of the teacher's objectives, amongst others, is to stimulate the acquisition, understanding and application of knowledge. It therefore seems perfectly reasonable and desirable that the teacher should also want to explore the extent to which these objectives have been achieved. Indeed, in any walk of life, a time comes when we have to expose our knowledge and have it evaluated. This assessment of attainment and its evaluation at any given time is one of the central aims of education.

Beyond the classroom there are employers and professions who require some assurances about the level of competence reached by prospective entrants. These assurances must be expressed as accurately as possible and in terms which are readily understood by all concerned. Examination marks in secondary and higher education are thought to provide one such criterion, although, as we shall see, marks can just as readily be misunderstood. When an organization external to the school is engaged, it adds a measure of objectivity and credibility to the marks obtained.

## Diagnosis

### The pupil

By comparing the attainments of a group of people who have taken the same examination, it is possible to draw some conclusions about the strengths and weaknesses of individuals. Of course, we have only measured the effects and not the causes of success or failure in the exam. Detecting the origins of failure is no easy task, particularly if the exam is not all that it should be. Essay-type papers, for example, are less useful when we want to see how extensively a pupil has covered the syllabus. An objective-type test which endeavours to cover a good portion of the syllabus is more likely to be of value in this kind of diagnosis. Also, the failure of a large number of pupils to give an adequate answer to particular questions could arise from inadequate teaching or question design.

### Evaluation of the teacher and the topic

It is part of the process of curriculum design for teachers to evaluate the effectiveness and efficiency of their methods and the suitability of the content. Care is clearly needed in making these judgements because so many variables, apart from considerations of the teacher's competence, impinge on pupil performance. Nevertheless, the methods of presentation and communication, the suitability and level of content, in fact all the learning experiences offered by the teacher will be reflected to some extent in the results of any evaluative programme.

The teacher's task of using examination scores as one source of pupil analysis and self-analysis, known as *feedback*, is very important and requires careful scrutiny of the scripts. Insufficient attention is given to the feedback made possible by this kind of analysis. In school examinations pupils should be allowed to see their scripts after they have been marked. The opportunity for pupils to see where they have gone wrong, to evaluate their competence and to set realistic goals is a most important function of well-designed examinations.

## Prediction

Success in public examinations opens the door to a number of careers. Whether or not we agree with the validity of this process, most external exams are used to assess the potential of the examinee. If a student obtains so many GCSE passes he or she is deemed suitable for 'A' Level studies; 'A' Level successes are taken as the basis for choosing an academic or professional course; merit in the form of authority and professional status is often placed in the hands of those who succeed in examinations (Young 1961). The tacit assumption is that examination results are valid predictors. The 11+ entrance examination was probably the most widespread prognostic device ever used in British educational history. Success in standardized tests of numerical, verbal and spatial ability was said to indicate those children who would benefit most from an academic schooling.

## Providing and maintaining standards – targets and benchmarks

A carefully devised examination can be set at whatever level one chooses. Attempts are made in GCSE exams, for example, to retain the same standard from one year to the next or from one examining board to the next, although that claim is hotly contested (e.g. press comments about the annual GCSE results; also see HMI Report 1992). Establishing standards of attainment is inevitable in a society which demands minimum levels of competence as a prerequisite for certain qualifications. How would we find our next generation of teachers if the last generation of teachers abandoned the idea of distinguishing between the qualities of their pupils? A public exam system is also an admission that we cannot trust each other. Its presence gives an air of impartiality and respectability to whatever standards are obtained.

The National Curriculum and accompanying Key Stage tests of Standard Assessment Tasks (SATs) are a clear example of public setting, maintaining and assessing standards. The disadvantageous effects of targets, particularly those using arbitrary demarcation lines (e.g., percentages of those passing GCSE 'O' level at C or better) are regularly challenged by some contemporary writers (see Pole 1998, Fitz-Gibbon 2001).

## Motivation

Learning is not easy. It requires self-discipline and hard work. Interest is obviously a good starting point, but this often comes as a product of becoming competent in a subject.

---

### Further reading

Some researches have shown little or no correlation between interest and attainment. Interest, by its very nature, is subject to change and does not always depend on competence. How many youngsters have started to learn the piano or violin only to discover that it requires hard effort to reach any level of competence? Rowlands back in 1961 showed low correlations for prospective scientists, non-scientists and early leavers. Cronbach (1984) in *Essentials of Psychological Testing* reports an extensive summary of this field of investigation and concludes that:

> Interests are poor academic predictors. . . . Out of 21 correlations of course mark with interest in that subject matter (expressed prior to the course), 17 were below + 0.3. (p. 431)

For a discussion of this topic see Bloom (1976).

---

One major source of motivation is the long-term prospect of obtaining a qualification and a good job. For example, it was thought by some teachers that the introduction of the CSE (Certificate of Secondary Education) injected new life and purpose into the work of moderately able secondary pupils who at one time would have impatiently played out their last school years longing to be wage earners at the end of the fourth form. The motivational qualities of exams need hardly be mentioned to student teachers, who have all experienced the annual retreat into studies and libraries (around Easter time, usually) and the feverish activity which preceded the exams.

---

### Further reading

There is ample evidence from social psychologists (summarized in Reid, 1989) that this ability to postpone an immediate gratification for a long-term goal such as a professional qualification is more characteristic of children from middle- than from working-class homes. This is one of many social reasons why early leavers come largely from working-class backgrounds.

---

## Development

Examinations have been said to bring out qualities of perseverance and industriousness. They are thought to give practice in expressing ideas lucidly, fluently and quickly. They compel students to organize their ideas and develop systems of study and concentration which may be adapted for service in later life.

## Social (and administrative) engineering

By making examinations available to anyone who feels capable of sitting them, it is possible for social mobility to take place (but see Young 1961). At one time, favouritism and patronage played a large part in the life-chances of young people entering schools, universities or business. Now nepotism (favouring relatives irrespective of their qualities) no longer has any significant effect. The 11+ was seen by many as promoting social justice and enabling bright children from less fortunate home backgrounds to enter grammar schools. Indeed, that was the original intention of Thomson in Northumberland (see Thomson's work in 'Selection tests', Chapter 9, p. 300). Robbins (1963), in a report on higher education, foresaw the existence of 'pools of ability' largely consisting of able youngsters leaving school before attempting to get into higher education. Government policy was set to increase the numbers entering higher and further education from 7 per cent in post Second World War Britain to 40 per cent by the turn of the last century. This target has been achieved and an even higher percentage is in prospect.

# Problems associated with assessment

There are many problems associated with conventional examinations, tests and assessments. Much research money and energy has been spent in discovering the problems and trying out or suggesting solutions. Government bodies such as the Schools Council, which produced a stream of *Examinations Bulletins*, and the successor bodies (the National Curriculum Council and the School Examinations and Assessment Council) have researched this area. So too has the National Foundation for Educational Research. A report by a task force, in the days of the DfE, called Task Group on Assessment and Testing (TGAT) set the pattern for the present National Curriculum assessments (DES 1988a and 1988b).

First amongst the limitations are fundamental requirements which apply to any test or assessment which is going to be used to make judgements about how much a person has learned, how performance compares from one testing occasion to the next, how a person's performance compares with that of comparable people and whether the test measures what it was designed to measure. There are three statistical requirements which play a particularly important part in defining the adequacy of assessments. They are *reliability, validity* and *comparability.* Here, we shall give the rudiments. For a sound introduction, see Satterly (1989).

## Reliability

Let us first define this term as applied to examinations. A reliable exam is one which will give a consistent score from one occasion to the next for the same individual or group irrespective of the person who marks it. We are dealing here with the adequacy of the measurement, and not the content. A simple example should suffice. If a teacher gives a primary-school class a home-made arithmetic test on two separate occasions and the two scores for individuals are irregular, the teacher would be justified in suspecting that the test was unreliable. If most of the scores increase on the second testing, it may mean that the children have had some practice in the meantime or that they have remembered some answers and left more time for the solution of other questions. If, on the other hand, the scores for some children are a mixture of some going higher and some lower, then it could mean that the questions are poor or the marking inconsistent. These are the kinds of inconsistency which give rise to unreliability of tests.

First, there are inconsistencies arising in one examiner's marks for a particular paper when it is marked on different occasions. This occurs primarily because of fatigue, mood, time of day and inadvertent changes in interpretation of an answer from one script to the next. Therefore, on marking the same batch of scripts on two occasions, two different sets of scores for each candidate or variations between candidates who have given similar answers could result.

Second, different examiners often have different interpretations and expectations of the candidates' answers. An essay-type answer is especially prone to varied interpretations because examiners can look for so many differing qualities. Some might be influenced by a fluent and witty style even when the content is thin; others might reward grammatical structure. An 'impression' mark is also decidedly open to criticism because of the high degree of subjective judgement involved.

To illustrate the fluctuations in essay marks between examiners, we shall use some material from a famous research in the 1930s by Hartog and Rhodes – just as appropriate today as then. For subjects like French, English essays, history and mathematics at levels from junior school to university, Hartog and Rhodes (1936) invited panels of expert examiners to mark sets of papers. Table 16.1 shows the marks awarded to six candidates in an Entrance Scholarship Examination to university by five examiners, (a) to (e). Five of these candidates were selected from a much larger table in Hartog and Rhodes because they all exhibited a discrepancy of 25 marks between the best and worst examiners' marks. The other selection (Candidate 25) is included as an illustration of a huge discrepancy of 36.

In a perfect world, all the examiners would give the same mark to a candidate. So candidate 25 would have had the same mark reading across the row. This has not happened

**Table 16.1** Disparity in examiners' marks in an essay question.

| Candidate | Examiner (a) | (b) | (c) | (d) | (e) | Discrepancy range | Average | Position |
|---|---|---|---|---|---|---|---|---|
| 25 | 60 | [32] | 65(1) | 50 | (68)(1) | 36 | 55.0 | 1 |
| 34 | (65) | 52(1) | [40] | 60(1) | 55 | 25 | 54.4 | 2 |
| 13 | (67)(1) | 50 | 45 | [42](6) | 52 | 25 | 51.2 | 3 |
| 23 | 42 | [35] | (60) | 58 | 47 | 25 | 48.4 | 4 |
| 9 | 48 | [30](6) | (55) | (55) | 40 | 25 | 45.6 | 5 |
| 47 | 32(6) | 36 | 35(6) | (55) | [30](6) | 25 | 37.6 | 6 |
| Mean score | 52.3 | 39.2 | 50.0 | 53.3 | 48.7 | | | |

Extracted from Table 96, p. 143 of *The Marks of Examiners* (1936) by P. Hartog and E. C. Rhodes. Reprinted with the kind permission of the publishers, Macmillan, London and Basingstoke.

and the best we can do is to find the average of the range of marks awarded to 25 by the five examiners. The averages and rank order are shown in the last two columns of Table 16.1. The candidates are also arranged in rank order.

Still reading the rows, there is no consistency in whom the examiners think is the best or the worst. The highest mark awarded to a candidate is in a circle and the lowest in a square. Candidate 25 gets 32 from Examiner (b) and 68 from (e) – a discrepancy of 36. Indeed, the candidate is second from the bottom for (b) and top for (e). Candidate 13 also presents the anomaly of being top for (a) with 67 and bottom for (d) with 42. Notice that Examiner (e) happens to have given marks which would arrange the candidates in the same order as the averages. However, overall, the candidates awarded (1)s or (6)s (shown in brackets) do tend to be towards the top and bottom respectively. Note that the range between the highest and lowest average mark is about 17 – less than the 25 from the original marks. Averaging marks does tend to contract the range (known as *regression to the mean*).

Reading the columns for each examiner's marks is also instructive. The mean for each examiner is at the bottom of the columns. The size of the means tells us how strictly they have marked. Examiner (d) is the most generous with an average of 53.3 and (b) the meanest with 39.2.

These results speak for themselves. There are several other ways of looking at these data, but they all display an unreliable ragbag of opinions about students' competence, and they also expose enormous differences in the marks allotted to candidates by different examiners for the same work.

Regrettably, these findings from the mid-1930s are still valid in today's exam scene. Satterly (1989, Table 7.7, p. 229), for instance, gives several additional examples of unreliability of marking essay-type tests. Despite progress in examination practices, we hear (annually) of the difficulties experienced by examination boards. We have to admit that examining essay-type questions is not an exact science and extra care is needed. Admittedly, teachers do not have time or resources to adopt the systems used by examining bodies, but they need to keep at the front of their minds the possible sources of inconsistency in their marking. At the very least, know clearly what points you are looking for in a piece of work and be consistent in awarding marks for these points.

A great deal has been done by bodies responsible for public examinations to overcome unreliability by making improvements in marking procedures. For example, it is now common practice for examiners in a subject to meet and co-ordinate a marking scheme. Decisions are made about the allocation of marks and the range of answers which the panel will accept, and these are adhered to by them all. Marked scripts are sampled and re-marked by a second examiner, usually the leader of the team. Borderline candidates' scripts are always re-examined. Nothing is now knowingly left to chance in public examinations.

Multiple marking and finding the average as in Table 16.1 has been one often used solution. Wiseman back in 1949 (also see 1956) suggested that several examiners should mark each paper, thus diluting the idiosyncrasies of individual examiners. Work published by the Schools Council (1966) on *multiple* marking in English composition at 'O' level, using a combination of marks for impression (three independent assessors) and mechanical accuracy (one assessor) reveals an improvement in reliability over the official mark awarded by an examining board. There was also closer agreement with a continuous assessment given by the schools of the candidates. In subjects where impression marking is prevalent and several people are used to make the assessment, there is a danger that the assessments will 'regress to the mean'. Because 'one person's meat is another person's poison', marks tend to head towards the average and the range is reduced as we saw in Table 16.1.

Even in a subject like mathematics, there can be variations from one sitting to the next. Dale (1954) found several disconcerting movements in the marks obtained by candidates at 'O' Level in successive June and September (resit) examinations. He gives four examples of increased marks which seem to go far beyond what one might reasonably expect as a result of concentrated effort in the time between the two exams. Table 16.2 is a reproduction of his findings.

**Table 16.2** Differences in mathematics marks between June and September (resit).

| Candidate | Marks as percentages | | Range |
| | June | September | |
| --- | --- | --- | --- |
| A | 27 | 58 | 31 |
| B | 25 | 63 | 38 |
| C | 32 | 59 | 27 |
| D | 36 | 76 | 40 |

Reproduced from *From School to University* (1954) by R. R. Dale, p. 141, with the kind permission of the publishers, Routledge and Kegan Paul, London.

This kind of unreliability is of particular interest, for it calls into question the comparability of test papers which, superficially at least, are thought to be similar. In mathematics there is an additional problem; candidates may spend disproportionate amounts of time on a few questions without necessarily being successful in solving them.

Apart from a stricter control of marking schemes and increasing the number of examiners, it is also possible to improve the reliability by increasing the length of the examination paper. This is usually the case in multiple-choice tests, as we shall see.

## Validity

If a test achieves what the originators intended it to achieve, it is a valid test. There are several kinds of validity (Satterly 1989), but our main concerns here are *content* and *predictive* validity. Before describing these, it ought to be noted that there is a connection between the validity and the reliability of a test or examination paper. If a test is unreliable, then plainly it cannot be valid for any purpose. On the other hand, if it is highly reliable it need not necessarily be valid; in other words, it might be highly reliable at measuring something which the designers never intended! Briefly, tests can be reliable and invalid, but they cannot be unreliable and valid.

### Content validity

For an examination to have content validity it must contain qualitative and quantitative representation in the sampling of the whole syllabus. This rests upon the judgement of the examiner in completing questions from the syllabus. Essay-type papers often fall short of this requirement. It is very difficult to cover a significant portion of a syllabus using only ten or so questions. Multiple-choice designs overcome this difficulty to some extent by setting a large number of short questions covering a major part of a syllabus. However, there is more to content validity than merely making sure the syllabus content has been sampled adequately. We also need to know whether the questions are set in such a way as to fulfil the purposes and aims of the course. The teaching has been geared to certain objectives (see Chapter 15). Have these objectives been realized in the choice of questions and the answers given? Unfortunately, there are no formulae for finding content validity. The teacher must make up his or her mind about it from experience with the material and by using, where possible, a second opinion, because this is a qualitative rather than a quantitative activity. Deciding on objectives and setting appropriate questions is a difficult business. In this respect, Bloom's *Taxonomy of Educational Objectives* (1956) is quite helpful in defining the scope and extent of the purposes we ascribe to educational procedures and in providing the kinds of questions appropriate for them (see Chapter 15).

### Predictive validity

We saw earlier that one function of many public examinations is to enable us to select people for certain occupational or scholastic pursuits. The predictive validity of an examination is characterized by its ability to forecast those who might succeed in these pursuits. For example, 'A' Level results are used by universities and colleges as a major source of evidence of a student's capacity for coping with the course requirements (Sherwin and Child 1970, Child *et al.* 1986, Sear 1983, Cook 1993b). A degree, for instance, is often taken as evidence that a person has the ability to cope in industry.

The results of research into the predictive value of examinations have not been encouraging. Investigations into the prognostic use of the 11+, 'O' and 'A' Levels, teachers' certificates and degree results have all, at one time or another, provided conflicting results. The reasons for this confused picture are complex, but one fairly obvious cause of low correlations is that some occupations demand qualities which are not disclosed by traditional written examination papers, and some qualities required in the preparation for, and competitive elements of, examinations are of little use in certain jobs.

## Comparability and value added

### Comparing examination marks

Comparability is closely linked with reliability, but it is so often neglected that a separate discussion is needed. Issues associated with comparisons of tests within the same subject were raised in the section above. Basically, if we want to compare the results of an individual on two or more tests or the results of several groups using the same test, we have to make sure that the comparisons are legitimate. For example, given two parallel forms of a French or arithmetic paper, are we justified in comparing the raw scores obtained by an individual on the two parts? This depends on a number of factors. Have the tests similar content? Do the scores for each group have similar means? Are the scores spread out in a similar fashion in both tests? The GCSE results in 1992 were the subject of criticism from the Inspectorate (HMI Report 1992a) for their lack of comparability across the examining bodies operating in England and Wales. This has led to government proposals (1996) for fewer examining bodies placed under central monitoring of standards.

A number of worries have been expressed (Nuttall 1989) about the comparability of the Standard Assessment Tasks (SATs) now in operation with the National Curriculum at the Key Stage ages of 7, 11, 14 and 16. One major problem is the aggregation of marks (see Chapter 18) by combining the results of each component of a child's performance (Shorrocks-Taylor 1998, Fitz-Gibbon 1998, 2001).

### School Performance (League) Tables

The advent of School Performance Tables has raised several important issues about valid and reliable methods of comparing the different performances of schools (Fitz-Gibbon 1997, 1998, Shorrocks-Taylor 1998). *Performance indicators* and measures of pupil and school progress, that is, value added, from one test to the next has become a critical area of research.

Perhaps the first thing to notice about 'whole school' performance is that variations between schools accounts for much less than 'whole class' performance or 'individual pupil' performance. In other words, if you want to learn more about sources of variation in the marks obtained by pupils, look at them and their subject teachers, not at the school. Vincent (1997), using a multi-level analysis of the 1994 Key Stage 3 mathematics and English results (the levels being school, class, individual), showed that in mathematics the school effects (influence of different kinds of school) are very small (15 per cent) when compared with department or classroom effects (influence of a teacher in a class teaching a particular subject – 43 per cent) and individual child effects (42 per cent). Therefore, comparisons between schools are not useful in measuring pupil progress or teacher competence. A similar pattern emerged for English.

Likewise, straight comparisons between subjects are not reliable (Chapter 18). Fitz-Gibbon (2001) gives some convincing results from her work on value-added effects between GCSE 'O' (or other standardized tests) and 'A' Level results. For instance, some subjects are harder than others. Therefore adding the raw marks or grades across subjects is not acceptable. League tables arising from added or averaged grades at 'A' Level will give a false impression. Using prior performance at GCSE 'O' Level or standardized test results, she has shown wide variations in the *difficulty* of different school subjects and its effect on recruitment and performance at 'A' Level.

Because of national policy in comparing school performance, the study of comparability has become one of the most important areas in assessment. Teachers are wise to keep a watchful eye on the topic.

## The examinee

There are many intellectual, personal and social reasons which impose limitations on the performance of students but which have little or nothing to do with the setting or marking of the papers. Whether we could in some way allow for these variables is an extremely difficult and unresolved matter. They exist, and we should at least be aware of them. There are several obvious reasons which need little comment. Some people are over-optimistic about their talents and do not really have the necessary skills. Choosing the wrong subject is at the root of some students' problems. Few people are entirely consistent in their mood from one examination to another. The physical and mental condition of a candidate can affect performance, and in some cases candidates do not do themselves justice. Others are capable, but do not work, often through lack of motivation or over-confidence. Poor study strategies, lack of guidance about the requirements or faulty examination technique, all of which can be remedied, are common sources of trouble. Sometimes a teacher has a style of presentation which is incompatible with the style of learning of the pupil (cognitive style). Student teachers out on school practice will have experienced those blank looks on a child's face when something is being described, even when the student is convinced that the presentation was simple and logical. The art of simplification, using metaphor and analogy, and discovering the modes of thinking of pupils are skills which every teacher has to cultivate.

Some have argued that examinations engender an unnecessary spirit of competition between pupils. However, in most public examinations where an external paper and examiner are employed, the pupil and the teacher are, in some respects, in partnership. They cooperate in an attempt to meet the external demands of the examination system.

Research (see Chapter 12 on personality) suggests that those who succeed in conventional written examinations may have particular personality predispositions. It would be surprising if this were not the case. Characteristics such as persistence, a theoretical turn of mind, fondness for books and other forms of written word, solitude and reflection are clearly beneficial to a student doing a theoretical course. These characteristics have been associated with the introverted personality, and research has shown that introverts abound in higher education, where theoretical, solitary study is at a premium.

Another influence arises from the fact that British exam systems tend to overemphasize the written word. Recently an effort has been made to introduce other means by which students can communicate their skills and knowledge, besides the two-hour or three-hour written paper. Practicals, vivas, project work and orals have been around for a while, but have usually made a minor contribution to the marks (Satterly 1989).

Finally, a word about *anxiety* and *stress* aroused by the tensions which accompany an examination system. Whenever there is a threat to one's self-esteem, anxiety is inevitable. In turn, anxiety states will have some influence on learning and performance. Intellectual and personal factors interact in a complex fashion not yet understood by psychologists, and the direction of influence is still not predictable. In some circumstances a moderate level of stress may provide drive energy which can be harnessed to good effect. In other cases, the level of stress may be so high as to be disruptive (driving tests have a habit of being this!). More detailed discussion of stress and performance can be found in Chapters 8 and 12.

The question of stress for both pupils and teachers in the SATs deserves a special mention. Tension has been raised by the spectre of endless testing. No matter how hard one tries to 'sugar the pill', most pupils and teachers feel they are under the microscope. The assessments which will attract the most attention will be the *high stakes* ones, that is, Key Stage assessments and any others which form an obvious part of any measures likely to be transformed into pupil, teacher, class or school benchmarks and league tables. Other kinds of assessment such as those for which subjective rating scales, checklists and self-assessment profiles by the pupils are in evidence are *low-stake* assessments with less chance of getting the attention thought, by some, to be due to them.

Most teachers soon discover those pupils who have a nervous disposition. It is up to teachers to put pupils at ease by showing sympathy and a willingness to talk through the problems. Teachers too need to talk through their anxieties with colleagues and any staff (in or outside the school) who have expertise in counselling. The anxiety generated by examinations, especially public exams ranging from SATs onwards to university on which one's future (next school, university, career) might hinge, is a regular source of trouble. It affects young and old alike. Teachers should do all in their power to allay excessive tension. Where possible, the test or examination should be held in familiar surroundings in the school, with familiar faces as invigilators; also, the examination should be fitted into the normal school routines if possible. The atmosphere in an examination room should not be unduly tense and distant, but relaxed, quiet and conducive to concentration. Pupils should have a clear idea of what is expected of them, and this can frequently be achieved by making sure they understand the rubric of their papers, without unduly prolonging the period of preparation before the exam.

## Curriculum

To what extent are syllabuses determined and restricted by the existence of an examination? How are teaching methods affected by syllabus demands? Are there important educational needs (social, moral and intellectual) which are not examinable and which have to be sacrificed in favour of examinable themes? It has been suggested by many teachers that both they and their pupils have to make many omissions in their work because they get caught up in the frenzied scramble towards the Key Stage examinations from SATs to GCSEs (Nuttall 1989, DES Report on TGAT 1988a and a DES digest of the Report for Schools 1988b, Pole 1998). For many years the teaching of mathematics and science was designed to provide routine strategies for problem-solving without arousing much exploratory interest in these subjects. The phenomenon of the examination dictating the content of the curriculum and methods of teaching is known as the 'backwash' effect. It is a subject with which every teacher should be familiar.

Question 'spotting' (guessing in advance the content of the exam questions) is commonly practised by pupils and teachers. Some teachers have developed the art to a high degree by juggling the questions on back papers with great dexterity. Unfortunately, it makes nonsense of a syllabus intended to give a comprehensive grounding in a subject.

## Sex differences in academic achievement

A great deal of confusion surrounds the issues of sex differences in academic achievement. Let us first refresh our memories about differences in biological and cognitive abilities.

From Chapter 2, the findings of behavioural geneticists, psychiatrists and psychologists confirm structural and functional differences between females and males and, consequently, the relationship of these findings to cognitive performance. In Chapter 8, we made the point that no matter how able a student is, he or she must also be willing to work at a subject. In Chapter 9, meta-analyses of psychometric intelligence test performance were reported. These showed no differences in overall performance, but significant differences of performance in certain specific cognitive abilities. On average, females do significantly better

**Table 16.3** Extract from government statistics: percentages of pupils achieving Level 5 or above at Stage 3 (England 2003/04).

| Subject | All (%) | Girls (%) | Boys (%) |
|---|---|---|---|
| English | 71 | 78 | 64 |
| Reading | 65 | 71 | 60 |
| Writing | 72 | 80 | 65 |
| Mathematics | 72 | 74 | 72 |
| Science | 66 | 67 | 65 |

in tasks requiring verbal skills such as verbal fluency, reading, spelling and verbal memory. Males, on average, do significantly better in visuo-spatial and some quantitative tasks.

What effect could these differences have on accomplishment in school subjects? Most school subjects are language based. Most forms of mathematics do not require spatial problem-solving ability and many problems depend as much on verbal as on numerical understanding. Therefore, on average, one would expect females to do better than males in most school subjects.

A browse through UK government statistics (see the end of the chapter for a DfES website address) quickly reveals the language advantage of females affects most subjects in most performance charts. Table 16.3 is taken from the Government Standards statistics (see website addresses) and shows the superiority of girls at Stage 3, Level 5 and above in English, Reading and Writing – very much as one would have predicted from the evidence mentioned previously. The differences in English, with girls 14 per cent higher than boys, Reading 11 per cent and Writing 15 per cent, look enormous and are, in statistical terms, highly significant.

Where the overall performance is more or less the same, as in Science and Mathematics (Science – girls 67%: boys 65%, Maths – girls 74%: boys 72%), where some aspects may depend on visuo-spatial skills (see the discussion in Chapter 9 of sex differences, Neisser *et al.* 1996) there is probably a moderating effect on the percentages.

Another impressive statistic is that the percentage of females gaining two or more GCE 'A' Levels has increased by 23 per cent (from 20% to 43%) between 1995/6 and 2001/2. For males the corresponding increase is quite a bit less at 16 per cent (from 18% to 34%).

The literature often quotes American statistics relating to their system of basing university selection partly on the results of a Scholastic Assessment Test (SAT). You will notice it has the same (confusing) acronym as the UK's Standard Assessment Tasks (SATs). Males score higher than females on the mathematical sections of this test (Gallagher and DeLisi 1994). But these assessments tend to contain some items not unlike those in IQ tests and possibly requiring spatial orientation solutions.

The gap between girls and boys in Table 16.3 has been widening over the years at all stages of SATs. Arnot *et al.* (1996) give details of the shift. There was little difference up to the mid 1980s after which the *gender gap* has slowly widened and continues to do so. But why has it increased over the years? There cannot be a biological explanation, for the gap would always have been there. We have to turn to a gender or sex-role explanation.

These gender distinctions applied throughout education; indeed they became overstated in the processes of guiding students into subjects and careers. 'Image' was all-important. In school subjects, languages and language-related subjects were 'sissy' and really for girls; maths, science, technical subjects, even ITC were 'macho' and for boys. Sex-role stereotyping in the last century was still in evidence until the 1980s. Legislation in equal opportunities for, and less discrimination against, females is beginning to have an effect, although they have not yet been achieved. This 'image' issue is closely related to motivation. Even when interest is high, where 'image' is involved it is often the most potent stimulus or repellent.

Do these differences matter to teachers? Yes, they do. By the early 1990s with declining sex-role stereotyping, girls and boys were not discouraged from pursuing subjects they wanted. To continue this advance, it is still crucial for teachers to get under the superficial skin of gender stereotypes and explore each child's strengths. Despite, 'on average', boys doing well and heading towards 'systemizing' (Baron-Cohen 2003) subjects and careers, some girls are also good at this and need to be spotted and encouraged. Though, 'on average', girls do well and choose 'empathic' subjects, some boys are good at these and need support.

# Methods of assessment in use

There has been a marked growth in alternatives to *conventional written examinations* over the years. The most important of these has been the *objective-type test*, of which the now familiar multiple-choice item is an example. Other forms in use are *continuous* (or, more accurately, *intermittent*) *assessment, orals, practicals, portfolio* and *performance*. The most recent innovations to be introduced with the new General Certificate of Secondary Education (GCSE) have *grade-related* criteria and SATs which include *rating scales* and *checklists*.

## Conventional written examinations

It is hardly necessary to remind readers of the design of traditional exam papers. We are all too familiar with the rubric 'Answer 3 from 7 in 3 hours: careless and untidy work will be penalized'. But a number of interesting variations have been tried. Some universities, for instance, are experimenting with 'open-book' methods where the candidate is allowed to take specified texts into the exam room (if time is found to use them). Some candidates have been given the actual questions in advance or have been allowed to set their own papers. Naturally, the tendency is to set questions which make greater demands on the students if they are being given the advantage of a preview. The questions require answers which are less factual, more analytical and not unlike essays.

## Objective-type examinations

In essay questions students are free to plan their own answers using whatever knowledge can be recalled, usually without any clues from the question. In objective questions the information given (or 'stem' of the question) is posed in such a way that there is only one acceptable answer, which either can be recalled from memory or recognized from a collection of probable answers. They are called 'objective' because the questions and answers are carefully predetermined, rendering the responses free from the personal biases of the examiner. Designing items is a skilled job, as we shall see in the next chapter. Hubbard and Clemans (1961), though dated, gives a very clear idea of how to construct questions. Item analysis is required to provide a measure of the difficulty of each item for a given ability group, and to determine the discriminative qualities of the item.

In the UK the use of objective tests has been gathering momentum. Examination papers now contain many items of this kind. The Schools Council was most prolific in the researches it has sponsored, and its publications relating to many important aspects of the whole field of educational assessment make important reading for both students and teachers.

Several examples are given below to give the student some idea of the scope of objective-test items now available. Answers appear at the end of the chapter. They by no means cover all the variations in use, but represent the commonest. For convenience, we might make a broad distinction between items requiring straightforward *recall* and those requiring the *recognition* (or choice response) of an answer, although some designs require both these mental activities.

### Recall items

As stated above, these require the candidate to remember a simple correct answer without it appearing on the answer sheet. Some factual essay questions require just this, except that the answers are buried in continuous prose. There are three basic kinds of recall item.

**Simple recall:** Here the candidate must recall a single fact (or series of facts), as in the following example which is typical of Key Stage 3 Mathematics (14-year-olds), Tier 4–6:

The following right-angle triangle is *not* to scale. One side is 14.5 cm long as shown.

Tony says, 'the perimeter of the triangle is about 25 cm.' How can you tell that he is wrong without measuring the other two sides?

**Open (or sentence) completion:**  The candidate fills in an incomplete sentence, phrase or equation. For example:

(1)  If          $m + 6 = 15$
     complete     $m + 9 = \ldots.$
     This example is about the standard of Key Stage 2 Mathematics (11 year-olds), Levels 3–5.
(2)  Jeremiah said that the Lord 'Will give all Judah into the Hand of . . .' Complete the sentence.
     (West Yorkshire and Lindsey Regional Examining Board for the Certificate of Secondary Education, Religious Knowledge, 1970.)

**The unlabelled diagram:**  This is used extensively in science, particularly biology, where candidates are asked to recall parts of an organ or apparatus. For example:

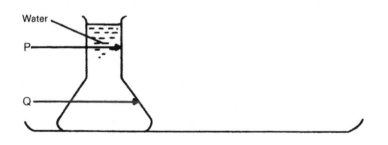

The diagram shows a conical vessel full of water. Show, on the diagram, the jets of water which occur when small holes are made in the vessel at the points marked P and Q; assume that air resistance is negligible.
(University of Cambridge Local Examinations Syndicate, GCE O level Physics, 1970.)

### Recognition items
Recognition items require the candidate to choose a correct answer from two or more possible answers which are given. There are several ways of presenting this kind of item, and four are illustrated below.

**True/false items:** The candidate is given a stem and is required to say whether it is true or false. For example:

Place a tick in either the 'True' or 'False' column after each statement depending on which you think is the appropriate answer.

|  | True | False |
|---|---|---|

1. Intelligence may be defined as inborn all-round mental efficiency.
2. Intelligence is largely a product of the culture in which a child is reared, and the stimulation he receives.
3. Intelligence is entirely distinct from attainments or acquired information, and education received.
4. The IQ (if tested by a reliable test) remains constant to within about 5 points either way throughout school life.

(Taken from a questionnaire by P. E. Vernon in *The Bearings of Recent Advances in Psychology on Educational Problems*, Evans, London, 1955.)

**Multiple-choice responses:** These are the commonest forms of objective test. Usually there are about five alternative answers provided for each item. It is possible to have more than one acceptable answer in some cases. The following are examples having one correct response:

You are asked to underline the appropriate item in each case.

1. The chief danger from FALL-OUT comes from

   Cosmic dust, fission fragments, fusion fragments, cosmic rays, disturbance of the atmosphere, any of these, none of these.

2. ALTAMIRA attracts visitors for the same reason as

   Palmyra, Nimes, Alicante, Bonn, Lisieux, Lascaux, Arles, none of these.

3. Which of these has the most complex MOLECULAR STRUCTURE?

   Salt, sugar, starch, protein, petroleum, potassium permanganate, nitrous oxide.

4. One of these Shakespearean characters is out of keeping with the others.

   Iago, Macbeth, Cassius, Claudius, Feste, Richard III, Timon.

(Taken from a 'culture test' by W. K. Richmond, in *Culture and General Education*, Methuen, London, 1963.)

Example having several correct responses:

> Solids, liquids and gases have different properties. The chart below shows some of these properties.
>
> *Complete the table by ticking (√) to show the properties of solids, liquids and gases. The first row has been done for you. Some rows may need more than one tick.*
>
> | Property | solid | liquid | gas |
> |---|---|---|---|
> | keeps its own shape | √ | | |
> | flows easily through a pipe | | | |
> | can make rigid or stiff structure | | | |
> | can be squashed in a much smaller volume | | | |
> | takes the shape of the container into which it is put | | | |
>
> (Taken, with permission, from 1995 Key Stage 2 Science (11-year-olds), Test A, (Levels 3–5), SCAA, London.)

Example using the 'best reason' method:

Answer the question implied in the following statement by selecting the answer A, B, C, D or E which best completes the sentence.

A metaphorical expression

A.  is allowable in poetry but not in prose
B.  is never used except for rhetorical ornament
C.  falsely likens one thing to another
D.  is always in the form 'A is B'
E.  implies a comparison

(Joint Matriculation Board, GCE A level General Studies – Paper I, 1968.)

**Matching items and rearrangement:** These are self-evident from the examples below. The following is an example of matching items:

> Draw lines to connect each raw material to the substance produced from it.
>
> | Raw material | Substance produced |
> |---|---|
> | clay ● | ● glass |
> | ore ● | ● metal |
> | sand ● | ● pottery |
> | wood ● | ● paper |
>
> (Taken, with permission, from 1995 Key Stage 3 Science (14-year-olds), Paper 1, (Tier 3–6), SCAA, London.)

---

**Example of rearrangement:**

Write in the box alongside the statement in the second column the letter which is given to the structures in the first column which is best related to that statement.

Also write in the name of the structure that has been omitted from the first column in the question.

| | | |
|---|---|---|
| (a) DNA | Carries information from nucleus to cytoplasm | ☐ |
| (b) Chloroplast | Combines loosely with oxygen | ☐ |
| (c) Haemoglobin | Every plant and animal has a fixed number of these structures in the nucleus | ☐ |
| (d) RNA | Contains 'coded information' from parents | ☐ |
| (e) ———— | Absorbs light energy for photosynthesis | ☐ |

(West Yorkshire and Lindsey Regional Examining Board for the Certificate of Secondary Education, Biology, 1970.)

The unlabelled diagram with separate labels which the candidate must place in the correct position is another variation of this method.

---

## Continuous (intermittent) assessment

Continuous assessment is now a popular method of assessment in universities and colleges of education. It usually involves essays, projects and perhaps some formal examination, but may include seminar papers marked for presentation and content. The actual assessment process most frequently adopted is a five-point literal grading system (A to E), or degree classification. It is possible to have in mind specific qualities such as facts, ability to write fluently or the extent of the literature covered, but these matters of detail often become submerged in the overall mark. The reliability of marking can be improved by operating a ranking system in which the points on the scale in use are first established using essays chosen so as to obtain one at each point on the grading system. The consequent marking is based upon these. But judging the quality of extended written work is arduous if it is properly done with the criteria clearly stated and weighted before marking commences. Anyone marking essays should be in a position to include what is being assessed and how much emphasis is being placed on different aspects of the answers.

The snares of intermittent assessment are legion (Satterly 1989), but not insurmountable. Marking is more subjective than in multiple-choice questions and attempts the very difficult task of measuring complex, ill-defined skills ('analytical' qualities, creativity, coherence, etc.) from what is usually a combined effort between the essay writer and his or her reference sources. Where a marker knows the writer, there can be tendencies towards self-fulfilling prophecy (see Chapter 8). This occurs when a general impression of the pupil's competence is allowed to colour *all* the work he or she does. Other qualities which have nothing to do with essay writing may intrude ('a nice person deserves a nice mark' – the halo effect). Lack of refinement in the marking scale or several markers, as mentioned above, causes the grades to cluster in the middle of the range. There tend to be fewer 'A's and 'E's than in conventional written exams. Further, when the marks for a course are compiled, the central tendency is exaggerated even more, particularly if several people have been responsible for the marking (either as moderators re-marking an essay or in separate essays). The pressures on pupils or students can be quite heavy. Therefore the setting of questions has to be worked out most carefully between all the teachers concerned to avoid log-jams of work at certain times in the course. Essays hurriedly put together often contain ideas which pass from a reference source to the essay without being considered by the writer. In fact this aspect of essay writing, that is, how much of the reference material is assimilated by the student and can be recalled or recognized at some future date, has not been researched thoroughly. It is also very important to choose suitable essay titles. Without care, it is easy to give essay titles which are unmanageable.

Nevertheless, with the sting of the three-hour unseen exam paper drawn, it is felt by some that learning is more effective and less anxiety-provoking. Essays allow us to expose our ability to produce, organize and express ideas, to integrate information from several sources, to pose and solve problems and evaluate ideas.

## Oral and practical examinations

Oral and practical assessment methods have been with us for many years. In the GCSE and 'A' Levels we have orals in language, and practical work and assessment in the sciences. The marking of orals depends on a variety of criteria hingeing on pronunciation, understanding of conversation and the accuracy of response. Some subjective judgement is needed, but the criteria of student performance are generally stated clearly. Similarly, in the science practicals, the expectations in student performance should be clearly mapped out (and generally are with the entire public examining boards). Some students find the face-to-face aspect of orals intimidating, and it is probable that a few do not do themselves justice.

In higher education these methods are used extensively. In teacher education the student has to carry out a school practice, under observation; in medicine and professions supplementary to medicine (physiotherapy, nursing) the student is observed in a variety of practical settings relating to professional skills in either real or simulated circumstances. Degrees and other professional qualifying courses in the performing arts and qualifications in, for instance, British sign language have huge practical components which have to be assessed. Making valid and reliable assessments of other people's activities is a very difficult process, not least because it involves the examiner in subjective judgements about *quality* as well as quantity. Other kinds of practical experience are found in technological courses ('sandwich' experience), dentistry and the law. The need for practical professional experience is regarded by most as crucial, but the accuracy of assessment of performance during this experience is still a matter of contention and research. Finding fair and replicable criteria of achievement for performers who are still learning is not at all easy.

## Case history and interpretive questions

These questions have particular relevance in examinations for applied fields such as medicine, teaching and management. The case-history technique provides the candidate with sufficient information about a case to enable diagnosis, indicate complications and offer treatment or decisions. Hubbard and Clemans (1961), in a book about multiple-choice examining in medicine, give a number of examples of this approach. The 'A' Level General Studies papers have also adopted a similar procedure. The questions are usually long-winded because a thorough exposition of all the symptoms or observations must be given in order for the student to select answers. Very complex and searching questions are possible using this design, chiefly when the candidate is required to recall and evaluate rather than recognize the answer.

A great deal of evidence is still required before we are able to evaluate the various kinds of assessment now being adopted. Several questions still need to be answered. Are all these methods measuring more or less the same qualities, thus obviating the need for such an elaborate array of methods, or do they inspire different modes of learning and thinking? Do continuous assessment methods have an inhibiting effect on students in fear of prejudicing their assessment? Nisbet (1969) makes the point that:

> The advantages of a prescribed examination over informal or continuous assessment are that the examination is, to some extent, a public occasion, revealing at least some of the bases of assessment; and that the examination identifies the occasions when the student is on trial and thus gives him freedom at other times. Examinations impose on students occasions of submission, but they also define areas of freedom.

Again, we might ask whether continuous methods are less reliable because they are more susceptible to manipulation than formal examinations. These and many other problems are the focus of research at present.

## Standardized tests

There are now many standardized tests of ability and attainment in a wide variety of subjects designed for use with children from 4 to 16 years of age. A detailed look at them is left to Chapter 18. Several of these tests are compiled with teachers in mind, so that the tests can be administered by the teacher in his or her own class, either individually or as group tests. For obvious reasons, the tests are available only to registered persons who have a need for them and who are able to use them properly. Of the publishing firms and organizations in this country, the National Foundation for Educational Research undoubtedly has built up a tradition as a designer and supplier of well-standardized test material. Its publications cover clinical, educational and psychometric materials (NFER-Nelson catalogues at http://www.nfer-nelson.co.uk/catalogue/catalogue.asp). They contain a comprehensive selection of ability and attainment tests covering reading, comprehension, word recognition, number, arithmetic or mathematics, verbal and non-verbal reasoning, interest and practical-skill tests. We have dealt more extensively with the concept of standardization in the previous chapter.

### Ability tests

Ability tests have already been mentioned in Chapter 9. They attempt to measure the all-round mental efficiency of a person, without necessarily indicating specific subject skills. Verbal and non-verbal reasoning tests are amongst those ability tests most used in schools. As we have seen, they have been used to define broad classifications of pupils for streaming or selection purposes in the belief that pupils so classified should, in general, be capable of coping with academic work of a given standard. But they do not tell us *in particular* if a child is better at physics than at history. They are most efficient when it comes to showing the extremes (high or low IQ) of mental functioning.

### Attainment tests

While they correlate to some extent with ability tests, attainment tests are designed principally to sample achievement in specific school subjects (see NFER-Nelson web reference above for a catalogue of tests available), having first been tested out on a large representative group of children. The sampling usually occurs over a fairly small age range (three or four years at the most) to enable a reasonably accurate estimate of attainment to be made. In the next chapter, on standardization, we shall look more closely at the method of standardizing the age norms. These are commonly used in primary schools as a means of estimating progress in specific basic subjects such as reading, arithmetic and word recognition. *Aptitude tests* are designed to predict success in future academic work and are said *not* to depend on the effects of instruction, that is, they are said to predict future learning despite previous learning.

### Diagnostic tests

Constructed in a similar way to attainment tests, they are intended to give a more detailed picture of the weaknesses in a school subject (see NFER-Nelson catalogue for examples). They are common in basic subjects such as reading and arithmetic, where they usually consist of several sub-tests constructed to show the finer details of the difficulties experienced by children. Their application is particularly helpful in cases of retarded development.

## Grade-related criterion tests

In Chapter 9 criterion-referenced testing was discussed. This method of testing was introduced under the heading of grade-related criterion testing to replace 'O' Level and

CSE examinations by the GCSE (General Certificate of Secondary Education), but it was discontinued. The Secondary Examinations Councils (SEC, replaced part of the activities of the Schools Council) established working parties to look in detail at the ten examination subjects with the largest entries. They were to identify six 'domains' to be assessed, specifying the skills and competencies which must be demonstrated by the candidates in order to obtain grades at specified levels on a seven-point scale from A to G. This means that the examiners would work from a set of statements about the level of performance required for the award of a grade within each of the six domains. As indicated in Chapter 9, candidates would have to demonstrate 'mastery' by reaching a predetermined level of skill or competence. Mastery would vary from topic to topic, but success rates of 70 to 80 per cent have been suggested. The criteria for achievement must be expressed in positive terms, that is, what the candidates know or can do, and not in negative terms based on what candidates do *not* know. The starting point for building up these criteria is taken to be the bottom two grades, F and G, so that the importance of positive knowledge and skill acquisition can be emphasized. Such a system has been adopted in the National Vocational Qualifications, but it has its critics (e.g. Smithers 1998).

## Checklists and rating scales

Checklists and rating scales are very much dependent on personal feelings and opinions. They are used chiefly by teachers as they observe their children in the performance of a task. The method is also popular in judging studies requiring performance, such as dance, drama or sign language.

What is a *checklist*? It is a list of activities, steps in a problem, which attempts to give a systematic progression. A child can ('yes') or cannot ('no') carry out a particular step in the list. The criterion-referencing mentioned earlier can be assessed using this method. It rests upon the ability of teachers to break down a procedure into sufficiently small and recognizable steps for an observation schedule to be drawn up, which is *not* an easy task. Try breaking down the mathematical steps in solving the problem: 'Express 0.007614 to two significant figures'.

- Does the child understand decimals?
- Does the child understand places of decimals?
- What is a significant figure?
- Are zeros significant *figures*?
- What happens to the other figures?

Careful analysis of errors is required to get at the root of pupils' difficulties in solving such a problem.

Profile reports frequently contain checklists, as we shall see later. An example is given below relating to secondary-school language skills. Each question requires a yes/no response.

- Has legible handwriting
- Can write simple sentences
- Can read and understand a popular newspaper
- Can use simple punctuation correctly
- Avoids elementary spelling mistakes
- Can write a personal letter
- Can give and take a telephone message
- Can accurately complete a passport application
- Regularly borrows from school or public library
- Can write a business letter
- Can make an accurate written report
- Can make a clear spoken report
- Can summarize accurately a notice or report
- Can understand simple instructions in a foreign language
- Can give a simple instruction in a foreign language.

*Rating scales* are slightly more sophisticated than the checklist alluded to above. Ratings are generally classified in graduations from one extreme to another, e.g. very good–very poor, easy–hard. Another example from a profile record used by a school or personal assessment is given below:

---

### Example

| Qualities | Rating |
|---|---|
| Standard of work presentation | |
| Perseverance in completing a task | |
| Making most of his/her ability | |
| Ability to work without supervision | |
| Initiative | |
| Etc. | |

The rating is (1) very good; (2) good; (3) average; (4) poor; (5) very poor. Again 'school effort' is frequently recorded in terms of grades: (1) excellent; (2) good; (3) satisfactory; (4) unsatisfactory; (5) poor.

---

## Impression marking

In the classroom, systems range from clinical analysis of question and answer (e.g. some kinds of maths and science marking) to unadulterated impressionistic (e.g. some aspects

of essays, the performing arts or even teaching competence, which could be regarded as a performing art). Unfortunately, the criteria for impression marking are not generally stated or indeed stable. Some systems have tried to use the checklist or rating-scale methods, but there always seems to be that bit left over which requires an overall personal judgement about 'quality' often based on previous experience in similar circumstances. Many claim that experience teaches them what a piece of work or performance is worth; but experiences differ, as do judgements, about 'worth'. Sad to say, research into impression marking is not at all encouraging. Whatever the implicit criteria are, they tend to vary from one marker to the next and very little consistent marking results. At the very least, teachers should attempt to define what it is that gives a good or bad impression.

Most teachers use a combination of impression and more solidly-based mark allocation for specified responses in essay-type and performing arts subjects. The problem is that a systematic analysis of questions and answers takes time, but it is time well spent in that it provides a useful framework by which to judge the sources of difficulties – and it assists the teacher in defining what he or she expects.

# Advantages and limitations of objective-type examinations

## Advantages

Many more questions can be set in a given time than is possible in essay examinations. It is suggested that about 100 items per hour, without a choice, is a reasonable pace. As a consequence, more extensive sampling of syllabus content is practicable, and this gives a corresponding increase in the reliability of the score. Marking is made easier because responses are short, to the point and systematically arranged on the answer sheet. Clearly there is complete impartiality in the marking, although mistakes are still possible, e.g. when adding is incorrect, two pages are turned by mistake or accidents occur in the marking. Test marking and totalling can now be automated.

Less time is spent by candidates in writing out their answers. This, one hopes, leaves more time for thinking! There is little opportunity for padding or writing long, elaborate answers to questions which the examiner has not set.

As we saw in the last chapter, the construction of objective tests enables a careful control of the difficulty levels associated with each item. In this way we can decide in advance the spread and frequency of each level of difficulty. With essay answers the level of difficulty experienced by candidates is discovered in retrospect once the marks have been awarded. Much time and skill are required to accumulate an 'item bank' containing questions of known difficulty for a given ability range.

By taking a large number of items covering small sections of a syllabus it is easier to detect and counsel a pupil's (or teacher's) weaknesses. This has an added advantage, in that students have not only knowledge of results but also a detailed analysis of the shortcomings. Essays are not easy to analyse in this way.

## Limitations

Although scoring is made easy, setting the questions is a difficult business. Badly constructed tests can have a disastrous effect on the study and morale of students. Poor design often reflects the subjective element which enters into the choice of questions. So we see that the position in 'objective' questions is the reverse of that in essay-type questions: the former require subjective judgement in the setting, the latter in the marking. Panels of judges for question-setting will overcome this problem to some extent.

There is something deceptively comforting about a paper which provides the answers as well as the questions. It is certainly easier to recognize an answer than to recall it from memory (see Chapter 7). But not all questions need be of this kind. In applied fields, medicine for example, the student can be given information from which he or she must provide evidence of not only knowledge but also reasoning and judgement (see the 'Case history and interpretive questions' section above). Advanced level General Studies papers contain many examples of questions requiring comprehension, interpretation and application of knowledge. Nevertheless, there is limited opportunity for disciplined expression.

The short, sharp question and answer requires a particular kind of behaviour which can be developed. Sophistication in answering these questions is also a criticism levelled at the IQ test, where concentrated practice can give increased scores. A corollary of this is the influence that practice may have on the whole pattern of study. There could be serious distortions if only this kind of question is used.

Little opportunity is afforded for imaginative and creative work. The emphasis is on fact rather than fancy and little, if any, account is taken of the *quality* of thought which has led to the answer. Consequently, only certain subjects, chiefly factual areas of mathematics, the sciences, history, geography etc., lend themselves to objective assessment. Skills such as organizing and presenting knowledge in a lucid, concise and fluent manner are not in evidence. In fact, the examinee spends rather more time reading than writing. The obvious way round this criticism is to ensure that essays are included somewhere in the examination.

*Guessing* is quite possible in multiple-choice answers, but it is not as great a problem as some people have supposed. It must first be made quite clear to the candidates that they must not attempt a question which they cannot answer and that guessing will be penalized. A formula can then be used to counteract guesswork. It is derived in the following way. Suppose a test consists of ten questions, each having five alternative answers, of which only one is correct. A candidate who can answer five correctly would obtain only five marks if the instructions were followed. However, with guesses at the remaining five answers the candidate would, by chance, obtain one more mark, because in a five-way choice with one correct choice there would be a one-in-five chance of being correct. The total, therefore, would be six. The formula devised to overcome guessing should give a total of five, because this extra mark was a guess.

$$\text{Total mark} = \text{number of correct items} - \frac{\text{number of incorrect items}}{\text{number of choices in an item} - 1}$$

In our example, number correct $= 6$
  number incorrect $= 4$
  number of choices in each item is 5
    $\therefore$ Total mark $= 6 - \frac{4}{5-1} = 6 - 1 = 5$

# Assessing, recording and reporting achievement

## Assessing (Open University series starting in 1993 – see 'Further reading')

Much of this chapter has been devoted to assessment. This is what teachers and schools are required to share with parents, authorities and government bodies. It is a time-consuming, but important, function for the teacher.

In standardized or well-designed teacher-made tests, the marking system is carefully laid down beforehand. Public examinations also aim to be well planned, especially those where particular facts, statements, solutions are sought.

All other forms of assessment in the classroom raise important questions which teachers should address when deciding on what to record and report. What key aspects should receive marks – should everything be 'marked'? How many marks should be allocated to each answer (they may not be of equal importance and therefore should not all receive the same weighting)? Are all the errors the child's fault and therefore should marks be automatically docked? Should some written comment or analysis accompany the mark? What use is going to be made of the response patterns for each child (i.e. if formative or diagnostic, the patterns will be most important; if summative assessment is the case, there need not be any analysis)? How is the mark to be fed back to the pupil (e.g. mark out of ten, grade, written comment only)? What follow up is necessary (e.g. remedial session needed with the class or individuals)? Will the marks form part of course-work assessment? How will progress be judged from one set of marks to the next? These and other questions have led to greater emphasis being placed on the responsibility of schools to provide consistent guidelines to all teachers. The 'whole school approach' is now a key element in the assessment process (Engel-Cough *et al.* 1984, James 1998).

## Profiles and records of achievement

Following the DES policy document on records of achievement in 1984, there has been considerable research into the most effective modes of presenting a pupil's progress. The issues and problems, not surprisingly, have not yet been resolved. Finding ways of showing a pupil's achievements which are relevant, accurate and carry some conviction that they are usable by teachers, parents and employers has not been easy. Following government initiatives on records of achievement (DES 1987 and 1988d), from 1991 onwards, all pupils leaving school had a *National Record of Achievement* (NRA). The Record was not well used and a review was carried out in 1997 from which a DfEE report appeared in 1999 (DfEE 1999a). The upshot was that the NRA was modified and appears as the National Record of Achievement/Progress File.

There are many technical issues relating to records (see Satterly 1989 for a good chapter on profiles and records). For example, what forms of presentation are available in showing profiles? Should the content be honest in presenting weaknesses as well as strengths? Should profiles be confidential or open? How credible will reports be where personal judgement has played a large part in the assessment? Can the profiles of, say, different children in the same class or school be compared with other children, classes or schools?

Most existing records contain the following information:

- biographical details – name, age, sex, birth date, address and general information about schools attended
- health and home conditions such as illness or handicaps which may affect a child's progress or require regular treatment
- attainments in general ability, verbal reasoning, word recognition, reading, comprehension and arithmetic taken at various ages in school along with the name of the test
- interests such as music, drama, sport, social activities or practical skills
- attendance
- behaviour and personality, including deviant behaviour (delinquency, truancy) and emotional disturbance
- other general comments by the teachers or headteacher
- a personal comment by the pupil.

To the new style profiles would be added the assessments from SATs at ages 7, 11, 14 and 16. The attainment targets for each subject are to be arranged in groups called profile components. An example of a profile component might be taken from English (5–11) in which one would find three such as speaking and listening, reading, writing. Not only will the results be available to parents, but also class profiles are to be made public.

During the 1980s, research began to appear relating to school reports, profiles and records of achievement.

---

**Further reading**

Considerable research was then devoted to the problems of record keeping and school reports. The Schools Council and NFER carried out a study of profiling and school reporting. An indication of their findings can be found in Balogh 1982; Goacher 1983; Broadfoot 1986; Goacher and M. I. Reid 1983; DES (1987); DES (1988d).

---

Since then, the emphasis has been on developing a national system of school records of achievement and in the early 1990s the Government produced a prototype National Record of Achievement (NRA) following the pilot study PRAISE (DES 1987 and 1988d). These records were voluntary and were to include the results of norm- and criterion-referenced assessment in school subjects, attendance, personal characteristics, leisure activities and, if relevant, work experience. These records were also to be carried into the workplace. The NRAs are summative and intended largely for post-school selection. Whatever else, the records of achievement are at a developmental stage and there is much research required to assess their validity and reliability (Broadfoot 1996).

The actual compilation of scores from the SATs at each stage has become a mathematical minefield because there are so many numbers of different weights to be handled at each level, all to be taken into account. For a discussion of this problem, see Pole (1993) and Shorrocks-Taylor (1998).

---

## Summary

Evaluating pupils' learning is a necessary step in any formalized educational system. Our system is such that we need to have some valid and reliable assessment of a child's personal progress, potential and standing relative to the peer group. At the same time, the assessment should be in a form which is readily understood by pupils, teachers, parents, government bodies and, where necessary, employers. Examinations provide, with varying degrees of success, an estimate of attainment and a means of diagnosing weaknesses and misdirections in the pupils' studies. They are also used with the intention of predicting aptitude for further study or entry to work. Examinations provide an opportunity for upward mobility for the successful, but they can produce feelings of inadequacy in the unsuccessful as an unfortunate spin-off. They are used, too, as a gauge in predetermining and maintaining standards as well as measuring the efficiency of the content of a teacher's work and methods used. Revision for examinations acts as a means of reinforcing the learning of the content.

These ambitious suggestions about the purposes of examinations must be considered along with two important criteria. Any assessment must measure what it is supposedly designed to measure – it must be valid; and if it is valid, the assessment must be consistent when used with the same or similar pupils – it must be reliable. But the potency of examinations also depends on conditions external to the design of the test material. Among these, the psychological condition of the pupil is paramount. Too little is known about the interaction of personality attributes and performance, although everyday experiences teach us that excessive anxiety can adversely affect achievement. The presence of unfamiliar people or conditions, lack of understanding of what is required and undue pressure from parents or teachers to perform well can all take their toll. Faulty learning strategies are also effective in depressing performance.

For these reasons, examination results should be treated with some caution. Given the findings of differences in cognitive ability between males and females, how might his affect performance in examinations? What was the condition of the examinee? How well prepared? Were there 'image' problems relating to the developmental age and peer group pressures?

The range of instruments and methods is now quite extensive. Among these are the essay-type tests, projects, vivas, practicals, rating scales, checklists, attainment tests and objective tests, of which the last mentioned are becoming very significant alternatives to the well-established unseen essay paper. The method does compensate for several criticisms levelled against essay-type questions, but the preparation of objective-type questions must be a highly technical and time-consuming job for the outcome to be of value. Assessment is used largely as a means of communication between pupil, teacher and parent. Therefore we should endeavour to give a pupil every opportunity of using as many communication media as possible. The emphasis in our system has been on the written word produced over a timed period. It seems equally important to encourage children to communicate their knowledge in oral or practical ways where this is feasible. Once assessments have been made, others, like teachers, parents, local education authorities and employers, need to have the information in a usable form. School reports are the commonest method of conveying the information to parents and considerable research effort has been applied to accurate and useful reporting. Many authorities now provide a cumulative school record card on which attainments, amongst other helpful details, are recorded by the school. Regular entries on these records enable an extremely useful profile to be compiled for each child. In the 1990s a system involving the National Record of Achievement (NRA) was introduced on a voluntary basis and the NRA/ Progress File has superseded this.

## Tutorial enquiry and discussion

(a) On school practice or school visits, investigate the following and bring the results back to a tutorial session for pooling and discussion:

   (i) School and local authority (LA) records and profiles of achievement – what are they for? How are they compiled? What use do teachers, LAs and employers make of them?

   (ii) Discuss with teachers their methods of assessing children, both in term time as part of continuous assessment and in end-of-term tests. What difficulties do they experience? What use do they make of these assessments? Are they reliable and valid? How does assessment vary with the subject?

   (iii) School reports and parents' days are routine features in most schools. How do teachers overcome the tricky task of telling parents about their children's shortcomings? How do parents respond? Do parents have difficulty in evaluating how their children are developing or how they are progressing in relation to others? (See text for useful references.)

   (iv) Discover pupils' views of the public examination system and continuous assessment.

(b) Examine the place of assessment in (1) primary or (2) secondary or (3) higher education. What forms might it take? What are the purposes served by such assessment? Are the purposes achieved? How might we overcome the difficulties mentioned in this chapter?

(c) League tables comparing school performance in England have become an annual event. Discuss in tutorial the problems associated with comparison tables. See, for example, the work of Carol Fitz-Gibbon in the references.

(d) Read, then write about or discuss the following:

   (i) the effects of anxiety or fear of failure in examinations

   (ii) the role of ambition in examination motivation

   (iii) methods for ensuring sex differences are not translated into sex-role discrimination

   (iv) validity and reliability of 'home-made' examinations in primary or secondary schools

   (v) the evaluation of project work or 'creative writing'

   (vi) the distinction between ability and attainment tests

   (vii) the advantages and limitations of Records of Achievement/Progress Files.

## References

Arnot, M., David, M. and Weiner, G. (1996), *Educational Reforms and Gender Equality in Schools*. Manchester: Equal Opportunities Commission.

Balogh, J. (1982), *Profile Reports for School-leavers*. Schools Council Programme 5: Longman.

Baron-Cohen, S. (2003), *The Essential Difference: Men, Women and the Extreme Male Brain*. London: Allan Lane (and Penguin Books).

Bloom, B. S. (1976), *Human Characteristics and School Learning*. New York: McGraw-Hill.

Broadfoot, P. (ed.) (1986), *Profiles and Records of Achievement*. London: Holt, Rinehart and Winston.

Child, D., Hatton, C. and Orde, A. (1986), 'A-levels as a predictor: the correlation between A-level and degree results for the 1981 entry to Leeds University', *Reporter*, Leeds University, No. 255.

Cook, M. (1993b), *Personnel Selection and Productivity* (2nd edn). Chichester: Wiley.

Cronbach, L. J. (1990), *Essentials of Psychological Testing* (5th edn). New York: Harper and Row.

Dale, R. R. (1954), *From School to University*. London: Routledge and Kegan Paul.

DES (1987), *Pilot Records of Achievement in Schools Evaluation (PRAISE): An Interim Report*. London: HMSO.

DES (1988a), *National Curriculum: Task Group on Assessment and Testing, and three supplementary reports*. London: HMSO. DES (1988b) *National Curriculum: Task Group on Assessment and Testing Report – A Digest for Schools*. London: HMSO.

DES (1988d), *Pilot Records of Achievement in Schools Evaluation (PRAISE): Final Report*. London: HMSO.

DfEE (1999a), *Evaluation of the Trial of Progress Profile: a Research Report*. London: HMSO.

DfES (1999), *Statistics of Education: Public Examinations GCSE and GCE in England, 1998–9*. London: HMSO.

Engel-Cough, E., Davis, P. with Sumner, R. (1984), *Assessing Pupils: a Study of Policy and Practice*. Windsor: NFER-Nelson.

Fitz-Gibbon, C. T. (1997), *The Value Added National Project Final Report: Feasibility Studies for a National System of Value Added Indicators*. London: School Curriculum and Assessment Authority.

Fitz-Gibbon, C. T. (1998), 'Indicator systems for schools: fire-fighting it is!', in D. Shorrocks-Taylor (ed.), *Directions in Educational Psychology*. London: Whurr.

Fitz-Gibbon, C. T. (2001), *Value Added for Those in Despair: Research Methods Matter*. The 20th Vernon-Wall Lecture. Leicester: British Psychological Society.

Gallagher, A. M. and DeLisi, R. (1994), 'Gender differences in scholastic aptitude test: Mathematics problem solving among high ability students', *Journal of Educational Psychology*, 86, 204–11.

Goacher, B. (1983), *Recording Achievement at 16+*. London: Longman/Schools Council.

Goacher, B. and Reid, M. I. (1983), *School Reports to Parents*. Windsor: NFER-Nelson.

Hartog, P. and Rhodes, E. C. (1936), *The Marks of Examiners*. London and Basingstoke: Macmillan.

HMI Report (1992), *GCSE Examinations: Quality and Standards*. London: HMSO.

Hubbard, J. P. and Clemans, W. V. (1961), *Multiple-choice Examinations on Medicine: A Guide for Examiner and Examinee*. London: Kimpton.

James, M. (1998), *Using Assessment for School Improvement*. Oxford: Heinemann Educational.

Neisser, U., Boodoo, G., Bouchard, T. J. (jnr), Boykin, A. W., Brody, N., Ceci, S. J., Halpern, D. F., Loehlin, J. C., Perloff, R., Sternberg, R. J. and Urbina, S. (1996), 'Intelligence: knowns and unknowns'. *American Psychologist*, 51, 77–101.

Nisbet, J. D. (1969), 'The need for universities to measure achievement', in Assessment of Undergraduate Performance, *Conference Report – Committee of Vice-Chancellors and Principals and the Association of University Teachers*, pp. 15–18.

Nuttall, D. L. (1989), 'National assessment: will reality match aspirations?', *Education Section Review* (British Psychological Society), 13, 1–2.

Pole, C. (1998), 'Assessing, recording and testing achievement: some issues in accountability, professionalism and educational markets', in D. Shorrocks-Taylor (ed.), *Directions in Educational Psychology*. London: Whurr.

Reid, Ivan (1989), *Social Class Differences in Britain: Life-chances and Life-styles* (3rd edn). London: Fontana.

Robbins Report, The (1963), *Higher Education*. London: HMSO.

Satterly, D. (1989), *Assessment in Schools* (2nd edn), in the series 'Theory and Practice of Education' (General editor, D. Child). Oxford: Blackwell.

Schools Council (1966), *Examinations Bulletin No. 12. Multiple Marking of English Compositions*. London: HMSO.

Sear, K. (1983), 'The correlation between A-level grades and degree results in England and Wales', *Higher Education*, 12(5), 609–19.

Sherwin, E. and Child, D. (1970), 'Predicting the performance of undergraduate chemists', *Education in Chemistry*, 7(4), 156–8.

Shorrocks-Taylor, D. (1998), 'Cross purposes: development and change in National Curriculum assessment in England and Wales', in D. Shorrocks-Taylor (ed.), *Directions in Educational Psychology*. London: Whurr.

Smithers, A. G. (1998), 'Improving vocational education: NVQ's and GNVQ's', in D. Shorrocks-Taylor (ed.), *Directions in Educational Psychology*. London: Whurr.

Vincent, L. (1997), *The Value Added National Project: Analysis of Key Stage 3 Data for 1994 Matched to GCSE Data for 1996*. London: School Curriculum and Assessment Authority.

Wiseman, S. (1949), 'The marking of English compositions in grammar school selection', *British Journal of Educational Psychology*, 19, 200–9.

Wiseman, S. (1956), 'The use of essays in selection at 11+. Reliability and validity', *British Journal of Educational Psychology*, 26, 172–9.

Young, M. (1961), *The Rise of the Meritocracy 1870–2033: An Essay on Education and Equality*. London: Penguin.

## Further reading

Broadfoot, P. (1996), *Education, Assessment and Society*. Milton Keynes: Open University Press.

Broadfoot, P., Grant, M., James, M., Nuttall, D. L. and Stierer, B. (1991), *Records of Achievement: Report of the National Evaluation of Extension Work in Pilot Schemes*. London: HMSO.

James, M. (1998), *Using Assessment for School Improvement*. Oxford: Heinemann Educational.

Open University A new series covering 'Assessing Assessment' contains several relevant titles.
 Butterfield, S. (1993), *Educational Objectives and National Assessment*;

Gipps, C. and Murphy, P. (1994), *A Fair Test? Assessment, Achievement and Equity*;

Gray, J. and Wilcox, B. (eds) (1995), *Good School, Bad School: Evaluating Performance and Encouraging Improvement*;

Ross, M., Radnor, H., Mitchell, S. and Bierton, C. (1993), *Assessing Achievement in the Arts*;

Torrance, H. (ed.) (1995), *Evaluating Authentic Assessment: Problems and Possibilities in New Approaches to Assessment*;

Wolf, Alison (1995), *Competence-based Assessment*. Buckingham: Open University Press.

Pole, C. (1993), *Assessing and Recording Achievement: Implementing a New Approach in School*. Buckingham: Open University Press.

Satterly, D. (1989) *Assessment in Schools* (2nd edn). Oxford: Blackwell.

Shorrocks-Taylor, D. (ed.) (1998) *Directions in Educational Psychology*. London: Whurr. There are five relevant chapters (7 to 10 and 17) in this volume by Youngman, Pole, Shorrocks-Taylor, Fitz-Gibbon and Smithers.

## Useful websites

NFER website is: http://www.nfer-nelson.co.uk/catalogue/catalogue.asp

DfES website for statistics is: http://www.dfes.gov.uk/rsgateway. For the data given in this chapter on GCSE 'O' and GCE 'A' level results, the appropriate 'update' was selected. But clicking 'other publications' will reveal many other statistics relevant to education..

Government standards website is: http://www. standards.dfes.gov.uk

## Answers to test items

## Recall

### Simple recall

For a correct answer, there has to be a valid explanation based on a calculation such as 'the sum of the other two sides cannot be less than the 14.5 cm side. But, $25 - 14.5 = 10.5$, which is less than 14.5. So Tony was wrong.'

### Open completion

(1) 18      (2) 'the king of Babylon' (Chapter 20).

### The unlabelled diagram

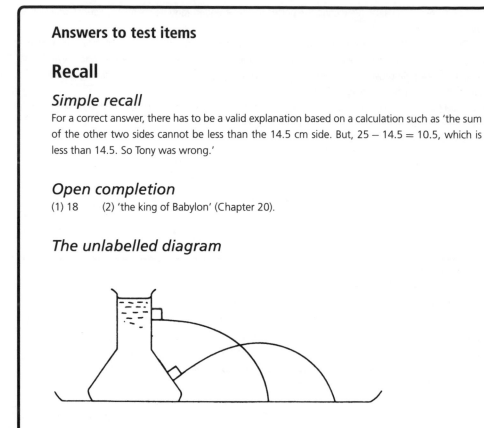

## Recognition

### True/false

(1) False; (2) True; (3) False; (4) False

### Multiple-choice: one correct

(1) Fission fragments; (2) Lascaux; (3) Protein; (4) Feste.

### Multiple-choice: several correct

| Property | solid | liquid | gas |
|---|---|---|---|
| keeps its own shape | ✓ | | |
| flows easily through a pipe | | ✓ | ✓ |
| can make rigid or stiff structure | ✓ | | |
| can be squashed in a much smaller volume | | | ✓ |
| takes the shape of the container into which it is put | | ✓ | ✓ |

⟶

*Multiple choice: best reason*
Response E.

*Matching items*

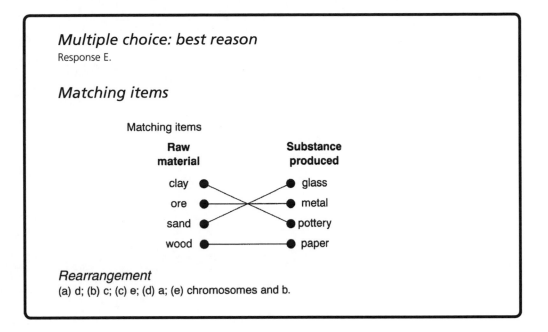

Matching items

| Raw material | Substance produced |
| --- | --- |
| clay | glass |
| ore | metal |
| sand | pottery |
| wood | paper |

*Rearrangement*
(a) d; (b) c; (c) e; (d) a; (e) chromosomes and b.

# Part Six
## Educational Research and Test Design

# Research in Education

## Implications for Teachers

- Avoid using first impressions or 'off-the-cuff' methods for deciding about your pupils' academic abilities, personalities or behaviour.
- Examine reports, whether government or otherwise, with a keen eye to their scientific soundness and treat even hard-won evidence with care.
- Make sure that any conclusions you may read in the media, educational literature, light or serious, are based on evidence.
- Keep up to date with the ever growing volume of information in textbooks, journals, government reports and the Internet.

Research findings form a substantial part of this book. Also many undergraduate and postgraduate student teachers are now required to produce a project or dissertation as part of their degree or teaching qualification. This chapter is intended to give a brief idea about how the findings are obtained in educational enquiries and some of the difficulties which accompany research in educational psychology.

# Studying human behaviour

There are several ways in which researchers have attempted to classify approaches to exploring human behaviour and experience in the behavioural sciences (which are psychology, sociology, political science, anthropology, economics). At its broadest, there are three traditions or *paradigms* (Cohen *et al.* 2000, Mertens 2004) and our personal beliefs often determine the paradigm which most appeals to us. The first, *scientific or experimental method,* is variously defined as *objective, positivist, normative* or *quantitative.* The second employs *naturalistic methods* and is sometimes called *subjective, anti-positivist, interpretive, humanist* or *qualitative.* A third broad category is *critical theory* or *emancipatory* (Mertens 2004) which adopts its own research style of *action research* as well as using the methods from the first two paradigms. This is less concerned with discovering what is and more interested in changing existing policies and practices by systematic intervention. The term 'emancipatory' is used because the issues of particular interest involve disadvantaged groups, for instance investigating physical, intellectual, ethnic and gender issues.

Despite the differing philosophies underpinning the scientific and naturalistic methodologies, the methods are not mutually exclusive. Many major contemporary researches involve both.

## Scientific method

The majority of researches over a century of theorizing and research in the psychology of education have employed the methods and assumptions of scientific method.

Dewey (1933) proposed the main stages of scientific method as follows:

- the recognition of a problem which has not been solved before
- an experiment is designed in such a way as to define the problem clearly, then information is accumulated through careful observations
- the information is organized to see whether regularities exist
- explanations for such regularities are suggested – this is known as setting up hypotheses (that is tentative theories)
- experiments are designed to test the hypotheses
- the hypotheses are used to predict new effects which in turn are put to the test.

These are general principles applied in the natural sciences (physics, chemistry and biology). They all attempt to arrive at generalizations, laws and theories, by which future behaviour might be predicted (Gall *et al.* 2002). Within psychology, as seen in previous chapters, the Behaviourist School comes closest to applying scientific method.

Probably very few experiments involving humans take this precise form. Apart from ethical issues when using human beings in experiments, we do not lie dormant waiting to be researched like inanimate objects. Consequently, there are limitations to the use of scientific method in education, including the fact that the kinds of questions of significance to practising teachers are not clear-cut. Indeed, some psychologists in education have questioned the suitability of scientific method in its purest form as the appropriate technique at this stage in our hazy knowledge of human behaviour. They ask, 'Are the highly sophisticated methods of science too refined for the uncharted realms of complex human conduct?'

However, some of the alternatives of guesswork, speculation or teaching folklore, though they might assist in the process of formulating testable ideas, are hardly likely to provide us with firm foundations from which decisions in the classroom are made possible. Evidence-based proposals for education (e.g. Fitz-Gibbon 1997 and http://www.cemcentre.org.uk), though in short supply, are more likely to give teachers usable information.

## Naturalistic research

Behaviourism and its adherence to scientific method brought a reaction from some psychologists in the twentieth century. They believed that humans were free agents in decision-making and not bound by conditioned responses. Therefore, in Chapter 6 we saw that cognitivists used methods involving close questioning of individuals about their thoughts and feelings. In Chapter 3 on perception and attention we were interested in how we interpret our surroundings. Each person, being unique, operates interactively in his or her environment and this can only be explored by asking individuals for their personal experiences. For this, several research strategies and tools were created.

These methods have special appeal in education. Teachers, for instance, are keen that observations should reflect classroom life as it actually exists by observing pupils, teachers, classrooms and schools *in situ*. The classroom environment lends itself to observation and analysis in an open-ended way. It can be done in 'fly-on-the-wall' ways which do not affect the processes being observed (called *non-participant observation*). Where the researcher 'joins the tribe' as a fully accepted member, this is referred to as *participant observation*.

It should not be thought that these subjective styles are unsystematic. There are ways of defining and organizing the collected material so that general principles can be created. Perhaps the most significant difference between scientific and naturalistic paradigms is that they are trying to tap human behaviour at different levels of complexity. Behaviourists are trying to work at the 'atomic' or 'molecular' level, believing that the whole can only be the sum of its parts, so let us find the parts; on the other hand, humanists are more concerned with the whole object and not its molecular structure, so for them the whole is more than the sum of its parts. These perspectives, in turn, give rise to different hypotheses, methods of data collection and analysis. The outcomes too tend to be more descriptive than predictive.

Sometimes, this method precedes the scientific approach in the hope that the open-ended, exploratory technique will expose the important variables for subsequent, quantitative analysis.

# Styles of educational research

Cohen *et al.* (2000; but for alternative ways of looking at this area, see Mertens 2004 and Kerlinger 1986) identify eight *research styles* which in varying degrees adopt scientific and naturalistic approaches. The styles are *experimental, correlational, ex post facto, survey, ethnographic, case study, historical* and *action research*.

In all of them, we meet with *variables*. These are qualities or attributes which can have differing values as we move from one person to the next. In psychology and education we create the variables. Some are complex such as type of school, motivational factors, aptitude, personality, achievement; others are specific like age and sex of pupil. Some are referred to as *independent variables* because they are the source of variation; for example, a state system such as comprehensive and grammar schools, the sex of a person or coaching can be the causes of variations in other variables. An important independent variable of special interest to the teacher includes the teaching methods employed in the classroom. *Dependent variables*, on the other hand, consist of measures which 'depend' for their value on independent variables. The most common dependent variable in education is achievement, or the amount of learning that has taken place as a consequence of, say, teaching methods.

The first four, that is, experimental, correlational, *ex post facto* and survey, employ mainly quantitative methods.

## Experimental research

In the experimental set-up we choose random samples from representative populations, carefully choose variables that can be measured, deliberately hold constant, or *control*, most of the independent variables and vary just one or two. For example, if we wanted to test the efficiency of a new method of teaching reading for those who are behind in reading (e.g. Clay 1993) compared with a traditional method, the two independent variables would be the new method and the traditional method of teaching reading. Two random samples from children behind for their reading age would be chosen. The relevant dependent variable, in this case, the children's reading ability, would have to be tested for the two samples, both before (*pre-test*) and after (*post-test*) a trial experiment of the new method with one of the samples, whilst all other independent variables which could influence children's reading performance, such as intelligence, home background and previous reading experiences with teachers would have to be comparable for both groups, that is, controlled.

The chances of being able to create such a tidy experiment are remote. Strict experimental control is rarely possible in educational research when we are dealing with real-life situations in which practical and ethical issues need to be considered. Therefore, psychologists are often forced to use 'quasi-experimental' designs for research (Campbell and Stanley 1963). One such method involves one child from each sample with identical or very similar characteristics. This is called pairing or pair matching. Another type of quasi-experimental design which is widely used in educational psychology is the 'single subject research design' (Barlow and Hersen 1984). In this kind of research each subject becomes his or her own control. Observations are repeated over many sessions so that changes in behaviour due to the interventions can be clearly seen when the data are graphically displayed.

Animals have frequently been the subjects of strict laboratory approaches. But there are obvious dangers in transferring the results of animal experiments to human situations. The presence of different levels of psychological organization, intellect and motivation, amongst other things, are all certain to give rise to difficulties when interpreting human in terms of animal behaviour.

## Correlational research

Although correlation is a statistical technique, it has also become a research style favoured, for example, by psychologists with an interest in the analysis of personality and intelligence (psychometrics in Chapters 9 and 12).

A question which teachers frequently ask is 'What can I do to bring about desired changes in achievement or behaviour in my students'? The 'what can I do' part of the question would be influences or *causes* and the 'desired changes' would be outcomes or *effects*. To find out which variables (the causes and effects) are related, *correlation* is used. Some examples are the relationship between reward or punishment and performance, intelligence and reading ability, or truancy and family attitudes. Each one of these, unfortunately, consists of several variables which would require to be identified and measured. Also, correlational techniques do not tell us which of the variables are causes and which are effects. The direction of the relationships has to be found by other means.

There are several methods of calculating correlation which are covered in any standard statistics textbook (e.g. Cohen and Holliday 1982, 1996). For those who just want a thumbnail sketch of correlation, the following may suffice.

Correlation is undoubtedly the most widely used statistical concept. It has even crept into common usage in a great variety of forms. Fundamentally, it tells us in a numerical form known as the *correlation coefficient* the extent to which two sets of measures for the same group of people are related. If we take as an illustration the length of people's legs compared with the length of their arms, we would expect tall people to have long limbs and small people to have short limbs. In other words, there is a direct connection between the two measures. If this relationship were perfect, that is, for each slight variation in arm length there is an exact corresponding variation in leg length as we pass from one person to another, the numerical value obtained would be a 'positive correlation' of +1. With two measures in which one increases while the other decreases in exact steps we obtain a 'negative correlation' of −1. But things are never that perfect. We will always find the 'sports' with long arms and short legs (or vice versa), tending to give a correlation somewhat less than +1. In fact the numerical value can be anything between +1 through 0 to −1. A value of 0 or thereabouts represents 'zero correlation', the sort of value we might obtain if we compared the size of shoe which a person takes with that person's personality profile.

To give some idea of typical values, if we gave a group intelligence test to a class of 100 pupils and retested them a week later, the correlation for a good, reliable test between the scores obtained on the first and second occasions by each person would be about +0.90 to +0.98, a very good value. If now we compared the marks obtained in a school physics examination with intelligence test scores we might get a value in the region of +0.50. In a study by the author the correlation between IQ and biology came to +0.14, positive but not high for a medium-sized sample (see later). In the chapter on personality a correlation of +0.30 was typical between self-concept and academic attainment. Negative correlations are less common in behavioural studies than in natural sciences, but one often-quoted example is the relationship between intelligence test scores and the number of children in a family. The value is around −0.25 and is taken to mean that the larger the family the lower the measured intelligence. Another topical negative correlation occurs between the cost of living (rising) and a person's spending power (falling), given a constant wage.

It is most important when interpreting a correlation coefficient to take the sample size into account. This is obvious, because if we obtained a correlation of +0.20 for a sample of five people we would not view it with the same confidence as for a sample of 500. In fact +0.20 for five sets of data is *not significant*; that means the correlation is no better than zero. For a sample of five we would have to obtain a correlation coefficient of + or −0.88 for us to place any reliance on its being a significant positive or negative correlation, i.e. significantly different from zero. For 500 the value need only reach ±0.12 for it to be significantly better than zero. The value of +0.14 between IQ and biology quoted above proved to be insignificant once the sample size was taken into account.

Another important point to watch is the interpretation we place on the underlying causes of the correlation. All the correlation tells us is the extent and direction of a relationship, and not the reason for it. As an example, just think of the many reasons for the negative correlation of −0.25 between family size and measured intelligence; it would be impossible to arrive at a single causal relationship from this information alone.

When all the inter-correlations between a number of variables are available (e.g., a with b, a with c, b with c) it is sometimes possible to group these into 'factors' (Child 2006). Indeed, several educational researchers (Youngman 1998) are now looking to *multivariate* techniques in which large numbers of inter-related activities are measured in natural settings on several occasions, thus allowing for nature to carry out the spontaneous manipulations in behaviour to be captured in the data. Two such procedures are factor and cluster analysis (Child 2006).

## *Ex post facto* research

The Latin words in the title mean 'retrospectively'. Frequently, it is not possible to set up an experiment from scratch. But, there are times when we can look at something that has already happened and try to work back to the causes. Forensic psychology offers good examples. The crime has already taken place. But is there evidence there which will take us back to causes and tell us something about the criminal? In effect, the manipulation of the independent variables has already happened. So the researcher makes a thorough examination of the outcome of events (dependent variables) in the hope that such examination will reveal a pattern from which we can deduce the causes.

Take as an illustration the study of juvenile delinquency (dependent variable). The delinquents already exist, so the starting point would be to take a group of attested delinquents and look, for example, at their life histories (presumed independent variables) in terms of family background, friendship networks, relationship with parents, personal and intellectual characteristics, criminal record pattern, school reports and so on, and compare these with a group of non-delinquents. Where there are differences, there may be a case for assuming some causal relationships.

Another topical example is provided by the increase in lung cancer (dependent variable) and the possibility that smoking (independent variable) is the cause. This is a very good case for *ex post facto* analysis. We cannot (ethically) manipulate the independent variable before cancer has appeared; we can only look in retrospect at the possibilities which might distinguish cancer from non-cancer sufferers. Kerlinger (1986) devotes a whole chapter to *ex post facto* research.

In some cases, it is no easy task to decide which of the possible independent variables are relevant, thus a large number is usually chosen at the outset. Research in education relies heavily on this method of analysis because of its convenience in cases where we cannot carry out controlled experiments with pupils as subjects.

Developmental studies provide another good example of *ex post facto* technique. Developmental studies involve a detailed description of selected variables at different stages in the lives of children and adults. We may look at the same group of people at particular ages, say ten-year intervals from 10 to 50; this is a *longitudinal study*. Or we may take five samples who are 10, 20, etc., years of age and test each sample on one occasion; this is a *cross-sectional* study. Developmental studies have been of great service in theories of the growth of thinking skills (Chapter 5), intelligence (Chapter 9) and vocational choice (Chapter 13).

## Survey research

In the survey technique, the results of which are now used extensively in educational policy-making at government level, the object is to collect information about readily obtainable facts from a total population or a representative sample of the population. A national census affords a well-known example of a fact-finding survey of existing conditions.

Most of the data collection and analysis consists of 'head counting' and frequency distribution. A statement of the distribution of scores obtained by children sitting SATs Stage 2 in mathematics for the year 2001 would be a fact obtainable from survey techniques. Successive governments have increasingly employed surveys to assist in the production of reports such as those of Plowden (1967), Warnock (1978) and the National Curriculum Task Group (1987) Committees.

HMSO (Her Majesty's Stationery Office) produces a huge amount of documentation containing survey material. The best known at present is *Statistics in Education*, produced annually in volumes about such topics as schools, public examination results and teachers (e.g., how many, doing what subject, where). *Statistical Bulletins* from the DfES appear throughout the year with short reports on such things as examinations, school absentee tables and special needs provision.

## Ethnographic research

So far, the research techniques have involved mainly data collected and been processed using quantitative methods. The next three research techniques of ethnographic, case and historical studies are largely qualitative. It is important to note that frequently the questions asked by those using these techniques are different from those who use scientific method, mainly because the purposes are more exploratory than confirmatory.

At first sight, many of the processes used seem to be the same. A location for the research is decided, a sample is chosen, data are collected and analysed and a report written. On closer inspection, there are profound differences.

Fields of interest for ethnographers range from total institutions (prisons, schools), complete cultures (remote tribes, small island nations, gangs) to individuals in clearly defined roles (headteachers, managers).

Samples are often hand-picked, not random, because they have certain desired qualities. Those chosen may be *typical* or *unique* examples or *cases* as they are called. They may possess all the qualities being investigated (*critical cases*) or the researcher may have to be satisfied with the sample on offer at the time and place of the research (*opportunity* or *convenience samples*). Sometimes a few people are chosen with the desired qualities and after the research they are asked to recommend another person with similar qualities – *snowball samples*.

These styles of research give rise to mountainous piles of data and it is important to begin the analysis during the research process. The commonest sources of data come from field and biographical notes, observation schedules, diaries and tape recordings of interviews. Using coding systems for the responses, these data are reduced to manageable proportions. Coding requires some categorization on the part of researchers; despite a build-up of experience in creating categories, the system is rarely free from value judgements. As with scientific research, the hope is to move from descriptions to theories by finding patterns and consistencies in the data (Miles and Huberman 1994).

Computer analysis has offered a quicker, alternative method of dealing with the large amounts of data (LeCompte and Preissle 1993). There are now many packages available (Kelle 1995).

There are many issues in education which lend themselves to this approach. The study of school ethos, classrooms, teachers, headteachers, indeed, any social setting with educational implications, lends itself to ethnographic exploration. For example, a feminist ethnographer (Mertens 2004) might be concerned to discover if sub-cultural beliefs exist in science classes which affect the performance of girls and boys.

## Case study research

Case study research focuses on either individuals or well-defined groups such as a family, school or community. Case studies are best used for intensive investigation of complex situations where there are many interacting variables. Case studies typically take more of a qualitative than a quantitative approach, allowing participants to speak for themselves, thereby enabling the situation to be seen through the eyes of participants. The main source of information for case studies is usually based on interviews with key participants, but documentary evidence, questionnaire data, observational data, even information from standardized tests has been included.

There are three main types of case studies referred to as *exploratory, descriptive* and *explanatory* (Yin 1984). Exploratory studies can be used as pilot studies for larger projects using a different form of research. A study of teacher attitudes to the inclusion of pupils with special needs, conducted in one school, in which teachers are asked to complete questionnaires and take part in interviews, would be an example. Feedback from this case study of one school is then used to plan a larger project involving a representative sample of schools from throughout the country.

The second type, descriptive studies, provides narrative accounts of a particular case. An example would be a focused study of a teenage girl with anorexia nervosa, which details the development and treatment of the disorder over a period of years from the perspectives of her parents, teachers and the girl herself. This is a typical method in psychoanalysis.

The third type of case study, explanatory, attempts to test hypotheses or theories using a single person or homogeneous group. For example, an intensive investigation following the exploratory example above might be used to track the effects of integrating students with disabilities into mainstream inclusive schools (Stakes and Hornby 2000).

## Historical research

Historical research involves using information from the past (e.g., documents, artifacts). It is intended to provide a systematic location, examination and synthesis of past evidence in order to achieve an accurate representation of past events. Historical research in education may focus on an individual, group, organization, institution, idea or movement. It is a form of *ex post facto* research for which the qualitative paradigm is most appropriate.

Data for historical research exist in the form of either *primary* or *secondary* sources. Primary sources are first-hand accounts of an event from someone who was there. It should be a pristine, accurate and original account. Sources include manuscripts (hand-written information) and published material (laws, reports, letters, archival material (e.g. family records), newspapers) and artifacts (e.g. actual materials used in schools over the centuries). Secondary sources, in effect, are accounts by people not directly involved in the original event. These accounts are assumed to be obtained from primary sources and usually appear in written form. The accuracy of secondary source material is always a problem and should be questioned.

As the data are largely written or verbal accounts of events, the analysis is similar in many ways to those described in ethnographic research above. It would involve classifying (coding), synthesizing and interpreting the data in a qualitative mode.

An example of historical research in education is an account of the development of provision for children with special educational needs in mainstream schools in England during the last century (Stakes and Hornby 1997). The study identified key factors in the evolution of positive change in mainstream provision for children with special needs.

## Action research

Action research is designed to bridge the gap between research and practice in the field of education. For a most readable introduction, see Macintyre (2000). Cohen *et al.* (2000) define action research as 'a small-scale intervention in the functioning of the real world and a close examination of the effects of such an intervention'. In education, the intention is to improve professional practice. It might, for example, attempt to improve an educational method in a classroom through practical interventions while learning from the effects of the resulting changes. But it has to be systematic (McNiff *et al.* 2003, Macintyre 2000). It can be used in any setting in which a problem has been identified and can be undertaken by an individual teacher or by teachers collaborating with colleagues, researchers or other education professionals. Action research can, for example, focus on improving teaching skills, assessment or management procedures.

Action research can involve any of the qualitative and quantitative methods mentioned above. In education, it focuses on problems which are of immediate concern to teachers. It encourages teachers to reflect on their practices and thereby should enhance the competencies of all the participants whether pupils or teachers.

An example of action research could be one designed by a teacher who was concerned about the effectiveness of the National Literacy Hour on children with learning difficulties. She could construct and teach an alternative programme to her group of children with learning difficulties and compare the results with those from the prescribed programme.

## Meta-analysis

When reviewing evidence from previous research, the commonest technique is to express the findings in words. Most students are used to this kind of literature review in essays and project work. But it is also possible to summarize previous researches in statistical form, provided certain conditions apply. In effect, we combine the results of several similar researches into one statistically acceptable single data set. The main advantages are an increase in sample size, therefore reducing size effects, and a greater prospect of representing the population from which the different research samples have been drawn.

But care has to be taken in choosing suitable research results. In meta-analysis, we must not try to compare 'chalk' and 'cheese'. The 'cases' across the studies, which are 'people' in most researches in educational psychology, should be drawn from the same population without bias. The variables used in the studies and their measurements have to be the same, similar or comparable. In some meta-analyses, the findings from previous studies are combined and subjected to special statistical processes; in others, the data are unpicked and all cases combined to form a single large sample. Two other problems may intrude. There is always a temptation only to submit statistically significant research results for publication. As meta-analyses are usually based on published work, it may not be representative of *all* (the full range of) research findings in a field (sometimes called the 'file drawer effect' because non-significant results tend to get filed away). Another problem is that poorly constructed studies sometimes get roped in to make up numbers. But be careful, because 'garbage in gives garbage out'.

There are several examples of meta-analysis in this text. In Chapter 5, we looked at Hillocks' work (1986) on teaching methods in composition writing. Chapter 9 gave two examples. Vernon *et al.* (2000) (see Chapter 9) looked at 11 studies linking brain size and intelligence. Erlenmeyer-Kimling and Jarvik (1963) and subsequently Bouchard and

McGue (1981) (summarized in Plomin *et al.*, 2001) combined most of the twin studies using psychometric intelligence tests to explore the size of the genetic component using correlational studies. The outcome, plus evidence since then, is illustrated in Table 9.3. In a meta-analysis of the genetic component for extraversion and neuroticism in trait personality, Loehlin (1992) looked at as many twin studies as he could find, generating a massive sample of 24,000. The resulting correlations and distribution of variance for genetic and environmental factors are discussed in Chapter 12.

Care has to be taken in the interpretation of meta-analyses. There are occasions when they can confuse rather than clarify. Sometimes, buried beneath an avalanche of data, specific information might be completely obscured. For example, huge samples of 'people' obtained for an analysis and showing, say, no correlation between two variables might disguise the fact that there are 'female/male' differences. This is always a risk in data analysis exaggerated by large-scale analysis. Therefore, it is important to try to account for all possible variables within the data. We saw a possible example of this in the discussion of sex differences in mathematics performance in Chapter 16.

# Limitations of research in educational pyschology

As we can see from the above brief outline, research in educational psychology is difficult. But even the natural sciences have their critics. Medawar (1963, 1969), in summarizing some of the problems facing scientists, put his finger on many shortcomings of 'scientific method'. According to him, the formulation of theories purporting to be scientific starts with, one assumes, the 'unvarnished and unembroidered' evidence of the senses. Initial observations should be simple, unbiased, unprejudiced, naïve and innocent. From evidence through the senses we should end up with simple declarations which express, in an orderly fashion, the laws of nature. The ornithologist unobtrusively watches birds in nature without disturbing the facts as they exist. In the same dispassionate way, the educational researcher attempting to use scientific method would like to be a 'human watcher'. But this is rarely possible.

These high aims are bedevilled by many setbacks which the cautious teacher should bear in mind when examining the research literature for its implications for teaching.

Some of the questions posed in education are as large as life itself. Psychological themes sometimes have this awkward habit of depending on so many independent variables as to render controlled research impossible. The terms of reference are never as clear-cut as those found in physics or chemistry. Our subject matter is cumbersome with variables; our methods are messy rather than elegant and clean; our results are tentative, often specific to our own situation and thereby rarely capable of direct application to all classroom practice.

These problems were the justification for looking at the alternative paradigms outlined above.

How unbiased can research be? The act of choosing a subject for research nearly always reflects a bias. Fashions come and go in educational research as the climate of opinion about values in education changes. With limited resources, this means that some topics have to be ignored. Selecting methods of measurement, analysis and interpretation requires decisions that often call for biased judgement. The experimenter brings to research a lifetime of prejudices and predispositions about human nature, thus making it difficult to be objective about research design and interpretation.

*Ex post facto* methods necessarily lead to an emphasis on the products of our behaviour rather than the processes by which these products came into being. For example, we look at the outcome of a perceptual task or examination results and make assumptions, in retrospect, about what might have been taking place in the process of perceiving or studying for the examination. On the other hand, many of the teacher's problems focus on processes, assumptions about which can be used to modify and make efficient the learning of children. This is where action research has a part to play.

In educational research, particularly ethnographic studies, there is a marked dependence on introspection. When questions of attitude or opinion are asked, the responses depend entirely on the selective memory of the person being asked. Some of our behaviour is moderated by attitudes of which we may not even be aware. The way in which the questions are posed may influence the answers given. The answers also depend on the communication skills of individuals, and this is particularly difficult with children.

# Decision-making from educational research

Given all the strictures of previous sections in this chapter, how can we make best use of research results in education? This has to be achieved bearing in mind that, no matter which paradigm is followed, we have a long way to go to reach the level of reliability reached in the natural sciences.

Ausubel (1953) sees three levels or ways in which we have attempted to use knowledge from research in educational decision-making. In the first, *basic science research*, the experimenter is concerned with discovering general principles as ends in themselves. In the case of education, the fundamental principles derived in psychology, sociology or philosophy would be the source of information. One problem here is that the principles are commonly discovered using controlled experimental designs which bear only a marginal, if any, similarity to the situation which exists in a classroom.

The level of complexity in a classroom frequently militates against the direct application of fundamental findings using animal or controlled human experiments. Again, the researcher is often not particularly concerned to find laws or generalities which have predetermined applications. In fact, where attempts are made to take the findings and apply them directly to classroom settings, they frequently fail because the level of generality is at a much higher point than is required in a classroom, where knowledge of individual differences is crucial.

One of the few examples of applying a basic scientific finding is the Yerkes–Dodson Law mentioned in Chapters 8 and 12. It shows that there is a predictable relationship between performance and drive, provided we can specify the conditions under which a task is being conducted. All manner of conclusions are possible which, from a knowledge of the law, are particularly relevant to classroom practices, but we still have some way to go in determining the details of the conditions which influence the relationship.

A second level defined by Ausubel is the *extrapolated basic science research* in which the experimenter sets out with a specific practical problem in mind and designs an analogous basic science research from which general principles can be extracted. The original research is rarely carried out in the applied setting for which it is being used and suffers from much the same shortcomings as in applying basic research. We draw on studies from the psychology of language acquisition and apply these to the classroom. For example, operant conditioning can be used in language learning in the primary school. However, one fault is the tendency to extrapolate from basic research and apply the results to pedagogical problems without first finding out the extent to which this link is valid (Bijou 1970). Much of the quantitative research now available falls into this category.

The third suggestion Ausubel calls *research at an applied level*, by which he means performing research *in situ* and in the conditions which normally pertain in schools. As we saw above, qualitative, ethnographic and action research in the classroom involve the identification and exploration of learning environments *as they exist* in schools. Naturally, this approach presents far more difficulties because of the complex nature of the task than would be the case in classical controlled researches. However, Ausubel believes that the pay-off for teachers would be much greater than that which exists at present.

There are the beginnings of a shift in emphasis from the study of individual differences to the study of learning environments in education (Marjoribanks 1991). Shulman (1970) makes the point that 'the language of education and the behavioural sciences is in great need of a set of terms for describing environments that is as articulated, specific and functional as those already possessed for characterizing individuals'. We need to know far more about the characteristics by which we can describe educational environments and the significance of these to the processes of behaviour change and the job of teaching. To some extent, the social psychologist in education has been concerned with detecting the influence of these environmental variables on individuals, but rarely has this occurred with the classroom as the environment. It is not just the content of lessons which the teacher manipulates, but the whole background of the classroom. We need to discover how these manipulations influence performance in different environmental structures and how this might be evaluated (Parlett 1974, Dockrell and Hamilton 1980).

# Reading the research literature

Keeping up to date or preparing for a project in a rapidly expanding market of research literature associated with the psychology of education is difficult for researchers, let alone teachers in training. Libraries are splitting at the seams with the onslaught of new periodicals and books reporting theory, research and practice. This, if nothing else, is a testimony to the increasing vitality and enthusiasm for pursuing answers to our many questions.

Sometimes the topic requires the use of standardized test materials such as diagnostic and progress tests in English, mathematics and science or various aspects of cognitive ability (Cohen 1976). It is no longer possible to obtain such tests without first showing that one has the necessary ability and credentials to use the tests. Users must now be registered with the test-publishing agency or the British Psychological Society (http://www.bps.org.uk). With some tests, this can be done through the tutor or project supervisor or the school in which the project is being undertaken. The NFER is also a useful resource for test materials (NFER in 'References'). Some can be used by teachers, but others can only be administered by registered users, speech therapists or educational psychologists.

Quite understandably, students may find some technical papers almost unreadable. Children become 'subjects'; classes of children become 'biased samples' of size '$N$'; 'variables' are manipulated using '$t$-tests', 'chi-square' or 'correlation coefficients', and so on. Fortunately, most journals use a similar format including an abstract or summary, consisting of a few hundred words, at the beginning or the end of an article. These try to be user friendly and are intended to give a brief idea of the article. Towards the end of a paper there is a discussion section which endeavours to summarize the findings and make suggestions about their implications. Summary and discussion sections do not normally contain too much statistical terminology, so provided students or teachers can pick their way through the technical jargon of the subject matter of the paper, they should gain something from the article.

The list of educational research journals relevant to educational psychology is very long indeed. To get an idea of the journals available, students or teachers should look at the *British Education Index* (BEI). For those with website facilities, look in at http://www.leeds.ac.uk/bei. The index lists many periodicals (hyperlink list of journals). It is also a most useful starting point for a project which requires recent research references. Most of the major journals to which it refers are usually available in college and university libraries. An international education index (ERIC – Education Resources Information Center) exists and is a most helpful source for further information on current research. The website is at http://www.eric.ed.gov/ but a summary can be found at http://www.kerlins.net/scott/ERIC.html. It covers the education indexes of Britain, Australia and Canada. Both BEI and ERIC indexes are available in book and disc form.

---

### Further reading

The number of journals widely available to students is extensive. A few examples will suffice to show the range of general and specialist texts available. General journals in psychology and education include the *British Journal of Educational Psychology, Child Development, Educational Psychologist, Educational Psychology, Educational Psychology in Practice, Journal of Educational Psychology, Psychology in the Schools, Psychology of Education Review, School Psychology International* and the *School Psychology Review.*

Specialist journals cover specific psychological topics as do *Applied Psycholinguistics, British Journal of Learning Disabilities, Personality and Individual Differences, British Journal of Developmental Psychology, Computer Assisted Language Learning, Education and Treatment of Children, Intervention in School and Clinic, Journal of Abnormal Child Psychology, Journal of Applied Behavior Analysis, Journal of Child Psychology and Psychiatry, Journal of Experimental Child Psychology and Preventing School Failure.*

Texts on sectors of the educational system include *Primary Teaching Studies, Journal of Adolescence, Higher Education*; and school subjects are covered by, for example, *Primary Science Review, Language Learning, Research in Reading, Mathematics Education, German Teaching, Psychology of Music.*

---

The major British learned society producing several specialist journals is the *British Psychological Society* (BPS). The journal circulated to the members of the BPS, *The Psychologist,* sometimes has articles of interest to teachers, for example a series of articles on the subject of psychology and education appeared in the March 1993 edition. Another of its journals, the *British Journal of Educational Psychology,* contains useful papers, although the statistical sophistication may limit some readers to the summary and discussion sections of the papers. The Education Section of the Society has its own journal, *The Psychology of Education Review.*

A government-supported body, the *National Foundation for Educational Research* (NFER), publishes a journal, *Educational Research,* which is a review of research for the benefit of teachers. The website for the NFER is http://www.nfer.ac.uk. Both the BPS and NFER produce a large number of books and tests that are often referred to in this book. For a sourcebook of test methods and materials, see Cohen (1976).

### Summary

General textbooks in educational psychology are dependent for their content on the findings of research. Students are also required to read and to use research methods in their degree studies. Therefore a short chapter has been included to introduce readers to the subject.

As a scientific enterprise, educational psychology still has a long way to go and consequently the message of this chapter has been one of cautious optimism for the application of research findings to the daily routines of the teacher. Quantitative, qualitative and action research were outlined and their uses considered. While these methods cannot provide unequivocal answers to the teacher's problems, nevertheless they do provide an essential ingredient in the decision-making processes met by teachers in classrooms.

## Tutorial enquiry and discussion

(a) It is said that the research styles chosen by people depend on their philosophy of life. Examine your own preferences in research methods.

(b) Action research has become an important part of teachers' examination of their classroom practices. McNiff, Lomax and Whitehead (2003) in 'Further reading' is a good starting point for you to examine your own classroom practices.

(c) In tutorial, take a current educational debate and determine how you would set about getting the information to enable you to make sound judgements in the debate.

## References

Ausubel, D. P. (1953), 'The nature of educational research', *Educational Theory*, 3, 314–20.

Barlow, D. H. and Hersen, M. (1984), *Single-case Experimental Designs: Strategies for Studying Behavior Change*. New York: Pergamon.

Bijou, S. W. (1970), 'What psychology has to offer education – now', *Journal of Applied Behavioral Analysis*, 3, 65–71.

Bouchard, T. J. and McGue, M. (1981), 'Familial studies of intelligence: a review', *Science*, 121, 1055–9.

Campbell, D. T. and Stanley, J. (1963), 'Experimental and quasi-experimental designs for research on teaching', in N. Gage (ed.), *Handbook of Research on Teaching*. Chicago: Rand McNally.

Child, D. (2006), *The Essentials of Factor Analysis* (3rd edn). London: Continuum.

Clay, M. M. (1993, revised 1995), *Reading Recovery: A Guidebook for Teachers in Training*. Auckland, NZ: Heinemann Educational.

Cohen, L. (1976), *Educational Research in Classrooms and Schools: A Manual of Materials and Methods*. London: Harper and Row.

Cohen, L. and Holliday, M. (1982), *Statistics for Education and Physical Education*. London: Harper and Row.

Cohen, L. and Holliday, M. (1996), *Practical Statistics for Students: An Introductory Text*. London: Chapman.

Cohen, L., Manion, L. and Morrison, K. (2000), *Research Methods in Education* (5th edn). London: Routledge Falmer.

Dewey, J. (1933), *How We Think*. Boston, MA: Heath.

Dockrell, W. B. and Hamilton, D. (eds) (1980), *Rethinking Educational Research*. Sevenoaks: Hodder and Stoughton.

Erlenmeyer-Kimling, L. and Jarvik, L. F. (1963), 'Genetics and intelligence', *Science*, 142, 1477–9.

Fitz-Gibbon, C. T. (1997), *The Value Added National Project Final Report: Feasibility Studies for a National System of Value Added Indicators*. London: School Curriculum Assessment Authority.

Gall, M. D., Borg, W. R. and Gall, J. (2002), *Educational Research: An Introduction* (7th edn). Glesne, CA: Allyn and Bacon.

Hillocks, G. (1986), *Research on Written Composition*. Proceedings of a conference on research on English, reading and communication skills. Urbana, IL. University of Illinois Press.

Kelle, U. (ed.) (1995), *Computer-aided Qualitative Data Analysis*. London: Sage.

Kerlinger, F. N. (1986), *Foundations of Behavioral Research: Educational and Psychological Inquiry* (3rd edn). London: Holt, Rinehart and Winston.

LeCompte, M. and Preissle, J. (1993), *Ethnography and Qualitative Design in Educational Research* (2nd edn). London: Academic Press Ltd.

Loehlin, J. C. (1992), *Genes and Environment in Personality Development*. Newbury Park: Sage.

Macintyre, C. (2000), *The Art of Action Research in the Classroom*. London: David Fulton Publishers.

Marjoribanks, K. (1991), 'Social theories of education', in K. Marjoribanks (ed.), *The Foundations of Students' Learning*. Oxford: Pergamon.

McNiff, J., Lomax, P. and Whitehead, J. (2003), *You and Your Action Research Project* (2nd edn). London: Routledge Falmer.

Medawar, P. B. (1963), 'Is the scientific paper a fraud?', *The Listener*.

Medawar, P. B. (1969), *Induction and Intuition in Scientific Thought*. London: Methuen.

Mertens, D. M. (2004), *Research Methods in Education and Psychology: Integrating Diversity with Quantitative and Qualitative Approaches* (2nd edn). Thousand Oaks, CA: Sage.

Miles, M. and Huberman, M. A. (1994), *Qualitative Data Analysis* (2nd edn) Beverly Hills, CA: Sage.

National Curriculum, The (1987), *Task Group in Assessment and Testing-Final and Supplementary Reports*. London: DES and Welsh Office.

Parlett, M. (1974), 'The new evaluation', *Trends in Education*, 34, 13–18.

Plomin, R., DeFries, J. C., McClearn, G. E. and McGuffin, P. (2001), *Behavioral Genetics* (4th edn). New York: Worth.

Plowden Report, The (1967), *Children and Their Primary Schools*. Vol. 1. London: HMSO.

Shulman, L. S. (1970), 'Reconstruction of educational research', *Review of Educational Research*, 40, 371–96.

Stakes, R. and Hornby, G. (1997), *Change in Special Education: What brings it about*? London: Cassell.

Vernon, P. A., Wickett, J. C., Bazana, P. G. and Stelmack, R. M. (2000), 'The neuropsychology and psychophysiology of human intelligences' in R. J. Sternberg (ed.), *Handbook of Intelligence*. Cambridge: Cambridge University Press.

Warnock Report, The (1978), *Special Educational Needs*. London: HMSO, Cmnd 7212.

Yin, R. K. (1984), *Case Study Research: Design and Methods*. Beverly Hills, CA: Sage.

Youngman, M. (1998), 'Trends in educational measurement and research methodology', in D. Shorrocks-Taylor (ed.), *Directions in Educational Psychology*. London: Whurr.

## Further reading

Gall, M. D., Borg, W. R. and Gall, J. (2002), *Educational Research: An Introduction* (7th edn). Glesne, CA: Allyn and Bacon.

Cohen, L. (1976), *Educational Research in Classrooms and Schools: A Manual of Materials and Methods*. London: Harper and Row.

Cohen, L., Manion, L. and Morrison, K. (2000), *Research Methods in Education* (5th edn). London: RoutledgeFalmer.

Kline, P. (2000), *The Handbook of Psychological Testing* (2nd edn). London: Routledge.

McNiff, J., Lomax, P. and Whitehead, J. (2003), *You and Your Action Research Project* (2nd edn) London: Routledge Falmer.

Mertens, D. M. (2004), *Research Methods in Education and Psychology: Integrating Diversity with Quantitative and Qualitative Approaches* (2nd edn). Thousand Oaks, CA: Sage.

## Useful websites

British Psychological Society at: http://www. bps.org.uk

*British Education Index* (BEI) at: http://www.leeds.ac.uk/bei

ERIC – (Educational Resources Information Center) is available at: http://eric.ed.gov and http://www. kerlins.net/scott/ERIC.html

Fitz-Gibbon at: http:// www.cemcentre.org.uk

NFER at: http://www.nfer.ac.uk

# 18 Standardization and Item Analysis

## Implications for teachers

- The increase in standardized tests at all levels in the educational system has made it important for teachers to understand the reasoning behind the published statistical information.

- Many psychological research papers contain data gathered from standardized tests.

- Frequent reference is made in this book to statistical data.

This chapter is offered as an optional extra for those who wish to know more about the statistics of standardizing test scores and the fundamentals of item analysis. It is not an attempt to introduce students to statistics. That would require a whole textbook. A good introduction for those still 'cutting teeth' in statistics is Satterly (1989; also see 'Further reading'). Even so, students without any mathematical background or with a phobia about mathematical concepts are likely to find this chapter somewhat intimidating. The author, nevertheless, believes that students should at least attempt to fathom basic statistical concepts in order to make their reading of the research literature more meaningful, as well as helping to expose for them some of the dangers inherent in the design and use of standardized tests. In this respect, colleges and departments have an important role to play in providing suitable introductory courses in statistics for students in educational studies. The current emphasis on standard assessments (SATs) at several ages in the school-life of children and the annual debate about mark distributions and declining standards following GCSE exams make it inevitable that teachers will be faced with statistical information applied to education.

# Standardization of examination marks

Teachers are often faced with the task of pooling several sets of marks, sometimes for the same school subject, sometimes between different subjects. But there are good reasons why it is not always justified simply to add all the marks together and use the total, or average, as a measure of the relative competence of pupils. The standard of marking varies for an individual from one occasion to the next. Standards also vary between teachers and between subjects. Often the marks are widely spread in subjects such as science and mathematics with well-defined expectations in the answers, whereas essay marks tend to bunch round the average mark. The average itself is also affected by the leniency or severity of the marker or the content of the examination questions. Even when the standards for each subject are the same, one may question the sense of adding the marks of such disparate subjects as French, arithmetic and needlework. What we shall do in this section is demonstrate a method for adjusting the marks in two subjects to make them comparable. This process of converting the raw marks to a common scale is known as *standardization*.

## Tabulation

Suppose a form teacher has received two sets of marks (variously referred to in the following text as raw marks and scores), one for arithmetic, the other for English. When the marks for each pupil are assembled, the list will have the chaotic appearance of Table 18.1. Gathering systemic information would be impossible from the confusion of figures as they appear in this table.

The first task is to rearrange the scores to provide us with a concise picture of the *distribution*, that is, the frequency with which successive scores occur. The best and most easily interpreted arrangement is a *tabulation* obtained by writing down all the possible scores in ascending or descending order. By working through the list of marks we *tally* each one against the appropriate mark to build up a tabulation looking something like Table 18.2. The fifth tally mark is drawn through the first four, like a gate, and a second

**Table 18.1** Marks for arithmetic and English (N = 50). (Maximum score = 10)

| Pupil | Arithmetic | English | Pupil | Arithmetic | English |
|---|---|---|---|---|---|
| 1 | 9 | 3 | 26 | 4 | 8 |
| 2 | 1 | 9 | 27 | 4 | 6 |
| 3 | 4 | 8 | 28 | 3 | 7 |
| 4 | 8 | 4 | 29 | 7 | 7 |
| 5 | 7 | 5 | 30 | 2 | 7 |
| 6 | 4 | 7 | 31 | 5 | 5 |
| 7 | 2 | 2 | 32 | 3 | 4 |
| 8 | 4 | 8 | 33 | 5 | 8 |
| 9 | 6 | 6 | 34 | 4 | 8 |
| 10 | 5 | 7 | 35 | 6 | 7 |
| 11 | 3 | 5 | 36 | 0 | 6 |
| 12 | 4 | 6 | 37 | 1 | 3 |
| 13 | 8 | 7 | 38 | 5 | 8 |
| 14 | 7 | 6 | 39 | 6 | 7 |
| 15 | 10 | 3 | 40 | 5 | 8 |
| 16 | 4 | 7 | 41 | 2 | 7 |
| 17 | 3 | 8 | 42 | 5 | 4 |
| 18 | 2 | 7 | 43 | 4 | 9 |
| 19 | 5 | 9 | 44 | 5 | 8 |
| 20 | 4 | 6 | 45 | 6 | 2 |
| 21 | 3 | 6 | 46 | 1 | 6 |
| 22 | 6 | 7 | 47 | 3 | 5 |
| 23 | 4 | 4 | 48 | 2 | 4 |
| 24 | 3 | 5 | 49 | 7 | 7 |
| 25 | 4 | 5 | 50 | 6 | 9 |

set is started with the sixth occurrence of the mark. This has the advantage of breaking the scoring into convenient units of five, thus giving easy addition at the completion of the tally. This process will be familiar to some who have done statistics as part of their maths GCSE.

Where the range of marks involved is extensive, as would most likely be the case for a percentage scale, the tabulation of single numbers is not sufficiently compressed to give a clear picture of the frequency distribution; nor is it convenient for the calculation of statistical quantities. In this case, we group the marks in useful *class intervals*. For a percentage scale the interval might be five consecutive marks such as 0 to 4, 5 to 9, 10 to 14 and so on. A score of 8 would be tallied in the class interval 5 to 9. In subsequent calculations the mid-point of the interval is then used to represent the interval. For example, the mid-points of 0 to 4 and 5 to 9 are 2 and 7 respectively – convenient whole numbers which result from taking class intervals containing an odd number of scale points such as five.

**Table 18.2** Tabulation of arithmetic and English marks

| | Arithmetic | | English | |
|---|---|---|---|---|
| Mark | Tally | Frequency | Tally | Frequency |
| 0 | I | 1 | | 0 |
| 1 | III | 3 | | 0 |
| 2 | IIII | 5 | II | 2 |
| 3 | IIII II | 7 | III | 3 |
| 4 | IIII IIII II | 12 | IIII | 5 |
| 5 | IIII III | 8 | IIII I | 6 |
| 6 | IIII I | 6 | IIII III | 8 |
| 7 | IIII | 4 | IIII IIII III | 13 |
| 8 | II | 2 | IIII IIII | 9 |
| 9 | I | 1 | IIII | 4 |
| 10 | I | 1 | | 0 |
| | | — | | — |
| | | Total 50 | | Total 50 |

## Graphical representation

Although we can now see some semblance of order, there is an even more graphic way of presenting the information. If the frequencies of Table 18.2 are plotted against the corresponding marks in the form of bars we have a *histogram*, as portrayed in Figure 18.1(a). For each mark along the horizontal axis of the graph we erect a block whose height represents the frequency of the mark. Figure 18.1(a) is the histogram for the arithmetic distribution. At a glance we can see that the frequencies for arithmetic accumulate around a mark of 4; for English the most frequent mark is 7.

An alternative method of presenting the frequencies is the *frequency polygon*. If, instead of drawing bars, we join up the mid-points at the top of each bar, as in Figure 18.1(b), a frequency polygon is generated. In the histogram the base of the bar is one mark unit wide, with the actual mark value at the centre of this base, while in the frequency polygon the points to be joined correspond to the centre of the base at the mark value. The lines joining the points are straight. However, with large numbers and a good spread of marks the lines joining the points take on the appearance of a continuous *curve*. For ease of presentation the subsequent illustrations will be smoothed; readers should appreciate that the curve will have been derived from a less regular distribution.

## Distributions

The shape of the curve tells us a lot about irregularities in the distributions. Many statistical formulae rely on the fact that the distribution of data is *normal*. A normal curve has a

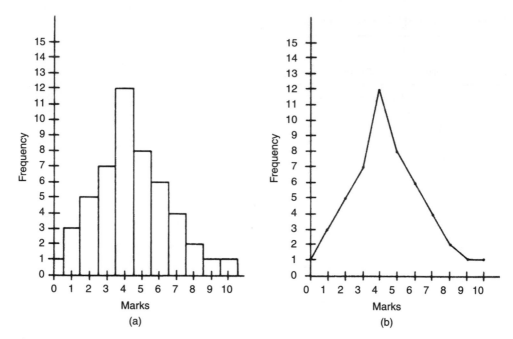

**Figure 18.1** (a) Histogram and (b) frequency for arithmetic.

symmetrical appearance of frequencies regularly diminishing on either side of the most frequent score. Figure 18.2(a) is a normal distribution; our distributions in arithmetic and English are close to normal. Intelligence tests are designed to give normal distributions when administered to a random sample of a population. Test items are chosen so as to give this kind of distribution. Consequently, it is meaningless to suppose that intelligence tests can 'prove' intelligence to be normally distributed in a population because the tests are manipulated to make normality inevitable.

The English marks tend to fall towards the high end of the distribution, and where this becomes exaggerated, as shown in Figure 18.2(b), it is known as a *negative skew*. A preponderance of scores towards the low end of the scale gives a *positive skew*, as in Figure 18.2(c). When two obvious maxima occur in a distribution, as would result if we plotted 1, 3, 7, 10, 17, 14, 14, 17, 11, 5, 1, a *bimodal* distribution is said to exist. Bimodal distributions are common where there are two clearly defined groups in the sample chosen – clearly defined because they give rise to conspicuously different maximum frequencies. The figures chosen above are in fact the totals of frequencies for the marks between 0 and 10 in arithmetic and English. As we saw in Table 18.2, the maxima for these subjects are different, and this is reflected in the overall distribution of the totals shown in Figure 18.2(d). Heights or weights of men and women, if combined, would also tend to give bimodal curves, one maximum connected with the men and the other with the women.

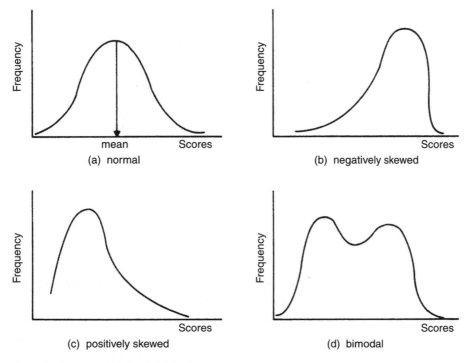

**Figure 18.2** Different kinds of distribution.

## Means

The difference in the distributions and maxima for arithmetic and English makes it highly improbable that we can make direct comparisons of the raw marks for each pupil. If we wanted an overall mark we could not simply add the raw scores. We must first convert the distributions to some common standard – a technique known as standardization and used, for example, in the 11+ examination where verbal, numerical and general ability scores were first adjusted before being added to get a grand total. Occasionally, it is achieved by altering one distribution to comply with the second (see the discussion of cumulative frequencies later) or, as in the following case, by converting the two scales to a third common scale. To do this, we need to know two things about the marks: we need (a) the *mean* or average of each distribution, sometimes known as a measure of central tendency (along with *mode* and *median*), see next section, and (b) the spread or *standard deviation* of the marks in a distribution, sometimes known as a measure of dispersion. These two important statistics are closely connected to the distribution and provide an accurate way of describing it. Where the scores give a small standard deviation, the curve is steep and high, whereas a large spread would give a flat curve; both are illustrated in Figure 18.3.

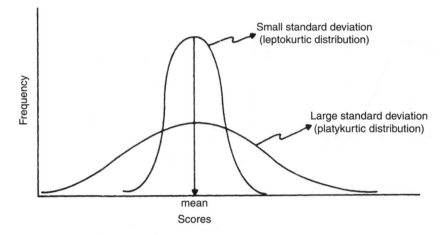

**Figure 18.3** Extreme kinds of normal distribution.

The popular way of finding a mean is to add all the figures and divide by the total number of figures involved. Unfortunately, this is a laborious job if there are numerous figures to contend with. One short cut is demonstrated in Table 18.3.

The weird and wonderful symbols employed are in very common usage. $X$ represents the raw mark, $\overline{X}$ (pronounced 'ex bar') is the mean, $\overline{X}_A$ (pronounced 'ex bar sub A') is the particular mean for arithmetic, $\Sigma$ means 'the sum of', so $\Sigma f$ is the 'sum of all the frequencies', which is bound to equal the sample size N. $\Sigma fX$ means 'the sum of all the separate *frequencies times the marks*'. If one inspects the table it will become clear that each $fX$ saves the trouble of having to add all the separate marks together, that is, instead of

**Table 18.3** Finding the mean for arithmetic.

| Mark (X) | Frequency (f) | fX |
|---|---|---|
| 0 | 1 | 0 |
| 1 | 3 | 3 |
| 2 | 5 | 10 |
| 3 | 7 | 21 |
| 4 | 12 | 48 |
| 5 | 8 | 40 |
| 6 | 6 | 36 |
| 7 | 4 | 28 |
| 8 | 2 | 16 |
| 9 | 1 | 9 |
| 10 | 1 | 10 |

$$\Sigma f = N = 50 \qquad \Sigma fX = 221$$

$$\text{The mean } \overline{X}_A = \Sigma fX/N = 221/50 = 4.42$$

**Table 18.4** Calculating a mean using class intervals for arithmetic marks

| Range | Mid-point | f | fX | (actual totals of fX) |
|---|---|---|---|---|
| 0–4 | 2 | 28 | 56 | 82 |
| 5–9 | 7 | 21 | 147 | 129 |
| 10 | 10 | 1 | 10 | 10 |
| | | | $\Sigma fX = 213$ | 221 |

adding twelve lots of the mark 4, one has $12 \times 4 = 48$. With our simple example not much saving is apparent, but if the numbers were larger there would be considerable economy of effort. The reader might like to calculate the mean for the English marks using the same technique as shown in Table 18.3. The value $\overline{X}_E$ should be 6.20.

Note that if a class interval system had been used, the mid-point of the interval would have been taken to represent the range of marks falling within the interval. Thus the interval 0 to 4 is represented by 2, 5 to 9 is represented by 7, and so on. The term $fX$ would then be found by multiplying the frequency of marks within a given interval by the mid-interval score. For any one interval this procedure may be slightly inaccurate, as we see in Table 18.4.

One would never dream of calculating a mean using the very small range in our example, but it does illustrate the effect on $fX$ of taking the mid-interval point. For the range 0–4, mid-point 2, the product $fX$ would be 56. In fact, it should be 82 if we consider the marks separately as in Table 18.3. The inaccuracy is lessened by the second range, and the total for $fX$ comes very close to the true value. With a greater number of class intervals the minor variations in $fX$ tend to cancel each other out.

In these days of high-speed hand and computer calculators, many students use their statistical packages and enter all the data as individual cases. The calculator does the rest in providing means, modes, medians, sample sizes and standard deviations. Some calculators will also give frequencies and cumulative frequencies.

## Modes and medians

Modes and medians are alternative ways of describing central tendency. The *mode* is the value which is most frequent in a distribution. The mode for marks in arithmetic (Table 18.2 and Figure 18.1) occurs at mark 4 where the frequency, 12, is higher than at any other point. The mode for English shown in the same table is at mark 7 with the largest frequency of 13. There can be more than one mode if the same, or nearly the same, maximum frequency occurs more than once. Hence we get the term *bimodal* for two maxima, *trimodal* for three and so on. Figure 18.2 shows an example of a bimodal distribution. Bimodal distributions in assignment marks are sometimes bad news. It can mean that one or more criteria have been consistently left out by the candidates in the lower mode. This could represent poor instructions about the requirements of the work, poor revision or understanding on the part of the candidates or even unfortunate teaching strategy. This latter is often spotted when a teacher has left out part of the curriculum for a national examination.

The *median* is the middle score in a distribution (the 50th percentile) and divides the sample into two equal halves above and below the median. Fortunately, having calculated and drawn the cumulative frequency curves for arithmetic and English (see Figure 18.5), all we need do is look for the marks at the 50th percentile. These are drawn on Figure 18.5 and give approximately 4.3 for arithmetic and 6.6 for English. Most of the time, we do not draw cumulative frequency curves and Satterly (1989) gives a clear description of how to calculate a value.

Where a distribution is normal, the mean, mode and median are identical. This is clearly not the case with the arithmetic and English distributions. The arithmetic mean = 4.42, mode = 4 and median = 4.25 (by calculation); for English we have mean = 6.20, mode = 7 and median = 6.58 (by calculation). Therefore, neither the arithmetic nor English distributions are normal.

## Standard deviation

The second important statistic we need to know is the standard deviation. A knowledge of the central tendency of the marks, the mean for instance, tells us nothing about the way in which the marks are distributed on each side of the mean and the next stage will be devoted to finding the dispersion of the marks. In the following, we will concentrate on the *method* of finding a standard deviation rather than the reasons for the procedures we adopt – in a similar manner to using a cookery book! As was observed above, one would really need a course in statistics to understand the reasoning behind the mathematical manoeuvres.

The stages necessary for the calculation are: (a) find the mean; (b) find the difference between the mean and each mark; (c) square the difference obtained in (b); (d) multiply the square from (c) by the frequency $f$ if this applies; (e) find the sum of the results from (d); (f) divide the answer from (e) by the number of pupils in the sample; (g) find the square root of the answer in (f). This gives the standard deviation of the marks. Using symbols again, let the mean be $\overline{X}$, let the raw mark be $X$, then (a) to (g) would be represented by:

(a) $\overline{X}$

(b) $\overline{X} - X$

(c) $(\overline{X} - X)^2$

(d) $f(\overline{X} - X)^2$

(e) $\sum f(\overline{X} - X)^2$

(f) $\sum f(\overline{X} - X)^2 / N$

(g) $\sqrt{\sum f(\overline{X} - X)^2 / N}$

The headings and calculations in Table 18.5 follow this pattern. Stage (f) is $\sum f(\overline{X} - X)^2 / N = 222.36/50 = 4.447$ and the standard deviation $\sigma$ (sigma) $= \sqrt{4.447} = 2.11$. Notice that we include the correct sign in the column $(\overline{X} - X)$ and when this is squared in the next column the sign becomes positive. Squaring, therefore, overcomes the

**Table 18.5** Finding the standard deviation for arithmetic ($\overline{X} = 4.42$).

| Mark (X) | Frequency (f) | $\overline{X} - X$ | $(\overline{X} - X)^2$ | $f(\overline{X} - X)^2$ |
|---|---|---|---|---|
| 0 | 1 | 4.42 | 19.54 | 19.54 |
| 1 | 3 | 3.42 | 11.70 | 35.10 |
| 2 | 5 | 2.42 | 5.86 | 29.30 |
| 3 | 7 | 1.42 | 2.02 | 14.14 |
| 4 | 12 | 0.42 | 0.18 | 2.16 |
| 5 | 8 | −0.58 | 0.34 | 2.72 |
| 6 | 6 | −1.58 | 2.50 | 15.00 |
| 7 | 4 | −2.58 | 6.66 | 26.64 |
| 8 | 2 | −3.58 | 12.82 | 25.64 |
| 9 | 1 | −4.58 | 20.98 | 20.98 |
| 10 | 1 | −5.58 | 31.41 | 31.14 |
| | $\Sigma f = N = 50$ | | | $\Sigma f(\overline{X} - X)^2 = 222.36$ |

problems of a negative sign. Readers may like to try a similar calculation for the standard deviation of the English marks. The answer should be $\sigma = 1.82$ using a mean, $\overline{X}_E$, of 6.20.

One interesting fact about standard deviations for distributions approaching normality is that the percentage of the sample falling within one standard deviation on both sides of the mean is approximately 68 per cent of the total sample. Figure 18.4 is a diagrammatical expression of this fact. The mean for arithmetic was 4.42 and one standard deviation of 2.11 above and below this value gives a range from 2.31 to 6.53. We were operating with whole numbers and this range would include values between 3 and 6. Reference to Table 18.2 shows that, for arithmetic, 33 pupils obtained scores between these limits, that is, 68 per cent of the sample. Two standard deviations on both sides of the mean would enclose

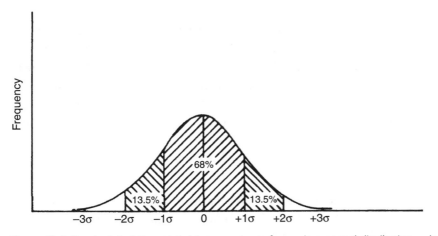

**Figure 18.4** Standard deviation related to percentage of cases in a normal distribution. $\sigma$ is the symbol for standard deviation. In the area between $-1\sigma$ and $+1\sigma$ there will be about 68 per cent of the cases.

about 95 per cent of the sample. Three standard deviations on both sides enclose almost the whole sample (99.7 per cent), as shown in Figure 18.4.

## Standardization

Armed with the means and standard deviations of the two subjects, we are now in a position to equate the two sets of marks. But what standard are we going to choose for the third scale? To make life easy in the transformation calculations, it is usual to take whole numbers for the new mean and standard deviation. A convenient mean would be 5, with standard deviation of 2. The common quantity which links all the scales together is the *standard score* (z). This is obtained by dividing $(\overline{X} - X)$ by the standard deviation $(\sigma)$. For the arithmetic marks

$$\frac{\overline{X}_A - X_A}{\sigma_A} = \frac{\overline{X}_S - X_S}{\sigma_S}$$

where $\overline{X}_S$, $X_S$ and $\sigma_S$ are the mean, new standardized mark and standard deviation for the new scale. The only unknown quantity in this equation is $X_S$ the new set of standardized scores. Rearranging the equation we get:

$$X_S = \overline{X}_S - \frac{(\overline{X}_A - X_A)\sigma_S}{\sigma_A}$$

Suppose we want to standardize a score of 9/10 in arithmetic, then substituting in the formula above for $\overline{X}_S = 5$, $\sigma_S = 2$, $\overline{X}_A = 4.42$, $X_A = 9$ and $\sigma_A = 2.11$, we obtain:

$$X_s = 5 - \frac{(4.42 - 9)2}{2.11} = 5 + 4.34 = 9.34$$

Referring to Table 18.1 will reveal that pupil 1 obtained 9/10 for arithmetic. He also managed 3/10 in English, which converts to 1.48 when standardized using $\overline{X}_E = 6.20$ and $\sigma_E = 1.82$. In fact, pupils 1, 4, 5, 9 and 10 have all obtained a raw score total of 12 when arithmetic and English are added. Yet on standardizing their marks, a rank order of the five pupils is created as shown in the last column of Table 18.6. Wider variations in the means and particularly the standard deviations than those cited here can produce conspicuous changes when scores are adjusted.

## Cumulative frequency

When there is some doubt regarding the normality of a distribution, it is possible to employ a *cumulative frequency graph* or *ogive* (usually pronounced 'ohjive'). For this solution the frequencies are arranged as in Table 18.2, but with the lowest score or mark at the bottom of the column. The frequencies are then added in succession, starting at the lowest score.

**Table 18.6** Marks before and after standardization.

| Pupil | Raw marks | | | Standardized marks | | |
|---|---|---|---|---|---|---|
| | Arithmetic | English | Total | Arithmetic | English | Total |
| 1 | 9 | 3 | 12 | 9.34 | 1.48 | 10.82 |
| 4 | 8 | 4 | 12 | 8.40 | 2.58 | 10.98 |
| 5 | 7 | 5 | 12 | 7.45 | 3.68 | 11.13 |
| 9 | 6 | 6 | 12 | 6.50 | 4.78 | 11.28 |
| 10 | 5 | 7 | 12 | 5.55 | 5.88 | 11.43 |

For arithmetic the cumulative frequency ($cf$) is given in Table 18.7. The highest $cf$ should equal the sample size, giving 50 in the present case. To construct a cumulative frequency graph, plot the marks along the horizontal axis against the $cf$ along the vertical axis. For our purposes a percentage cumulative frequency graph is required. To convert $cf$ into percentage $cf$, simply divide the value of $cf$ by the sample size and multiply the result by 100. At a mark of 5 in arithmetic the $cf$ is 36. Hence the percentage $cf$ to this point in the distribution is $36/50 \times 100$ which gives 72. The graph of percentage $cf$ against marks from Table 18.7 has the appearance of Figure 18.5. Note the characteristic shallow S-shaped curve of the ogive.

To produce a conversion graph, first draw percentage cumulative frequency curves for arithmetic and English on the same graph (Figure 18.5). In this case we are going to convert marks on one subject to a comparable scale in the other subject. To convert 5/10 in arithmetic so that it has a comparable mark in English, first draw a vertical line from 5 on the mark scale upwards until it reaches the curve for arithmetic, marked B on the graph. Then draw a

**Table 18.7** Cumulative frequency of arithmetic marks.

| Mark | Frequency (f) | Cumulative frequency (cf) | Percentage (cf) |
|---|---|---|---|
| 10 | 1 | 50 | 100 |
| 9 | 1 | 49 | 98 |
| 8 | 2 | 48 | 96 |
| 7 | 4 | 46 | 92 |
| 6 | 6 | 42 | 84 |
| 5 | 8 | 36 | 72 |
| 4 | 12 | 28 | 56 |
| 3 | 7 | 16 | 32 |
| 2 | 5 ← plus gives → 9 | | 18 |
| 1 | 3 ← plus gives → 4 | | 8 |
| 0 | 1 | 1 | 2 |

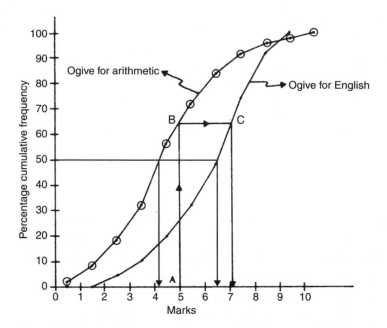

**Figure 18.5** Standardizing scores using a cumulative frequency method.

line horizontally from B until it meets the curve for English, marked C. Drop a line from C onto the mark scale and this reading gives the corresponding mark, which for English is 7.1. Notice that both these marks occur at the 64th percentile, as indicated on the percentage cumulative frequency axis.

## Standard scores and percentage of a population

Whenever we have a normal distribution of ten scores it is possible to calculate the percentage of cases (number of people, for instance) falling between given scores on the scale. This is a very useful piece of information, particularly when we want to discover the number of people who, for example, might have IQ scores greater or less than given values. Figures 18.4 and 9.1 (in Chapter 9) were both calculated using this knowledge.

The first stage involves the calculation of the standard score corresponding to the range of scores required and using this standard score to determine the percentage for the range chosen. Table 18.8 gives a series of standard scores and the corresponding percentages of

**Table 18.8** Percentage of cases under a normal curve using standard scores from the mean.

| Standard score | 0.5 | 1.0 | 1.5 | 2.0 | 2.5 | 3.0 | 3.5 |
|---|---|---|---|---|---|---|---|
| Percentage of cases | 19.15 | 34.13 | 43.32 | 47.72 | 49.38 | 49.87 | 49.98 |

the population falling in the range *between the mean and a point along the scale of scores* which would give the standard score.

Let us suppose we wanted to know how many in a population of children would obtain IQ scores between 100 and 115 on a test which has a mean of 100 and a standard deviation of 15. The standard score for 115 is:

$$\frac{100 - 115}{15} = -1$$

Ignoring the negative sign, which merely tells us which side of the mean we are operating on, the percentage of cases falling between the mean of 100 and one standard score higher (115), according to Table 18.8, is 34.13. From the mean to the far end of the distribution on either one side or the other would incorporate half or 50 per cent of the population. Thus, if we wanted to know the percentage from a point along the scale to the end, let us say 115 and greater, we could subtract the percentage obtained in the method just described from 50 per cent. Hence we would find $50.00 - 34.13 = 15.87$ per cent above 115 IQ points on a scale with a mean of 100 and a standard deviation of 15.

# Item analysis

Several references have already been made to item design and analysis as the starting point in the production of multiple-choice (Haladyna 1994) test papers. In the next few pages we cannot do more than suggest some important considerations which are taken into account when these tests are required. It is not anticipated that students will be able to construct their own items after reading this brief description. For details the reader is referred to the Schools Council's publications and other references made at the end of this chapter. One particularly relevant description appears in the work of a research unit at the University of London which investigated test materials for the Nuffield Science Teaching Project (1967). We shall draw on the team's work in 'O' Level chemistry to introduce the student to item design and analysis.

## Test blueprint (Wood and Skurnik 1969)

Before we can design a set of items we must have a clear idea of the aims, objectives and scope of the subject matter (see Chapter 15) as well as making explicit the kinds of student ability and behaviour we wish to exploit. Rather than pulling topics out of a hat or dreaming up essay titles while watching television, it is essential to make a detailed map of the nature and content of the whole paper, with regard to the activities and abilities being tapped. We have to decide if our pupils are required to use comprehension or evaluative techniques in the questions posed. Are they to apply knowledge to novel problems? What proportions of these skills do we hope to represent in the questions? In a nutshell, we have created a syllabus to bring about the growth and development of behavioural skills in our pupils; the examination should aim at testing these skills.

Once these skills and the subject matter through which they are expressed have been defined, a *blueprint* which incorporates all the essential features of test design is required. The blueprint consists of a grid which must include all the attributes so defined. For the purposes of building this grid, the Nuffield Project team decided to use some of the educational objectives proposed by Bloom (1956) as a workable classification of student behaviour.

The categories chosen were knowledge (recalling facts), comprehension (calculating, translating, interpreting and making deductions to solve problems with familiar solutions), application (applying knowledge to unfamiliar situations) and analysis/evaluation (analysing information for the purpose of making value judgements). These skills represent one important dimension to be accounted for in item design.

A second dimension is, clearly, the content of the syllabus, and this should be divided into conveniently discrete areas of similar material. A third possibility results when the content is classified according to the operations of 'activities' required by the wording of the problem. In Nuffield chemistry the activities postulated were: composition and change in materials; practical techniques; patterns in the behaviour of materials; essential measurements; and concepts. These can be seen as broader groupings of the syllabus content.

If we consider the 'activities' and 'abilities' dimensions as shown in Figure 18.6 a grid is generated. The cells of the grid are used to guide us in accounting for whichever combinations of the categories we desire. Not all cells will necessarily be represented. It may transpire that some topics cannot be expressed in all forms of activity. The important point to remember is that we can scrutinize in detail the distribution of the syllabus content and the behaviour we wish to evoke from the questions. Sorting out the proportion of items to appear in each cell is complex and rests on value judgements made by the test designer. Weighting of specific categories along the two-way table is a starting point, and these have

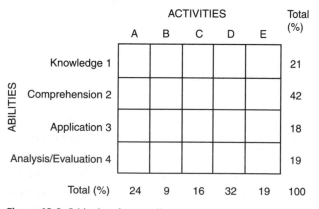

**Figure 18.6** Grid taken from Nuffield Chemistry Project (page 4).

been inserted along the sides of the grid. By judicious manipulation of these marginal proportions we obtain the individual proportions to be assigned to each cell, according to the emphases we wish to observe. If nothing else, blueprint design is a most effective way of getting a teacher to examine and define his or her purposes in providing a particular course.

## Test item design

Having created a ground plan of the skills, topics and activities we wish to examine in a predetermined proportion we must devise appropriate items. The chances of creating items which are all entirely satisfactory is remote. There will be wastage in the design process. Therefore, it is important to create more than necessary for the final version. This is called a *bank* or *pool* of items. Some researchers create about three times as many as might be needed in the final version by repeating (using different wording or numbers) item content. Tests should not be too long and daunting for the respondent; surveys, for example, have become so commonplace these days that most of them find their way into wastebins. Allow about 30 seconds per item and have in mind an approximate length for the final version. It is not a bad idea to have someone with a keen eye looking at the items for poor wording, ambiguity, grammatical errors, inconsistencies, etc. Trial the items on a representative sample of the population you are ultimately going to examine.

There are two important indices which help in forecasting the suitability of test items. These are the *facility index*, which shows whether the candidates have found an item easy or difficult, and the *discrimination index*, which shows how far an item distinguishes the high-scoring from the low-scoring candidates. In all that follows we are assuming that large samples are involved, certainly more than 30 individuals.

### Facility (or difficulty) index (F)

It is plainly important to know the level of difficulty experienced by a group of candidates in answering each item. In setting traditional examination questions chance plays a major part in the choice of easy or difficult questions. What appears easy to a teacher in the setting may be very difficult for the pupil in the execution. The teacher's comprehension of a subject often makes it difficult for him or her to assess, before the fact, the quality of the answers that will be received. To overcome this problem, the questions are initially tried out with a similar group of pupils, referred to as a *pilot sample*. Usually a teacher has neither the time nor the resources to embark on this kind of venture. Consequently, research has been done to test the feasibility of creating 'libraries' or 'banks' of items covering specified ability levels and school subjects (Wood and Skurnik 1969).

For an examination of the facility and discrimination indices, the following example has been taken from the Nuffield Science Teaching Project (1967).

Directions: the group of questions below consists of five lettered headings followed by a list of numbered phrases. For each numbered phrase select the one heading which is most closely related to it. Each heading may be used once, more than once, or not at all.

Classify the following changes into one of the categories, A–E

A   Radioactive decay
B   Catalysis
C   Hydrolysis
D   Cracking
E   Oxidation

1   The conversion by heat alone of an organic liquid consisting of one compound only, into a mixture of compounds which are gaseous at room temperature.
2   The production of thermal energy from the fossil fuels.
3   Changes in the nuclei of atoms.

The originators of this item are testing comprehension, their argument being that the questions require not just simple recall but an understanding of the chemistry in the example and the terms used for sorting out the type of change involved. Note also that the activity involved in questions 1 and 2 is 'composition and changes in materials'; for question 3 it is 'concepts'.

To deal only with question 1, 348 candidates took the paper and 8 did not respond to this question. The remaining candidates gave one of the alternatives A to E as set out in Table 18.9.

The step before this table was built required the pupils to be arranged in rank order according to the total mark obtained on the whole paper. The order was then divided into five equal, or almost equal, groups shown as fifths in the table.

Look first of all at the column totals. Not surprisingly, alternative D attracted the highest proportion of respondents because it was the correct answer. Expressed as a percentage,

**Table 18.9** Distribution of responses to question 1 $N = 348$.

| Students classified by total test score | Alternative | | | | | | |
|---|---|---|---|---|---|---|---|
| | A | B | C | D[a] | E | Omits[b] | Total |
| Lowest fifth | 5 | 17 | 11 | 13 | 21 | 3 | 70 |
| Next lowest fifth | 4 | 7 | 7 | 33 | 16 | 3 | 70 |
| Middle fifth | | 8 | 8 | 37 | 15 | 2 | 70 |
| Next highest fifth | 2 | 3 | 7 | 47 | 11 | | 70 |
| Highest fifth | 1 | 2 | 4 | 56 | 5 | — | 68 |
| Total | 12 | 37 | 37 | 186 | 68 | 8 | 348 |

[a] Correct answer.
[b] Number of students who reached question but did not answer it (i.e. omitted the question).

53 per cent of the total sample ($186 \times 100/348$) got the question right. The proportion (0.53) of respondents giving the correct solution is known as the *facility index* ($F$ or $p$). If only 20 per cent had managed to get the right answer, the question would clearly be a difficult one. Higher percentages or $F$ values would signify easy questions. The inverse of the facility index is known as the *difficulty index*. Whether items are included which give a wide distribution of facility levels depends on the purposes of the test. Nevertheless, indices which are lower than 0.10 or higher than 0.90 are often caused by badly worded questions or, as we shall see, because alternative answers may distract the respondent. The inclusion of a few easy items may help the less confident to settle down or the less able to gain some benefit from the test; difficult items, which are frequently analytical or evaluative, may reveal the 'high fliers' in a group. But most papers possess a substantial proportion of items with near to average facility levels (ranging from roughly 0.30 to 0.70).

The totals for the alternative answers are also very important. An incorrect answer which attracts a large proportion of respondents is known as a *distracter* and should be treated with caution. In multiple-choice items it is common practice to select alternatives which give the appearance of being plausible. If the alternatives were superficial and ridiculous, the candidate could arrive at the correct solution by a process of elimination. On the other hand, the inaccurate answers should not readily draw the candidate off the scent. There is a very real danger that distracters arise through poor and inaccurate teaching or ambiguity in the wording of the question. In our example, alternative E has the largest response rate, apart from the correct answer, and claims some 20 per cent of answers. There are no hard and fast rules governing the limits set for distracters, and test designers create their own standards from experience. If distracters are appealing to better candidates they should certainly be replaced. Ideally, in the multiple-choice item we are looking for alternatives which would be equally attractive to someone with little knowledge of the subject being tested. Thus if the brighter candidates are being fooled by distracters it is wiser to discard and replace them.

## Discrimination index (D)

It seems obvious that an item should be answered correctly most often by those with the highest overall mark. It would be a curious question indeed if it were answered correctly by poorer candidates and incorrectly by the better ones. The *discrimination index* gives us a measure of how far an item distinguishes between high-scoring and low-scoring candidates. A formidable collection of methods now exists for estimating discrimination. Of these, it will suffice to mention two and to direct the student to Anastasi's book in (Further reading) for a thorough exposition of the subject.

The simplest measure can be used when the numbers involved are high (certainly not less than 30 and preferably over 100) and when the high-scoring and low-scoring groups contain the same number of individuals. The formula is $p_1 - p_2$, where $p_1$ is the proportion of high scorers getting the question correct and $p_2$ the proportion of low scorers getting the question right. The number of high and low scorers must be the same. So we could find $p_1$ from the highest 2/5 and $p_2$ from the lowest 2/5. Extracting the values from Table 18.9:

$$p_1 = \frac{\text{number getting questions right in highest 2/5}}{\text{total in the highest 2/5}}$$

$$\text{thus } p_1 = 103/138 = 0.747$$

$$\text{and } p_2 = 46/140 = 0.328$$

$$\text{then } p_1 - p_2 = 0.747 - 0.328 = 0.419 = D$$

The closer this $D$ value is to 0.5, the better is the discriminative power of the item. Again no statistical rule about limits exists, but many test constructors avoid $D$ values outside 0.3 to 0.7.

A second, more sophisticated measure of discrimination can be obtained by correlating an individual's correct or incorrect response to an item with his or her total score. When this is performed for the whole sample, a high correlation means that, generally speaking, those who obtained the correct answer to the item also obtained a high overall score (and vice versa for the low scorers). For a discussion of correlation see Chapter 17. The value obtained from Table 18.9 is +0.54. Interpreting the significance of the correlation coefficient depends on the size of the sample. For $N = 100$ or more a value of at least 0.20 is needed, although most item users would look for somewhat higher values than this if at all possible. With a $D$ value of 0.419 by the first method and 0.54 by the second, question 1 appears to discriminate satisfactorily whichever method is applied.

The final decisions in fabricating a test paper depend largely on the bank of items available. It pays to start with a large number of well-formulated questions in order to create a store of items with adequate facility and discrimination levels. The final test can be assembled with an eye to satisfying the blueprint and at the same time introducing questions with known standards of difficulty. But there are many pitfalls which confront the would-be test designer. These are discussed in the books recommended for further reading at the end of the chapter.

## Summary

In an age when every teacher is involved in standardized assessments, it is crucial to have some knowledge of the statistics underlying the procedures. SATs and GCSEs are the subjects of statistical analysis and they involve almost every teacher in the land. In marking one's own work and reporting to the school or parents, it may be necessary to standardize the marks. The technique of standardization is also used in the design of objective and intelligence tests (see Chapter 9). In this chapter we have touched lightly on some of the basic statistics involved in standardization processes to help students in their interpretation of marks and scores obtained from examination and test material. Such fundamental concepts as tabulation, distribution, mean and standard deviation are mentioned. Item analysis is also mentioned in the hope that it will serve as an aid in the understanding of objective test construction and as a preliminary to our further discussions of curriculum design in Chapter 17.

## Tutorial enquiry and discussion

(a) On school practice or school visits, investigate the following:

   (i) What system the school uses for mark standardization. How do the teachers view the prospect of standardizing the marks for the terminal or annual reports?

   (ii) How do teachers *actually* devise examination questions? What attempts are made to sample the syllabus and the skills required in answering questions?

   (iii) What measures are taken to ensure that course work, portfolios and other forms of continuous assessment are standardized?

(b) Investigate:

   (i) methods used in creating SATs at the Stages of particular interest to you

   (ii) the problems of aggregating SATs marks for the National Curriculum (see Shorrocks-Taylor 1998)

   (iii) the design methods and problems in NVQ and GNVQ skill-based competence tests (see Smithers (1998) for a critical starting point for your search).

(c) It has been suggested that children with IQs less than 70 on a scale having a mean of 100 and SD of 15 would usually require some special form of education. What percentage of the population of children would this involve? Using the same scale, and taking 145 IQ and above as the criterion of giftedness, what percentage of children would you expect to be gifted, assuming always that intelligence is normally distributed? Again with the same scale, what percentage of the population would you find between IQ 85 and 115? Compare your answer with the value quoted in Figure 18.4. You should now be in a position to check the other values in this figure. Refer to Chapter 9 on intelligence and Chapter 11 on special educational needs for some recent data on these questions. (*Answers*: number of cases less than 70 IQ = 2.28 per cent

   number of cases greater than 145 IQ = 0.13 per cent

   number of cases between 85 and 115 IQ = 68.26 per cent.)

## References

Bloom, B. S. (ed.) (1956), *Taxonomy of Educational Objectives. Handbook I: Cognitive Domain*. London: Longman.

Haladyna, T. M. (1994), *Developing and Validating Multiple-Choice Test Items*. Hillsdale, NJ: Erlbaum.

*Nuffield Science Teaching Project in Chemistry at O level* (1967), London: Research Unit of the School Examinations Department, University of London.

Shorrocks-Taylor, D. (1998), 'Cross purposes: development and change in National Curriculum assessment in England and Wales', in D. Shorrocks-Taylor (ed.), *Directions in Educational Psychology*. London: Whurr.

Wood, R. and Skurnik, L. S. (1969), *Item Banking*. Slough: NFER.

## Further reading

Aiken, L. R. and Groth-Marnat, G. (2006), *Psychological Testing and Assessment* (12th edn). Boston: Allyn and Bacon.

Anastasi, A. (1996), *Psychological Testing* (7th edn). New York: Macmillan.

Cohen, L. and Holliday, M. (1996), *Practical Statistics for Students: An Introductory Text*. London: Chapman.

Cronbach, L. J. (1990), *Essentials of Psychological Testing* (5th edn). New York: Harper Row.

Satterly, D. (1989), *Assessment in Schools* (2nd edn). Oxford: Blackwell.

# Index of Names

# Index of Subjects

Page numbers in *italics* refer to illustrations or tables